International Child Law

This book examines the rights of the child using the global framework of the United Nations International *Convention on the Rights of the Child* 1989. Analysing both public and private international legal aspects, this cross-disciplinary text promotes a holistic understanding of the ongoing development of child law, children's rights and the protection of the child. In-depth analyses of the following topic areas are included: Childhood in the digital age; Child labour; International parental child abduction; Inter-country adoption; Child sexual exploitation; Children and armed conflict; and Indigenous children. These topics are contextualised with further chapters on the concept of childhood and children's rights, the international legal framework in which the Convention operates and a substantive chapter on the Convention itself.

This fourth edition has been updated and revised, including a new chapter dealing with issues arising from childhood in the age of unprecedented digital technological advancements; a crucial issue for childhood experiences in modern times. This edition also includes new case studies, recent legal developments in the field of international child law, and inclusion of broader scholarship to capture diverse views on international law and child law. The aim of this book is to provide the reader with an accessible, informed, critical and scholarly account of the international law framework relating to children.

Drawing on a range of legal and other disciplines, this book remains a valuable resource for those in the course of study and research in this area.

Dr Rajnaara C. Akhtar is a Senior Lecturer at De Montfort University, UK. Her main teaching and research interests include family law, international law, child law, gender and law and human rights. She received her PhD from the University of Warwick in 2013, and holds a Masters degree in Human Rights Law from the University of Nottingham.

Dr Conrad Nyamutata is a lecturer at De Montfort University, UK. His main teaching and research interests include broadly public international law, with specialisms in international child law, international human rights law, international humanitarian law and media and mass communications. He holds an MA in Mass Communication (University of Leicester) and an LLM in international human rights and international humanitarian law from Lancaster University. He received his PhD at De Montfort University in 2015.

International Child Law

Fourth edition

Rajnaara C. Akhtar and
Conrad Nyamutata

Routledge
Taylor & Francis Group
LONDON AND NEW YORK

First published 2020
by Routledge
2 Park Square, Milton Park, Abingdon, Oxon OX14 4RN

and by Routledge
52 Vanderbilt Avenue, New York, NY 10017

Routledge is an imprint of the Taylor & Francis Group, an informa business

© 2020 Rajnaara C. Akhtar and Conrad Nyamutata

The right of Rajnaara C. Akhtar and Conrad Nyamutata to be identified as authors of this work has been asserted by them in accordance with sections 77 and 78 of the Copyright, Designs and Patents Act 1988.

All rights reserved. No part of this book may be reprinted or reproduced or utilised in any form or by any electronic, mechanical, or other means, now known or hereafter invented, including photocopying and recording, or in any information storage or retrieval system, without permission in writing from the publishers.

Trademark notice: Product or corporate names may be trademarks or registered trademarks, and are used only for identification and explanation without intent to infringe.

British Library Cataloguing-in-Publication Data
A catalogue record for this book is available from the British Library

Library of Congress Cataloging-in-Publication Data
Names: Akhtar, Rajnaara, author. | Nyamutata, Conrad, author.
Title: International child law/Rajnaara Akhtar and Conrad Nyamutata.
Description: 4th edition. | Milton Park, Abingdon, Oxon; New York, NY: Routledge, 2019. | Includes bibliographical references and index.
Identifiers: LCCN 2019056985 | ISBN 9781138585188 (hardback) | ISBN 9781138585195 (paperback) | ISBN 9780429505485 (ebook)
Subjects: LCSH: Children (International law) | Children – Legal status, laws, etc.
Classification: LCC K639.B83 2019 | DDC 346.01/35 – dc23
LC record available at https://lccn.loc.gov/2019056985

ISBN: 978-1-138-58518-8 (hbk)
ISBN: 978-1-138-58519-5 (pbk)
ISBN: 978-0-429-50548-5 (ebk)

Typeset in Baskerville
by Apex CoVantage, LLC

For my parents – Rajnaara C. Akhtar
For my father (1942–2017) – Conrad Nyamutata

Contents

Preface xiii
Table of cases xv
Table of international legal instruments xix
List of figures and tables xxxvi
Case studies xxxviii

1 Childhood and children's rights — 1

1.1 Childhood — 1
    1.1.1 Historical perspectives — 2
    1.1.2 Psychological perspectives — 6
    1.1.3 Sociological perspectives — 9
    1.1.4 Social policy perspectives — 14
1.2 Human rights — 18
    1.2.1 Children's rights — 21
    1.2.2 International children's rights — 35
1.3 Childhood, children's rights and cultural relativism — 36
1.4 Concluding remarks — 39

2 Introduction to international law sources and institutions — 40

2.1 Introduction — 40
2.2 Sources of international law — 41
    2.2.1 International treaties and conventions — 41
    2.2.2 International customary law — 46
    2.2.3 General principles of law recognised by civilised nations — 49
    2.2.4 Judicial decisions and publicists' writings — 50
    2.2.5 Hierarchy of sources and *jus cogens* — 51
    2.2.6 'Soft law' — 52
2.3 The relationship between domestic and international law — 52

	2.4	International organisations and institutions	55
		2.4.1 The United Nations (UN)	55
		2.4.2 The Hague Conference on Private International Law	70
		2.4.3 The International Criminal Court	72
	2.5	Human rights protection	74
		2.5.1 Global protection – UN machinery	74
3	**The *United Nations Convention on the Rights of the Child***		**86**
	3.1	Introduction	86
	3.2	Background and history	88
	3.3	Failure to ratify the *Convention on the Rights of the Child*	90
	3.4	The Committee on the Rights of the Child	93
	3.5	The reporting process under the Convention	97
	3.6	The Optional Protocols	106
		3.6.1 *Optional Protocol to the Convention on the Rights of the Child on the Sale of Children, Child Prostitution and Child Pornography* (OPSC)	107
		3.6.2 *Optional Protocol to the Convention on the Rights of the Child on the Involvement of Children in Armed Conflict* (OPAC)	109
		3.6.3 *Optional Protocol to the Convention on the Rights of the Child on a Communications Procedure* (OPIC)	111
	3.7	The implementation of the *Convention on the Rights of the Child*	120
		3.7.1 General measures of implementation: articles 4, 42 and 44(6)	121
		3.7.2 Definition of the child: article 1	129
		3.7.3 General principles: articles 2, 3, 6 and 12	134
		3.7.4 Civil rights and freedoms: articles 7, 8, 13–17, 28(2) and 37(a)	155
		3.7.5 Family environment and alternative care: articles 5, 18(1), (2), 9–11, 19–21, 25, 27(4) and 39	170
		3.7.6 Violence against children: articles 19, 37 (a), 34 and 39	179
		3.7.7 Disability, basic health and welfare: articles 6, 18(3), 23, 24, 26, 27(1), (2) and (3), and 33	189
		3.7.8 Education, leisure and cultural activities: articles 28, 29 and 31	204
		3.7.9 Special protection measures: articles 22, 30, 32–36, 37(b)–(d), 38–40	210
	3.8	Concluding remarks	232

4	**Childhood in the digital age**		**233**
	4.1 Introduction		233
	4.2 Children and the internet: an overview		234
	4.3 Children and trends in internet usage		237
		4.3.1 Digital divide	238
	4.4 Gender gap in digital access		240
	4.5 Theories of childhood in the digital context		242
		4.5.1 Risk-based approach	248
		4.5.2 Rights-based approach	265
		4.5.3 UNCRC in the digital era	268
		4.5.4 Digital space and the 'best interests' principle	271
	4.6 Concluding remarks		273
5	**Child labour**		**275**
	5.1 The phenomenon of child labour		275
		5.1.1 Difficulties of definition and types of child labour	276
		5.1.2 Identifying the causes of child labour	280
		5.1.3 The 'poverty and education' thesis	281
		5.1.4 TWAIL, cultural relativism and child labour	284
		5.1.5 The extent and location of exploitative child labour	286
		5.1.6 Forced labour and marriage	291
		5.1.7 Child labour and armed conflict	292
		5.1.8 Covert nature of child labour	293
		5.1.9 Measuring the extent of child labour	294
	5.2 International legal protection of child labour		296
		5.2.1 The *Minimum Age Convention* of 1973	297
		5.2.2 The *UN Convention on the Rights of the Child and Child Labour*	304
		5.2.3 Elimination of the *Worst Forms of Child Labour Convention of 1999*	305
		5.2.4 Other international instruments relating to child labour	313
		5.2.5 The wider role of the International Labour Organization (ILO)	316
		5.2.6 ILO reporting, representation and complaints procedures	319
	5.3 Progressing the elimination of exploitative child labour		323
		5.3.1 Child labour in international law: assessing the role of law and the enforceability problem	324
		5.3.2 Partnership and coordination	325

	5.3.3	Linking trade and labour standards		326
	5.3.4	Corporate social responsibility		328
5.4	Concluding remarks			334

6 International parental child abduction — 335

6.1	International parental child abduction		335
6.2	Introduction to the international legal instruments		338
	6.2.1	*UN Convention on the Rights of the Child*	339
	6.2.2	*European Convention on Recognition and Enforcement of Decisions Concerning Custody of Children and on Restoration of Custody of Children of 1980*	340
	6.2.3	The *Revised Brussels II Regulation of 2003*	341
6.3	The *Hague Convention on the civil aspects of international child abduction* (1980)		344
	6.3.1	Wrongful removal or retention	348
	6.3.2	The duty to make a return order	361
	6.3.3	Exceptions from the duty to make a return order	363
	6.3.4	Exercising discretion	376
6.4	International parental abduction and non-convention countries		380
6.5	The use of mediation in international parental child abduction		383
6.6	Concluding remarks		386

7 Intercountry adoption — 387

7.1	Introduction		387
	7.1.1	Intercountry adoption: the statistics	390
	7.1.2	The sending and receiving countries	393
7.2	The need for international legal regulation		394
	7.2.1	The *Hague Convention of 1965*	394
	7.2.2	Adoption and the *UN Convention on the Rights of the Child*	395
	7.2.3	The Special Commission and the *Hague Convention of 1993*	396
	7.2.4	UNICEF's position	399
7.3	The *Hague Convention on Intercountry Adoption of 1993*		400
	7.3.1	The best interests of the child are paramount	403
	7.3.2	Subsidiarity principle	406
	7.3.3	Safeguards to protect children from abduction, sale and trafficking	407

		7.3.4	Cooperation between States and within States	410
		7.3.5	Automatic recognition of adoption decisions	410
		7.3.6	Competent authorities, Central Authorities and accredited bodies	412
	7.4	\multicolumn{2}{l}{*Hague Conference International Centre for Judicial Studies and Technical Assistance*}	414
	7.5	\multicolumn{2}{l}{Decline in intercountry adoptions}	419
	7.6	\multicolumn{2}{l}{Conflicting perceptions on intercountry adoption}	420
	7.7	\multicolumn{2}{l}{Concluding remarks}	428

8 Child sexual exploitation — 429

	8.1	Introduction		429
		8.1.1	What is child sexual exploitation?	429
		8.1.2	Emerging issues: the trafficking of children and 'modern slavery'	431
	8.2	International action		435
		8.2.1	Global bodies	435
		8.2.2	Regional bodies	440
		8.2.3	Industry	442
	8.3	International instruments		449
		8.3.1	*UN Convention on the Rights of the Child*	449
		8.3.2	*Convention on the Worst Forms of Child Labour* (1999)	451
		8.3.3	*Optional Protocol to the Convention on the Rights of the Child on the sale of children, child prostitution and child pornography of 2000* (OPSC)	452
		8.3.4	*Optional Protocol to Prevent, Suppress and Punish Trafficking in Persons Especially Women and Children 2000*	454
	8.4	States' responsibilities		456
		8.4.1	Criminalisation	456
		8.4.2	Establishing jurisdiction	464
		8.4.3	International cooperation and support	467
		8.4.4	Assisting victims	467
	8.5	Reporting mechanisms		469
	8.6	Concluding remarks		470

9 Children in armed conflict — 471

	9.1	Children and armed conflict: the international law framework	471
		9.1.1 Child soldiering	472
		9.1.2 International human rights law	481

9.2		The United Nations and children associated with armed forces or armed groups	493
	9.2.1	Security Council resolutions	493
	9.2.2	The 'Paris Principles'	498
	9.2.3	The Special Representative of the Secretary-General for children and armed conflict	499
9.3		International courts and tribunals	502
	9.3.1	The International Criminal Tribunal for the former Yugoslavia (ICTY)	503
	9.3.2	International Criminal Tribunal for Rwanda (ICTR)	504
	9.3.3	Special Court for Sierra Leone (SCSL)	505
	9.3.4	International Criminal Court (ICC)	508
	9.3.5	Child soldiers: victims or perpetrators?	512
9.4		Concluding remarks	520

10 Indigenous children — 521

10.1	Introduction	521
	10.1.1 Who are indigenous peoples?	521
10.2	Indigenous peoples: international law and policy	524
	10.2.1 United Nations Human Rights Treaties	524
	10.2.2 *Convention on the Rights of the Child*	527
	10.2.3 *ILO Indigenous and Tribal Peoples Convention*	532
	10.2.4 *United Nations Declaration on the Rights of Indigenous Peoples*	535
10.3	Indigenous peoples and United Nations mechanisms	538
	10.3.1 United Nations Permanent Forum on Indigenous Peoples	539
	10.3.2 The Special Rapporteur on the situation of human rights and fundamental freedoms of Indigenous people	540
	10.3.3 Expert Mechanism on the Rights of Indigenous Peoples	546
10.4	Concluding remarks	547

Bibliography — 549
Index — 583

Preface

Trevor Buck's *International Child Law* has been a core text for teaching this subject area in many Law Schools in the UK and globally. We extend our special thanks to Trevor for giving us the opportunity to continue with this great work. The Fourth Edition stays true to previous editions in structure and content, updated throughout and incorporating a brand new chapter covering the key issues of 'Childhood in the digital age'. This edition also includes new case studies and recent legal developments in the field of international child law. An effort has been made to broaden consulted scholarship to capture diverse views on international law and child law. The aim of this book has been to provide the reader with an accessible, informed, critical and scholarly account of the international law framework relating to children. Chapter 1 (Childhood and children's rights) and Chapter 2 (International law sources and institutions) set the scene with introductions to the key disciplinary perspectives on the nature of childhood, the international movement and theoretical debates about children's rights and a narrative account of international law sources and institutions. Chapter 3 (*UN Convention on the rights of the child*) includes detailed commentary on the articles of this landmark Convention which has established comprehensive normative legal standards of international child law. Chapters 4 to 10 focus on more specialist concerns: Childhood in the digital age; Child labour; International parental child abduction; Inter-country adoption; Child sexual exploitation; Children in armed conflict; and Indigenous children. These chapters examine the social phenomenon under discussion and then provide an account of the relevant matrix of international law and its institutional regimes. Some aspects of child law are consistent throughout each specialist area, most notably the concept of the 'best interests of the child'. The addition of a chapter on childhood in the digital age was necessary to provide a complete picture of the changing nature of childhood itself, and the new globalised context of childhood experiences today. Our hope is that the reader will be provoked to question whether the international law frameworks established have been appropriate responses to the phenomena examined, and how accessible resolutions are. Thanks are due to a number of individuals who have, in different ways, contributed to the production of this edition: in particular to Trevor Buck for his work on the three previous editions of this book and his review of Chapter 4; to

Dr Elizabeth Faulkner (University of Hull) who has updated Chapter 8; and to Dr Rachel Heah (Lancaster University) and Dr Joseph Savirimuthu (University of Liverpool) for their invaluable comments on Chapter 4. A number of staff members at Routledge have been extremely helpful in bringing this project to completion. Our thanks in particular to: Chloe James (Routledge Editorial Assistant), Sarah Hall (copy editor) and the Routledge production team.

Dr Rajnaara C. Akhtar and Dr Conrad Nyamutata
De Montfort University, United Kingdom
April 2020

Table of cases

Australia
Director-General, Department of Families, Youth and Community Care v Rhonda May Bennett [2000] Fam CA 253, HC/E/AU 275 375

Canada
AC v Manitoba (Director of Child and Family Services, 2009 SCC 30 (2009), 26 June 2009 28–9
Canada (Prime Minister) v Khadr, 2010 SCC 3, [2010] 1 SCR 44 231–2
Crnkovich v Hortensius [2009] WDFL 337, 62 RFL (6th) 351, 2008; HC/E/CA1028... 373
W(V) v S(D), (1996) 2 SCR 108, (1996) 134 DLR 4th 481m, HC/E/CA 17 .... 345, 350

European Court of Human Rights and European Court of Justice
Ahmed v Turkey (1997) 24 EHRR 278.. 466
J McB v LE Case C-400/10 PPU HC/E/ 1104, 5 October 2010..................... 350
Neulinger and Shuruk v Switzerland (Application No 41615/07), Grand Chamber, 6 July 2010; (2012) 54 EHRR 31, HC/E/ 1323... 340, 350, 368–9, 370, 371
Šneersone and Kampanella v Italy (Application no 14737/09), 12 July 2011 340
Soering v United Kingdom (1989) 11 EHRR 439 466
Vladimir Ushakov v Russia (Application No 15122/17), Third Section, 18 June 2019 340

India
Lakshmi Kant Pandey v Union of India, A I R 1984 (S C) 469................................ 421

Ireland
HI v MG [1999] 2 ILRM 1; [2000] 1 IR 110; HC/E/IE 284......................... 349
Re H (A Minor) (Abduction: Rights of Custody) [2002] 2 AC 291 351
WPP v SRW [2001] ILRM 371, HC/E/IE 271 350

Japan
2017 *(Ju) No 2015* 373–4

Malawi
Re Justin H: Hansen v Hansen, No 12062 (17th Jud Dist Tenn May 17, 2012) 425
Re Adoption of Children Act (Cap26:01); In Re: David Banda (Adoption Case
  No2 o 2006) (of) [2008] MWHC 243 (27 May 2008) 421–2
*Re Adoption of Children Act CAP 26:01; In Re: CJ (A Female Infant) of C/o Mr Peter
  Baneti, Zomba (Adoption Case No 1 of 2009) ((A Female Infant))* [2009]
  MWHC 3 (02 April 2009) 422–3
Re CJ A Female Infant of C/o PO Box 30871, Chichiri, Blantyre 3 (Msca
  Adoption Appeal No 28 of 2009) [2009] MWSC 1 (12 June 2009) 421

New Zealand
Anderson v Paterson [2002] NZFLR 641; HC/E/NZ 471 349
Fairfax v Ireton [2009] NZFLR 433 (NZ CA), HC/E/NZ 1018 352
RCL v APBL [2012] NZHC 1292; HC/E/NZ 1231 354–7

South Africa
Re A D & Another v D W & Others 2008 (3) SA 183 (CC) (S Afr) 421
Sonderup v Tondelli 2001 (1) SA 1171 (CC) (Constitutional Court of
  South Africa) 372

United Kingdom
AQ v JQ Outer House of the Court of Session (Scotland), 12 December
  2001, HC/E/UK 415 373
Cannon v Cannon [2004] EWCA Civ 1330; [2005] 1 FLR 169; HC/E/UKe
  598 364
Derbyshire County Council v Times Newspapers Ltd [1992] QB 770 54
Director-General, Department of Child Safety v Stratford [2005] Fam CA 1115,
  HC/E/UKe 830 367
Garland v British Rail Engineering Ltd [1983] 2 AC 751 54
Gillick v West Norfolk and Wisbech Area Health Authority [1986] AC 112, [1985]
  3 All ER 402 .... 26–8, 29
In the Matter of C (Children) [2018] UKSC 8, (on appeal from: [2017] EWCA
  Civ 980) 347, 358–61
JSC v Wren (1986), 76 AR 115 (CA) 28
M (Children) (Abduction: Rights of Custody) [2007] UKHL 55, [2008] 1 AC
  1288, HC/E/UKe 937 .... 363, 365, 372, 374, 375–6
NJC v NPC [2008] CSIH 34, 2008 SC 571 375
Nottinghamshire County Council v KB and KB [2011] IESC 48, HC/E/IE 1139 376
O v O 2002 SC 430; HC/E/UKs 507 366
R v Bow Street Metropolitan Stipendiary Magistrate ex p Pinochete Ugarte (No3)
  [2000] 1 AC 147, 276 (House of Lords) 53
R v D [1984] AC 778 336

Table of cases xvii

R v Secretary of State for the Home Department ex p Brind [1991] 1 AC 696................54
Re B (A Minor) (Abduction) [1994] 2 FLR 249; HC/E/UKe 4............................349
Re D (A Child)(Abduction: Rights of Custody) [2006] UKHL 51; [2007] 1 AC
  619; HC/E/UKe 880... 342, 350, 351, 374, 375
Re F (Abduction: Child's Wishes) [2007] EWCA Civ 468..343
Re G (Child Abduction) (Unmarried Father: Rights of Custody) [2002] EWHC 2219
  (Fam); [2002] ALL ER (D) 79 (Nov); [2003] 1 FLR 252; HC/E/UKe
  506 349
Re H (Abduction: Acquiescence) [1998] AC 72 367
Re HB (Abduction: Child's Objections) (No 2) [1998] 1 FLR 564..............................373
Re I (Abduction: Acquiescence) [1999] 1 FLR 778...367
Re J (A Child) (Return to Foreign Jurisdiction: Convention Rights) [2005] UKHL 40,
  [2006] 1 AC 80, HC/E/UKe 801..381–2
Re K (Abduction: Consent) [1997] 2 FLR 212; HC/E/UKe 55...............................367
Re M (A Child) (Abduction: Child's Objections to Return) [2007] EWCA Civ 260,
  [2007] 2 FLR 72 342
Re M (Children) (Abduction: Rights of Custody) [2007] UKHL 55, [2008] 1 AC
  1288, HC/E/UKe 937............................... 363, 365, 372, 374, 375–6, 377–9
Re R (a minor) (wardship: consent to treatment) [1992] Fam 11, [1991] 4 All ER
  177 28
Re S (A Child) (Abduction: Grave Risk of Harm) [2002] EWCA Civ 908, [2002]
  3 FCR 43; HC/E/UKe 469...372
Re S (A Child) (Abduction: Rights of Custody) [2012] UKSC 10, [2012] 2 AC
  257 .... 380, 370–1
Re V-B (Abduction: Custody Rights) [1999] 2 FLR 192, HC/E/UKe 261 350
Re W (a minor) (medical treatment: court's jurisdiction) [1993] Fam 64, [1992] 4 All
  ER 627... 28
Re W (Abduction: Procedure) [1995] 1 FLR 878; HC/E/UKe 37 .... 367, 366
Regulation: Re A (Custody Decision after Maltese Non-Return Order) [2006] EWHC
  3397 (Fam), [2007] 1 FLR 1923 343
S v S, 2003 SLT 344; HC/E/UKs 577...366
TB v JB (formerly JH) (Abduction: Grave Risk of Harm) [2001] 2 FLR 515 372
W v W [2004] 2 FLR 499 372

United States
Abbot v Abbott, 130 S Ct 1983 (2010), HC/E/USf 1029.......................................350
Chafin v Chafin133 S Ct 1017, 185 L Ed 2d 1 (2013); HC/E/US 1206 346
Dana v The Hershey Company et al United States District Court Northern
  District of California Case No15-cv-04453-JCS....................................333–4
John Doe, I; John Doe, II; John Doe, III; John Doe, IV; John Doe, V; and John Doe,
  VI, each individually and on behalf of proposed class members v Nestle, SA; Nestle
  USA, inc; Nestle Ivory Coast; Cargill Incorporated Company; Cargill Cocoa;
  Cargill West Africa, S A; Archer Daniels Midland Company, No 17-55435 DC
  no 2:05-cv-05133- svw-mrw 331–3
Re Gault 387 US 1, 13 (Fortas J) (1967).. 33

Re JS (Private International Adoption) [2000] 2 FLR 638 351
Re: Justin H: Hansen v Hansen, No 12062 (17th Jud DistTenn May 17, 2012) 425
Roper v Simmons, 543 US 551 (2005) 92
State of Washington v Carri Darlene Williams, Court of Appeals-State of Washington Division One No 71193-81-26 February 2015 424
State of Washington v Larry Williams, Court of Appeals-State of Washington Division OneNo 71112-1-I 6 August 2015 424–5
United States v William Irey, UNODC No: USA062 442–3
Walsh v Walsh No 99–1747 (1st Cir July 25, 2000) (US Court of Appeals for the First Circuit) 372
Whallon V Lynn, 230 F3d 450 (1st Cir October 27, 2000); HC/E/USf 388 350

International processes
CRC Communications Procedure
CE v Belgium, CRC/C/79/D/12/2017 116
IAM v Denmark, CRC/C/77/D/3/2016 .... 116, 117–18
NBF v Spain, CRC/C/79/D/11/2017 116–17
International Court of Justice
Application of the Convention of 1902 Governing the Guardianship of Infants (Netherlands v Sweden) (Judgment) [1958] ICJ Rep 55 (aka the *Boll Case*) 50, 63–4
Corfu Channel Case (UK v Albania) (Merits) [1949] ICJ Rep 4 62
Nicaragua v United States (Military and Paramilitary Activities in and against Nicaragua) (Judgement) [1986] ICJ Rep 14 48–9
Legal Consequences of the Construction of a Wall in the Occupied Palestinian Territory, Advisory Opinion of 9 July 2004, [1994] ICJ Rep 136 and 155 65
Legality of the Use by a State of Nuclear Weapons in Armed Conflict, Advisory Opinion of 8 July 1996, [1996] ICJ Reports 226 64
Nuclear Tests (NewZealand v France) (Judgment) [1974] ICJ Rep 457 50

International Criminal Court
Prosecutor v Dominic Ongwen Pre-trial Chamber II No: ICC-02/04-01/15, 23 March 2016 .... 516, 520
Prosecutor v Dominic Ongwen 'Third Public Redacted Version of 'Defence Brief for the Confirmation of Charges Hearing", filed on 18 January 2016 as ICC-02/04-01/15-404-Conf ICC-02/04-01/15' 25 May 2016 .... 516, 518, 519, 520
Prosecutor v Dominic Ongwen Trial hearing Opening Session: Defence Opening Statements Criminal CourtICC-02/04-01/15 18 September 2018 518

Table of international legal instruments

Hague Conference on Private International Law
Guide to Good Practice: Mediation 2012 385
Guide to Good Practice No 1: The Implementation and Operation of the
   1993 Hague Intercountry Adoption Convention 402–3, 416, 417, 419
Guide to Good Practice No 2: Accreditation and Adoption Accredited
   Bodies 2012 .... 398, 413, 418
Hague Convention on the Civil Aspects of International Child Abduction
   1980 .... 44, 45–6, 71, 335, 339, 340,
                                       341, 347, 356, 357, 358–60, 361, 368, 369, 380,
                                       381, 382, 383, 386, 395, 398
    Preamble 353
    art 1 344–5
    art 2 345
    art 3 .... 348–9, 352, 353, 361, 366, 367
    art 3(a) 349, 351
    art 3(b) 350
    art 4 .... 345, 352, 353
    art 5 366
    art 5(a) 349
    art 6 412
    art 7 .... 383, 385
    art 7(c) 367
    art 8 351
    art 10 385
    art 11 345
    art 11(2) 345
    art 11(3) 345
    art 12 .... 361–2, 366, 370, 371, 378
    art 12(1) 362
    art 12(2) 343, 362, 363, 364, 377
    art 13 .... 343, 362, 364–5, 376, 377, 378, 386
    art 13(1)(a) 363

art 13(1)(b) 363, 372, 375
art 13(2) 363
art 13(a) 366, 367
art 13(b) 343, 370, 371
art 15 351–2
art 18 .... 364, 377
art 20 .... 343, 362, 363, 375–6, 377, 386
art 24 46
art 26 46
art 42 45
Hague Convention Concerning the Powers of Authorities and the Law Applicable in Respect of the Protection of Infants 1961 64
Hague Convention on the International Recovery of Child Support and Other Forms of Family Maintenance 2007 .... 71, 397
Hague Convention on Jurisdiction, Applicable Law and Recognition of Decrees Relating to Adoptions 1965 .... 42, 394
    art 2(b) 394
    art 6 395
Hague Convention on Jurisdiction, Applicable Law, Recognition, Enforcement and Co-operation in respect of Parental Responsibility and Measures for the Protection of Children 1996 .... 50, 63, 71, 360, 397
Hague Convention on Protection of Children and Co-operation in respect of Intercountry Adoption 1993 .... 42, 44, 45, 71, 178, 389, 397, 399–400, 402–3, 414, 415–16, 418, 419, 428
    Preamble 406
    art 1 421
    art 1(a) 140
    art 1(b) 407, 410
    art 1(c) 410
    art 2(1) 401
    art 2(2) 410
    art 3 404
    art 4 410
    art 4(a) 404, 408
    art 4(b) 403, 406, 408
    art 4(c) 402, 408
    art 4(c)(3) 408
    art 4(c)(i) 407
    art 4(c)(ii)–(iv) 407
    art 4(d) 408
    art 5 410
    art 5(a) 404, 408
    art 5(b) 404
    art 5(c) 404
    art 6 412

art 7	412, 417
art 7(1)	410
art 7(2)	410
art 7(2)(b)	412
art 8	408, 412
art 9	412
art 9(a)	404
art 10	409
art 11	409
art 12	409
art 13	409
art 14	404
art 15(1)	405
art 16(1)(a)	405
art 16(1)(b) & (c)	405
art 16(1)(d)	403, 405
art 16(2)	405
art 17	405
art 17(c)	411
art 18	405
art 19(2)	405
art 20	406
art 21	406
art 22	413
art 23	410
art 25	411
art 26	411
art 26(1)	411
art 26(2)	411
art 26(3)	411
art 27	412
art 29	408
art 30	404
art 32	408
art 32(2)	396
art 40	45
art 42	397, 398
art 46(1)	42
art 46(2)(a)	42
Hague Convention Protocol on the Law Applicable to Maintenance Obligations 2007	71, 397
Hague Convention on the Settlement of Guardianship of Minors 1902	50, 63–4
Statute of the Hague Convention on Private International Law 1955	70
art 1	70

xxii Table of international legal instruments

International Labour Organization
Abolition of Forced Labour Convention 1957 (No 105) 307
Constitution of the International Labour Organisation 1919 .... 68, 69, 317, 319
    art 19(5)(b) 321
    art 19(6)(b) 321
    art 22 319–20
    art 23 320
    art 24 321
    art 25 321
    arts 26–28 321
    art 26 .... 321, 322
    art 29 322
    art 30 321
    art 31 322
    art 32 322
    art 33 322
    art 34 322
Decent Work for Domestic Workers 2011 (No 189) 220, 313
    art 3(2)(b) & (c) 313
    art 4(1) & (2) 313
Declaration on Fundamental Principles and Rights at Work and its Followup
    1998 .... 305, 306–7, 318, 320, 326
Declaration of Philadelphia 1944 .... 68, 317
Discrimination (Employment and Occupation) Convention 1958 (No 111) 307
Employment Policy Convention 1964 (No 122) 320
Equal Remuneration Convention 1951 (No 100) 307
Forced Labour Convention 1930 (No 29) 291, 307, 322
    art 29 310
Freedom of Association and Protection of the Right to Organise Convention
    1948 (No 87) 307
Indigenous and Tribal Peoples Convention 1989 (No 169) .. 521, 532, 533–5, 547
    Preamble 533
    Parts II to VI 534
    art 1(2) 533
    art 1(3) 533
    art 1(a) 533
    art 2 534
    art 3 534
    art 4 534
    art 6 534
    art 7 534
    art 8(1) 534
    art 15 534
    art 34 534

Table of international legal instruments   xxiii

Indigenous and Tribal Populations Convention 1957 (No 107) 532–3
Labour Inspection (Agriculture) Convention 1969 (No 129) 320
Minimum Age (Agriculture) Convention 1921 (No 10) 297
Minimum Age Convention 1973 (No 138) 220, 296, 297–8, 303–4, 305, 306,
307, 309, 313, 315, 321, 323, 326
    art 1 298
    art 2 .... 302, 304
    art 2(1) 298
    art 2(3) 298
    art 2(4) 298
    art 3 302
    art 3(1) 301–2, 308–9
    art 3(2) 302
    arts 4–7 298
    art 4 299
    art 4(2) 299
    art 5 299
    art 5(2) 299
    art 5(3) 299
    art 6 299–300
    art 7 .... 300, 303
    art 7(3) 300, 301
    art 7(4) 300
    art 8 301
    art 8(2) 301
    art 9 302
    art 9(2) 302
    art 9(3) 302
    art 10 303
Minimum Age (Fishermen) Convention 1959 (No 112) 297
Minimum Age (Industry) Convention 1919 (No 5) 297, 316
Minimum Age (Industry) Convention (Revised) 1937 (No 59) 297
Minimum Age (Non-Industrial Employment) Convention 1932 (No 33) 297
Minimum Age (Non-Industrial Employment) Convention (Revised) 1937
    (No 60) 297
Minimum Age Recommendation 1973 (R146) 302
    para 5 298
    para 7 298
    para 9 302
    para 10 302
    para 12(2) 300
    paras 14–16 303
Minimum Age (Sea) Convention 1920 (No 7) 297
Minimum Age (Sea) Convention (Revised) of 1936 (No 58) 297

xxiv Table of international legal instruments

Minimum Age (Trimmers and Stokers) Convention 1921 (No 15).................... 297
Minimum Age (Underground Work) Convention 1965 (No 123)..................... 297
Right to Organize and Collective Bargaining Convention 1949 (No 98)......... 307
Tripartite Consultation (International Labour Standards) Convention of
    1976 (No 144) 320
        Worst Forms of Child Labour Convention 1999 (No 182)........ 220, 280, 296,
                303–4, 305–7, 312, 313, 315,
                323, 326, 451, 460, 472
            Preamble 306
            art 1 307
            art 2 .... 307, 308, 451
            art 3 .... 278, 307–9, 451
            art 3(a)–(c) 310
            art 3(a) 485
            art 3(b) 451
            art 3(d) 308, 309, 310, 451
            art 4(2) 309
            art 4(3) 309
            art 5 310
            art 6(1) 310
            art 7 452
            art 7(1) 309, 310
            art 7(2) 311
            art 7(2)(c) 311
            art 8 311–12
Worst Forms of Child Labour Recommendation 1999 (R190)................ 295, 309
        para 2 310
        para 4 309
        para 5(1) 295, 309–10
        paras 8–11 310
        para 11 310–11
        para 12 .... 310, 452
        para 12(a) 485
        para 13 310
        para 14 310
        para 15(j) 311
        para 16(b) & (c) 312

Regional International Instruments
Africa
African Charter on Human and Peoples' Rights (Banjul Charter) 1981.... 19, 266
African Charter on the Rights and Welfare of the Child 1990 .... 38, 422, 423,
                440, 472, 482–3, 506, 518
    art 7 267
    art 22 483

Table of international legal instruments xxv

America
American Convention on Human Rights (Pact of San Jose) 1969 19

Asia
Asian Human Rights Charter: A Peoples Charter 1998 20
South Asian Association for Regional Co-operation (SAARC) Convention on Preventing and Combating Trafficking in Women and Children for Prostitution 440

Europe
(i) Council of Europe
Convention on Action against Trafficking in Human Beings 2005 441
Convention on the Adoption of Children 1967 14
Convention on the Adoption of Children (revised) 2007 14
Convention on Contact Concerning Children 2003 14
Convention on Cybercrime 2001 .... 14, 441
    art 9 .... 441, 459
    art 9(1)(e) 459
    art 9(4) 459
Convention on the Exercise of Children's Rights 1996 14
Convention on the Legal Status of Children Born out of Wedlock 1975 14
Convention on the Protection of Children against Sexual Exploitation and Sexual Abuse 2007 .... 14, 441, 453
    art 20 459
    art 25 447
Convention for the Protection of Human Rights and Fundamental Freedoms 1950 .... 14, 19, 26, 33, 54, 340, 375, 440
    art 8 .... 15, 340, 368–9, 462
Convention on Recognition and Enforcement of Decisions Concerning Custody of Children and on Restoration of Custody of Children 1980
.... 14, 340–1, 347

European Social Charter 1961 14
European Social Charter (revised) 1996 14

(ii) European Union
Charter of Fundamental Rights of the European Union 2007
    art 24 343
Council Decision 2000/375/JHA of 29 May 2000 to Combat Child Pornography on the Internet [2000] OJ L138/1 441
Council Framework Decision 2004/68/JHA of 22 December 2003 on Combating the Sexual Exploitation of Children and Child Pornography [2004] OJ L13/44 .... 441, 456
Council Regulation (EU) 2201/2003 (Revised Brussels II Regulation) 339, 341–4, 360, 372, 383
    Preamble 343
    art 10 342

art 11(2) 342, 344, 374
art 11(4) 343
art 11(6)–(8) 343
art 55 384
Directive 2011/92/EU of 13 December 2011 on Combating the Sexual Abuse and Sexual Exploitation of Children and Child Pornography and replacing Council Framework Decision 2004/68/JHA [2011] OJ L335/1 441
Treaty on European Union (Maastricht Treaty) 1992 .... 441, 442

United Nations

2030 Agenda for Sustainable Development 56
Charter of the United Nations 1945 .... 18, 55, 74, 82
    Chp VII 503, 504
    art 1(2) 533
    art 2(1) 324
    art 2(2) 49
    art 2(7) 324
    art 3(1) 66
    arts 9–22 56
    art 13(1) 79
    arts 23–32 57
    art 27 57
    art 51 49
    art 57 60
    art 60 59
    arts 61–72 58
    art 62(2) 79
    art 63 60
    art 68 18–19
    arts 92–96 .... 59, 62
    art 96 64
    arts 97–101 60
    art 100 60
Convention against Torture and Other Cruel, Inhuman and Degrading Treatment or Punishment 1984 .... 84, 89, 527
Convention on the Elimination of All Forms of Discrimination against Women 1979 .... 66, 84, 137, 454
Convention on the Elimination of All Forms of Racial Discrimination 1965 .... 84, 91, 526
Convention on the High Seas 1958 67
Convention on the Law of the Sea 1982 48
Convention on Psychotropic Substances 1971 222
Convention on the Reduction of Statelessness 1961 .... 160, 212

Convention Relating to the Status of Refugees 1951 212
Convention Relating to the Status of Stateless Persons 1954 212
Convention on the Rights of the Child 1989 .... 1, 5, 6, 17, 20–1, 22, 23,
35, 37, 38, 42, 43, 46, 49, 54, 64, 65–6,
71, 84, 86–7, 110, 111, 113, 137, 196,
236, 237, 267, 271, 272, 296, 304, 320,
336, 386, 395, 399, 400, 422, 423–4, 428,
437, 449, 452, 454, 457, 460, 469–70,
472, 481, 506, 518, 524, 547

    Preamble 92, 133, 134
    arts 1–41 268
    art 1 .... 89, 107, 129, 133, 404, 451
    art 2 .... 122, 134, 135, 192, 217, 269, 531
    art 3 .... 29, 30, 116, 117, 134, 140
    art 3(1) 141, 142, 483
    art 4 .... 121, 124–5, 126, 127, 218, 488
    art 5 .... 29, 129, 151, 163, 170–1
    art 6 .... 134, 146, 147, 149, 189, 269
    art 6(2) 35
    art 7 .... 108, 122, 156–7, 160, 161, 162, 214
    art 8 .... 157, 160, 161, 165, 214, 269
    arts 9–10 122
    arts 9–11 .... 338, 340
    art 9 214
    art 9(1) 140, 171, 338, 339
    art 9(2) 171
    art 9(3) 140, 338, 339
    art 10 .... 116, 214
    art 10(1) 171
    art 10(2) 171, 339
    art 11 .... 107, 214, 339
    art 11(1) 171, 339
    art 11(2) 339, 380
    arts 12–17 122
    art 12 .... 29–30, 31–2, 116, 117, 134, 150–1, 155, 213, 270, 342
    art 12(2) 152
    arts 13–17 162–3
    art 13 .... 36, 151, 155, 163, 165, 270
    art 14 .... 29, 36, 89, 164–5, 270
    art 14(1) 165
    art 15 .... 36, 155, 165, 166, 270
    art 16 .... 155, 165, 167–8, 214, 269
    art 17 .... 169, 270, 531
    art 17(1) 528

art 17(a)–(d)	269
art 17(d)	521, 528
art 17(e)	269
art 18	214
art 18(1)	140, 170
art 18(2)	170, 174, 214
art 18(3)	174, 189
art 19	117, 122, 179–80, 183, 188, 214, 248, 269, 271
art 20	165, 214
art 20(1)	140, 171, 214
art 20(2)	171
art 20(3)	171
art 21	89, 107, 140, 172, 177, 178, 395–6, 403, 421, 424
art 21(a)	172, 179
art 21(b)	172, 177, 406
art 21(d)	408
art 21(e)	178
art 22	122, 210
art 22(1)	211–12
art 22(2)	212, 484
art 23	138, 191, 214
art 23(1)	189
art 24	35, 36, 193–4, 214, 423
art 24(1)	189, 315
art 25	171
art 26	36, 189, 214
art 27	35, 36, 217
art 27(1)	189, 202
art 27(2)	174, 202
art 27(3)	203
art 27(4)	171, 214
arts 28–31	214
art 28	122, 165, 205, 269, 495–6
art 28(1)(a)	204, 205, 282
art 29	269, 529, 531
art 29(1)	205, 207–8
art 29(1)(a)–(e)	205
art 29(1)(a)	140, 204
art 29(1)(c)	528
art 29(1)(d)	528
art 30	165, 210, 216–17, 218, 269, 521, 527–8, 531
art 31	204, 208–10, 269, 270
arts 32–36	107, 214
art 32	122, 210, 214, 277, 304, 305

art 32(1) 220
art 32(2) 220
art 33 .... 189, 210, 222
art 34 .... 185, 211, 223, 269, 271, 429, 449–50, 453, 460, 469
art 35 .... 211, 223, 269, 339–40, 449, 450–1, 469
art 36 .... 211, 224–5, 269
art 37 .... 122, 132, 213, 226, 269
art 37(a) 181–3, 211, 229
art 37(b)–(d) 211, 228–9
art 37(b) 229
art 37(c) 123, 140, 143
art 38 .... 89, 109, 211, 230–1, 308, 482, 483, 485, 487
art 38(1) 482
art 38(2) 482, 483
art 38(3) 482, 483, 487
art 38(4) 483
art 39 .... 188, 211, 214, 230, 231, 269, 306, 311, 483–4
art 40 .... 122, 132, 211, 213, 226, 227, 512
art 40(2) 227
art 40(3) 132, 227, 228
art 40(3)(a) 131
art 40(3)(b) 461
art 40(4) 227
art 41 .... 108, 111
arts 42–54 268
art 42 .... 121, 128, 528
art 42(b)(iii) 140
arts 43–45 97
art 43 93
art 43(8) 97
art 44 .... 97, 102
art 44(1) 83
art 44(5) 105, 107
art 44(6) 121, 128
art 45(a) 99
art 45(b) 106
art 45(c) 105
art 45(d) 106
art 49(1) 89
art 51 38
art 51(2) 46, 123
Convention on the Rights of Persons with Disabilities 2006 .... 85, 190, 193
art 3(h) 190
art 7 191

Declaration on the Protection of Women and Children in Emergency and
    Armed Conflict 1974 478–9
Declaration of the Rights of the Child 1924.............................. 21–2, 64, 88, 481
Declaration of the Rights of the Child 1959.......22, 64, 88, 134, 140, 156, 208, 314
Declaration on the Rights of Indigenous People 2007 .... 52, 217, 521, 535–8,
    540, 542, 547
Declaration on Social and Legal Principles relating to the Protection and
    Welfare of Children, with special reference to Foster Placement and
    Adoption, Nationally and Internationally 1986 178
Durban Declaration and Programme of Action adopted at the World
    Conference against Racism, Racial Discrimination, Xenophobia and
    Related Intolerance 2001 140
Forced Labour Convention 1930 (No 29) 291, 307, 310, 322
    art 29 310
Geneva Convention IV: Relative to the Protection of Civilian Persons in
    Time of War 1949 .... 472, 474
    art 3 .... 477–8, 504
    arts 13–26 474
    art 14 474
    art 23 475
    art 24 475
    art 24(3) 476
    arts 27–141 474
    art 50 476
    art 82 476
    art 89 476
    art 94 477
    art 132 477
    art 136 476
Guidelines on Justice in Matters Involving Child Victims and Witnesses of
    Crime 2005 .... 108, 211
Guidelines for the Prevention of Juvenile Delinquency (Riyadh Guidelines)
    1990 .... 132, 226
ILC Draft Articles on the Responsibility of States for Internationally
    Wrongful Acts 2001 67
ILC Guide to Practice on Reservations to Treaties (2011) 67
International Bill of Human Rights 19, 35, 61, 74, 89, 163,
    166, 167, 182
International Code of Marketing of Breast-milk Substitutes 1981 197
International Convention for the Protection of All Persons from Enforced
    Disappearance 2006 .... 85, 161
International Convention on the Protection of the Rights of All Migrant
    Workers and Members of their Families 1990 .... 85, 289–90
    art 29 157

International Covenant on Civil and Political Rights 1966............. 19, 61, 74, 84, 89, 94, 130
    art 1 524
    art 2 134
    art 6(1) 146
    art 6(5) 480
    art 7 182
    art 14(3)(d) 512
    art 17 167
    art 18 164
    art 19 .... 163, 266
    arts 21–22 166
    art 23 22
    art 24 .... 22, 157
    art 24(2) 157
    art 24(3) 157
    art 27 .... 216, 525, 527, 528
International Covenant on Economic, Social and Cultural Rights 1966 .... 19, 61, 74, 84, 89, 537
    art 1 525
    art 2 134
    art 10(3) 22, 315
    art 12 22
    art 13 22
Millennium Declaration 2000 56
Minamata Convention on Mercury 2013 315
    Annexure C 1(i) 316
Optional Protocol of the Convention against Torture 2002 83
Optional Protocol of the International Covenant on Economic, Social and Cultural Rights 2008 19
Optional Protocol to the Convention on the Rights of the Child on a Communications Procedure 2012 .... 36, 45, 93, 106, 107, 116, 188, 271
    Preamble 140
    art 2 .... 112, 140
    art 3(2) 140
    art 4 113
    art 5 .... 36, 112, 113
    art 6 .... 115, 117
    art 7(d) & (e) 114
    art 8 115
    art 9 115
    art 11 115
    art 12 112
    art 12(1) 119

art 12(2) 119
art 12(3) 119
art 13 .... 112, 119
art 13(2) 119
art 13(3) 119
art 13(7) 118
art 13(8) 118
art 14 119
art 16 .... 105, 107
Optional Protocol to the Convention on the Rights of the Child on the Involvement of Children in Armed Conflict 2000 .... 36, 93, 103, 104, 106, 109, 113, 231, 271, 454, 472, 481, 485–6, 494, 518
    Preamble 109, 110, 140, 188, 488
    art 1 .... 110, 486
    art 2 .... 110, 140, 487
    art 3 .... 110, 140, 487
    art 3(2) 487
    art 3(3) 487
    art 3(5) 110
    art 4 111
    art 4(1) 488
    art 4(2) 488
    art 4(3) 488
    art 5 .... 108, 111, 488
    art 6(1) 111, 488
    art 6(2) 488
    art 6(3) 111, 188, 488
    art 7 .... 110, 488
    art 7(1) 488
    art 7(2) 489
    art 8 .... 102, 111
Optional Protocol to the Convention on the Rights of the Child on the Sale of Children, Child Prostitution and Child Pornography 2000 .... 36, 93, 103, 104, 106, 107, 113, 180, 223, 271, 336, 437, 452–4, 457, 460, 470
    Preamble 107, 140
    art 1 107
    art 2 .... 107, 453, 457, 458
    art 2(c) 459
    art 3 .... 456, 458, 459, 466
    art 3(1) 108, 456, 457, 459, 464, 466
    art 3(1)(b) 458
    art 3(1)(c) 459

art 3(2) 456
art 3(3) 456
art 3(4) 466
art 4 464
art 4(2) 464, 466
art 4(2)(a) & (b) 464
art 4(3) 465–6
art 5 .... 465, 466
art 5(1) 466
art 5(2) 466
art 5(3) 466
art 5(4) 466
art 6 .... 108, 448, 467
art 7 467
art 7(1) 467
art 7(2) 467
art 8 .... 108, 140, 449, 468
art 8(1) 468
art 8(2) 468
art 8(3) 461
art 8(6) 468
art 9 108
art 9(3) 188
art 10 .... 108, 448
art 10(1) 467
art 10(2) 188, 468
art 10(3) 108, 468
art 10(4) 468
art 11 .... 108, 111
art 12 .... 101–2, 108
art 12(2) 469
art 13(1) 469
Optional Protocol to the Convention on the Rights of Persons with
 Disabilities 2006
 art 1 190
Paris Commitments to Protect Children Unlawfully Recruited or Used by
 Armed Forces or Armed Groups 2007 498
Paris Principles and Guidelines on Children associated with Armed Forces
 or Armed Groups 2007 .... 232, 498–9, 518
Principles Relating to the Status of Independent National Human Rights
 Institutions (Paris Principles) 1993 .... 128, 490
Protocol Additional to the Geneva Conventions of 12 August 1949, the
 Protection of Victims of International Armed Conflicts (Protocol I)
 1977 .... 472, 479, 518

art 68 480
art 77(1) 479
art 77(2) 479
art 77(3) 480
art 77(4) 480
art 77(5) 480
art 78 480
Protocol Additional to the Geneva Conventions of 12 August 1949, the Protection of Victims of Non-International Armed Conflicts (Protocol II) 1977 .... 472, 480, 482, 518
art 1(2) 481
art 4(3) 480–1
art 4(3)(c) 481
Protocol relating to the Status of Refugees 1967 212
Rome Statute of the International Criminal Court 1998 ..... 43, 72, 231, 486, 512
art 5(1)(d) and (2) 72
art 6 72
art 7 72
art 8 .... 72, 514
art 8(2)(b)(xxvi) 110, 508
art 8(2)(e)(vii) 110, 508, 509, 510
art 12 73
art 13 73
art 15 73
art 17 73
art 26 514
Rules for the Protection of Juveniles Deprived of their Liberty (Havana Rules) 1990 226
Single Convention on Narcotic Drugs 1961 222
Standard Minimum Rules for the Administration of Juvenile Justice (Beijing Rules) 1985 226
r 4 132
Standard Rules on the Equalization of Opportunities for Persons with Disabilities 1993 193
Statute of the International Court of Justice 1945 62
art 38 .... 41, 49, 50, 51
art 38(1)(c) 50
art 38(2) 41
art 59 .... 41, 50
Statute of the International Criminal Tribunal for the Former Yugoslavia 2002 504
Statute of the International Law Commission 1947 67
Supplementary Convention on the Abolition of Slavery, the Slave Trade and Institutions and Practices Similar to Slavery 1956 313–14
art 1(d) 314

Treaty of Versailles 1919 68
Universal Declaration of Human Rights 1948 .... 19, 22, 37, 47, 61,
74, 82, 88, 89
    art 1 19
    art 5 182
    art 12 .... 20, 167
    art 16(3) 20
    art 18 164
    art 19 .... 163, 266
    art 20 166
    art 25(2) 20
    art 26 20
    art 27(1) 524
Vienna Convention on Diplomatic Relations 1961 67
Vienna Convention on the Law of Treaties 1969 .... 42, 67, 123
    art 18 .... 43, 89, 90
    arts 19–23 45
    art 26 43
    art 31 .... 43–4, 272
    art 31(3)(c) 340
    art 53 51
Vienna Declaration and Programme of Action 1993 75
Vienna Guidelines for Action on Children in the Criminal Justice System
    1997 226

Figures and tables

Figures

1.1	The orb web model	12
3.1	*United Nations Convention on the Rights of the Child:* Signatures (140), Ratifications (196), Accessions (47) and Successions (8) by Year	87
4.1	Percentage of under-15 children using the internet, selected countries and territories, 2012–2016	239
5.1	Changes in rates of progress against child labour since 2000	287
5.2	Percentage of children in employment, child labour and hazardous work, 5–17 years age range, globally and in countries affected by armed conflict, 2016	288
6.1	The structure of the Hague Convention of 1980	347
7.1	Estimated numbers of children adopted via intercountry adoption 1948–2010 – total 970,000 adoptions	390

Tables

2.1	International Human Rights Treaty Bodies	83
2.2	International Human Rights Treaty Bodies: communication/complaints procedures	84
3.1	General Comments of the Committee on the Rights of the Child	94
3.2	Numbers of state and individual reports considered by the Committee on the Rights of the Child in 2018 and 2019, under the Convention and the three Optional Protocols	102
4.1	Typology of ICT-related harms	250
4.2	Selected articles of the UNCRC of particular relevance to the digital age	269
5.1	Number and percentage of children in child labour and hazardous work, by national income grouping, 2016	281
5.2	Number and percentage of children in child labour and hazardous work, by region, 2016	288

5.3	Child labour by sector	289
6.1	Outcome of return applications 1999–2015	338
6.2	Reasons for judicial refusal in 2015	362
7.1	International adoption by continent	390
7.2	Top 5 states of origin 2004–2017	391
7.3	Top 5 receiving countries	392

Case studies

Chapter 1

Case study 1.1 27–8
Gillick v. West Norfolk and Wisbech Area Health Authority [1986] AC 112, [1985] 3 All ER 402

Case study 1.2 28–9
A.C. v. Manitoba (Director of Child and Family Services, 2009 SCC 30 (2009), 26 June 2009

Chapter 2

Case study 2.1 63–4
The *Boll Case (1958)*[1] in the International Court of Justice (ICJ)

Case study 2.2 76–9
United Nations: Youth Assembly on 'Malala Day', in New York, 12 July 2013

Chapter 3

Case study 3.1 117–18
I.A.M. v. Denmark (CRC/C/77/D/3/2016)

Chapter 4

Case study 4.1 253–58
London Borough Tower Hamlets v B [2016] EWHC 1707 (Fam)

Chapter 5

Case study 5.1 331–33
Extract from: John Doe, I; John Doe, II; John Doe, III; John Doe, IV; John Doe, V; and John Doe, VI, each individually and on behalf of proposed class members, v. Nestle, S.A.; Nestle USA, INC.; Nestle Ivory Coast; Cargill Incorporated Company; Cargill Cocoa; Cargill

---

1 *Application of the Convention of 1902 Governing the Guardianship of Infants (Netherlands v Sweden) (Judgment)* [1958] ICJ Rep 55 (aka the Boll Case).

West Africa, S. A.; Archer Daniels Midland Company. Appeal from the United States District Court or the Central District of California Stephen V. Wilson, District Judge, Presiding Argued and Submitted June 7, 2018 Pasadena, California No. 17–55435 D.C. No. 2:05-cv-05133-SVW-MRW Filed October 23, 2018 Amended July 5, 2019

Chapter 6

Case study 6.1   354–56
High Court of New Zealand, *RCL v. APBL* [2012] NZHC 1292; HC/E/NZ 1231, per J W Gendall J, Judgment 11 June 2012

Case study 6.2   358–61
Supreme Court UK, Judgement In the matter of C (Children) [2018] UKSC 8, 14 February 2018

Case study 6.3   370–71
In re S (A Child) (Abduction: Rights of Custody) [2012] UKSC 10, [2012] 2 A.C. 257

Case study 6.4   378–79
Re M. (Children) (Abduction: Rights of Custody) [2007] UKHL 55, [2008] 1 AC 1288, HC/E/UKe 937

Case study 6.5   381–382
Re J. (A child) (Return to foreign jurisdiction: convention rights), [2005] UKHL 40, [2006] 1 AC 80, HC/E/UKe 801

Chapter 7

Case study 7.1   415–19
Extract from: Hague Conference of Private International Law, *Report of Mission to Kazakhstan (9–12 May 2011)*, Jennifer Degeling and Laura Martínez-Mora, July 2011, Permanent Bureau: The Hague, Netherlands.

Case study 7.2   426–27
Re Justin H. No. M2013–02517-COA-R3-JV Court of appeals of Tennessee at Nashville Decided May 29, 2015.

Chapter 8

Case study 8.1   445–49
Child sex tourism

Case study 8.2   461–63
Aziz & Others v Secretary of State for the Home Department [2018] *EWCA Civ 1884*

Chapter 9

Case study 9.1   489–93
Extract from: Concluding observations on the initial report of China submitted under article 8 of the Optional Protocol to the Convention on the Rights

of the Child on the involvement of children in armed conflict, adopted by the Committee at its sixty-fourth session (16 September – 4 October 2013), CRC/C/OPAC/CHN/CO/1 (29 October 2013).

Case study 9.2 **516–17**

Extract from: *Prosecutor v. Dominic Ongwen* ICC-02/04–01/15

Chapter 10

Case study 10.1 **541–46**

End of mission Statement by the Special Rapporteur on the rights of indigenous peoples on her mission to Mexico Victoria Tauli-Corpuz 17 November 2017

Chapter 1
Childhood and children's rights

The international law relating to children is best understood by considering at the outset what we mean when we talk about 'childhood' and 'children's rights'. At first sight, these two concepts seem straightforward, but on closer examination they turn out to be contestable notions. 'Childhood' assumes some kind of understanding of what it means to be a child, and, by implication, an adult. 'Children's rights' assumes a background framework of knowledge about 'human rights' of which children's rights can be considered an integral part. To an extent, the project of international law relating to children is one which is predicated on the existence of a universally held definition of 'child',[1] and yet it is self-evident that 'childhood' is experienced very differently by groups of children even within the same nation state. Furthermore, the way in which we perceive childhood and children's rights will have a highly significant bearing on how we view international child law and the international community's approach to legal regulation and standard-setting in this area. This chapter seeks to introduce the reader to these two important concepts.

1.1 Childhood

The following sections include a brief overview of the historical, psychological, sociological and social policy perspectives on childhood. The study of childhood has become a truly multi-disciplinary activity. However, while the focus on childhood tends to be favoured within the academic community, research initiatives that are more highly linked to policy and specific projects have, since the 1990s, tended to concern themselves primarily with child protection (Ennew 2008). Indeed, there are many research centres dedicated to the study of childhood,[2] and the number of 'childhood studies' programmes in higher education has grown.

---

1 The *UN Convention on the Rights of the Child* (1989) defines the child thus: 'For the purposes of the present Convention, a child means every human being below the age of eighteen years unless under the law applicable to the child, majority is attained earlier.'
2 Numerous major UK universities host research centres focused on the study of children and childhood, including the University of Suffolk: www.uos.ac.uk/content/centre-for-study-children-childhood (accessed 20 February 2020), the University of Oxford: www.history.ox.ac.uk/centre-history-childhood (accessed 20 February 2020).

1.1.1 Historical perspectives

As one commentator has observed, '[f]or much of history children have not been of particular interest to academics or policy-makers' (Kelly 2005: 375). However, Ariès's (1962) work was the classic historical study of the notion of childhood and his analysis is often referred to in the literature as simply the 'Ariès thesis'. Ariès examined the iconography in art and literature over several centuries to identify an emerging 'discovery of childhood'. He suggested famously that 'in mediaeval society the idea of childhood did not exist'. He stated that there had been no distinctive vocabulary of childhood, nor any distinct dress or games. He argued that infants below seven years old were recognised as physically vulnerable, but their parents were largely indifferent to them, probably because of the high levels of infant mortality. After seven years of age, the child was simply regarded as another (smaller) adult. By contrast, from about the fifteenth to the seventeenth century, Ariès suggested a transition had occurred in the prevalent notion of childhood: the child was perceived as a significant family member, to be nurtured and protected. Change started, first, in wealthy households where there were increasing concerns for the moral and educational development of children. Children were becoming creatures to be nurtured and reformed by a combination of rationality and discipline. Ariès reinforced his views by pointing to the historical development of education for the young and the establishment of the 'child' as a central figure in the appearance of the 'family', itself a newly developing institution emerging over the centuries. Ariès argued that these new attitudes to children were then transmitted to the bourgeois class where there was additionally concern for the health and hygiene of children as well as their education. The expansion of the school system brought with it a lengthening in the period of childhood.

Some later studies reinforced these views by examining the history of child-rearing practices. For example, Stone (1990) asserted that in earlier centuries high infant mortality had prompted a low level of affection for children by their parents/carers. In the eighteenth century a new, more affectionate style of child-rearing emerged and traditional practices such as wet-nursing, swaddling and excessive punishment declined. However, by the mid-nineteenth century a reaction, caused by the Methodist revival, had set in, whereby the child was perceived as naturally tending towards sinful behaviour and in need of correction by parents and other adults by means of stern discipline designed to break the will (and wilfulness) of a child. This reversion to a more authoritarian family type in turn gave way to a more permissive style in the later Victorian era.

> Only in the closing decades of the Victorian period was there a gradual return to child-centredness and permissiveness caused by a variety of new influences – the decline of religiosity, women's emancipation, family limitation and the new psychological theories of child development. These trends ultimately affected all social classes in the twentieth century, resulting in the small, modern family characterised by high concentration of affection, a

decline in paternal authority, more 'natural' child-rearing practices and more democratic sharing of roles.

(Burnett 1983: 1)

Subsequent commentators have questioned Ariès's thesis and methodology (Pollock 1983), and indeed some of his conclusions do not appear to be sufficiently supported by the evidence. In short, his work:

sparked off a whole series of strictly historical debates: on whether the mediaeval period did in fact have an awareness of childhood, on the key periods in 'the discovery of childhood', on the nature of parent – child relations at various periods, and on the role of the schools to name a few.

(Heywood 2001: 5)

Both Ariès and another historian, Lloyd De Mause, believed in essence that the further one went back in history the worse would be the level of treatment of children. Indeed, De Mause stated that '[t]he history of childhood is a nightmare from which we have only recently begun to awaken' and that '[t]he further back in history one goes, the lower the level of child care, and the more likely children are to be killed, abandoned, beaten, terrorised, and sexually abused' (De Mause 1976: 1–2).

Archard (1993), among others, has provided a carefully crafted deconstruction of Ariès's influential thesis. He points not only to the weak evidential basis but also to Ariès's 'predisposition to interpret the past in the light of present-day attitudes, assumptions and concerns'. Furthermore, he argues that Ariès subscribes (wrongly) to a historical understanding of 'modernity' as a linear progression to moral enlightenment. Instead, Archard argues, one can employ a distinction between a 'concept' and a 'conception' to better analyse Ariès's thesis. The argument, in brief, is that to have a 'concept' of childhood is to recognise that there is a distinction between children and adults. To have a 'conception' of childhood is a specification of what the distinguishing attributes are. Archard concludes that all societies at all times have had a concept of childhood, but there have been a number of different conceptions. Historically, we cannot be confident about the reliability of our knowledge in relation to these conceptions. He therefore concludes that Ariès's thesis is flawed by what he refers to as an 'ill judged leap' from 'concept' to 'conception'.

Archard also provides an interesting conceptual framework to accommodate the examination of different 'conceptions' of childhood. He introduces three elements to the notion of childhood: its 'boundaries', 'dimensions' and 'divisions'. The boundary for childhood he defines as the point at which it ends. He argues that any particular society's conception of this boundary may differ according to its culture. Conceptions of childhood frequently locate the relevant boundary in relation to cultural 'rites of passage or initiation ceremonies which celebrate the end of childhood and beginning of adulthood'; according to Archard, '[t]hese are likely to be associated with permission to marry, departure from the parental home or assumption of the responsibility to provide for oneself ' (Archard 1993: 23).

Conceptions of childhood may also differ according to their 'dimensions'. Archard suggested that a number of perspectives would render a distinction between children and adults; for example, moral, juridical, philosophical and political. Each society will have its own particular value system which may at any one time favour one or more of these perspectives. Sometimes a society sets the legal age of majority according to a view about one or more of these dimensions. A majority age need not necessarily be consistent with the 'boundary' implied by other dimensions. By way of illustration of this point, Archard points to the origins (in Europe) of the age of majority, which was fixed in the Middle Ages by the capacity of a young boy to bear arms and changed as armour became increasingly heavier and thus demanded greater strength to wear it (Archard 1993: 25). If, however, rationality is the key dimension, then the acquisition of reason is a better test of majority age. Similarly, in societies that focus on the overriding importance of sustaining and reproducing life, 'the ability to work and bear offspring is a strikingly obvious mark of maturity' (Archard 1993: 26).

Archard argues that conceptions of childhood will also depend on how its 'divisions' are ordered and managed. There are in most societies a number of subcategories between birth and adulthood. Most cultures recognise a period of very early infancy where the child is particularly vulnerable and deserving of adult care; a point that is consistent with the findings of developmental psychology outlined in the following discussion. Some cultures attach importance to weaning; the point where close maternal care finishes. Some societies put particular significance on the point at which a child acquires speech. Roman law specified three age periods of childhood: *infantia* (child incapable of speech); *tutela impuberes* (pre-pubescent child requiring a tutor); and *cura minores* (post-pubescent young person requiring the care of a guardian prior to attaining majority).

At any rate, the notion of 'adolescence' or 'youth' in the modern conception of childhood is widely recognised as a period usually involving an apprenticeship for the roles to be required of adulthood. Indeed, the inclusion of the 'middle-aged child', that is, the post-infantile seven-year-old to the pre-adolescent 12-year-old, is arguably a key element of the modern conception of childhood. Archard (1993: 27) concluded that:

> any conception of childhood will vary according to the ways in which its boundaries are set, its dimensions ordered and its divisions managed. This will determine how a culture thinks about the extent, nature and significance of childhood. The adoption of one conception rather than another will reflect prevailing general beliefs, assumptions and priorities. Is what matters to a society that a human can speak, be able to distinguish good from evil, exercise reason, learn and acquire knowledge, fend for itself, procreate, participate in running the society or work alongside its other members?

In an influential and controversial work, Pollock (1983) challenged what had become the orthodoxy of Ariès, De Mause and Stone. She argued that the experience of childhood was not as unremittingly gloomy as had been portrayed. Her study was based on her doctoral work which examined over 500 published diaries and autobiographies. She rebutted the notion that there were any fundamental changes in the way parents viewed or reared their children in the period 1500–1900: '[t]he texts reveal no significant change in the quality of parental care given to, or the amount of affection felt for infants for the period 1500–1900' (Pollock 1983: 3).

The controversies in historical research about childhood are not made easier by the difficulties in locating reliable source materials. One commentator puts it thus:

> Ideas about childhood in the past exist in plenitude; it is not so easy to find out about the lives of children. There are sources which can tell us about their numbers in relation to adults, their life expectancy, the ages at which they were likely to start work and leave home and so on, but those seeking to recapture the emotional quality of the lives of children in the past encounter formidable hurdles. The letters and diaries of parents seem to be one way of surmounting the hurdles, but they tend to be written only by the articulate and well-to-do, and in them our view of the child is mediated through the perceptions of the adult. Children themselves have sometimes left behind written materials, but too often what they write in their diaries tells us more about the genre of diary writing and the desires and expectations of adult readers than about the experience of being a child.
>
> (Cunningham 2005: 2)

In essence, what emerges from the historical analyses is that the notion of childhood is a culturally transmitted idea that may have changed significantly over past centuries, though there is little consensus about the detail of how and why these changes in perception have occurred. At the least, this brief survey of the historical perspective of childhood ought to suggest that the aim of universal norm-creation underlying international human rights instruments, such as the *United Nations Convention on the Rights of the Child*,[3] may not necessarily be consistent with the core notion of childhood prevalent in any one society at any one time in history. In recent years there appears to be some renewed academic interest in the history of childhood. Indeed, in 2003, the History Faculty at the University of Oxford established the first Centre for the History of Childhood in the United Kingdom, which continues to promote links between historians and childcare professionals.[4]

---

3 *Convention on the Rights of the Child*, opened for signature 20 November 1989, 1577 UNTS 3 (entered into force 2 September 1990). See generally, Chapter 3 in this volume.
4 Centre for the History of Childhood: available at: <www.history.ox.ac.uk/research/centre/centre-for-the-history-of-childhood.html> (accessed 20 February 2020).

The definition of the 'child' contained in the *Convention on the Rights of the Child*[5] is, in Archard's terminology, a 'boundary' of the conception of childhood. Given the high degree of 'cultural relativity' (see section 1.3 below) inherent in the conception of childhood, it is perhaps surprising that the international community was ever able to agree on this important age limit of 18 years. Equally, the definition contained in article 1 of the *Convention on the Rights of the Child* (see further, section 3.7.2 in this book) does also allow for a majority age of less than 18 years, a result achieved partly by virtue of sensitivity to cultural diversity and in part by the diplomatic awareness that such flexibility would encourage a maximum number of States that could ratify the Convention. International human rights instruments, aimed at achieving a universalist code, are likely to be vulnerable to the criticism that the negotiation and implementation of such agreements will carry the cultural preferences of the most powerful actors responsible for their creation and implementation. If we view the Convention as a paradigm of international norm-creation, then equally we must address carefully the cultural relativist critique (Harris-Short 2001). The issue of cultural relativity is examined in more detail in section 1.3 below.

1.1.2 Psychological perspectives

Sigmund Freud emphasised the significance of an individual's experiences in childhood, and much of his work focused on mental disorders rather than normal functioning. He conceptualised child development as a series of 'psychosexual' stages: oral, anal, phallic, latency and genital. Libidinal desire could be satisfied at each stage, but if not, an individual would be at risk of developing a range of personality and behavioural disorders in later life (Freud 1920). Erik Erikson, much influenced by Freud and also by cultural anthropology, later devised a theory of eight 'psychosocial' stages of development. At each stage, Erikson thought that an individual would experience a conflict that had the potential to become a beneficial or damaging developmental turning-point. In addition to Freud's reliance on universal drives within the psyche to explain development, Erikson also pointed to the way in which an individual's personality could be shaped by the wider society and culture in which that person lived (Erikson 1995).

As we have seen in the previous section, Ariès pointed to the development of education as historical evidence of a major shift in historical attitudes towards the nature of childhood. Similarly, an understanding of the developmental psychology of children has been enhanced by the adoption of universal education, at least in some countries. It is perhaps unsurprising that such an investment of resources is based upon some pre-existing theory of learning. The particular shape of an education system in any society must be based on a view about the ability of children to receive and process knowledge, in other words, cognitive development.

---

5 See n. 3 above.

Piaget (1952, 1960) provided a highly influential analysis of how the processes of thought were structured through his theory of learning. He realised that a child's mind was different from merely being a small version of an adult's mind. In essence, Piagetian theory attempts to explain how humans adapt to their environment via the process of the child's 'assimilation' (taking in new encounters) and 'accommodation' (revising cognitive constructs) of experience. Piaget suggested that the developmental process involved the individual in a search to achieve a balance between assimilation and accommodation. This balance is what Piaget describes as 'equilibrium'.

On the basis of empirical studies, Piaget identified a model of the child's intellectual growth through separate chronological stages. First, the sensory-motor stage (infancy) immediately after birth. In this period, which he asserted lasted until around two years old, the infant's adaptation to his/her environment is shown by motor activity without the use of abstract reasoning. At first, infants use motor reflexes to interact with their environment. The infant relies on seeing, feeling, sucking and touching to learn about his/her environment. Infants eventually learn that their environment is not simply an extension of themselves, and they develop a sense of causation in learning to move an object by hand.

Children acquire the concept of 'object permanence' at about seven months old, that is, an understanding that an object (or person) still exists when not in view. For example, a young infant will lose interest in a toy when it is covered up, but an older infant will actively seek it out. Following an understanding of object permanence, the infant performs motor experiments ('directed groping') and learns how to manipulate objects. An increase in the child's physical mobility allows the child to develop new intellectual abilities. Some symbolic abilities, for example language, are developed at the end of this stage.

Piaget's second 'pre-operational stage' (toddler and early childhood) lasts until the child is around two to seven years old. In this period, a child will acquire language skills, and memory and imagination are developed, but thinking is done in a non-logical, non-reversible manner. This stage is characterised by what Piaget terms egocentric thinking; that is, they will only view the outside world from their own perspective. For example, a three-year-old may well hide behind a chair in the belief that, as s/he cannot see anyone else, no one else can see him/her. Pre-operational children will develop an internal representation of the outside environment that allows them to provide a description of people, events and feelings. Children can be observed using memory and imagination during this stage.

Piaget's third stage, 'concrete operations' (elementary and early adolescence), was said to last for children from around seven to twelve years old. Such children are capable of taking into account another person's point of view and can appreciate more than one perspective at the same time. The beginning of this period is marked by the acquisition of the principle of 'conservation'. This is an understanding that the number, volume, mass, liquid, weight, area and length of objects does not change when the particular configuration of the object(s) is changed. For example, a child will appreciate that two identical lengths of ribbon, one rolled up into a ball and the other laid flat, retain the same length.

Children also acquire the idea of reversibility; that is, some changes can be undone by reversing an earlier action. For example, one can regain the flat ribbon by rolling out the ball. Children become capable of mentally visualising this type of action without the need to see it actually performed. Egocentric thought decreases. A child develops the ability to coordinate two dimensions of an object simultaneously, arrange structures in sequence, and transpose differences between items in a series, and will have a better idea of time and space. During this stage, a child begins to reason logically, but can only think about actual, concrete, physical objects; they cannot yet manage abstract reasoning.

The final stage of Piaget's theory is 'formal operations' (adolescence and adulthood), acquired by children from around 11 or 12 years old into adulthood. Children at this stage will be capable of thinking logically and in the abstract and can reason theoretically, though some people may never reach this stage. Early on at this stage there is a return to egocentric thought processes. However, thinking is not tied exclusively to events that can be observed. The stage is characterised by the ability to construct hypotheses and systematically test these to resolve a problem. In particular, the ability to reason hypothetically or contrary to the known facts, appears. For example, an argument based on the premise that the world is flat could be processed.

The impact of thinkers such as Freud, Erikson and Piaget has been profound. Piaget's theory in particular has had a significant influence in shaping education curricula. The lasting influence of Piaget can be seen in the proliferation of 'Early Childhood Studies' courses available in university education and other departments.[6] One key point to his theory should be noted. This is that a child could only pass from one stage to another when the appropriate levels of maturity and external stimuli were present. The theory thus acknowledges both the importance of the child's biological maturation and the differential influence of the external environment; in other words, 'nature and nurture'. In the absence of good conditions to sustain both, a child is unlikely to progress to his or her fullest potential.

However, subsequent researchers in developmental psychology do not accept Piaget's theory uncritically. For example, the theory does not clearly explain why development from one stage to another happens. The theory largely ignores individual differences in cognitive development and provides little explanation for why some individuals may proceed faster than others from one stage to another. Also, the actual functioning of a person at a particular time may vary considerably in relation to the understanding of spatial, mathematical and other concepts, to the point where placing that individual in one of Piaget's stages becomes artificial. In order to remove some of these weaknesses scholars, known as 'neo-Piagetian'

---

6 A UCAS search in the UK produced 476 such courses available in 2019, an increase from 249 in 2013. See: <www.ucas.ac.uk/students/coursesearch/2013searcheu/> (accessed 10 August 2019).

theorists – for example, Demetriou et al. (2000) – have adapted Piaget's theory to develop new understanding of cognitive and developmental psychology.

Indeed, there is an increasing body of evidence in the last 30 years that young babies, for example, do far more representational 'thinking' than merely the motor reflexes which Piaget underlined at his first 'stage' (Sutherland 1992). Nevertheless, Piaget's contribution has been enduring and indeed the very concept of the cognitive development of the child makes much sense when applied, as in the *Gillick* case (see Case Study 1.1 below) in the United Kingdom, to determine the point at which teenagers can be regarded as sufficiently mature to understand the meaning and consequences of important decision-making which may have significant effects upon their lives. As we shall see, one of the key dilemmas in discussions of 'children's rights' (section 1.2.1 below) is the nature and extent of the child's autonomy across a range of decision-making areas. The insights of developmental psychology have much to contribute towards a more rounded understanding of children's ability to conduct and understand fully the consequences of their own independent action.

1.1.3 Sociological perspectives

In the 1980s and 1990s, academic societies started to pay specific attention to an emerging *sociology of childhood*. For example, in 1998 a research committee of the International Sociological Association was dedicated to the study of childhood.[7]

One explanation for the side-lining of interest in children is their general marginalisation in society. Adult perspectives on children often focus on what children are to become rather than appreciate what they are. Since all children are expected to grow up, there is a tendency to focus on the end product, that is, the adult, rather than to concentrate on the child and the 'here and now' aspects of childhood. Children are often viewed as passive consumers of a culture already established by adults. Society can be seen, within traditional social theory, as maintaining its integrity through a process of 'socialisation'. Individuals are in effect guided into suitable roles via a wide range of institutional and other processes. The notion of socialisation itself involves society's values being lodged into individuals' personalities. Social theory has often recognised the child as particularly in need of such socialisation in order to provide the appropriate induction into the adult world.

However, it is the family that has the expected primary role to ensure that this process of socialising the child is carried out effectively. It is useful in this context to distinguish two different versions of the socialisation process: the deterministic and constructivist models (Corsaro 2017: 7–9).

The deterministic model is based on the idea that the child is essentially appropriated by society, that is, trained into becoming a useful member of society.

---

[7] International Sociological Association: Research Committee 53 Sociology of Children. Available at: <www.isa-sociology.org/rc53.htm> (accessed 20 February 2020).

On the one hand, the child's potential future contribution to society is recognised. On the other hand, the underlying assumption is that without the appropriate application of socialisation the child will remain a threat to the good order of society. The child's role in this conceptualisation is essentially a passive one. Furthermore, there are 'functionalist' and 'reproductive' models contained within this deterministic approach.

The functionalist approach in the 1950s and 1960s emphasised the need to maintain order and balance in society and therefore looked at children in terms of how they can be best prepared to take up useful places in the adult world. Theorists such as Talcott Parsons advocated such an approach and viewed the child as a threat to the intricate balance required to maintain society. Parsons saw the child as a 'pebble "thrown" by the fact of birth into the social pond' (Parsons and Bales 1956).

The child's point of origin, the family, will be the first element to feel the effects of this potential disruption, followed by schools and then other social institutions and processes. Eventually, the child internalises the values, norms and standards of the wider society. A key criticism of the functionalist approach was that the internalisation of the requirements for society's good order could simply be viewed as a sophisticated method of social control. It assumed that the status quo would be maintained. In other words, these socialisation processes were viewed as a means to reproduce social inequalities.

The reproductive model of society therefore tended to analyse the nature of such inequality in a more critical manner and not just assume that the function of society was merely to reproduce itself without improvement or any fundamental change. As regards the impact on children, such an approach takes greater note of the existence and nature of social conflict and inequality. The deterministic approach as a whole can be criticised in that it will tend to overemphasise the outcomes of socialisation and underestimate the active roles played by the individual. Some advocates of the deterministic approach have advanced a behaviourist understanding of childhood, emphasising the value of training in skills needed for functional living and the need for a clear system of rewards and punishment which would determine appropriate socialisation.

In contrast to the notion of society appropriating the child, the 'constructivist' model focuses on how the child appropriates society. The contribution of developmental psychology, in particular Piagetian theory, is particularly important here. The child is conceptualised as extracting information from his or her environment in order to construct their own interpretation of society. Piaget's 'stage' analysis of intellectual development (see section 1.1.2 above) confirms children's differing qualitative understandings of their environment and their interactions with it as compared to adults. Piaget's concept of 'equilibrium' also provides a view of the child as being more active and self-determining than a picture of the child determined by irresistible societal forces. Though Piaget believed there was an inherent tendency for children to compensate for environmental intrusions (he termed this 'equilibrium'), nevertheless, 'the nature of the compensations is dependent on the activities of children in their social-ecological worlds' (Corsaro 2017: 11).

Lev Vygotsky is another significant constructivist theorist who underlined children's active rather than passive roles. He believed that their social development was based on *collective* rather than individual action. He argued that language and other cultural tools are developed collectively by societies over the course of history and are acquired by children in order to actively participate and contribute to that culture. Vygotsky had a notion of 'internalisation' whereby every function in the child's development appeared not only on the social level at first, that is *between* people (interpsychological), but also on the individual level, that is *inside* the child (intrapsychological) (Vygotsky 1962). The following commentary provides a useful illustration of how such a conception can be seen to operate.

> Consider Vygotsky's conceptions of self-directed and inner speech. With *self-directed speech*, Vygotsky is referring to the tendency of young children to speak out loud to themselves, especially in problematic situations. Piaget saw such speech as egocentric or emotional and serving no social function. Vygotsky, on the other hand, saw self-directed speech as a form of interpersonal communication, except that in this case the child is addressing himself as another. In a sense, the child is directing and advising himself on how to deal with a problem. In experimental work, Vygotsky found that such speech increased when children were given tasks such as building a car with construction toys or were told to draw a picture. Vygotsky believed that over time, self-directed speech was transformed or internalized from the interpersonal to the intrapersonal, becoming inner speech or a form of thought. We can grasp his ideas when we think about how we first learn to read. Most of our early reading as young children is done out loud as we read to ourselves and others. Over time we begin to mumble and then to mouth the words as we read, and eventually we read entirely at a mental level. In short, the intrapsychological function or skill of reading has its origins in social or collective activity – reading out loud for others and oneself. For Vygotsky internalization occurs gradually over an extended period of time.
>
> (Corsaro 2017: 14)

In addition, Vygotsky posed a model of development in which children were constantly in between their actual and potential developmental levels (the 'zone of proximal development'), interacting with others in order to acquire more skills and information. Children gradually appropriated the norms and values of society through this collective process of sharing and creating culture. Although constructivist models are capable of providing a picture of the child as a more active participant in society, there are two essential weaknesses with this general approach. First, most constructivist theory focuses on *individual* child development. Even Vygotsky's notion of *collective* action at the interpersonal level becomes obscured with an overemphasis on the intrapersonal level, the process of an individual child's internalisation of culture. Second, the focus is usually on the endpoint of the developmental cycle, the transition from immaturity to adult maturity. Corsaro offers the notion of 'interpretive reproduction' as a theoretical perspective which refocuses attention on collective interactions and children's own creative generation of culture:

> The term *interpretive* captures the innovative and creative aspects of children's participation in society. In fact, . . . children create and participate in their own unique peer cultures by creatively taking or appropriating information from the adult world to address their own peer concerns. The term *reproduction* captures the idea that children are not simply internalizing society and culture, but are actively contributing to cultural production and change. The term also implies that children are, by their very participation in society, constrained by the existing social structure and by societal reproduction. That is, children and their childhoods are affected by the societies and cultures of which they are members. These societies and cultures have, in turn, been shaped and affected by processes of historical change.
>
> (Corsaro 2017: 18)

Corsaro has produced a graphic representation of his model (Figure 1.1). The spokes represent a range of fields that comprise various social institutions. Cultural information flows to all parts of the web along these spokes.

The child enters their culture at the point of origin, the family. Children begin, however, to participate in relations outside the family from an early age, as is represented in the figure by the spiral lines. They 'begin to produce and participate in a series of peer cultures' (Corsaro 2017: 25). There are four distinct peer cultures

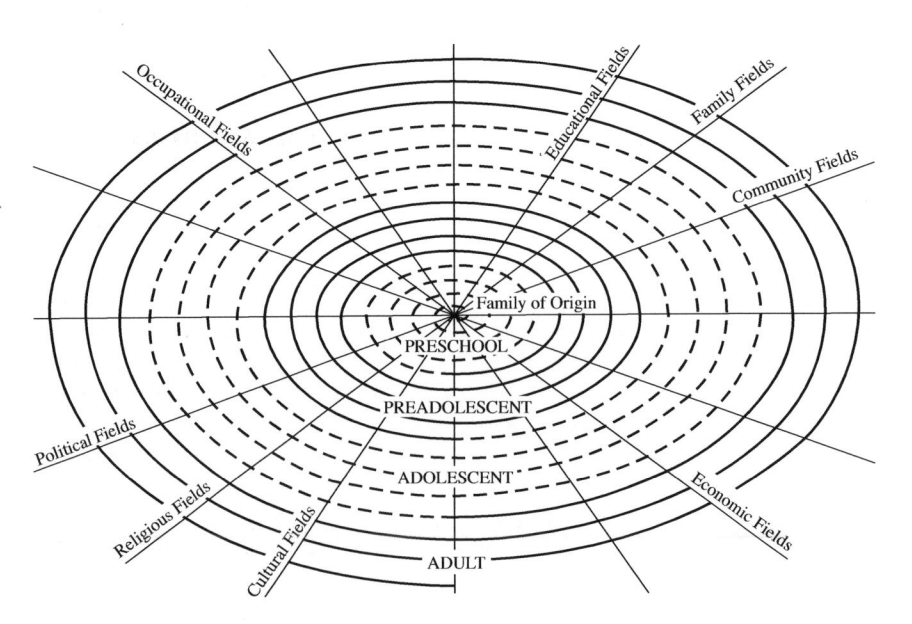

Figure 1.1 The orb web model.

Source: Corsaro (2017: 26).

represented: preschool, pre-adolescent, adolescent and adult. Corsaro argues that these peer cultures are not stages through which children progress. They are not, for the most part, pre-existing structures, but are produced and participated in by the children themselves. It can be seen that one key element of the recent sociological theorising about childhood has been the focus on the child as an active social agent:

> In sociology this has been codified . . . as a call for children to be understood as social actors, shaping as well as shaped by their social circumstances. This represents a definitive move away from the more or less inescapable implication of the concept of socialization: that children are to be seen as a defective form of adult, social only in their future potential but not in their present being. And yet this rallying point of children's agency is embedded in and related to a much wider process through which the individual voices and presence of children is now being recognised and accounted for.
> (James et al. 1998: 6)

Consequently, this approach avoids viewing children as somehow outside of the mainstream of society and also avoids any marginalisation of children by viewing them only as emerging members of the wider community.

Another key theme in the sociological perspective on childhood, sometimes referred to as 'generational order', has been the way in which children are categorised by age for different purposes which does not necessarily reflect children's own needs but instead may be seen as structural requirements in society to maintain social order (Mayall 2003). Consequently, social inequalities are also intimately related to the sociological understanding of childhood. Some sociological work focuses on the accounts that children themselves have of their lives and relations with parents and other adults. Children themselves make important points on questions relating to autonomy and interdependence. Some commentators have called for more attention to be paid to children's own perspectives:

> Whilst Western liberal thinkers have regarded the autonomous, independent moral agent as the highest form of life, children regard relationships as the cornerstone of their lives. It is of crucial importance to them to work with and through family relationships, to care about those who live elsewhere as well as those they live with . . . . Thus any account of how the social order works, in terms of values ascribed by varying social groups to dependence, independence, and inter-dependence, needs to take account of children's views.
> (Mayall 2000: 256)

One commentator has observed that the 'new sociology of childhood'[8] has become 'the dominant theoretical framework, for anyone seeking a sociological

---

8 For example, Corsaro (2017), James and Prout (2015), James et al. (1998), Jenks (1996) and Qvortrup et al. (1994).

understanding of childhood and children' (King 2007: 194). He observes that the new sociology of childhood is distinct from the socialization and development psychology research of previous decades. It can also be seen that this renewed sociological emphasis on the child's competence, autonomy and active agency and 'voice' fits comfortably around the legal-oriented perspective of 'children's rights' which is examined in further detail in section 1.2.1 below. Indeed, as King observes, 'One of the difficulties faced by the new sociology of childhood has been that of establishing a clear demarcation line between what claims to be a new theoretical understanding of children and the discourse of children's rights' (King 2007: 194).

1.1.4 Social policy perspectives

The way in which the concept of childhood has been viewed historically, the theories of child development, and the constructivist account of childhood from the sociological perspective, discussed above, cannot provide a complete picture without an understanding of society's approach to formulating and developing social policy in child-related matters. To an extent, the approach to building social policy relating to children will reflect a society's distilled understanding (derived from many disciplines) of how children fit into the overall order of that society. An understanding of international child law is enhanced by an ability to locate it within the context of the wider social policy framework at the international, regional or national level. At the international level, this can be identified in the programmes pursued by the United Nations, for example, via the United Nations Children's Fund (UNICEF) (see section 2.4.1.2 in this book). At the regional level; in Europe for example one needs to look at the key institutions – the Council of Europe and the European Union (EU) – to determine how policy is determined and delivered. Indeed, there are indications that both these latter institutions are becoming active participants in progressing child policy. The Council of Europe has issued a number of conventions related to family and child matters.[9] The EU

---

9 *Convention for the Protection of Human Rights and Fundamental Freedoms*, opened for signature 4 November 1950, CETS No. 005 (entry into force 3 September 1953); *European Social Charter*, opened for signature 18 October 1961, CETS No. 035 (entry into force 26 February 1965); *European Convention on the Adoption of Children*, opened for signature 24 April 1967, CETS No. 058 (entry into force 26 April 1968); *European Convention on the Legal Status of Children born out of Wedlock*, opened for signature 15 October 1975, CETS No. 085, (entry into force 11 August 1978); *European Convention on Recognition and Enforcement of Decisions concerning Custody of Children and on Restoration of Custody of Children*, opened for signature 20 May 1980, CETS No. 105 (entry into force 1 September 1983); *European Convention on the Exercise of Children's Rights*, opened for signature 25 January 1996, CETS No. 160 (entry into force 1 July 2000); *European Social Charter* (revised), opened for signature 3 May 1996, CETS No. 163 (entry into force 1 July 1999); *Convention on Cybercrime*, opened for signature 23 November 2001, CETS No. 185 (entry into force 1 July 2004); *Convention on Contact concerning Children*, opened for signature 15 May 2003, CETS No. 192 (entry into force 1 September 2005); *Convention on the Protection of Children against Sexual Exploitation and Sexual Abuse*, opened for signature 25 October 2007, CETS No. 201 (entry into force 1 July 2010); *European Convention on the Adoption of Children (Revised)*, opened for signature 25 October 2007, CETS No. 202 (entry into force 1 July 2010).

has in the past sidelined child-related issues on the basis that they are not directly related to the overall EU project of the single market. However, this appears to be changing.

> In recent years, the pendulum has swung from a steadfast resistance on the part of the EU and nation States to EU intervention in children's rights, towards a growing eagerness to engage the institutions in a range of issues affecting children. Indeed, the broadening scope of EU activity has made it increasingly difficult to justify maintaining a hands off approach; all aspects of EU law and policy have a direct or indirect impact on children's lives such that it is no longer a question of why the EU should be enacting child-focused provision, but rather, what it should be doing to minimise the adverse effects of EU law and policy for children.
>
> (Stalford and Drywood 2009: 170–1)

Finally, at the national level, government activity in the relevant ministries, in addition to local government organs and voluntary agencies, will implement policy and feedback both strategic and operational lessons learned from such implementation.

It would appear that a key driver of social policy formulation in relation to children is a society's dominant perception of the *State – family* relationship. Fox Harding (1996) has described seven potential models describing this relationship. At one end of this typology there is an authoritarian model, where the State sets out to compel and prohibit certain family behaviour, thereby severely limiting personal freedom. At the other end there is a laissez-faire model, where State intervention is minimal and where family life is seen as a private matter unsuitable for legal intervention. It is arguable that at present the British government, for example, best reflects one of Fox Harding's models located between these two extremes, in which the state will substitute for and support families when they fail. In this model the State recognises that, in the normal course of affairs, the family should be left alone and is the best place for children to be raised. However, when the family breaks down a State duty arises to mitigate the resulting damage, protect family members and support the formation of a substitute family, for example, by arranging an adoption. Indeed, this approach is probably comparable to the position in several other European States and elsewhere. The way in which the right to respect for private and family life, home and correspondence in the *European Convention on Human Rights*[10] (ECHR) is drafted, and its practical operation, are based on the assumption that the individual is in need of protection from arbitrary interference by the State and therefore any State interference must be justified on specified grounds. It can be seen that those grounds in effect may describe circumstances where private and family life have become dysfunctional and therefore

---

10 *Convention for the Protection of Human Rights and Fundamental Freedoms*, opened for signature 4 November 1950, CETS No. 005 (entry into force 3 September 1953), art. 8.

justify a higher degree of State involvement, subject always to the proportionality principle that requires the particularities of State interference to be commensurate with the overall aims of that interference.

In countries where this type of State – family relationship prevails, the social policies in relation to children have tended to focus on interventions deemed necessary to address situations where families fail. The classic example is where parents, for a variety of reasons, are no longer perceived as capable or available to look after their children properly. Consequently, in many countries child policy has often tended to gravitate towards a concentration on the State's social services for children. A comparable child welfare approach is also found in the education and health sectors. In these sectors, the State only intervenes, at least with coercive techniques, when clear dysfunctions are evident.

Furthermore, social policy relating to children is often viewed as either 'welfarist' or 'rights-based', though these two approaches are not necessarily mutually exclusive. The former usually refers to an underlying policy aimed at protecting children who are seen as vulnerable members of society in need of guidance and control. The role of parents, schools, social services and the State is to protect, nurture and provide fulfilling opportunities for children's development. Rights-based policy is designed to support children's own participation in decision-making and is based on a conception of children having distinct rights that can be asserted, both morally and legally. As we have seen, this approach also very much resonates with the dominant sociological image of the child as a competent, autonomous and active social agent. The dichotomy in current debates between welfarist and rights-based policy should not hide other complexities of child welfare policy and the subtle changes in perception of the acceptability of State intervention in the family. For example, Hendrick showed, in an examination of British child welfare, that there was a shift in around the 1870s 'from a simple concern with child reformation and rescue, usually by placing children in either philanthropic or Poor Law institutional care, to a far more complex notion and practice of welfare' (Hendrick 1997: 41).

The precise boundaries of State intervention also depend on the way in which the major social problems involving children are perceived. If the physical, emotional or sexual abuse of children is regarded as a manifestation of the individual pathology of the abuser, then detection, treatment and/or punishment of the offender are likely to be of central concern in social policy initiatives. On the other hand, if child abuse can be explained to an extent by a social structure that harbours poverty and inequality, then other initiatives are required.

Child protection policy that is based on intervention only in circumstances where the family unit has broken down obviously raises issues about the extent of family dysfunction that might justify such intervention, for example by means of family care and supervision orders.[11] In addition, our understanding of the

---

11 In some countries the legal threshold test that will trigger state power to take a child into care is a 'significant harm' formulation: e.g. in the United Kingdom's Children Act 1989, s.31(2).

background State – family configuration will also impact upon the decision-making involved in placing children once they are ingested into the public care system. Consistently with the standards about the family environment set out in the *Convention on the Rights of the Child* (1989) (see section 3.7.5 in this book), planning the child's future will take place initially on the understanding that the ultimate aim is to rehabilitate the family unit. Where this is not possible 'permanency planning' will follow, that is, placing the child with a new adoptive family. However, such decision-making is of course fraught with difficulties; in what circumstances does the underlying aim of rehabilitation become a hopeless cause and the alternative of adoption a realistic one?

At the international level, a significant landmark in setting social policy goals was the adoption by the United Nations General Assembly of the *Sustainable Development Goals* (SDGs) in September 2015.[12] The 17 SDGs and 169 targets commit all countries and all stakeholders to act on eradicating poverty, including extreme poverty, as a means of shifting the world to a sustainable and resilient path. Of the 169 targets, 44 are child-related indicators. As a result, the SDGs have particular relevance in providing a broad framework for child policy formulation. For example: SDG 1 (end poverty in all its forms everywhere) aims to 'reduce at least by half the proportion of men, women and children of all ages living in poverty'; SDG 4 (ensure inclusive and equitable quality education and promote lifelong learning opportunities for all) aims to 'ensure that all girls and boys have access to quality early childhood development, care and pre-primary education so that they are ready for primary education'; SDG 5 (achieve gender equality and empower all women and girls) aims to '[e]liminate all forms of violence against all women and girls in the public and private spheres, including trafficking and sexual and other types of exploitation'.

UNICEF undertakes important development and other work for children and reports annually on the state of the world's children (see section 2.4.1.2 in this book). A recent report, for example, focuses on tracking progress of the child-related indicators in the SDGs (UNICEF 2019).

It may often be difficult to identify clearly what is the social policy of a particular community towards its children. Sometimes this is precisely because the policy, if it exists at all, is relatively incoherent and uncoordinated. As we shall see, the 'concluding observations' emanating from the Committee on the Rights of the Child (section 3.4 in this book) in response to States parties' reports are full of such criticisms. States parties' reports submitted to the Committee and the latter's 'concluding observations' are a useful source of information about a State's policy on child-related matters. Another informative source is the official documentation, along with critical commentary from non-governmental organisations (NGOs) and academic commentary.

---

12 UNGA Res 70/1 (21 October 2015) UN Doc. A/RES/70/1, *Transforming our World, the 2030 Agenda for Sustainable Development*. The General Assembly (see section 2.4.1 below) is the chief deliberative, policy-making and representative organ of the United Nations.

1.2 Human rights

Children's rights can be properly understood only in the context of the wider human rights framework. The devastating impact of the Second World War and the founding of the United Nations in its aftermath have been the most recent modern inspiration behind the human rights movement in the twentieth century. Early legal codes in medieval times, which appear to include 'rights', on closer inspection turn out merely to reflect how powerful groups in that society at that time were realigning themselves. Thus, the *Magna Carta* (1215)[13] in England, for example, is concerned more with the privileges of the barons and Church – State relationships than with matters of common humanity. Similarly, the English *Bill of Rights* in the seventeenth century[14] set out the ground rules for a new constitutional settlement between King and Parliament. Philosophers in the eighteenth and nineteenth centuries generated thinking about 'natural rights' and 'natural law', that is, the rights attached to a human by virtue of nature, rather than by status or any other classification. The American (1776) and French (1789) Revolutions drew on such ideas for their inspiration. The *US Declaration of Independence* (4 July 1776) famously stated that 'we hold these truths to be self-evident; . . . that all men are created equal, that they are endowed by their Creator with certain unalienable Rights, that among these are Life, Liberty and the pursuit of Happiness.' John Locke (1632–1704), the English philosopher, believed there was a natural-law right to life, liberty and property. The French Republic produced its *Declaration of the Rights of Man and of Citizens* (26 August 1789) and the *US Constitution and Bill of Rights* (15 December 1791) followed shortly after.

In the nineteenth century a number of recognisable human rights issues were becoming increasingly controversial, for example, slavery, serfdom, bad working conditions and child labour. Social movements sprang up in response; for example, labour unions, racial and religious minority groups, women's rights and national liberation movements. The idea that every human being was equally deserving of respect and dignity and could be regarded as a right holder was emerging. Individuals were recognised as capable of asserting rights against other individuals and the State and governments had a duty to respect, promote and protect such rights.

The political consensus achieved by the Allies in the immediate post-war period allowed the conditions necessary for a synthesis of these ideas to emerge. There are several references in the *United Nations Charter* of 1945[15] to human rights, in particular in the preamble, where it is stated that the peoples of the United Nations are determined 'to reaffirm faith in fundamental human rights, in the dignity and worth of the human person, in the equal rights of men and women and of nations large and small'. Article 68 of the *Charter* required the UN's Economic and Social

---

13 Confirmed and reissued in the reign of King Edward I, Magna Carta 1297, c.9.
14 1688 (c.2) 1 Will and Mar Sess 2.
15 *Charter of the United Nations*, 24 October 1945, 1 UNTS XVI.

Council (ECOSOC) to set up a UN Commission on Human Rights (UNCHR).[16] Its first task, through the chairmanship of Eleanor Roosevelt, was to produce an International Bill of Human Rights. It was decided that this should be in the form of a Declaration (not binding in international law) rather than a binding Treaty. It was envisaged that the document should be short, inspirational and accessible, and would be followed at a later date with more detailed (and binding) treaty provisions. The result was the *Universal Declaration of Human Rights of 1948* (UDHR).[17] Article 1 stated that '[a]ll human beings are born free and equal in dignity and rights. They are endowed with reason and conscience and should act towards one another in a spirit of brotherhood.' Eighteen years later the (binding) treaty provisions appeared in the form of the *International Covenant on Civil and Political Rights of 1966* (ICCPR) and the *International Covenant on Economic, Social and Cultural Rights of 1966* (ICESCR).[18] The ICCPR and the ICESCR together with the (non-binding) UDHR are now collectively referred to as the *International Bill of Rights*. The two international covenants reflect respectively the so-called 'first generation' (civil and political) and 'second generation' (economic, social and cultural) rights. Human rights scholars have questioned the justiciability of the latter type of rights as they necessarily vary according to the resources available to State authorities. Following the adoption of an *Optional Protocol* that established a communication/complaint procedure under ICESCR[19] in 2008 'it became more difficult to sustain objections to the justiciability of economic, social and cultural rights' (Buck and Wabwile 2013: 207). This approach is consistent with the general view that human rights are: 'interdependent', i.e. the full range of rights constitutes a complementary framework in which the exercise of one right affects the exercise of others; and the rights are 'indivisible', i.e. each individual right is equally important – there should be no 'hierarchy' of rights.

Despite its formal non-binding status, the UDHR has become the accepted universal standard of international human rights. It has almost certainly become part of what is termed 'international customary law' (see section 2.2.2 below). It has inspired similar human rights instruments to be produced at the regional level. For example, the *European Convention on Human Rights* (Rome, 1950), the *American Convention on Human Rights* (the 'Pact of San Jose', Costa Rica, 1969) and the *African Charter on Human and Peoples' Rights* (the 'Banjul Charter', Nairobi, 1981). The 50th

---

16 The UNCHR was replaced by a United Nations Human Rights Council (UNHRC) in 2006: see section 2.5.1.1 below.
17 UN General Assembly, *Universal Declaration of Human Rights*, 10 December 1948, 217 A (III). The UDHR was adopted by the then 56 members of the United Nations; the vote was unanimous, although eight nations chose to abstain.
18 *International Covenant on Civil and Political Rights*, opened for signature 16 December 1966, 999 UNTS 171 (entered into force 23 March 1976); *International Covenant on Economic, Social and Cultural Rights*, opened for signature 16 December 1966, 993 UNTS 3 (entered into force 3 January 1976).
19 *Optional Protocol of the International Covenant on Economic, Social and Cultural Rights*, opened for signature 10 December 2008, UN Doc. A/RES/63/117 (entered into force 5 May 2013).

anniversary of the UDHR was celebrated by the adoption of the *Asian Human Rights Charter: A Peoples Charter* (Kwangju, South Korea 1998). Individual countries too are increasingly incorporating these now well-known human rights standards into their own domestic law.[20]

Some of the provisions of the UDHR relate to the family and children. Article 12, for example, states that '[n]o one shall be subjected to arbitrary interference with his privacy, family, home or correspondence, nor to attacks upon his honour and reputation. Everyone has the right to the protection of the law against such interference or attacks.' Article 16(3) states that '[t]he family is the natural and fundamental group unit of society and is entitled to protection by society and the State.' Article 25(2) interestingly provides that '[m]otherhood and childhood are entitled to special care and assistance. All children, whether born in or out of wedlock, shall enjoy the same social protection.' Article 26 contains a right to education which should be free and compulsory at the elementary stage and 'directed to the full development of the human personality and to the strengthening of respect for human rights and fundamental freedoms'.

The historical development of human rights outlined in the preceding discussion and the emergence of the UN 'Treaty bodies' (section 2.5.1.2 and Table 2.1) that now deal with particular categories of human rights issues, including the Committee on the Rights of the Child supervision and monitoring of the *Convention on the Rights of the Child* (1989), have raised the issue of how far *children's* rights should be differentiated from the general international human rights instruments. The problem with the latter is that they have tended to focus on the rights of *parents*. There may also be obligations on parents and institutions towards children but these are likely to be unenforceable by children. Arguably, the recognition of children's rights may lead to an assumption that children have different rights from adults, with different justifications, rather than accommodating children as an integral part of the same human rights protection regime. However, it would seem preferable to regard children as part of the human family with each individual equally entitled to rights. Any special or additional formulations of human rights would need to be premised on children's particular vulnerability or inexperience (Sawyer 2006: 13).

This reinforces the point that in order to be effective, any instrument that purports to provide for children must be child-centred and independent of adult bias. Hence the view that a more appropriate way forward in providing for children would be to grant them defined 'rights'; a trend that became increasingly popular following the end of the First World War and which eventually led to a fully-fledged code of children's rights in the form of the *Convention on the Rights of the Child* (1989).

As will be seen in Chapter 3 below, the *Convention on the Rights of the Child* contains some particular principles customised to apply to children (e.g. the 'best interests'

---

20 For example, the UK's Human Rights Act in 1998 and the Australian Capital Territory produced Australia's first Bill of Rights in its Human Rights Act of 2004.

and 'participation' principles) as distinct to adults and there are a number of rights that resonate with general human rights instruments but are formulated in a way that provides a child-centred focus or context to those rights. It is interesting to note that the same arguments raised in opposition to the *Convention on the Rights of the Child* on the basis that general international human rights law applied equally to the whole human family irrespective of their age, continue to be revisited in relation to the on-going debate in the UN about whether to adopt a UN 'Convention on the Rights of Older Persons'.[21] The delineation of a meaningful category of 'older persons' is arguably, even more difficult than the definition of the 'child' in the *Convention on the Rights of the Child*. Could such a Convention 'age-proof' human rights in the way that the *Convention on the Rights of the Child* provides an attempt to 'child-proof' human rights?

1.2.1 Children's rights

Even before the modern development of international human rights law, as outlined in the preceding section, the League of Nations (1919–1946) had shown an interest in protecting and providing welfare services for children, in particular those orphaned and displaced following the First World War. In 1919 a Committee for the Protection of Children was set up by the League of Nations. Eglantyne Jebb (1876–1928), the founder of the British Save the Children Fund and the Save the Children International Union in Geneva, was an early campaigner for children and succeeded in getting the League of Nations to adopt a *Declaration on the Rights of the Child* (1924).[22]

This was in fact the first declaration of human rights adopted by any inter-governmental organisation and preceded the UDHR by 24 years. The *Declaration* was reaffirmed by the League of Nations in 1934. It contains five principles directed to creating the conditions necessary for children to be protected and to enable them to develop into citizens who will contribute to their communities. However, the text of this document implies that the child is a *passive* object of concern rather than as an *active* subject capable of asserting rights against others.

The intention behind the *Declaration* of 1924 was not to create a binding treaty but merely to create guiding principles for those working in international child welfare. The *Declaration* reflects a paternalistic view of child welfare where adults are clearly in total control of children's destinies. There is no suggestion here about welcoming or encouraging children's participation in decision-making or other aspects of children's self-determination.

---

21 *Strengthening Older People's Rights: Towards a UN Convention: A resource for promoting dialogue on creating a new UN Convention on the Rights of Older Persons*. Available at: <https://social.un.org/ageing-working-group/documents/Coalition%20to%20Strengthen%20the%20Rights%20of%20Older%20People.pdf> (accessed 20 February 2020).
22 *Geneva Declaration of the Rights of the Child*, adopted 26 September 1924, League of Nations OJ Spec. Supp. 21, at 43 (1924).

The *Declaration* was revisited and revised by the United Nations in the form of the *Declaration of the Rights of the Child* (1959).[23] A much more robust language of rights is deployed in this *Declaration*. It sets out ten principles in a more expanded form than the 1924 document. Indeed, some commentators have regarded the *Declaration* of 1959 as the 'conceptual parent' to the *UN Convention on the Rights of the Child* of 1989 (Van Bueren 1998: 14). Although the UDHR contains some material specifically addressed to children, there are more specific formulations of rights directly affecting family and child issues contained in the ICCPR and ICESCR.

The ICCPR contains a robust right of the child to be protected from discrimination, a right to a name and nationality:

1 Every child shall have, without any discrimination as to race, colour, sex, language, religion, national or social origin, property or birth, the right to such measures of protection as are required by his status as a minor, on the part of his family, society and the State.
2 Every child shall be registered immediately after birth and shall have a name.
3 Every child has the right to acquire a nationality.[24]

The status of the family as 'the natural and fundamental group unit of society' referred to in the UDHR is reaffirmed in article 23, which also sets out a principle of equality of spouses during marriage and at dissolution and that '[i]n the case of dissolution, provision shall be made for the necessary protection of any children.' The ICESCR contains a strongly worded provision giving protection to children against economic and social exploitation, in particular setting out standards to regulate child labour. State parties to the Covenant recognise that, *inter alia*:

> Special measures of protection and assistance should be taken on behalf of all children and young persons without any discrimination for reasons of parentage or other conditions. Children and young persons should be protected from economic and social exploitation. Their employment in work harmful to their morals or health or dangerous to life or likely to hamper their normal development should be punishable by law. States should also set age limits below which the paid employment of child labour should be prohibited and punishable by law.[25]

Rights to health (article 12) and education (article 13) are also included in detailed formulations in the ICESCR.

In short, the modern human rights movement in the post-war era has involved an increased concern for the rights of children. This has been reflected both in the

---

23 *Declaration of the Rights of the Child*, GA res. 1386 (XIV), 14 UN GAOR Supp (No 16) at 19, UN Doc A/4354 (1959).
24 *International Covenant on Civil and Political Rights*, opened for signature 16 December 1966, 999 UNTS 171 (entered into force 23 March 1976), art. 24.
25 *International Covenant on Economic, Social and Cultural Rights*, opened for signature 16 December 1966, 993 UNTS 3 (entered into force 3 January 1976), art. 10(3).

development of the more robust textual formulations found in the two International Covenants of 1966 and in the further development of UNICEF and other inter-governmental organisations and NGOs working for improvements in children's lives. The account of how the UN's International Year of the Child in 1979 eventually led to the production of the *Convention on the Rights of the Child* in 1989, which has become, in effect, the template for the international legal rights of the child, is taken up in more detail in section 3.2 below. For the purposes of this Chapter, however, it is useful to consider further what 'children's rights' means.

There is now a considerable academic literature relating to the subject of children's rights. As Fortin (2009: 3) notes, the literature gravitates around three themes: how to identify children's rights; how to balance one set of rights against another in the event of a conflict between them; and how to mediate between children's rights and those of adults.

1.2.1.1 Theories of children's rights

It is useful to make a preliminary distinction between positive 'legal rights' and 'moral rights', the latter being ones that are recognised by a moral theory.[26] Most States readily acknowledge children's legal rights, as evidenced by the near-universal ratification of the *Convention on the Rights of the Child*. The controversy about children's rights usually gravitates around more fundamental questions whether there is a credible account of children's moral rights. Furthermore, '[t]hat children have 'positive' rights does not then settle the question of whether they do or should have moral rights' (Archard 2010).

There are two fundamental, moral philosophical debates that have exercised theorists who have grappled with the notion of children's rights. First, there is a 'choice' or 'will' theory of rights.[27] This theory assumes that the person asserting those rights will have a choice as to when and whether to exercise them. As children at various levels of maturation will not be likely to have the capacity or competence to exercise such choices in all circumstances, it has been questioned whether they can properly be described as having 'rights' at all. If rights are basically premised on the notion that the right holder must be capable and competent to make such choices, then it might follow that, at least in circumstances where it is clear that a child would lack competence to choose, that child could not be properly described as a right holder. There are a number of difficulties with this approach. As Fortin (2009: 12) remarks, '[t]he assertion that children, who are too young and incompetent to claim rights, therefore have no rights, has an unattractive logic.' Indeed, if one applied the same approach to, for example, the position of a severely mentally ill or disabled adult, the 'unattractiveness' of the logic is exposed. In order to circumnavigate such a stark conclusion, it could be conceded

---

26 See generally Freeman (1983: ch. 2); Fortin (2009: 3–30); Archard (2010).
27 Advocates of the 'choice' theory include: Feinberg (1980); Hart (1984); Sumner (1987); and Steiner (1994).

that there may be correlative duties on parents and other adults or institutions to provide a remedy for children (or severely mentally ill or disabled adults) who are not competent to make their own choices. Put another way, the choice theory can still be seen as delivering rights for children if one accepts that adults act in effect as proxies for the choices a child would make if endowed with sufficient capacity or competence. Thus a child's right might obtain some, albeit indirect, recognition from the existence of such correlative duties placed on adults in respect of (incompetent) children. However, this theory can be criticised on the basis that it over-emphasises the existence of remedies. MacCormick (1982), for example, argues that it is only because a child has a right to care and nurture that the legal imposition on adults and institutions to provide such protection is justified; the existence of the right presupposes the remedy. In addition, the will/choice theory fails to provide children with a secure standpoint in the face of parents or institutions who are failing in their correlative duties to protect. Furthermore, how should the identification of representatives of children's choices be tested? Parents would not necessarily be the best option. As we know from the considerable literature on child abuse, it is frequently the case that the greatest threat to a child's emotional, physical and sexual integrity comes from parents and other close family members and friends.

Second, there is the 'interest' theory of rights[28] intended to address some of the problems of the 'choice' theory. According to this theory, rights are based upon whether a child has an interest that is in need of protection rather than merely based upon whether the right holder is actually capable of asserting or waiving their claim. If society generally recognises that children have a need for care and protection, then it ought to be possible to construct rights upon such foundations. It is also convenient to think about the distinctions between choice and interest theories in parallel to a distinction of the content of rights into categories of 'liberty rights' and 'welfare rights'. Archard (2010) characterises liberty rights as 'rights to choose, such as to vote, practise a religion, and to associate' and welfare rights as 'rights that protect important interests such as health'. Even if children lack the capacity or competence to 'choose' they surely have fundamental interests worthy of protection and thus have 'welfare rights' (Brighouse 2002).

Once children's 'interests' have been identified it can be seen that it should not be too difficult to formulate a credible set of 'moral rights' applying to children. One formulation of a moral right is 'a good of such importance that it would be wrong to deny it or withhold it' from any member of a given class (MacCormick 1982: 160). However, this does not assist greatly in the task of identifying which interests can be transformed into moral rights and on what basis; it appears merely to beg the same question using different terminology. What constitutes a 'good' of 'such importance' that it would be 'wrong' to deny or withhold it? Even if a set of

---

28 Advocates of the 'interest' theory include: MacCormick (1982); Campbell (1992); Raz (1996); and Kramer (1998).

moral rights can be reliably formulated, there still remains the issue of the basis upon which moral rights ought to be transformed into concrete legal rights. Many commentators accept that such transformation occurs 'if there is some recognition of their importance by the rest of society and consequently the imposition of correlative legal duties on others regarding the fulfilment of those rights' (Fortin 2009: 15).

The core point of the interest theory is that children ought not to be denied access to concrete legal rights merely because some children will not be sufficiently mature to make informed choices in their exercise and operation. However, the proponents of the interest theory would not claim that all children's interests are suitable to be transformed into moral rights and subsequently legal rights. A weakness of the interest theory is the uncertainty involved in identifying the relevant interests and the mechanisms that might operate to transform such interests into moral and then into legal rights. Which 'interests' should be rights-protected and why? By what criteria are we to assess the various interests of children for inclusion in a list of potential moral and legal rights?

Although there is no definitive resolution to this problem, Eekelaar at least provides a practical classification of children's interests which might be capable of transformation into moral/legal rights. In order to meet the problem that children might not be competent to properly formulate their interests, he suggested that the adult should 'make some kind of imaginative leap and guess what a child might retrospectively have wanted once it reaches a position of maturity' (Eekelaar 1986: 170). He ordered children's interests into three groups: 'basic', 'developmental' and 'autonomy' interests. Children's basic interests refer to the child's need for immediate physical, emotional and intellectual care. Children's developmental interests are concerned with children's needs to optimise their full developmental potential by having equal access to appropriate resources. A child's autonomy interests relate to the need for children to be free to make independent decisions about their lives. Eekelaar argued that where autonomy interests conflicted with basic and/or developmental interests the latter interests should prevail.

> The problem is that a child's autonomy interest may conflict with the developmental interest and even the basic interest. While it is possible that some adults retrospectively approve that they were, when children, allowed the exercise of their autonomy at the price of putting them at a disadvantage as against other children in realizing their life-chances in adulthood, it seems improbable that this would be a common view. We may therefore rank the autonomy interests subordinate to the basic and the developmental interests. However, where they may be exercised without threatening these two interests, the claim for their satisfaction must be high.
>
> (Eekelaar 1986: 171)

So, for example, the autonomy demonstrated by a child's decision to smoke cigarettes would be overridden by the recognition of basic (and development) health interests. Using the 'imaginative leap' notion referred to earlier, Eekelaar justifies this view on the basis that adults would be unlikely to retrospectively approve behaviour that would clearly prejudice their life-chances in adulthood.

As regards the underlying debate between the application of 'choice/will' or 'interest' theory, Fortin has argued that the emerging case law under the Human Rights Act 1998 has suggested that a young person's claim to exercise autonomy based on Convention rights has been dependent on that person's ability to comprehend what is involved in the decision itself. This is an approach that conforms to the 'choice/will' theory, but in practice, it is neither a logical nor a safe approach. On the other hand, an interest theory of rights 'allows conceptions of the child's welfare to be accommodated within conceptions of his interests or rights', and the interest theory does not compel any rejection of the idea of children making choices.

> Children may indeed have some rights to self-determination based on their interest in choice, without having a right to complete autonomy. An analysis based on an interest theory of rights withholds the right to complete autonomy, including the right to make all fundamental decisions regarding his future, until the teenager reaches a required level of maturity, measured not only by reference to his powers of comprehension. At this level, he is deemed to be on a par with adult rights holders, with no paternalistic interventions available to protect him from the hazards of dangerous decision- making. Before then the courts are entitled to deny him the right to reach decisions which will materially threaten his adult wellbeing. Such a stance is a morally coherent one, reflecting the view that the status of minority carries a legal significance. It is designed to protect children from the dangers of adulthood, more particularly from making life-threatening decisions.
>
> (Fortin 2006: 325)

1.2.1.2 Autonomy, paternalism and participation

The review of theories of children's rights above exposes significant issues relating to the capacity and competence of children to make choices that justify the attribution of rights. A key controversy in child law and policy is the extent to which the child can be properly regarded as having a right to autonomy or self-determination. This reflects the focus on the active *agency* of the child identified in our discussion of the sociological perspective on childhood (section 1.1.3 above). It also reflects the way in which childhood is a 'social construction', a point brought out by our discussion of the historical perspective on childhood (section 1.1.2 above). The notion of active agency has been increasingly recognised and supported by the strengthening of a global human rights culture since the UDHR in 1948.

In the United Kingdom, for example, the process of the legal recognition of children's autonomy was given a significant boost in the landmark case of *Gillick*.

Case study 1.1

Gillick v. West Norfolk and Wisbech Area Health Authority [1986] AC 112, [1985] 3 All ER 402.

Facts: In this case, the Department of Health and Social Security had issued guidance to area health authorities on family planning which contained a section dealing with contraceptive advice and treatment for young people. It stated that attempts would always be made to persuade children under the age of 16 who attended clinics to involve their parent or guardian at the earliest stage of consultation, and that it would be most unusual to provide contraceptive advice to such children without parental consent. However, the guidance underlined the need not to abandon the principle of confidentiality between doctor and patient, and stated that in exceptional cases it was for a doctor exercising his or her clinical judgment to decide whether to prescribe contraception. The plaintiff, who was the mother of five girls under the age of 16 years, wrote to her local area health authority seeking an assurance from them that no contraceptive advice or treatment would be given to any of her daughters without her knowledge and consent. The area health authority refused to give such an assurance and stated that in accordance with the guidance the final decision must be for the doctor's clinical judgment. The plaintiff challenged the legality of the guidance.

Held: The House of Lords held that the National Health Service legislation indicated that Parliament regarded contraceptive advice and treatment as essentially medical matters and that there was no statutory limit on the age of the persons to whom contraceptive facilities might be supplied; and that a girl under the age of 16 years had the legal capacity to consent to medical examination and treatment, including contraceptive treatment, if she had sufficient maturity and intelligence to understand the nature and implications of the proposed treatment; that the parental right to control a minor child deriving from parental duty was a dwindling right which existed only in so far as it was required for the child's benefit and protection; that the extent and duration of that right could not be ascertained by reference to a fixed age, but depended on the degree of intelligence and understanding of that particular child and a judgment of what was best for the welfare of the child; that the parents' right to determine whether a child under 16 should have medical treatment terminated when the child achieved sufficient intelligence and understanding to make that decision itself; that although in the majority of cases parents were the best judges of matters concerning the child's welfare, there might be exceptional cases in which a doctor was a better judge of the medical advice and treatment that would conduce to a child's welfare and where it might be desirable for a doctor to give a girl, in her own best interests, contraceptive advice and treatment, if necessary without the consent or even the knowledge of the parents; and that, accordingly, the department's guidance did not contain advice that was an infringement of parents' rights.

The support which this case appeared to give to a child's autonomy of decision-making, subject to being recognised as of sufficient understanding and maturity in relation to the decision, was much heralded at the time, and the appearance of the iconic 'Gillick-mature child' in public debate in the United Kingdom and elsewhere has persisted.[29] Shortly after the House of Lords' decision in *Gillick*, the 'mature minor' doctrine was applied in Canada.[30] More recently, the Supreme Court of Canada, in *A.C. v. Manitoba (Director of Child and Family Services)*, had to grapple with the question of a child's autonomous decision-making in the context of a life-threatening scenario.

Case study 1.2

A.C. v. Manitoba (Director of Child and Family Services, 2009 SCC 30 (2009), 26 June 2009.

Facts: C, a devout Jehovah's Witness, was admitted to hospital when she was 14 years and 10 months old, suffering from lower gastrointestinal bleeding caused by Crohn's disease. She refused consent to the receipt of blood. The Director of Child and Family Services apprehended her as a child in need of protection, and sought a treatment order from the court under section 25(8) of the Manitoba Child and Family Services Act, by which the court may authorise treatment that it considers to be in the child's 'best interests'. There is a presumption in section 25(9) of the Act that the best interests of a child 16 or over will be most effectively promoted by allowing the child's views to be determinative, unless it can be shown that the child

---

29 *Gillick* was followed in the early 1990s by two decisions that arguably diminished the child's right to make autonomous decisions: see *Re R (a minor) (wardship: consent to treatment)* [1992] Fam. 11, [1991] 4 All ER 177; and *Re W (a minor) (medical treatment: court's jurisdiction)* [1993] Fam. 64, [1992] 4 All ER 627. The Court of Appeal ruled that the court could override a young person's decision to withhold consent from life-saving treatment (anti-psychotic drug treatment and treatment for anorexia nervosa respectively).
30 *J.S.C. v. Wren* (1986), 76 A.R. 115 (C.A.), a 16-year-old girl had received medical approval for a therapeutic abortion, but her parents sought an injunction to prevent it because the age of majority was 18. Based on *Gillick*, Kerans J.A. concluded that the girl was capable of consenting to the abortion on her own behalf.

does not understand the decision or appreciate its consequences. Where the child is under 16, however, no such presumption exists. The applications judge ordered that C receive blood transfusions, concluding that when a child is under 16 there are no legislated restrictions of authority on the court's ability to order medical treatment in the child's 'best interests'. C and her parents appealed the order, arguing that the legislative scheme was unconstitutional because it unjustifiably infringed C's rights under sections 2(a), 7 and 15 of the Canadian Charter of Rights and Freedoms. The Court of Appeal upheld the constitutional validity of the impugned provisions and the treatment order.

Held: The Supreme Court of Canada held (Binnie J. dissenting) that the appeal should be dismissed and that sections 25(8) and 25(9) of the Child and Family Services Act were constitutional. The majority (LeBel, Deschamps, Charron and Abella JJ) found that when a young person's best interests are interpreted in a way that sufficiently respects his or her capacity for mature, independent judgment in a particular medical decision-making context, the constitutionality of the legislation was preserved. The statutory scheme struck a constitutional balance between what the law has consistently seen as an individual's fundamental right to autonomous decision-making in connection with his or her body, and the law's equally persistent attempts to protect vulnerable children from harm. The 'best interests' standard in section 25(8) operated as a sliding scale of scrutiny, with the child's views becoming increasingly determinative depending on his or her maturity. The more serious the nature of the decision and the more severe its potential impact on life or health, the greater the degree of scrutiny required. Interpreting the 'best interests' standard in this way navigates the tension between an adolescent's increasing entitlement to autonomy as he or she matures and society's interest in ensuring that young people who are vulnerable are protected from harm. The Supreme Court took the view that this approach brought the 'best interests' standard in line with the evolution of the common law (including Gillick) and with international principles.

The mention of 'international principles' here was a reference to the *Convention on the Rights of the Child*, in which article 3 describes 'the best interests of the child' as a primary consideration in all actions concerning children (section 3.7.3.2 below). Articles 5 and 14 of the *Convention on the Rights of the Child* require State parties to respect the responsibilities, rights and duties of parents to provide direction to the child in exercising his or her rights 'in a manner consistent with the evolving capacities of the child'. Similarly, article 12 requires State parties to 'assure to the child who is capable of forming his or her own views the right to express those views freely in all matters affecting the child, the views of the child being given due weight in accordance with the age and maturity of the child' (section 3.7.3.4 below). Parkes (2013: 12) found that children in Europe feel that the right to participation is the least respected of their human right, as they are excluded from important decisions affecting their lives. Archard pinpoints a 'central tension' between two of the foundational principles of the *Convention on the Rights of the Child*, the best interests principle (article 3) and the child's right to be heard (article 12):

> The tension between a best interest principle and a child's right to express her own views on matters affecting her interests is not simply an abstract or theoretical conflict of attitudes toward the child. It is a tension that yields conflicting practical recommendations in those situations where we must decide what to do in respect of a child, and where what the child wants is at odds with what adults who must make that decision judge is best.
> (Archard 2012: 329)

In essence, this reflects the need for a balance between the elements of *protection* and *empowerment* in the Convention.

There are, of course, a number of legal duties to take into account children's views in child law in many countries.[31] Although these may fall short of full participation rights in decision-making, at least they indicate a fuller acknowledgment of children's capacities and autonomy. It may be inappropriate, even positively damaging, to give a younger child the final decision about which parent they want to live with, in the context of a parental dispute, it may be suitable to ensure some consultation with the child to ascertain their wishes and feelings in order to improve the overall decision-making process. After all, the airing of a child's views is good practice for more central participation in decision-making to be undertaken later in adulthood.

If a child cannot be regarded as fully autonomous, then it follows that there is a need for some adult or State constraint on a child's autonomy, commensurate with the maturity and competence of the developing child and the prevalent view within that society of the respective responsibilities of parents, the wider family and the State. Most commentators now accept the justification for at least some paternalistic intervention. Raz (1996) justifies paternalistic coercion on the basis that it may be grounded on the general trust reposed by

---

31 For example, under the 'welfare principle' contained in section 1 of the Children Act 1989, when a court is considering making, varying or discharging an order under Part IV of the Act, or making etc. a section 8 order, where that order is opposed, it must have regard in particular to a welfare checklist which includes 'the ascertainable wishes and feelings of the child concerned (considered in the light of his age and understanding)' (s.1(3)(a)).

the child in the person or body exercising such coercion. Thus a child may trust and respect their parents to understand at least the legitimacy of their coercive action in relation to specific behaviours. Paternalism is often identified as an agent of oppression; paternalistic structures of society are frequently used to explain sex discrimination and gender-based inequalities. In the context of the child-parent relationship, however, paternalism is arguably a key component once it has been accepted that the best interests of children lie in both welfarist protection and the encouragement of participatory decision-making. Fortin argues that the theories of rights 'provide a substantial body of wisdom supporting the view that paternalism can be justified as a means of protecting children's long term interests' (Fortin 2006: 325). Other advocates of children's rights, while affirming that '[t]he language of rights can make visible what has for too long been suppressed' (Freeman 2007: 6), have had little difficulty in retaining a suitable place for liberal paternalistic intervention, particularly in relation to life-threatening decision-making by adolescents (Freeman 1983: 54–60; Freeman 2007: 15).

If the principle of the need for at least some paternalistic intervention is accepted, then the argument will often turn to how the occasions on which such intervention is appropriate can be properly identified. This has remained an almost irresolvable issue in the literature. On the one hand, there is a need to respect children's interests in making choices, in deploying their autonomy. On the other hand, there is a need to override some of their decisions which would otherwise damage their lives. The problem is particularly acute at the threshold of adult responsibility seen in older teenagers. Most parents of adolescents will have experienced the dilemma of when to exert authority over their child on the basis that this is in their best interests, or to allow the child to follow his or her own choices which, though disapproved, will provide the child with a sense of being taken seriously and an opportunity to learn better the practice of autonomous decision-making. As Fortin wisely puts it: 'The ideal formula would authorise paternalistic interventions to protect adolescents from making life-threatening mistakes, but restrain autocratic and arbitrary adult restrictions on their potential for autonomy. Finding it may prove problematic' (Fortin 2009: 29).

Perhaps a more pragmatic way to examine children's rights is to focus on their 'participation rights'. This phrase refers to the way in which a child may participate in a range of decision-making. The advantage of using this type of language is that it allows a finer calibration of the extent to which a child may participate in any one particular decision according to the child's own maturity and the nature of the decision in question. Article 12 of the *Convention on the Rights of the Child* obliges state parties to assure to the child who is capable of forming their own views a right to express views about matters affecting them; it also confers on the child a right to be heard in any judicial or administrative proceedings affecting the child (section 3.7.3.4 below). As will be seen, this right is one of the foundational principles of the *Convention*, and its importance has been underlined by the

Committee on the Rights of the Child's production of recommendations following a *Day of General Discussion*[32] and a detailed and analytical *General Comment* (section 3.4 below).[33]

A widespread practice has emerged in recent years, which has been broadly conceptualised as 'participation', although this term itself does not appear in the text of article 12. The term has evolved and is now widely used to describe ongoing processes, which include information-sharing and dialogue between children and adults based on mutual respect, and in which children can learn how their views and those of adults are taken into account and shape the outcome of such processes.[34]

This idea of a continuum of children's participation has an immediate practical appeal and indeed has been taken up enthusiastically by child advocates and practitioners. Hart (1992: 8) produced a useful model of a 'ladder of participation'.[35] The first three rungs of the ladder ('manipulation', 'decoration' and 'tokenism') are not categorised as true child participation. 'Manipulation' refers to situations where children may be used as a means to an (adult) end. 'Decoration' refers, 'for example, to those occasions when children are given T-shirts related to some cause' and this rung is distinguishable from 'manipulation' in that 'adults do not pretend that the cause is inspired by children; they simply use the children to bolster their cause in a relatively indirect way' (Hart 1992: 9). 'Tokenism' refers to situations where children are apparently given a voice but have little or no choice about the subject or style of communicating it and little or no opportunity to formulate their own opinions. The remaining five rungs of the ladder are categorised as constituting differing degrees of children's participation.

A useful critique of Hart's 'ladder of participation' and related theories of children's participation is provided by Thomas (2007). He concludes that the components of a theory of children's participation should:

a) encompass all the sites where children's participation may or may not take place;
b) be located in a broader context of inter-generational relations;
c) understand the distinction between 'participation' meaning activity that children engage in conjointly with adults, and children and young people's autonomous activity;

---

32 Committee on the Rights of the Child, *Day of General Discussion on the right of the child to be heard*, Report on the 43rd session, CRC/C/43/3 (16 July 2007) [980–1041].
33 Committee on the Rights of the Child, *General Comment No 12: The right of the child to be heard*, 51st session, UN Doc. CRC/C/GC/12 (20 July 2009).
34 Ibid., para. 3.
35 This model was based on Arnstein's (1969) model relating to adult participation in the political process.

d) accommodate the new kinds of participatory practice with children and young people that have been developed (particularly in countries of the majority world);
e) account for the demands for children and young people to have the same political rights as adults.

(Thomas 2007: 215)

1.2.1.3 Children's rights movement

The growing international recognition of children's rights can be regarded as one element of a more general interest in human rights that followed the Second World War. In Europe this was characterised by the *European Convention on Human Rights* in 1950,[36] prompted by the previous experience of arbitrary State interference with individual liberties. There has been an increased awareness of sex and race discrimination issues. Indeed, the civil rights movement in the United States demonstrated a broad concern about the 'rights' of minority groups. The US Supreme Court had ruled in *Re Gault* that 'neither the Fourteenth Amendment nor the Bill of Rights is for adults alone'[37] and that children could likewise benefit from the US Constitution's procedural safeguards.

The minority legal status of children came to be regarded in some quarters as oppressive and as a means to conceal the abuse of power over children, both by parents and the State. The American so-called 'child liberationists' took this to extremes. They suggested that it was essentially a form of oppression to exclude children from the adult world and adult freedoms. Holt (1974), for example, argued that children of any age should have the vote, they should be able to work for money, direct their own education and be paid a guaranteed minimum State income. Thus the movement for children's rights was unfortunately closely associated with simply giving adult freedoms to children. This was a gross distortion of the true position, as any cursory examination of the structure and content of the *Convention on the Rights of the Child* would reveal.

Some commentators now believe that the liberationists did little to serve the cause of children's rights precisely because of this lasting association (Fortin 2009: 4). However, other social movements have equally gone through stages of militant ideology in their development. Such militant interludes have arguably performed the valuable function of challenging conventional orthodoxies, but also have acted as precursors to more measured responses.

In retrospect, the liberationists' views do appear to have been formulated without due regard to the obvious facts of varying physical and mental competence

---

36 *European Convention for the Protection of Human Rights and Fundamental Freedoms*, opened for signature 4 November 1950, 213 UNTS 221 (entered into force 3 September 1953).
37 *Re Gault* 387 US 1, 13 (Fortas J.) (1967).

found in children. Their views ignore, for example, all the carefully worked and tested body of knowledge concerning children's cognitive development. The liberationists' views can also be regarded as potentially damaging to the extent that they may encourage children to shoulder adult responsibilities before proper preparation for such roles. Campbell (1992), for example, stressed the need for children not to have their experience of childhood stolen from them under the guise of offering them adult responsibilities. On one view, the focus on the need for children to make their own decisions and exercise autonomy, if taken too far, would inevitably lead to the boundary of adulthood and childhood being redefined. However, the radical approach of the liberationists has at least established that children are not inherently incapable of informed and rational decision-making, at even quite young ages, contrary to what many people might have otherwise thought.

Some commentators, in particular Goldstein et al. (1973, 1980), have argued strongly for family autonomy from the State, that is, a model of minimum State interference in the privacy of family life.[38] There have been recent public debates influenced by this orientation. An authoritative historian of childhood has noted the significant differences between the experience of childhood now and in past centuries: 'Children in the past have been assumed to have capabilities that we now rarely think they have . . . . So fixated are we on giving our children a long and happy childhood that we downplay their abilities and their resilience' (Cunningham 2006: 245).

Gill further develops this picture of children and argues that childhood is becoming undermined by 'risk aversion'. For example, a range of childhood activities previously enjoyed by children have been 'relabelled as troubling or dangerous, while the adults who still permit them are branded as irresponsible'. He detected 'a pattern of growing adult intervention to minimise risk at the expense of childhood experience' (Gill 2007: 10–11).

The assumption of those advocating a minimalist State intervention role is that parents should be entitled to raise their children as they think best. While this perspective is reflective of the general human rights drive to prevent arbitrary state interference, it also poses a threat to the integrity of children's rights. If legal systems are premised on minimum State intervention in family life, as many are, there equally may be little opportunity for supporting children's choices where these conflict with parental views. The assumption underlying the minimalist State intervention model of the centrality of parental roles, may be in danger of being translated into a parental immunity from any type of appropriate accountability. But these positions need not be mutually exclusive. It is no doubt possible to constrain both State and parental authority within reasonable limits, thus reflecting a desired balance of authority in relation to children.

---

38 A similar position to the laissez-faire model of Fox Harding (1996) outlined in section 1.1.4 above.

1.2.2 International children's rights

Although it is reassuring to find theoretical justifications for children's rights, the approach of legal positivism has simply been to point to the existence of such rights in contemporary legal instruments. At the international level one can identify, in addition to the references contained in the *International Bill of Rights*, 40 substantive rights as set out in the 54 articles of the *Convention on the Rights of the Child*. The speed at which the *Convention on the Rights of the Child* was ratified (Table 3.1), and the number of States parties involved, strengthen the argument, at least on a pragmatic basis, that this Convention has established itself as the key international instrument that sets out the fundamental principles of international children's rights. Indeed, that argument is further advanced by the view that the Convention may constitute a special form of international law which can be regarded as having a 'fundamental' status, that is, *jus cogens* (see section 2.2.5 below). On the other hand, it has been said that the Convention, and indeed other international treaties, are vehicles for 'manifesto' rights, that is, rights that reflect mere aspirations. Some commentators note that the proliferation of international human rights instruments may have led to a 'devaluation' in the currency of rights talk (Wellman 1999). Fortin identifies article 27 of the *Convention on the Rights of the Child* (the child's right to an adequate standard of living – see section 3.7.7.6 below) as a provision that it is difficult to imagine could ever be legally enforced due to its 'extreme vagueness' (Fortin 2009: 18). However, once we move away from expectations of concrete legal enforceability, even such provisions as article 27 may be seen as offering more than mere rhetoric. Upon closer examination, article 27 does at least provide a useful normative legal standard, namely that parents have the 'primary responsibility' for securing favourable living conditions, and the State by implication has a secondary responsibility to assist parents and other carers in these tasks and 'in case of need provide material assistance and support programmes, particularly with regard to nutrition, clothing and housing'. It thus provides a useful structure, defining the relationship between parents and State, in which the right to an adequate standard of living can be operationalised. It also contains a more detailed obligation on States to secure the recovery of maintenance for children.[39]

Lawyers and policy-makers are often concerned more with the way in which legal rights, that is, those contained in valid international and domestic instruments, are formulated and structured, rather than their philosophical pedigree. How do individual rights relate to other associated rights in the same or related instrument? For example, article 27 of the *Convention on the Rights of the Child* is linked to article 6(2) ('child's right to survival and development') and article 24 ('the right to enjoyment of the highest attainable standard of health'). Inevitably most rights, especially social, economic and cultural rights, can only be successfully

---

39 *Convention on the Rights of the Child*, art. 27(2–4).

implemented by balancing them against other rights and interests. One of the reasons for the wide recognition of the important status of the *Convention on the Rights of the Child* is precisely its form and structure and the origins of its drafting. Chapter 3 of this book deals with this in greater detail, but suffice it to say here that the Convention combines civil and political rights ('first generation rights') – for example, articles 13, 14 and 15 – with social, economic and cultural rights ('second generation rights') – for example, articles 24, 26 and 27. Indeed, consistently with the structure of general human rights instruments, securing second generation rights often proved to be a necessary precondition for meeting first generation rights. Freedom of expression, for example, can be conducted more effectively only when a society has created reasonable conditions of economic security and social order. The way in which the international community continues to perceive children's rights through its legal instruments and programmes provides a unique opportunity to examine how that community is constantly revising and setting its priorities in relation to children.

As will be seen (section 3.5 below), the 'Concluding Observations' of the Committee on the Rights of the Child on States parties' periodic reports give specific direction to State parties about the shortcomings that need to be addressed in order to further the cause of children's rights as formulated in the *Convention on the Rights of the Child*. One of the key weaknesses in the system was the perceived lack of 'teeth' if the state party is somewhat dilatory in addressing these issues. The addition of the *Optional Protocol to the UN Convention on the Rights of the Child on a Communications Procedure*[40] to the Committee's remit was intended to enhance the implementation of children's rights (Buck and Wabwile 2013). This third Optional Protocol to the *Convention on the Rights of the Child* is procedural, allowing individual children to submit complaints regarding violations of rights under the Convention and its first two Optional Protocols.[41]

1.3 Childhood, children's rights and cultural relativism

The discussion of both the concepts of childhood and children's rights in this Chapter also raises the issue of 'cultural relativism'; a term first used in anthropological research, implying that human beliefs and activities can only be understood in terms of their own culture. It should be noted that this concept should not be confused with 'moral relativism'; a belief that all cultures are both separate and equal and that any value system, however different from another, is equally valid. The problem of cultural relativism in international human rights law was highlighted at the time the United Nations was in the process of preparing the

---

40 *Optional Protocol to the UN Convention on the Rights of the Child on a Communications Procedure*, 28 February 2012, UN Doc. A/RES/66/138 (entered into force 14 April 2014).
41 Article 5.

UDHR in 1947–1948. The Executive Board of the American Anthropological Association produced a statement on human rights and put the question thus:

> The problem is thus to formulate a statement of human rights that will do more than just phrase respect for the individual as an individual. It must also take into full account the individual as a member of the social group of which he is a part, whose sanctioned modes of life shape his behavior, and with whose fate his own is thus inextricably bound.
>
> Because of the great numbers of societies that are in intimate contact in the modern world, and because of the diversity of their ways of life, the primary task confronting those who would draw up a Declaration on the Rights of Man is thus, in essence, to resolve the following problem: How can the proposed Declaration [UDHR] be applicable to all human beings, and not be a statement of rights conceived only in terms of the values prevalent in the countries of Western Europe and America?
>
> (American Anthropological Association 1947: 539)

Consequently, one can see how any international human rights instrument, such as the *Convention on the Rights of the Child* which seeks to achieve a universal standard, may be significantly weakened in terms of its legitimacy and ultimately its implementation if it is seen to be an exclusive product of the cultural values held principally by the powerful nations who were in a position to manage and direct its drafting. It would appear, for example, that at least in the early years of the drafting process of the Convention, '[t]he industrialised countries were significantly over-represented at all stages' and fears that the outcome would be 'a heavily Northern-oriented text were widespread and justified' and only mitigated by the participation of a few developing countries in combination with a last-minute surge of delegates from the South, many from States with Islamic law (Cantwell 1992: 23).

Equally, although cultural differences must be respected, conversely this must not become an excuse for practices that are widely perceived as unacceptable (Harris-Short 2001: 306). International human rights law has frequently been criticised in two respects: first, that it lacks universality and in fact has been construed according to an ethnocentric view of the world usually associated with the influence of the more powerful nations of the North; second, it is conceded that the normative standards may be culturally 'neutral', but consequently they will lack any substantial meaning in terms of their practical implementation. It is certainly true that any perusal of the Convention's preparatory works (*travaux préparatoires*) (Detrick 1992) shows the negotiated and mediated nature of some of the legal standards that eventually emerged in the final text. Some would argue, that a high number of active State participants in the drafting process should ensure that there is reasonable attention to cultural diversity in framing such standards in the first place.

Cultural relativism is also a significant aspect of how international legal standards are viewed by individual nations and put into practice. For example, a State that has become politically and economically weak, which may have suffered years of warfare, civil strife, poverty and hunger, is likely to have very different priorities from some of the well-established and relatively secure industrialised nations. There will not only be a difference in the resources available for deployment on appropriate programmes, but there will also be differences in how such States may construe the key underlying assumptions, relationships and concepts behind the standards. For example, it can be seen that the African nations, in their production of the *African Charter on the Rights and Welfare of the Child*,[42] have proceeded on the basis of a different view about the nature of the family unit and the relationship of individuals to the family and to the wider community.

The way in which the *Convention on the Rights of the Child* was drafted, the nature of the standards finally agreed, and the way in which the Committee on the Rights of the Child has interacted with State parties in their examination of reports, are all alive with cultural implications. As will be seen in the detailed discussion of the *Convention on the Rights of the Child* in Chapter 3, it contains an ideological commitment to a relatively modest extent of State interference in family affairs, shown both by the way in which certain articles of the Convention have been framed and the Committee's comments in respect of countries that appear to have a quite different view of the relationship between the State and the family (section 3.7.5 below). 'Traditional and customary practices' are also frequently criticised by the Committee as obstacles in achieving the standards set out in the Convention – for example, in relation to another foundational principle of the Convention, the right to life, survival and development (section 3.7.3.3 below). Yet anthropologists may well point out that such practices can have a positive influence, underwriting the community's social solidarity and shared belief systems.

In theory, the ability to make *declarations* and *reservations* (section 2.2.1 below) on ratifying the Convention[43] allows room to accommodate such differences, but within a unified international framework. It can be argued that a generous provision for reservations and declarations in international treaties should be a mandatory element of the required consensus-building in the international community. Equally, the way in which the Committee on the Rights of the Child probes individual States parties for their reasons and justifications for such departures from international normative standards reflects a mechanism of dialogue that is actively exploring cultural sensitivities but remains within the overall international framework. The balance to be achieved in advancing concrete international rights in this area and allowing sufficient flexibility to encompass cultural sensitivity is not an easy one to strike.

---

42 See *African Charter on the Rights and Welfare of the Child*, adopted 11 July 1990, OAU Doc. CAB/LEG/24.9/49 (1990) (entered into force 29 November 1999).
43 See *Convention on the Rights of the Child*, art. 51.

1.4 Concluding remarks

Understanding the concept of childhood and the development process children undergo as they mature into adults is key to understanding the need for a human rights framework which focuses solely on the rights of children. This chapter outlines the various historic and modern day approaches to childhood and children's rights, demonstrating how these notions are in fact contestable. Advent of the Convention was precipitated by recognition that protecting children was key to their healthy development. While childhood norms and experiences are not homogenous for all children in all states, nor indeed all children within a single state, the lofty goals of the Convention seek to provide a benchmark towards which all states should aspire.

Chapter 2

Introduction to international law sources and institutions

2.1 Introduction

This chapter provides an outline of some of the key sources, concepts and institutions that are necessary for an understanding of the international law relating to children. Those already familiar with international law sources and institutions might wish to omit this chapter, though it contains references to child law-related examples that illustrate some of the general international law points discussed. A number of topics, discussed in some detail in general international law textbooks (e.g. Kaczorowska 2010; Crawford 2012; Shaw 2017), are omitted here as they have little connection specifically with the realm of international child law. Thus, the reader will find little about the law of the sea, territorial sovereignty, State succession and other concepts and institutions which do not relate directly to the subject of this book. However, an understanding of international child law will require some basic knowledge of the international legal system, how disputes are resolved and the nature of some of the key international institutions that have an important role to play in this field.

The study of international law is characteristically divided into private international law (more accurately described as 'conflict of laws') and public international law. 'Conflict of laws' refers to the body of laws that regulate private relationships across national borders. It deals largely with cases within legal systems where there is a foreign element to consider. It has been described as 'the body of rules the domestic law of a State that is applicable when a legal issue contains a foreign element, and it has to be decided whether a domestic rule should apply foreign law or relinquish jurisdiction to a foreign court' (Aust 2010: 1). Public international law, on the other hand, deals mainly with relations between States and the operation of international bodies. International child law in fact encompasses both subdivisions of international law. For example, there are a number of conventions emanating from the Hague Conference on Private International Law (section 2.4.2 below) that seek to enhance judicial and administrative cooperation on inter-country adoption and child abduction. There are also a number of human rights standards from the United Nations and from regional institutions that are directly relevant to children.

2.2 Sources of international law

Unlike most domestic legal orders that are based on the existence, in some form or another, of a distinct legislature, an executive and a judicial power, the international legal order is not constructed in this way. As yet there is no unified world government with law-making and executive authority to issue international laws that will be applied and interpreted by a global court system. The arrangement of international institutions does have some similar features to State governance, but there are important points of distinction. There is an authoritative statement of the sources of international law to be found in article 38 of the *Statute of the International Court of Justice* (1945),[1] which most commentators would agree has been universally accepted, even though it technically applies only to the sources that the International Court of Justice (ICJ) (section 2.4.1.1 below) must apply.

(1) The Court, whose function is to decide in accordance with international law such disputes as are submitted to it, shall apply:

   (a) international conventions, whether general or particular, establishing rules expressly recognised by the contesting states;
   (b) international custom, as evidence of a general practice accepted as law;
   (c) the general principles of law recognised by civilized nations;
   (d) subject to the provisions of article 59, judicial decisions and the teachings of the most highly qualified publicists of the various nations, as subsidiary means for the determination of rules of law.

(2) This provision shall not prejudice the power of the Court to decide a case *ex aequo et bono*, if the parties agree thereto.[2]

These sources of international law, i.e. conventions/treaties, international customary rules, the general principles, judicial decisions and teachings, are discussed in the following sections.

2.2.1 International treaties and conventions

'Treaties' are known by a number of different names: e.g. Agreements, Statutes, Declarations, Pacts, Conventions, Charters, Covenants and Protocols, etc. In essence, they involve the creation of a written agreement with which the States participating in them will be bound in international law. The procedural and other matters relating to the making of treaties have developed over time into

---

1 *Charter of the United Nations and Statute of the International Court of Justice*, concluded 26 June 1945, 1 UNTS XVI, (entered into force 23 October 1945).
2 *Statute of the International Court of Justice*, art. 38. Article 59 states: 'The decision of the Court has no binding force except between the parties and in respect of that particular case.' The Latin phrase in art. 38(2) means 'according to what is right and good; in equity and good conscience'.

rules of customary international law which have been consolidated and extended by the *Vienna Convention on the Law of Treaties*[3] (1969) (hereafter '*Vienna Convention*'). Treaties are traditionally divided into two types: there are 'law-making treaties' that are intended to have a general relevance; and 'treaty-contracts' intended only as binding between two or a few states. A good example of a lawmaking treaty in this context is the *United Nations Convention on the Rights of the Child*[4] (1989) (hereafter the 'CRC'). The CRC is, as we shall see in Chapter 3, a comprehensive statement of an agreed international vision of children's rights. An example of a treaty-contract is any one of the many bilateral extradition treaties that regulate the surrender by one government to another of an accused or convicted person. The United Kingdom, for example, has extradition relations with more than a hundred territories by way of both multilateral extradition conventions and agreements, or under bilateral extradition treaties. Extradition relations are regulated in the United Kingdom by the Extradition Act 2003.

It is in the nature of a multi-lateral law-making treaty that its success in establishing anything approaching a global or general effect will often depend on the political support that it receives from the nations of the world. Thus, for example, although the *Hague Convention on Jurisdiction, Applicable Law and Recognition of Decrees Relating to Adoptions*[5] (1965) represented an attempt to manage certain adoption issues at the international level, the lack of State ratifications deprived this instrument of ever having any significant impact. This convention has now been 'denounced' by each of the ratifying countries and has ceased to have effect in international law. A new international instrument, the *Hague Convention on Protection of Children and Co-operation in respect of Intercountry Adoption*[6] (1993) (see Chapter 7 below), has superseded it.

A treaty will normally specify two commencement dates: first, when it comes into force in international law; and second, the date when any particular ratifying State is bound by it in international law. For example, the *Hague Convention on Protection of Children and Co-operation in respect of Intercountry Adoption* specifies, first, that it will enter into force in international law 'on the first day of the month following the expiration of 3 months after the deposit of the third instrument of ratification, acceptance or approval'. Second, it will 'thereafter' enter into force 'for each State ratifying, accepting or approving it subsequently, or acceding to it, on the first day of the month following the expiration of 3 months after the deposit of its instrument of ratification, acceptance, approval or accession'.[7] All other things being

---

3 Opened for signature 23 May 1969, 1155 UNTS 331 (entered into force 27 January 1980).
4 Opened for signature 20 November 1989, 1577 UNTS 3 (entered into force 2 September 1990).
5 Hague Conference on Private International Law, concluded 15 November 1965 (denounced and ceased to have effect 23 October 2008). Austria, Switzerland and the United Kingdom were the only States to have ratified this Convention.
6 Hague Conference on Private International Law, concluded 29 May 1993 (entered into force 1 May 1995).
7 *Hague Convention on Protection of Children and Co-operation in respect of Intercountry Adoption 1993*, arts 46(1), (2)(a). This Convention has been ratified by 101 States at the time of writing (20 February 2020).

equal, the greater the international support for such international instruments, the more likely their underlying aims will be realised.

States that have not ratified a treaty will not be bound by its terms in international law. Thus, the United States is not bound by the CRC as it is the only country which has failed to ratify it. Remarkably, all the other (196) countries of the world have ratified this convention. However, even if a State has not ratified an international treaty there are two ways in which it might nevertheless be bound by it, or at least by parts of the treaty. First, the treaty may contain some provision(s) that could be regarded as 'international customary law' (section 2.2.2 below) which is deemed to bind all nations. Second, a State may have appended their 'signature' to the treaty but then failed to follow this with the next usual step of final 'ratification'. The act of signature is not without any legal effect. The *Vienna Convention* provides that once a State has signed a treaty it is 'obliged to refrain from acts which would defeat the object and purpose of a treaty' at least until it has made clear its intention not to become a party to the treaty; this is often referred to as the 'compatibility test'.[8] The United States did in fact sign the CRC in 1995. States will normally 'sign' treaties as a preliminary step to indicate their forthcoming agreement in the later 'ratification'. Signature in effect qualifies the State to proceed to ratification and creates an obligation of good faith not to 'defeat the object and purpose of a treaty'.

The use of treaties as a primary means of international law-making has been so widespread that there was a need for an authoritative statement of the principles and formalities of treaty-making. This was achieved in the *Vienna Convention* which reflected and codified pre-existing international customary law relating to the machinery of treaty-making, for example, the basic international law principle that treaties bind the parties to them and must be performed in good faith, '*pacta sunt servanda*'.[9] It also contains some general guidance about the approach to be taken to the interpretation of treaties.

Article 31
General rule of interpretation

1 A treaty shall be interpreted in good faith in accordance with the ordinary meaning to be given to the terms of the treaty in their context and in the light of its object and purpose.

---

8 Article 18. A state may deposit an instrument expressly clarifying that, despite its signature, it does not intend to become a party to the treaty and that accordingly it 'has no legal obligations arising from its signature'. An example of this is the United States' signature (31 December 2000) of the *Rome Statute of the International Criminal Court* (1998) followed by its later statement (6 May 2002) that it did not intend to become a party to this treaty.
9 'Every treaty in force is binding upon the parties to it and must be performed by them in good faith': *Vienna Convention* art. 26.

2   The context for the purpose of the interpretation of a treaty shall comprise, in addition to the text, including its preamble and annexes:

   (a) any agreement relating to the treaty which was made between all the parties in connection with the conclusion of the treaty;
   (b) any instrument which was made by one or more parties in connection with the conclusion of the treaty and accepted by the other parties as an instrument related to the treaty.

3   There shall be taken into account, together with the context:

   (a) any subsequent agreement between the parties regarding the interpretation of the treaty or the application of its provisions;
   (b) any subsequent practice in the application of the treaty which establishes the agreement of the parties regarding its interpretation;
   (c) any relevant rules of international law applicable in the relations between the parties.

4   A special meaning shall be given to a term if it is established that the parties so intended.

The *Vienna Convention* also permits recourse to 'supplementary means' of interpretation, including 'preparatory works' (*travaux préparatoires*), in three cases:

1   To confirm the meaning resulting from the application of article 31.
2   To determine the meaning when the interpretation according to article 31 leaves the meaning ambiguous or obscure.
3   To determine the meaning when the interpretation according to article 31 leads to a result which is manifestly absurd or unreasonable.

Preparatory works can provide an authoritative source of background and contextual information relating to the origins, objects and purpose and drafting history of the treaty in question. For example, Detrick's (1992) work on the CRC. Background documentation on International Labour Organisation (ILO) Conventions is now collected on a website[10] containing texts of the preparatory reports, discussions at the International Labour Conference, committee reports, votes and texts of all up-to-date ILO Conventions. There are also 'explanatory reports' available in respect of the Hague Conventions: e.g. the reports by Pérez-Vera (1980) on child abduction and by Parra-Aranguren (1994) on inter-country adoption. Regional international organisations also produce explanatory reports in relation to their legal instruments.

International law and international relations are closely entwined and the process of a State agreeing to any particular treaty is often influenced by political

---

10 Available at: <https://libguides.ilo.org/c.php?g=526073&p=3652268> (accessed 20 February 2020).

considerations at the domestic, regional and international level. Multilateral treaties between a larger number of countries will often involve both compromise in the drafting process and some flexibility in the treaty text as to the extent to which States are bound with respect to some specific provisions. Such flexibility is achieved by two methods. First, the text of the treaty may stipulate that States can opt in or opt out of a particular provision.[11] Second, States may make certain 'reservations', 'understandings' or 'declarations' upon signature and/or ratification of a treaty. A separate instrument containing such statements are usually lodged by States with the depositary of the treaty and then communicated to the other contracting States.[12] Such statements may affect the degree to which a State is bound by any particular provision of the treaty in question. Where such a statement is formulated expressly as a 'reservation' this indicates that the State intends that it should not be bound by a particular article of the treaty. A State reserving its agreement to a particular article may withdraw its reservation subsequently.[13]

Some ground rules about reservations have been formulated in the *Vienna Convention*.[14] Usually, the facility and procedure for making reservations in a treaty are set out expressly in the text of the individual treaty. Consequently, it is important to read any relevant provisions of the particular treaty at issue alongside the *Vienna Convention* to understand fully the precise scope of reservation-making that is available to contracting States. The *Vienna Convention* provides authority for States to formulate any reservations when signing or ratifying a treaty, subject to three exceptions:

1   Where the reservation is prohibited by the treaty.
2   Where the treaty provides that only specified reservations may be made.
3   Where the reservation is 'incompatible with the object and purpose' of the treaty.

An example of the first exception can be found in the *Hague Convention on Protection of Children and Co-operation in respect of Intercountry Adoption*, which stipulates that 'no reservation to the Convention shall be permitted'.[15] An illustration of the second exception is contained in the *Hague Convention on the Civil Aspects of International Child Abduction*[16] (1980), which specifies that reservations are only permitted in two

---

11 For example, there is provision to *opt in* to the interstate communications procedure and provision to *opt out* of the inquiry procedure in the *Optional Protocol to the Convention on the Rights of the Child on a Communications Procedure* (2012). See further Chapter 3.
12 The depositary for the CRC is the Secretary-General of the UN; the depositary for ILO conventions is the Director-General of ILO.
13 For example, the UK made four reservations upon its ratification; they had all been withdrawn by November 2008.
14 Arts 19–23.
15 Hague Conference on Private International Law, concluded 29 May 1993 (entered into force 1 May 1995), art. 40. This was required because of the 'the mandatory character of the Convention's rules' (Parra-Aranguren 1994: para. 578).
16 Hague Conference on Private International Law, concluded 25 October 1980 (entered into force 1 December 1983), art. 42.

rather narrow areas[17] and furthermore re-iterates the customary provision that a State can 'at any time withdraw a reservation it has made' (Pérez-Vera 1980: para. 150). The third exception articulates the customary rule that prohibits making a reservation which is incompatible with the object and purpose of the treaty. Some treaties expressly adopt this formula. For example, the CRC provides that a 'reservation incompatible with the object and purpose of the present Convention shall not be permitted'.[18] Of course, this begs the question as to which reservations can be regarded as striking sufficiently at the root of a treaty's 'object and purpose'. In this regard, the Committee on the Rights of the Child (hereafter 'the Committee') has expressed concerns that some reservations are plainly incompatible with the CRC's 'object and purpose'; for example, those suggesting 'that respect for the Convention is limited by the State's existing Constitution or legislation, including in some cases religious law'.[19] There have also been general concerns at the widespread use of reservations, declarations and understandings in relation specifically to multilateral human rights treaties, including the CRC.[20] International human rights treaties tend to provide a minimum standard of protection, and any departure from these is often criticised as contributing to a weakening of their overall legitimacy and effectiveness.

2.2.2 International customary law

The law on international treaties was first developed by the emergence of rules of 'international customary law' relating to a wide range of subject matter. It is tempting to think in modern times that the role of custom as a source of law is merely a residual one. This is generally the case within many municipal (i.e. domestic) legal systems of developed nations. However, at the international level, the role of custom as a source of law has remained creative rather than merely residual, precisely because the international legal order lacks the better defined and authoritative institutional framework generally found in domestic legal orders. The appearance of international customary law can be a flexible and responsive mode of law-making in a changing world; and one that may be necessary to preserve international legal order. In essence, two requirements are needed for a rule of international customary law to be recognised:

1 The material facts of the alleged customary rule must be found in *State practice*.
2 States must subjectively believe that such practice is binding (*'opinio juris'*).

---

17 In relation to the choice of language translation into French or English of documents sent to the Central Authority of the requested state (art 24); and in relation to the assumption of costs and expenses of proceedings (art 26)
18 CRC, art. 51(2).
19 Committee on the Rights of the Child, *General Comment No 5: General Measures of Implementation of the Convention on the Rights of the Child (Arts 4, 42 and 44, para. 6)*, UNCRC/GC/2003/5, 34th session, 27 November 2003. On reservations to the CRC, see generally, Schabas (1996).
20 At the time of writing there were 74 States parties to the CRC that had lodged reservations or declarations.

General international customary rules ought normally to be uniform and consistent in relation to both the above requirements, though a rigid prescription of these requirements should be avoided. The context and nature of the customary rule may give a different emphasis as to how these requirements are viewed. In domestic legal systems, the *duration* of an alleged custom is often of importance.[21] In international law, customs can appear instantly. For example, the customary rule about State sovereignty over air space appeared around the time of the First World War and the rule of non-sovereignty of space appeared at the time the first satellites were being launched in the 1950s and 1960s (Haanappel 2003).

In theory, all States can participate in the formation of international customary law. However, the influence and power of particular nations on specific issues may mean that an individual State's contribution to international discussion on certain issues will lead the direction of international law-making on those issues. For example, the United Kingdom, a powerful maritime nation in the nineteenth century, had a key influence on the formation of the international law of the sea, and prize law. Russia and the United States had a crucial influence on the formation of space law. However, matters affecting human rights generally, and children's rights in particular, are unlikely to be viewed explicitly in this way. The core ethic of human rights law is the recognition of the dignity of an individual person irrespective of their national identity. In principle, it would seem ironic if only the economically powerful nations had a significant influence in designing the structure of international human rights law. On the other hand, the postwar emergence of the United Nations system and the *Universal Declaration of Human Rights* (UDHR) of 1948 can be seen as international architecture heavily influenced by the victor nations of the Second World War. As one commentator puts it, 'scholars should not jump too quickly to the conclusion . . . that altruism must motivate the establishment of morally attractive international norms' (Moravcsik 2000: 48). It would be difficult, and ethnocentric, to assert that there might be some principled basis for certain nations to claim some special distinctive role or superior moral authority in relation to forming legal standards that are relevant specifically to children's rights. On the other hand, to ignore the influence of power relations embedded in the international community in this field would be naïve. The drafting process of a multilateral treaty is ultimately a diplomatic one not immune from the influence of power politics. The way in which such instruments are perceived and acted upon (or not acted upon) after they subsequently emerge into the body of international law is also a process often more driven by the shape of international relations than a result of applying principles from the legal text of an international instrument.

As we have seen, the first requirement for a rule to have the status of customary law is to show a *State practice*. The State practice must be uniform and consistent

---

21 One of the tests to identify custom as a recognised source of English law is famously whether it has been so regarded since 'time immemorial', the latter being a reference to 3 September 1189, the date of the coronation of King Richard I (Ward and Akhtar 2011).

with the alleged rule of customary law, and a range of materials may evidence this. For example, the State's official publications, diplomatic exchanges, resolutions made by the General Assembly of the United Nations, drafts produced by the International Law Commission and the cumulative practice of international organisations may be good evidence of customary law. Some States have produced extensive Digests and Yearbooks containing their own State practices relevant to the international community which have particular authority, for example, the *British Yearbook of International Law* (Lowe and Crawford 2012), and the *Digest of US Practice in International Law* (Guymon 2012). The domestic law of a State may, in certain circumstances, be evidence of a State practice. Ultimately, the identification of State practice which may form the basis of customary law is a somewhat circular exercise.

The requirement to establish *opinio juris* involves a subjective belief by a State that its practice is binding. As might be expected, a high threshold is required to prove it. Objections by other States may interrupt the legitimising process of custom formation. It is difficult to be prescriptive about this process; sometimes State protests may themselves contain the seeds of a new customary rule. Two customary rules may coexist for a while side by side. For example, in the 1960s some countries used the customary three-mile rule, that is, national rights were limited to waters extending from the coast to three nautical miles (the 'cannon shot' rule). Others used the customary 12-mile rule that had developed in the post-war period onwards as nations laid claim to mineral resources, to protect fishing and to enforce pollution control in their territorial waters.[22]

An important feature of rules of international customary law is that they will be binding on *all* States unless a State has objected to it from the start. In some States, including the United Kingdom, international customary law may be regarded as being automatically incorporated into domestic law according to the 'incorporation doctrine' (section 2.3 below). It can therefore be very important from both a national and an international perspective to determine whether an international rule has become part of customary law.

The relationship and status of treaties and customary law has been a difficult issue in international law discourse. Historically, custom preceded the more modern liking for formal treaty-making. On the other hand, treaties, though often desired because they promised greater certainty, often include some codification of existing customary law. However, where a treaty has effectively codified a part of customary law, the treaty provision has not necessarily substituted the customary source of law. The ICJ (see section 2.4.1.1 below) held in the *Nicaragua Case*[23] that a customary rule about a State's right of self-defence had not been superseded by

---

22 Maritime international customary rules have been codified in the *UN Convention on The Law of The Sea*, opened for signature 10 December 1982, 1833 UNTS 3 (entered into force 16 November 1994).
23 *Nicaragua v United States (Military and Paramilitary Activities in and against Nicaragua) (Judgement)* [1986] ICJ Rep 14.

a provision of the *United Nations Charter* (1945);[24] these two sources of law coexisted. In the context of international child law, for example, it is arguable that international customary law protects the child against sexual, economic and other forms of exploitation analogous to slavery, similar to the protection offered in some of the articles relating to such exploitation contained in the CRC (Van Bueren 1998).

2.2.3 General principles of law recognised by civilised nations

The international legal order will inevitably have significant gaps where it may appear there is no law, or where the law is silent on a particular matter. Where there is no treaty or customary law rule, case law may well fill some of these gaps. But in the international legal system there is often a lack of case law in particular areas, either because the subject has not been litigated or because there is no court-like forum that forms part of the international arrangements at issue. This is so in relation to the operation of the CRC, a treaty which does not have an international court forum comparable to the ICJ. However, an accepted standard of international law is that every international situation is, as a matter of law, capable of being determined (Shaw 2017: 51–52). One of the functions therefore of the 'general principles of law' in the context of article 38 of the *Statute of the International Court of Justice* is to fill such gaps where necessary. The provenance and content of these general principles are contested by scholars, but it is thought that they may include legal principles that are common to a large number of domestic law systems. However, it is much more difficult precisely to identify these principles, and indeed some commentators regard them as a sub-category of either treaties or custom rather than a discrete but limited source of law. On one view, general principles tend to be preconditions for the operation and efficiency of the international legal system as a whole. For example, the key general principle that international agreements are binding and must be carried out in good faith (*pacta sunt servanda*) is a presupposition without which the whole of treaty law would lack the key quality of legal obligation. Similarly, 'equity' and 'equitable principles' are often regarded as part of the 'general principles' of international law. There is also the fundamental principle of 'good faith' in the *UN Charter* which provides that 'all Members, in order to ensure to all of them the rights and benefits resulting from membership, shall fulfil in good faith the obligations assumed by them in accordance with the present Charter.'[25] Again, principles of equity and good faith can

---

24 'Nothing in the present Charter shall impair the inherent right of individual or collective self-defence if an armed attack occurs against a Member of the United Nations, until the Security Council has taken measures necessary to maintain international peace and security. . . . .' *Charter of the United Nations and Statute of the International Court of Justice*, concluded 26 June 1945, 1 UNTS XVI, (entered into force 23 October 1945), art. 51.
25 *Charter of the United Nations and Statute of the International Court of Justice*, concluded 26 June 1945, 1 UNTS XVI, (entered into force 23 October 1945), art. 2(2).

be viewed as preconditions for a well-ordered international legal order. A leading British authority on international law concludes:

> Although generalised principles or concepts that may be termed community value-judgments inform and pervade the political and therefore the legal orders in the broadest sense, they do not themselves constitute as such binding legal norms. This can only happen if they have been accepted as legal norms by the international community through the mechanisms and techniques of international law creation. Nevertheless, 'elementary principles of humanity' may lie at the base of such norms and help justify their existence in the broadest sense, and may indeed perform a valuable role in endowing such norms with an additional force within the system.
>
> (Shaw 2017: 81)

In practice, the appeal to the so-called 'general principles of law' may derive either from domestic law analogies or from international law. However, the extraction of principles from domestic law will need to be at a sufficient level of generality to come within the formulation in article 38(1)(c) of the *Statute of the International Court of Justice*. The ICJ and its predecessor, the Permanent Court of International Justice (PCIJ), have managed on occasion to extract general principles from domestic legal systems.[26]

2.2.4 Judicial decisions and publicists' writings

Article 38 of the *Statute of the International Court of Justice* appears to establish a hierarchy of sources; judicial decisions and the writings of publicists are said to be a 'subsidiary' means for the determination of rules of law. There is no binding doctrine of precedent in international law. Even the decisions of the ICJ are expressly stated to have no binding force except as between the parties and in relation to the case in hand.[27] Nevertheless, some of these cases do have considerable influence and authority. The intellectual content of some decisions of the ICJ and PCIJ have found their way subsequently into the text of treaties. In any event, court decisions may provide useful interpretations of existing treaty provisions. An example is the *Boll Case*,[28] a rare child law case heard by the ICJ, which had to consider various provisions of the *Hague Convention on Guardianship*[29] (1902) (see further, section 2.4.1.1 below).

---

26 For example, *Factory at Chorzów (Germany v Poland) (Merits)* [1928] PCIJ, Ser. A, No. 17, 29. It is thought one of the most significant general principles is that of good faith: see *Nuclear Tests (New Zealand v. France) (Judgment)* [1974] ICJ Rep 457, 473.
27 *Statute of the International Court of Justice*, art. 59.
28 *Application of the Convention of 1902 Governing the Guardianship of Infants (Netherlands v Sweden) (Judgment)* [1958] ICJ Rep 55 (aka the *Boll Case*).
29 Hague Conference on Private International Law, *Hague Convention on the Settlement of Guardianship of Minors*, concluded 12 June 1902 (entered into force 30 July 1904, replaced by the *Hague Convention on Jurisdiction, Applicable Law, Recognition, Enforcement and Co-Operation in Respect of Parental Responsibility and Measures for the Protection of Children*, concluded 19 October 1996 (entered into force 1 January 2002).

The phrase 'judicial decisions' in article 38 also includes international arbitration awards and the rulings of national courts. Supreme Court decisions in federal states, for example, may be considered when examining the issue of border disputes. In some areas, certainly in the past, writers have had a key influence on the formation of the law. Shaw (2017: 84) comments that authorities such as Gentili, Grotius, Pufendorf, Bynkershoek and Vattel 'were the supreme authorities in the sixteenth to eighteenth centuries and determined the scope, form and content of international law'. Their influence has waned, in part because of the proliferation of treaty law.[30] Though the historical importance to international law of the writings of jurists as a source in its own right has declined, the leading textbooks are routinely consulted by States, courts and international organisations, perhaps more so than in the past given the increased growth in international law instruments and their increasing significance in international affairs.

2.2.5 Hierarchy of sources and jus cogens

If there is a hierarchy of sources in international law, then one can say that judicial decisions and juristic writings are given a 'subsidiary' role under the terms of article 38 of the *Statute of the International Court of Justice*. The 'general principles of law' appear to function as a limited supplement to custom and treaty. The priority order between custom and treaty is generally that the later in time will have priority. However, there are some rules of international law that are regarded as so fundamental that the usual relationship between custom and treaty will be disrupted. The theoretical basis is that there are some obligations that each State has towards the international community as a whole, for example, outlawing aggression, genocide, prohibition of torture, protection from slavery and racial discrimination. The *Vienna Convention on the Law of Treaties* provides that a treaty will be void if 'it conflicts with a peremptory norm of general international law'.[31] The rule, known as *jus cogens* ('compelling law'), also applies to customary rules. Such a peremptory norm cannot be derogated from by local custom. In short, such norms are binding on all nations; they cannot be derogated from, nor can they be usurped by treaty provision. In the context of child law, this is an important issue. An argument can be made that the CRC contains norms of the character fulfilling the requirements of *jus cogens*. Van Bueren (1994a: 55–6), for example, argues by analogy that the sexual and economic exploitation of children is comparable to slavery and should therefore be recognised as a 'peremptory norm of general international law' capable of overriding conflicting treaty provision and binding nations that have not ratified the treaties that provide protection against such exploitation of children.

---

30 The United Nations Treaty Series (UNTS) (December 1946 – March 2010) collection contains over 200,000 treaties and related subsequent actions, published in hard copy in over 2,660 volumes.
31 Opened for signature 23 May 1969, 1155 UNTS 331 (entered into force 27 January 1980), art. 53.

2.2.6 'Soft law'

Although not a formal source of law, 'soft law' is a term often used to describe non-binding international instruments or documents. These are often called 'guidelines', 'principles', 'declarations', 'codes of practice' or 'recommendations', but the legal status of such an instrument is determined by the intention of States parties to create legal relationships rather than the instrument's title. Some of these instruments/documents may be part of, or lead up to, a treaty negotiating process; others may impact on the practice of States leading to the creation of international customary law. The main advantage of soft law is that it provides States with a flexible means to indicate areas of policy agreement without the full commitment of treaty law. The organic growth of soft law in relation to particular policy areas can be seen as a testing ground for conversion at a later stage into a fully-fledge legal norm in the form of a treaty or customary law. International soft law has been particularly prevalent in the areas of international economic and environmental law, though the increasing volume and range of soft law has been observed in the human rights arena too; for example, the *UN Declaration on the Rights of Indigenous Peoples* (2007).[32] However, the definition and analytical coherence of the term 'soft law' remains controversial in international legal scholarship. One commentator concludes:

> soft law is best understood as a continuum, or spectrum, running between fully binding treaties and fully political positions. Viewed in this way, soft law is something that dims in importance as the commitments of states get weaker, eventually disappearing altogether.
>
> (Guzman and Meyer 2010: 173)

2.3 The relationship between domestic and international law

The details of the relationship between domestic and international legal orders are complex: see further, Shaw (2017: 96–154). There are two debates to consider. First, a debate concerning 'monist' and 'dualist' doctrines of international law. Second, a debate about the 'transformation' and 'incorporation' doctrines of international law. As regards the first debate, the older, monist doctrine asserts that domestic and international law are part of a single, integral legal order and, if there is a conflict between the two, international law ('the law of nations') should prevail. The dualist doctrine, by contrast, asserts that the two systems exist separately; they do not affect each other, and it therefore follows that neither system prevails over the other. The two systems have different fundamental concerns. International law, it is argued, is primarily about the legal relationships *between* States, whereas domestic law is mainly concerned with the horizontal legal relationships between

---

32 UNGA Res 61/295, UN Doc. A/Res/61/295 (13 September 2007).

citizens and the vertical relationships between the sovereign State and its citizens. A third strand of thought, a modification of the dualist doctrine, has emerged which acknowledges the separate realms of domestic and international law and concludes that there is therefore little conflict of obligation possible between the two systems. A State's practice on a particular issue may well be in breach of its obligations under international law. This will be a matter for remedial action, if there is any available, in the international community. However, any 'conflicting' domestic legislation of a sovereign State will remain supreme unless specifically repealed in response to international 'naming and shaming' and other pressures. In fact, the practice of legislatures and the courts is sometimes thought to be a more reliable way to understand the relationship between domestic and international law.

The second area of contention, concerning the doctrines of transformation and incorporation, focuses on the practical problems of how domestic courts should deal with international legal standards. The doctrine of transformation (which is based on a 'dualist' understanding of the separate realms of domestic and international law) asserts that domestic law will not be able to fully digest rules of international law unless there has been an explicit (transformative) act of adoption. This will be achieved according to the constitutional machinery appropriate for the nation concerned.

In the United Kingdom, for example, it will be by the passage of an Act of Parliament. By contrast, the doctrine of incorporation (based on a 'monist' understanding of the unity of domestic and international law) holds that international law is automatically part of domestic law without the need for a constitutional ratification procedure. However, it should be noted immediately that the doctrine of incorporation is only to be applied to international customary law. The position with international treaties is treated differently. A lengthy case law development, dating back to the eighteenth century, has produced an acceptance of the doctrine of incorporation (of international customary law) in English common law. The landmark case was *Trendtex Trading Corp v. Central Bank of Nigeria*.[33] The Court of Appeal confirmed that the incorporation doctrine was the correct one and that international law did not know a rule of *stare decisis* (binding precedent). The domestic courts could implement changes in international customary law without waiting for any binding case precedents to be overturned in the Supreme Court. Later cases have reaffirmed that '[c]ustomary international law is part of the common law'.[34] However, the certainty in choice of doctrine does nothing to resolve the problem that domestic courts may still have in identifying clearly what the relevant international customary rule is.

---

33 [1977] QB 529.
34 *R v. Bow Street Metropolitan Stipendiary Magistrate ex p Pinochete Ugarte (No. 3)* [2000] 1 AC 147, 276 (House of Lords).

In dualist nations treaties are not incorporated automatically within the domestic legal system. In the United Kingdom, for example, the constitutional position is that, although the executive authority (the Government Ministers on behalf of the Crown) signs and ratifies international treaties,[35] which then will have effect within international law, there is an additional need for the legislature (Parliament) to produce an Act, before that treaty will have binding legal effect recognised by the domestic courts. Depending on the government's political will on the matter, and the terms stated in the treaty to be met for it to enter into force, a long period of time might expire between international ratification and domestic enactment. For example, the UK Government was one of the first countries to sign (4 November 1950) and ratify (8 March 1951) the *European Convention on Human Rights*.[36] Although this Convention came into force in *international law* in 1953, the British courts only started to apply the Convention directly in the UK, by virtue of domestic legislation nearly half a century later.[37] As will be seen in Chapter 3, the CRC was signed and ratified by the UK Government in 1989, but it has not yet been enacted through Parliament and therefore does not have binding legal effect in UK courts.[38]

However, an unincorporated international treaty does usually have some, albeit limited, significance in domestic law. Under English law, for example, a rule of statutory interpretation has developed to assist with possible conflicts between unincorporated international treaty provisions and domestic legislation. The rule presumes that Parliament could not, at least without express words, have legislated contrary to the State's international obligations.[39] However, this presumption can be relied upon only in cases of ambiguity, not in cases where the statute offers a discretion. On the other hand, some cases have been more proactive in pointing to an unincorporated treaty provision to resolve a gap in domestic law.[40] However,

---

35 This executive power is not entirely without Parliamentary oversight. A constitutional convention arose from 1924 – the 'Ponsonby Rule' – which required that most international treaties should be laid before Parliament for 21 days before ratification. This was placed on a statutory footing by the Constitutional Reform and Governance Act 2010 which has further strengthened Parliament's scrutiny role. The Government must now lay most treaties subject to ratification before Parliament for 21 sitting days before it can ratify them. If either House objects, the government must give reasons why it wants to ratify before it can proceed, but the Commons can block ratification indefinitely (Thorp 2011).
36 *European Convention for the Protection of Human Rights and Fundamental Freedoms*, opened for signature 4 November 1950, 213 UNTS 221 (entered into force 3 September 1953).
37 By virtue of its domestic legislation, the *Human Rights Act 1998*, which came into force on 2 October 2000.
38 It is interesting to note, however, the gathering political pressures to incorporate the CRC in the United Kingdom. A Children's Rights Bill [HL Bill 8] contained provisions that would incorporate the CRC on much the same basis as the Human Rights Act 1998 incorporated the ECHR. The Bill was a Private Member's Bill moved by Baroness Joan Walmsley and received a first reading in the House of Lords on 19 November 2009, to coincide with the 20th anniversary of the adoption of the CRC. It has not progressed any further since then.
39 *Garland v. British Rail Engineering Ltd* [1983] 2 AC 751; *R v. Secretary of State for the Home Department ex p Brind* [1991] 1 AC 696.
40 *Derbyshire County Council v. Times Newspapers Ltd* [1992] QB 770, 830.

this approach to utilising unincorporated treaties as an 'aid to construction' in statutory interpretation in the United Kingdom falls a long way short of allowing international law to properly enter the body of domestic law.

2.4 International organisations and institutions

The following sections contain some basic information about the main international organisations and institutions, in particular those that are connected to international children's rights. The references in this section should provide the reader with signposts to more specialist reading if required. Section 2.4.1 deals generally with the UN system, section 2.4.2 with the Hague Conference on Private International Law, and section 2.4.3 with the International Criminal Court. The international human rights charter and treaty bodies within the United Nations system are dealt with in more detail in section 2.5.

2.4.1 The United Nations (UN)[41]

The United Nations was established on 24 October 1945 by 51 nations in response to the Second World War, to preserve peace through international cooperation and collective security. UN membership is now global: all 195 States are members of the UN. The membership of the UN is divided into five (informal) groups for the purposes of nominating candidates for election to UN organs and subsidiary bodies: African (54), Asian (including the Middle East) (55), Eastern European (23), Latin American and Caribbean (33), and Western European and others (WEOG) (29). Kiribati is not a member of any regional group and Palestine is a non-Member observer state.[42] Membership of the UN involves accepting the obligations of the *UN Charter*[43] (1945), a treaty that sets out some principles of international relations. The *UN Charter* provided for six principal organs:

1   General Assembly
2   Security Council
3   Economic and Social Council
4   Trusteeship Council
5   International Court of Justice (ICJ)
6   Secretariat

In fact, there are now only five active organs. The Trusteeship Council30 suspended operations on 1 November 1994.[44] All of the principal organs are based

---

41 See generally, Weiss et al. (2016).
42 UNGA Res 67/19 (29 November 2012) UN Doc. A/RES/67/19
43 *Charter of the United Nations and Statute of the International Court of Justice*, concluded 26 June 1945, 1 UNTS XVI, (entered into force 23 October 1945).
44 It was originally established to provide international supervision of eleven Trust Territories. All of these territories have now achieved independence or self-government.

at the UN headquarters in New York, other than the ICJ which is located at The Hague in the Netherlands.

The General Assembly, established under the *UN Charter*,[45] is the main deliberative and policy-making organ of the UN and is made up from representatives of all (193) Member States. In essence, this is the UN's debating chamber. Peterson (2007: 97) identifies two key functions: 'a forum for deliberation among member governments providing collective legitimation (or de-legitimation) of norms, rules, and actions; and a provider of some administrative oversight of the UN system'. It provides a unique forum for multilateral discussion of all the international issues covered by the *Charter*. It meets in regular session from September to December each year, and thereafter as required. Each Member State in the Assembly, however powerful, has one vote. Votes taken on certain key issues, such as recommendations on peace and security and the election of Security Council members, require a two-thirds majority of Member States. Other questions are decided by simple majority. In recent years there has been an effort to achieve consensus without the need to make decisions by way of a formal vote in order to strengthen the legitimacy of the Assembly's decisions.

The landmark *Millennium Declaration*[46] was adopted by the Assembly in 2000 and reflected the Member States' commitment to create a new global partnership and to attain specific goals. In 2015, the 2030 Agenda for Sustainable Development was then agreed,[47] as a plan of action for 'people, planet and prosperity.' 17 Sustainable Development Goals (SDGs) and 169 targets[48] were agreed, with a recognition that extreme poverty is the greatest global challenge to be overcome and indispensible for the achievement of sustainable development. The SDGs built upon the *Millennium Development Goals* and were in some parts, a continuation of those targets which were not achieved. With the close of the general debate, the Assembly allocates items among its six main committees. The committees then prepare and present draft proposals and decisions for consideration at a plenary meeting of the Assembly. The six main committees[49] and the Secretariat carry the General Assembly's work forward when it is not in session.

The General Assembly is also authorised to establish 'subsidiary organs' as deemed necessary. This includes a number of boards, commissions, committees, councils, panels and working groups; for example, the UN Human Rights Council (UNHRC) established in 2006.[50] The UNHRC is elected by and reports to the

---

45 Chapter IV, arts 9–22.
46 UNGA Res 55/2 (8 September 2000) UN Doc. A/RES/55/2.
47 UNGA Res 70/1 (21 October 2015) UN Doc. A/RES/70/1.
48 Preamble.
49 First Committee (Disarmament and International Security); Second Committee (Economic and Financial); Third Committee (Social, Humanitarian and Cultural); Fourth Committee (Special Political and Decolonization); Fifth Committee (Administrative and Budgetary); and Sixth Committee (Legal).
50 The United Nations Human Rights Council (UNHRC) is the successor body to the United Nations Commission on Human Rights (UNCHR).

Assembly and its 'special procedures' (section 2.5.1.1 below) are overseen by the Third Committee (the Social, Humanitarian and Cultural Committee). A number of programmes, funds and other bodies, for example, the United Nations Children's Fund (UNICEF) and the Office of the High Commissioner for Human Rights (OHCHR), report directly to the General Assembly.

The Third Committee interacts with various special rapporteurs, independent experts and chairpersons of working groups of the UNHRC. It discusses the advancement of women, the protection of children, indigenous issues, the treatment of refugees, the promotion of fundamental freedoms through the elimination of racism and racial discrimination, and the promotion of the right to self-determination. This Committee also addresses important social development questions such as issues related to youth, family, ageing, persons with disabilities, crime prevention, criminal justice and drug control.

The General Assembly's resolutions are not strictly binding in international law, but they may have great moral authority, particularly where there is a unanimous resolution, or a resolution is passed consensually without the need for a vote. Nevertheless, they remain recommendatory in nature, except for decisions on internal matters, and 'over time the substance of certain resolutions may become accepted as reflecting customary international law' (Aust 2010: 190).

The Security Council[51] has the onerous task of maintaining international peace and security and convenes when necessary. It is organised so as to be able to function continuously; a representative of each of its members must be present at all times at UN Headquarters. There are five permanent Council members (known as the 'P-5'): China, the Russian Federation, the United Kingdom, France and the United States, 'chosen on the basis of power politics in 1945' (Shaw 2017: 926). There are also an additional ten members elected by the General Assembly for periods of two years. In practice, the non-permanent membership is distributed according to the regional groups: Africa (3), Asia (2), Eastern Europe (1), Latin America and the Caribbean (2) and WEOG (2). Decisions of the Council, other than procedural matters, require nine votes and the absence of a veto by any of the five permanent members. It has been declared that the issue of whether a matter was procedural or not was itself subject to a veto.[52] The Council attempts to resolve disputes peacefully and in some cases will itself undertake investigation and mediation. The Council has frequently issued cease-fire directives and it also sends United Nations peacekeeping forces to troubled areas, often to keep opposing forces apart and to facilitate peaceful settlements (Malone 2007). The Council can impose economic sanctions and trade and arms embargoes, and has

---

51 *Charter of the United Nations*, Chapter V, arts 23–32.
52 'This "double-veto" constitutes a formidable barrier. Subsequent practice has interpreted the phrase "concurring votes of the permanent members" in article 27 in such a way as to permit abstentions. Accordingly, permanent members may abstain with regard to a resolution of the Security Council without being deemed to have exercised their veto against it' (Shaw 2017: 926).

authorised the use of collective military action to ensure its decisions are carried out. A recalcitrant Member State may be suspended from exercising the rights of UN membership by the General Assembly on the recommendation of the Council, and a persistent violator of the principles of the *Charter* may be expelled from the United Nations by the Assembly on the Council's recommendation. The Presidency of the Council rotates monthly, according to the listing of its Member States. The Council has a number of subsidiary bodies, including the Counter-Terrorism Committee, established by Council resolutions[53] following the attack on the twin towers of the World Trade Center in New York City on 11 September 2001.

The Economic and Social Council[54] (ECOSOC) has a remit under article 62 of the *UN Charter* in two broad areas: economic and social matters, and human rights. It also coordinates the work of the UN's 'specialized agencies' (see below). It has a potentially important role of interaction with non-government organisations (NGOs), acting as their main 'portal of entry' to the UN system, and has an oversight role in relation to an array of subsidiary bodies including the functional and regional commissions. Its decisions and resolutions are not binding on Member States nor even the specialised agencies indicative of its powerlessness (Rosenthal 2018). It has 54 member governments elected by the General Assembly for overlapping periods of three years. Seats on ECOSOC are allotted according to the five regional groupings: Africa (14), Asia (11), Eastern Europe (6), Latin America and Caribbean (10), WEOG (13). ECOSOC holds several short sessions and preparatory meetings with members of civil society throughout the year. It holds a four-week substantive session in July, alternating between New York and Geneva. This is organised in five segments (High-level, Coordination, Operational Activities, Humanitarian Affairs, and General). A ministerial declaration is generally adopted on the theme of the High level Segment, which provides policy guidance and recommendations for action. ECOSOC has a number of functional and regional commissions and standing committees and expert bodies that report to it, for example,[55] the Economic Commission for Africa. At the 2005 World Summit, heads of State and government mandated ECOSOC to hold annual Ministerial Reviews and a biennial Development Cooperation Forum. The objective of the former was to assess progress in achieving internationally agreed development goals. The objective of the latter was to enhance the coherence and effectiveness of activities of different development partners. ECOSOC has generally been regarded as of decreasing importance in the UN system, in part because of the ambiguities surrounding its relationship with the General Assembly. ECOSOC has 'principal organ' status

---

53 UNSC Res 1373 [on threats to international peace and security caused by terrorist acts], (28 September 2001) UN Doc. S/RES/1373.
54 *Charter of the United Nations*, Chapter X, arts 61–72.
55 Also, the Commission on Human Rights which came to an end in 2006.

under the *UN Charter*, although the UN function of international economic and social cooperation is 'vested in the General Assembly and, under the authority of the General Assembly, in the Economic and Social Council'.[56] This raises 'the vexing problem of the respective responsibilities' of the General Assembly and ECOSOC (Rosenthal 2018: 172). The various reviews which have taken place to assess possible reform initiatives of ECOSOC have varying emphases on its global policy review and institutional coordination roles. One commentator concluded:

> A close reading of the Charter suggests that ECOSOC was never intended to be the center of global policy coordination. Rather, the main powers emerging from World War II preferred to concentrate global policymaking in organizations that reflected their weight in world affairs. The right to exert a veto in the Security Council provided such a UN mechanism in the area of peace and security, while in the area of economic policymaking the weighted voting arrangements at the Bretton Woods institutions made the World Bank and the IMF far more attractive alternatives to the UN General Assembly and ECOSOC, where each sovereign state has one vote.
>
> (Rosenthal 2018: 174)

One significant alteration to ECOSOC's balance of responsibilities has been the General Assembly's decision in 2006[57] to replace the UN Commission on Human Rights (UNCHR) with the UN Human Rights Council (UNHRC), transferring this important oversight from ECOSOC to the General Assembly. However, the iteration of reform proposals and plans to strengthen ECOSOC[58] have not yet produced the coherence and clarifications that is required.

The ICJ,[59] sometimes referred to as the 'World Court', consists of 15 judges elected by the General Assembly and the Security Council; they sit for a renewable term of nine years. The ICJ decides claims between States, but the States' participation in this process is voluntary. It should be noted that the ICJ has no criminal jurisdiction nor is it a court of appeal. The ICJ also provides Advisory Opinions to the General Assembly and the Security Council (see further, section 2.4.1.1 below).

---

56 *Charter of the United Nations*, art. 60.
57 UNGA Res. 60/251 (15 March 2006) UN Doc. A/RES/60/251. A recorded vote on this resolution was requested: adopted by 170 votes; against 4 (Israel, Marshall Islands, Palau and the USA); abstentions 3 (Belarus, Islamic Republic of Iran, Bolivarian Republic of Venezuela).
58 ESC Res. 212/30 'Role of the Economic and Social Council in the integrated and coordinated implementation of and follow-up to the outcomes of the major United Nations conferences and summits, in the light of relevant General Assembly resolutions, including resolution 61/16' (27 July 2012) UN Doc. E/RES/2012/30.
59 *Charter of the United Nations*, Chapter XIV, arts 92–96.

The Secretariat[60] is headed by the Secretary-General of the UN,[61] currently António Guterres (Portugal), the ninth Secretary-General,[62] who took office on 1 January 2017. The Secretariat conducts the administrative work of the UN, as directed by the other organs of the United Nations. It derives from the concept of an international civil service developed during the period of the League of Nations (1920–46). The Secretariat has some 37,505 staff members around the world.[63] There are UN offices at the headquarters in New York, and also in a number of other locations. Two important themes can be identified throughout the life of the Secretariat, 'a battle over its independent nature and an almost constant restructuring accompanied by calls for its reform' (Jonah 2007: 160). The *UN Charter* specifically provides that the Secretary-General and the staff of the Secretariat 'shall not seek or receive instructions from any government or from any other authority external to the Organization' and that each Member State must respect the 'exclusively international character of the responsibilities of the Secretary-General and the staff and not to seek to influence them in the discharge of their responsibilities'.[64]

The principal organs of the United Nations are also linked to the 'specialised agencies' through cooperative agreements. The specialised agencies are established by inter-governmental agreement and have 'relationship agreements' with the UN, and are linked to the coordinating machinery of ECOSOC.[65] There are currently 17 such agencies.[66] The oldest of these agencies, the International Labour Organization (ILO); see section 2.4.1.4 below. Many of the specialised agencies have developed methods to ensure that their decisions are practically

---

60 *Charter of the United Nations*, Chapter XV, arts 97–101.
61 See generally, Newman (2018) 'Secretary-General', Chapter 12, in Weiss, T. G. and Daws, S. (eds) (2018) *The Oxford Handbook on the United Nations*, 2nd edn. Oxford: Oxford University Press, pp. 131–249.
62 Ban Ki Moon (Korea) 2007–2016, Kofi A. Annan (Ghana) 1997–2006; Boutros Boutros-Ghali (Egypt) 1992–1996; Javier Perez de Cuellar (Peru) 1982–1991; Kurt Waldheim (Austria) 1972–1981; U Thant (Myanmar) 1961–1971; Dag Hammarskjöld (Sweden) 1953–1961; and Trygve Lie (Norway) 1946–1953.
63 As at 31 December 2018, the total population of the staff of the Secretariat was 37,505, down from 42,887 in 2012. 'Composition of the Secretariat: staff demographics, Report of the Secretary-General' (22 April 2019) UN Doc. A/74/82.
64 *Charter of the United Nations*, art. 100.
65 See *Charter of the United Nations*, arts 57 and 63.
66 Food and Agriculture Organization (FAO); International Atomic Energy Agency (IAEA); International Civil Aviation Organization (ICAO); International Fund for Agricultural Development (IFAD); International Labour Organization (ILO); International Maritime Organization (IMO); International Monetary Fund (IMF); International Telecommunications Union (ITU); United Nations Educational, Scientific and Cultural Organization (UNESCO); United Nations Industrial Development Organization (UNIDO); Universal Postal Union (UPU); World Bank (WB); World Food Programme (WFP); World Health Organization (WHO); World Intellectual Property Organization (WIPO); World Meteorological Organization (WMO); World Tourism Organization (WTO).

binding on their members (Shaw 2008: 1285). The specialised agencies, together with the UN and its principal organs, are sometimes known collectively as the 'UN family' or the 'UN system'.

The work of the United Nations in establishing the UDHR in 1948 and the two *International Covenants* (the ICCPR and ICESCR) in 1966, collectively referred to as the *International Bill of Human Rights* has been outlined already in Chapter 1 of this book. In recent years, the United Nations has changed its focus from providing international legal 'standard setting' to ensuring that human rights standards are implemented. The Office of the United Nations High Commissioner for Human Rights (OHCHR) was created in 1993 as part of a package of wider reforms to the United Nations. The OHCHR is a subsidiary body of the UN's Secretariat. It supports the work of the various human rights mechanisms such as the UNHRC and the core treaty bodies (e.g. the Committee on the Rights of the Child). It also coordinates UN human rights education and public information activities. The High Commissioner has the rank of Under-Secretary and reports to the General-Secretary of the United Nations and to the General Assembly. The OHCHR seeks to prevent violations of human rights and works with governments to further the observance of human rights standards. The UN's system for human rights protection is explored in further detail in section 2.5 below.

The importance of the United Nations for the development of children's rights was underlined in a 'Special Session on Children' of the General Assembly held in May 2002.[67] It was the first session devoted exclusively to children and the first to include children as official delegates. The aim of the session was to review progress since the World Summit for Children[68] in 1990 and to revitalise commitment to children's rights. The document later derived from this special session, 'A World Fit for Children', was adopted by a resolution of the General Assembly,[69] included a (non-binding) declaration that reaffirmed a commitment to promoting and protecting the rights of children and to a number of principles and objectives aimed at eradicating child poverty, discrimination, poor education, protection from harm, exploitation, disease and war. 'A World Fit for Children' also contained a detailed plan of action that recognised chronic poverty remained the 'single biggest obstacle' to meeting children's needs and protecting their rights. It recognised that poverty hit children hardest and should be a central aim of development activities 'because it strikes at the very roots of their potential for development – their growing bodies and minds'.[70]

---

67 See the archived materials of this Session at: <www.unicef.org/specialsession/> (accessed 20 February 2020).
68 World Summit for Children, United Nations, New York, 29–30 September 1990: <www.unicef.org/wsc/> (accessed 20 February 2020).
69 UNGA Res S-27/2 (10 May 2002) UN Doc. A/RES/S-27/2.
70 Ibid., para. 18.

2.4.1.1 The International Court of Justice (ICJ)

The ICJ, the successor body to the Permanent Court of International Justice (PCIJ) (1922–46), is the principal judicial organ of the United Nations. It is located at The Hague in the Netherlands. The *Statute of the International Court of Justice* (annexed to, and an integral part of the UN Charter[71]) is the main constitutional document constituting and regulating the Court. The General Assembly and Security Council elect the 15 judges of the ICJ to a nine-year term of office. The Court cannot have more than one judge of each nationality and these judges must have the relevant qualifications for high judicial office in their respective countries. A judge of the nationality of a party to a case before the Court retains the right to sit on that case, and a State party to a case without a national judge of the Court, may designate a judge ad hoc. Consequently, in some cases there may be as many as 17 judges sitting. The President and the Vice-President of the Court[72] are elected by the Members of the Court every three years by secret ballot.

The Court has two main roles: to hear and decide *Contentious Cases* between States, and to give *Advisory Opinions* on legal questions referred to it by authorised international bodies. As regards Contentious Cases, it is only States parties that may appear before the Court, which is only competent to hear a case if the States concerned have accepted its jurisdiction. Consent to jurisdiction may be given:

(i) generally in advance;
(ii) by treaty with respect to a defined class of cases;
(ii) by special agreement in relation to a dispute that has already arisen; or
(iv) by ad hoc consent.

Although there is an underlying principle of consent of the parties, the Court's jurisdiction has been described as 'quasi-compulsory' in cases (i) and (ii) above (Crawford and Grant 2007: 195). The Court's procedure is defined in its *Statute* and in essence includes a written and an oral stage, after which the Court deliberates in private and then delivers its judgment in public. The Court is competent to appoint individuals or bodies to provide an expert opinion or carry out an inquiry. There is no appeal from the judgment of the ICJ. Failure to comply with a judgment may result in the other party having recourse to the Security Council.

The first case entered in the General List of the Court was submitted on 22 May 1947.[73] From 1947 to 2019, there have been a total of 177 cases entered in the General List.[74] These have concerned a number of issues, for example, territorial

---

71 *Charter of the United Nations and Statute of the International Court of Justice*, concluded 26 June 1945, 1 UNTS XVI, (entered into force 23 October 1945), Chapter XIV, articles 92–96.
72 The current President is Judge Abdulqawi Ahmed Yusuf (Somalia) and current Vice-President Judge Xue Hanqin (China), elected on 6 February 2018.
73 See *Corfu Channel Case (UK v Albania) (Merits)* [1949] ICJ Rep. 4.
74 Comprising 150 'contentious' cases and 27 'advisory' proceedings. See the ICJ website: <www.icj-cij.org/docket/index.php?p1=3&p2=2> (accessed 20 February 2020).

Introduction to international law sources and institutions   63

sovereignty, land and marine boundary disputes, diplomatic relations, hostage taking and the right of asylum. The Court has gone through periods of inactivity; for example from 1965 to 1985 relatively few cases were brought. The Court's cases expanded in volume and breadth in the 1980s and 1990s from a focus on land and maritime boundary disputes to military and paramilitary activities, compensation for the environmental effects of mining operations, diplomatic immunities and international criminal law. The 2000s and 2010s have continued to see cases concerning maritime boundaries and land border disputes, nuclear arms and disarmament, sovereignty and the legality of the use of force.

There is, however, only one judgment to date directly relevant to children, and that concerned the issue of guardianship: see the *Boll Case* (1958) below. This also remains the only case in which a Hague Convention was the principal subject of interpretation by a court with worldwide jurisdiction.

Case study 2.1

The *Boll Case (1958)*[75] in the International Court of Justice (ICJ)

Facts: A Dutch girl, Marie Elizabeth Boll, was the child of a Dutch seaman and his deceased Swedish wife. She had lived in Sweden with her mother before her mother's death, but only had Dutch nationality. On her mother's death the Dutch authorities assigned guardianship under their procedures. However, the Swedish authorities overrode this and placed her under their protective upbringing regime on the basis of her continuing residence in Sweden with her maternal grandparents. The Netherlands claimed that the Swedish measure of protective upbringing was incompatible with the obligations under the *Hague Convention of 1902*.[76] Under this Convention the application of the national law of the child was expressly extended to both the person and the property of the child. On the facts, this would have led to the child being handed over to a Dutch guardian.

Held: The ICJ construed the concept of guardianship narrowly. It held that the *Convention of 1902* did not cover the social purpose of the Swedish protective upbringing regime; therefore there was no failure by Sweden to

---

75 *Application of the Convention of 1902 Governing the Guardianship of Infants (Netherlands v Sweden) (Judgment)* [1958] ICJ Rep. 55 (aka the Boll Case).
76 Hague Conference on Private International Law, *Hague Convention on the Settlement of Guardianship of Minors*, concluded 12 June 1902 (entered into force 30 July 1904, replaced by the *Hague Convention on Jurisdiction, Applicable Law, Recognition, Enforcement and Co-Operation in respect of Parental Responsibility and Measures for the Protection of Children*, concluded 19 October 1996 (entered into force 1 January 2002).

> observe its obligations under this Convention and the Netherlands' claim was rejected (by twelve votes to four).
>
> **Commentary:** In effect, this decision 'allowed a state to void a guardianship established by another state with presumed jurisdiction by adopting a domestic public law measure voiding it of content' (Dyer 1997: 631). The Hague Conference responded to correct the result in *Boll* by drafting a further Convention in 1961[77] which recognised a new concept, 'measures directed to the protection of [the child's] person or property', a notion sufficiently broad to cover both a State's private law measures and public care orders. The Convention of 1961 focussed on the 'interests of the child' as the basis upon which the state of the child's nationality could override measures taken by another state (usually the state of the child's 'habitual residence').
>
> This emphasis upon the interest of the child, a concept that appeared only for emergency measures in the 1902 Convention, reflected the intervening shift of attitudes that had been internationally expressed in the 1924 Declaration of the Rights of the Child and in the 1959 United Nations Declaration on the Rights of the Child. This was a recognition at the international level of a shift taking place in the domestic laws of many countries, from an emphasis on paternal or parental authority towards an emphasis on protecting the child, even from the child's parents. This concept foreshadowed the ideas reflected in the later 1989 *Convention on the Rights of the Child*, that a child should be viewed as a subject of rights and not merely as an object of rights or of protective action. (Dyer 1997: 633)

The ICJ's function to provide Advisory Opinions is available only to international organisations. The *UN Charter* provides that it is only the General Assembly or the Security Council that may request Advisory Opinions of the Court. Other organs of the United Nations and the 'specialised agencies' authorised by the General Assembly may also request Advisory Opinions on legal questions within the scope of their activities,[78] though more often it is the General Assembly that requests Advisory Opinions. In one case,[79] the Court held that the request from the World Health Organization (WHO) did not fall within the remit of WHO and refused jurisdiction.

---

77 Hague Conference on Private International Law, *Hague Convention Concerning the Powers of Authorities and the Law Applicable in Respect of the Protection of Infants*, concluded 5 October 1961 (entered into force 4 February 1969).
78 *Charter of the United Nations*, art. 96.
79 *Legality of the Use by a State of Nuclear Weapons in Armed Conflict*, Advisory Opinion of 8 July 1996, [1996] ICJ Reports 226.

Introduction to international law sources and institutions   65

There have been suggestions that the power to request Advisory Opinions could be given to the Secretary-General and to States parties and national courts (Schwebel 1984, 1988). The Court has made it clear that it will not decline a request for an Advisory Opinion on the basis only that the legal questions at issue also implicate political issues.[80] In principle, the Court's Advisory Opinions are not binding in character, but there is provision to agree in advance that the Advisory Opinion will be binding. The Court has processed 27 Advisory Opinion proceedings since 1946, concerning, for example: the conditions of admission of a State to membership in the United Nations; reparation for injuries suffered in the service of the United Nations; the international status of South West Africa (Namibia); certain expenses of the United Nations; certain judgments rendered by the United Nations administrative tribunal; Western Sahara; questions relating to the privileges and immunities of human rights rapporteurs; the legality of the threat or use of nuclear weapons; and the legal consequences of the construction of a wall in the Israeli-occupied Palestinian territory. In general, it would seem that the ICJ is now playing a more central role within the international legal system.

2.4.1.2   The United Nations Children's Fund (UNICEF)[81]

The United Nations Children's Fund was created by the General Assembly on 11 December 1946 to provide emergency food and healthcare for children in countries that had been devastated by the Second World War. In 1953, UNICEF became a permanent part of the UN system and its name was shortened (from the original 'United Nations International Children's Emergency Fund'), but it has continued to be known by the popular acronym based on the old name. UNICEF's 36-strong executive board is elected by ECOSOC to guide its work. Members are elected for three-year terms and the board regularly makes reports to ECOSOC. UNICEF has a strong presence in most countries. In the past nearly seven decades its role has evolved into broader development work to tackle poverty in order to meet the needs of children. The organisation was awarded the Nobel Peace Prize in 1965. In the 1980s there was a policy focus on addressing child mortality rates that was implemented by simple, low cost, primary health care activities to tackle the range of infections prevalent in early childhood.[82] UNICEF also participated in the late 1980s in the establishment of the CRC. The CRC is fundamental to UNICEF's mission which shifted in the 1990s from the promotion of the child's survival and development to supporting children's rights under the

---

80 Ibid., pp. 233–4; *Legal Consequences of the Construction of a Wall in the Occupied Palestinian Territory*, Advisory Opinion of 9 July 2004, [1994] ICJ Rep. 136 and 155 (para. 41).
81 See generally, Black (1986, 1996) for a history of UNICEF. Available at: <www.unicef.org/about/history/index_publications.html> (accessed 16 October 2013).
82 The techniques deployed were known as 'GOBI': 'G' for growth monitoring, 'O' for oral rehydration therapy, 'B' for breastfeeding and 'I' for immunisation.

CRC. This approach broadened UNICEF's operation and 'has led the organization to address some of the most difficult issues of our times, such as children in armed conflict, child labor, and sexual exploitation of children' (Rios-Kohn 1998: 191). UNICEF has, it is argued, 'taken steps to integrate the principles of the CRC into all aspects of its activities' (Oestreich 1998: 184). This rights-based approach remains a key element of UNICEF's mission, though not without criticism in so far as this focus may detract from its child survival and mortality work (Horton 2004).

Its humanitarian work was also strengthened by the *Core Commitments for Children in Humanitarian Action* (UNICEF 2010), a global framework for humanitarian action for children undertaken by UNICEF and its partners. In all its activities UNICEF's approach prioritises children who are most vulnerable and in greatest need. In recent years, 'a renewed emphasis on equity for children has become a cornerstone of the organization's programme, policy and advocacy work' (Mullerbeck and Anthony 2011). UNICEF previously produced a flagship annual publication entitled *The State of the World's Children*,[83] which focused on a particular issue in detail, for example, children in an urban world (UNICEF 2012) and children with disabilities (UNICEF 2013).

There are a number of national committees that raise funds for UNICEF. Each country office initiates a five-year programme in collaboration with the host government, and focuses on practical ways in which to achieve the rights of children and women in accordance with the principles laid down in the CRC and the UN's *Convention on the Elimination of All Forms of Discrimination against Women* (1979).[84] A situation report is produced at the beginning of each programme cycle. The overall policy on children is made at the UN headquarters. UNICEF helps to provide humanitarian aid in times of civil commotion and war, supplying food, safe water, medicine and shelter. It has also advanced the idea of 'children as zones of peace' and 'corridors of peace' to help protect children where there is armed conflict. On 22 December 2017, Henrietta H. Fore became the seventh Executive Director of the United Nations Children's Fund.[85]

2.4.1.3 The International Law Commission (ILC)

When the United Nations was established, there was little support by those framing the *UN Charter* to give the United Nations direct law-making powers. However, there was support for a power to undertake studies and make recommendations for 'encouraging the progressive development of international law and its codification'.[86] The General Assembly established the ILC for this purpose in 1947,

---

83 Available at: <www.unicef.org/sowc/> (accessed 16 September 2019). Last issue dated 2017.
84 Opened for signature 1 March 1980, 1249 UNTS 13 (entered into force 3 September 1981).
85 See <www.un.org/sg/en/content/profiles/henrietta-fore> (accessed 20 February 2020) for a short biography.
86 *Charter of the United Nations*, art. 3(1).

along with a *Statute of the International Law Commission*.[87] The ILC meets annually and is composed of 34 members elected by the General Assembly for five-year terms; members act as individuals and not as State representatives. The members serve in an individual capacity, reflecting their expertise, rather than as mandated government representatives. The topics for their work are sometimes referred to them by the General Assembly or ECOSOC, or requested either by a government, an inter-governmental organisation or a UN agency, and they are also initiated by the ILC itself.

It is provided that the ILC 'shall concern itself primarily with public international law, but is not precluded from entering the field of private international law'.[88] In fact, it has predominantly dealt with public international law matters. The *Statute of the International Law Commission* also makes a distinction between its two main tasks. 'Progressive development' means 'the preparation of draft conventions on subjects which have not yet been regulated by international law or in regard to which the law has not yet been sufficiently developed in the practice of States'. 'Codification' means 'the more precise formulation and systematisation of rules of international law in fields where there already has been extensive State practice precedent and doctrine'.[89]

The ILC's work has resulted in a number of treaties that have made a significant contribution to the international legal order, for example, the *Convention on the High Seas* (1958),[90] the *Vienna Convention on Diplomatic Relations* (1961),[91] and the *Vienna Convention on the Law of Treaties* (1969),[92] It has also produced some significant 'soft law' instruments; for example, the *Draft Articles on the Responsibility of States for Internationally Wrongful Acts* (2001),[93] and the *Guide to Practice on Reservations to Treaties* (2011).[94]

Once a topic has been identified, a special rapporteur is usually appointed by the Commission who will analyse it and report back to the Commission. States will have an opportunity to comment on the Commission's progress and their report will be further debated by the Sixth Committee (legal). Draft articles are then generally submitted in final form to the General Assembly with a recommendation that it convenes a diplomatic conference to adopt the draft articles as a convention.

---

87 UNGA, A-RES-174(II), 21 November 1947. Amended on 12 December 1950, 3 December 1955 and 18 November 1981.
88 *Statute of the International Law Commission*, art. 1(2).
89 Ibid., art. 15.
90 Opened for signature 29 April 1958, 450 UNTS 11 (entered into force 30 September 1962).
91 Opened for signature 18 April 1961, 500 UNTS 95 (entered into force 24 April 1964).
92 Opened for signature 23 May 1969, 1155 UNTS 331 (entered into force 27 January 1980).
93 International Law Commission, *Draft Articles on Responsibility of States for Internationally Wrongful Acts*, November 2001, Supplement No. 10 (A/56/10), chp.IV.E.1, available at: <www.unhcr.org/refworld/docid/3ddb8f804.html> (accessed 20 February 2020).
94 International Law Commission, *Report on the Work of its Sixty-third Session*, UN GAOR, 66th Sess., Supp. No. 10, UN Doc. A/66/10 (2011), para. 75). The report will appear in *Yearbook of the International Law Commission, 2011*, vol. II, Part Two.

However, there are a number of questions (McCrae 2012) arising about the present and future practice of the ILC: are codification and progressive development separate or interrelated enterprises; what are the selection criteria and the evidence base for the analyses of the various topics under consideration; what is the appropriate relationship between the ILC and States and other international actors; can the Commission deal with politically controversial issues; and should the outcome of ILC work be formalised as draft articles ready for treaty-making or should it generate more soft law instruments? A general criticism that is emerging (McCrae 2012) is that the days of major codification, the core of the Commission's work in the past, may be over, thus highlighting the current lack of a clearly defined role for the ILC. On the other hand, a shift to progressive development will bring the ILC into a more politicised environment rather than an expert forum. In ILC held its 71st session in Geneva for 11 weeks between June and August 2019.

2.4.1.4 The International Labour Organization (ILO)[95]

The 'specialised agencies' of the UN are a privileged and integral part of the UN system. The ILO is of particular interest to international child lawyers as one of its mainstream concerns is the problem of child labour (see Chapter 5 of this book). ILO became the first 'specialised agency' of the UN system in 1946. It was originally founded in 1919 and is the only surviving creation of the *Treaty of Versailles* (1919) that established the League of Nations.

Its principal task is to establish international labour standards in the field of employment rights. It also provides technical assistance, for example, in the fields of employment policy, labour law and industrial relations, working conditions and labour statistics. Its general aims and purpose were set out in the *Declaration of Philadelphia* (1944) and this document is now annexed to the *ILO Constitution* (1946).[96] ILO has a unique tripartite structure: workers' and employers' organisations participate as equal partners, along with governments, in its principal organs. The tripartite structure is reflected in all three of its main bodies; the International Labour Conference, the Governing Body and the International Labour Office.

There are three principal elements to ILO's work. First, ILO adopts a range of international labour standards ('*ILO Conventions*' and '*ILO Recommendations*') for implementation by ILO's Member States. These conventions and recommendations contain guidelines on child labour, protection of women workers, hours of work, labour inspection, vocational guidance and training, social security protection,

---

95 See generally, Kott and Droux (2013).
96 The General Conference of the International Labour Organization, *Declaration concerning the aims and purposes of the International Labour Organisation* ('Declaration of Philadelphia'), 26th session, 10 May 1944, Philadelphia, § I. International Labour Organization, *Constitution of the International Labour Organisation (ILO)*, 1 April 1919. Adopted by the Peace Conference in April 1919, Constitution became Part XIII of the Treaty of Versailles (1919).

workers' housing, occupational health and safety, conditions of work at sea and the protection of migrant workers. They also encompass basic human rights such as; freedom of association, collective bargaining, the abolition of forced labour, the elimination of discrimination in employment, and the promotion of full employment. At the time of writing, ILO had adopted 189 Conventions and 202 Recommendations. Eight of these conventions have been identified by ILO as 'fundamental',[97] and in 1995 ILO started a campaign aimed at achieving universal ratification of these conventions. Second, it provides a programme of technical cooperation in conjunction with the United Nations Development Program and other agencies to assist developing nations. Finally, international labour standard-setting and technical cooperation is further enhanced by an extensive research, training, education and publications programme.

ILO operates a significant enforcement procedure. The *ILO Constitution* requires member states to make annual reports on the measures they have taken to implement the conventions they have adopted. Such reports are closely scrutinised by a committee of experts which may follow up issues with the relevant governments. There is also a developed complaints system available to member states: see further details in sections 5.2.5 and 5.2.6 below).

The Member States of ILO (currently 187) meet in Geneva at the International Labour Conference in June of each year. Two government representatives and one worker delegate and one employer delegate represent each Member State. Delegations are usually headed by Cabinet-rank ministers, but individual delegates can vote freely, even against their own delegation. The conference plays a key role in discussing and adopting international labour standards. It elects the Governing Body and adopts the budget. The Governing Body is the executive council; it consists of 28 government, 14 worker and 14 employer member representatives, and 66 deputy members. Ten of the government seats are permanently held by States of chief industrial importance,[98] and representatives of the remaining government seats are elected at the conference every three years. It meets three times a year in Geneva. It sets the agenda for ILO's policy and presents the programme and budget for approval by the conference. It will also elect a Director-General for a five-year term to lead the International Labour Office.[99] This body is ILO's permanent secretariat and carries out the work of the organisation under the scrutiny of the Governing Body. The Office employs some 2,700 officials of over 150 nations at its Geneva headquarters and in 40 field offices. In addition, some 900 experts undertake missions in all regions of the world under the programme of technical cooperation.

---

97 See Chapter 5.
98 Brazil, China, France, Germany, India, Italy, Japan, the Russian Federation, the United Kingdom and the United States.
99 Guy Ryder CBE (born Liverpool, UK, 3 January 1956) was elected the 10th Director General of ILO in October 2012.

2.4.2 The Hague Conference on Private International Law

The Hague Conference on Private International Law (hereafter the 'Hague Conference') is *not* part of the UN system; its origins predate the formation of the League of Nations in 1919. The Hague Conference is an intergovernmental organisation whose main purpose is 'to work for the progressive unification of the rules of private international law'.[100] Relationships of a personal, family or commercial nature between individuals and companies in more than one country have become increasingly common in the modern world. One main function of the Hague Conference is to resolve the differences that may occur between the various legal systems involved through the formulation and adoption of 'private international law' rules. The Hague Conference has also developed its role as a centre for international judicial and administrative cooperation in the area of private law, especially in the fields of protection of the family and children, civil procedure and commercial law.

The first session of the Hague Conference was convened in 1893 by the Netherlands government. Six sessions were held prior to the Second World War and the seventh session, held in 1951, saw the introduction of a *Statute of the Hague Conference on Private International Law*,[101] which made the Hague Conference a permanent intergovernmental organisation. There were, at the time of writing, 75 Members of the Hague Conference comprised of 74 Member States and one Regional Economic Integration Organisation (the European Union). In 1980, the Conference opened its doors to non-Member States where the subject matter of the convention at issue indicated this was appropriate. This decision was taken with international trade law in mind, but there has been an increasing tendency for non-Member States[102] both to participate in proceedings and to ratify Hague Conference Conventions across the whole range of subject matter (Van Loon 2000: 231).

The work of the Hague Conference has been to draw up multilateral conventions over a number of private international law fields including conflict of laws issues, the recognition of companies, jurisdiction and foreign judgments, and international judicial and administrative cooperation. Hague Conference activities are organised by a secretariat, the 'Permanent Bureau', headed by a Secretary General. The Permanent Bureau's main role is to make the necessary preparations for the plenary sessions and for the Special Commissions. The Permanent Bureau will undertake some of the preliminary research on a convention or treaty

---

100 *Statute of the Hague Convention on Private International Law* (1955), art. 1.
101 The *Statute* was adopted during the Seventh Session of the Hague Conference on Private International Law on 31 October 1951 and entered into force on 15 July 1955. Amendments were adopted during the Twentieth Session on 30 June 2005 (Final Act, C), approved by Members on 30 September 2006 and entered into force on 1 January 2007.
102 At the time of writing there were additionally 69 non-member states which had signed, ratified or acceded to one or more Hague Conventions.

and then refer it to a Special Commission made up of government experts. The drafts are then discussed and adopted at the plenary session. These sessions meet roughly every four years and additional 'Extraordinary Sessions' are convened on an ad hoc basis. The Standing Government Committee of Private International Law formally sets the agenda for the plenary session under the *Statute*. However, more direct influence by Member States has evolved so that recommendations are made by the Special Commissions and then to the plenary sessions. At the plenary session each Member State has one vote, and non-Member States, invited to participate on an equal footing, also have a vote. By tradition, the President of the plenary session has always been the person leading the Netherlands delegation, reflecting its historical origins. The Conference has adopted 39 conventions since 1951.

Special Commissions are also used frequently to monitor the operation of particular conventions. This has occurred, for example, in relation to the conventions aimed at child protection.[103] The Hague Conference has also been active in its outreach activities. It has organised international judicial seminars, for example, on child custody and the international protection of children.

The Hague Conference has increasingly become a centre for international judicial and administrative cooperation in the area of private law, especially in the fields of protection of the family and children, of civil procedure and commercial law. There are several modern Hague conventions that have been particularly influential in the development of international child law and have been very successful Hague conventions in their own right. These are the Hague Conventions on: the *Civil Aspects of International Child Abduction* (1980) (see Chapter 6 of this book); the *Protection of Children and Cooperation in respect of Intercountry Adoption* (1993) (see Chapter 7 of this book).[104]

As the globalisation of human rights standard-setting increases, there arises a need to ensure the complementarity of Hague Conventions with other international legal regimes. One commentator observes that in relation, for example, to the Hague *Child Abduction Convention* and *Intercountry Adoption Convention*, the CRC 'provides the general framework' while the Hague Conventions 'implement the framework's principles, and provide coordination of the diversity of legal systems' (Van Loon 2011: 184).

---

103 For example, *Conclusions and Recommendations of Part I and Part II of the Special Commission on the practical operation of the 1980 Child Abduction Convention and the 1996 Child Protection Convention*, April 2012, Hague Conference.

104 Other relevant Hague Conventions are: *Convention on Jurisdiction, Applicable Law, Recognition, Enforcement and Cooperation in Respect of Parental Responsibility and Measures for the Protection of Children*, concluded 19 October 1996 (entered into force 1 January 2002); *Convention on the International Recovery of Child Support and Other Forms of Family Maintenance*, concluded 23 November 2007 (entered into force 1 January 2013); *Protocol on the Law Applicable to Maintenance Obligations*, concluded 23 November 2007 (entered into force 1 August 2013).

2.4.3 The International Criminal Court

The International Criminal Court (ICC) began operating on 1 July 2002 following international discussions initiated by the General Assembly and established by the *Rome Statute of the International Criminal Court* (1998) (hereafter the *'Rome Statute'*).[105] Its official seat is in The Hague but its proceedings may take place anywhere. It is the first permanent international court charged with trying those who commit the most serious crimes under international law, that is, 'crimes against humanity', 'war crimes' and 'genocide'.[106] It may in the future exercise jurisdiction over the crime of 'aggression', once a definition of this crime has been agreed by States parties and an amendment to the *Rome Statute* is made.[107] It should be noted that it does not have a *general* criminal jurisdiction; it does not, for example, have jurisdiction over terrorism or drug trafficking.

The ICC is *not* part of the UN system. It is functionally independent of the UN in terms of personnel and financing, but some meetings of the ICC governing body, the Assembly of States Parties to the *Rome Statute*, are held at the UN. There is an agreement between the ICC and the United Nations that governs how the two institutions work with each other.[108] Although at the time of writing 122 countries are parties to the *Rome Statute*,[109] its authority is weakened by the absence of China, India, Russia and the United States from membership.[110] There have also been criticisms of the ICC relating to its power to assume jurisdiction over the nationals of non-States parties without those States' consent, in particular where the nationals are military personnel (Akande 2003).

The Court comprises four organs: the Presidency, the judicial Divisions, the Office of the Prosecutor, and the Registry. The Presidency consists of three judges of the Court elected by their fellow judges for a three-year term. The President and two Vice-Presidents of the Court are responsible for its overall administration. The judicial Divisions consist of 18 judges in three Divisions: Pre-Trial, Trial and Appeals. The Office of the Prosecutor has responsibility for receiving referrals and information on crimes within the Court's jurisdiction and for conducting investigations and prosecutions before the Court. The Registry is responsible for the non-judicial administration of the Court. The Registrar, who is elected by the judges for a term of five years, performs his/her functions under the authority of the President of the Court.

---

105 *Rome Statute of the International Criminal Court*, opened for signature 17 July 1998, 2187 UNTS 90 (entered into force 1 July 2002).
106 Closely defined in the *Rome Statute*, arts 6, 7 and 8.
107 See *Rome Statute*, art. 5(1)(d) and (2).
108 International Criminal Court, *Negotiated Relationship Agreement between the International Criminal Court and the United Nations*, Doc. No ICC-ASP/3/Res. 1 (entry into force 22 July 2004).
109 Of these, 33 are African States, 18 are Asia-Pacific States, 18 are from Eastern Europe, 28 are from Latin American and Caribbean States, and 25 are from Western European and other States.
110 The Russian Federation and the United States both signed the *Rome Statute*, but the United States expressly clarified later that it did not intend to ratify this treaty.

Introduction to international law sources and institutions 73

There are three routes available to the Prosecutor to undertake an investigation into a 'situation':

(a) on the basis of a referral from any state party;
(b) a referral from or the UN's Security Council; and
(c) by the Prosecutor's own motion (*proprio motu*) on the basis of information received from individuals or organizations.[111]

Under routes (a) and (b) the Court can exercise jurisdiction only if: (i) the State on whose territory the crime was committed, or (ii) the State of the nationality of the accused person; is a States party to the *Rome Statute*. If neither is a States party, either can voluntarily accept the Court's jurisdiction.[112] The jurisdiction of the Court is also constrained by a 'complementarity' rule. The Court will determine a case is inadmissible where:

(a) The case is being investigated or prosecuted by a State which has jurisdiction over it, unless the State is unwilling or unable genuinely to carry out the investigation or prosecution;
(b) The case has been investigated by a State which has jurisdiction over it and the State has decided not to prosecute the person concerned, unless the decision resulted from the unwillingness or inability of the State genuinely to prosecute;
(c) The person concerned has already been tried for conduct which is the subject of the complaint, . . .;
(d) The case is not of sufficient gravity to justify further action by the Court.[113]

It should be noted however, that a State must have incorporated in their domestic legislation, the crimes envisaged in the *Rome Statute*, in order to rely on the complementarity principle.

To date, 11 'situations' have been brought before the International Criminal Court. Uganda, the Democratic Republic of the Congo and the Central African Republic have referred situations occurring on their territories to the Court. In addition, the Security Council has referred the situation in Darfur, Sudan and the situation in Libya (both non-state parties). The Court granted the Prosecutor authorisation to open an investigation proprio motu (own one's own motion/initiative) in the situations of Kenya in 2010 and in Côte d'Ivoire in 2011. In addition, the Office of the Prosecutor is currently conducting preliminary examinations in a number of situations including Afghanistan, Georgia, Guinea, Colombia, Honduras, Korea and Nigeria. There were, at the time of writing, 27 cases before

---

111 *Rome Statute*, arts 13 and 15.
112 Ibid., art. 12.
113 *Rome Statute*, art. 17.

74 Introduction to international law sources and institutions

the Court.[114] The ICC's first trial to be brought to a judgment concerned the Congolese militia leader, Lubanga. On 10 July 2012, he was sentenced to a total period of 14 years of imprisonment for the war crime of enlisting and conscripting children under the age of 15 years into armed forces. He appealed the decision and the Appeals Chamber confirmed both the decision and the sentence on 1 December 2014. See Chapter 9 in this book for further details.

2.5 Human rights protection

The overview of the development of human rights protection in Chapter 1 provides some detail about the introduction of the *Universal Declaration of Human Rights* (UDHR) (1948) and the two *International Covenants* (1966) (section 1.2.1 above), dealing respectively with (civil and political) and (economic, social and cultural) rights. The UDHR, made by resolution of the General Assembly, is not strictly binding in international law. However, it is generally treated as having entered into international customary law. The UDHR and the two (binding) Covenants are often referred to collectively as the *International Bill of Human Rights*.[115] It is thought to have three main elements: a declaration of principles (UDHR), a Convention (the two *International Covenants* of 1966 and their Optional Protocols), and the means of implementation: for example, periodic reports, technical assistance, global studies and the appointment of a High Commissioner for Human Rights (Hobbins 2001: 38–9). The *International Bill of Human Rights* has laid the modern foundation of international human rights law, and their provisions have found their way into the written Constitutions of a number of States and subsequent human rights treaties. There have also been further UN treaties dealing with particular subject areas of human rights concerns, for example, racial discrimination, discrimination against women, the prevention of torture, the protection of migrant workers, enforced disappearances, the rights of persons with disabilities, and the rights of the child.

2.5.1 Global protection – UN machinery

There are two types of body generally within the UN system of global protection that promote and protect human rights. First, those created under the *UN Charter*, and second, those established by international human rights treaties. 'Charter bodies' are established under provisions of the *UN Charter*, or by bodies which themselves are created by the *UN Charter*. They are the political UN human rights institutions, made up of representatives of governments. The 'treaty bodies' are

---

114 These 27 cases concerned the situations in: Uganda (2 cases); Democratic Republic of the Congo (6); Darfur, Sudan (5); Central African Republic (3); Kenya (4); Libya (3); Côte d'Ivoire (2); Mali (2).
115 See further: 'The International Bill of Human Rights', *Fact Sheet No. 2 (Rev. 1)*, Geneva, United Nations. Available at: <www.ohchr.org/Documents/Publications/FactSheet2Rev.1en.pdf> (accessed 20 February 2020).

'the quasi-judicial arm of UN human rights supervision' (Joseph and Kyriakakis (2010: 5) established under one of the international human rights Conventions (see Table 2.1 below).

Most of these entities receive administrative support and coordination from the Office of the High Commissioner for Human Rights (OHCHR), a subsidiary body of the UN's Secretariat. The interrelationship between the range of human rights and the need for the United Nations to treat human rights pervasively within all its activities was recognised in the *Vienna Declaration and Programme of Action* adopted by the General Assembly in 1993,[116] following a World Conference on Human Rights in the same year. This *Declaration* emphasised that all human rights were universal, indivisible and interrelated; and it called for, *inter alia*, the creation of OHCHR to spotlight and coordinate human rights activities. The OHCHR was established some months later, and the first incumbent took office in 1994. The OHCHR is based at the Palais Wilson in Geneva and the UN headquarters in New York City. The idea was to have a centre with strong moral authority to lead the human rights movement and to enhance the UN's ability to implement human rights standards. The OHCHR has forged links with non-government organisations (NGOs), academic institutions and others to promote human rights education, in addition to its involvement in preventative work. One of the aims of the OHCHR is to assist in *mainstreaming* human rights thinking throughout the UN system. The OHCHR is broadly tasked with a liaison role between all the human rights bodies within the UN and beyond.

The OHCHR acts as the principal focal point of human rights research, education, public information, and advocacy activities in the United Nations system. It also provides assistance to Governments and others, in the areas, for example, of administration of justice, legislative reform, and electoral process, to help implement international human rights standards on the ground. It works with governments, civil society, national human rights institutions and other international bodies to promote and protect human rights. It undertakes three principal functional activities: standard-setting, monitoring, and implementation on the ground. It offers substantive and secretariat support to the different United Nations human rights bodies as they discharge their standard-setting and monitoring duties. OHCHR, for example, serves as the Secretariat of the key 'charter body', the UN Human Rights Council (UNHRC) (see below). It also supports the work of 'special procedures' – including special rapporteurs, independent experts, and working groups – appointed by UNHRC to monitor human rights in different countries or in relation to specific issues. OHCHR also supports the core human rights 'treaty bodies'.

Finally, OHCHR works towards the implementation of international human rights standards on the ground through greater country engagement and its field presences. OHCHR employs around 1,300 staff, based in Geneva and New York

---

116 UNGA, *Vienna Declaration and Programme of Action*, UN Doc. A/CONF.157/23, 12 July 1993. Endorsed by General Assembly resolution: UNGA Res 48/121, UN Doc. A/RES/48/121, 20 December 1993.

and in 12 country offices and 12 regional offices around the world, including a workforce of some 235 international human rights officers serving in UN peace missions. The High Commissioner is currently Michelle Bachelet of Chile.[117] She took up the post on 1 September 2018. It has been observed that the High Commissioner is called upon to fulfil somewhat contradictory roles – 'moral leadership, political sensitivity, and bureaucratic-managerial duties' (Ramcharan 2007: 452).

It should not be forgotten that the United Nations system provides, from time to time, a world stage upon which the message of human rights protection generally, and children's rights in particular can be communicated with a powerful impact on a global audience.

Case study 2.2

United Nations: Youth Assembly on 'Malala Day', in New York, on 12 July 2013:
Pakistani schoolgirl Malala Yousafzai marked her 16th birthday by delivering a speech at the UN headquarters as part of her campaign to ensure free compulsory education for every child.

Malala's Speech:
'Honourable UN Secretary General Mr Ban Ki-moon, respected president of the General Assembly Vuk Jeremic, honourable UN envoy for global education Mr Gordon Brown, respected elders and my dear brothers and sisters: Assalamu alaikum.

Today is it an honour for me to be speaking again after a long time. Being here with such honourable people is a great moment in my life and it is an honour for me that today I am wearing a shawl of the late Benazir Bhutto. I don't know where to begin my speech. I don't know what people would be expecting me to say, but first of all thank you to God for whom we all are equal and thank you to every person who has prayed for my fast recovery and new life. I cannot believe how much love people have shown me. I have received thousands of good-wish cards and gifts from all over the world. Thank you to all of them. Thank you to the children whose innocent words encouraged me. Thank you to my elders whose prayers strengthened me. I would like to thank my nurses, doctors and the staff of the hospitals in Pakistan and the UK and the UAE government who have helped me to get better and recover my strength.

I fully support UN Secretary General Ban Ki-moon in his Global Education First Initiative and the work of UN Special Envoy for Global Education

---

117 Previous High Commissioners were: Mr Zeid Ra'ad Al Hussein, Jordan, 2014–2018; Ms Navanethem Pillay South Africa, 2008–2014; Ms Louise Arbour, Canada, 2004–2008; Mr Bertrand Ramcharan (Acting High Commissioner), August 2003 – July 2004); Mr Sergio Vieira de Mello, Brazil, 2002–2003; Mrs Mary Robinson, Ireland, 1997–2002; Mr José Ayala-Lasso, Ecuador, 1994–1997.

Gordon Brown and the respectful president of the UN General Assembly Vuk Jeremic. I thank them for the leadership they continue to give. They continue to inspire all of us to action. Dear brothers and sisters, do remember one thing: Malala Day is not my day. Today is the day of every woman, every boy and every girl who have raised their voice for their rights.

There are hundreds of human rights activists and social workers who are not only speaking for their rights, but who are struggling to achieve their goal of peace, education and equality. Thousands of people have been killed by the terrorists and millions have been injured. I am just one of them. So here I stand, one girl among many. I speak not for myself, but so those without a voice can be heard. Those who have fought for their rights. Their right to live in peace. Their right to be treated with dignity. Their right to equality of opportunity. Their right to be educated.

Dear friends, on 9 October 2012, the Taliban shot me on the left side of my forehead. They shot my friends, too. They thought that the bullets would silence us, but they failed. And out of that silence came thousands of voices. The terrorists thought they would change my aims and stop my ambitions. But nothing changed in my life except this: weakness, fear and hopelessness died. Strength, power and courage was born. I am the same Malala. My ambitions are the same. My hopes are the same. And my dreams are the same. Dear sisters and brothers, I am not against anyone. Neither am I here to speak in terms of personal revenge against the Taliban or any other terrorist group. I am here to speak for the right of education for every child. I want education for the sons and daughters of the Taliban and all the terrorists and extremists. I do not even hate the Talib who shot me.

Even if there was a gun in my hand and he was standing in front of me, I would not shoot him. This is the compassion I have learned from Mohamed, the prophet of mercy, Jesus Christ and Lord Buddha. This is the legacy of change I have inherited from Martin Luther King, Nelson Mandela and Mohammed Ali Jinnah.

This is the philosophy of nonviolence that I have learned from Gandhi, Bacha Khan and Mother Teresa. And this is the forgiveness that I have learned from my father and from my mother. This is what my soul is telling me: be peaceful and love everyone.

Dear sisters and brothers, we realise the importance of light when we see darkness. We realise the importance of our voice when we are silenced. In the same way, when we were in Swat, the north of Pakistan, we realised the importance of pens and books when we saw the guns. The wise saying, "The pen is mightier than the sword." It is true. The extremists are afraid of books and pens. The power of education frightens them. They are afraid of women. The power of the voice of women frightens them. This is why they killed 14 innocent students in the recent attack in Quetta. And that is why they kill female teachers.

That is why they are blasting schools every day because they were and they are afraid of change and equality that we will bring to our society. And I remember that there was a boy in our school who was asked by a journalist: "Why are the Taliban against education?" He answered very simply by pointing to his book, he said: "A Talib doesn't know what is written inside this book."

They think that God is a tiny, little conservative being who would point guns at people's heads just for going to school. These terrorists are misusing the name of Islam for their own personal benefit. Pakistan is a peace-loving, democratic country. Pashtuns want education for their daughters and sons. Islam is a religion of peace, humanity and brotherhood. It is the duty and responsibility to get education for each child, that is what it says. Peace is a necessity for education. In many parts of the world, especially Pakistan and Afghanistan, terrorism, war and conflicts stop children from going to schools. We are really tired of these wars. Women and children are suffering in many ways in many parts of the world.

In India, innocent and poor children are victims of child labour. Many schools have been destroyed in Nigeria. People in Afghanistan have been affected by extremism. Young girls have to do domestic child labour and are forced to get married at an early age. Poverty, ignorance, injustice, racism and the deprivation of basic rights are the main problems, faced by both men and women.

Today, I am focusing on women's rights and girls' education because they are suffering the most. There was a time when women activists asked men to stand up for their rights. But this time we will do it by ourselves. I am not telling men to step away from speaking for women's rights, but I am focusing on women to be independent and fight for themselves. So dear sisters and brothers, now it's time to speak up. So today, we call upon the world leaders to change their strategic policies in favour of peace and prosperity. We call upon the world leaders that all of these deals must protect women and children's rights. A deal that goes against the rights of women is unacceptable.

We call upon all governments to ensure free, compulsory education all over the world for every child. We call upon all the governments to fight against terrorism and violence. To protect children from brutality and harm. We call upon the developed nations to support the expansion of education opportunities for girls in the developing world. We call upon all communities to be tolerant, to reject prejudice based on caste, creed, sect, colour, religion or agenda to ensure freedom and equality for women so they can flourish. We cannot all succeed when half of us are held back. We call upon our sisters around the world to be brave, to embrace the strength within themselves and realise their full potential.

Dear brothers and sisters, we want schools and education for every child's bright future. We will continue our journey to our destination of peace and education. No one can stop us. We will speak up for our rights and we will bring change to our voice. We believe in the power and the strength of our

> words. Our words can change the whole world because we are all together, united for the cause of education. And if we want to achieve our goal, then let us empower ourselves with the weapon of knowledge and let us shield ourselves with unity and togetherness.
>
> Dear brothers and sisters, we must not forget that millions of people are suffering from poverty and injustice and ignorance. We must not forget that millions of children are out of their schools. We must not forget that our sisters and brothers are waiting for a bright, peaceful future.
>
> So let us wage a glorious struggle against illiteracy, poverty and terrorism, let us pick up our books and our pens, they are the most powerful weapons. One child, one teacher, one book and one pen can change the world. Education is the only solution. Education first. Thank you.

2.5.1.1 *Charter bodies: the United Nations Humans Rights Council (UNHRC)*

Two of the UN's 'principal organs' have a wide mandate in relation to human rights. The General Assembly may 'initiate studies and make recommendations . . . assisting in the realization of human rights and fundamental freedoms for all without distinction as to race, sex, language, or religion'.[118] All the UN human rights bodies report back to the General Assembly. It can make (non-binding) resolutions or declarations. ECOSOC is also tasked with a human rights mandate; it 'may make recommendations for the purpose of promoting respect for, and observance of, human rights and fundamental freedoms for all'.[119] ECOSOC 'effectively delegated its human rights functions to the Commission on Human Rights' (UNCHR) in 1946 (Joseph and Kyriakakis 2010: 6). Most of the UN human rights documents were drafted by the UNCHR up until 2006 when it was replaced with the United Nations Human Rights Council (UNHRC). In addition to its standard-setting it also laid the foundations for the development of complaints mechanisms and 'special procedures'[120] including country-specific mandates. However, its credibility waned.

> A number of key problems were widely recognised. Cynical manipulation of the [UN]CHR's mechanisms by Member States in order to avoid scrutiny

---

118 *Charter of the United Nations*, art. 13(1).
119 *Charter of the United Nations*, art. 62(2).
120 Despite an earlier resolution by ECOSOC in 1947 that UNCHR had 'no power to take any action in regard to any complaints concerning human rights' (ECOSOC Res 75 (V)), the Commission came under pressure from petitions from South Africa objecting to the apartheid regime. It departed from previous practice, and established in 1965 an ad hoc working group of experts to investigate the situation of human rights in Southern Africa (UNCHR resolution 2 (XXIII)). The ad-hoc working group can be considered as the first 'special procedure' of the UNCHR.

and possible public censure or to score political points against other States, the increasing 'politicisation' of the CHR and in particular the selectivity reflected in the choice of States singled out for country-specific measures, and a number of high-profile elections to the CHR of States with particularly poor human rights records.

(Joseph and Kyriakakis 2010: 9)

The United Nations Human Rights Council (UNHRC) was established in 2006[121] and is the successor body to the UNCHR, but unlike its predecessor which was a sub-commission of ECOSOC, it is a higher status as a direct subsidiary body of the General Assembly. The UNHRC is now the principal Charter body with responsibility for human rights, and comprises 47 Member States elected for a term of three years by secret ballot by an absolute majority of the General Assembly. There is provision for periodic reviews of membership with the possibility of suspension for any state accused of systematic human rights violations.[122] The 47 seats are distributed among the UN's regional groups: Africa (13); Asia (13); Eastern Europe (6); Latin America and the Caribbean (8); and Western Europe and others (7). The Council meets in regular session three times annually and in special session as needed, and reports to the General Assembly.

In September 2007 an Advisory Committee was established[123] (replacing the Sub-Commission on the Promotion and Protection of Human Rights, a part of the former UNCHR regime) which provides expert advice and serves as the UNHRC's think tank. The Advisory Committee has 18 members: Africa (5); Asia (5); Latin America and Caribbean (3); Western Europe and others (3); and Eastern Europe (2). The expert nature of the Advisory Committee ought in principle to act 'as an important counter-balance to the political machinations that necessarily take place in the Council', though regrettably it does not have the powers of own initiative that the Sub-Commission had (Joseph and Kyriakakis 2010: 15).

There is also a complaints procedure, established in 2007, that allows individuals and organisations to bring complaints about human rights violations to the attention of the UNHRC. It has a wide mandate 'to address consistent patterns of gross and reliably attested violations of all human rights and all fundamental freedoms occurring in any part of the world and under any circumstances'.[124] The procedure retains its confidential nature, with a view to enhancing cooperation with the State concerned. A 'Working Group on Communications', consisting of five independent experts (serving for three-year terms) and representative of the five regions, make determinations whether a complaint deserves investigation. If it does, the complaint is passed to the 'Working Group on Situations', which

121 UNGA Res. 60/251, UN Doc. A/RES/60/251 (15 March 2006).
122 Ibid., paras 7–9.
123 *Institution-building of the United Nations Human Rights Council* HRC Res. 5/1, 5th sess., UN Doc. A/HRC/RES/5/1 (18 June 2007) [65 to 84].
124 Ibid. [85].

again consists of five members (for a term of one year) representative of the five regions.[125] This group then reports to the UNHRC and makes recommendations about the course of action to be taken.

'Special procedures' is the general name given to the mechanisms established by the UNHRC's predecessor body to address either specific country situations or thematic issues. They involve independent human rights experts with mandates to report and advise on human rights from a thematic or country-specific perspective. These have been retained in a similar form by UNHRC despite fears that the new structure would limit the independence and methods of special procedures. As of 1 October 2013 there were 37 thematic and 14 country mandates. Special procedures report annually to the Human Rights Council; the majority of the mandates also report to the General Assembly. Their tasks are defined in the resolutions creating or extending their mandates. Special procedures consist of either an individual (a 'Special Rapporteur' or 'Independent Expert') or a working group consisting of a member from each of the five regional groupings, who are appointed by UNHRC and serve in their personal capacity. Mandate holders undertaking country visits typically send a letter to the State requesting cooperation with a visit. Some countries have issued 'standing invitations' indicating they are, in principle, prepared to receive a visit from any special procedures mandate holder.[126] The UNHRC adopted a resolution in 2007 containing a Code of Conduct for special procedures mandate holders.[127] In 2011, the UNHRC undertook a review of its work and functioning.[128] The review reaffirmed and strengthened essential principles, such as the obligation of States to cooperate with special procedures. Member States also confirmed their strong opposition to reprisals against persons cooperating with United Nations human rights mechanism.

As part of the UNHRC's institution-building efforts in 2007, it also committed to undertaking a 'Universal Periodic Review' (UPR) to assess human rights situations in all the UN Member States in four-year cycles.[129] Forty-two states are reviewed each year during three Working Group Sessions dedicated to 14 states each. This is an innovative procedure designed to be a cooperative, non-confrontational and non-political process. The stated objectives of the review are:

(a) The improvement of the human rights situation on the ground;
(b) The fulfilment of the State's human rights obligations and commitments and assessment of positive developments and challenges faced by the State;

---

125 Ibid. [91–9].
126 As of 16 September 2019, 121 Member States and 1 non-Member Observer State had extended standing invitations to the special procedures.
127 *Code of Conduct for Special Procedures Mandate-holders of the Human Rights Council* HRC Res 5/2, 5th sess., UN Doc. A/HRC/RES/5/2 (18 June 2007).
128 *Review of the Work and Functioning of the Human Rights Council* HRC Res 16/21, 16th sess., UN Doc. A/HRC/RES/16/21 (12 April 2011).
129 *Institution-building of the United Nations Human Rights Council* HRC Res 5/1, 5th sess., UN Doc. A/HRC/RES/5/1 (18 June 2007) [1–38].

(c) The enhancement of the State's capacity and of technical assistance, in consultation with, and with the consent of, the State concerned;
(d) The sharing of best practice among States and other stakeholders;
(e) Support for cooperation in the promotion and protection of human rights;
(f) The encouragement of full cooperation and engagement with the Council, other human rights bodies and the Office of the United Nations High Commissioner for Human Rights.[130]

The records of States are assessed against the standards contained in the *UN Charter*, the UDHR, any human rights instrument to which the State is a party, any voluntary commitments, and any applicable humanitarian law. The utility of this new procedure remains contentious. UPR has been viewed as the remedy for the problems of the (discredited) UNCHR, in particular the problem of 'politicisation' of that body (Gaer 2007). It remains to be seen whether it will produce substantive outcomes in terms of human rights implementation, or whether it will have 'no consequences beyond embarrassment' in terms of the implementation of the review recommendations (Komanovics 2012).

2.5.1.2 UN human rights treaty bodies[131]

In addition to the 'Charter' bodies, there are also a number of human rights 'treaty bodies'. There are currently ten such bodies established under their respective treaties[132] and tasked with monitoring the implementation of the principal human rights treaties. These are set out in Table 2.1 below. The treaty bodies carry out various functions in accordance with the provisions in the treaties that established them. They have three main functions:

1 the consideration of States parties' reports;
2 issuing 'General Comments' and organising thematic discussion;
3 the consideration of complaints ('communications').

The OHCHR makes efforts to coordinate the work of the various treaty bodies where necessary, and there is also an annual meeting of the chairpersons of the treaty bodies. This provides a forum for members of the ten human rights treaty bodies to discuss their work, share best practices, and consider ways to enhance the effectiveness of the treaty body system as a whole.

When a State has ratified one of these treaties it is obliged to implement the provisions of the treaty, including an obligation to submit periodic reports to the

---

130 *Institution-building of the United Nations Human Rights Council*, HRC Res 5/1, 5th sess., UN Doc. A/HRC/RES/5/1 (18 June 2007) [4].
131 See generally, Office of the High Commissioner for Human Rights (2012).
132 The exception is the Committee on Economic, Social and Cultural Rights which was set up under the authority of an ECOSOC resolution: see ECOSO Res. 1985/17 (28 May 1985).

Table 2.1 International Human Rights Treaty Bodies

Committee	Committee Abbreviation	Monitoring Treaty
Committee on the Elimination of Racial Discrimination	CERD	International Convention on the Elimination of All Forms of Racial Discrimination (1965)
Human Rights Committee	CCPR	International Covenant on Civil and Political Rights (1966)
Committee on Economic, Social and Cultural Rights	CESCR	International Covenant on Economic, Social and Cultural Rights (1966)
Committee on the Elimination of Discrimination Against Women	CEDAW	Convention on the Elimination of all forms of Discrimination against Women (1979)
Committee Against Torture	CAT	Convention against Torture and Other Cruel, Inhuman or Degrading Treatment (1984)
Committee on the Rights of the Child	CRC	Convention on the Rights of the Child (1989)
Committee on Migrant Workers	CMW	International Convention on the Protection of the Rights of All Migrant Workers and Members of their Families (1990)
Subcommittee on Prevention of Torture and other Cruel, Inhuman or Degrading Treatment or Punishment	SPT	Optional Protocol of the Convention against Torture (2002)
Committee on the Right of Persons with Disabilities	CRPD	International Convention on the Rights of Persons with Disabilities (2006)
Committee on Enforced Disappearances	CED	International Convention for the Protection of All Persons from Enforced Disappearance (2006)

relevant treaty body reporting on how the treaty rights have been implemented.[133] For example, states parties to the CRC are obliged to produce an 'initial' report after two years from ratification and then every five years.[134] Following problems of delay, both by States parties to produce their reports, and by the Committees to process State reports expeditiously, there are now revised reporting requirements.[135] Two documents are presented by States parties to the treaty bodies for scrutiny: a 'core document' containing background information and information relating to provisions across a number of treaties; and, a 'treaty-specific document' dealing with information customised to the State's obligations under a specific

---

133 The exception is the Subcommittee on Prevention of Torture etc. (SPT), as the *Optional Protocol of the Convention against Torture* does not contain any reporting requirement.
134 CRC art. 44(1).
135 *Compilation of Guidelines on the Form and Content of Reports to be Submitted by States Parties to the International Human Rights Treaties*, UN Doc. HRI/GEN/2/Rev. 5 (29 May 2008).

84 Introduction to international law sources and institutions

treaty. The treaty bodies also benefit from the information that often accompanies these reporting cycles from national human rights institutions (NHRIs), national and international civil society organisations, and other UN intergovernmental organisations, in addition to professional groups and academic institutions. There are some variations across the treaty bodies in the procedure governing the consideration of reports but in essence they enter into a written and oral dialogue with the State party delegation culminating in the treaty body publishing its 'concluding observations' on the States party's report.

The jurisprudence of each treaty is also assisted by the *General Comments* that each treaty body may issue.[136] These are published interpretations of the content of human rights provisions on thematic issues or methods of work.

The competence of the treaty bodies includes a range of available 'communications procedures' (complaints). See Table 2.2 below. Most of the treaty bodies[137]

Table 2.2 International Human Rights Treaty Bodies: communication/complaints procedures

Committee	Treaty	Inter-state	Individual	Inquiry
CERD	International Convention on the Elimination of All Forms of Racial Discrimination (1965)	Yes Art. 11–13	Yes Art. 14	No
HRCttee	International Covenant on Civil and Political Rights (1966)	Yes Arts 41–3	Yes 1st Optional Protocol	No
CESCR	International Covenant on Economic, Social and Cultural Rights (1966)	Yes Optional Protocol Art. 10	Yes Optional Protocol	Yes Optional Protocol Art. 11
CEDAW	Convention on the Elimination of all forms of Discrimination against Women (1979)	No	Yes Optional Protocol	Yes Optional Protocol Art. 8
CAT	Convention against Torture and Other Cruel, Inhuman or Degrading Treatment (1984)	Yes Art. 21	Yes Art. 22	Yes Art. 20
CRC	Convention on the Rights of the Child (1989)	Yes* 3rd Optional Protocol Art. 12	Yes* 3rd Optional Protocol Art. 5	Yes* 3rd Optional Protocol Arts 13–14

---

136 For example, the Committee on the Rights of the Child has issued 21 General Comments. Available at: <https://tbinternet.ohchr.org/_layouts/15/treatybodyexternal/TBSearch.aspx?Lang=en&TreatyID=5&DocTypeID=11> (accessed 20 February 2020).
137 CCPR, CERD, CAT, CEDAW, CRPD and CED all have individual communication procedures entered into force. The CRC, CMW and CESCR have individual communication procedures, but these three have not yet entered into force.

Committee	Treaty	Inter-state	Individual	Inquiry
CMW	International Convention on the Protection of the Rights of All Migrant Workers and Members of their Families (1990)	Yes* Art. 76	Yes* Art. 77	No
CRPD	International Convention on the Rights of Persons with Disabilities (2006)	No	Yes Optional Protocol Art. 1	Yes Optional Protocol Art. 6
CED	International Convention for the Protection of All Persons from Enforced Disappearance (2006)	Yes Art. 32	Yes Art. 31	Yes Art. 33

(*) = procedure not yet entered into force

now have an 'individual complaints' procedure and can, under certain conditions, receive petitions (aka 'communications') from individuals alleging that their rights have been violated. The decisions and recommendations of the treaty bodies made in response to such complaints are quasi-judicial in nature and may be regarded as a form of authoritative jurisprudence in relation to the interpretation of the treaties.

Some of the treaty bodies[138] also have provisions for 'inter-state complaints' where one States party may, under certain conditions, complain about violations of the treaty rights by another States party. It should be noted however, that no *inter-state communication* under these procedures to date has been made. Most of the treaty bodies[139] have, additionally, a procedure for investigating 'inquiry complaints' where they receive reliable information about *grave or systemic* violations of rights by a States party. For further details of the communication/complaints procedures available under the *Convention on the Rights of the Child*, see section 3.6.3.

---

138 CCPR, CERD and CAT all have inter-state communication procedures in force. CED, CRC and CMW have such procedures but they have not yet entered into force. CEDAW, CRPD and CESCR do not have an inter-state communication procedure.
139 CESCR, CAT, CEDAW, CRPD, CED, CRC.

Chapter 3

The *United Nations Convention on the Rights of the Child*

3.1 Introduction

The *United Nations Convention on the Rights of the Child*[1] (1989) ('the Convention') is in many ways distinctive among international treaties and unique in terms of international law generally. It was produced after a lengthy drafting process that started in 1978. The participation of non-governmental organisations (NGOs) in both the drafting process and the reporting mechanism set up under the Convention is also significant. Another remarkable feature has been the way in which States have been eager to sign and ratify the Convention. On the first day the Convention was opened for signature (26 January 1990), no fewer than 61 States parties signed, somewhat of a record for an international treaty: see Figure 3.1 below. The Convention entered into force in international law on 2 September 1990. A remarkable feature of the Convention is quite simply the near-global ratification it has received. There are currently 196 parties to the Convention; only the United States has failed to ratify it (see section 3.3). Detrick, who has provided a detailed and authoritative annotation of each of the substantive articles of the Convention, concluded:

> While the Convention on the Rights of the Child may not be the last – or complete – word on children's rights, it is the first universal instrument of a legally binding nature to comprehensively address those rights. As such, it forms a universal benchmark on the rights of the child – a benchmark against which all future claims for evolution will and must be answered.
>
> (Detrick 1999: 721)

The Convention contains not only civil and political rights but also social, economic and cultural rights. International law discourse used to refer to these as, 'first-' and 'second-generation' rights respectively. Lately, these labels have been dropped in deference to an increasing recognition that there should be no hierarchy of human rights, and that such rights are indivisible and interdependent.

---

1 Opened for signature 20 November 1989, 1577 UNTS 3 (entered into force 2 September 1990).

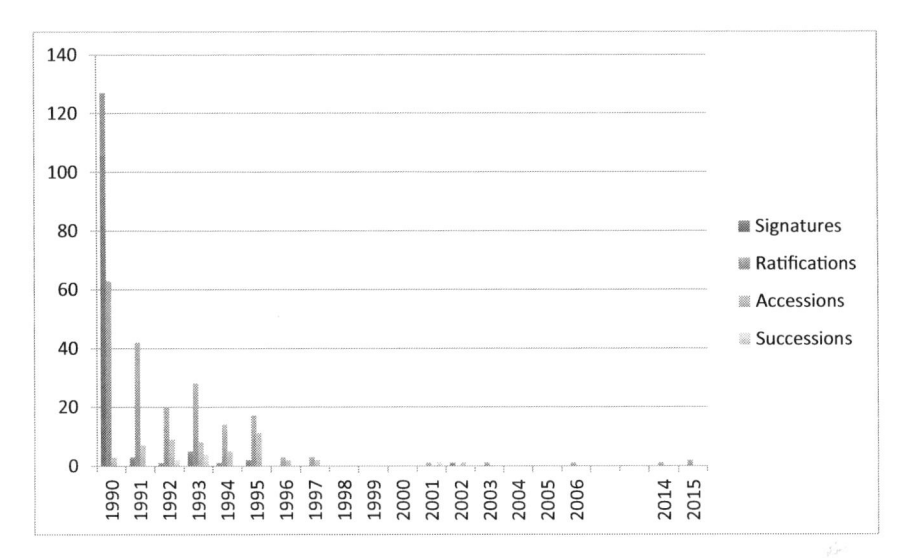

Figure 3.1 United Nations Convention on the Rights of the Child: Signatures (140), Ratifications (196), Accessions (47) and Successions (8) by Year.

The figures given for 'ratifications' add up to 196. The combination of figures for signatures, accessions and successions adds up to 197 as the US has signed the Convention but has not yet ratified it.

The Convention is the first, comprehensive, rights-based international treaty specifically constructed to protect and enhance the position of children. It marks a step-change in the international law of children's rights. Prior to this treaty, the international community had begun to recognise the child at least as a legitimate 'object' of international law. The Convention goes further and recognises the child as a more active 'subject' of international law who can be a holder of rights and participate in important decision-making.

The Convention is a good example of the 'globalisation' process as applied in the international legal realm; it signals the worldwide convergence of normative legal standards. In its relatively short existence, it has established itself as the central international instrument on children's rights and has influenced the operation of international, regional and domestic law and policy. It can be reasonably claimed that the appearance of the Convention justifies the study of 'international child law' as a discrete subject in its own right. The Convention does more than establish an authoritative text of children's rights; it has also provided the international community with a powerful vehicle to institute programmes of action and shape policy initiatives to further advance their practical implementation. However, as will be seen, the Convention, along with the machinery it has established and the way in which it has been received by the international community, has not been immune from various defects and weaknesses.

3.2 Background and history

The *Declaration of the Rights of the Child*[2] (1924), emanating from the old League of Nations, was in fact the first human rights document approved by an inter-governmental institution and preceded the *Universal Declaration of Human Rights*[3] (1948) itself by 24 years. The *Declaration* of 1924 was merely a non-binding resolution of the League of Nations, though it carried significant moral force. It was reaffirmed by the League of Nations in 1934. The General Assembly of the United Nations unanimously adopted a new text of the *Declaration of the Rights of the Child*[4] (1959), containing 10 major principles. This document did not have international legal binding force either, but its *unanimous* adoption by the General Assembly enhanced its authority. The language used in the text of the *Declaration* of 1959 reflects the conception of a child as more than merely a passive recipient of international humanitarian aid, but rather as an active participant in the enjoyment of human rights and freedoms.

However, the States that accepted the *Declaration* of 1959 also opposed the creation of a legally binding treaty on the subject of children's rights. Interest in such a treaty was not to arise until 20 years later when the General Assembly proclaimed 1979 as the 'International Year of the Child'. In 1978, Poland submitted a draft text for a *Convention on the Rights of the Child*. Various States took the view that the Polish text merely replicated the *Declaration* of 1959 and did not provide an adequate update given the changes in social, economic and cultural development that had occurred in the previous two decades. Furthermore, it was thought that the revision of the 1959 principles was worded too vaguely for a Convention that was now intended to be legally binding. In 1979, the United Nations Commission on Human Rights (UNCHR)[5] organised an open-ended working group to review and expand the original Polish text. Any of the States that were then represented in the UNCHR could participate; other UN members could send observers and contribute from the floor, and inter-governmental organisations could also contribute. NGOs could also send observers but with no absolute right to speak, but their requests to take the floor were rarely refused (Detrick 1999). In order to encourage State ratification of the treaty, the working group adopted a principle of consensus working, so that no votes were taken during the course of the Convention's drafting. A report was issued on each of the working group's sessions and discussed by UNCHR, and in turn through the Economic and Social Council (ECOSOC) and by the General Assembly (section 2.4.1). The working group

---

2 League of Nations, *Official Journal*, Special Supplement No. 23, Records of the Fifth Assembly, Geneva, 1924, at 177.
3 UN General Assembly, *Universal Declaration of Human Rights*, 10 December 1948, 217 A (III).
4 General Assembly, *Declaration of the Rights of the Child*, 14th session, UN Doc. A/RES/1386 (XIV) (20 November 1959).
5 The United Nations Commission on Human Rights (UNCHR) was abolished and replaced by the United Nations Human Rights Council (UNHRC) in 2006, in part because the former body had been discredited for including countries with poor human rights records: see further, section 2.5.1.1 in this book. The UNHRC has 47 State Members (October 2019).

held 11 sessions between 1979 and 1988. The industrialised countries were overrepresented in the drafting process, giving rise to criticisms that the Convention was a 'Northern' oriented document. However, there were active contributions from some of the developing countries, in particular Algeria, Argentina, Senegal and Venezuela, and in 1988 there was a 'sudden last minute surge of delegates from the South, many from States with Islamic law' (Cantwell 1992: 23). The general thaw in East – West relations in the mid-1980s made a significant difference to the atmosphere of debate in these working group sessions. In the early 1980s, the delegations working on the drafts of the Convention and the Convention against Torture were working, literally, along the corridor from each other, and on occasion the delegations traded concessions in their respective groups: 'The NGOs' contributions were in many respects remarkable. It is generally acknowledged in the international community that the NGOs had a direct and indirect impact on [the CRC] that is without parallel in the history of drafting international instruments' (Cantwell 1992: 24).

The ad hoc group of NGOs was able to identify no less than 13 substantive articles for which they claimed primary responsibility, and a further similar number of articles to which they had a less direct but nevertheless important input. Although every clause of the Convention was fully debated, Cantwell (1992: 26) has identified four key areas of principal controversy that occurred during the drafting process:

1   the definition of the minimum age of the child (article 1);
2   freedom of religion (article 14);
3   adoption (article 21); and
4   the age at which children should be permitted to participate in armed conflict (article 38).

The working group finally adopted a text in December 1988 and it was then transmitted to the General Assembly for approval and adoption through the UNCHR and ECOSOC. After ten years of negotiation the Convention emerged, its wording clearly influenced by the *Universal Declaration of Human Rights* (1948) and the two *International Covenants* (1966) (these three documents also known as the *International Bill of Rights*). The UN General Assembly unanimously adopted the *Convention on the Rights of the Child* on 20 November 1989. It was opened for signature on 26 January 1990. The Convention entered into force on 2 September 1990.[6]

---

6 Thirty days after the deposit of the 20th instrument of ratification or accession: see CRC, art. 49(1). The difference between ratification and accession (as regards the CRC) is that those initially 'signing' must *ratify* whereas States that have *not* signed *accede*. The act of signature does not bind the party to ratify, though in practice this does usually follow. However, the act of signature on its own is not without legal effect. Such a State is bound not to do anything that would defeat the object and purpose of the relevant treaty until the State has made its intention not to ratify clear: see the *Vienna Convention on the Law of Treaties* (1969), art. 18.

There are at least two elements that go towards the explanation of how children's issues emerged at the top of the international agenda in the 1990s (Black 1996): first, the movement for children's rights, culminating in the Convention in 1989 (section 1.2.1.3 in this book); and second, the child survival campaign resulting in the World Summit for Children in 1990. The latter was concerned mainly with health and other issues relating to children. In September 1990, a large gathering of world leaders; 71 heads of State and 88 other senior officials, mostly at ministerial level, assembled at the United Nations headquarters in New York. The summit adopted a *Declaration on the Survival, Protection and Development of Children* and a *Plan of Action for Implementing the Declaration* in the 1990s.[7] The *Declaration* and *Plan of Action* contained a number of targets for improving both the survival of children and their opportunities for positive growth and development. These included: the reduction of infant and under-five child mortality, the reduction of maternal mortality, the reduction of severe and moderate malnutrition among under-five children, universal access to safe drinking water, greater food supply and sanitary means of sewage disposal, universal access to basic education, the completion of primary education, the reduction of the adult illiteracy rate, and the improved protection of children in difficult circumstances. These targets were revisited by the international community in the form of the Millennium Development Goals (MDGs) in 2000, and the Sustainable Development Goals (SDGs) in 2015.

3.3 Failure to ratify the *Convention on the Rights of the Child*

The United States is the only country that has not ratified the Convention, although it is a signatory.[8] The act of signature is not without some legal effect.

> Where signature is subject to ratification, acceptance, or approval . . . signature does not establish consent to be bound. However, signature qualifies the signatory state to proceed to ratification, acceptance, or approval and creates an obligation of good faith to refrain from acts calculated to frustrate the objects of the treaty.
>
> (Brownlie 2008: 610)

Article 18 of the *Vienna Convention on the Law of Treaties*[9] (1969) provides that States are bound not to do anything that would defeat the object and purpose of the relevant treaty until the State has made its intention *not* to ratify clear. The most recent ratifications occurred in 2015 by both Somalia and the newly independent Republic of South Sudan. Somalia was a signatory to the Convention in 2002, but did not ratify for some years due to continuing civil unrest. South Sudan did not

---

7 Available at: <www.unicef.org/wsc/declare.htm> (accessed 2 October 2019).
8 On 16 February 1995.
9 Opened for signature 23 May 1969, 1155 UNTS 331 (entered into force 27 January 1980).

gain independence from the Republic of Sudan until 2011. These states exemplify the need for stable government to facilitate international treaty engagement. The third of the recent states to ratify was Palestine, which became a non-Member Observer State of the UN in 2012[10] and ratified the Convention in 2014.

The failure of the United States to ratify the Convention is a significant weakness, given its global power and influence. In the 1990's, President Clinton decided that the United States would sign the Convention but that, in sending it to the Senate for their 'advice and consent' to ratification, he would

> ask for a number of reservations and understandings . . . [to] protect the rights of the various states under the nation's federal system of government and maintain the country's ability to use existing tools of the criminal justice system in appropriate cases.[11]

Madeleine Albright, acting as the US delegate to the United Nations, signed the Convention on behalf of the United States on 16 February 1995.

To an extent, the failure of the USA to ratify the Convention reflects the general policy of US foreign relations to strike up *bilateral* relations with other countries rather than participate at the *multilateral* level. This approach has had an enduring impact on the USA's disconnection generally from the UN human rights system. As one commentator put it, the failure to ratify the Convention 'is just one example of the United States' inability to marshal the United Nations convention system and place it in the service of U.S. foreign Policy' (Engle 2011: 800).

Rutkow and Lozman (2006) usefully explain the USA's failure to ratify the Convention in terms of four areas of concern: sovereignty, federalism, reproductive and family planning, and parental rights. In terms of sovereignty, the United States has often been very cautious about agreeing to international human rights treaties; for example, the *International Convention on the Elimination of All Forms of Racial Discrimination*[12] (1965) was only ratified by the USA 28 years after being signed by President Lyndon B. Johnson.[13] In essence, there are some structural and constitutional difficulties that have posed obstacles to US ratification (Kilbourne 1998), though increasingly commentators argue that such obstacles are either misconceived or have been superseded by subsequent developments. The concern about federalism is based on the fact that family law matters generally fall within the competence of the State legislatures rather than the Federal government,[14] so there are fears that ratification would federalise an area of law traditionally within the States'

---

10 GA Resolution A/RES/67/19, 4 December 2012.
11 *Press Release*, The White House, 'White House Statement on U.S. Decision to Sign UN Convention on Rights of the Child' (10 February 1995).
12 Opened for signature 7 March 1966, 660 UNTS 195 (entered into force 4 January 1969).
13 Signed by USA on 28 September 1966, ratified on 21 October 1994.
14 The Tenth Amendment to the US Constitution: 'The powers not delegated to the United States by the Constitution, nor prohibited by it to the States, are reserved to the States respectively, or to the people.' This restricts the Federal government's authority to legislate in this area.

competence. Under article VI of the *US Constitution* (the 'supremacy clause'),[15] an international treaty ratified by the United States should be applied as part of the 'law of the land'; that is, it would be binding in State and Federal courts. In principle, therefore, such ratification would result in American courts being able to cite provisions of the Convention. However, in recent times, when the Senate has given its consent to the ratification of human rights treaties, it has often included a declaration that the rights-guarantee provisions are not 'self-executing' (Quigley 2002). The lower courts have relied on these declarations as depriving litigants of the right to rely on the guarantee provisions. However, it has been pointed out that: 'This Senate practice, and the deference given by courts, remain controversial. No court has yet explained in constitutional terms how a Senate declaration of non-self-execution acquires the force of law' (Quigley 2002).

Even if there were elements of the Convention that were 'self-executing', i.e. automatically given domestic effect, the United States could deploy reservations to avoid their applicability (Engle 2011: 814). One particular sticking point has been the conflict between the 'right to life' in the Convention and the existence of the death penalty applicable to under-18-year-olds in some states in the USA. However, the US Supreme Court in 2005 abolished juvenile executions.[16] There have also been concerns about reproductive and family planning matters, mainly on the basis of religious beliefs and that the Convention does not expressly offer protection of the foetus (Smolin 2006). The identification of the beginning of childhood proved problematic in drafting the Convention, and the combination of the text of article 1 and the ninth preambular paragraph[17] in effect provides an opportunity for States parties to interpret the Convention as providing legal protection either from the moment of live birth or from conception, as the case may be.

The failure to ratify can also be explained by reference to certain objections in principle, in particular the issue of how far 'children's rights' might threaten 'parental rights' (Lee 2017). It has been thought also that the inclusion of economic rights in the Convention might be inconsistent with American concepts of the limits of government. Finally, there are political and social factors to consider, particularly the influence of 'moral rearmament' groups that have often been prompted to resistance in particular by the emphasis in the Convention on children's participation rights (Rutkow and Lozman 2006: 165).

---

15 'This Constitution, and the Laws of the United States which shall be made in Pursuance thereof; and all Treaties made, or which shall be made, under the Authority of the United States, shall be the supreme Law of the Land; and the Judges in every State shall be bound thereby, any Thing in the Constitution or Laws of any State to the Contrary notwithstanding': *US Constitution 1787*, article VI, clause 2.
16 *Roper v. Simmons*, 543 U.S. 551 (2005).
17 CRC, Preamble §9: 'Bearing in mind that, as indicated in the *Declaration of the Rights of the Child*, "the child, by reason of his physical and mental immaturity, needs special safeguards and care, including appropriate legal protection, before as well as after birth".'

The influence of the Convention in the USA has been significant despite its failure to ratify to the extent that, arguably, 'the CRC is seen by U.S. courts as codifying customary international law, or at least as evidence of customary international law' (Engle 2011: 794). It is a matter of regret generally in the international community that the United States, though it signed the Convention in 1995, has still failed to transmit it to the US Senate for ratification, particularly in the light of its active interest and participation in the original drafting process and its support and ratification of the two substantive Optional Protocols (section 3.6 in this book) to the Convention. The USA will remain outside the deliberations of the international Committee until it ratifies. It has also been an important strand to US foreign policy to encourage human rights observance in other States, a policy made more difficult by its own delays in ratifying such instruments. The emergence of the Obama administration gave some early hope to reformers that the United States might eventually ratify the Convention. When President Obama was on the campaign trail preceding his first term of office, he responded to questions about US ratification thus:

> It's important that the United States return to its position as a respected global leader and promoter of Human Rights. It's embarrassing to find ourselves in the company of Somalia, a lawless land. I will review this and other treaties and ensure that the United States resumes its global leadership in Human Rights.
> (20 October 2008, Presidential Youth Debate, Walden University, USA)[18]

Since that time, Somalia has in fact ratified the Convention.

3.4 The Committee on the Rights of the Child

The Convention provides for the establishment of a specialist Committee, the purpose of which is to examine the progress made by States in achieving the realisation of the obligations established under the Convention.[19] In addition, since the entry into force of the *Optional Protocol to the Convention on the Rights of the Child* on a communications procedure in April 2014,[20] the Committee is able to hear individual complaints alleging violation of the Convention and its first two Optional Protocols. There was originally a Committee of ten child law and policy experts elected by the States parties. The membership of the Committee was increased to 18 by an amendment to the Convention that came into force in 2003. Members of the Committee serve in their 'personal capacity' as experts;

---

18 Text available from: <www.youthdebate2008.org/debate-transcript> (accessed 2 October 2019).
19 CRC, art. 43.
20 *Optional Protocol to the Convention on the Rights of the Child on a Communications Procedure*. Adopted and opened for signature, ratification and accession by General Assembly resolution A/RES/66/138 of 19 December 2011, entered into force on 14 April 2014.

they do not hold a representative mandate from their respective countries. Each member is an independent expert of 'high moral standing and recognised competence in the field'. Nevertheless, an equitable geographical distribution and representation of the principal legal systems is taken into consideration in their selection.[21]

The Committee has a small permanent secretariat at the Office of the High Commissioner for Human Rights (OHCHR) in Geneva. Its primary function is to receive and comment upon the States parties' periodic country reports. It meets in Geneva for three sessions each year, normally in January, May and September. The Committee held its first session in October 1991.

The Committee publishes its interpretation of the content of human rights provisions in the form of *General Comments*. As with the *General Comments* emanating from the other international human rights treaty bodies, these are increasingly taken to contain authoritative interpretation of the relevant Convention. Indeed, at least in relation to the key Human Rights Committee (which monitors the *International Covenant of Civil and Political Rights* (1966)), *General Comments* that receive wide support 'may be regarded as a secondary source of international law' (Aust 2010: 233). Table 3.1 below sets out the *General Comments* that the Committee have issued up to the end of 2019.

Table 3.1 General Comments of the Committee on the Rights of the Child

No.	Title	Reference	Date
1	The aims of education	CRC/GC/2001/1	17 April 2001
2	The role of independent human rights institutions	CRC/GC/2002/2	15 November 2002
3	HIV/AIDS and the rights of the child	CRC/GC/2003/3	17 March 2003
4	Adolescent Health	CRC/GC/2003/4	01 July 2003
5	General measures of implementation for the *Convention on the Rights of the Child*	CRC/GC/2003/5	03 October 2003
6	Treatment of unaccompanied and separated children outside their country of origin	CRC/GC/2005/6	01 September 2005
7/Rev.1	Implementing child rights in early childhood	CRC/C/GC/7/Rev.1	20 September 2006
8	The right of the child to protection from corporal punishment and other cruel or degrading forms of punishment	CRC/C/GC/8	02 March 2007

---

21 CRC, art. 43(2).

No.	Title	Reference	Date
9	The rights of children with disabilities	CRC/C/GC/9	27 February 2007
10	Children's rights in Juvenile Justice	CRC/C/GC/10	25 April 2013
11	Indigenous children and their rights under the Convention	CRC/C/GC/11	12 January 2009
12	The right of the child to be heard	CRC/C/GC/12	20 July 2009
13	The right of the child to freedom from all forms of violence	CRC/C/GC/13	18 April 2011
14	The right of the child to have his or her best interests taken as a primary consideration (art. 3, para. 1)	CRC/C/GC/14	29 May 2013
15	The right of the child to the enjoyment of the highest attainable standard of health (art. 24)	CRC/C/GC/15	17 April 2013
16	On State obligations regarding the impact of the business sector on children's rights	CRC/C/GC/16	17 April 2013
17	The right of the child to rest, leisure, play, recreational activities, cultural life and the arts	CRC/C/GC/17	17 April 2013
18	Harmful practices	CRC/C/GC/18[22]	14 November 2014
19	Public budgeting for the realization of children's rights	CRC/C/GC/19	21 July 2016
20	Rights of the child during adolescence	CRC/C/GC/20	6 December 2016
21	Children in street situations	CRC/C/GC/21	21 June 2017
22	The human rights of children in the context of international migration	CRC/C/GC/22[23]	16 November 2017
23	State obligations regarding the human rights of children in the context of international migration in countries of origin, transit, destination and return	CRC/C/GC/23[24]	16 November 2017
24	Children's rights in the child justice system	CRC/C/GC/24	18 September 2019

Note: See the Committee's website for an up-to-date account of the *General Comments*: <https://tbinternet.ohchr.org/_layouts/15/treatybodyexternal/TBSearch.aspx?Lang=en&TreatyID=5&DocTypeID=11> (accessed 3 October 2019).

22 This is a joint general comment, with General Comment No. 31 of the Committee on the Elimination of Discrimination Against Women.
23 This is a joint general comment, with General Comment No. 3 (2017) of the Committee on the Protection of the Rights of All Migrant Workers and Members of Their Families.
24 This is a joint general comment, with General Comment No. 4 (2017) of the Committee on the Protection of the Rights of All Migrant Workers and Members of Their Families.

General Comments are also specifically referred to as relevant sources which must be taken into account when States parties are preparing their periodic reports to the Committee.[25] The Committee also holds, in accordance with its rules of procedure,[26] a *Day of General Discussion* on a thematic issue in its September session. These used to be held every year, but at its 61st session (17 September to 5 October 2012) it resolved to hold general discussion days on a biennial basis.[27] These are public meetings open to representatives of States parties, UN agencies and bodies, NGOs, national human rights institutions, professional groups, academics, youth groups and other interested parties. The Committee sometimes chooses to develop a *General Comment* from an article, provision or theme that has been discussed earlier in one of its *Days of General Discussion*.

The Committee also, from time to time, adopts *Recommendations* which, in recent years, have been referred to as *Decisions*.[28] Of the 11 Recommendations issued to date, seven are concerned with procedural matters relating to the reporting process. For example, *Decision No. 10*[29] requests the General Assembly to provide appropriate financial support to enable it to work in two chambers at pre-sessional working group meetings due to take place in 2012 and at a session in 2013.

Although, as detailed below, the reporting and communications processes are the central activity of the Committee, it should not be thought that Members of the Committee do not contribute outside of the formal sessions. Members regularly engage in numerous activities; e.g. conferences, seminars, lectures and courses, and may be involved in 'the follow-up to the Committee's Concluding Observations in a number of countries upon invitation from States, civil society organizations and the United

---

25 See *Treaty-specific guidelines regarding the form and content of periodic reports to be submitted by States parties under article 44, paragraph 1 (b), of the Convention on the Rights of the Child*, CRC/C/58/Rev. 3, 3 March 2015, paras 13, 21, 27, 30, 32, 36, 38 and 40.

26 *Rules of Procedure*, Committee on the Rights of the Child, CRC/C/4/Rev. 5, 1 March 2019, Provisional rules of procedure were adopted at the Committee's first session and revised subsequently at its 33rd, 55th, 62nd, 67th and 79th sessions. Available at: <https://tbinternet.ohchr.org/_layouts/15/treatybodyexternal/Download.aspx?symbolno=CRC/C/4/Rev.5&Lang=en> (accessed 3 October 2019). Rule 79 states that: 'In order to enhance a deeper understanding of the content and implications of the Convention, the Committee may devote one or more meetings of its regular sessions to a general discussion on one specific article of the Convention or related subject.'

27 The last *Day of General Discussion* on the issue of 'Protecting and Empowering Children as Human Rights Defenders' took place in September 2018 during the 76th session of the Committee at Palais des Nations.

28 See the Committee's website: <www.ohchr.org/EN/HRBodies/CRC/Pages/Decisions.aspx> (accessed 3 October 2019). This book will refer to the first six issued as *Recommendations* and the seventh and subsequent ones as *Decisions*.

29 'Decision of the Committee on the Rights of the Child to request approval from the General Assembly at its sixty-sixth session to work in two chambers once per year', *Decision No. 10*, Committee on the Rights of the Child, 11 February 2011.

Nations Children's Fund (UNICEF)'.[30] The Committee has also been active in the process initiated by the OHCHR in 2009 on strengthening the treaty body system.[31]

3.5 The reporting process under the Convention

The Committee normally holds three regular sessions lasting for three weeks each in and around January, May and September each year. In addition, a pre-sessional working group meeting is convened, lasting one week, following each of the plenary sessions. The sessions of the Committee are held at the United Nations Office at Geneva.

The legal framework for the reporting process is contained in articles 43–45 of the Convention and in the Committee's *Rules of Procedure*[32] that have been established under article 43(8) of the Convention. The Secretary-General provides the necessary staff and administrative facilities to service the work of the Committee. There is a primary legal duty for States parties to submit reports to the Committee both on the measures they have adopted to give effect to the Convention and on the progress made on the enjoyment of those rights.[33] The 'initial report' must be submitted within two years of the date the Convention entered into force for that State and thereafter a periodic report every five years. The Convention emphasises that these reports should contain 'sufficient' information to provide the Committee with a 'comprehensive' understanding of its implementation of the Convention, but need not repeat basic data in subsequent periodic reporting cycles. As at October 2019, the Committee had received 814 reports pursuant to article 44 of the Convention.

The guidelines for States parties on producing the 'initial report'[34] make it clear that such reports shall 'contain sufficient information to provide the Committee with a comprehensive understanding of the implementation of the Convention in the country concerned', and provides 'an important occasion for conducting a comprehensive review of the various measures undertaken to harmonize national law and policy with the Convention and to monitor progress'.[35] These guidelines and practice also established nine groupings (referred to as 'clusters') under which States parties were expected to provide relevant information in both their initial and subsequent periodic reports. These are:

1 General measures of implementation
2 Definition of the child

---

30 General Assembly, *Report of the Committee on the Rights of the Child*, A/67/41, 21 June 2012, para. 16.
31 Ibid., para. 17. The Committee was 'the first treaty body to endorse as a whole the Dublin II outcome document.'
32 *Rules of Procedure*, Committee on the Rights of the Child, CRC/C/4/Rev. 5, 1 March 2019.
33 CRC, art. 44.
34 *General Guidelines regarding the form and content of initial reports to be submitted by States parties under Article 44, paragraph 1(a), of the Convention*, CRC/C/5, 30 October 1991.
35 Ibid., paras 2 and 3.

3   General principles
4   Civil rights and freedoms
5   Family environment and alternative family care
6   Violence against children
7   Disability, basic health and welfare
8   Education, leisure and cultural activities
9   Special protection measures

The guidelines on periodic reports[36] have now developed according to harmonised guidelines on reporting to the international human rights treaty bodies.[37] States parties' reports are now constituted in two parts: a 'common core' document, and a document that specifically relates to the implementation of the Convention and its Optional Protocols (known as a 'treaty-specific report').[38] The combination of both of these documents constitutes the full report under the Convention.[39]

The common core document contains general statistical and other information about the reporting State, the general framework of human rights, including information on non-discrimination, equality and remedies.[40] This general information should not normally be repeated in the treaty-specific report, though the Committee can request that the common core document is updated.[41]

The treaty-specific report[42] should make specific reference to the previous recommendations of the Committee and include details on how the recommendations have been addressed in practice along with an account of obstacles encountered and any measures envisaged to overcome such obstacles.[43] Furthermore, it should contain information specific to the implementation of the Convention and its Optional Protocols including 'information of a more analytical nature on how laws, legal systems, jurisprudence, the institutional framework, policies and programmes impact on children within the jurisdiction of the State party'.[44] The guidelines emphasise that:

> While general statistical information should be included in the common core document, the treaty-specific report should include specific data and statistics,

---

36 *Treaty-specific guidelines regarding the form and content of periodic reports to be submitted by States parties under article 44, paragraph 1 (b), of the Convention on the Rights of the Child*, CRC/C/58/Rev.3, 3 March 2015.
37 HRI/GEN/2/Rev.6.
38 *Treaty-specific guidelines regarding the form and content of periodic reports to be submitted by States parties under article 44, paragraph 1 (b), of the Convention on the Rights of the Child*, CRC/C/58/Rev.3, 3 March 2015, para. 5.
39 See 'Periodicity and Format of Reports – to supersede previous related decisions', *Decision No. 9*, 55th session, Committee on the Rights of the Child, 1 October 2010.
40 Ibid., para. 7. The common core document should not exceed 60–80 pages.
41 Ibid., para. 8.
42 The treaty-specific report should be limited to 60 pages. Ibid., para. 11.
43 Ibid., para. 12.
44 Ibid., para. 13.

disaggregated by age, sex and other relevant criteria, that are pertinent to the implementation of the Convention and of the Optional Protocols, if applicable. States parties should include statistical information as indicated in the annex to the present guidelines. (*Treaty-specific guidelines* . . ., CRC/C/58/Rev.3)

(3 March 2015, para. 14)

The treaty-specific report should also provide information organised according to the various clusters of rights, identified above, indicating the 'progress and challenges in achieving full respect for the provisions of the Convention and Optional Protocols'. Information on actions taken to implement the recommendations from previous Concluding Observations of the Committee as they relate to each cluster is particularly welcome.[45]

As stated earlier in this chapter, one of the distinctive features of the Convention machinery is that NGOs have had a more intense impact, as compared with other international human rights treaty bodies, both at the stage of drafting the Convention and their input into the reporting and monitoring activity of the Committee. The Committee has acknowledged the key role of the coalition of NGOs in supporting the reporting process.[46] Additional guidelines for the participation of NGOs and individual experts in the pre-sessional working group of the Committee make it clear that the reference to 'other competent bodies' in the Convention[47] includes NGOs, they announce that this Convention is 'the only international human rights treaty that expressly gives NGOs a role in monitoring its implementation'.[48] Requests by national, regional and international NGOs (INGOs) to participate should be submitted to the Committee through its secretariat at least two months prior to the pre-sessional working group. Based on the written information received, the Committee then selects NGOs to participate in the pre-sessional working group meeting (which is closed to the public). Detailed guidance on NGO submissions is provided by the *NGO Group* (NGO Group for the *Convention on the Rights of the Child* 2006). This Group was established in 1983 to influence the drafting of the Convention. The NGO Group is now known as *Child Rights Connect* and its website indicates the Group's reach is currently made up of a registered network of 86 national and international NGOs committed to children's rights. *Child Rights Connect* holds special ECOSOC consultative status at

---

45 Ibid., para. 17.
46 See Committee on the Rights of the Child, *General Comment No. 5: General measures of implementation for the Convention on the Rights of the Child*,, CRC/GC/2003/5, para. 59.
47 '(a) . . . The Committee may invite the specialized agencies, the United Nations Children's Fund and other competent bodies as it may consider appropriate to provide expert advice on the implementation of the Convention in areas falling within the scope of their respective mandates . . . ' CRC, art. 45(a). See also Detrick (1992: 25).
48 See 'Guidelines for the participation of partners (NGOs and individual experts) in the pre-sessional working group of the Committee on the Rights of the Child', *Report on the twenty-second session*, CRC/C/90, 7 December 1999, Annex VIII, para. 1.

the United Nations, and its core mission is 'the realisation of Children's Rights through the United Nations human rights system'.[49]

There is nothing in the Convention itself to indicate any consequence or sanction for the non-submission of reports. The Committee's *Rules of Procedure* state that non-submission will result in the Committee sending to the States party 'a reminder concerning the submission of such report or additional information and undertake any other efforts in a spirit of dialogue between the State concerned and the Committee', and if the party remains recalcitrant the Committee can report this to the General Assembly.[50]

Currently, around nine States parties are invited to submit reports to be considered at each of its regular plenary sessions. Priority is given, to the examination of Initial Reports and the Committee will take into account the criterion of the chronological order of submissions. A States party's report will first be sent to the Secretariat of the Committee at the Office of the High Commissioner for Human Rights (OHCHR) in Geneva. The Committee will examine it at the next available session and attempts to examine reports within one year of receipt. Following receipt of the country report, the Committee will seek written information from other sources, such as NGOs National Human Rights Institutions (NHRIs) and inter-governmental organisations. This information is then reviewed during the Committee's pre-sessional working group. This is a *private* session composed of Committee members, where an initial review of the States party's report is carried out. NGOs and inter-governmental organisation representatives may be invited to attend the pre-sessional working group. The working group will then prepare a 'list of issues' that is submitted to the States party, to indicate the areas which the Committee considers to be priorities for discussion. States parties are requested to respond to these questions in writing, prior to the plenary session which currently usually takes place within around seven months of the pre-sessional meeting.

During the plenary session, which (in contrast to the pre-sessional working group meeting) is held in *public*, the Committee examines the country report in the presence of the government representatives, who are invited to respond to the questions and comments made by Committee members. The Committee recommends that representatives of the government who are directly involved at the national level with the implementation of the Convention be present for the examination of the report. If the States party delegation has genuine participation and responsibility for strategy relating to children's rights the dialogue generated at the session is more likely to have impact on the formulation of policy and implementation activity.

The Committee devotes one day (two meetings of three hours each) to its public examination of States parties' reports and will usually appoint two Committee

---

49 *Child Rights Connect* website: < www.childrightsconnect.org/ > (accessed 6 October 2019).
50 *Rules of Procedure*, Committee on the Rights of the Child, CRC/C/4/Rev. 5, 1 March 2019, rule 71.

members to act as 'country rapporteurs' and lead the discussion with the States party delegation. Journalists are free to attend in addition to NGO representatives and any interested individual. The order of play of the session procedure is described as follows:

> After a brief introductory statement by the head of delegation the interactive dialogue starts. The Chairperson of the Committee will request the country rapporteur(s) to provide a brief overview of the state of child rights in the concerned State party. Thereafter the Chairperson will invite the Committee members to ask questions or make comments on the first cluster of rights, and the delegation may respond. The discussion moves step by step through the next group of issues identified in the reporting guidelines.
> Towards the end of the discussion, the country rapporteurs summarize their observations on the report and the discussion itself and may also make suggestions and recommendations. Lastly, the State delegation is invited to make a final statement.
> ('Working Methods', Committee's website: <www.ohchr.org/EN/HRBodies/CRC/Pages/WorkingMethods.aspx> (accessed 7 October 2019))

After this dialogue, the Committee prepares, in a closed meeting at the end of the session, its Concluding Observations, which summarise the main points of discussion and pinpoint the key issues requiring further action and follow-up by the States party. It usually takes between two and three hours for its discussion of each set of Concluding Observations. Concluding Observations usually contain the following elements: an introduction; positive aspects including the progress achieved; factors impeding implementation; main subjects for concern; suggestions and recommendations addressed to the States party. The Concluding Observations are made public on the last day of a Committee session during the adoption of the session report. It is assumed that the concerns indicated in the Committee's Concluding Observations will be addressed in the country's next periodic report. All the relevant documentation of the reporting process is available from the Committee's website. For the purposes of maintaining an up-to-date register of the status of States parties' submission of reports and the adoption of related Concluding Observations, the Committee regularly issues a document that contains information on the exceptional measures taken to address late or non-reporting States parties.

The throughput of States party reports has been around the same level for a number of years. Table 3.2 below shows the number of report examinations brought to a Concluding Observation in each of the sessions planned to take place in 2018 and 2019 respectively.

There is also a comparable reporting regime to the reporting process under the main Convention in relation to the obligations imposed by the *Optional Protocol to the Convention on the Rights of the Child on the Sale of Children, Child Prostitution and*

102   The *United Nations Convention on the Rights of the Child*

Table 3.2 Numbers of state and individual reports considered by the Committee on the Rights of the Child in 2018 and 2019, under the Convention and the three Optional Protocols

Session No.	Month	CRC	OPSC	OPAC	Individual	Sub-totals
		Year 2018				
77th session	January	8	0	0	3	11
78th session	May	5	2	2	3	12
79th session	September	4	3	2	2	11
Total 2018						34
		Year 2019				
80th session	January	6	1	0	1	8
81st session	May	6	1	0	3	10
82nd session	September	5	1	2	1	9
Total 2019						27

Child Pornography[51] (OPSC), and the *Optional Protocol to the Convention on the Rights of the Child on the Involvement of Children in Armed Conflict*[52] (OPAC). It is required that each States party must submit an initial report within two years following the entry into force for that States party, providing information on the measures it has taken to implement the provisions of the Protocol(s). Following the submission of this 'comprehensive' initial report, States parties are then obliged to submit any further information with respect to the implementation of the Protocol(s), in the periodic reports submitted to the Committee in accordance with article 44 of the main Convention. States parties to the Optional Protocol(s) who are *not* parties to the main Convention (e.g. the USA) must submit subsequent reports every five years. The two sets of guidelines for OPSC[53] and OPAC[54] set out the categories of information requested from States parties. These obviously differ in their detail, but share the following generic categories: general measures of implementation; prevention; prohibition; protection; international assistance and cooperation. These guidelines are aptly summarised by the *NGO Group*:

> The guidelines . . . request States parties to provide information on progress and obstacles encountered in fulfilling obligations under the Protocols,

---

51   25 May 2000, 2171 UNTS 227 (entered into force 18 January 2002), art. 12.
52   25 May 2000, 2173 UNTS 222 (entered into force 12 February 2002), art. 8.
53   *Revised Guidelines Regarding Initial Reports to be Submitted by States parties under Article 12, Paragraph 1, of the Optional Protocol to the Convention on the Rights of the Child on the Sale of Children, Child Prostitution and Child Pornography*, CRC/C/OPSC/2, 3 November 2006.
54   *Revised Guidelines Regarding Initial Reports to be Submitted by States parties under Article 8, Paragraph 1, of the Optional Protocol to the Convention on the Rights of the Child on Involvement of Children in Armed Conflict*, CRC/C/OPAC/2, 19 October 2007.

budget allocation, and detailed disaggregated statistical data. Reports should also provide information on legal status, coordination, dissemination and awareness-raising and whether, and in what ways, the implementation of the Protocols are in line with the general principles of the Convention. It should also provide information on the involvement of non-governmental organizations in the preparation of the report.

(NGO Group for the *Convention on the Rights of the Child* 2006: 6)

The Committee issued a *Recommendation* in 2005 on the consideration of reports under the two Optional Protocols.[55] The procedures for reporting under the main Convention apply to the examination of country reports on the Optional Protocols. If a States party submits reports under both Optional Protocols at the same time, they will be considered at the next session of the Committee and given a maximum of six hours to consider both reports. If a States party only submits its report under OPSC it will receive a half-day slot at the next available session. However, where a States party only submits its report under OPAC, the Committee will not automatically examine it except where it determines that the States party is 'facing or had recently faced serious difficulties in respecting and implementing [OPAC]'.[56] Other States parties are given the option of oral examination with a government delegation, or a technical review (a closed meeting), and the latter will take place in private without any governmental delegation present. As at September 2016, the Committee had processed 109 initial reports and two periodic reports under OPAC, and 98 initial reports and two periodic reports under OPSC.[57]

A significant weakness of the Committee, as with some of the other international human rights treaty bodies, has been the delays in managing the States party reporting process. This is all the more serious in the context of the Committee's work because, as explained earlier, the reporting process remains the core sanctioning mechanism available under the Convention, in conjunction with the communications procedure under the third Optional Protocol (section 3.6.3 in this book). The problem of delay is twofold. First, there has been delay by the Committee itself in managing the reporting process. Second, there have been delays by some States parties in producing their initial and periodic reports. The Committee has made some efforts to manage the reporting process more efficiently. In January 2000, it increased its workload to examine 27 reports per year, compared to the 18 per annum previously. Several of the Committee's *Recommendations*[58] to date have been concerned with trying to address the delays experienced

---

55 'Consideration of reports under the two Optional Protocols of the Convention on the Rights of the Child', *Decision No. 8*, Committee on the Rights of the Child, *Report on the Thirty-Ninth Session*, CRC/C/150, 21 December 2005.
56 Ibid., rule 3(a).
57 *Status of the Convention on the Rights of the Child, Report of the Secretary-General*, A/71/413, 71st session, 27 September 2017, para. 7.
58 *Recommendation No. 3* (2002); *Recommendation No 4* (2002); *Recommendation No. 5* (2003), *Recommendation No. 6* (2003); *Decision No. 8* (2005); *Decision No. 9* (2010); *Decision No. 10* (2011).

in the reporting cycle. In January 2002, the Committee recommended a system of 'combined reports' for States where the reporting cycle had been delayed. In May 2002, the Committee recommended that reports should not be too lengthy and should focus more on key developments and progress in actual implementation. In January 2003, the Committee added an additional rule requiring a combined second and third report where the second periodic report was due between one and two years following the dialogue with the Committee about its initial report. In September 2003, a *Recommendation* acknowledged that there was a two-year delay between the submission of reports and consideration by the Committee, and noted there were 13 initial reports and around 100 second periodic reports overdue.[59] It also acknowledged the extra workload caused by the reporting procedures under the two (substantive) Optional Protocols that would be expected from January 2004. The Committee proposed to work in two chambers in order to clear a target of 48 reports a year rather than the target of 27 set in 2000.[60] However, it can be seen from Table 3.2 (above) that this target has not been achieved. In 2010, the Committee continued its practice to allow States parties whose reports have been delayed to submit combined periodic reports and that, in compliance with the adoption of the Harmonized Treaty Specific Guidelines,[61] future States party reports should not exceed 60 pages. Finally, the Committee adopted another *Decision* in 2011 requesting approval from the General Assembly to work in two chambers in one of its three sessions every year. The request in 2004, implemented in 2006 to work in two chambers had resulted in clearing the backlog of reports awaiting review. However, '[w]hen the Committee resumed single-chamber sessions, a backlog again began to accumulate'. In 2008, the Committee requested a further four two-chamber sessions and three were approved and held in 2010 (which led to the highest number of reports processed to date of 54 in that year). However, *Decision No. 10* noted that since the previous double-chamber sessions in October 2010, 'the backlog has again begun to increase and currently stands at approximately 90 reports'.[62] The Committee concluded that it would require one of its three annual sessions to be held in two chambers every year. The Committee, sitting in two parallel chambers, each consisting of nine Members would, the Committee calculated, increase the number of reports to be examined from 10 to 18 during one annual session, resulting in a yearly increase from 30 to 38 reports per year.[63] *Decision No. 11* in 2014[64] enhanced these provisions by adopting 'a simplified reporting procedure', and reducing the

---

59 *Recommendation No. 5* (2003).
60 *Recommendation No. 6* (2003).
61 CRC/C/58/Rev. 2.
62 'Decision of the Committee on the Rights of the Child to request approval from the General Assembly at its sixty-sixth session to work in two chambers once per year', *Decision No. 10*, Committee on the Rights of the Child, 11 February 2011.
63 Ibid.
64 'Follow-up of resolution 68/268 on Strengthening and enhancing the effective functioning of the human rights treaty body system', *Decision No. 11*, Committee on the Rights of the Child, 19 September 2014.

word-length of Concluding Observations by 20%.[65] It also acknowledged a continuing backlog of reports awaiting consideration. This simplified reporting procedure is voluntary, and became available to States parties from 1 September 2019, through quarterly invitations. This is intended to reduce the significant workload of producing and considering reports.

> The Committee sends to the State party that accepted the simplified reporting procedure a request for specific information, known as List of Issues Prior to Reporting (LOIPR) containing up to 30 questions. The State party's replies to the LOIPR constitute the State party's report to the Committee.
>
> Differently from the standard reporting procedure, under the LOIPR States parties are no longer required to submit to the Committee both a State party report and written replies to a list of issues, thus reducing the two reporting steps to one.[66]

The twofold problem of delay – prevarication in the submission of country reports, and the Committee's own inability to process work expeditiously – remains a significant challenge in the Committee's work. If this problem of delay in the reporting process is not successfully managed, the impact is likely to be corrosive of the underlying aims of the Convention, and the resulting demoralisation within the international community may threaten the legitimacy of this type of international human rights instrument. The new simplified reporting procedure had merely commenced at the time of writing, and its success remains to be seen.

In addition to managing the periodic reporting cycle, the Committee must also submit reports about its own activities every two years to the General Assembly through ECOSOC.[67] These biennial reports[68] provide an update on the organisation and activities of the Committee, the submission of reports, membership and officers of the Committee, and some analysis of the overall progress achieved in the period under review. The Committee may also recommend to the General Assembly that the Secretary-General undertakes on its behalf a study on a specific issue relating to children's rights.[69] In addition, there is a requirement under the *Optional Protocol to the UN Convention on the Rights of the Child on a Communications Procedure*[70] (OPIC) for the Committee to include in its report to the General Assembly a summary of its activities under that Protocol[71] and individual communications

---

65 Ibid.
66 *Committee on the Rights of the Child, Simplified Reporting Procedure. Information note for States parties*. Available at <www.ohchr.org/EN/HRBodies/CRC/Pages/ReportingProcedure.aspx> (accessed 6 October 2019)
67 CRC, art. 44(5). The *Rules of Procedure*, r. 68, n 18 above, add that the Committee may also 'submit such other reports as it considers appropriate'.
68 See, for example: *Report of the Committee on the Rights of the Child*, A/67/41, General Assembly, 21 June 2012.
69 CRC, art. 45(c).
70 28 February 2012, UN Doc. A/RES/66/138.
71 OPIC, art. 16.

under OPIC commenced in 2016. A further provision of the Convention requires the Committee to submit to specialised agencies, UNICEF and 'other competent bodies' any reports from States parties 'that contain a request, or indicate a need, for technical advice or assistance, along with the Committee's observations and suggestions, if any, on these requests or indications'.[72] The Committee decided in one of its sessions in 1993 that, when appropriate, it would indicate the possible need for technical assistance in its Concluding Observations on States parties' reports.[73]

Finally, the Committee is also empowered to make 'suggestions and general recommendations' based on the information received via the reporting process[74] and transmit these to any States party concerned.

3.6 The Optional Protocols

There are three Optional Protocols to the Convention:

(i) *The Optional Protocol to the Convention on the Rights of the Child on the Sale of Children, Child Prostitution and Child Pornography* (OPSC);[75]
(ii) *The Optional Protocol to the Convention on the Rights of the Child on the Involvement of Children in Armed Conflict* (OPAC);[76] and
(iii) *The Optional Protocol to the Convention on the Rights of the Child on a Communications Procedure* (OPIC).[77]

It should be noted that an Optional Protocol is *not* an amendment to the text of a UN Convention. It is an *addition* to the main Convention on any topic relevant in the original treaty. Such Protocols are 'optional' as States may not wish to have the burden of additional duties to those in the main Convention that they have already ratified. In this text we shall refer to OPSC and OPAC as the two 'substantive' Optional Protocols, whereas OPIC provides a 'procedural' process. As will be seen, OPIC establishes three procedures enabling complaints to be addressed to the Committee in relation to the violation of children's rights contained in the main Convention and/or either of the two substantive Optional Protocols. The reporting regime applicable for the two substantive Optional Protocols

---

72 CRC, art. 45(b).
73 *Implementation Handbook*, p. 656, citing Committee on the Rights of the Child, 3rd session, CRC/C/16, January 1993, paras 139–45.
74 CRC, art. 45(d).
75 25 May 2000, 2171 UNTS 227 (entered into force 18 January 2002). OPSC had 121 signatories and 176 ratifications as at 8 October 2019.
76 25 May 2000, 2173 UNTS 222 (entered into force 12 February 2002). OPAC had 130 signatories and 170 ratifications as at 8 October 2019.
77 28 February 2012, UN Doc. A/RES/66/138 (entered into force 14 April 2014). OPIC has 52 signatories and 46 ratifications as at 8 October 2019.

has been referred to above. As the third Optional Protocol (OPIC) is essentially a procedural instrument there is no country reporting system as such, but there is a requirement for the Committee to include a summary of its activities under OPIC in its biennial report to the General Assembly.[78] The Rules of procedure under OPIC also require the Secretary General to maintain a permanent record of all individual communications, information of state violations, and inter-State communications which are brought to the attention of the Committee.[79]

It should also be observed that the USA, which has conspicuously failed to ratify the main Convention to date, nevertheless *has* ratified both OPAC and OPSC. The following sections provide an overview of each Optional Protocol. OPAC and OPSC are discussed in further detail in Chapters 7 and 8 respectively.

3.6.1 Optional Protocol to the Convention on the Rights of the Child on the Sale of Children, Child Prostitution and Child Pornography (OPSC)

The overall aim of OPSC[80] is to better achieve the implementation of various provisions in the Convention[81] relating to the prevention of a range of sexual and economic forms of exploitation. There was particular concern about the practice of 'sex tourism', the vulnerability of the girl child and the growing availability of child pornography on the Internet and other social media. The drafting of OPSC was prompted by an increasing international concern[82] about the traffic in children for the purposes of the sale of children, child prostitution and child pornography. OPSC was developed in parallel with the *Protocol to Prevent, Suppress and Punish Trafficking in Persons, Especially Women and Children*[83] that supplements the *UN Convention against Transnational Organized Crime*.[84] In short, OPSC was drafted in order to ensure the criminalisation of certain behaviours and better to provide for the protection of child victims. The 'sale of children', 'child prostitution' and 'child pornography' are given definitions in OPSC, and States parties are enjoined to 'prohibit' such activities.[85] In particular, each State party must ensure 'as a minimum' that these activities, so defined, are 'fully covered under its criminal or penal law, whether such offences are committed domestically or transnationally or on an

---

78 OPIC, art. 16; CRC, art. 44(5).
79 Rule 5. *Rules of procedure under the Optional Protocol to the Convention on the Rights of the Child on a communications procedure.* CRC/C/62/3, 16 April 2013.
80 25 May 2000, 2171 UNTS 227 (entered into force 18 January 2002). OPSC had 121 signatories and 176 ratifications as at 8 October 2019.
81 The Preamble to OPSC, refers to CRC, arts 1, 11, 21, 32–6.
82 The Preamble to OPSC refers to: the International Conference on Combating Child Pornography on the Internet, Vienna, 1999; and, a programme of action and Declaration adopted at the World Congress against Commercial Sexual Exploitation of Child, Stockholm, 1996.
83 15 November 2000, 2237 UNTS 319 (entered into force 25 December 2003).
84 15 November 2000, 2225 UNTS 209 (entered into force 29 September 2003).
85 OPSC, arts 1 and 2.

individual or organized basis'.[86] OPSC also contains a general provision ensuring that nothing in the Protocol will affect any element of either domestic or international law that may be 'more conducive to the realization of the rights of the child'.[87] States parties are obliged to take necessary measures to establish jurisdiction over such defined offences, when the offences are committed in its territory, or when the offender or victim is a national of that State.[88] OPSC also deems these offences to be included as extraditable offences in any extradition treaties between States parties.[89] States parties are further enjoined to provide measures of assistance with one another in respect of the Protocol offences including obtaining evidence at their disposal.[90] International cooperation is also supported in OPSC by provisions encouraging States parties to strengthen their cooperation around relevant multilateral, regional and bilateral arrangements, and between their own authorities and NGO, INGO and international organisations.[91]

OPSC also establishes a set of legal normative standards to guide States parties in adopting measures to protect the rights and interests of *child victims*.[92] This ensures, *inter alia*, that the 'best interests of the child shall be a primary consideration' in their treatment by the criminal justice system.[93] The protection of child victims and witnesses was also given more detailed attention in *Guidelines* proposed by the International Bureau of Children's Rights[94] and adopted by ECOSOC in 2005.[95] The focus in OPSC on the protection of child victims is further strengthened by obligations on States parties to take all feasible measures to ensure assisting such victims, including 'their full social reintegration and their full physical recovery', and that they have access to adequate procedures to seek compensation.[96] A country reporting regime,[97] comparable to the one under the main Convention, is also established under OPSC, as discussed above.

---

86 OPSC, art. 3(1).
87 OPSC, art. 11. Comparable provisions also appear in CRC, art. 41 and OPAC, art. 5.
88 OPSC, art. 4.
89 OPSC, art. 5.
90 OPSC, art. 6. States parties are additionally obliged, subject to their national law, to take measures to provide for the seizure and confiscation of certain goods and proceeds relating to the Protocol offences and to take measures aimed at closing premises used to commit such offences (CRC, art. 7).
91 OPSC, art. 10. The promotion of international cooperation is formulated explicitly 'to address the root causes, such as poverty and underdevelopment' contributing to children's exploitation; see OPSC 10(3).
92 Or 'child survivors', the term preferred by NGOs.
93 OPSC, art. 8.
94 An international non-governmental organisation, based in Montreal, Canada, established in 1994. It was given consultative status with ECOSOC in 2005: see <www.ibcr.org/en/> (accessed 8 October 2019).
95 ECOSOC 'Guidelines on Justice in Matters involving Child Victims and Witnesses of Crime' Res. 2005/20 (22 July 2005).
96 OPSC, art. 9.
97 OPSC, art. 12.

It is interesting to note, however, that the proposal for an OPSC was not actively supported by the Committee, unlike its support for OPAC. Hodgkin and Newell provide the following explanation:

> It was felt that the issues were already addressed within the Convention, that they should not be seen in isolation but holistically within the broad range of children's human rights, and that energies should rather be put into strengthening the implementation of existing rights than into the creation of new instruments. Nonetheless the desire for more detailed state responsibilities to tackle these forms of child abuse, particularly as regards the prosecution and extradition of 'sex tourists', ultimately ensured the Optional Protocol's adoption.
>
> (Hodgkin and Newell 2007: 669)

3.6.2 Optional Protocol to the Convention on the Rights of the Child on the Involvement of Children in Armed Conflict (OPAC)

The age at which children should be permitted to participate in armed conflict, as stated earlier in this chapter, was one of four key issues that were the subject of controversy during the drafting of the Convention. Article 38 of the Convention obliges States parties: to respect the rules of international humanitarian law relevant to children; to take all feasible measures to ensure that persons under *15 years of age* do not 'take a direct part in hostilities'; to refrain from recruiting persons under the age of 15 years into their armed forces; and, to protect the civilian population in armed conflicts, including taking feasible measures to protect children affected by armed conflict. A proposal for a Protocol to strengthen this provision was proposed in the Committee's first *Day of General Discussion* in 1992.[98] OPAC[99] was prompted by the international community's concern about 'the harmful and widespread impact of armed conflict on children and the long-term consequences it has for durable peace, security and development'.[100] Given the basic definition of a child in the Convention of an individual below the age of 18 years, it is not surprising that there was international discomfort with the age limitation of the protection in article 38 to only those under 15 years of age. However, some consistency was achieved with the inclusion of the definition of the war crime of conscripting or enlisting children, again under the age of 15 years, or using them to participate actively in hostilities (in both inter- and intra-State conflicts), in the

---

98 *Report of the second session*, Committee on the Rights of the Child, CRC/C/10, 19 October 1992, para. 75(c). Available at: <http://www2.ohchr.org/english/bodies/crc/docs/discussion/conflict.pdf> (accessed 8 October 2019).
99 25 May 2000, 2173 UNTS 222 (entered into force 12 February 2002). OPAC had 130 signatories and 170 ratifications as at 8 October 2019.
100 OPAC, Preamble, §3.

text of the *Rome Statute of the International Criminal Court* (1998).[101] Nevertheless, setting the threshold at 18 years gained in popularity, and, as the Preamble to OPAC notes, the 26th International Conference of the Red Cross and Red Crescent recommended in 1995 that 'parties to conflict take every feasible step to ensure that children below the age of 18 years do not take part in hostilities'.[102]

Reflecting a paradigm shift in the global pattern of armed conflicts from inter-state conflicts to a preponderance of intra-state conflicts, OPAC also contains a more explicit recognition of the need to expand the coverage of international law to not only recruitment into the State's armed forces, but also recruitment by non-State militias into 'armed groups distinct from the armed forces of a State, and recognizing the responsibility of those who recruit, train and use children in this regard'.[103] In addition, it also recognises the need to strengthen international cooperation in the implementation of the Protocol as well as the 'physical and psychosocial rehabilitation and social reintegration of children who are victims of armed conflict'.[104]

OPAC requires States parties to take 'all feasible measures' to ensure that members of their *armed forces* under the age of 18 years 'do not take a direct part in hostilities',[105] and must ensure that those under 18 years of age 'are not compulsorily recruited into their armed forces'.[106] A key provision requires States parties to raise the minimum age for voluntary recruitment into their national armed forces from 15 years as required by the Convention, by means of a declaration to be made upon ratification or accession, setting out a raised minimum age for these purposes, in addition to 'a description of the safeguards it has adopted to ensure that such recruitment is not forced or coerced'. A number of minimum standards relating to these safeguards are set out in this provision.[107] Many States made declarations asserting that 18 is the State's minimum age for either voluntary recruitment or conscription, thus complying with the position taken by the Committee and some States parties that failed to reach a consensus in the drafting process. But there are other States which have specified minimum ages of 16 years (e.g. United Kingdom, Canada, India), or 17 years (e.g. USA, Australia, France, Germany, Israel, New Zealand): see Hodgkin and Newell (2007: 662) for a list of minimum ages for recruitment.

---

101 Opened for signature 17 July 1998, 2187 UNTS 90 (entered into force 1 July 2002), arts 8(2)(b)(xxvi) and 8(2)(e)(vii).
102 OPAC, Preamble, §9.
103 OPAC, Preamble §11.
104 OPAC, Preamble §17. OPAC, art. 7 obliges States parties to cooperate with each other in the implementation of the Protocol.
105 OPAC, art. 1.
106 OPAC, art. 2.
107 OPAC, art. 3, and see also CRC. There is an exception prescribed from the requirement to raise the minimum age in relation to 'schools operated by or under the control of the armed forces of the States parties': see OPAC, art. 3(5). Some of the States parties' declarations indicate that children may be enrolled in military schools earlier than the prescribed minimum age.

By contrast, OPAC requires that *armed groups* (as distinct from State-sponsored *armed forces*) 'should not, under any circumstances, recruit or use in hostilities persons under the age of 18 years'. States parties are obliged to take all feasible measures to prevent such recruitment or use, including the criminalisation of such practices.[108] OPAC also contains a provision clarifying that the Protocol is without prejudice to any provisions in domestic, international or humanitarian law that may be 'more conducive to the realization of the rights of the child'.[109] In addition to a general duty placed on States parties to 'take all necessary legal, administrative and other measures to ensure the effective implementation and enforcement' of OPAC, they are also obliged to take all feasible measures 'to ensure that persons within their jurisdiction recruited or used in hostilities' contrary to the Protocol 'are demobilized or otherwise released from service', and to provide such persons with 'appropriate assistance for their physical and psychological recovery and their social reintegration'.[110] A country reporting regime,[111] comparable to the one under the main Convention, is also established under OPAC, discussed above.

Many stakeholders in the working group drafting the Protocol wanted protection of all under-18 year olds from any involvement in hostilities, direct or indirect, and any recruitment into the armed forces, irrespective of whether this was conscription or voluntary. But, as Hodgkin and Newell comment:

> The resulting text is a compromise which does improve the protection offered by article 38 of the Convention, but falls short of the clear standards sought by the Committee on the Rights of the Child, many States parties and many non-governmental organizations concerned with children's rights.
>
> (Hodgkin and Newell 2007: 660).

3.6.3 Optional Protocol to the Convention on the Rights of the Child on a Communications Procedure (OPIC)

The *Convention on the Rights of the Child* was the last international human rights treaty to have a communication/complaints procedure attached to it. Leading up to this, the Human Rights Council (HRC) had established an open-ended working group (OEWG)[112] in 2009 to discuss the parameters of such a procedure.[113] It

---

108 OPAC, art. 4.
109 OPAC, art. 5. Comparable provisions also appear in CRC, art. 41 and OPSC, art. 11.
110 OPAC, art. 6(1) & (3).
111 OPAC, art. 8.
112 Human Rights Council, *Report of the open-ended working group to explore the possibility of elaborating an optional protocol to the Convention on the Rights of the Child to provide a communications procedure*, first session report, UN Doc. A/HRC/13/43 (21 January 2010, adopted 18 December 2009) [28]. (Hereafter, 'OEWG 2010').
113 Human Rights Council, UN Doc. A/HRC/11/L.3 (12 June 2009).

appears that, as with the main Convention, the NGOs had a significant influence on international agenda-setting in this context (Türkelli et al. 2013; Buck and Wabwile 2013), and Child Rights Connect in particular claims an 'instrumental' role in the creation of OPIC.[114,115] The new Protocol implements child-sensitive procedures in compliance with the principles and policy of the main Convention, and in acknowledgement that 'the effectiveness of the procedure would depend to a large extent on its accessibility by children'.[116,117] The OEWG recorded its aims of providing a remedy where the national system fails; developing its own jurisprudence to contribute to the interpretation of the Convention; and, independence from national jurisdictions achieved by requiring applications to exhaust domestic remedies before cases can be referred to it. The report also noted that the procedure would 'give content to the right to be heard' and would be 'a child sensitive mechanism'.[118]

OPIC was open for signature on 28 February 2012 and entered into force on 14 April 2014. The *Rules of Procedure* ('OPIC RoP') appeared in April 2013.[119]

OPIC established three complaint procedures:

- Article 5 – individual communications;
- Article 13 – inquiry procedure; and
- Article 12 – inter-state communications.

OPIC and the OPIC RoP set out some general principles and methods of work that apply to all three procedures.[120] The Committee, in fulfilling its functions under OPIC, shall be guided by the 'best interests' principle and also have regard to the rights and views of the child(ren). It must also take appropriate measures to ensure that children are 'not subject to improper pressure or inducement' by those acting on their behalf.[121] There is also a general 'principle of expeditiousness' that applies to the Committee's handling of communications and it must also encourage the parties to avoid unnecessary delays.[122] In order to reduce the risk that complainants may suffer repercussions from their initiation of a communication, their identity shall not be revealed publicly without their express

---

114 28 February 2012, UN Doc. A/RES/66/138 (entered into force 14 April 2014). OPIC has 52 signatories and 46 ratifications as at 8 October 2019.
115 See <www.childrightsconnect.org/optional-protocol-on-communications-protocol-opic/> (accessed 8 October 2019).
116 Drahoslav Štefánek (Slovakia): OEWG 2010, [40].
117 OEWG 2010, [20].
118 OEWG 2010, [31].
119 *Rules of procedure under the Optional Protocol to the Convention on the Rights of the Child on a communications procedure*, CRC/C/62/3, 8 April 2013 (hereafter, 'OPIC RoP').
120 OPIC RoP, rules 1 to 11.
121 See OPIC, art. 2, and OPIC RoP, rule 1.
122 OPIC RoP, rule 2.

consent.[123] The protection measures established in OPIC which oblige States parties to take appropriate steps to ensure that individuals are not subject to such negative repercussions are further supported in the *OPIC RoP* which specify that in the event of a States party's failure to comply in this regard, the Committee may request the States party to take appropriate measures 'urgently to stop the breach reported' and submit written responses to the Committee.[124] As regards methods of work, the Secretary-General is obliged to maintain permanent records of violations under all three procedures, and this information must be made available to any member of the Committee.[125] The Committee may also consult with independent experts, at its own initiative, or at the request of any of the parties.[126]

3.6.3.1 Individual communications

Individual communications may be submitted 'by or on behalf of an individual or group of individuals' within a States party, claiming to be victims of breaches by that States party of any of the rights (to which the State is a party) in the main Convention, OPSC and OPAC. Where a communication is submitted *on behalf of* an individual or group of individuals, this must be with their consent 'unless the author can justify acting on their behalf without such consent'.[127] 'Working methods to deal with individual communications received under the Optional Protocol to the Convention on the Rights of the Child on a communications procedure' based on the OPIC RoP[128] were adopted in 2015 and updated in 2017.[129] This provides for a permanent Working Group[130] composed of nine members, with four or five rotating biannually. The Working Group operates permanently providing a constant mechanism for the processing of complaints outside of Committee sessions.[131] A Petitions Unit/Secretariat receives all correspondence under OPIC, and acts in a record keeping capacity.[132] All communications submitted by children to the Petitions Unit will be forwarded to the working group for consideration,[133] whereas communications from adults are to be vetted through a screening process to confirm admissibility, relevance to the CRC and Optional Protocols, that the communication relates to a States party and that the grounds are not unfounded.[134]

---

123 OPIC RoP, rule 3; and OPIC, art. 4.
124 OPIC RoP, rule 4.
125 OPIC RoP, rule 5.
126 OPIC RoP, rule 10.
127 OPIC, art. 5.
128 (CRC/C/62/3).
129 Adopted by the Committee on the Rights of the Child on 2 October 2015 and revised by the Working Group on communications on 2 June 2017.
130 Established under Rule 6 of the OPIC RoP.
131 Working method (6).
132 Working method (7).
133 Working method (9).
134 Working method (13).

Notice of receipt of the communication must be sent to the author within two weeks of the communication.[135] Domestic remedies must have been exhausted prior to a communication being made under OPIC unless 'the application of remedies is unreasonably prolonged or unlikely to bring effective relief'.[136]

Third party written information and/or documentation may be submitted to both the Working Group and the Committee to assist in the examination of a communication,[137] and acceptance of such materials shall be decided by the Working Group.[138] Friendly settlements can be initiated by the Committee or the Working Group.[139] The Working Group decisions shall be reached by a majority vote, with interim measures being adopted by at least three members of the Working Group[140] within 24 hours.[141] Each communication shall be appointed a case rapporteur from within the Working Group who shall be responsible for a full appraisal of the case, making recommendations and assessing the merits of the case. Such assessment shall then be open for comment from the other members.[142] Following consultation, and the possible engagement of independent experts[143] or relevantly informed Committee members with experience on either the specific country or thematic issue concerned, the case rapporteur is responsible for consolidating the views and opinions into a recommendation for the Committee for further discussion and final adoption.[144] This must be written in language that is appropriate and comprehensible for the child victim involved in the case.[145] This should be a consensus decision of the Working Group, failing which, a majority decision will apply.[146] The Committee may choose to seek additional clarifications and information from experts, UN documentation and other sources before formulating its final View.[147] Finally, implementation of Views where violations of the Convention or Optional Protocols are found or friendly agreements reached, shall be monitored by the case rapporteur and any members of the Committee who possess relevant expertise on the issues raised by the case.[148] The procedure is described by Child Rights Connect as follows:

> It is a quasi-judicial mechanism: the decisions of the Committee on the communications it receives are not legally binding on the State concerned.

---

135 Working method (11).
136 See OPIC, art. 7(d) & (e).
137 Working method (17).
138 Working method (18).
139 Working method (15) and (16).
140 Working method (20).
141 Working method (21). Very urgent cases can be decided by the Chair of the Working Group by immediate executive decision.
142 Working method (22).
143 OPIC RoP, Rule 10.
144 Working method (26).
145 Working method (28).
146 Working method (24).
147 OPIC RoP, Rule 10.
148 Working method (29).

However, this does not mean that the State concerned should not comply with them: by becoming a party to OP3 CRC, the State has indeed committed to follow them and provide redress to the victim.[149]

The Committee also has a power, following receipt of the communication and prior to determination on the merits, to request that the States party take 'interim measures as may be necessary in exceptional circumstances to avoid possible irreparable damage' to the victim(s) of the alleged violation.[150] The Committee must bring the communication *confidentially* to the attention of the States party concerned as soon as possible, and the latter must submit a written response within six months.[151] The complaint can be dealt with either through a merits hearing or a 'friendly settlement'.[152] The OPIC RoP make it clear that the Committee can, in effect, hold oral hearings inviting the complaint and/or alleged victim(s) and representatives of the States party.[153] The principle of confidentiality is further supported in the OPIC RoP which establishes a presumption that all the working documents 'shall be confidential unless the Committee decides otherwise'.[154] Furthermore, the names of complainants and victims of a communication shall not be published in an inadmissibility or merits decision, or a decision closing its consideration following a friendly settlement, except where express consent is forthcoming. However, subject to the requirements to obtain express consent of individuals concerned, the complainant or the States party is free to make public any submission or information bearing on the proceedings.[155] Following receipt of the Committee's views and recommendations, the States party must submit a written response 'including information on any action taken and envisaged' as soon as possible and within six months.[156]

Despite only being in force since 2014, it currently ranks fifth in terms of the numbers of communications registered with 300 individual communications received and 98 of these being registered as cases.[157] The Committee has made decisions in 23 of these cases to date, with Convention violations found in six cases,[158] a further six cases being discontinued and 11 cases deemed inadmissible.[159]

---

149 Child Rights Connect Information Pack about the Optional Protocol to the Convention on the Rights of the Child on a Communications Procedure (OP3 CRC) (2018) Fact Sheet 1, para. 1.1. Available at: <www.childrightsconnect.org/wp-content/uploads/2018/01/CRC_OP3_info_pack_web.pdf> (accessed 8 October 2019).
150 OPIC, art. 6.
151 OPIC, art. 8.
152 OPIC, art. 9.
153 OPIC RoP, rule 19.
154 OPIC RoP, rule 29.
155 Ibid.
156 OPIC, art. 11.
157 *Recent developments in the Individual communications received under the Optional Protocol to the Convention on the Rights of the Child on a Communications Procedure ('OPIC-CRC')*, September 2019.
158 Details available here <www.ohchr.org/documents/hrbodies/crc/adoptedcases.docx> (accessed 9 October 2019).
159 As at October 2019.

Further cases were not registered at all, including those where the events occurred prior to OPIC being in force, where the actors were non-state, domestic remedies had not been adequately exhausted or the cases were deemed to be unfounded.[160] Most of the states against whom complaints were received were European including Spain, Denmark, Switzerland, Finland, Belgium, Germany, France, Ireland, Slovakia and Georgia; with further complaints against Central and South American states of Argentina, Chile, Costa Rica, Panama and Paraguay. The cases have mainly involved issues of migration, including non-refoulment, determination of age (of child migrants), and family reunification.[161]

The 'follow-up' process provides a mechanism to track the effectiveness of OPIC and the first Report on Follow-up to Views was adopted during the Committee's 82nd Session.[162] The follow-up progress report on individual communications[163] used the newly agreed assessment criteria of 'compliance', 'partial compliance', 'non-compliance' and 'no reply' in updates on three cases.[164] In the case of *I.A.M. v. Denmark*[165] the Committee found Denmark to be in partial compliance (see Case Study 3.1 below). In *C.E. v. Belgium*,[166] concerning the denial of a visa to a Moroccan child who was fostered under the Islamic *khafalah* system by a Belgian – Moroccan couple, the measures taken by the state were deemed to be compliant with the Committee's requirements and the case was closed. The case concerned the denial of a visa to the child, and the authors of the complaint argued that it violated Articles 3, 10 and 12 of the Convention. The Committee found a violation, and urged the state to reconsider its decision 'in a positive spirit, while ensuring that the best interests of the child' were a primary consideration.[167] It also called on the state to take steps to prevent similar violations in future. The state therefore re-examined the visa application and included oral evidence from the child concerned, as well as wider investigations of the family situation, to ensure it was a suitable environment for the child. While shortcomings were identified, including in basic housing provisions, the state granted a six-month temporary visa; imposing conditions for improvement in housing and appropriate schooling for the child. The third case, *N.B.F. v. Spain*[168] concerned undocumented child migrants, and tests for determining age. In this case, the use

---

160 *Recent developments in the Individual communications received under the Optional Protocol to the Convention on the Rights of the Child on a Communications Procedure ('OPIC-CRC')*, September 2019.
161 A full list of considered cases can be found here: <https://juris.ohchr.org/en/search/results?Bodies=5&sortOrder=Date> (accessed 9 October 2019).
162 9–27 September 2019.
163 CRC Follow-up progress report on individual communications. CRC/C/82/1, 4 October 2019.
164 I.A.M. v. Denmark (CRC/C/77/D/3/2016), N.B.F. v. Spain (CRC/C/79/D/11/2017), C.E. v. Belgium (CRC/C/79/D/12/2017).
165 (CRC/C/77/D/3/2016).
166 (CRC/C/79/D/12/2017).
167 CRC Follow-up progress report on individual communications. CRC/C/82/1, 4 October 2019, 8.
168 (CRC/C/79/D/11/2017).

of a test involving an x-ray of the complainant's hand resulted in a determination that he was over 19 years of age. He argued that the test was not correct and not the appropriate test, and also that he was not appointed a representative to support him during the process. He claimed a breach of Articles 3 and 12 of the Convention and article 6 of the Optional Protocol on a communications procedure. The remedy proposed by the Committee was to reiterate the state's obligation to prevent similar violations in the future by ensuring that processes for ascertaining age are consistent with the Convention, and that appropriate legal or other representation is provided in a timely manner. The state responded by detailing procedures it had undertaken in response to the Committee's Views, however, much of this was disputed by the counsel of the author of the complaint, resulting in the Committee deciding to maintain follow-up dialogue and request regular updates from the state. The case remains open.

Case study 3.1

I.A.M. v. Denmark (CRC/C/77/D/3/2016)

Views adopted: 25 January 2018

Subject matter: Deportation of a single mother and her baby daughter to the Puntland, Somalia. The author claimed that, as a single mother, she would be unable to resist social and family pressure to subject her daughter to female genital mutilation against her will.

Articles violated: Articles 3 and 19 of the Convention.

Remedy: The State party is under an obligation to refrain from deporting the author and her daughter to Puntland. The State party is also under an obligation to take all steps necessary to prevent similar violations from occurring in the future. The State party is requested to publish the present Views and to have them widely disseminated in the official language of the State party.

State party's response: In its submission dated 5 September 2018, the State party observes that it is standard practice for the Refugee Appeals Board to reopen cases in which a United Nations treaty body has found that the decision made by the Board is contrary to an international convention. However, the Board found no basis for reopening the case at hand given that the author and her daughter had left Denmark and the Danish authorities are not aware of their whereabouts. Even though the Government and the Board suspended the time limit for the departure of the author and her daughter, the Board accepted as a fact that the author and her daughter had left Denmark, given their unknown location since early 2017. In reference to the request to publish the Committee's Views, the State party reports that the Views and decisions of the United Nations treaty bodies in cases against

> Denmark involving the Refugee Appeals Board and information on further measures taken by the Board are uploaded to the Board's website as quickly as possible after the Views and decisions have been adopted. The Views and information on the present case were posted on 9 February 2018. In addition, the Board publishes in its annual report the Views and decisions of the committees in cases against Denmark. The Ministry of Foreign Affairs has also made the Committee's views publicly available on its website. The State party asserts that, given the prevalence of English language skills in Denmark, the Government sees no reason for full translation of the Committee's Views into Danish.
>
> Counsel's comments: In his comments dated 26 April 2019, the author's counsel states that he was not informed by the author of her new location or residence. However, he notes that the Government has refrained from responding to the Committee's Views in relation to the prevention of similar violations in the future. He notes that a press release was published on the Refugee Appeals Board's website stating that the Board was maintaining its practice despite criticism from the Committee. In that press release, the Board explains that the decision of the Committee is against its practice and against the jurisprudence of the European Court of Human Rights, and that the decisive factor must therefore be whether the family can be assumed to be capable of protecting the child from circumcision.
>
> Decision of the Committee: The Committee notes the absence of information about the author and her daughter's whereabouts and the lack of contact between the author and her counsel since early 2017, and accepts that it was not possible to implement the individual remedy. However, with regard to the general remedy, the Committee notes the absence of information on any measures taken by the State party to prevent similar violations in the future. In light of all the above, the Committee decides to close the follow-up dialogue with a "B" assessment.

3.6.3.2 Inquiry procedure

States parties may declare upon signature or ratification of OPIC that they are opting out of the inquiry procedure.[169] Many delegations in the OEWG sessions supported an opt-out facility as it would promote wider acceptance of the Protocol.[170] The procedure obliges the Committee, upon receipt of 'reliable information indicating grave or systematic violations' by a State party of rights set forth in the Convention or either of the two substantive Optional Protocols, to invite

---

169 OPIC, art. 13(7). Such States parties may at any time withdraw the declaration to opt-out of the inquiry procedure: OPIC, art. 13(8).
170 OEWG 2011, [86].

the States party to cooperate in an inquiry, conducted by one or more of the Committee members.[171] In the case of such 'reliable information' it may 'on its own initiative' commence an inquiry.[172] The inquiry shall be conducted confidentially and may include a visit to the States party territory.[173] The Committee may designate one or more of its members to conduct an inquiry and report back to the Committee.[174] It would seem that the member(s) conducting the inquiry will have liberty 'to determine their own methods of work'.[175] The principle of confidentiality is further supported in the OPIC RoP which protects all documents and proceedings of the Committee relating to the inquiry, and provides that meetings will be closed.[176] The Committee must transmit its findings to the States party together with any comments or recommendations, and the States party is obliged to respond with its observations within six months of receiving the Committee's findings. The Committee may then, if necessary, follow-up by inviting the States party to inform it of the measures taken and envisaged in response to the inquiry, and also request further information in the States party's subsequent reports under the main Convention or either of the two substantive Optional Protocols.[177]

3.6.3.3 Inter-state communications

This procedure is initiated where one States party claims that another States party is not fulfilling its obligations under the main Convention and/or either of the two substantive Optional Protocols.[178] By contrast to the *opt-out* provision of the inquiry procedure discussed above, the inter-state communications procedure requires States parties to *opt-in* by making a declaration 'at any time' recognising the competence of the Committee in this respect.[179] Furthermore, *both* States parties must have made such opt-in declarations for the Committee to have competence to consider the case.[180] Like the individual communications procedure, the inter-state communications procedure also has provision for the States parties to arrive at a 'friendly solution' of the matter by availing themselves of the Committee's good offices.[181] The OPIC RoP expands on this latter point

---

171 OPIC, art. 13.
172 OPIC RoP, rule 31.
173 OPIC, art. 13(2) & (3). On visits to the States party territory, see further OPIC RoP, rules 38 and 39.
174 OPIC RoP, rule 36(1).
175 OPIC RoP, rule 36(3).
176 OPIC RoP, rule 33.
177 OPIC, art. 14.
178 OPIC, art. 12(1).
179 Of the 46 States parties that had ratified OPIC, at the time of writing, 12 (Albania, Belgium, Chile, Czech Republic, Finland, Germany, Italy, Liechtenstein, Portugal, Slovakia, Slovenia and Switzerland) had opted in to the inter-state communication procedure.
180 OPIC, art. 12(2); OPIC RoP, rule 45.
181 OPIC, art. 12(3).

by providing that the Committee may establish 'an ad hoc conciliation commission' to deal with the case.[182] The *Rules* envisage two outcome documents arising from this procedure. First, if a 'friendly solution' is reached then the Committee will adopt a report confined to 'a brief statement of the facts and of the solution reached'. Second, if such a solution cannot be reached, then a more fulsome report by the Committee is envisaged, including its own views on the matter along with the written submissions by each party.[183]

It should be noted that this procedure, although it has precedents in the international law relating to other international human rights treaties, nevertheless has 'an uninspiring track record' (Buck and Wabwile 2013: 216), as the mechanism has never been used in practice in relation to the other UN human rights treaty bodies.[184] The underlying risks of this procedure being captured and politicised by more general inter-State rivalries are obvious, and may account for States' unwillingness to subscribe to the procedure, a consideration which no doubt led to the insertion of the opt-in facility in order to forestall wholesale rejection of the Protocol by States.

3.7 The implementation of the *Convention on the Rights of the Child*

The Committee's *Guidelines* on how to prepare 'initial'[185] and 'periodic' state reports[186] group the provisions of the Convention into nine thematic clusters and request responses using this structure. This approach reflects the Convention's holistic perspective of children's rights, an approach that is consistent with the general human rights law principle that such rights are indivisible and interrelated, and that equal importance should be attached to each and every right. A further 'simplified reporting procedure' was proposed by the United Nations General Assembly in 2014,[187] to facilitate a less burdensome reporting process for states, to enhance their responsiveness to treaty reporting obligations. The Committee adopted such a reporting process for the Convention beginning with reports due on 1 September 2019 onwards. Those states that have accepted the simplified reporting procedure will receive a request for a List of Issues Prior to

---

182 OPIC RoP, rule 47.
183 OPIC RoP, rule 49.
184 OEWG 2011, above n. 118, [89]. However, they have been used under the *European Convention for the Protection of Human Rights and Fundamental Freedoms*, opened for signature 4 November 1950, 213 UNTS 221 (entered into force 3 September 1953).
185 *General Guidelines regarding the form and content of initial reports to be submitted by States parties under Article 44, paragraph 1(a), of the Convention*, CRC/C/5, 30 October 1991.
186 *Treaty-specific guidelines regarding the form and content of periodic reports to be submitted by States parties under article 44, paragraph 1 (b), of the Convention on the Rights of the Child*, CRC/C/58/Rev. 3, 3 March 2015.
187 'Strengthening and enhancing the effective functioning of the human rights treaty body system', General Assembly Resolution A/RES/68/268.

Reporting (LOIPR) with 30 questions; the answers to which form the State party's report to the Committee.

There is a detailed account of the legal provenance of each article of the Convention given in Detrick (1999). In the following sections (3.7.1 to 3.7.9) however, an account of each of these nine 'clusters', as defined in the *Guidelines*, is given with reference to the interactions between the States parties and the Committee in the reporting process.

In this section, all the Committee's Concluding Observations on reports submitted under article 44 of the Convention in the 80th, 81st and 82nd sessions[188] have been reviewed to prepare a summary and illustrative examples of the points discussed under each theme. It is hoped that this will enable the reader to obtain an understanding not only of the standard-setting achieved by the text of the Convention, but also of the way in which it is actually being implemented in practice across a wide range of countries.

3.7.1 General measures of implementation: articles 4, 42 and 44(6)

These Convention articles contain strongly worded provisions emphasising States parties' duties to *implement* and *disseminate* the principles and provisions of the Convention. Article 4 of the Convention obliges States parties to 'undertake all appropriate legislative, administrative, and other measures for the implementation of the rights recognized' in the Convention. However, the text of article 4 also makes it clear that with regard to *economic, social and cultural rights*, the States parties' obligation to action implementation measures shall be undertaken 'to the maximum extent of their available resources and, where needed, within the framework of international co-operation'. Article 42 obliges States parties to 'make the principles and provisions of the Convention widely known, by appropriate and active means, to adults and children alike'. Article 44(6) places a duty on States parties to 'make their reports widely available to the public in their own countries'. The Committee has set out useful advice to States parties in its *General Comment No. 5*[189] in 2003 on how these obligations can be pursued. It commends the development of a comprehensive and rights-based strategy built on the framework of the Convention. The Committee takes the view that economic, social and cultural rights, as well as civil and political rights, 'must be regarded as justiciable'.[190]

The 'general measures' cluster in the Committee's Concluding Observation usually opens with a commentary on the extent to which its recommendations and

---

188 80th session – 14 January to 1 February 2019; 81st session – 13 May to 31 May 2019; 82nd session – 9 to 27 September 2019.
189 Committee on the Rights of the Child, *General Comment No. 5: General measures of implementation of the Convention on the Rights of the Child (arts 4, 42 and 44, para. 6)* 34th sess., CRC/GC/2003/5 (27 November 2003).
190 Ibid., [25].

concerns in the previous reporting round have been addressed. The Committee will usually be able to find specific areas from the previous reporting cycle which it considers the States party has not sufficiently addressed. For example, it expressed disappointment that Singapore had failed to withdraw any of its declarations to articles 12–17, 19 and 37, and reservations to articles 7, 9–10, 22, 28 and 32 of the Convention.[191] Similarly, it noted that Belgium had failed to withdraw its declaration regarding articles 2 and 40 of the Convention.[192] In the case of Syria, it reminded the state of the 'indivisibility and interdependence of the rights enshrined in the Convention' and further emphasised that all recommendations being made were of equal import.[193]

Clearly, the assessment of the extent to which specifically 'legislative' measures have contributed towards successful implementation of the Convention is a significant task that is performed in the reporting process. The Committee will welcome countries that proactively amend their national laws[194] or even their Constitution[195] to accommodate the legal standards set out in the Convention. In the case of Malta, the Committee referred to the domestic Minor Protection (Alternative Care) Bill, recommending that the adoption of this bill be expedited in order to enable compliance with the Convention, and provide adequate human, technical and financial resources for implementation.[196] Equally, the Committee will express concern, for example in respect of Japan, the Committee strongly recommended the adoption of a 'comprehensive law on children's rights' and for the state to take steps to 'harmonize its existing legislation with the principles and provisions of the Convention'.[197] The Committee can frequently be seen to encourage States parties to bring their domestic law into conformity with the Convention and to strengthen their efforts towards formal recognition of it in domestic law, and will express concern where the Convention is not directly applicable by courts and cited in court judgements.[198] There are often challenges with countries that have a federal/state constitutional structure in receiving the Convention into their domestic systems in ways which are acceptable to the Committee and avoid disparate application of the Convention depending on whether this occurs within the federal, state or district levels of government jurisdiction. The Committee found, for example,

---

191 CRC/C/SGP/CO/4–5 (31 May 2019) [7].
192 CRC/C/BEL/CO/5–6 (28 February 2019) [6].
193 CRC/C/SYR/CO/5 (6 March 2019) [5].
194 E.g. the Committee welcomed the adoption of the Children's Act in 2009 and the amendments to the Penal Code in 2018 by Botswana to align it with the Convention, but noted several other laws relevant to children did not conform to the Convention, namely the Adoption of Children Act, the Marriage Act, the Affiliations Proceedings Act, the Deserted Wives and Child Protection Act and the Wills Act. CRC/C/BWA/CO/2–3 (26 June 2019) [6].
195 CRC/C/SYR/CO/5 (6 March 2019) [8](b).
196 CRC/C/MLT/CO/3–6 (26 June 2019) [8].
197 CRC/C/JPN/CO/4–5 (5 March 2019) [7].
198 CRC/C/UZB/CO/3–4 (14 June 2013) [8].

that in the case of Australia, the Assistant Minister for Children and Families was lacking a clear mandate and had insufficient 'authority to coordinate all of the activities related to implementing the Convention at cross-sectoral, federal, state, territory and local levels'.[199] Equally, the Committee has expressly stated that the Convention provisions must prevail over both domestic legislation and 'common practice' where there is a conflict between these respective provisions.[200] Domestic customary law is often viewed by the Committee as an obstacle to the implementation of the Convention.

However, the Committee will go much further than a mere paper audit of child-friendly legislation. It will want to see that the legislation in question has a substantial impact in the real world. Regrettably, implementation is often measured by some States according to a rather narrow focus on the compatibility of its municipal legal system with Convention standards. Some countries have incorporated the Convention into their domestic laws, but the relationship between municipal and international law is often a subtle one. France's *Cour de Cassation*, for example, has recognised the direct applicability of the Convention to domestic law, and the *Conseil d'État* followed suit, but the Committee had to express concern that only a limited number of provisions of the Convention were recognised to have such direct effect.[201]

There were, at the time of writing, around 58 States parties that had current declarations and/or reservations on ratifying the Convention. The Committee routinely urges States to withdraw reservations; for example, it recommended that Japan should promptly withdraw its reservation to article 37(c).[202] Over the years, many reservations have been withdrawn, for example, all four of the UK's reservations made upon ratification have now been withdrawn.[203] The facility to make reservations is often a useful diplomatic tool to persuade countries to ratify an international instrument. However, there are some limits to making them. Any reservation that is against the 'object and purpose' of the Convention would not be allowed,[204] and even if such reservations were not expressly prohibited in the Convention, they would be prohibited under the *Vienna Convention on the Law of Treaties*[205] (1969). The

---

199 CRC/C/AUS/CO/5–6 (30 September 2019) [9].
200 CRC/C/MOZ/CO/3–4 (1 October 2019) [6](b).
201 CRC/C/FRA/CO/4 (11 June 2009) [10].
202 'In applying paragraph (c) of article 37 of the Convention on the Rights of the Child, Japan reserves the right not to be bound by the provision in its second sentence, that is, "every child deprived of liberty shall be separated from adults unless it is considered in the child's best interest not to do so", considering the fact that in Japan as regards persons deprived of liberty, those who are below twenty years of age are to be generally separated from those who are of twenty years of age and over under its national law.' CRC/C/JPN/CO/4–5 (5 March 2019 [6].
203 These reservations concerned: children's hearings in Scotland, younger workers, nationality and immigration issues, and child detention. They were withdrawn in respectively: 1997, 1999, 2008 and 2008. See Buck (2011: 99–102) for details of the UK's reservations.
204 CRC, art. 51(2).
205 Opened for signature 23 May 1969, 1155 UNTS 331 (entered into force 27 January 1980).

Committee has been concerned that some reservations plainly breach the Convention 'by suggesting, for example, that respect for the Convention is limited by the State's existing Constitution or legislation, including in some cases religious law'.[206]

The Committee rarely misses an opportunity to recommend:

> [T]hat the State party ensure the realization of children's rights in accordance with the Convention, the Optional Protocol on the involvement of children in armed conflict and the Optional Protocol on the sale of children, child prostitution and child pornography throughout the process of implementing the 2030 Agenda for Sustainable Development. It urges the State party to ensure the meaningful participation of children in the design and implementation of policies and programmes aimed at achieving the 17 Sustainable Development Goals as far as they concern children.[207]

It also encourages States to mainstream children's rights across all relevant sectors. In its quest to encourage States parties to develop comprehensive national policies, the Committee emphasises the need for coordination and collaboration by different government entities and the clear identification of the lead government Ministry in managing a coordinated response. Even where there is an identifiable lead agency, the Committee will often find that it lacks sufficient authority or resources to meet an overall coordination role. For example, it noted that in the cases of Malta, Syria and Singapore respectively, each had allocated a relevant Ministry/body to oversee implementation of the Convention, however, in each case it was lacking 'a clear mandate'. Further, Malta and Syria lacked 'adequate human, technical and financial resources' and Singapore required 'sufficient authority to coordinate all activities related to the implementation of the Convention'.[208] The Committee has pointed out that the decentralisation of government power does not in any way reduce States parties' direct responsibility to fulfil their responsibilities. Equally, such decentralisation or devolution may require safeguards to protect groups from discrimination. The Committee has encouraged States to adopt a continuous process of 'child impact assessment' and evaluation to be built into the policy-making process itself.

The requirement in the Convention for States parties to commit the 'maximum extent' of their available resources in pursuit of economic, cultural and social rights, under article 4 is given further elaboration and substantiation in *General Comment No. 19* (2016) on public budgeting for the realisation of children's rights (art. 4),[209]

---

206 Committee on the Rights of the Child, *General Comment No. 5: General measures of implementation of the Convention on the Rights of the Child (arts. 4, 42 and 44, para. 6)* 34th sess., CRC/GC/2003/5 (27 November 2003) [15].
207 CRC/C/CPV/CO/2 (27 June 2019) [4].
208 CRC/C/MLT/CO/3–6 (26 June 2019) [10], CRC/C/SGP/CO/4–5 (31 May 2019) [10], CRC/C/SYR/CO/5 (6 March 2019) [10].
209 CRC/C/GC/19 (20 July 2016). This builds on General Comment No. 5 (2003) detailing general measures for implementation of the Convention, and the day of general discussion held in 2007 on the responsibility of States regarding resources for the rights of the child [6].

which 'provides States parties with a framework to ensure that public budgets contribute to the realization of those rights'.[210] The *General Comment* provides a detailed overview of the legal obligations arising from article 4[211] in relation to public budgets and 'makes recommendations on how to realize all the rights under the Convention, especially those of children in vulnerable situations, through effective, efficient, equitable, transparent and sustainable public budget decision-making'.[212] The *General Comment* is informed by 'several United Nations resolutions'[213] which elaborate budget related principles for the realisation of human rights goals, and extensive engagement with states, NGOs, experts and a survey of 2,693 children in 71 countries.[214] The engagement with children in particular reflects the spirit of the Convention and enabled the identification of clear child-focused goals including governments' consultation with children to ensure their actual needs are being met, inclusion of children with special needs in budget allocation, efficient use of resources, viewing resource allocation to children as investments for the future, countering corruption and transparency in governance including transparent record keeping, and providing budget information 'to all children in ways that are easily understood'.[215] The Committee has historically aimed to encourages States parties to consider legislating a specific proportion of public expenditure to be allocated to children and to make children a priority in budgetary allocations and consider using rights-based monitoring and analysis in addition to child impact assessments on how investments in any sector may serve children's best interests.[216]

The *General Comment* responds to States parties' failure to adequately prioritise the rights of the child in its budget allocation,[217] and emphasises that 'States parties have no discretion as to whether or not to satisfy their obligation to undertake the appropriate legislative, administrative and other measures necessary to realize children's rights, which includes measures related to public budgets'.[218] Thus, *all* branches of government involved in devising budgets are expected to pay particular attention to the general principles of the Convention, and be provided with access to the necessary 'information, data and resources' relating to children to enable adequate planning.[219] States are expected to take numerous steps under

---

210 Ibid., [2].
211 States parties shall undertake all appropriate legislative, administrative and other measures for the implementation of the rights recognised in the Convention. With regard to economic, social and cultural rights, States parties shall undertake such measures to the maximum extent of their available resources and, where needed, within the framework of international cooperation.
212 CRC/C/GC/19 (20 July 2016), [1].
213 Ibid., [7].
214 Ibid., [8].
215 Ibid.
216 *Day of General Discussion on 'Resources for the Rights of the Child – Responsibility of States'*, [23, 30].
217 CRC/C/GC/19 (20 July 2016), [12].
218 Ibid., [18].
219 Ibid., [19],[20].

article 4, including 'legislative' to ensure sufficient budgets are allocated for the realisation of children's rights; 'administrative' such as the development of programs to further the Convention aims; and 'other measures' such as 'the development of public budget participation mechanisms, and data or policies related to children's rights'.[220] Additionally, states are required to show the impact of the investments in terms of positive outcomes in terms of children's rights.[221] Thus, all four stages of the public budget process are included: 'planning, enacting, executing and follow-up'.[222] The General Comment envisages children's rights under the Convention being placed in a pivotal position in States parties' national priorities. However, it is clear from evidence in numerous concluding observations that states are failing to adequately strategise on this issue.

As with other matters, but especially in relation to questions about resources, the Committee will often apply higher standards and expectations of more affluent countries.[223] It will also identify any discrepancy in treatment of different groups of children, as it did with Australia, singling out 'Aboriginal and Torres Strait Islander Children' for particular attention.[224] Where data is available, discriminatory allocation is sometimes exposed. For example, the Committee previously noted with concern that the average spending per child in Israel in Arab areas was estimated to be more than a third lower than in Jewish localities.[225]

The Committee will pinpoint where there are weaknesses; for example, where there is no adequate tracking system for the allocation of resources as in the case of Cabo Verde.[226] The Committee makes specific reference to *General Comment No. 19* tracking or other monitoring process in every Concluding Observation of 2019,[227] reflecting a keen focus on the allocation of resources by states to enable the Convention aims to be met. States' responses have been varied, including Belgium's 'child budgeting' policy which the Committee welcomed in principle,

---

220 Ibid., [23].
221 For example, the Committee advised Malta to set up 'budget classification systems that allow expenditures related to the rights of the child to be reported, tracked and analyzed'. CRC/C/MLT/CO/3–6 (26 June 2019), [11](c).
222 CRC/C/GC/19 (20 July 2016), [26].
223 In relation to Canada, it observed: 'Bearing in mind that the State party is one of the most affluent economies of the world and that it invests sizeable amounts of resources in child-related programmes, the Committee notes that the State party does not use a child-specific approach for budget planning and allocation in the national and provinces/territories level budgets, thus making it practically impossible to identify, monitor, report and evaluate the impact of investments in children and the overall application of the Convention in budgetary terms': CRC/C/CAN/CO/3–4 (5 October 2012) [16].
224 CRC/C/AUS/CO/5–6 (30 September 2019), [10](b).
225 CRC/C/ISR/CO/2–4 (14 June 2013) [13].
226 CRC/C/CPV/CO/2 (27 June 2019), [12].
227 Bahrain, Belgium, Italy, Japan, Syria, Botswana, Cabo Verde, Cote d'Ivoire, Malta, Singapore, Tonga, Australia, Bahrain, Bosnia and Herzegovina, Mozambique, Portugal and Republic of Korea.

however, found to be implemented irregularly with an overall concern that the budget was inadequate especially with regards to vulnerable children.[228]

The Committee has acknowledged that the obligations of the Convention, though placed on States parties, in practice stretch beyond State institutions and services and require the cooperation of civil society and the family. It urges governments to give NGOs non-directive support and develop sound links with them, and will often comment on the quality of cooperation with civil society organisations. The Committee has also stressed that article 4 requires *international* cooperation and urges States to meet internationally agreed targets.

The Committee's Concluding Observations to each state include a statement regarding data collection, reiterating the need for a system of coordinated data collection enabling disaggregation by 'age, sex, disability, geographic location, ethnic origin, migration status and socioeconomic background' covering the entire period of childhood to age 18.[229] This data should be shared with relevant government ministries and relevant stakeholders, and used to analyse the effectiveness of the state's implementation of the Convention. Even where countries have established national statistics institutions that collect data on a regular basis, the Committee will pinpoint areas where the statistics are weak, for example, in Australia, where it specified the need to collect data on 'violence, alternative care, natural disasters and children in conflict with the law'.[230]

While approving governments' self-monitoring and evaluation, the Committee also regards the *independent* monitoring of progress as essential. It encourages this, in particular, by recommending the establishment of independent human rights institutions. The Committee issued *General Comment No. 2* on this subject and it 'considers the establishment of such bodies to fall within the commitment made by States parties upon ratification to ensure the implementation of the Convention and advance the universal realization of children's rights'.[231] However, such independent institutions should be seen as complementary to government structures; governments ought not merely to delegate their monitoring functions to them. The Committee typically recommends the establishment of a Children's Commissioner or Ombudsman where there is none. Some States parties do not have a functional independent national human rights institution.[232] Where there is a general national human rights institution it may lack an explicit mandate to investigate children's complaints,[233] or simply lack the required human and financial resources to operate

---

228 CRC/C/BEL/CO/5–6 (28 February 2019) [10].
229 E.g. Portugal, CRC/C/PRT/CO/5–6 (27 September 2019) [11](a); Botswana, CRC/C/BWA/CO/2–3 (26 June 2019) [13](a).
230 CRC/C/AUS/CO/5–6 (30 September 2019) [11](a).
231 Committee on the Rights of the Child, *General Comment No. 2: The role of independent national human rights institutions in the promotion and protection of the rights of the child*, 32nd sess., CRC/GC/2002/2 (15 November 2002) [1].
232 For example, Singapore: CRC/C/SGP/CO/4–5 (31 May 2019) [13]; Belgium: CRC/C/BEL/CO/5–6 (28 February 2019) [12].
233 CRC/C/CPV/CO/2 (27 June 2019)[15](b).

successfully.[234] The Committee generally raises criticisms where it perceives that the body in question falls below the standard of independence as indicated in *General Comment No. 2*[235] and the 'Paris Principles'.[236] In the past, it has expressed concern with States parties, like Slovenia, whose Ombudsman Office was only credited with a 'B' status by the International Coordinating Committee of National Institutions for the Promotion and Protection of Human Rights.[237]

The duties to disseminate and publicise the Convention in articles 42 and 44(6) are especially important. These duties often require relevant language translations for minority or indigenous groups, and programmes of rights awareness including targeted awareness raising for 'the judiciary, the police, the army and other law enforcement professionals, as well as school, health and social workers'.[238] The Committee notes some of the positive efforts made; for example, measures taken in Belgium to improve children's knowledge of the Convention, 'in particular by its integration into education for citizenship in democratic society'.[239] The involvement of NGOs and children in such advocacy campaigns has become a hallmark of such activity. Indeed, the Committee has concluded that: '[o]ne of the satisfying results of the adoption and almost universal ratification of the Convention has been the development at the national level of a wide variety of new child-focused and child-sensitive bodies, structures and activities'.[240] However, the reporting process is still revealing low levels of awareness of the Convention, as noted by the Committee in the case of Botswana[241] and Cabo Verde,[242] as well as others in 2019.

---

234 CRC/C/PRT/CO/5–6 (27 September 2019) [12](b).
235 Committee on the Rights of the Child, *General Comment No. 2: The role of independent national human rights institutions in the promotion and protection of the rights of the child*, 32nd sess., CRC/GC/2002/2 (15 November 2002).
236 General Assembly, 'Principles Relating to the Status of Independent National Human Rights Institutions', General Assembly RES/48/134 (20 December 1993) (the 'Paris Principles').
237 CRC/C/SVN/CO/3–4 (14 June 2013) [18]. The International Coordinating Committee of National Institutions for the Promotion and Protection of Human Rights (ICC) is a representative body of national human rights institutions established in 1993 and aims to assist in establishing and strengthening independent and effective National Human Rights Institutions (NHRIs), which meet the international standards set out in the Paris Principles. One of its key functions is to provide accreditation of an 'A' status to NHRIs which comply fully with the Paris Principles. These are eligible to become voting members of the ICC and to hold governance positions. NHRIs which only partially comply with the Paris Principles – and which have been granted 'B status' by the ICC Bureau – can participate in meetings of the ICC but are not eligible to vote or to hold governance positions.
238 CRC/C/SYR/CO/5 (6 March 2019) [14].
239 CRC/C/BEL/CO/5–6 (28 February 2019) [13].
240 Committee on the Rights of the Child, *General Comment No. 5: General measures of implementation of the Convention on the Rights of the Child (arts. 4, 42 and 44, para. 6)* 34th sess., CRC/GC/2003/5 (27 November 2003) [9].
241 The Committee repeated its previous recommendations to increase nationwide awareness of the Convention. CRC/C/BWA/CO/2–3 (26 June 2019) [16](a).
242 The Committee recommended 'systematic and continuous' awareness raising. CRC/C/CPV/CO/2 (27 June 2019), [18].

The Committee frequently recommends that all professional groups working for and with children receive adequate and systematic training, in particular law enforcement officials, teachers, health workers, social workers, religious leaders and those working in alternative care.

The Committee issued *General Comment No. 16*[243] in 2013 regarding the impact of the business sector on children's rights. This establishes that States parties are not relieved of their general obligations under the Convention 'when their functions are delegated or outsourced to a private business or non-profit organization' and a State will be in breach of its obligations 'where it fails to respect, protect and fulfil children's rights in relation to business activities and operations that impact on children.'[244] The Committee has called, for example, for a clear regulatory framework to be established in Bosnia and Herzegovina and Singapore in relation to the business sector operating in the States party to ensure their activities do not 'negatively affect human rights or endanger environmental and other standards, especially those relating to children's rights'.[245] Further, in the case of Singapore, the Committee also recommended that the state require companies to complete due diligence in their operations and across supply chains to assess the harmful effects of environmental degradation on the rights of children.[246]

3.7.2 Definition of the child: article 1

Article 1
For the purposes of the present Convention, a child means every human being below the age of eighteen years unless under the law applicable to the child, majority is attained earlier.

The issue of the definition of a child was a crucial and contentious part of the negotiations in the original drafting of the Convention (Cantwell 1992: 26). Article 1 was essentially a compromise: it sets the international legal definition of a child as a person below 18 years, but subject to the proviso that a domestic law that sets legal majority at an earlier age will not be compromised. In its *General Comment No. 4*, the Committee underlined that:

> adolescents up to 18 years old are holders of all the rights enshrined in the Convention; they are entitled to special protection measures, and, according to their evolving capacities, they can progressively exercise their rights (art. 5).[247]

---

243 Committee on the Rights of the Child, *General Comment No. 16: State obligations regarding the impact of the business sector on children's rights*, 62nd sess., CRC/C/GC/16 (17 April 2013).
244 Ibid. [25].
245 CRC/C/BIH/CO/5–6 (30 September 2019) [16](a).; CRC/C/SGP/CO/4–5 (31 May 2019) [16](a).
246 CRC/C/SGP/CO/4–5 (31 May 2019) [16](d).
247 Committee on the Rights of the Child, *General Comment No. 4: Adolescent health and development in the context of the Convention on the Rights of the Child*, CRC/GC/2003/4 (1 July 2003) [1].

The Human Rights Committee has also stated that protective ages must not be set 'unreasonably low', and that in any case a States party cannot absolve itself under the *International Covenant on Civil and Political Rights* (1966) (ICCPR)[248] from obligations to children under 18 years old, even if they have reached the age of majority under domestic law.[249] *General Comment No. 20*[250] further reaffirms that the minimum age for marriage; recruitment to armed forces and involvement in hazardous or exploitative work should be 18 years.[251] In some countries an age lower than 18 years is used to define the child. For example, in Namibia, the Constitution defines 'child' as anyone under the age of 16 years.[252] Where the general legal majority age is lower than 18, the Committee encourages States parties to raise it to 18 years where possible. In some countries there is no clearly defined age of majority.

In many countries the general age of majority is 18 years, for example, in Norway, Germany, Italy, China and the United Kingdom. However, such countries will also have specific legislation that offers legal capacity in particular areas. However, the setting of the upper age limit of 18 years for the definition of a child remains an important target for some countries, particularly those states that still have problems with the prevalence of child marriages.[253] In the case of Tonga, the Committee noted its serious concern at the minimum age of marriage being set at 15 years.[254]

In some countries there is no uniform definition of the child in laws and policies. The Committee observed, for example, that in Malta there were numerous areas of legislation where the States party did not provide for children above the age of 16 years 'resulting in a de facto definition of the child being a person under 16 years of age'.[255] There may also be, for example, conflicting legal minimum ages of children for marriage according to whether civil law or religious and customary laws apply, as in the case of Botswana where the Committee noted that the state prohibition on child marriages in the Marriage Act does not apply to customary and religious marriages.[256]

---

248 *International Covenant on Civil and Political Rights*, opened for signature 16 December 1966, 999 UNTS 171 (entered into force 23 March 1976).
249 Human Rights Committee, *General Comment No. 17: Rights of the child (Art. 24)* UN Doc. HRI/GEN/1/Rev. 8 (4 July 1989) [4].
250 Committee on the Rights of the Child, *General Comment No. 20 (2016) on the implementation of the rights of the child during adolescence*, CRC/C/GC/20 (6 December 2016).
251 Ibid., [40].
252 CRC/C/NAM/CO/2–3 (16 October 2012) [27].
253 Of the 14 concluding observations issued by the Committee in 2019, 12 included recommendations that the State parties remove all exceptions that allow marriage under the age of 18 years.
254 CRC/C/TON/CO/1 (2 July 2019) [19].
255 CRC/C/MLT/CO/2 (5 February 2013) [26].
256 CRC/C/BWA/CO/2–3 (26 June 2019) [19].

In its *General Comment No. 4* the following observations aptly summarise the objections to early marriage and the Committee's recommendations to address this issue.

> The Committee is concerned that early marriage and pregnancy are significant factors in health problems related to sexual and reproductive health, including HIV/AIDS. Both the legal minimum age and actual age of marriage, particularly for girls, are still very low in several States parties. There are also non-health-related concerns: children who marry, especially girls, are often obliged to leave the education system and are marginalized from social activities. Further, in some States parties married children are legally considered adults, even if they are under 18, depriving them of all the special protection measures they are entitled under the Convention. The Committee strongly recommends that States parties review and, where necessary, reform their legislation and practice to increase the minimum age for marriage with and without parental consent to 18 years, for both girls and boys. The Committee on the Elimination of Discrimination against Women has made a similar recommendation
> (General Comment No. 21 of 1994).[257]

The differential definitions of legal majority within a country can often deprive older children of essential services and care. For example, in Kyrgyzstan, assistance to families with children with HIV/AIDS has been provided only to children under the age of 16, and children aged 16 and over have been transferred to adult psychiatric care.[258]

Article 40(3)(a) of the Convention provides that:

> States parties shall seek to promote the establishment of laws, procedures, authorities and institutions specifically applicable to children alleged as, accused of, or recognized as having infringed the penal law, and, in particular:

> The establishment of a minimum age below which children shall be presumed not to have the capacity to infringe the penal law;

In the Committee's *General Comment No. 10* in 2007 it observes:

> *The minimum age of criminal responsibility*
> The reports submitted by States parties show the existence of a wide range of minimum ages of criminal responsibility. They range from a very low level of

---

257 Committee on the Rights of the Child, *General Comment No. 4: Adolescent health and development in the context of the Convention on the Rights of the Child*, CRC/GC/2003/4 (1 July 2003) [20]. See also: Committee on the Elimination of Discrimination against Women, *General Recommendation No. 21: Equality in marriage and family relations*, HRI/GEN/1/Rev. 8 (1994) [36].
258 CRC/C/15/Add.244 (3 November 2004) [24].

age 7 or 8 to the commendable high level of age 14 or 16. Quite a few States parties use two minimum ages of criminal responsibility. Children in conflict with the law who at the time of the commission of the crime are at or above the lower minimum age but below the higher minimum age are assumed to be criminally responsible only if they have the required maturity in that regard. The assessment of this maturity is left to the court/judge, often without the requirement of involving a psychological expert, and results in practice in the use of the lower minimum age in cases of serious crimes. The system of two minimum ages is often not only confusing, but leaves much to the discretion of the court/judge and may result in discriminatory practices. In the light of this wide range of minimum ages for criminal responsibility the Committee feels that there is a need to provide the States parties with clear guidance and recommendations regarding the minimum age of criminal responsibility.[259]

This was further strengthened by the Committee's *General Comment No. 20* in 2016:

> States parties are urged to introduce comprehensive juvenile justice policies that emphasize restorative justice, diversion from judicial proceedings, alternative measures to detention and preventive interventions, to tackle social factors and root causes, consistent with articles 37 and 40 of the Convention, and the United Nations Guidelines for the Prevention of Juvenile Delinquency. The focus should be on rehabilitation and reintegration . . . The Committee emphasizes the imperative to ban the death penalty and prohibit life imprisonment for anyone convicted of a crime committed when under the age of 18 years. The Committee is seriously concerned at the number of States seeking to lower the age of further responsibility. It calls on States to maintain the age of criminal majority at 18 years.[260]

There is also a comparable recognition in *The United Nations Standard Minimum Rules for the Administration of Juvenile Justice*, (the 'Beijing Rules'), that the minimum age of criminal responsibility should 'not be fixed at too low an age level, bearing in mind the facts of emotional, mental and intellectual maturity'.[261] Article 40(3) of the Convention requires States parties to promote a minimum age (unspecified) below which children will be presumed to lack capacity to break penal law. Children above the minimum age but below 18 years can be charged but the criminal justice process must be in full compliance with the Convention and *General*

---

259 Committee on the Rights of the Child, *General Comment No. 10: Children's rights in juvenile justice*, CRC/C/GC/10 (25 April 2007) [30].
260 Committee on the Rights of the Child, *General Comment No. 20 (2016) on the implementation of the rights of the child during adolescence*, CRC/C/GC/20 (6 December 2016) [88].
261 *The United Nations Standard Minimum Rules for the Administration of Juvenile Justice* (the 'Beijing Rules'), General Assembly, 96th plen. UN Doc. A/RES/40/33 (29 November 1985), rule 4.

Comment No. 10, which concludes that 'a minimum age of criminal responsibility below the age of 12 years is considered by the Committee not to be internationally acceptable', and States parties are encouraged to increase this minimum age threshold to higher levels over time.[262] However, there are still diverse rules relating to the age of criminal responsibility across different countries. In the United Kingdom, for example, the age of criminal responsibility in England, Wales and Northern Ireland is ten years old. In Scotland, the age of criminal responsibility has been raised from eight to the internationally acceptable (minimum) standard of 12 years.[263] The Committee recommended in 2008[264] that the UK should raise the minimum age of criminal responsibility in accordance with *General Comment No. 10*.

It is of greater difficulty to determine when childhood *begins*. Van Bueren (1994b: 33) notes that States 'hold such fundamentally conflicting views when childhood begins that they cannot be reconciled simply by the device of a treaty'. She concludes that there is no universally agreed point of time when childhood begins, but it would appear that international law protects the beginning of childhood, at least from the moment of a live birth. States are not prevented from extending their definition of childhood to include periods in the womb, but such protection cannot be read into customary international law or into treaty provisions that protect the right to life. The combination of the text of article 1 and a preambular paragraph of the Convention[265] in effect provides an opportunity for States parties to interpret the Convention as providing legal protection either from the moment of live birth or from conception, as the case may be. The *Implementation Handbook* explains the key point from the drafting history of the Convention:

> The preambular statement [. . .] caused difficulties within the Working Group that drafted the Convention. In order to reach consensus, the Group agreed that a statement should be placed in the *travaux préparatoires* to the effect that 'In adopting this preambular paragraph, the Working Group does not intend to prejudice the interpretation of article 1 or any other provision of the Convention by States parties.' (E/CN.4/1989/48, pp. 8 to 15; Detrick, p. 110).
>
> (Hodgkin and Newell 2007: 2)

Some States have registered a number of reservations or declarations in order to clarify their country's position in relation to this question. For example, the United Kingdom has made an interpretative declaration in respect of article 1.[266]

---

262 Ibid. [32].
263 See respectively: Crime and Disorder Act 1998, s.34; Criminal Justice (Northern Ireland) Order 1998, s.3; and Criminal Justice and Licensing (Scotland) Act 2010, s.52.
264 CRC/C/GBR/CO/4 (20 October 2008) [78].
265 CRC, Preamble §9. See n. 18a above.
266 'The United Kingdom interprets the Convention as applicable only following a live birth.'

However, other countries, for example Argentina, have specifically appealed to the (ninth) preambular paragraph of the Convention and the (third) preambular paragraph of the *Declaration of the Rights of the Child* (1959) in support of the contention that the Convention confers rights on the human foetus.

3.7.3 General principles: articles 2, 3, 6 and 12

These are the foundational principles of the Convention. Article 2 (non-discrimination principle), article 3 (best interests principle), article 6 (right to life, survival and development) and article 12 (participation rights according to evolving capacities) are fundamental to an understanding of the Convention. States parties are expected to provide information not only in respect of these general principles but also, pervasively, in relation to how these principles may impact on the implementation of other specific rights contained in the Convention.

3.7.3.1 The non-discrimination principle

Article 2
1. States parties shall respect and ensure the rights set forth in the present Convention to each child within their jurisdiction without discrimination of any kind, irrespective of the child's or his or her parent's or legal guardian's race, colour, sex, language, religion, political or other opinion, national, ethnic or social origin, property, disability, birth or other status.

2. States parties shall take all appropriate measures to ensure that the child is protected against all forms of discrimination or punishment on the basis of the status, activities, expressed opinions, or beliefs of the child's parents, legal guardians, or family members.

The grounds for discrimination in article 2 of the Convention are similar to those contained in ICCPR[267] and ICESCR,[268] with the addition of 'ethnic original' and 'disability'. There is no definition of 'discrimination' within the text of the Convention, nor is there a dedicated *General Comment* on the non-discrimination principle. However, it is clear from *General Comment No. 5* that an *active approach* to implementation is envisaged. The non-discrimination obligation requires States actively to identify individual children and groups of children, the recognition and realisation of whose rights may demand special measures. For example, the Committee highlights, in particular, the need for data collection to be disaggregated to enable discrimination or potential discrimination to be identified. Addressing

---

[267] *International Covenant on Civil and Political Rights*, opened for signature 16 December 1966, 999 UNTS 171 (entered into force 23 March 1976), art. 2.
[268] *International Covenant on Economic, Social and Cultural Rights*, opened for signature 16 December 1966, 993 UNTS 3 (entered into force 3 January 1976), art. 2.

discrimination may require changes in legislation, administration and resource allocation, as well as educational measures to change attitudes. It should be emphasised that the application of the non-discrimination principle of equal access to rights does not mean identical treatment. A *General Comment* by the Human Rights Committee has underlined the importance of taking special measures in order to diminish or eliminate conditions that cause discrimination.[269]

The language of article 2 further supports this active approach to the non-discrimination principle. The obligation to 'ensure' goes beyond the obligation to 'respect' and implies an affirmative obligation on States to take the necessary measures to enable individuals to enjoy and exercise the relevant rights (Alston 1992: 5). This approach has been confirmed in *General Comment No. 14* relating to the 'best interests principle'.

> The right to non-discrimination is not a passive obligation, prohibiting all forms of discrimination in the enjoyment of rights under the Convention, but also requires appropriate proactive measures taken by the State to ensure effective equal opportunities for all children to enjoy the rights under the Convention. This may require positive measures aimed at redressing a situation of real inequality.[270]

The non-discrimination principle applies in conjunction with all the substantive rights in the Convention, but does not provide an *independent* right to freedom from discrimination (Detrick 1999: 72). The words 'birth or other status' cover discrimination in relation to children born out of wedlock. The prohibition of discrimination does not of course 'outlaw the legitimate differentiation between children in implementation – for example to respect the "evolving capacities" of children' (Hodgkin and Newell 2007: 26).

The Committee takes note of Target 10.3 of the Sustainable Development Goals (SDGs) in numerous concluding observations in 2019: 'Ensure equal opportunity and reduce inequalities of outcome, including by eliminating discriminatory laws, policies and practices and promoting appropriate legislation, policies and action in this regard.'

In order to meet these objectives, some states were encourages by the Committee to undertake in-depth and sweeping revisions to legislation in order to fully guarantee and uphold non-discrimination in law and practice.[271] Some states had implemented legislation in order to ameliorate their record on non-discrimination, such as Cabo Verde's Special Law on Gender-Based Violence in 2011; Japan's Act

---

269 Human Rights Committee, *General Comment No. 18: Non-discrimination*, 37th sess. (10 November 1989) [5].
270 Committee on the Rights of the Child, *General Comment No. 14: on the right of the child to have his or her best interests taken as a primary consideration (art. 3, para. 1)*, CRC/C/GC/14 (29 May 2013) [41].
271 For example Singapore and Japan.

of Partial Revision of the Civil Code in 2013 and revised Penal Code in 2017; and Portugal's Act 93/201 to prevent and combat discrimination on the grounds of racial and ethnic origin, colour, nationality, descent and country of origin. However, the majority of states required further action. For example, section 118 of Tonga's Criminal Offences Act does not recognise boy victims of rape leading to discriminatory outcomes for boy and girl victims of rape;[272] a situation which also persisted in Japan before revisions to the Penal Code were made in 2017.

The range of characteristics giving rise to discrimination vary, and the Committee identified state specific concerns ranging from open hostility to restrictions on access to services by certain groups. In Australia, the Aboriginal and Torres Strait Islanders' children suffered prejudice,[273] while in Singapore, flashpoints for discrimination arise 'in law or in practice' against children without Singaporean citizenship, as well as girls, children with disabilities, or those born to unmarried parents or same sex couples.[274] Poverty continues to give rise to discrimination,[275] resulting in a lack of access to essential services such as safe drinking water.[276] In Bahrain, the Committee expressed deep concerns about the persistent 'de facto discrimination' effecting girls, disabled children, Baharna and Ajam children, and children whose father are foreign or stateless.[277] Tonga's land ownership laws continue to discriminate against girls and children whose parents are unmarried.[278] In Mozambique, other categories including children with albinism, in street situations, rural area and asylum-seeking/ refugee children were all identified as suffering discrimination.[279] In the Republic of Korea, North Korean refugee children were identified as experiencing particular forms of discrimination including accessing birth registration, childcare facilities, education, healthcare, welfare, leisure and state protection.[280] In Syria, mothers are unable to pass on their citizenship to their children nor have their fathers name recorded where the parents are unmarried.[281] There have been moves to facilitate the assimilation of the legal status of legitimate and illegitimate children, however the Concluding Observations in 2019 demonstrate that discrimination against children born out of wedlock persists. In the case of Belgium, the Committee expressed concern about the issue of prejudice and hatred of children with migrant backgrounds, particularly following terrorist attacks in 2014 and 2016, placing an obligation on the state to counter such discrimination.

272 CRC/C/TON/CO/1 (2 July 2019) [21].
273 CRC/C/AUS/CO/5–6 (30 September 2019) [19](a).
274 CRC/C/SGP/CO/4–5 (31 May 2019) [19].
275 Belgium: CRC/C/BEL/CO/5–6 (28 February 2019) [16].
276 Syria.
277 CRC/C/BHR/CO/4–6 (27 February 2019) [16].
278 CRC/C/TON/CO/1 (2 July 2019) [22].
279 CRC/C/MOZ/CO/3–4 (1 October 2019) [16].
280 CRC/C/KOR/CO/5–6 (27 September 2019) [16].
281 CRC/C/SYR/CO/5 (6 March 2019) [17].

Awareness raising and preventative activities[282] against discrimination were encouraged of numerous states including Australia, Malta, Botswana, Singapore and Portugal; including through the school curricula, and affirmative action. The range of actions encouraged to tackle a lack of awareness and to change attitudes included collaboration with mass media, social networks and engagement with community and religious leaders,[283] and education on cultural diversity and inter-ethnic understanding.[284] Addressing negative impacts of stereotypes and discriminatory attitudes in media discourse was raised in particular for Bosnia and Herzegovina by encouraging a code of conduct for media.[285]

The State reports to the Committee often expose the persistence of discrimination in relation, particularly, to the 'girl child'. The Committee held a *Day of General Discussion* on this subject.[286] This emphasised that the *Convention on the Rights of the Child* and the *Convention on the Elimination of All Forms of Discrimination Against Women*[287] needed to be regarded as mutually reinforcing and complementary instruments. Furthermore:

> Within the larger movement for the realization of women's rights, history had clearly shown that it was essential to focus on the girl child in order to break down the cycle of harmful traditions and prejudices against women. Only through a comprehensive strategy to promote and protect the rights of girls, starting with the younger generation, would it be possible to build a shared and lasting approach . . .[288]

Discrimination is often directed against the girl child, and this usually reflects more fundamental discriminatory attitudes on gender within a State. For example, the Committee raised concerns about the prevalence of 'discrimination against girls rooted in patriarchal attitudes and stereotypes concerning the role of women and men' in Cabo Verde.[289] Further, the '[d]iscriminatory provisions excluding girls from landownership and inheritance rights' in Tonga,[290] and the 'legal provisions that discriminate against girls' in Syria including unequal inheritance rights.[291] Such pervasive gender discrimination has historically drawn strong criticism from the Committee. The Committee's Concluding Observations have identified evidence

---

282 CRC/C/AUS/CO/5–6 (30 September 2019) [19](b).
283 Singapore.
284 Portugal.
285 CRC/C/BIH/CO/5–6 (30 September 2019) [18] (b).
286 Committee on the Rights of the Child, *Day of General Discussion on 'The Girl Child'*, Report on the eighth session, CRC/C/38 (27 January 1995) [275–99].
287 *Convention on the Elimination of All Forms of Discrimination against Women*, opened for signature 18 December 1979, 1249 UNTS 13 (entered into force 3 September 1981).
288 Ibid. [284].
289 CRC/C/CPV/CO/2 (27 June 2019) [25].
290 CRC/C/TON/CO/1 (2 July 2019) [21].
291 CRC/C/SYR/CO/5 (6 March 2019) [17].

of multiple, gender-based discrimination in relation to the girl child; for example, in Guinea-Bissau, practices such as female, genital mutilation and cutting (FGM/C) and child marriage.[292] As the Committee observed in its *Day of General Discussion*:

> There was a need to ensure that a woman's life cycle would not become a vicious cycle, where the evolution from childhood to adulthood would be blighted by fatalism and a sense of inferiority. Only through the active involvement of girls, who are at the root of the life cycle, would it be possible to initiate a movement for change and betterment.[293]

The Committee has frequent cause to express its concern about discrimination against children belonging to particular minority ethnic groups within a State. For example, it noted concern at discrimination faced by Aboriginal and Torres Strait Islander children in Australia[294] and Ainu Buraku children in Japan.[295] Refugee children have also been identified as a particular group of children needing protective provisions, including North Korean refugee children in the Republic of Korea,[296] and 'asylum seeking, refugee and migrant children' in Malta.[297] On occasion, the Committee has used emotive language such as concern about 'hatred' of migrant children in Belgium following terrorist attacks in the country.[298] The Committee responds to these various concerns with a range of possible recommendations. These often include urging the country in question to ensure that their domestic legislation is Convention-compliant, to adopt awareness-raising campaigns and to embark upon training programmes with the relevant professionals including law enforcement officials and within school environments.

As regards discrimination against children with disabilities, it should be noted that the Convention was the first international human rights treaty to contain a specific reference to 'disability' and article 23 is exclusively dedicated to the rights and needs of children with disabilities. The Committee also issued *General Comment No. 9* on this topic.

> [T]he Committee on the Rights of the Child . . . has paid sustained and particular attention to disability based discrimination while other human rights treaty bodies have paid attention to disability based discrimination under 'other status' in the context of articles on non-discrimination of their relevant Convention.[299]

---

292 CRC/C/GNB/CO/2-4 (14 June 2013) [24].
293 Committee on the Rights of the Child, *Day of General Discussion on 'The Girl Child'*, Report on the eighth session, CRC/C/38 (27 January 1995) [285].
294 CRC/C/AUS/CO/5-6 (30 September 2019) [19]. The plight of indigenous children is discussed in more detail in Chapter 10.
295 CRC/C/JPN/CO/4-5 (5 March 2019) [18].
296 CRC/C/KOR/CO/5-6 (27 September 2019) [16].
297 CRC/C/MLT/CO/3-6 (26 June 2019) [19].
298 CRC/C/BEL/CO/5-6 (28 February 2019) [16].
299 Committee on the Rights of the Child, *General Comment No. 9: The rights of children with disabilities*, 43rd session, CRC/C/GC/9 (27 February 2007) [2].

General Comment No. 9 recommends that States parties should take the following measures to combat discrimination against disabled children.

(a) Include explicitly disability as a forbidden ground for discrimination in constitutional provisions on non-discrimination and/or include specific prohibition of discrimination on the ground of disability in specific anti-discrimination laws or legal provisions.
(b) Provide for effective remedies in case of violations of the rights of children with disabilities, and ensure that those remedies are easily accessible to children with disabilities and their parents and/or others caring for the child.
(c) Conduct awareness-raising and educational campaigns targeting the public at large and specific groups of professionals with a view to preventing and eliminating de facto discrimination against children with disabilities.[300]

The Committee regularly expresses its concern about the harassment and stigmatisation of children with disabilities in some States parties, and referred to discrimination against children with disabilities in its Concluding Observations in the reports of Singapore, Botswana, Belgium, Japan, Portugal, Bahrain, Tonga, Australia, Mozambique, and the Republic of Korea in 2019 alone. As pointed out by Hodgkin and Newell:

> the barrier [to the full enjoyment of rights] is not the disability itself but rather a combination of social, cultural, attitudinal and physical obstacles which children with disabilities encounter in their daily lives. The strategy for promoting their rights is therefore to take the necessary action to remove these barriers.
>
> (Hodgkin and Newell 2007: 29)

The way in which the principle of non-discrimination applies in the context of education rights is given some detailed treatment in *General Comment No. 1*.

> Discrimination on the basis of any of the grounds . . . offends the human dignity of the child and is capable of undermining or even destroying the capacity of the child to benefit from educational opportunities . . . To take an extreme example, gender discrimination can be reinforced by practices such as a curriculum which is inconsistent with the principles of gender equality, by arrangements which limit the benefits girls can obtain from the educational opportunities offered, and by unsafe or unfriendly environments which discourage girls' participation. Discrimination against children with disabilities

---
300 Ibid. [9].

is also pervasive in many formal educational systems and in a great many informal educational settings, including in the home. Children with HIV/AIDS are also heavily discriminated against in both settings. All such discriminatory practices are in direct contradiction with the requirements in article 29(1)(a) that education be directed to the development of the child's personality, talents and mental and physical abilities to their fullest potential.[301]

The Committee routinely draws States parties' attention to the principles of the *Declaration and Programme of Action* (Durban Declaration 2001), in addition to the outcome document[302] adopted at the 2009 Durban Review Conference. The Committee typically welcomes warmly the establishment of a national body with responsibility to remedy problems of discrimination, particularly where it has the power to receive individual complaints

3.7.3.2 The best interests principle

Article 3

1. In all actions concerning children, whether undertaken by public or private social welfare institutions, courts of law, administrative authorities or legislative bodies, the best interests of the child shall be a primary consideration.

This principle first appeared, at the international level, in principles 2 and 7 of the *Declaration of the Rights of the Child* (1959).[303] The principle has appeared in various forms in different countries and over a range of international legal instruments. For example, one objective of the *Hague Convention on Protection of Children and Co-operation in respect of Intercountry Adoption*[304] is, 'to establish safeguards to ensure that intercountry adoptions take place in the best interests of the child and with respect for his or her fundamental rights as recognised in international law'.[305] In addition to its appearance in article 3, the 'best interests' principle is also referred to elsewhere in the Convention and in all three Optional Protocols.[306]

---

301 Committee on the Rights of the Child, *General Comment No. 1: Article 29(1) – The Aims of Education*, 26th session, CRC/GC/2001/1 (17 April 2001) [10].
302 UN Office of the High Commissioner for Human Rights, *Outcome document of the Durban Review Conference*, 24 April 2009. Available at: <www.refworld.org/docid/49f584682.html> (accessed 12 September 2019).
303 General Assembly, *Declaration of the Rights of the Child*, 14th session, UN Doc. A/RES/1386 (XIV) (20 November 1959). Principle 2 of the *Declaration* of 1959 provides the stronger legal threshold, that is, 'the best interests of the child shall be the paramount consideration' in contrast to the 'primary consideration' in the *Convention*. It has sometimes been argued that the 'paramountcy' standard should be the basic rule in international child law.
304 Hague Conference on Private International Law, concluded 29 May 1993 (entered into force 1 May 1995).
305 Ibid., art. 1(a). See Chapter 6.
306 See CRC, arts 9(1)(3), 18(1), 20(1), 21, 37(c) and 42(b)(iii); OPSC, preamble, art. 8; OPAC, preamble, arts 2 and 3; OPIC, preamble, arts 2 and 3(2).

The principle has been controversial, not least because of the difficulties in pinpointing its core meaning and implementation with any intellectual precision. One persistent criticism of the best interests principle is that any one country's construction of its normative meaning will 'enable cultural considerations to be smuggled by States into their implementation of the rights recognised in the CRC' (Detrick 1999: 89). In addition to its referencing in earlier *General Comments*, the Committee issued *General Comment No. 14*[307] in 2013 which is dedicated to interpreting and analysing the best interests principle contained in article 3(1).[308] The appearance of this *General Comment* has, to an extent, provided an answer to the criticisms of 'vagueness' that have been levelled against it. *General Comment No. 14* makes it clear that '[t]he concept of the child's best interests is aimed at ensuring both the full and effective enjoyment of all the rights recognized in the Convention and the holistic development of the child'.[309] Furthermore, the Committee asserts that it is a 'threefold concept':

(a) *A substantive right*: The right of the child to have his or her best interests assessed and taken as a primary consideration when different interests are being considered in order to reach a decision on the issue at stake, and the guarantee that this right will be implemented whenever a decision is to be made concerning a child, a group of identified or unidentified children or children in general. Article 3, paragraph 1, creates an intrinsic obligation for States, is directly applicable (self-executing) and can be invoked before a court.

(b) *A fundamental, interpretative legal principle*: If a legal provision is open to more than one interpretation, the interpretation which most effectively serves the child's best interests should be chosen. The rights enshrined in the Convention and its Optional Protocols provide the framework for interpretation.

(c) *A rule of procedure*: Whenever a decision is to be made that will affect a specific child, an identified group of children or children in general, the decision-making process must include an evaluation of the possible impact (positive or negative) of the decision on the child or children concerned. Assessing and determining the best interests of the child require procedural guarantees. Furthermore, the justification of a decision must show that the right has been explicitly taken into account. In this regard, States parties shall explain how the right has been respected in the decision, that is, what has been considered to be in the child's best

---

307 Committee on the Rights of the Child, General Comment No. 14: on the right of the child to have his or her best interests taken as a primary consideration (art. 3, para. 1), CRC/C/GC/14 (29 May 2013).
308 *General Comment No. 14* does not deal with articles 3(2) and (3). A commentary on these provisions can be found in Hodgkin and Newell (2007: 40–2).
309 CRC/C/GC/14 (29 May 2013), para. 4.

interests; what criteria it is based on; and how the child's interests have been weighed against other considerations, be they broad issues of policy or individual cases.[310]

In addition, *General Comment No. 14* identifies three different types of obligations for States parties.[311] First, they must ensure that the child's best interests are appropriately integrated and applied in every action taken by public institutions. Second, States parties must ensure that all judicial and administrative decisions and policies and legislation concerning children demonstrate that the child's best interests have been a primary consideration. Finally, States parties must ensure that the child's interest have been equally attended to as a primary consideration in decisions and actions taken by the private sector. In order to ensure compliance, *General Comment No. 14* advises that States parties should undertake a number of 'implementation measures', for example, reviewing and amending domestic legislation and other sources of law so as to incorporate article 3(1).[312] The 'actions' referred to in article 3(1) 'does not only include decisions, but also all acts, conduct, proposals, services, procedures and other measures' and also omissions and failure to take action.[313] It is also clear that the best interests principle should be applied 'to children not only as individuals, but also in general or as a group'.[314] *General Comment No. 14* also makes an attempt to define 'the best interests of the child'. It states that the concept is 'flexible and adaptable' to the specific situation of children, and its content can be best clarified, in making both individual and collective assessments, on a 'case-by-case basis'.[315] However, the *General Comment* also implies a warning deriving from the inherent flexibility of the concept:

> [I]t may also leave room for manipulation; the concept of the child's best interests has been abused by Governments and other State authorities to justify racist policies, for example; by parents to defend their own interests in custody disputes; by professionals who could not be bothered, and who dismiss the assessment of the child's best interests as irrelevant or unimportant.[316]

The expression 'a primary consideration' means 'that the child's best interests may not be considered on the same level as all other considerations'.[317] Inevitably,

---

310 Ibid., para. 6.
311 Ibid., para. 14.
312 Ibid., para. 15(a), and see also sub-paras (b) to (h).
313 Ibid., paras 17 and 18.
314 Ibid., para. 23.
315 Ibid., para. 32.
316 Ibid., para. 34.
317 Ibid., para. 37.

children's interests will need to be weighed against other interests though 'a larger weight must be attached to what serves the child best'.[318]

> Viewing the best interests of the child as 'primary' requires a consciousness about the place that children's interests must occupy in all actions and a willingness to give priority to those interests in all circumstances, but especially when an action has an undeniable impact on the children concerned.[319]

General Comment No. 14 contains a detailed account of the approach that should be taken to the *assessment* and *determination* of a child's best interests and the necessary *procedural safeguards* required to guarantee its implementation. As regards assessment, it recommends in particular that decision-makers 'draw up a non-exhaustive and non-hierarchical list of elements that could be included in a best-interests assessment',[320] and sets out (seven) elements to take into account.[321] There are: the child's views; the child's identity; preservation of the family environment and maintaining relations; care, protection and safety of the child; situations of vulnerability; the child's right to health; the child's right to education. Of course, '[n]ot all the elements will be relevant to every case, and different elements can be used in different ways in different cases', and such elements 'may be in conflict when considering a specific case and its circumstances'.[322] As regards procedural safeguards, the Committee suggests that States parties and others pay special attention to a list of (seven) safeguards/guarantees: the right of the child to express his or her own views; the establishment of facts; time perception; qualified professionals; legal representation; legal reasoning; mechanisms to review or revise decisions; child-rights impact assessment (CRIA).[323] This is a welcome prompt for States parties which the Committee has had cause to criticise on the basis of 'the absence of guidelines and procedures for ensuring that the [best interests principle] is applied continuously throughout the State party's policies, legislation and programmes'.[324]

The best interests principle is applied in subsequent General Comments including *General Comment No. 24* (2019) on children's rights in the child justice system,[325] reiterating the principle to be applied in decisions, for example, concerning the placement of children in adult prisons where it is permitted only if in the child's best interests. In this case, the best interests provision of article 37(c) is to be construed narrowly. *General Comment No. 22* (2017) on the general principles regarding

---

318 Ibid., para. 39.
319 Ibid., para. 40.
320 Ibid., para. 50.
321 Ibid., paras 52–79.
322 Ibid., paras 80 and 81.
323 Ibid., paras 89–99.
324 CRC/C/GUY/CO/2–4 (5 February 2013) [26].
325 CRC/C/CG/24 (18 September 2019) [92].

the human rights of children in the context of international migration[326] also reiterates the applicability of the best interest principle, stating that 'a larger weight must be attached to what serves the child best.'[327] It asserts the following.

> 29. States parties shall ensure that the best interests of the child are taken fully into consideration in immigration law, planning, implementation and assessment of migration policies and decision-making on individual cases, including in granting or refusing applications on entry to or residence in a country, decisions regarding migration enforcement and restrictions on access to social rights by children and/or their parents or legal guardians, and decisions regarding family unity and child custody, where the best interests of the child shall be a primary consideration and thus have high priority.
>
> 30. In particular, the best interests of the child should be ensured explicitly through individual procedures as an integral part of any administrative or judicial decision concerning the entry, residence or return of a child, placement or care of a child, or the detention or expulsion of a parent associated with his or her own migration status.[328]

The fundamental nature of the best interests principle has encouraged some countries to include the principle in their Constitutions, though of course this is never a guarantee that the principle is actually fully integrated with the country's national laws or policies.[329] On occasion, the Committee will recommend that the principle ought to be included in a State's Constitution.[330] The Committee, in its Concluding Observations, frequently has cause to comment on the failure of States parties to fully incorporate the best interests principle in major pieces of legislation and/or in key policies, programmes and decision-making processes.[331] For example, in the case of Japan, the Committee found that the principle was not appropriately or consistently applied in a range of settings, including 'education, alternative care, family disputes and juvenile justice'.[332] Further, the Committee observed that 'the judicial, administrative and legislative bodies do not take into account the best interests of the child in all decisions relevant to children'.[333] They

---

326 CRC/C/GC/22 (16 November 2017), with Joint General Comment No. 3 (2017) of the Committee on the Protection of the Rights of All Migrant Workers and Members of Their Families, CMW/C/GC/3.
327 Ibid., [28].
328 Ibid., [29] – [30].
329 CRC/C/NAM/CO/2-3 (16 October 2012) [32]; CRC/C/AUT/CO/3-4 (5 October 2012) [26].
330 For example, in Slovenia: CRC/C/SVN/CO/3-4 (14 June 2013) [29].
331 See, for example: Malta: CRC/C/MLT/CO/3-6 (26 June 2019); Bosnia and Herzegovina: CRC/C/BIH/CO/5-6 (30 September 2019; Belgium: CRC/C/BEL/CO/5-6 (28 February 2019).
332 CRC/C/JPN/CO/4-5 (5 March 2019) [19].
333 Ibid.

therefore recommended reforms to overcome these failings, including the establishment of 'compulsory processes for ex ante and ex post impact assessments of all laws and policies relevant to children',[334] and that all assessment of the child's best interests are conducted by a 'multidisciplinary team with the obligatory participation of the concerned child'.[335]

Weaker legal formulations of the principle, for example, the 'legitimate interests' of the child, are likely to be criticised by the Committee as falling below the expected standard.[336] However, the Committee's Concluding Observations also record successful amendments to national laws, for example, Singapore's positive measures to integrate the principle in developing a 'child-sensitive approach to child abuse victims in police investigations and hearings in youth courts.[337] In this case, the Committee recommended that the state continue to integrate this principle to facilitate consistent interpretation in all 'legislative, administrative and judicial proceedings', as well as new legislation, and 'all policies, programmes and projects that are relevant to and have an impact on children'.[338]

The Committee's Concluding Observations also provide some evidence of the negative perceptions of the best interests principle that may be present in some States parties. One of the (eight) 'implementation measures' set out in *General Comment No. 14* specifically identifies:

> (h) Combating all negative attitudes and perceptions which impede the full realization of the right of the child to have his or her best interests assessed and taken as a primary consideration, through communication programmes involving mass media and social networks as well as children, in order to have children recognized as rights holders.[339]

For example, the Committee expressed its concern in the case of Botswana of a discrepancy between the High Court judgements and that of lower courts as well as professionals who work with or for children.[340]

As mentioned above, one of the (seven) procedural safeguards contained in *General Comment No. 14* is the 'child-rights impact assessment' (CRIA). The need for child impact assessment and evaluation was first advocated in an earlier *General Comment*.[341] What is envisaged is a 'continuous process' of CRIA, which should be designed to

---

334 Ibid.
335 Ibid.
336 For example, in Uzbekistan and Armenia: CRC/C/UZB/CO/3-4 (14 June 2013) [22]; CRC/C/ARM/CO/3-4 (14 June 2013) [20].
337 CRC/C/SGP/CO/4-5 (31 May 2019) [21].
338 Ibid.
339 *General Comment No. 14*, para. 15(h).
340 CRC/C/BWA/CO/2-3 (26 June 2019) [23].
341 Committee on the Rights of the Child, *General Comment No. 5: General measures of implementation of the Convention on the Rights of the Child* (arts. 4, 42 and 44, para. 6) 34th sess., CRC/GC/2003/5 (27 November 2003) [45-7].

'predict the impact of any proposed policy, legislation, regulation, budget or other administrative decision which affect children and the enjoyment of their rights'.[342]

> CRIA needs to be built into Government processes at all levels and as early as possible in the development of policy and other general measures in order to ensure good governance for children's rights. Different methodologies and practices may be developed when undertaking CRIA. At a minimum, they must use the Convention and its Optional Protocols as a framework, in particular ensuring that the assessments are underpinned by the general principles and have special regard for the differentiated impact of the measure(s) under consideration on children.[343]

The Republic of Korea was praised for its establishment of the Child Impact Assessment System.[344]

3.7.3.3 The right to life, survival and development

Article 6
1. States parties recognize that every child has the inherent right to life.

2. States parties shall ensure to the maximum extent possible the survival and development of the child.

The right to life, like its counterpart in the ICCPR,[345] is the only right in the Convention described as an 'inherent' right. Indeed, some commentators take the view that this is one of the 'peremptory norms of general international law', in other words, the *jus cogens* rule comes into play (see Chapter 2). The right to life differs, however, from its counterpart in other major human rights treaties, as it additionally requires States to ensure 'to the maximum extent possible' the child's 'survival and development'. These were seen as complementary elements, implying, for example, the need for State measures to reduce infant mortality. Given the difficulties experienced in the drafting process to arrive at a satisfactory definition of the child (see section 3.7.2 above), it is not surprising that a few countries have made declarations or reservations to ensure that the interpretation of article 6 will not conflict with national abortion and family planning legislation. For example, China's reservation[346] aims to protect its 'one child' policy. Luxembourg, Tunisia

---

342 *General Comment No. 14*, paras 35 and 99.
343 Ibid., para. 99.
344 CRC/C/KOR/CO/5–6 (27 September 2019) [18].
345 'Every human being has the inherent right to life. This right shall be protected by law. No one shall be arbitrarily deprived of his life.' ICCPR, art. 6(1).
346 '[T]he People's Republic of China shall fulfil its obligations provided by article 6 of the Convention under the prerequisite that the Convention accords with the provisions of article 25 concerning family planning of the Constitution of the People's Republic of China and in conformity with the provisions of article 2 of the Law of Minor Children of the People's Republic of China.'

and France have made declarations ensuring that article 6 does not interfere with their abortion legislation.[347]

The Committee has not yet issued a *General Comment* on this general principle, in part perhaps because the Human Rights Committee has already developed a jurisprudence around the earlier, comparable provision in ICCPR. It issued a *General Comment* in 1982 which stated:

> [T]he [Human Rights] Committee has noted that the right to life has been too often narrowly interpreted. The expression 'inherent right to life' cannot properly be understood in a restrictive manner, and the protection of this right requires that States adopt positive measures. In this connection, the Committee considers that it would be desirable for States parties to take all possible measures to reduce infant mortality and to increase life expectancy, especially in adopting measures to eliminate malnutrition and epidemics.[348]

However, article 6 has been referenced in some of the Committee on the Rights of the Child's *General Comments*. For example, in *General Comment No. 22*, the following paragraph appears:

> [40]. Article 6 of the Convention on the Rights of the Child highlights the States parties' obligations to ensure the right of life, survival and development of the child, including the physical, mental, moral, spiritual and social dimensions of his or her development. At any point during the migratory process, a child's right to life and survival may be at stake owing to, inter alia, violence as a result of organized crime, violence in camps, push-back or interception operations, excessive use of force of border authorities, refusal of vessels to rescue them, or extreme conditions of travel and limited access to basic services. Unaccompanied and separated children may face further vulnerabilities and can be more exposed to risks, such as gender-based, sexual and other forms of violence and trafficking for sexual or labour exploitation. Children travelling with their families often also witness and experience violence. While

---

347 'The Government of Luxembourg declares that article 6 of the present Convention presents no obstacle to implementation of the provisions of Luxembourg legislation concerning sex information, the prevention of back-street abortion and the regulation of pregnancy termination.'

'The Government of the Republic of Tunisia declares that the Preamble to and the provisions of the Convention, in particular article 6, shall not be interpreted in such a way as to impede the application of Tunisian legislation concerning voluntary termination of pregnancy.'

'The Government of the French Republic declares that this Convention, particularly article 6, cannot be interpreted as constituting any obstacle to the implementation of the provisions of French legislation relating to the voluntary interruption of pregnancy.'

348 Human Rights Committee, *General Comment No. 6, Article 6 (Right to life)*, 16th sess., HRI/GEN/1/Rev. 8 (1982) [5].

migration can provide opportunities to improve living conditions and escape from abuses, migration processes can pose risks, including physical harm, psychological trauma, marginalization, discrimination, xenophobia and sexual and economic exploitation, family separation, immigration raids and detention. At the same time, the obstacles children may face in gaining access to education, adequate housing, sufficient safe food and water or health services can negatively affect the physical, mental, spiritual, moral and social development of migrant children and children of migrants.[349]

The specific threat to children's lives presented by HIV/AIDS is highlighted in the Committee's *General Comment No. 3*.

State obligation to realize the right to life, survival and development also highlights the need to give careful attention to sexuality as well as to the behaviours and lifestyles of children, even if they do not conform with what society determines to be acceptable under prevailing cultural norms for a particular age group. In this regard, the female child is often subject to harmful traditional practices, such as early and/or forced marriage, which violate her rights and make her more vulnerable to HIV infection, including because such practices often interrupt access to education and information.[350]

The Committee will often express its most 'grave', 'deep' or 'serious' concern in relation to the loss of children's lives resulting from military conflicts. For example, in the case of the Arab Syrian Republic, the Committee was 'deeply concerned about the impact that armed conflict has on the right to life, survival and development of children', drawing particular attention to the 'thousands of children killed and injured as a result of attacks' including airstrikes, and indiscriminate use of weapons including unlawful ones.[351] Children's right to life, survival and development are violated as a consequence of being the most vulnerable of victims in hostilities. Added hazards of war include the psychological impact on children of witnessing bombings and other attacks, as well as the impact of suffering a deprivation of liberty. In the case of girl victims, the Committee made express reference to the 'sexual slavery by non-state armed groups' of Yazidi girls.[352] Further to this, it noted that millions of children in the Syrian conflict suffered from denial of food, education, health care, water, sanitation and a minimum standard of living', arising due to deliberate siege tactics employed in the warfare.[353] The

---

349 CRC/C/GC/22 (16 November 2017) [40].
350 Committee on the Rights of the Child, *General Comment No. 3: HIV/AIDS and the rights of the child*, CRC/GC/2003/3 (17 March 2003) [11].
351 CRC/C/SYR/CO/5 (6 March 2019) [19].
352 Ibid.
353 Ibid.

Convention's preambular paragraphs recognise the particular difficulties faced by children 'living in exceptionally difficult conditions', acknowledging the need for special consideration in such situations. There are overlaps between the aims of the Convention and other human rights instruments, including in reference to war crimes. The Committee identifies a range of specific situations in the Syrian conflict which require addressing, including 'potential threats posed by explosive hazards', 'psychological needs of children whose survival and development are affected by bombings and attacks', the investigation of war crimes and crimes against humanity, the release of girls 'held in captive' and protocols for their care, and to enable children and families to 'leave areas affected by the conflict to reach safety and access basic humanitarian assistance'.[354]

Other concerns relating to article 6 rights include the high neonatal and infant mortality rates and child malnutrition in some States.[355] The objective assessment of neonatal mortality is usually carried out in accordance with an internationally recognised World Health Organization (WHO) definition of a live birth. Causes of death in infants and children vary from state to state, and a range of concerns was raised in 2019, including poverty, ante- and post-natal care, conflict, and preventable diseases. The Committee expressed concern over the rate of child mortality in Mozambique, arising from preventable diseases.[356] Health and wellbeing are linked to the right to life, and in the case of the Republic of Korea, the specific issue of health damage caused by humidifier disinfectants was raised, in addition to asbestos dust in settings where children spend time including schools.[357] In Portugal, the Committee called on the state to 'extend legal framework on safety of children in swimming pools, including the obligation to have a protective fence'.[358] Traffic accidents too have remained a major cause of fatal injuries of children and young people in some States. In the case of Bahrain, the Committee responded to the 'continuing high rate of deaths and injuries among children due to traffic accidents', recommending prevention measures including traffic awareness campaigns and the strict enforcement of traffic laws.[359] Road traffic accidents were also identified as a cause for serious concern in Tonga[360] and Mozambique.[361]

In its Concluding Observation to the Republic of Korea, the Committee expressed grave concerns about the 'high rates of child suicide', which represented a leading cause of death among children. This was identified as arising due to family problems, depression, academic pressure and bullying.[362] The Committee

---

354 CRC/C/SYR/CO/5 (6 March 2019) [21].
355 For example, Botswana: CRC/C/BWA/CO/2–3 (26 June 2019) [25].
356 CRC/C/MOZ/CO/3–4 (1 October 2019) [18].
357 CRC/C/KOR/CO/5–6 (27 September 2019) [19].
358 CRC/C/PRT/CO/5–6 (27 September 2019) [19].
359 CRC/C/BHR/CO/4–6 (27 February 2019) [19].
360 CRC/C/TON/CO/1 (2 July 2019) [25].
361 CRC/C/MOZ/CO/3–4 (1 October 2019) [18].
362 CRC/C/KOR/CO/5–6 (27 September 2019) [19].

acknowledged that the state had established a National Plan for Suicide Prevention in light of these issues. In the case of Japan, similarly, the Committee urged research into the 'root causes for suicide amongst children', calling for the implementation of preventative measures.[363] In the case of Australia, the Committee called for the state to 'support the work of the Australia and New Zealand Child Death Review and Prevention Group'.[364] In the case of Belgium, the Committee called for 'the fullest possible review and control of decisions on euthanasia in relation to children'.[365]

In previous years, the Committee expressed concern about a range of other threats to the life and development of children, including 'widespread and increasing problem of honour killings'.[366] An earlier *General Comment* noted the problem of honour killings and the need for States parties to 'take all effective measures to eliminate all acts and activities which threaten the right to life of adolescents, including honour killings'.[367] In a similar vein, it has expressed concern about 'the persistence of "blood feuds" [in Albania] resulting from the application of customary law known as "Kanun" and in particular the killing of children . . .',[368] and the Committee 'remains seriously concerned at the persistence of ritualistic killings of children [in Liberia]'.[369] On occasion, extreme instances of ritual killing has been identified. More recently, in the case of Tonga, the Committee expressed serious concern that the minimum age for the death penalty is 15 years under the Criminal Offences (Amendment) Act, and urged the state to raise this to 18 years.[370]

3.7.3.4 The right to express views and participate in decisions

Article 12

1. States parties shall assure to the child who is capable of forming his or her own views the right to express those views freely in all matters affecting the child, the views of the child being given due weight in accordance with the age and maturity of the child.

2. For this purpose, the child shall in particular be provided the opportunity to be heard in any judicial and administrative proceedings affecting the child, either directly, or through a representative or an appropriate body, in a manner consistent with the procedural rules of national law.

---

363 CRC/C/JPN/CO/4–5 (5 March 2019) [20].
364 CRC/C/AUS/CO/5–6 (30 September 2019) [21].
365 CRC/C/BEL/CO/5–6 (28 February 2019) [18].
366 CRC/C/PAK/CO/3–4 (15 October 2009) [37].
367 Committee on the Rights of the Child, *General Comment No. 4: Adolescent health and development in the context of the Convention on the Rights of the Child*, CRC/GC/2003/4 (1 July 2003) [24].
368 CRC/C/ALB/CO/2–4 (5 October 2012) [31].
369 CRC/C/LBR/CO/2–4 (5 October 2012) [37].
370 CRC/C/TON/CO/1 (2 July 2019) [25–6].

One of the continuing concerns for children's rights advocacy has been the extent to which important decisions are made about children without children's own participation. This article is one of the four general principles of the Convention identified by the Committee. When read together with articles 5 and 13, it reflects a move away from merely identifying what decisions children are not competent to take, to the consideration of how children *can* participate. Its importance has been underlined by the Committee's production of recommendations following a *Day of General Discussion*[371] which are now contained in *General Comment No. 12*[372] which provides a comprehensive legal analysis of article 12.

As regards the first paragraph of article 12, *General Comment No. 12* points out that the words 'shall assure' in article 12 'is a legal term of special strength, which leaves no leeway for State parties' discretion'.[373] The phrase 'capable of forming his or her own views' is a phrase that 'should not be seen as a limitation, but rather as an obligation for States parties to assess the capacity of the child to form an autonomous opinion to the greatest extent possible'.[374] Furthermore, as regards the phrase 'to express those views freely':

> 22. [. . .] 'Freely' means that the child can express her or his views without pressure and can choose whether or not she or he wants to exercise her or his right to be heard. 'Freely' also means that the child must not be manipulated or subjected to undue influence or pressure. 'Freely' is further intrinsically related to the child's 'own' perspective: the child has the right to express her or his own views and not the views of others.
>
> 23. States parties must ensure conditions for expressing views that account for the child's individual and social situation and an environment in which the child feels respected and secure when freely expressing her or his opinions.[375]

It is also clear that the phrase 'in all matters affecting the child' should be 'respected and understood broadly'.[376] Furthermore, '[a]rticle 12 stipulates that simply listening to the child is insufficient; the views of the child have to be seriously considered when the child is capable of forming his or her own views'.[377]

---

371 Committee on the Rights of the Child, *Day of General Discussion on the right of the child to be heard*, Report on the 43rd session, CRC/C/43/3 (16 July 2007) [980–1041].
372 Committee on the Rights of the Child, *General Comment No. 12: The right of the child to be heard*, CRC/C/GC/12 (20 July 2009).
373 Ibid., para. 19.
374 Ibid., para. 20. Furthermore, States parties should presume that a child has such capacity.
375 Ibid., paras 22–3.
376 Ibid., paras 26–7.
377 Ibid., para. 28.

As regards the second paragraph of article 12:

> The Committee emphasizes that this provision applies to all relevant judicial proceedings affecting the child, without limitation, including, for example, separation of parents, custody, care and adoption, children in conflict with the law, child victims of physical or psychological violence, sexual abuse or other crimes, health care, social security, unaccompanied children, asylum-seeking and refugee children, and victims of armed conflict and other emergencies. Typical administrative proceedings include, for example, decisions about children's education, health, environment, living conditions, or protection. Both kinds of proceedings may involve alternative dispute mechanisms such as mediation and arbitration.[378]

General Comment No. 12 sets out five steps that can be taken to implement the child's right to be heard. First, the need for *preparation*, for example, the need for decision-makers to ensure that the child is informed about their right to express views and the option of communicating directly or through a representative. Second, the context of the *hearing* needs to be enabling and encouraging. Third, the need for developing good practice in the *assessment of the capacity of the child*. Fourth, *information about the weight given to the views of the child (feedback)* needs to be provided to ensure that the child's views have been heard and taken seriously. Finally, legislation is required to provide *complaints, remedies and redress* routes for children whose rights to be heard have been disregarded or violated.[379]

The *General Comment* also outlines how article 12 relates to other important provisions of the Convention, and examines the implementation of the child's right to be heard in different settings and situations. It concludes that States parties should avoid tokenistic approaches to the implementation of this article. Children's *participation*[380] should be understood as a process, not a one-off event. The *General Comment* recommends that all processes in which children are heard and participate must conform to a number of benchmarks.[381] They must be given accessible information about their right to express their views freely, how this participation will take place and its scope, purpose and potential impact. This should be a voluntary process and children's views should be treated with respect. The issues on which children have a right to express their views must be of real

---

378 Ibid., para. 32.
379 Ibid., paras 41–7.
380 'A widespread practice has emerged in recent years, which has been broadly conceptualized as "participation", although this term itself does not appear in the text of article 12. This term has evolved and is now widely used to describe ongoing processes, which include information-sharing and dialogue between children and adults based on mutual respect, and in which children can learn how their views and those of adults are taken into account and shape the outcome of such processes'. Ibid., para. 3.
381 *General Comment No. 12*, paras 134(a) to (i).

relevance to their lives; children should be enabled to address issues they themselves identify as relevant. Environments and working methods should be adapted to accommodate children's evolving capacities. Participation should be inclusive, encouraging opportunities for marginalised children to be involved. Adults need support and training to facilitate children's participation. In certain situations, expression of views may expose children to risks and every precaution should be made to minimise any harmful risks. There is a need for accountability. Any research or consultative process involving children should provide some evaluation and follow-up in order to inform children how their views have been interpreted and used and, where necessary, provide opportunities for children to challenge and influence the analysis of findings.

General Comment No. 20 (2016) on the implementation of the rights of the child during adolescence refers to article 12 and asserts:

> States parties should introduce measures to guarantee adolescents the right to express views on all matters of concern to them, in accordance with their age and maturity, and ensure they are given due weight, for example, in decisions relating to their education, health, sexuality, family life and judicial and administrative proceedings. States should ensure that adolescents are involved in the development, implementation and monitoring of all relevant legislation, policies, services and programmes affecting their lives, at school and at the community, local, national and international levels. The online environment provides significant emerging opportunities for strengthening and expanding their engagement. The measures should be accompanied by the introduction of safe and accessible complaint and redress mechanisms with the authority to adjudicate claims made by adolescents, and by access to subsidized or free legal services and other appropriate assistance.[382]

Further to this entrenchment of the right to be heard, the Committee recognised that in order for adolescents to exercise this right, it is adults who must understand the provisions. In order to achieve this, it called for training and awareness-raising campaigns spearheaded by states, aimed at those in caring, policy or decision-making roles involving adolescents.[383]

The Committee's Concluding Observations on States parties' reports reflect some of the practical ways in which the child's right to be heard is being taken forward and, in some cases, the limitations on its progress. For example, the Committee has generally welcomed the creation of Youth or Children's Parliaments (in Mozambique, Cabo Verde, Tonga) as an obvious indicator of progress in the democratisation of children's voices, though on further analysis some of these new institutions lack resources and are insufficiently consulted and heard. In

---

382 CRC/C/GC/20 (6 December 2016) [23].
383 CRC/C/GC/20 (6 December 2016) [25].

the European Context, the Committee referred to the Council of Europe Child Participation Assessment Tool, which seeks to standardise the participation and consultation mechanisms for involving children in decisions, which affect them.[384] The pivotal issue raised is the need to ensure that those working with children in a range of capacities systematically receive 'appropriate training on hearing and taking into account children's views in all decisions effecting them and in accordance with the child's age and maturity'.[385]

Some states were far from achieving a basic level of child participation, for example Syria. In other cases, the state was limiting the extent of the child's right to be heard based on academic performance.[386] The Committee urged the state to ensure all children are given the opportunity to express their views, regardless of their performance at school and to abolish any arbitrary age limits being placed on the child's right to express their view, either in law or in practice.[387]

The Concluding observations identify a range of areas where children have the right to be heard including family services (both judicial and non-court based),[388] migration processes,[389] environmental matters,[390] criminal processes.[391]

As with the other general principles of the Convention, the Committee will commend States parties that have placed the rights contained in article 12 into their own constitutional or ordinary legislative regimes. The Committee will also be critical of States parties that have not passed laws or regulations establishing explicitly the child's right to be heard in any judicial and administrative proceedings affecting him or her.[392] Where a States party has passed laws purporting to incorporate the child's freedom of expression the Committee will comment where it detects that the national laws fall short of international standards.[393] For example, Botswana set up its own Children's Consultative Forum to facilitate child participation at the village and national levels.[394] Similarly, Japan amended its Child Welfare Act and Domestic Relations Case Procedure Act.[395] However, in both cases the Committee was concerned that such mechanisms or amendments did not facilitate meaningful and empowered participation of children in matters that concern them.

The Committee's overall task, as indicated in *General Comment No. 12*,[396] to build a 'culture of respect' for children's views, is undoubtedly a challenging one. One

---

384 CRC/C/MLT/CO/3–6 (26 June 2019 [21]).
385 Malta: CRC/C/MLT/CO/3–6 (26 June 2019).
386 Republic of Korea.
387 CRC/C/KOR/CO/5–6 (27 September 2019) [21]; CRC/C/BEL/CO/5–6 (28 February 2019) [19].
388 CRC/C/AUS/CO/5–6 (30 September 2019) [22].
389 Ibid.
390 CRC/C/TON/CO/1 (2 July 2019) [28].
391 CRC/C/PRT/CO/5–6 (27 September 2019) [20].
392 CRC/C/PRT/CO/5–6 (27 September 2019) [20].
393 For example, in Bahrain: CRC/C/BHR/CO/4–6 (27 February 2019) [20].
394 CRC/C/BWA/CO/2–3 (26 June 2019) [27].
395 CRC/C/JPN/CO/4–5 (5 March 2019) [21].
396 *General Comment No. 12*, para. 136.

key obstacle identified in its Concluding Observations is the prevalence of traditional and societal attitudes that appear to limit children in freely expressing their views in schools, communities and within the family. For example, tackling persistent traditional societal attitudes towards children, particularly girls, resulting in the limitation of free expression of views.[397] While undoubtedly some States parties are making better progress in developing a culture of respect for children's views, there are intransigent obstacles in others. For example, the Committee had cause to urge Japan 'to assure to any child who is able to form views the right to freely express those views, without age limitations, in all matters affecting the child, and that due weight be given to the child's views, while providing safeguards against intimidation and punishment of the child'.[398] Some states were called on to 'develop toolkits for the consultation of children on national policy development that affects them to standardise such consultation at a high level of inclusiveness and participation'.[399]

It is interesting to note that the *General Comment* states that 'in most societies around the world, implementation of [article 12] continues to be impeded by many long-standing practices and attitudes, as well as political and economic barriers'.[400] The *General Comment* acknowledges that the comprehensive fulfilment of the obligations required by article 12 is likely to be a challenge for many States parties:

> Achieving meaningful opportunities for the implementation of article 12 will necessitate dismantling the legal, political, economic, social and cultural barriers that currently impede children's opportunity to be heard and their access to participation in all matters affecting them. It requires a preparedness to challenge assumptions about children's capacities, and to encourage the development of environments in which children can build and demonstrate capacities. It also requires a commitment to resources and training.[401]

3.7.4 Civil rights and freedoms: articles 7, 8, 13–17, 28(2) and 37(a)

During the drafting process of the Convention, there was a general move to incorporate provisions from the ICCPR (Detrick 1992: 233). The US delegation had proposed a single provision to include a child's right to civil and political freedoms, in particular a right to privacy (now article 16), a right to freedom of association (now article 15) and the right to freedom of expression (now article 13). The US

---

[397] Mozambique: CRC/C/MOZ/CO/3–4 (1 October 2019) [19].
[398] CRC/C/JPN/CO/4–5 (5 March 2019) [22].
[399] For example, Portugal: CRC/C/PRT/CO/5–6 (27 September 2019) [20].
[400] *General Comment No. 12*, para. 4.
[401] Ibid., para. 135.

delegation stated that children not only had the right to expect certain benefits from governments but they also had civil and political rights to protect them from abusive actions by governments. The consensus view during the drafting process had been that children should have broadly the same civil and political rights as applied to adults, other than the right to vote. However, the identity rights contained in article 7, which first appeared in the *Declaration of the Rights of the Child* (1959),[402] were a novel addition in a major human rights treaty. The duty on States parties to ensure that systems are in place for the registration of every child at or immediately after birth is also a key provision.

3.7.4.1 Birth registration and identity rights (articles 7 and 8)

> *Article 7*[403]
> 1. The child shall be registered immediately after birth and shall have the right from birth to a name, the right to acquire a nationality and. as far as possible, the right to know and be cared for by his or her parents.

The existence of an enduring and robust birth registration system is a necessary precondition to the formulation of child policy and planning; a reliable and accurate demographic profile will be a valuable tool in national planning. Furthermore, where a child remains unregistered it is easier to abduct, sell or induce that child into prostitution, and a child may become stateless as a result of non-registration and consequently prevented from accessing health, education and other social services.

> Registration is the State's first official acknowledgement of the child's existence; it represents recognition of each child's individual importance to the State and of the child's status under the law. Where children are not registered, they are likely to be less visible, and sometimes less valued. Children who are not registered often belong to groups who suffer from other forms of discrimination.
>
> (Hodgkin and Newell 2007: 98)

In a *Day of General Discussion* held in 2004, the Committee recommended to States parties

> to undertake all necessary measures to ensure that all children are registered at birth, inter alia, by using mobile registration units and make birth registration free of charge. The Committee also reminds States parties of the

---

402 'The child shall be entitled from his birth to a name and a nationality': *Declaration of the Rights of the Child of 1959*, Principle 3.
403 See generally, Hodgkin and Newell (2007: 97–112) for a detailed analysis of article 7.

importance of facilitating late registration of birth, and to ensure that children, despite being not yet registered, have equal access to health care, education and other social services.[404]

Article 7 resonates with the text of article 24(2) and (3) of the ICCPR,[405] and also contains an additional right 'to know and be cared for by his or her parents'. The Human Rights Committee issued a *General Comment* on article 24 of ICCPR[406] which states that the right to be registered immediately after birth and to have a name is of special importance in relation to children born out of wedlock; and that '[t]he main purpose of the obligation to register children after birth is to reduce the danger of abduction, sale of or traffic in children, or of other types of treatment'. Special attention was also needed in relation to the child's right to acquire a nationality in order to prevent a child becoming stateless.

The registration of a birth becomes more imperative in the context of migration, and the 'right to a name, identity, and a nationality' (under article 29 of the International Convention on the Protection of the Rights of All Migrant Workers and Members of Their Families and articles 7 and 8 of the *Convention on the Rights of the Child*) are contained in the joint *General Comment No. 23 (2017)* on State obligations regarding the human rights of children in the context of international migration in countries of origin, transit, destination and return.[407] This provides that:

> [20] The lack of birth registration may have many negative impacts on the enjoyment of children's rights, such as child marriage, trafficking, forced recruitment and child labour. Birth registrations may also help to achieve convictions against those who have abused a child. Unregistered children are at particular risk of becoming stateless when born to parents who are in an irregular migration situation, due to barriers to acquiring nationality in the country of origin of the parents as well as to accessing birth registration and nationality at the place of their birth.

---

404 Committee on the Rights of the Child, *Day of General Discussion on Implementing Child Rights in Early Childhood*, Report on the 37th session, CRC/C/143 (12 January 2005) [532–63, at 547].

405 '1. Every child shall have, without any discrimination as to race, colour, sex, language, religion, national or social origin, property or birth, the right to such measures of protection as are required by his status as a minor, on the part of his family, society and the State.'
2. Every child shall be registered immediately after birth and shall have a name.
3. 'Every child has the right to acquire a nationality.' ICCPR, art. 24.

406 Human Rights Committee, *General Comment No. 17: Rights of the child (Article 24)*, 35th session (7 April 1989) [7–8].

407 *Joint general comment No. 4* (2017) of the Committee on the Protection of the Rights of All Migrant Workers and Members of Their Families and No. 23 (2017) of the Committee on the Rights of the Child on State obligations regarding the human rights of children in the context of international migration in countries of origin, transit, destination and return. CMW/C/GC/4 – CRC/C/GC/23 (16 November 2017) [20].

[21] The Committees urge States parties to take all necessary measures to ensure that all children are immediately registered at birth and issued birth certificates, irrespective of their migration status or that of their parents. Legal and practical obstacles to birth registration should be removed, including by prohibiting data sharing between health providers or civil servants responsible for registration with immigration enforcement authorities; and not requiring parents to produce documentation regarding their migration status. Measures should also be taken to facilitate late registration of birth and to avoid financial penalties for late registration. Children who have not been registered should be ensured equal access to health care, protection, education and other social services.

The Committee also draws on the Sustainable Development Goals target 16.9, which calls for 'legal identity for all, including birth registration' by 2030. In making recommendations to States parties in pursuit of this goal, the Committee has suggested a number of methods for improved registration including more efficient processes, such as online registration, more physical registration centres, and positive obligations to identify unregistered births.[408] The adoption of mobile registration units, particularly in rural areas, and the establishment of national electronic birth registration databases are encouraged where necessary. There is particular concern about the birth registration in rural areas[409] and for nomadic communities.[410] Further in the case of the Republic of Korea, the Committee called for an end to 'baby boxes' in which children can be anonymously abandoned into the care of religious organisations. The Committee called instead for confidential hospital births as a last resort.[411]

During the reporting process, the Committee will often encourage States parties to enshrine their birth registration systems into legislation. It welcomed the introduction of an 'electronic civil registry system, the elimination of geographical restrictions for registration and the expansion of registration centres' in the case of Mozambique.[412] However, remained concerned about a number of factors which hindered registration including children born in remote areas where access to registration infrastructure is limited, the late fee for births registered after 120 days, the lack of effective methods for ensuring the registration of *all* children including girls and those born to unmarried parents, and finally the continuing lack of awareness of the importance of registration.[413]

---

408 For example: CRC/C/KOR/CO/5-6 (27 September 2019) [22].
409 For example: Cabo Verde, Mozambique, Botswana, Tonga, Bahrain.
410 For example, in Botswana.
411 CRC/C/KOR/CO/5-6 (27 September 2019) [21].
412 CRC/C/MOZ/CO/3-4 (1 October 2019) [20].
413 Ibid.

In terms of the registration itself, Hodgkin and Newell comment:

> [T]he Convention does not specify what must be registered, other rights (to name and nationality, to know parentage, family and identity) imply that registration ought, as a minimum, to include:
>
> - the child's name at birth,
> - the child's sex,
> - the child's date of birth,
> - where the child was born,
> - the parents' names and addresses,
> - the parents' nationality status.
>
> (Hodgkin and Newell 2007: 101)

The Committee welcomes States parties' efforts to improve national systems of birth registration. For example, it commended Cabo Verde on its 'almost universal birth registration' success, however also raised concern about the discrepancy in birth registration rate between urban and rural areas.[414] Similarly, Botswana's measures to improve registration were welcomed, while noting that significant numbers of children, especially children in remote areas, were not registered.[415]

There are often particular concerns about birth registration of minority groups and indigenous children as greater proportions of such children remain unregistered, and therefore are also at a high risk of becoming stateless. The issue of statelessness is keenly linked to birth registration access and therefore, the Committee encourages states to adopt international (regional or global) conventions on statelessness. Linked to this, the stability of the state is key to achieving an effective birth registration system, and the Committee expressed serious concern regarding Syria, where the armed conflict has resulted in children not being registered and not having access to birth certificates.[416] In the case of Malta, the Committee recognised the amendment to the Civil Code to enable 'children who were born at sea on board unregistered vessels to be registered in the State party for humanitarian reasons', while expressing serious concern for the lack of birth registration facilities for asylum-seeking, refugee and migrant children.[417] In the case of Bosnia and Herzegovina, the Committee further recommended the provision of 'special support to illiterate or undocumented persons in order to facilitate birth registration of their children.[418] The Committee also urged states to ratify the 2009 Council of Europe Convention on the Avoidance of Statelessness in relation to State

---

414 CRC/C/CPV/CO/2 (27 June 2019) [31].
415 CRC/C/BWA/CO/2-3 (26 June 2019) [29].
416 CRC/C/SYR/CO/5 (6 March 2019) [23].
417 CRC/C/MLT/CO/3-6 (26 June 2019) [22].
418 CRC/C/BIH/CO/5-6 (30 September 2019) [22].

Succession[419] or the Convention relating to the Status of the Stateless Persons and the Convention on the Reduction of Statelessness.[420]

Children's rights at birth to a 'name and to acquire nationality' are of course prejudiced where the States party withholds granting citizenship on a discriminatory basis. In the case of Bahrain, the Committee raised concerns regarding the lack of guarantee of citizenship to all children of Bahraini mothers (regardless of who the father is).[421] The Committee noted that a large number of children are at risk of being stateless including 'Baharna, Ajam and Bidoon children . . . whose citizenship has been revoked and children born to parents whose citizenship has changed or been revoked'.[422] The Committee called on Bahrain to expeditiously amend its Citizenship Act to ensure the right of nationality to all such children.

The Committee has been tireless in its encouragement of *free* birth registration. It criticises those States parties where birth registration is not free. Fines for late registration were identified by the Committee as unhelpful in increasing the rate of registration, and the fees may result in children not being registered.[423] In the case of Malta, the Committee called on the State to abolish all birth registration fees to ensure that all children are registered.[424]

The text of article 7 also contains the child's right to know and be cared for by his or her 'parents'. This latter term is perhaps contentious in terms of its scope. The Committee certainly interprets this to include the child's right to know their *biological* parents. Some commentators argue for a much wider interpretation:

> [A] reasonable assumption is that, as far as the child's right to know his or her parents is concerned, the definition of 'parents' includes genetic parents (for medical reasons alone this knowledge is of increasing importance to the child) *and* birth parents, that is the mother who gave birth and the father who claimed paternity through partnership with the mother at the time of birth (or whatever the social definition of father is within the culture: the point being that such social definitions are important to children in terms of their identity). In addition, a third category, the child's psychological parents – those who cared for the child for significant periods during infancy and childhood – should also logically be included since these persons too are intimately bound up in children's identity and thus their rights under article 8.
>
> (Hodgkin and Newell 2007: 105–6)

---

419 In the case of Bosnia and Herzegovina, Malta.
420 In the case of Japan, Malta, Cabo Verde.
421 CRC/C/BHR/CO/4–6 (27 February 2019) [21].
422 CRC/C/BHR/CO/4–6 (27 February 2019) [21].
423 CRC/C/SYR/CO/5 (6 March 2019) [23].
424 CRC/C/MLT/CO/3–6 (26 June 2019) [21].

The issue of assisted reproduction, identity and access to information by the children involved were raised in the case of Belgium[425] and Australia.[426] In both cases, the Committee called on the States to ensure the children had access to information about their origins. Where national adoption systems include a mother's right to conceal her identity and remain anonymous, this is likely to be criticised.[427] Nevertheless, Luxembourg's reservation to article 7 seems to contradict this interpretation.

> The Government of Luxembourg believes that article 7 of the Convention presents no obstacle to the legal process in respect of anonymous births, which is deemed to be in the interest of the child, as provided under article 3 of the Convention.[428]

Article 8 of the Convention provides that:

1. States parties undertake to respect the right of the child to preserve his or her identity, including nationality, name and family relations as recognized by law without unlawful interference.
2. Where a child is illegally deprived of some or all of the elements of his or her identity, States Parties shall provide appropriate assistance and protection, with a view to re-establishing speedily his or her identity.

The drafting of article 8 was originally proposed by Argentina (Detrick 1992: 292–3) and was prompted by the enforced disappearance of children and adults in that country under the previous military junta regime. The Committee commended the work done by Argentina's 'National Commission for the Right to an Identity' to recover children who had disappeared during the military regime (1976–83), and noted that, out of an estimated 500 cases of disappearance of children, 73 had been found.[429] In 2006 the General Assembly adopted an *International Convention for the Protection of All Persons from Enforced Disappearance*.[430]

Article 8 protects three elements of a child's identity: nationality, name and family relations. A child's nationality may be derived from his or her parents' nationality. Consequently, laws that prohibit children from inheriting nationality

---

425 CRC/C/BEL/CO/5–6 (28 February 2019) [20].
426 CRC/C/AUS/CO/5–6 (30 September 2019) [24].
427 CRC/C/FRA/CO/4 (11 June 2009) [43].
428 Committee on the Rights of the Child website: <http://www2.ohchr.org/english/bodies/crc/> (accessed 1 August 2013).
429 CRC/C/15/Add.187 (9 October 2002) [34].
430 General Assembly, *International Convention for the Protection of All Persons from Enforced Disappearance*, opened for signature 20 December 2006, UN Doc. A/RES/61/177 (entered into force 23 December 2010). This Convention had 98 signatories and 62 parties as at February 2020.

from their parents might not be compliant with the Convention. Where a child's nationality is derived from residence, laws that prohibit the acquisition of nationality by means of lengthy periods of residence might also fall below the standard set in this article. The protection of a right to a name derives in part from an aversion to the dehumanising impact of ascribing numbers to the mass movements of refugees or migrants. Most countries have prescriptive rules for the registration of names and what names should be used. Many of these systems are uncontroversial and are aimed to protect, in particular, children born outside of marriage. Of necessity, parents are the most likely persons to decide a child's name, but arguably, this should not be an absolute right.

> Domestic laws should have appropriate mechanisms to prevent registration of a name that might make a child an object of ridicule, bad luck or discrimination, as for example in Malawi's 'practice of derogatory names being assigned to some children such as children born out of wedlock', which the Committee recommended the government abolish (Malawi CRC/C/15/ Add.174, paras 31 and 32).
>
> (Hodgin and Newell 2007: 103)

The element of identity relating to 'family relations' reflects a growing recognition of the importance of children's relationships not only with their immediate family but also with the wider family. The right to acquire a nationality and a name has important implications for the right to obtain a passport and the right to vote. In general, under international law, nationality rules fall within the domain of municipal law, a point emphasised in the United Arab Emirates' reservation to article 7.[431] This has led to nations adopting different rules on nationality, and consequently there are persons who may fall between the various rules and become stateless.

3.7.4.2 The rights to freedom of expression, thought, conscience, religion, association, no interference with privacy and access to information (articles 13–17)

The following commentary from the *Manual of Human Rights Reporting* (OHCHR 1997) provides an overview of these provisions:

> Articles 13 to 17 constitute an important chapter of the Convention which clearly indicates the need to envisage the child not simply as a vulnerable and weak human being, but also as an active subject of rights . . . It is important to stress that these rights had already generally been recognized by previous

---

[431] 'The United Arab Emirates is of the view that the acquisition of nationality is an internal matter and one that is regulated and whose terms and conditions are established by national legislation.'

international instruments to 'every human being', thus also including children. The prevailing reality was however, and to a certain extent still is, that children, in view of their evolving maturity, are in practice not recognized as having the necessary capacity or competence to exercise them.

(OHCHR 1997: 434–45)

These articles are, to an extent, a reflection of the desire during the drafting process of the Convention to ensure that existing rights in the ICCPR were explicitly applied to children. The Human Rights Committee confirmed in a *General Comment* that 'as individuals, children benefit from all of the civil rights enunciated in the Covenant'.[432]

Article 13
1   The child shall have the right to freedom of expression; this right shall include freedom to seek, receive and impart information and ideas of all kinds, regardless of frontiers, either orally, in writing or in print, in the form of art, or through any other media of the child's choice.
2   The exercise of this right may be subject to certain restrictions, but these shall only be such as are provided by law and are necessary:
    (a) For respect of the rights or reputations of others; or
    (b) For the protection of national security or of public order (ordre public), or of public health or morals.

This article is based on similar provisions in the *International Bill of Human Rights*.[433] During the drafting process the question of the parents' role in relation to the child's civil rights arose, and an earlier draft of article 13 (Detrick 1992: 230) explicitly protected the child's right from limiting or otherwise affecting 'the authority, rights or responsibilities of a parent'. It was agreed that this would not be necessary because, 'while children might need direction and guidance from parents or guardians in the exercise of these rights, this does not affect the contents of the rights themselves' (Hodgkin and Newell 1997: 181). Parents' rights and responsibilities to provide appropriate direction and guidance, where consistent with 'the evolving capacities of the child', are protected instead by article 5.

The Committee's Concluding Observations have raised a number of issues in recent years. In the case of Australia, the Committee highlighted restrictions on freedom of expression, calling on the State to 'promote the right to freedom of expression, paying particular attention to Aboriginal and Torres Strait Islander children, children with disabilities, children with a refugee or migrant background, and children living in rural or remote areas'.[434] Children in Botswana are

---

432 Human Rights Committee, *General Comment No. 17: Rights of the child (Article 24)*, 35th session, Annex IV (7 April 1989) (pp. 173–5) [2].
433 See UDHR, art. 19 and ICCPR, art. 19.
434 CRC/C/AUS/CO/5–6 (30 September 2019) [25].

guaranteed freedom of expression under the State Children's Act, however, the Committee noted that 'prevailing traditional cultural and societal attitudes make it difficult for children to freely express their views'.[435]

Freedom of expression is often in jeopardy during periods of political and other crises in a States party. However, it is often also restricted in times of stability. The Committee in the case of Singapore consistently identified severe restrictions on freedoms. In its most recent Concluding Observations, the Committee reiterated its concerns regarding undue limitations which have serious repercussions for children, limiting them from expressing themselves including via mediums such as the internet.[436]

Article 14
1   States parties shall respect the right of the child to freedom of thought, conscience and religion.
2   States parties shall respect the rights and duties of the parents and, when applicable, legal guardians, to provide direction to the child in the exercise of his or her right in a manner consistent with the evolving capacities of the child.
3   Freedom to manifest one's religion or beliefs may be subject only to such limitations as are prescribed by law and are necessary to protect public safety, order, health or morals, or the fundamental rights and freedoms of others.

The text of article 14[437] protects the child's right to 'freedom of thought, conscience and religion'. Freedom of religion was one of the four principal areas of controversy in the drafting process of the Convention (Cantwell 1992). An earlier draft of article 13 included 'the freedom to have or to adopt a religion . . . of his choice'. It was pointed out that a child's right to *choose* a religion did not exist under Islamic law; it could only apply to adults.

> This put the drafters in a delicate situation. What attitude was to be taken towards the elimination of a right of the child in the future Convention which was already conferred by a well established international human rights instrument [the International Covenant on Civil and Political Rights, article 18] without restriction as to the age of the beneficiary? Reluctantly, in the end, the proponents of retaining the full right agreed to drop all reference to choice, 'in the spirit of compromise'.
>
> (Cantwell 1992: 26)

---

435 CRC/C/BWA/CO/2–3 (26 June 2019) [31].
436 CRC/C/SGP/CO/4–5 (31 May 2019) [24].
437 See UDHR, art. 18 and ICCPR, art. 18. '[ICCPR,] Article 18 protects theistic, non-theistic and atheistic beliefs, as well as the right not to profess any religion or belief': Human Rights Committee, *General Comment No. 22: Article 18 (Freedom of thought, conscience or religion)*, 48th session, CCPR/C/21/Rev. 1/Add. 4 (30 July 1993) [2].

This uneasy compromise has not resolved all differences, and perhaps explains why more States parties have made reservations and declarations concerning article 14 than any other article. The Belgian government, for example, made an interpretative declaration that article 14(1) 'implies also the freedom to choose his or her religion or belief'. Similarly, the Netherlands made a declaration that the article 'shall include the freedom of a child to have or adopt a religion or belief of his or her choice as soon as the child is capable of making such choice in view of his or her age or maturity'. Whereas the Holy See declared that it

> interprets the articles of the Convention in a way which safeguards the primary and inalienable rights of parents, in particular insofar as these rights concern education (articles 13 and 28), religion (article 14), association with others (article 15) and privacy (article 16).

The government of the Republic of Maldives made a reservation to article 14(1) on the basis that 'the Constitution and the Laws of the Republic of Maldives stipulate that all Maldivians should be Muslims'. Nevertheless, most commentators would agree that:

> The wording of article 14 and the Convention articles identified as general principles certainly do not support the concept of children automatically following their parent's religion until the age of 18, although article 8 (preservation of identity), article 20 (preservation of religion when deprived of family environment), and article 30 (right to practice religion in community with members of the child's group) support children's right to acquire their parents' religion.
>
> (Hodgkin and Newell 2007: 188)

The child's right to freedom of thought, conscience and religion has been challenged in the context of France's constitutional arrangements that require a strict separation of Church and State (Eva 2006). French laws which support a strictly secular public education system, by prohibiting the wearing of religious signs or symbols in public schools, have been a cause for concern for the Committee. The Committee's Concluding Observation on France in 2009 stated:

> The Committee notes that the States party has undertaken measures to attenuate the consequences of the Law No. 2004–228 of 15 March 2004 banning the wearing of 'signs or dress through which pupils ostensibly indicate which religion they profess in public, primary and secondary schools', including the establishment of a mediator in the national public education system. Nevertheless, the Committee endorses the concluding observations of [the Committee on the Elimination of Discrimination against Women] CEDAW, that the ban should not lead to a denial of the right to education for any girl and their inclusion into all facets of the States party's society (CEDAW/C/FRA/

CO/6, para. 20), as well as those adopted by the Human Rights Committee noting that respect for a public culture of laïcité would not seem to require forbidding wearing such common religious symbols

(CCPR/C/FRA/CO/4, para. 23).[438]

The Committee more recently expressed concern at reports that schools are placing a ban on the wearing of religious symbols, including headscarves worn by Muslim girls in Belgium. The Committee stated that this 'stigmatises and discriminated against school children, particularly girls of Muslim faith, and may influence their choice of school, further studies and employment'.[439]

Article 15
1 States parties recognize the rights of the child to freedom of association and to freedom of peaceful assembly.
2 No restrictions may be placed on the exercise of these rights other than those imposed in conformity with the law and which are necessary in a democratic society in the interests of national security or public safety, public order (ordre public), the protection of public health or morals or the protection of the rights and freedoms of others.

The Committee encourages States parties, as with other civil rights, to incorporate this article within their own legislation. It has acknowledged positively, in a *Day of General Discussion*, the increasing number of youth-led organisations in States.[440] Although these rights are based upon the texts of the *International Bill of Rights*[441] it would seem that article 15 remains relatively undeveloped in the context of children's rights.

It should be noted that, in general, the law concerning contracts and administration of organizations may pose obstacles for children below the age of majority or the age of legal capacity acting as directors or trustees of public associations. It seems that few countries have as yet explored this from the perspective of the full implementation of article 15.

(Hodgkin and Newell 2007: 198)

In the spirit of this article, the Committee recommended lowering the age of voting in Korea where it is currently 19 years, to enable membership of political parties and political participation sooner.[442] The Committee also raised serious concerns about political engagement through peaceful assembly with regards

---

438 Concluding Observations of the Committee on the Rights of the Child: France. CRC/C/FRA/CO/4 (11 June 2009) [45].
439 CRC/C/BEL/CO/5–6 (28 February 2019) [21].
440 Committee on the Rights of the Child, *Day of General Discussion on the right of the child to be heard*, Report on the 43rd session, CRC/C/43/3 (16 July 2007) [1016].
441 See UDHR, art. 20 and ICCPR, arts 21–2.
442 CRC/C/KOR/CO/5–6 (27 September 2019) [24].

to Bahrain, where a child under age 15 who participates in a 'demonstration, a march, a public gathering or a political sit-in' can be classed as delinquent, and children can face arrest if they participate in public demonstrations, or insult or criticise public officials.[443] The Committee reminded the State of the Convention provisions guaranteeing freedom of expression, association and peaceful assembly. It further called for raising awareness and building capacity of 'families, teachers, and government officials to respect the exercise of those freedoms by children'.[444] The Committee went further in the case of Mozambique, encouraging the state to support children in forming their own associations and initiatives, governed by state regulations which safeguard and protect the children's best interests.[445]

Article 16
1 No child shall be subjected to arbitrary or unlawful interference with his or her privacy, family, home or correspondence, nor to unlawful attacks on his or her honour and reputation.
2 The child has the right to the protection of the law against such interference or attacks.

The wording of this right is based on the texts contained in the *International Bill of Rights*.[446] The Human Rights Committee issued a *General Comment* on the right as formulated in article 17 of ICCPR.[447] These states, as regards the term 'privacy':

> As all persons live in society, the protection of privacy is necessarily relative. However, the competent public authorities should only be able to call for such information relating to an individual's private life the knowledge of which is essential in the interests of society as understood under the Covenant. Accordingly, the Committee recommends that States should indicate in their reports the laws and regulations that govern authorized interferences with private life.[448]

Article 16 of the *Convention on the Rights of the Child* has figured in an increasing amount of adverse commentary by the Committee on the relationship between the media, privacy and children. Children's breach of privacy can occur in numerous settings, including the school environment. In the case of the Republic of Korea, the Committee called for respect of children's privacy including data on smartphone devices and personal information such as grades and disciplinary history.[449]

---

443 CRC/C/BHR/CO/4–6 (27 February 2019) [23].
444 CRC/C/BHR/CO/4–6 (27 February 2019) [24].
445 CRC/C/MOZ/CO/3–4 (1 October 2019) [22].
446 UDHR art. 12, ICCPR, art. 17.
447 Human Rights Committee, *General Comment No. 16: Article 17 (Right to Privacy), The Right to Respect of Privacy, Family, Home and Correspondence, and Protection of Honour and Reputation*, 32nd session (8 April 1988) [7].
448 Ibid. [7].
449 CRC/C/KOR/CO/5–6 (27 September 2019) [25].

The Committee has taken a wide view on article 16 rights, and has recommended the amendment of state legislation such as the Personal Data Protection Act of Singapore to include special provisions regarding children,[450] tighter controls on internet service providers regarding unsuitable content and 'strengthening the mechanisms for monitoring and prosecuting ICT-related violations of children's rights'.[451] Cabo Verde's Statute of the Child and Adolescent was a concern to the Committee due to its failure to provide for children's rights to privacy. The Committee also encouraged cooperation between the state and the media to 'eliminate practices that violate' children's privacy.[452] While these two states already provided for some legislative safeguards, albeit inadequate, in other cases, no such frameworks are in place. For example, the Committee's Concluding Observations to Mozambique included the sweeping recommendations that

> the State party take all measures necessary to fully protect the right of the child to privacy, in particular by the media, by amending legislation to explicitly protect the right of the child to privacy; developing guidelines regarding the use of images of children and the disclosure of their identities in all forms of media; sensitizing media professionals on children's rights; and establishing child friendly mechanisms for children to report breaches of their privacy.[453]

The *General Comment* issued by the Human Rights Committee states that:

> The gathering and holding of personal information on computers, data banks and other devices, whether by public authorities or private individuals or bodies, must be regulated by law.
>
> Effective measures have to be taken by States to ensure that information concerning a person's private life does not reach the hands of persons who are not authorized by law to receive, process and use it, and is never used for purposes incompatible with the Covenant. In order to have the most effective protection of his private life, every individual should have the right to ascertain in an intelligible form, whether, and if so, what personal data is stored in automatic data files, and for what purposes. Every individual should also be able to ascertain which public authorities or private individuals or bodies control or may control their files. If such files contain incorrect personal data or have been collected or processed contrary to the provisions of the law, every individual should have the right to request rectification or elimination.[454]

---

450 CRC/C/SGP/CO/4-5 (31 May 2019) [25].
451 Ibid.
452 CRC/C/CPV/CO/2 (27 June 2019) [36].
453 CRC/C/MOZ/C)/3-4 (1 October 2019) [23].
454 Human Rights Committee, *General Comment No. 16: Article 17 (Right to Privacy), The Right to Respect of Privacy, Family, Home and Correspondence, and Protection of Honour and Reputation*, 32nd session (8 April 1988) [10].

The Committee has expressed its concern about the proliferation of databases in which personal data of children are gathered, stocked and used for a lengthy period, and that parents cannot oppose and/or are not informed of the registration of their children's data.[455] The Committee will want to ensure that such databases are lawfully regulated with clear aims, that the information cannot reach unauthorised recipients and that there are suitable rights of access by children and their parents to such data.

3.7.4.3 Access to appropriate information (article 17)

Article 17 (first paragraph)
States parties recognize the important function performed by the mass media and shall ensure that the child has access to information and material from a diversity of national and international sources, especially those aimed at the promotion of his or her social, spiritual and moral well-being and physical and mental health . . .

To this end, the article sets out five strategies to deliver these aims (article 17(a) to (e)). The original draft of this article had been formulated in negative language, providing protection for children from the mass media, but was eventually reworked in more positive terms and acknowledged the educational role of mass media (Detrick 1992: 279). It has been stated that article 17 'addresses in an innovative way the important area of the role of mass media, and of information in general, in the realization of children's rights' (OHCHR 1997: 439).

The Committee held a *Day of General Discussion* in 1996 that explored the relationship of the child with media,[456] and made 12 specific recommendations largely focussing on ways in which children's participation, portrayal and education in the media could be improved, State support to media for children and encouraging agreements with media companies to protect children from harmful influences. Since then, access to digital media has become a way of life for children in many parts of the world, and radically altered childhood experiences (see Chapter 4 in this book).

The Committee's Concluding Observations in 2019 provide examples of state's responses to obligations concerning access to appropriate information. Only four of the 16 Concluding Observations included comments on access to appropriate information, and these were Australia, Mozambique, Syria and Cabo Verde. The Committee recommended that Syria, Mozambique and Cabe Verde each takes steps to improve children's access to appropriate information from a diverse range of sources including the internet; and from a plurality of perspectives, both

---

455 CRC/C/FRA/CO/4 (11 June 2009) [50].
456 Committee on the Rights of the Child, *Day of General Discussion on the Child and the Media*, Report on the thirteenth session, CRC/C/15/Add.65 (7 October 1996) [242–57].

national and international.[457] In the case of Cabo Verde, the Committee further emphasized the nature of the information, including that 'aimed at promotion of the child's social, spiritual and moral well-being and physical and mental health'.[458] In the case of Australia and Mozambique in particular, the Committee also highlighted the needs of children in remote or rural areas where access to information is more challenging. Finally, the need for awareness and teaching on appropriate online behavior, including how to avoid online abuse and/or exploitation were identified as necessary.[459]

In previous years, the Committee was prompted to voice its concern about materials such as violent and pornographic imagery that children were exposed to on TV, the internet and other media in Azerbaijan.[460] It was concerned that, in relation to Albania, 'inappropriate movies are routinely broadcasted during hours when children can be expected to watch television whereas quality educative programmes are rare'.[461] These specific concerns were not raised in 2019 reports.

3.7.5 Family environment and alternative care: articles 5, 18(1), (2), 9–11, 19–21, 25, 27(4) and 39

This cluster of rights relates to the integrity of the family unit and the way in which the State intervenes both to support families and to provide alternative care where the family environment has failed to function properly. The framework of the Convention provides that *parents* (or, as the case may be, legal guardians) will have 'the primary responsibility for the upbringing and development of the child' and the best interests of the child will be 'their basic concern'.[462] The State's responsibilities will generally be to give parents appropriate assistance to perform their child-rearing responsibilities and 'ensure the development of institutions, facilities and services for the care of children'.[463] The important relationship between the respective obligations of States parties and parents/other carers in relation to children's exercise of rights is set out in the following key article of the Convention.

> *Article 5*
> States Parties shall respect the responsibilities, rights and duties of parents or, where applicable, the members of the extended family or community as provided for by local custom, legal guardians or other persons legally responsible for the child, to provide, in a manner consistent with the evolving capacities

---

457 CRC/C/SYR/CO/5 (6 March 2019) [26]; CRC/C/AUS/CO/5–6 (30 September 2019) [27]; CRC/C/CPV/CO/2 (27 June 2019) [38].
458 CRC/C/CPV/CO/2 (27 June 2019) [38].
459 CRC/C/AUS/CO/5–6 (30 September 2019) [27].
460 CRC/C/AZE/CO/3–4 (12 March 2012) [43].
461 CRC/C/ALB/CO/2–4 (5 October 2012) [37].
462 CRC, art. 18(1).
463 CRC, art. 18(2).

of the child, appropriate direction and guidance in the exercise by the child of the rights recognized in the present Convention.

The primacy of the family unit is further supported in the Convention by the principle that the State must ensure the non-separation of children from their parents against their will 'except when competent authorities subject to judicial review determine, in accordance with applicable law and procedures, that such separation is necessary for the best interests of the child'.[464] A child who is separated from his or her parents has a right 'to maintain personal relations and direct contact with both parents on a regular basis, except if it is contrary to the child's best interests'.[465] States are under a further obligation to deal with cases of family reunification, 'in a positive, humane and expeditious manner', where for example the child or parents have applied to enter or leave the State,[466] and a child whose parents reside in different States have the right to maintain on a regular basis 'direct contacts with both parents'.[467] States are also obliged to 'take measures to combat the illicit transfer and non-return of children abroad'.[468] States parties are also obliged to 'take all appropriate measures to secure the recovery of maintenance for the child from the parents or other persons having financial responsibility for the child, both within the State party and from abroad'.[469]

Where a child is 'temporarily or permanently deprived of his or her family environment' the Convention provides that the child will be 'entitled to special protection and assistance provided by the State'.[470] In particular, States are obliged to 'ensure alternative care for such a child' in accordance with their national laws.[471] This could include, 'foster placement, *kafalah* of Islamic law, adoption or if necessary placement in suitable institutions for the care of children'.[472] A child who has been placed by the competent authorities in foster care or in other protective arrangements has a right 'to a periodic review of the treatment provided . . . and all other circumstances relevant to his or her placement'.[473] If adoption is the chosen route for a particular States party, the Convention provides that the State must

---

464 CRC, art. 9(1).
465 CRC, art. 9(2).
466 CRC, art. 10(1).
467 CRC, art. 10(2).
468 CRC, art. 11(1).
469 CRC, art. 27(4).
470 CRC, art. 20(1).
471 CRC, art. 20(2).
472 CRC, art. 20(3). 'Placing children in *Kafalah* is similar to adoption, but not necessarily with the severing of family ties, the transference of inheritance rights, or the change of the child's family name. Traditional Muslim law does not appear to allow formal adoption because it refuses to accept the legal fiction which an adoption creates, namely that an adopted child can become equal to a blood relative of the adopting father' (Pearl and Menski 1998: 408).
473 CRC, art. 25.

ensure that 'the best interests of the child shall be the paramount consideration'.[474] This is a stronger legal formulation than the general 'best interests' principle in article 3(1) where it is formulated as 'a primary consideration'. The Convention further provides that adoptions must be authorized by the competent authorities that will determine whether the adoption is permissible according to applicable law and procedure.[475] States are also obliged to recognise that inter-country adoption may also be an appropriate alternative care solution for a child who cannot be adopted, fostered or placed in any suitable manner in the child's country of origin.[476] Article 19 obliges States parties to protect children from all forms of violence, including sexual abuse'. This provision is discussed in more detail in section 3.7.6.1 below.

Some of the relevant standards within this cluster of rights have been given further focus by the Committee's *Decision No. 7*[477] adopted in 2004, which recognised, *inter alia*, the frequency with which its Concluding Observations addressed 'serious difficulties regarding the provision of care for children in informal or formal fostering, including kinship care and adoption, or in residential facilities, often recommending the strengthening and regular monitoring of alternative care measures'.[478] The Committee has also convened a *Day of General Discussion* on the subject of children without parental care adopted in 2005.[479] This confirmed that 'the family, as the fundamental group of society, is the natural environment for the survival, protection and development of the child', and the need for States parties to develop 'a comprehensive national policy on families and children which supports and strengthens families'.[480] It noted, however, that in many States parties 'the number of children separated from their parents and placed in alternative care is increasing and at a high level. It is concerned that these placements are not always a measure of last resort and therefore not in the best interests of the child'.[481] Interestingly, the Committee raised the question whether a 'new paradigm' was needed to replace the traditional institutional model of children's out-of-home placement and to challenge 'the deep-rooted ideology behind the institutional model' by, for example, establishing smaller specialised units within institutions.[482] The Committee also emphasised its approval of a 'principle of individualization' in this field:

> Every child is unique and the separation from parents and the placement into out-of-home care should always be looked at case by case. There is no one

---

474 CRC, art. 21.
475 CRC, art. 21(a).
476 CRC, art. 21(b).
477 Committee on the Rights of the Child, *Decision No. 7: Children without parental care*, 37th session, CRC/C/143 (12 January 2005), 4–5.
478 Ibid., 4.
479 Committee on the Rights of the Child, *Day of General Discussion on 'Children without parental care'*, Report on the fortieth session, CRC/C/153 (17 March 2006) [636–89].
480 Ibid. [644–5].
481 Ibid. [654].
482 Ibid. [660–1].

solution which fits all situations. The individualization of solutions means more tailored solutions based on the actual situation of the child, including her/his personal, family and social situation. This provides better opportunities for the assessment of the child's long-term development and it respects the principle of the best interests of the child, e.g. what are the actual needs of the child, how to keep a close relationship with the biological family.[483]

A key theme underlying the Committee's Concluding Observations on this cluster of rights is the appropriate balance to be struck between the State's obligations and family responsibilities for children (see section 1.1.4 in this book). In some countries there is evidence that the family unit has been fundamentally and structurally weakened, often as a result of civil strife, war, HIV/AIDS and poverty. The Committee noted with concern in the *Day of General Discussion* that these factors resulted in a significant number of children being orphaned, or otherwise separated from their parents.[484]

The Committee also noted at the *Day of General Discussion* that 'precise guidance available to States working to meet their obligations with respect to suitable alternative care remains partial and limited', and it recommended that 'a set of international standards for the protection and alternative care of children without parental care' be developed for the General Assembly to consider.[485] Detailed *Guidelines for the Alternative Care of Children* were adopted by a General Assembly resolution celebrating the 20th anniversary of the Convention.[486] The *Guidelines* set out 'desirable orientations for policy and practice', and seek in particular:

(a) To support efforts to keep children in, or return them to, the care of their family or, failing this, to find another appropriate and permanent solution, including adoption and *kafala* of Islamic law;

(b) To ensure that, while such permanent solutions are being sought, or in cases where they are not possible or are not in the best interests of the child, the most suitable forms of alternative care are identified and provided, under conditions that promote the child's full and harmonious development;

(c) To assist and encourage Governments to better implement their responsibilities and obligations in these respects, bearing in mind the economic, social and cultural conditions prevailing in each State; and

(d) To guide policies, decisions and activities of all concerned with social protection and child welfare in both the public and the private sectors, including civil society.[487]

---

483 Ibid. [667].
484 Ibid. [687].
485 Committee on the Rights of the Child, *Day of General Discussion on 'Children without parental care'*, Report on the 40th session, CRC/C/153 (17 March 2006) [687–8].
486 General Assembly, *Guidelines for the Alternative Care for Children*, 64th sess., UN Doc. A/RES/64/142 (24 February 2010).
487 Ibid. [2].

General Comment No. 20 (2016) on the implementation of the rights of the child during adolescence also reinforces the role of the family in the life of children on the cusp of adulthood.[488] In this regard, the Committee reaffirmed States parties' obligations to provide appropriate support to parents and caregivers under articles 18(2) and (3), and article 27(2) of the Convention, and to assist parents in providing support to adolescents.[489] Of course, 'such support should respect the rights and evolving capacities of adolescents and the increasing contribution they make to their own lives. States should ensure that they do not, in the name of traditional values, tolerate or condone violence, reinforce unequal power relations within family settings and, therefore, deprive adolescents of the opportunity to exercise their basic rights.[490] *General Comment No. 20* also pays attention to the intergenerational gap in the form of the digital era and globalisation, which impacts on the experiences of children and adolescents as they grow up, and which is often very different to the experiences of parents' and caregivers' youth.[491]

> This changing context poses challenges to the capacity of parents and caregivers to communicate effectively with adolescents and provide guidance and protection in a manner that takes into account the current realities of their lives. The Committee recommends that States undertake research with adolescents and their parents and caregivers into the nature of guidance, assistance, training and support needed to help address the intergenerational divergence of experience.[492]

Such recommendations are sensible, however, the pace of change in technology may serve to make new research out of date as soon as it is published.

Where adolescents end up in alternative care, *General Comment No. 20* outlines particularly poor outcomes where the care is long-term and in a large institutional setting:

> These adolescents experience lower educational attainment, dependency on social welfare and higher risk of homelessness, imprisonment, unwanted pregnancy, early parenthood, substance misuse, self-harm and suicide. Adolescents in alternative care are commonly required to leave once they reach 16–18 years of age and are particularly vulnerable to sexual abuse and exploitation, trafficking and violence as they lack support systems or protection and have been afforded no opportunities to acquire the skills and capacities to protect themselves. Those with disabilities are often denied opportunities for community living and are transferred to adult institutions, where they are at increased risk of being subjected to continuing violations of their rights.[493]

---

488 CRC/C/GC/20 (6 December 2016).
489 Ibid., [50].
490 Ibid.
491 Ibid., [51].
492 Ibid.
493 Ibid., [52].

In order to counteract some of these negative outcomes, the *General Comment* urges states to only use such institutions as measures of absolute last resort, and with regular reviews of the adolescents' situation, providing them with a voice in the process.[494]

3.7.5.1 Family environment

The Committee welcomes States parties' efforts to strengthen family environments through investment in education, health and social services. Where there is no state social welfare service, the Committee recommends that state's prioritise establishing 'a network of services for children'.[495] In some States, there are no alternative care institutions available. The *Guidelines for the Alternative Care of Children*[496] recognises that 'residential care facilities and family-based care complement each other in meeting the needs of children' but where such large residential (institutional) facilities remain, 'alternatives should be developed in the context of an overall deinstitutionalization strategy'.[497] In the case of Tonga, an absolute lack of state infrastructure results in care being provided by extended family, with no alternative care options available should this option be unsuitable or fail.[498] The lack of even a minimum standard regulating the alternative care of children counters the Convention aims and the Committee recommended setting up a formal alternative care system, social welfare services and support of extended families.[499] Japan, on the other hand, has raised serious concerns due to an overzealous approach to institutional care, with the Committee noting that children may be removed from their homes and placed in 'guidance centres' for up to two months without a court order in place.[500] Parents are disempowered through this process and children are deprived of contact with biological parents once removed. The high numbers of children in institutions raises concerns due to inadequacy in standards, and the 'alleged' strong financial incentive for guidance centres to receive more children imbues suspicion. Further, these centres are not upholding the best interests of the child principle.[501] The Committee drew the State's attention to *Guidance for the Alternative Care of Children*, and made a number of recommendations including the introduction of 'mandatory judicial review for

---

494 Ibid., [53].
495 Tonga: CRC/C/TON/CO/1 (2 July 2019) [38].
496 General Assembly, *Guidelines for the Alternative Care for Children*, 64th sess., UN Doc. A/RES/64/142 (24 February 2010) [14].
497 General Assembly, *Guidelines for the Alternative Care for Children*, 64th sess., UN Doc. A/RES/64/142 (24 February 2010) [23].
498 Tonga: CRC/C/TON/CO/1 (2 July 2019), [39].
499 Ibid.
500 CRC/C/JPN/CO/4–5 (5 March 2019) [28].
501 Ibid.

determining whether a child should be removed from the family, setting up clear criteria for removal of the child and ensuring that children are separated from their parents as a measure of last resort only, when it is necessary for their protection and in their best interests, after hearing the child and its parents'.[502]

Other states, for example Malta are praised by the Committee for improving the 'system of alternative care for children left without parental care'.[503] However, residential care homes continue to be used, giving rise to potential harms; which the Committee highlights, recommending a reduction in use of these facilities. Similarly, Bosnia and Herzegovina's deinstitutionalisation process was encouraged, eased by the state 'supporting and facilitating family-bases care for children and harmonizing the foster care system at all levels of government'.[504] In order to end institutional care, other state mechanisms require capacity building such as social workers and foster carers.

The Committee has reiterated that the removal of children from families is a measure of last resort only, taking account of the views and best interests of the child, and ensuring the placement meets the needs of the child, including placing siblings together.[505]

The particular context pertaining to the State under scrutiny may impact dramatically on issues relating to the family environment. The Committee urges States to provide more assistance to families in some disadvantaged communities in crisis situations due to poverty and other factors. For example, in the case of Portugal, widespread use of institutional care was identified, including that of children aged below three years, for reasons of poverty and disability.[506] In this case, the Committee stated that poverty or financial concerns should never be the sole justification for the removal of a child from the care of parents.[507]

The limited degree to which fathers take parental responsibility for their children is sometimes a cause for concern. In the case of Cabo Verde, mothers are the main caregivers in 80% of families, and most single parent families headed by women are affected by poverty.[508] Here, the Committee recommended that the state promote 'equal parental responsibilities of fathers and mothers in a continuous and sustained manner'.[509] Further, financial support for single-parent households was identified as a means of ensuring a basic standard of living conditions for children.

---

502 Ibid., [29].
503 CRC/C/MLT/CO/3–6 (26 June 2019) [30].
504 CRC/C/BIH/CO/5–6 (30 September 2019) [30].
505 For example, Malta, Japan.
506 CRC/C/PRT/CO/5–6 (27 September 2019) [30].
507 Ibid., [31].
508 CRC/C/CPV/CO/2 (27 June 2019) [52].
509 Ibid., [53].

3.7.5.2 Adoption

Article 21

States parties that recognize and/or permit the system of adoption shall ensure that the best interests of the child shall be the paramount consideration and they shall:

(a) Ensure that the adoption of a child is authorized only by competent authorities who determine, in accordance with applicable law and procedures and on the basis of all pertinent and reliable information, that the adoption is permissible in view of the child's status concerning parents, relatives and legal guardians and that, if required, the persons concerned have given their informed consent to the adoption on the basis of such counselling as may be necessary;

(b) Recognize that inter-country adoption may be considered as an alternative means of child's care, if the child cannot be placed in a foster or an adoptive family or cannot in any suitable manner be cared for in the child's country of origin;

(c) Ensure that the child concerned by inter-country adoption enjoys safeguards and standards equivalent to those existing in the case of national adoption;

(d) Take all appropriate measures to ensure that, in inter-country adoption, the placement does not result in improper financial gain for those involved in it;

(e) Promote, where appropriate, the objectives of the present article by concluding bilateral or multilateral arrangements or agreements, and endeavour, within this framework, to ensure that the placement of the child in another country is carried out by competent authorities or organs.

In essence, article 21 establishes the stronger legal formulation of a *paramountcy principle* with regard to the consideration of children's best interests, and also sets out a series of (five) safeguards. Inter-country adoption is recognised as a potential option of alternative care in article 21(b) subject to an important 'subsidiarity principle', that is, it is acceptability only where suitable arrangements cannot be made in the child's country of origin: see further Chapter 7. The requirement that, in matters of adoption, the best interests of the child must be the 'the paramount' (in contradistinction to 'a primary') consideration is commented on in the *Implementation Handbook*:

> The provision establishes that no other interests, whether economic, political, state security or those of the adopters, should take precedence over, or be considered equal to, the child's.
>
> [...]
>
> The paramountcy principle should be clearly stated in law. Any regulation that fetters the principle could lead to a breach of the Convention – for

example inflexible rules about the adopters, such as the setting of age limits, or about the child, for example requiring a lengthy period before an abandoned child can be adopted.

(Hodgkin and Newell 2007: 295)

Article 21 was one of the four principal issues of controversy in the drafting of the Convention identified by Cantwell (1992: 26). Since the Western notion of adoption – the full severing of the legal relationship between parent and child – is not recognised under Islamic law, the aim was to ensure that the text did not compel the Islamic States to recognise or establish systems of adoption. However, new thinking on adoption had already emerged in the form of a *Declaration*[510] approved by the General Assembly in 1986.

This Declaration contained a number of fundamental principles that deserved inclusion in the Convention, and indeed translated the new thinking on inter-country adoption in particular, whereby emphasis was to be placed on guaranteeing the protection of the children concerned rather than on facilitating the process. The revised text of Article 21 took due account of all these questions.

(Cantwell 1992: 26)

Inter-country adoption (see further, Chapter 7) was given finer international focus several years after the *Declaration* with the adoption of the *Hague Convention on Protection of Children and Co-operation in respect of Intercountry Adoption*[511] (1993). The Committee, consistently with article 21(e) of the Convention, promotes the adoption of such treaties by States parties. For example, while welcoming measures taken by the Republic of Korea to regulate adoptions including establishing a court of authorisation, the Committee recommended that the State party acceded to the Hague Convention.[512] Similarly, with respect to Singapore, Tonga and Japan the Committee recommended the States parties expedite the ratification of the *Hague Convention*.[513]

Article 21 of the Convention, together with a number of other international instruments, is aimed to provide a more orderly regulation of adoption, particularly inter-country adoption, in order to protect children from a range of exploitative behaviours that can surround these transactions. For example, in the case

---

510 *Declaration on Social and Legal Principles relating to the Protection and Welfare of Children, with special reference to Foster Placement and Adoption, Nationally and Internationally*. General Assembly, 95th plenary meeting, UN Doc. A/RES/41/85 (3 December 1986).
511 Hague Conference on Private International Law, *Hague Convention on Protection of Children and Co-operation in respect of Intercountry Adoption*, concluded 29 May 1993 (entered into force 1 May 1995).
512 CRC/C/KOR/CO/5–6 (27 September 2019)[33].
513 CRC/C/SGP/CO/4–5 (31 May 2019) [33]; CRC/C/TON/CO/1 (2 July 2019) [42]; CRC/C/JPN/CO/4–5 (5 March 2019) [30].

of Japan, the Committee recommended that all adoptions, 'including those by a lineal relative of the person of the guardian, are subject to judicial authorization and are in accordance with the best interests of the child'.[514] In the case of Portugal, the Committee also recommended strengthened 'support and counseling' for adoptive parents to prepare them fully for the adoption and to assist them in the integration process of the adopted child into the adopted family.[515] Finally, in the case of Tonga, the Committee noted that most adoptions occur through customary practices, and there are no comprehensive State adoption laws or guidelines for the adoption process.[516] The Committee called on the State to enact its current draft adoption laws and produce formal guidelines for adoption processes. At the community level, an information and public awareness campaign would be required to transition from customary practices to formal legal adoptions.

The regulation of adoptions generally, envisaged in article 21(a), enables the Committee to assess the overall picture of domestic and inter-country adoption laws and procedures. For example, in the cases of Bosnia and Herzegovina, the Committee recommended that the State 'develop and adopt a comprehensive legal framework on adoption',[517] and consider ratifying the *Hague Convention*. It also encouraged the use of a universal integrated database for use by social welfare centres as a tool for matching potential adopters with adoptees.

3.7.6 Violence against children: articles 19, 37 (a), 34 and 39

3.7.6.1 Freedom of the child from all forms of violence

Article 19
1. States parties shall take all appropriate legislative, administrative, social and educational measures to protect the child from all forms of physical or mental violence, injury or abuse, neglect or negligent treatment, maltreatment or exploitation, including sexual abuse, while in the care of parent(s), legal guardian(s) or any other person who has the care of the child.
2. Such protective measures should, as appropriate, include effective procedures for the establishment of social programmes to provide necessary support for the child and for those who have the care of the child, as well as for other forms of prevention and for identification, reporting, referral, investigation, treatment and follow-up of instances of child maltreatment described heretofore, and, as appropriate, for judicial involvement.

---

514 CRC/C/JPN/CO/4–5 (5 March 2019) [30].
515 CRC/C/PRT/CO/5–6 (27 September 2019)[32].
516 CRC/C/TON/CO/1 (2 July 2019) [41].
517 CRC/C/BIH/CO/5–6 (30 September 2019) [31].

Article 19 has been given further focus in *General Comment No. 13*[518] issued in 2011, with the stated rationale that 'the extent and intensity of violence exerted on children is alarming'.[519] The link between article 19 and OPSC is also recognised by the Committee, but 'the Committee holds that article 19 forms the core provision for discussion and strategies to address and eliminate all forms of violence in the context of the Convention more broadly'.[520] This *General Comment* contains, *inter alia*, a detailed legal analysis of the text of article 19. For example, it explains the phrase '. . . all forms of . . .' thus:

> *No exceptions.* The Committee has consistently maintained the position that all forms of violence against children, however light, are unacceptable. 'All forms of physical or mental violence' does not leave room for any level of legalized violence against children. Frequency, severity of harm and intent to harm are not prerequisites for the definitions of violence. States parties may refer to such factors in intervention strategies in order to allow proportional responses in the best interests of the child, but definitions must in no way erode the child's absolute right to human dignity and physical and psychological integrity by describing some forms of violence as legally and/or socially acceptable.[521]

The Committee frequently referenced the *UN Study on Violence against Children*, led by Professor Paulo Sergio Pinheiro, in its Concluding Observations.[522] This Study was influential in guiding strategy and policy in this field, and in particular it was stated that the Study 'should mark a turning point – an end to adult justification of violence against children, whether accepted as "tradition" or disguised as "discipline"'.[523] The Study addressed violence against children in five settings: the family, schools, alternative care institutions and detention facilities, places where children work and communities. It called for urgent action to prevent and respond to all forms of violence and presented a set of strategic recommendations. In addition, it suggested the appointment of a *Special Representative of the Secretary General on Violence against Children* (SRSG), which was realised by a General Assembly resolution in 2008.[524] The SRSG reports directly to the UN Secretary General, and collaborates closely with a wide range of partners, within and beyond the UN system.[525]

From the basis of the material contained in *General Comment No. 13*, the UN Study and the activities of the SRSG, the Committee characteristically proceeds

---

518 Committee on the Rights of the Child, *General Comment No. 13: The right of the child to freedom from all forms of violence*, CRC/C/GC/13 (18 April 2011).
519 Ibid. [2].
520 Ibid. [7].
521 Ibid. [17].
522 E.g. CRC/C/AND/CO/2 (9 October 2012) [36].
523 General Assembly, *Rights of the child: note / by the Secretary-General*, Study on Violence against Children, UN Doc. A/61/299 (29 August 2006) [2].
524 General Assembly, *Rights of the child: resolution*, UN Doc. A/RES/62/141 (22 February 2008).
525 See generally: <http://srsg.violenceagainstchildren.org/> (accessed 26 September 2013).

to a number of recommendations in this field. For example, in relation to Bahrain, it recommended that the States party: take all necessary measures to prevent and prohibit, and to protect children from, all forms of torture and other cruel, inhuman or degrading treatment or punishment; strengthen independent monitoring of child detention facilities; provide adequate reparation, rehabilitation and recovery programmes for child victims; ensure that children can access existing mechanisms for receiving complaints.[526]

General Comment No. 20 (2016) on the implementation of the rights of the child during adolescence[527] further reiterated protection for children from all forms of violence:

> [49] The Committee refers States parties to the recommendations in general comments No. 13 (2011) on the right of the child to freedom from all forms of violence and No. 18 (2014) on harmful practices for comprehensive legislative, administrative, social and educational measures to bring an end to all forms of violence, including a legal prohibition on corporal punishment in all settings, and to transform and bring an end to all harmful practices. States parties need to create more opportunities for scaling up institutional programmes on prevention and rehabilitation, and the social reintegration of adolescent victims. The Committee highlights the need to involve adolescents in the development of prevention strategies and protective responses to victims of violence.

The Committee will sometimes pinpoint particular areas of concern. It raised concern, for example in relation to Syria, about children detained during armed conflict. It called on the state to ensure they were transferred to appropriate civilian prisons for children and only detained as a measure of last resort and for the shortest time period possible, and protected from ill treatment.[528]

3.7.6.2 The right not to be subjected to torture or other cruel, inhuman or degrading treatment or punishment: in particular, corporal punishment (article 37(a))

Article 37(a)
States parties shall ensure that:

(a) No child shall be subjected to torture or other cruel, inhuman or degrading treatment or punishment. Neither capital punishment nor life imprisonment without possibility of release shall be imposed for offences committed by persons below eighteen years of age;

[. . .]

---

526 CRC/C/BHR/CO/4–6 (27 February 2019) [27].
527 CRC/C/GC/20 (6 December 2016).
528 CRC/C/SYR/CO/5 (6 March 2019) [28].

This article resonates with similar provision in the *International Bill of Rights*.[529] A *Day of General Discussion* held in 2000,[530] recommended, *inter alia*, that:

> States parties review all relevant legislation to ensure that all forms of violence against children, however light, are prohibited, including the use of torture, or cruel, inhuman or degrading treatment (such as flogging, corporal punishment or other violent measures), for punishment or disciplining within the child justice system, or in any other context. The Committee recommends that such legislation incorporate appropriate sanctions for violations and the provision of rehabilitation for victims.[531]

Protection from corporal punishment has also been the subject of a dedicated *General Comment (No. 8)*[532] which contains a useful analysis of the child's right not to be tortured or suffer cruel, inhuman or degrading treatment including corporal punishment in a variety of settings: for example, at school, in the family, in alternative cases and in justice institutions. The *General Comment* acknowledges that there is 'widespread acceptance or tolerance of corporal punishment of children' and its elimination is not only mandated under the Convention but 'is also a key strategy for reducing and preventing all forms of violence in societies'.[533] The *General Comment* further notes that the elimination of violent and humiliating punishment of children has been reflected in the views of some of the other international human rights treaty bodies,[534] and regional human rights mechanisms.[535] As regards the core meaning of article 37(a):

> The Committee defines 'corporal' or 'physical' punishment as any punishment in which physical force is used and intended to cause some degree of pain or discomfort, however light. Most involves hitting ('smacking', 'slapping', 'spanking') children, with the hand or with an implement – a whip, stick, belt, shoe, wooden spoon, etc. But it can also involve, for example, kicking,

---

529 See UDHR, art. 5 and ICCPR, art. 7.
530 Committee on the Rights of the Child, *Day of General Discussion on Violence against Children*, Report on the 25th session, CRC/C/97 (22 September 2000), Annex IV; and Report on the 25th session, CRC/C/100 (14 November 2000), [666-88].
531 CRC/C/100 (14 November 2000), [688, sub-para. 8].
532 Committee on the Rights of the Child, *General Comment No. 8: The right of the child to protection from corporal punishment and other cruel or degrading forms of punishment (arts. 19; 28, para. 2; and 37, inter alia)*, CRC/C/GC/8 (2 March 2007).
533 Ibid. [3].
534 Ibid. [22]. Specifically, the Human Rights Committee, the Committee on Economic, Social and Cultural Rights and the Committee against Torture.
535 See the references to the European Court of Human Rights decisions, an Advisory Opinion of the Inter-American Court of Human Rights, and a decision on an individual communication to the African Commission on Human and People's Rights, in *General Comment No. 8: The right of the child to protection from corporal punishment and other cruel or degrading forms of punishment* [23-5].

shaking or throwing children, scratching, pinching, biting, pulling hair or boxing ears, forcing children to stay in uncomfortable positions, burning, scalding or forced ingestion (for example, washing children's mouths out with soap or forcing them to swallow hot spices). In the view of the Committee, corporal punishment is invariably degrading. In addition, there are other non-physical forms of punishment that are also cruel and degrading and thus incompatible with the Convention. These include, for example, punishment which belittles, humiliates, denigrates, scapegoats, threatens, scares or ridicules the child.[536]

The *General Comment* clarifies that the rejection of violence 'is not in any sense rejecting the positive concept of discipline'.[537] The Committee also make the distinction between the use of force to punish and the (legitimate) use of force motivated by the need to protect a child from harm.[538] It further underlines that the wording of article 19 makes it clear that *legislative* and other measures are required to fulfil States' obligation to protect children from all forms of violence. The Committee notes that provisions such as the long-standing (common law) defence of 'lawful', 'reasonable' or 'moderate' chastisement or the 'right of correction' in French law should be removed.[539] The *General Comment* notes that, given the pervasive traditional acceptance of corporal punishment, 'simply repealing authorization of corporal punishment and any existing defences is not enough'; explicit prohibition in civil and criminal law, in sectoral legislation and in professional codes of ethics and guidance is also required.[540] Implementation will require a range of awareness-raising, guidance and training.[541] The *General Comment* further emphasises the need for systematic monitoring by States parties through the development of appropriate indicators and reliable data collection.[542]

General Comment No. 8 is frequently cited in the Committee's Concluding Observations. The Committee will routinely urge States parties to enact legislation that explicitly prohibits all forms of corporal punishment in the family, schools, alternative care settings and penal institutions.[543] Sometimes, countries will make corporal punishment prohibited in schools while it remains lawful in the home and alternative care settings. The Committee will positively support national legislation or case law development that prohibits corporal punishment and will deplore the continuance of the 'reasonable chastisement' defence, where it occurs.[544]

---

536 *General Comment No. 8: The right of the child to protection from corporal punishment and other cruel or degrading forms of punishment* [11].
537 Ibid. [13].
538 Ibid. [15].
539 Ibid. [31].
540 Ibid. [34–5].
541 Ibid. [38].
542 Ibid. [50].
543 For example, in Mozambique: CRC/C/MOZ/CO/3–4 (1 October 2019) [25].
544 For example, in Namibia and Canada: CRC/C/NAM/CO/2–3 (16 October 2012) [38]; CRC/C/CAN/CO/3–4 (5 October 2012) [45].

The Concluding Observations reveal many countries that continue the extensive use of corporal punishment, with legal provisions being 'interpreted as justification for such forms of discipline'.[545] Even where countries have made serious efforts to eliminate corporal punishment from institutional settings, the Committee will comment adversely where corporal punishment remains widespread in the State party.[546] The reports reveal evidence of the persistence of traditional views about disciplining children. For example, in Cabo Verde, the Committee was seriously concerned 'that, despite the prohibition of corporal punishment in the family environment, beatings remains a prevalent disciplinary measure for children and corporal punishment of children is not explicitly prohibited in all settings in all circumstances'.[547] In some countries, for example Singapore, despite repeated recommendations from international human rights mechanisms, 'corporal punishment remains legal in all settings, except in early childhood development centres'.[548] The Committee's Concluding Observations provide examples of violations: for example in Tonga, 'whipping is used as a judicial corporal punishment for a crime';[549] and in Cabo Verde, the Committee expressed concern about 'police brutality against children, particularly children in street situations, as a form of extrajudicial punishment, and the absence of measures to duly record and investigate such complaints, prosecute and sanction perpetrators and provide redress to child victims'.[550] In the case of the Republic of Korea, despite the adoption of the Act on Special Cases Concerning the Punishment, etc. of Child Abuse Crimes and an increase in the budget for child abuse prevention, concerns were raised by the Committee regarding a plethora of serious issues.[551] These included a high prevalence of abuse of children including violence in schools, repeated child abuse in families without adequate legal provisions against reoffenders, corporal punishment remaining legal, underreporting of child abuse, and a shortage of local child protection agencies and other infrastructure required to minimise damage on children including shelters, counsellors, psychologists and trained legal representation.[552]

In the case of Bahrain, the Committee noted the State's implementation of awareness campaigns on 'positive forms of child-rearing'; however, despite these efforts, corporal punishment was still permitted in a range of settings including the home, alternative care settings and in the administration of justice.[553] The Committee recommended various measures to tackle this, including the explicit

---

545 For example, in Mozambique: CRC/C/MOZ/CO/3–4 (1 October 2019) [25].
546 CRC/C/BEL/CO/5–6 (28 February 2019) [22].
547 CRC/C/CPV/CO/2 (27 June 2019) [41].
548 CRC/C/SGP/CO/4–5 (31 May 2019) [26].
549 CRC/C/TON/CO/1 (2 July 2019) [31].
550 CRC/C/ CPV/CO/2 (27 June 2019) [39].
551 CRC/C/KOR/CO/5–6 (27 September 2019) [26].
552 Ibid.
553 CRC/C/BHR/CO/4–6 (27 February 2019) [28].

prohibition of corporal punishment through legislative and administrative provisions coupled with adequate monitoring and enforcement.[554]

The Committee made extensive recommendations to states on the issue of violence against children in its Concluding Observations in 2019, and also highlighted the *Sustainable Development Goals* Target 16.2 to 'end abuse, exploitation, trafficking and all forms of violence and torture against children'. In accordance with *General Comment No. 8*, the Committee continued to recommend the strengthening and expansion of awareness-raising campaigns 'among children, parents, legal guardians and teachers, on the illegality of all forms of corporal punishment'.[555]

3.7.6.3 Sexual exploitation and abuse (article 34)

Article 34
States parties undertake to protect the child from all forms of sexual exploitation and sexual abuse. For these purposes, States parties shall in particular take all appropriate national, bilateral and multilateral measures to prevent:

(a) The inducement or coercion of a child to engage in any unlawful sexual activity;
(b) The exploitative use of children in prostitution or other unlawful sexual practices;
(c) The exploitative use of children in pornographic performances and materials.

The Committee characteristically advises States partics to implement appropriate policies and programmes in accordance with the *Declaration and Agenda for Action and the Global Commitment* adopted at the 1996, 2001 and 2008 *World Congresses against Commercial Sexual Exploitation of Children* (see Chapter 7 in this book). The Committee examines carefully States parties' criminal/penal codes to ensure compliance with the Convention in this area, and identifies areas of concern in the State's responses. For example, the Committee identified low levels of awareness and the absence of 'defined procedures for the professional response to child sexual abuse' in Portugal.[556] It also identified low levels of reporting of online grooming, insufficient resource allocation for the investigation of sexual abuse of children, and insufficient data on the issue.[557] In order to redress the problems identified and meet the Convention aims, the Committee made several recommendations to the State including the adoption of an 'independent mechanism of inquiry' into child sexual exploitation, and a 'child-friendly and multiagency response to avoid secondary victimization and measures to provide

---

554 Ibid.
555 For example, in Portugal: CRC/C/PRT/CO/5-6 (27 September 2019) [23].
556 CRC/C/PRT/CO/5-6 (27 September 2019) [25].
557 Ibid.

appropriate support to victims'.[558] Further to this, raising awareness with parents, children, teachers and other relevant professionals; an increase in resource allocation including personnel and technical support for 'effective prevention, identification, investigation and prosecution' of child sexual abuse; and the collection and publication of relevant data, were all recommended by the Committee to facilitate a reduction in abuse.[559]

The Committee raised concerns, in relation to Japan, about insufficient measures to encourage child victims to report instances of abuse, recommending the rapid establishment of a reporting, complaint and referral mechanism for child victims.[560] As regards Belgium, the Committee welcomed its efforts to combat child exploitation and abuse, but noted the prevalence of sexual harassment in public spaces and drew particular attention to the Adriaenssens Commission report on the persistence of sexual abuse of children by religious personnel in the Catholic church.[561] The Committee made several recommendations including rapid adoption of new criminal legislation to combat such exploitation, and the strengthening of 'alternative measures to prevent sexual abuse of children by religious personnel and to support victims, such as by means of arbitration centres'.[562] This latter recommendation attempts to draw on existing dispute resolution forums; however, the suitability of such forums to deal with serious abuses is perhaps problematic.

The Committee's recommendations are broad ranging and responsive to individual country contexts. These have included urging activities which combat the stigmatisation of victims of sexual exploitation;[563] awareness-raising programmes to prevent sexual exploitation;[564] research of the scope and root causes of the vulnerability of children to sexual exploitation and abuse in order to develop a national plan of action for prevention;[565] establishing family protection units which provide shelter and specialised services to child victims in conflict zones;[566] among others.

In the case of Syria in the context of armed conflict, the Committee expressed deep concern about girls and boys suffering sexual abuse including rape and exploitation, and girls facing situations of forced marriages; with perpetrators from both the State security forces and non-State armed groups.[567] The context of armed conflict adds complexity and state responses are often inadequate. The

---

558 Ibid., [26].
559 Ibid.
560 CRC/C/JPN/CO/4–5 (5 March 2019) [24].
561 CRC/C/BEL/CO/5–6 (28 February 2019) [24].
562 Ibid.
563 Belgium: CRC/C/BEL/CO/5–6 (28 February 2019) [24].
564 Botswana: CRC/C/BWA/CO/2–3 (26 June 2019) [37].
565 Mozambique: CRC/C/MOZ/CO/3–4 (1 October 2019) [27].
566 Syria: CRC/C/SYR/CO/5 (6 March 2019) [31].
567 Syria: CRC/C/SYR/CO/5 (6 March 2019) [31].

Committee recommended the prompt investigation and prosecution of members of security forces found to be perpetrators of such abuse, however, where infrastructure is lacking, reliance on the State may prove insufficient.

The Committee raised serious concerns regarding Bahrain's treatment of offenders and victims of sexual exploitation, in particular the exemption from prosecution and punishment of perpetrators of rape who marry their victims.[568] Further, the Committee noted that child victims are often treated as offenders rather than victims and also stated that penalties for so called 'honour'-based crimes tend to be reduced. This speaks to an impression of leniency in the treatment of serious offences by the state. The Committee made several recommendations, including the repeal of articles 353 and 334 of the Penal Code to remove the exemption provision where the offender marries the victim, and the reduction in penalties for so called 'honour' crimes respectively.[569] Further, it also recommended the criminalisation of all forms of sexual abuse of children and the treatment of such children as victims and not subject to criminal sanctions. In response to the lack of statistical data on such abuses, the Committee also recommended mandatory reporting of child sexual abuse and exploitation with openly accessible, child-friendly and confidential reporting channels.[570]

States which allow child marriages generate another layer of complexity to the issue of child sexual exploitation. In the case of Singapore, the Committee welcomed legislative measures strengthening the protection of children from sexual exploitation and abuse and the bolstered support for child victims.[571] However, section 375(4) of the Penal Code enables a man to have sexual intercourse with a child under the age of 16 if she is his wife and consents. The Committee called on the State to abolish this provision.[572]

In response to the broad range of contexts in which child sexual abuse may occur, the Committee will characteristically recommend that the States party: conduct a national study on sexual abuse of children to determine root causes and assess its scale; strengthen its legislation; develop a long-term societal behaviour change campaign to reduce sexual abuse and its acceptability; address harmful cultural practices involving child abuse and exploitation; ensure mandatory reporting of child sex abuse; ensure that it has programmes and policies for the prevention, recovery and reintegration of child victims in accordance with the outcome documents adopted at the 1996, 2001 and 2008 *World Congresses against Sexual Exploitation of Children*.[573]

---

568 CRC/C/BHR/CO/4–6 (27 February 2019) [30].
569 Ibid., [31].
570 Ibid.
571 CRC/C/SGP/CO/4–5 (31 May 2019) [29].
572 Ibid.
573 CRC/C/GUY/CO/2–4 (5 February 2013) [37].

3.7.6.4 Recovery and reintegration of child victims

Article 39
States parties shall take all appropriate measures to promote physical and psychological recovery and social reintegration of a child victim of: any form of neglect, exploitation, or abuse; torture or any other form of cruel, inhuman or degrading treatment or punishment; or armed conflicts. Such recovery and reintegration shall take place in an environment which fosters the health, self-respect and dignity of the child.

One corollary of the obligations in article 19 (section 3.7.6.1 above) is the further duty placed on States parties contained in article 39. The Committee has indicated that 'the wording of article 39 requires consideration of a wide range of potential child victims' (Hodgkin and Newell 2007: 590). Following its *Day of General Discussion* on State violence against children,[574] the Committee made various recommendations on the rehabilitation of child victims. These included encouraging the existing 'United Nations human rights mechanisms with a mandate to consider individual complaints concerning violations of human rights to identify ways to respond more effectively to individual complaints concerning violence against children'.[575] This is now a part of the Convention reporting mechanism following the entry into force of OPIC. It also recommended that States parties review all relevant legislation to prohibit 'all forms of violence against children, however light', and that such legislation ought to 'incorporate appropriate sanctions for violations and the provision of rehabilitation for victims', and to 'ensure that children under 18, who are in need of protection are not considered as offenders' but are dealt with under child protection mechanisms.[576] OPSC also contains a provision which obliges States parties to 'take all feasible measures with the aim of ensuring all appropriate assistance to victims of [the Protocol] offences, including their full social reintegration and their full physical and psychological recovery' and States must 'promote international cooperation to assist child victims in their physical and psychological recovery, social reintegration and repatriation'.[577] OPAC contains a reference in its Preamble of the need for 'the physical and psychosocial rehabilitation and social reintegration of children who are victims of armed conflict' and the Protocol obliges States parties to provide, 'when necessary . . . all appropriate assistance for their physical and psychological recovery and their social reintegration'.[578]

---

574 Committee on the Rights of the Child, *Day of General Discussion on 'State Violence against Children'*, Report on the twenty-fifth session, CRC/C/97 (22 September 2000) [666–88].
575 Ibid. [688(4)].
576 Ibid. [688(8–9)].
577 OPSC, arts 9(3), 10(2).
578 OPAC, Preamble, §17; art. 6(3).

3.7.7 Disability, basic health and welfare: articles 6, 18(3), 23, 24, 26, 27(1), (2) and (3), and 33

Article 6 of the Convention (the right to life, survival and development) has been discussed above (section 3.7.3.3). Article 23 establishes rights relating to disabled children.

> *Article 23(1)*
> 1. States Parties recognize that a mentally or physically disabled child should enjoy a full and decent life, in conditions which ensure dignity, promote self-reliance and facilitate the child's active participation in the community.
> [...]

Article 24 sets out the child's right to health.

> *Article 24(1)*
> 1. States Parties recognize the right of the child to the enjoyment of the highest attainable standard of health and to facilities for the treatment of illness and rehabilitation of health. States Parties shall strive to ensure that no child is deprived of his or her right of access to such health care services.

The child's enjoyment of health facilities is complemented by the obligation on States parties to take 'all appropriate measures to ensure that children of working parents have the right to benefit from child-care services and facilities for which they are eligible' in article 18(3). A further important right of the child is the right to an adequate standard of living.

> *Article 27(1)*
> 1. States Parties recognize the right of every child to a standard of living adequate for the child's physical, mental, spiritual, moral and social development.

Related to this right is the right of every child 'to benefit from social security, including social insurance' in article 26. Finally, further protection is offered in article 33.

> *Article 33*
> States Parties shall take all appropriate measures, including legislative, administrative, social and educational measures, to protect children from the illicit use of narcotic drugs and psychotropic substances as defined in the relevant international treaties, and to prevent the use of children in the illicit production and trafficking of such substances.

Under this cluster of rights there has been an accretion of 'soft law' instruments (section 2.2.6) to guide States parties in their focus in reporting to the Committee on these issues. States parties are requested to take into account a number of relevant *General Comments* of the Committee:

- *General Comment No. 3* on HIV/AIDS[579]
- *General Comment No. 4* on adolescent health[580]
- *General Comment No. 9* on the rights of children with disabilities[581]
- *General Comment No. 15* on the right to health[582]

3.7.7.1 Children with disabilities

The Committee has noted the historical exclusion of disabled children from participation in 'normal' childhood activities and the fact that 'their plight rarely figured high on the national or international agenda, and they tended to remain invisible' in a *Day of General Discussion* held in 1997,[583] which recommended, *inter alia*, that the Committee consider the possibility of drafting a *General Comment* on disabled children.[584] *General Comment No. 9* appeared in 2006.[585] In the same year the United Nations also produced a new *Convention on the Rights of Persons with Disabilities* (2006),[586] along with an Optional Protocol[587] that will allow the Committee on the Rights of Persons with Disabilities (CRPD) 'to receive and consider communications from or on behalf of individuals or groups of individuals subject to its jurisdiction who claim to be victims of a violation by that States party of the provisions of the Convention'.[588] One of the eight general principles of the *Convention on the Rights of Persons with Disabilities* is '[r]espect for the evolving capacities of children with disabilities and respect for the right of children with disabilities to preserve their identities'.[589] There is also a discrete provision in the *Convention on the*

---

579 Committee on the Rights of the Child, *General Comment No. 3: HIV/AIDS and the rights of the child*, CRC/GC/2003/3 (17 March 2003).
580 Committee on the Rights of the Child, *General Comment No. 4: Adolescent health and development in the context of the Convention on the Rights of the Child*, CRC/GC/2003/4 (1 July 2003).
581 Committee on the Rights of the Child, *General Comment No. 9: The rights of children with disabilities*, 43rd session, CRC/C/GC/9 (27 February 2007).
582 Committee on the Rights of the Child, *General Comment No. 15: The right of the child to the enjoyment of the highest attainable standard of health (art. 24)*, 62nd session, CRC/C/GC/15 (17 April 2013).
583 Committee on the Rights of the Child, *Day of General Discussion on 'The Rights of Children with Disabilities'*, Report on the 16th session, CRC/C/69 (26 November 1997) [310–38, at 312].
584 Ibid. [338].
585 Committee on the Rights of the Child, *General Comment No. 9: The rights of children with disabilities*, 43rd session, CRC/C/GC/9 (27 February 2007).
586 *Convention on the Rights of Persons with Disabilities* opened for signature 13 December 2006, 2514 UNTS 3 (entered into force 3 May 2008). This Convention had 138 parties at the time of writing (October 2013).
587 *Optional Protocol to the Convention on the Rights of Persons with Disabilities*, opened for signature 13 December 2006, UN Doc. A/61/611 (entered into force 3 May 2008). This Optional Protocol had 78 parties at the time of writing (October 2013).
588 Ibid., article 1.
589 *UN Convention on the Rights of Persons with Disabilities*, art. 3(h).

Rights of Persons with Disabilities relating to children with disabilities which complements article 23 of the *Convention on the Rights of the Child*:

> *Children with disabilities*
> 1. States parties shall take all necessary measures to ensure the full enjoyment by children with disabilities of all human rights and fundamental freedoms on an equal basis with other children.
>
> 2. In all actions concerning children with disabilities, the best interests of the child shall be a primary consideration.
>
> 3. States parties shall ensure that children with disabilities have the right to express their views freely on all matters affecting them, their views being given due weight in accordance with their age and maturity, on an equal basis with other children, and to be provided with disability and age- appropriate assistance to realise that right.[590]

As stated in *General Comment No. 9*:

> The Committee, in reviewing State party reports, has accumulated a wealth of information on the status of children with disabilities worldwide and found that in the overwhelming majority of countries some recommendations had to be made specifically to address the situation of children with disabilities.[591]

As regards the barriers to the full enjoyment of the rights in the Convention experienced by children with disabilities, the Committee emphasised that 'the barrier is not the disability itself but rather a combination of social, cultural, attitudinal and physical obstacles which children with disabilities encounter in their daily lives'.[592] Access to education services is clearly an important part of the overall objective to include children with disabilities into mainstream society and provide them with the skills and means to contribute economically as an adult. The Committee encourages states to ensure that children with disabilities have access to education, for example, in the case of Malta, recommending stronger implementation of 'the Policy on Inclusive Education in Schools' to ensure that students with a range of disabilities including intellectual and psychosocial, are reasonably accommodated, and specialist teachers and professionals are trained to provide the necessary support and attention required by these children.[593] In the case of Singapore, the Committee noted 'the persistence of discriminatory attitudes and behaviours

---

590 *UN Convention on the Rights of Persons with Disabilities*, art. 7.
591 Committee on the Rights of the Child, *General Comment No. 9: The rights of children with disabilities*, 43rd session, CRC/C/GC/9 (27 February 2007) [3].
592 Ibid. [5].
593 CRC/C/MLT/CO/3–6 (26 June 2019) [31].

against children with disabilities' and further mentioned that despite the inclusion of all children with moderate to severe special educational needs in the Compulsory Education Act, some children with disabilities remained excluded.[594] Further to this, those children with disabilities who were not citizens of the State experienced less protection than Singaporean children. The Committee recommended that the State strengthen the implementation of its inclusive education policy and increase the availability of places at pre-school for children with disabilities, without any discrimination.[595] It also called for stronger awareness-raising campaigns 'targeting government officials, the public and families to combat stigma and prejudice against children with disabilities and promote a positive image of children with disabilities'.[596]

Recommendations to combat stigmatisation were made in the cases of Mozambique, Botswana, Australia, Bosnia and Herzegovina, Japan, Malta, Republic of Korea and Cabo Verde, with the Committee consistently advocating awareness-raising campaigns to combat prejudice and stigmatisation against children with disabilities, aimed at government officials, the public and families.[597] Numerous states have implemented legislation in order to achieve equality, including Belgium which adopted the 'M decree' in 2014, resulting in a reduction in the number of children with disabilities in segregated schools,[598] however, in French-speaking communities, higher numbers of children remain in specialised education. The Committee also noted that support for families by the State were insufficient leading to high levels of institutionalisation, exacerbated by long care waiting lists for limited respite care of poor quality.[599] In addition, the lack of precise data on the numbers of children with disabilities results in a lack of appropriate and responsive solutions. The Committee made several recommendations including 'immediate measures to ensure that children with disabilities have access to quality and timely health care'.[600]

The Convention was the first international human rights treaty to refer explicitly in its non-discrimination principle (article 2) to 'disability' as a discrete heading of discrimination (section 3.7.3.1 above). *General Comment No. 9* suggests that States parties, in their efforts to eliminate disability discrimination, should include explicitly disability as a forbidden ground in their Constitutional and/or their specific anti-discrimination laws; provide effective and accessible remedies; and, conduct awareness-raising and educational campaigns.[601]

---

594 CRC/C/SGP/CO/4–5 (31 May 2019) [35].
595 Ibid.
596 Ibid.
597 For example: CRC/C/CPV/CO/2 (27 June 2019) [59].
598 CRC/C/BEL/CO/5–6 (28 February 2019) [29].
599 Ibid.
600 Ibid. [30].
601 Committee on the Rights of the Child, *General Comment No. 9: The rights of children with disabilities*, 43rd session, CRC/C/GC/9 (27 February 2007) [19].

During the reporting process, the Committee recommends that States parties ratify the related international instruments referred to above, if they have not already done so.[602] It will, of course, welcome States parties' ratification of the *Convention on the Rights of Persons with Disabilities* (2006), but will also express its concern where 'no concrete steps have been taken to establish a clear legislative definition of disability' and the States party has failed to align its national and regional jurisdictions with these international standards. The Committee's Concluding Observations frequently refer to the need for the States party to take into account *General Comment No. 9* and the *Standard Rules on the Equalization of Opportunities for Persons with Disabilities*.[603] *General Comment No. 9* further notes the need to develop a widely accepted definition for disabilities 'that guarantees the inclusion of all children with disabilities so that children with disabilities may benefit from the special protection and programmes developed for them'.[604] The 'lack of detailed and disaggregated data hindering the State party formulating and taking effective measures to address the needs of children with disabilities' is a frequent refrain in the Committee's Concluding Observations.[605] *General Comment No. 9* emphasises the need to set up and develop robust mechanisms for data collection, an issue which is often overlooked and not viewed as a priority. In accordance with this, in the case of Malta, the Committee recommended that the state collect data

> on children with disabilities and develop, with the participation of organizations of persons with disabilities, including children with disabilities, an efficient system for disability assessment, which is necessary for putting in place appropriate budgets, policies and programmes for children with disabilities.[606]

3.7.7.2 Health and access to health services

General Comment No. 15 explains further the normative content of the right to health in article 24:

> The notion of 'the highest attainable standard of health' takes into account both the child's biological, social, cultural and economic preconditions and the State's available resources, supplemented by resources made available by other sources, including non-governmental organizations, the international community and the private sector.

---

602 For example, Tonga: CRC/C/TON/CO/1 (2 July 2019) [46]
603 General Assembly, *Standard rules on the equalization of opportunities for persons with disabilities*, A/RES/48/96, 48th session (20 December 1993).
604 Committee on the Rights of the Child, *General Comment No. 9: The rights of children with disabilities*, 43rd session, CRC/C/GC/9 (27 February 2007) [19].
605 CRC/C/GUY/CO/2–4 (5 February 2013) [45].
606 CRC/C/MLT/CO/3–6 (26 June 2019) [31].

Children's right to health contains a set of freedoms and entitlements. The freedoms, which are of increasing importance in accordance with growing capacity and maturity, include the right to control one's health and body, including sexual and reproductive freedom to make responsible choices. The entitlements include access to a range of facilities, goods, services and conditions that provide equality of opportunity for every child to enjoy the highest attainable standard of health.[607]

Child mortality rates have been a cause for deep concern by the Committee, and indeed the reduction of child mortality is one of the UN's Sustainable Development Goals (SDGs). SDG Indicator 3.2 sets out to

end preventable deaths of newborns and children under 5 years of age, with all countries aiming to reduce neonatal mortality to at least as low as 12 per 1,000 live births and under-5 mortality to at least as low as 25 per 1,000 live births

by 2030. There has been an overall improvement in child mortality figures, and between 1990 and 2017, it decreased by 51%, from 36.6 deaths per 1,000 live births to 18.0 live births (Hug et al., 2019: e713). However, an increasing proportion of child deaths are in sub-Saharan Africa, where in 2017, 32.2 deaths per 1,000 live births was recorded (ibid.). Furthermore, although the overall under-five deaths figure is declining, the proportion that occurs during the first month after birth is increasing. In 2019, the Committee noted with concern child mortality rates in Tonga and Bahrain[608] and welcomed the reduction of the child mortality rate in Cabo Verde and Mozambique.[609] The Committee noted with regard to the State of Tonga that the high rate of child deaths was due to 'perinatal and neonatal causes, as well as child mortality due to non-communicable diseases'.[610]

SDG Indicator 2.1 aims to 'end hunger and ensure access by all people, in particular the poor and people in vulnerable situations, including infants, to safe, nutritious and sufficient food all year round' by 2030. SDG Indicator 3.8 aims to 'achieve universal health coverage, including financial risk protection, access to quality essential health-care services and access to safe, effective, quality and affordable essential medicines and vaccines for all' by 2030. These goals are referred to by the Committee in numerous Concluding Observations, as supplementing the provisions of *General Comment No. 15*.

Malnutrition accounts for many child deaths and a number of associated health problems, often exacerbated in remote or rural areas in the States party.

---

607 Committee on the Rights of the Child, *General Comment No. 15: The right of the child to the enjoyment of the highest attainable standard of health (art. 24)*, 62nd session, CRC/C/GC/15 (17 April 2013) [23–4].
608 Tonga: CRC/C/TON/CO/1 (2 July 2019) [47]; Bahrain: CRC/C/BHR/CO/4–6 (27 February 2019)[37].
609 Cabo Verde: CRC/C/CPV/CO/2 (27 June 2019)[60]; Mozambique: CRC/C/MOZ/CO/3–4 (1 October 2019) [32].
610 Tonga: CRC/C/TON/CO/1 (2 July 2019) [47].

The Concluding Observations of the Committee draw attention to malnutrition, awareness of healthy food choices and obesity in a number of States parties.[611] In the case of Bahrain, the Committee recommended intensive measures to combat obesity, by promoting nutritional awareness and healthy eating habits.[612] Regarding general health, the Committee encouraged continued 'targeted interventions to prevent and treat iron-deficiency anemia and sickle-cell anemia among children'.[613] The expansion of a programme in the country to fortify flour with iron and folic acid was encouraged. Immunisation programmes are encouraged and the Committee welcomed Botswana's Expanded Programme on Immunization.[614] However, the Committee also noted concerns about health and wellbeing, including the limited access to healthcare for children in remote areas, and the prevalence of malnutrition and stunting, as well as a rise in childhood obesity. Overall, an insufficient availability of child-friendly healthcare services was also noted.[615] Immunisation programmes, nutritional awareness and child healthcare services were also identified as areas of concern in the case of Bosnia and Herzegovina.[616] Here, the Committee recommended the allocation of adequate 'human and financial resources to fully implement policies and programs' in early childhood health services; raise awareness of the importance of vaccines, and the regular assessment of 'the effectiveness of policies and programmes' focused on childhood nutrition.[617]

In context of armed conflict, the Committee raises serious concerns about the devastating impact that this can have on healthcare provisions. In the case of Syria, the Committee condemned 'the attacks carried out against health facilities and medical staff'.[618] In light of *General Comment No. 15* (2013) on the right of the child to the enjoyment of the highest attainable standard of health, the committee urged the State to take action to 'halt attacks against medical facilities and personnel by all parties to the conflict'; increase the budgetary allocation for healthcare provisions to enable the restoration of services with a particular focus on children's facilities; and 'ensure access to health services for all children without discrimination' whether they reside in State or non-State armed groups' controlled territory.[619] Further to this, the destruction of infrastructure leads to greater outbreaks of preventable diseases, setting back the State's progress. In the case of Syria, the Committee highlighted outbreaks of typhoid, acute diarrhoea and cholera.[620]

---

611 For example, Portugal: CRC/C/PRT/CO/5–6 (27 September 2019) [34]; Botswana: CRC/C/BWA/CO/2–3 (26 June 2019) [45]; Bahrain: CRC/C/BHR/CO/4–6 (27 February 2019) [37].
612 CRC/C/BHR/CO/4–6 (27 February 2019)[37].
613 Ibid.
614 CRC/C/BWA/CO/2–3 (26 June 2019) [45].
615 Ibid.
616 CRC/C/BIH/CO/5–6 (30 September 2019) [34].
617 Ibid.
618 CRC/C/SYR/CO/5 (6 March 2019) [37].
619 Ibid.
620 Ibid.

In addition to the early childhood diseases there are also cases of environmental threats to children's health. For example, the Committee noted with concern, in relation to Belgium, 'a high level of air pollution, particularly from road transport, in the State party and its negative impact on the climate and on children's heath, contributing to an increase in asthma and respiratory diseases'.[621] It encouraged assessments of the impact of such air pollution on the health of children with a view to regulating 'maximum concentrations of air-pollutant emissions'.[622] It also encouraged 'awareness raising of environmental health and climate change among children, with the active participation of schools'.[623] In light of the global anti-climate change movement *Extinction Rebellion*,[624] largely led by young people, such awareness-raising may play a key role in future global policies on the environment. In the case of Cabo Verde, the Committee was concerned about a 'lack of information' on climate change and its impact on children, noting that the State 'is already experiencing a shortage of freshwater, an increase in sea level, changes in rainfall patterns, desertification and an increase in temperatures'.[625] The Committee recommended a number of steps in response to this threat, including the development of policies and programmes which address climate change, taking children's special vulnerabilities into account; and increasing children's 'awareness and preparedness for climate change'.[626] In the case of Australia, the Committee was concerned that the State party takes the position that 'the Convention does not extend to protection from climate change',[627] and strongly reinforced its position that the 'the effects of climate change have an undeniable impact on children's rights' including the right to life, development, health and adequate standard of living.[628] The Committee further noted the State's negative response to child anti-climate-change protestors, which it believes 'demonstrates disrespect for their right to express their views on this important issue'.[629] The issue of children's rights and climate change will undoubtedly become a more central issue for the Committee in the coming years.

The poverty, hunger and consequent mortality and health problems associated with developing economies may not be present in developed economies, at least not to the same extent. The issue of unequal access to healthcare and services often arises as a consequence of underlying discriminatory practice and is frequently a cause for the Committee's concern.

---

621 CRC/C/BEL/CO/5–6 (28 February 2019) [35].
622 Ibid.
623 Ibid.
624 See <https://rebellion.earth/> (accessed 15 October 2019).
625 CRC/C/CPV/CO/2 (27 June 2019) [72].
626 Ibid., [73].
627 CRC/C/AUS/CO/5–6 (30 September 2019) [40].
628 Ibid.
629 Ibid.

3.7.7.3 Breastfeeding

The Committee urges States parties to encourage the exclusive breastfeeding of infants up to the age of six months, and sustain breastfeeding for two years or more as recommended by WHO.[630] States parties that fall below this standard are urged to adopt legislation and monitor compliance based on the *International Code of Marketing of Breast-milk Substitutes*[631] and the *Baby-friendly Hospital Initiative*.[632]

The Committee commented on the breastfeeding practices of a number of states within its Concluding Observations in 2019, including Portugal, where it recommended that the State 'reinforce action for the promotion of breastfeeding practices during the first six months of life'.[633] It further welcomed Malta's National Breastfeeding Policy and Action Plan (2015–2020), and encouraged campaigns promoting the long-term benefits of breastfeeding to mothers.[634]

The Committee expressed concern regarding the lack of available data from Cabo Verde on the breastfeeding practices promoted by the state, and the lack of monitoring mechanisms for compliance with the *International Code*.[635] Singapore also received recommendations for the adoption of the *International Code* and *Baby-friendly Hospital Initiative*.[636] Further, the Committee encouraged a national initiative for the 'protection, promotion and support of breastfeeding through comprehensive campaigns', supporting mothers in hospitals, clinics, and communities. It also recommended the ratification of the ILO Maternity Protection Convention 2000 (No. 183).[637]

3.7.7.4 Adolescent health

General Comment No. 4 sets out a useful description of the challenges posed by adolescence in the context of the Convention rights.

> Adolescence is a period characterized by rapid physical, cognitive and social changes, including sexual and reproductive maturation; the gradual building up of the capacity to assume adult behaviours and roles involving new

---

630 World Health Organization and UNICEF (2003) *The Global Strategy for Infant and Young Child Feeding*, Geneva: WHO. Available at: <www.who.int/nutrition/publications/infantfeeding/9241562218/en/index.html> (accessed 15 October 2019).
631 World Health Organization (1981) *International Code of Marketing of Breast-milk Substitutes*, Geneva: WHO. Available at: <www.who.int/nutrition/publications/code_english.pdf> (accessed 9 September 2013).
632 World Health Organization and UNICEF (1991) Available at: <www.who.int/nutrition/topics/bfhi/en/> (accessed 15 September 2019).
633 CRC/C/PRT/CO/5–6 (27 September 2019) [37].
634 CRC/C/MLT/CO/3–6 (26 June 2019) [36].
635 CRC/C/CPV/CO/2 (27 June 2019) [70].
636 CRC/C/SGP/CO/4–5 (31 May 2019) [37].
637 Ibid.

responsibilities requiring new knowledge and skills. While adolescents are in general a healthy population group, adolescence also poses new challenges to health and development owing to their relative vulnerability and pressure from society, including peers, to adopt risky health behaviour. These challenges include developing an individual identity and dealing with one's sexuality. The dynamic transition period to adulthood is also generally a period of positive changes, prompted by the significant capacity of adolescents to learn rapidly, to experience new and diverse situations, to develop and use critical thinking, to familiarize themselves with freedom, to be creative and to socialize.[638]

General Comment No. 20 (2016)[639] further reiterates the particular positioning of adolescent's rights under the Convention, on the basis of evolving capacity.

[2] Adolescence is a life stage characterized by growing opportunities, capacities, aspirations, energy and creativity, but also significant vulnerability. Adolescents are agents of change and a key asset and resource with the potential to contribute positively to their families, communities and countries. Globally, adolescents engage positively in many spheres, including health and education campaigns, family support, peer education, community development initiatives, participatory budgeting and creative arts, and make contributions towards peace, human rights, environmental sustainability and climate justice. Many adolescents are at the cutting edge of the digital and social media environments, which form an increasingly central role in their education, culture and social networks, and hold potential in terms of political engagement and monitoring accountability.

The *General Comment* intends to provide 'an overview on how the Convention in its entirety needs to be understood and implemented in respect of all adolescents',[640] and acknowledges the lack of state attention to the particular needs of adolescents, noting that '[g]eneric policies designed for children or young people often fail to address adolescents in all their diversity and are inadequate to guarantee the realization of their rights'.[641]

In some countries, the nature and extent of adolescent health problems are not well understood, and the Committee will characteristically advise that a comprehensive study is made as a basis for the formulation of adolescent health policies and practices. The Committee will encourage States parties to develop

---

638 Committee on the Rights of the Child, *General Comment No. 4: Adolescent health and development in the context of the Convention on the Rights of the Child*, CRC/GC/2003/4 (1 July 2003) [2].
639 Committee on the Rights of the Child, *General Comment No. 20 (2016) on the implementation of the rights of the child during adolescence*, CRC/C/GC/20 (6 December 2016) [2].
640 Ibid., [6].
641 Ibid., [3].

appropriate data collection mechanisms and '[w]here appropriate, adolescents should participate in the analysis to ensure that the information is understood and utilized in an adolescent-sensitive way'.[642]

It welcomed Singapore's compulsory sex education programme in schools, however, expressed concern that the state emphasised abstinence, and provided only limited information on contraception and sexually transmitted diseases.[643] The Committee called for a more comprehensive programme of sex education which is gender sensitive, non-discriminatory, and includes full attention of the use of contraception including emergency contraception and the treatment of sexually transmitted diseases.[644] In the cases of Portugal and Cabo Verde, the Committee made recommendations in response to high rates of teenage pregnancies.[645] The committee recommended studies to assess the causes of early pregnancy in order to understand the phenomenon and devise methods to reduce its incidence' in Portugal.[646] Further to this, the Committee called on the State to ensure access to 'safe abortions and post-abortion care services' for adolescent girls, ensuring they are fully part of the decision-making process.[647] In the case of Cabo Verde, the state recognised a discrepancy in sexual and reproductive health services provided in urban and rural settings, and called for quality and accessibility of services 'paying attention to rural areas'.[648]

The Committee will characteristically recommend a number of measures, usually referenced in *General Comment No. 4 and No. 20*, for example, the provision of access to adolescent-sensitive and confidential counselling and care services, which also include access to contraceptive services; awareness programmes on the consequences of substance abuse, particularly alcohol, tobacco and drugs;[649] and the promotion of healthy lifestyle education at schools and other children's institutions, including information on reproductive health and services.[650]

In *General Comment No. 4*, the Committee set out its concerns about the problems of mental health and suicide that some adolescents will be vulnerable to.

> The Committee is also very concerned about the high rate of suicide among this age group. Mental disorders and psychosocial illness are relatively common among adolescents. In many countries symptoms such as depression, eating disorders and self-destructive behaviours, sometimes leading to self-inflicted

---

642 *General Comment No. 4* [13].
643 CRC/C/SGP/CO/4-5 (31 May 2019) [36].
644 Ibid.
645 CRC/C/PRT/CO/5-6 (27 September 2019) [36]; CRC/C/CPV/CO/2 (27 June 2019) [64].
646 CRC/C/PRT/CO/5-6 (27 September 2019) [36].
647 Ibid.
648 CRC/C/CPV/CO/2 (27 June 2019) [64]-[65].
649 CRC/C/MLT/CO/3-6 (26 June 2019) [33]-[34]; CRC/C/KOR/CO/5-6 (27 September 2019) [39].
650 CRC/C/CPV/CO/2 (27 June 2019) [64]-[65].

injuries and suicide, are increasing. They may be related to, inter alia, violence, ill-treatment, abuse and neglect, including sexual abuse, unrealistically high expectations, and/or bullying or hazing in and outside school. States parties should provide these adolescents with all the necessary services.[651]

This is echoed and expanded in *General Comment No. 20*:

Mental health and psychosocial problems, such as suicide, self-harm, eating disorders and depression, are primary causes of ill health, morbidity and mortality among adolescents, particularly among those in vulnerable groups. Such problems arise from a complex interplay of genetic, biological, personality and environmental causes and are compounded by, for example, experiences of conflict, displacement, discrimination, bullying and social exclusion, as well as pressures concerning body image and a culture of 'perfection'. The factors known to promote resilience and healthy development and to protect against mental ill health include strong relationships with and support from key adults, positive role models, a suitable standard of living, access to quality secondary education, freedom from violence and discrimination, opportunities for influence and decision-making, mental health awareness, problem-solving and coping skills and safe and healthy local environments. The Committee emphasizes that States should adopt an approach based on public health and psychosocial support rather than overmedicalization and institutionalization. A comprehensive multisectoral response is needed, through integrated systems of adolescent mental health care that involve parents, peers, the wider family and schools and the provision of support and assistance through trained staff.

Mental health provisions vary from state to state, and in the case of Japan, the Committee identified insufficient attention with 'negative attitudes towards mental health issues in society and the shortage of child psychologists and other specialized personnel'.[652] The Committee was deeply concerned about children's mental health in the case of Syria, consequential to the armed conflict within the State, leading to gross violations of children's rights including 'torture and ill-treatment, sexual violence and abuse, child marriage, gender based violence, displacement, recruitment by parties to the conflict and use in hostilities'.[653] In response, the Committee called for a number of interventions including increased mental health provisions throughout the State, without discrimination, with a particular focus on children in areas previously under siege or retaken by the State.[654]

---

651 *General Comment No. 4* [22].
652 CRC/C/JPN/CO/4–5 (5 March 2019) [34].
653 CRC/C/SYR/CO/5 (6 March 2019) [38].
654 Ibid., [39].

3.7.7.5 The prevalence of HIV/AIDS

The prevalence of HIV/AIDS has been a source of profound concern in many nations. *General Comment No. 3* provides a detailed commentary about this issue and its relevance in the context of the Convention. It is noted, for example, that: 'Initially children were considered to be only marginally affected by the epidemic. However, the international community has discovered that, unfortunately, children are at the heart of the problem.'[655]

General Comment No. 20 further provides:

> [62] Adolescents are the only age group in which death due to AIDS is increasing. Adolescents may face challenges in gaining access to antiretroviral treatment and remaining in treatment; the need to gain the consent of guardians in order to access HIV-related services, disclosure and stigma are some barriers. Adolescent girls are disproportionately affected, representing two thirds of new infections. Lesbian, gay, bisexual and transgender adolescents, adolescents who exchange sex for money, goods or favours and adolescents who inject drugs are also at a higher risk of HIV infection.

> [63] The Committee encourages States to recognize adolescents' diverse realities and ensure that they have access to confidential HIV testing and counselling services and to evidence-based HIV prevention and treatment programmes provided by trained personnel who fully respect the rights of adolescents to privacy and non-discrimination. Health services should include HIV-related information, testing and diagnostics; information on contraception and the use of condoms; care and treatment, including antiretroviral and other medicines and related technologies for the care and treatment of HIV/AIDS; advice on suitable nutrition; spiritual and psychosocial support; and family, community and homebased care. Consideration should be given to reviewing HIV-specific legislation that criminalizes the unintentional transmission of HIV and the non-disclosure of one's HIV status.

In addition to recommending that States parties attend to the guidance in *General Comment No. 3 and No. 20*, SDG Indicator 3.3;[656] the Joint United Nations Programme on HIV/AIDS (UNAIDS) and OHCHR produced the *International Guidelines on HIV/AIDS and Human Rights* (UNAIDS 2006). The formulation of these guidelines represented a culmination of a number of international, regional and national declarations and activities. Many of these confirmed that discrimination on the basis of actual or presumed HIV/AIDS status was prohibited by

---

655 Committee on the Rights of the Child, *General Comment No. 3: HIV/AIDS and the rights of the child*, CRC/GC/2003/3 (17 March 2003) [2].
656 'By 2030, end the epidemics of AIDS, tuberculosis, malaria and neglected tropical diseases and combat hepatitis, water-borne diseases and other communicable diseases.'

existing international human rights standards, and clarified that the term 'or other status' used in the non-discrimination clauses of such texts 'should be interpreted to include health status, such as HIV/AIDS' (UNAIDS 2006: 108). This, and other, human rights aspects of the HIV/AIDS pandemic have proved to be key elements in preventing a stigmatisation and marginalisation process that might otherwise prevent open access to healthcare services. The Committee expressed concern, for example in relation to Botswana, that HIV/AIDS and tuberculosis remain persistently high, despite measures to address the prevalence of the diseases.[657] The State has implemented a national antiretroviral programme, a 'prevention of mother-to child transmission programme and an early infant diagnosis programme'.[658] Despite these measures, obstacles remain in place, including the limited access to antiretroviral treatment in particular by children with foreign nationalities, and the general limited access faced by children to 'basic HIV services, antiretroviral treatment and sexual and reproductive health services and education, including access to condoms'.[659] In light of these shortcomings, the Committee recommended the adoption of new national plans to tackle the diseases, informed by evaluations of the existing frameworks.[660] For adolescents in particular, the Committee called for the availability of 'confidential HIV testing and counseling services without the need for parental consent', respecting their rights to privacy and non-discrimination.[661]

Similarly, in the case of Mozambique, the committee expressed its deep concern at the high prevalence rate of HIV among adolescents, noting a much higher rate among girls than boys.[662] It called for youth-friendly services providing access to antiretroviral treatment; capacity building 'of community and health workers to provide care and support for children living with HIV/AIDS'; and an awareness campaign disseminating accurate information about the disease to reduce stigma and discrimination.[663] The need for 'quality, age-appropriate HIV/AIDS services' was also raised in the case of Japan.[664]

3.7.7.6 Standard of living

The child's right to an adequate standard of living under article 27(1) is complemented by the recognition in article 27(2) that parents have the *primary responsibility* to secure living conditions necessary for a child's development. States parties are in turn obliged to take appropriate measures to assist parents and others

---

657 CRC/C/BWA/CO/2–3 (26 June 2019) [48].
658 Ibid.
659 Ibid.
660 Ibid., [49].
661 Ibid.
662 CRC/C/MOZ/CO/3–4 (1 October 2019) [36].
663 Ibid.
664 CRC/C/JPN/CO/4–5 (5 March 2019) [35].

responsible for the child to implement this right, and 'in case of need provide material assistance and support programmes, particularly with regard to nutrition, clothing and housing'.[665] Child poverty is therefore a key concern. These provisions of the Convention resonate with some of the SDGs.[666] In particular, child poverty impacts frequently on marginalised and minority groups of children. Recommendations by the Committee to tackle child poverty and improve living standards include calling on states to ensure 'all children, irrespective of nationality' are able to access child benefits.[667] This conforms to SDG Indicator 1.3 to 'implement nationally appropriate social protection systems and measures for all, including floors, and by 2030 achieve substantial coverage of the poor and the vulnerable'. This was echoed in the Concluding Observations to Bosnia and Herzegovina, where the Committee recommended the harmonisation of policies and legislation relating to 'child allowance and social welfare services'.[668] Further, in recognition of structural impediments to equality, it called for poverty reduction strategies at the community levels by 'entity and cantonal governments to ensure equitable access to basic services, including water and sanitation, social services, healthcare and education'.[669] The need to increase employment opportunities for families was also highlighted,[670] and it also called on the Republic of Korea to collect data on children's living conditions in order to better respond to the needs of children in poverty.[671] These solutions often involve support for whole families. In other cases, such as in Australia, child homelessness, particularly of children who were previously alone without families and in alternative care arrangements, was identified as a concern.[672]

In some states, despite state family benefits being available, poverty persists. In the case of Belgium, the Committee expressed concern that notwithstanding the availability of family benefits, it has not had the desired poverty reduction impact:[673] 18.6% of children in the state are at risk of poverty, with the risk higher in families with unemployed adults, or single-parent families. It also noted that families whose origins are outside the European Union are also more likely to be in poverty.[674] The intersection of several issues can worsen the poverty, with the Committee noting that the 'extent of inadequate housing, homelessness and

---

665 CRC, art. 27(3).
666 Sustainable Development Goal Targets: 1.1 eradicate extreme poverty; 1.2 reduce at least by half, the numbers of men, women and children living in poverty; 1.3 implement social protection systems; 2.1 end hunger and ensure access to safe and sufficient food all year round; 2.2 end all forms of malnutrition.
667 CRC/C/KOR/CO/5–6 (27 September 2019) [40].
668 CRC/C/BIH/CO/5–6 (30 September 2019) [38].
669 Ibid.
670 Ibid.
671 Ibid.
672 CRC/C/AUS/CO/5–6 (30 September 2019) [42].
673 CRC/C/BEL/CO/5–6 (28 February 2019) [36].
674 Ibid.

forced evictions, as well as the cuts in welfare benefits . . . make some children vulnerable to begging'.[675] The Committee made several recommendations, including adequate housing for all children in the state, with Roma children provided with housing 'suited to their lifestyle'.[676]

In situations of armed conflict, children often become the most vulnerable victims. In the case of Syria, the Committee was concerned about the number of children lacking access to minimum standards of living and facing poverty directly attributable to the armed conflict. It recommended that the State take measures to address these issues by 'substantially' increasing investment in social welfare policies to provide children with adequate financial support and 'free, accessible services without discrimination'. It called for the prioritisation of drinking water, sanitation, housing and availability of affordable food.[677]

3.7.8 Education, leisure and cultural activities: articles 28, 29 and 31

Article 28(1)(a)

1   States Parties recognize the right of the child to education, and with a view to achieving this right progressively and on the basis of equal opportunity, they shall, in particular:

   (a)   Make primary education compulsory and available free to all;

[. . .]

Article 29(1)(a)

1   States Parties agree that the education of the child shall be directed to:

   (a)   The development of the child's personality, talents and mental and physical abilities to their fullest potential;

[. . .]

Article 31

1   States Parties recognize the right of the child to rest and leisure, to engage in play and recreational activities appropriate to the age of the child and to participate freely in cultural life and the arts.
2   States Parties shall respect and promote the right of the child to participate fully in cultural and artistic life and shall encourage the provision of appropriate and equal opportunities for cultural, artistic, recreational and leisure activity.

---

675   Ibid.
676   Ibid., [37].
677   CRC/C/SYR/CO/5 (6 March 2019) [42].

3.7.8.1 The right to education

The Convention's prescription for primary education in article 28(1)(a) is also reflected in the SDGs.[678] The various aims of education, which States parties agree children should be directed to, are contained in article 29(1)(a) to (e) and have been given a detailed commentary by the Committee in *General Comment No. 1*.[679] The *General Comment* states that this provision is 'of far-reaching importance' and that the aims of education 'are all linked directly to the realization of the child's human dignity and rights'.[680] In particular, the *General Comment* states that:

> Article 29(1) not only adds to the right to education recognised in article 28 a qualitative dimension which reflects the rights and inherent dignity of the child; it also insists upon the need for education to be child-centred, child-friendly and empowering, and it highlights the need for educational processes to be based upon the very principles it enunciates.[681]

While article 28 refers to matters of access to education, article 29(1) provides a framework of substantive *values* in which the content of education can be firmly rooted. The *General Comment* notes that education policies and programmes all too often seem to miss the elements embodied in article 29(1).[682] Furthermore, this provision serves to highlight, in the context of the Convention, the following dimensions:

- The indispensable *interconnected nature* of the Convention's provisions;
- The *importance of the process* by which the right to education is to be promoted;
- The individual and subject right to a specific *quality of education*;
- A *holistic and balanced approach* to education;
- The need for education to be *designed to reflect a range of specific ethical values* enshrined in the Convention; and
- The vital role of appropriate educational opportunities in *promoting all other human rights* and the understanding of their indivisibility.[683]

The Committee also urges States parties to consider and understand the critical importance of education and implementing children's rights specifically in

---

678 Sustainable Development Goal Targets: 4.1 ensure that all girls and boys complete free, equitable and quality primary and secondary education; 4.2 ensure that all girls and boys have access to quality early childhood development, care and pre-primary education so that they are ready for primary education.
679 Committee on the Rights of the Child, *General Comment No. 1: Article 29(1) – The Aims of Education*, 26th session, CRC/GC/2001/1 (17 April 2001).
680 Ibid., [1].
681 Ibid., [2].
682 Ibid., [3].
683 Ibid., [6–14].

early childhood. *General Comment No. 7*[684] arose from the Committee's experience of reviewing States parties' reports, where it identified that 'very little information had been offered about early childhood'.[685] Finally, the Committee has further considered, in a *Day of General Discussion*,[686] how the right to education should be viewed in 'emergency situations'.[687] It concurred with the general principle that the right to education should be upheld 'as a priority and an integral component of humanitarian relief response in emergency situations'.[688]

The Committee's Concluding Observations often identifies failures by States parties to allocate sufficient resources to education including providing free education. For example, in Tonga, the primary education is not free by law and enrolment of children in both primary and secondary schools has dropped.[689] The enrolment in early childhood education is also very low with limited accessibility 'on the outer islands and rural areas'.[690] In order to redress these issues, the Committee recommended a raft of measures including State provision of free primary education and funding for early childhood education. Further, it called for analysis of the root causes of the drop in child school enrolment in order to adequately redress the issues,[691] however it is unclear how such analysis can be undertaken in a comprehensive way. Where gender equality is concerned, the Committee called for 'complete equitable and quality primary and secondary education' for boys and girls.[692] Gender inequality in education can give rise to numerous concerns, and in the case of Bahrain, the Committee welcomed the advances achieved by the state regarding education and vocational training of girls, however, remained 'concerned about the persistent gender stereotypes regarding certain areas of education'.[693] It recommended a review of curricula and texts to eliminate discrimination and gender stereotypes and the tackling of structural causes for gender discrimination in education provision.[694] This acknowledges the fact that gender stereotypes can often lead to a limited number of career options for girls.

Where education provisions by the State are broadly effective, discrepancies may still arise regarding children's individual experiences. For example, the

---

684 Committee on the Rights of the Child, *General Comment No. 7: Implementing child rights in early childhood*, CRC/C/GC/7/Rev. 1 (20 September 2006).
685 Ibid., [1].
686 Committee on the Rights of the Child, *Day of General Discussion on 'The Right of the Child to Education in Emergency Situations'*, Report on the forty-ninth session, CRC/C/49/3 (3 October 2008, 25 February 2010) [37–94].
687 '[D]efined as all situations in which anthropogenic [human-made] or natural disasters destroy, within a short period of time, the usual conditions of life, care and education facilities for children.' Ibid. [61].
688 CRC/C/49/3 (3 October 2008, 25 February 2010) [63].
689 CRC/C/TON/CO/1 (2 July 2019) [55].
690 Ibid.
691 Ibid., [56].
692 Ibid.
693 CRC/C/BHR/CO/4–6 (27 February 2019) [39].
694 Ibid.

Committee commended Cabo Verde 'for achieving almost universal free primary education' and 'adopting eight years of compulsory schooling'.[695] However, it was concerned about regional differences in access to education, with children in rural areas and remote islands facing greater barriers to accessing provisions.[696] In addition, a high rate of repetition and dropouts was disproportionately experienced by girls, with links to teenage pregnancies and adolescent mothers.[697] The Committee recommended support for this group of children, to enable them to continue their education in mainstream schools.[698] Similarly, in the case of Belgium, the Committee expressed serious concerns about 'children from socially and economically disadvantaged families and children with migrant backgrounds', who experienced barriers to accessing quality education, and discrimination from peers and teachers in schools contexts.[699] Bullying and violence in schools was also identified as being pervasive, perpetrated by both peers and teachers. This leads to 'underperformance, overrepresentation in technical and vocational education, dropout, expulsions and failure to obtain a school diploma'.[700] These outcomes will carry lifelong consequences for the children. Solutions recommended by the committee were broad ranging, including strengthening the diversity training received by teachers and empowering them as facilitators of integration of children from diverse backgrounds. This would also require training to improve intercultural competence and effective conflict mediation.[701] Other recommendations included strengthening measures to combat bullying, including cyber-bullying.[702]

Barriers to accessing education result in a number of difficulties in delivering the rights envisaged in the Convention. Reasons for inaccessibility depends on the particular contexts of each state, and in the case of Portugal, the Committee identified children in vulnerable groups such as of Roma background, children of African descent, children with disabilities, children living in poverty and those living in rural areas; as all requiring increased access to education, especially in secondary and tertiary levels. The Committee recommended hiring of teachers from these communities to help overcome some of the issues.[703]

The integration of human rights education, including the principles contained within the Convention, are a common theme in the Committee's Concluding Observations.[704] *General Comment No. 1* notes that article 29(1) can also be seen as 'a

---

695 CRC/C/CPV/CO/2 (27 June 2019) [76].
696 Ibid., [77].
697 This was also identified as an issue in Mozambique: CRC/C/MOZ/CO/3-4 (1 October 2019) [41].
698 Ibid., [76]-[77].
699 CRC/C/BEL/CO/5-6 (28 February 2019) [38].
700 Ibid.
701 Ibid., [39].
702 Ibid.
703 CRC/C/PRT/CO/5-6 (27 September 2019) [40].
704 For example: Mozambique CRC/C/MOZ/CO/3-4 (1 October 2019) [41]; Bahrain CRC/C/BHR/CO/4-6 (27 February 2019) [39].

foundation stone for the various programmes of human rights education' called for by the World Conference on Human Rights, held in Vienna in 1993.[705]

> Human rights education should provide information on the content of human rights treaties. But children should also learn about human rights by seeing human rights standards implemented in practice, whether at home, in school, or within the community. Human rights education should be a comprehensive, life-long process and start with the reflection of human rights values in the daily life and experiences of children.[706]

This is further strengthened by SDG Indicator 4.7:

> By 2030, ensure that all learners acquire the knowledge and skills needed to promote sustainable development, including, among others, through education for sustainable development and sustainable lifestyles, human rights, gender equality, promotion of a culture of peace and non-violence, global citizenship and appreciation of cultural diversity and of culture's contribution to sustainable development.

The Committee has welcomed the introduction of human rights education in some States parties, for example Bahrain,[707] taking note of SDG Indicator 4.7 and human rights education as recommended in the framework of the *World Programme for Human Rights Education*.[708]

3.7.8.2 The right to rest, leisure, play, recreational activities, cultural life and the arts: article 31

The importance of play and recreation for children was referred to in the *Declaration of the Rights of the Child* (1959).[709] The *Convention on the Rights of the Child* contains a more detailed provision. During the drafting process the German and Japanese delegates doubted whether it was advisable to proclaim a universal right of the child to rest and leisure. The German representative 'indicated his preference for dealing with the issue in the context of the provision against economic and social

---

705 See: <www.ohchr.org/EN/ABOUTUS/Pages/ViennaWC.aspx> (accessed 17 September 2013).
706 Committee on the Rights of the Child, *General Comment No. 1: Article 29(1) – The Aims of Education*, 26th session, CRC/GC/2001/1 (17 April 2001) [15].
707 CRC/C/BHR/CO/4–6 (27 February 2019) [39]
708 General Assembly, 59th session, UN Doc. A/RES/59/113 (10 December 2004).
709 'The child shall have full opportunity for play and recreation, which should be directed to the same purposes as education; society and the public authorities shall endeavour to promote the enjoyment of this right.' General Assembly, *Declaration of the Rights of the Child*, 14th session, UN Doc. A/RES/1386 (XIV) (20 November 1959), Principle 7(3).

exploitation' (Detrick 1992: 416). Nevertheless, the text of article 31 was agreed and no country has entered a reservation in relation to this article.

It had been noted in *General Comment No. 7* in 2006 that 'insufficient attention has been given by States parties and others to the implementation of the provisions of article 31'.[710] *General Comment No. 7* attempted to highlight the importance of these rights in the context of early childhood.

> Play is one of the most distinctive features of early childhood. Through play, children both enjoy and challenge their current capacities, whether they are playing alone or with others. The value of creative play and exploratory learning is widely recognized in early childhood education. Yet realizing the right to rest, leisure and play is often hindered by a shortage of opportunities for young children to meet, play and interact in child-centred, secure, supportive, stimulating and stress-free environments.[711]

The poor recognition by States parties of the rights contained in article 31 prompted the Committee to issue *General Comment No. 17*[712] in 2013 focusing specifically and in detail on this article. This *General Comment* notes that, where States do invest in this area, 'it is in the provision of structured and organized activities, but equally important is the need to create time and space for children to engage in spontaneous play, recreation and creativity'.[713] It also refers to a number of 'profound changes' in the world that impact upon children's opportunities to enjoy these rights, for example a global increase in urbanisation and violence.[714] *General Comment No. 17* contains a detailed legal analysis of the text of article 31. For example, it delineates the concepts of 'rest', 'leisure', 'play', 'recreational activities', and 'cultural life and the arts'. But it goes much further than textual analysis and also supplies a detailed commentary addressing the creation of the context for the realisation of article 31, for example, the growing role of electronic media.

> Information and communication technologies are emerging as a central dimension of children's daily reality. Today, children move seamlessly between offline and online environments. These platforms offer huge benefits – educationally, socially and culturally – and States are encouraged to take all necessary measures to ensure equality of opportunity for all children to

---

710 Committee on the Rights of the Child, *General Comment No. 7: Implementing child rights in early childhood*, CRC/C/GC/7/Rev. 1 (20 September 2006) [34].
711 Ibid.
712 Committee on the Rights of the Child, *General Comment No. 17: The right of the child to rest, leisure, play, recreational activities, cultural life and the arts (art. 31)*, 62nd session, CRC/C/GC/17 (17 April 2013).
713 Ibid., [2].
714 Ibid., [4].

experience those benefits. Access to the Internet and social media is central to the realization of article 31 rights in the globalized environment.[715]

The appearance of *General Comment No. 17* prompted states to respond and the Committee's concluding observations duly began to make mention of article 31 provisions. In 2019, of the 16 Concluding Observations issued, nine specifically referred to *General Comment No. 17*.[716] The Committee's recommendations to the states were largely consistent, calling on States parties to strengthen 'efforts to guarantee the right of the child to rest and leisure and to engage in age appropriate recreational activities, cultural life and arts, based on the principles of inclusion, participation and non-discrimination'.[717] In other cases it extended the parameters, specifically including reference to 'children from disadvantaged families, children with disabilities, and refugee and migrant children' and expanded the parameters to include 'sufficient time to engage in play and recreational activities that are safe, accessible, inclusive, reachable by public transport, smoke free and age appropriate'.[718]

3.7.9 Special protection measures: articles 22, 30, 32–36, 37(b)–(d), 38–40

Under this cluster of rights, States parties are requested in the reporting guidelines[719] to provide relevant information on the following matters.

(a) Children outside their country of origin seeking refugee protection (article 22), unaccompanied asylum-seeking children, internally displaced children, migrant children and children affected by migration;
(b) Children belonging to a minority or an indigenous group (article 30);
(c) Children in street situations;
(d) Children in situations of exploitation, including measures for their physical and psychological recovery and social reintegration:

   (i) Economic exploitation, including child labour (article 32), with specific reference to applicable minimum ages;
   (ii) Use of children in the illicit production and trafficking of narcotic drugs and psychotropic substances (article 33);

---

715 Ibid., [45].
716 These related to Bosnia and Herzegovina, Syria, Japan, Tonga, Belgium, Cabo Verde, Bahrain, Mozambique and Botswana.
717 CRC/C/BWA/CO/2–3 (26 June 2019) [59].
718 CRC/C/BEL/CO/5–6 (28 February 2019) [40]. Similar provisions were included in the Concluding Observations to Bahrain: CRC/C/BHR/CO/4–6 (27 February 2019) [41].
719 *Treaty-specific guidelines regarding the form and content of periodic reports to be submitted by States parties under article 44, paragraph 1 (b), of the Convention on the Rights of the Child*, CRC/C/58/Rev. 3, 3 March 2015

(iii) Sexual exploitation and sexual abuse (article 34);
(iv) Sale, trafficking and abduction (article 35);
(v) Other forms of exploitation (article 36);

(e) Children in conflict with the law, child victims and witnesses of crimes and juvenile justice:

(i) The administration of juvenile justice (article 40), the existence of specialized and separate courts and the applicable minimum age of criminal responsibility;
(ii) Children deprived of their liberty and measures to ensure that any arrest, detention or imprisonment of a child shall be used a measures of last resort and for the shortest amount of time and that legal and other assistance is promptly provided (article 37 (b) – (d));
(iii) The sentencing of children, in particular the prohibition of capital punishment and life imprisonment (article 37 (a)) and the existence of alternative sanctions based on a restorative approach;
(iv) Physical and psychological recovery and social reintegration (article 39);
(v) The training activities developed for all professionals involved with the system of juvenile justice, including judges and magistrates, prosecutors, lawyers, law enforcement officials, immigration officers and social workers, on the provisions of the Convention, the Optional Protocols as applicable, and other relevant international instruments in the field of juvenile justice, including the Guidelines on Justice in Matters involving Child Victims and Witnesses of Crime (Economic and Social Council resolution 2005/20, annex);

(f) Children in armed conflicts (article 38), including physical and psychological recovery and social reintegration (article 39).

The guidelines further provide that 'under this cluster, States parties should take into account the Committee's *General Comments No. 6* (2005) on the treatment of unaccompanied and separated children outside their country of origin; *No. 10* (2007) on children's rights in juvenile justice; and *No. 11* (2009) on indigenous children and their rights under the Convention.[720]

The following sub-sections below follow this categorisation.

3.7.9.1 Children outside their country of origin seeking refugee protection (article 22)

Article 22(1)
1. States parties shall take appropriate measures to ensure that a child who is seeking refugee status or who is considered a refugee in accordance with

---

720 Ibid., [40].

applicable international or domestic law and procedures shall, whether unaccompanied or accompanied by his or her parents or by any other person, receive appropriate protection and humanitarian assistance in the enjoyment of applicable rights set forth in the present Convention and in other international human rights or humanitarian instruments to which the said States are Parties.

In this context, 'other international . . . instruments' refers to, *inter alia*: the *Convention relating to the Status of Refugees*[721] (1951) and its *Protocol*[722] (1967) – these two provide the international definition of 'refugee'; the *Convention relating to the Status of Stateless Persons*[723] (1954) and the *Convention on the Reduction of Statelessness*[724] (1961). A Handbook[725] produced by the Office of the United Nations High Commissioner for Refugees (UNHCR) is widely regarded as an authoritative interpretation of international refugee law.[726] The Committee will remind States parties that they need to conform to these standards, and/or ensure that they ratify these various instruments.[727] Article 22(2) of the Convention further obliges States parties to provide as they consider appropriate 'co-operation' in the efforts of the UN and other inter-governmental and non-governmental organisations to protect and assist such children, including family tracing to obtain the necessary information for reunification. States parties are requested to take into account the Committee's *General Comment No. 6* issued in 2005 on aspects of this article.[728] The general objectives of this detailed *General Comment* were: to draw attention to the particularly vulnerable situation of unaccompanied and separated children; to outline the challenges faced by States parties and other actors in ensuring that such children are able to access and enjoy their rights; and, to provide guidance on the protection, care and proper treatment of unaccompanied and separated children based on the entire legal framework provided by the Convention. An increasing number

---

721 *Convention Relating to the Status of Refugees*, opened for signature 28 July 1951, 189 UNTS 137 (entered into force 22 April 1954).
722 *Protocol Relating to the Status of Refugees*, opened for signature 31 January 1967, 606 UNTS 267 (entered into force 4 October 1967).
723 *Convention Relating to the Status of Stateless Persons*, opened for signature 28 September 1954, 360 UNTS 117 (entered into force 6 June 1960).
724 *Convention on the Reduction of Statelessness*, opened for signature, 989 UNTS 175 (entered into force 13 December 1975).
725 UNHCR, *Handbook and Guidelines on Procedures and Criteria for Determining Refugee Status under the 1951 Convention and the 1967 Protocol Relating to the Status of Refugees*, December 2011, HCR/1P/4/ENG/REV. 3. Available at: <www.refworld.org/docid/4f33c8d92.html> (accessed 20 February 2020).
726 See also: UNHCR, *Summary Note: UNHCR's Strategy and Activities Concerning Refugee Children*, October 2005, available at: <www.refworld.org/docid/439841784.html> (accessed 20 February 2020).
727 See CRC/C/ARM/CO/3-4 (14 June 2013) [47]; and CRC/C/UZB/CO/3-4 (14 June 2013) [62]; and CRC/C/RWA/CO/3-4 (14 June 2013) [58].
728 Committee on the Rights of the Child, *General Comment No. 6: Treatment of Unaccompanied and Separated Children Outside their Country of Origin*, 39th sess., CRC/GC/2005/6 (1 September 2005).

of children are engaged in an asylum-seeking or refugee situation, prompted by a number of factors; for example, persecution of the child or the parents, armed conflicts, trafficking, and the search for better opportunities. There are a number of protection gaps, including the greater risks for such children of sexual exploitation, military recruitment, child labour and detention. They often face discrimination and may be denied access to food, shelter, housing, health services and education. They may also find difficulty in accessing appropriate identification, registration and similar documentation. They may be denied entry to or detained by border or immigration officials. In other cases they may be admitted but are denied access to asylum procedures or their asylum claims are handled inappropriately.[729] There has also been a *Day of General Discussion* in 2012 on the subject of children and international migration.[730]

The Committee issued two further General Comments more recently, *Joint general comment No. 3 (2017) of the Committee on the Protection of the Rights of All Migrant Workers and Members of Their Families and No. 22 (2017) of the Committee on the Rights of the Child on the general principles regarding the human rights of children in the context of international migration*;[731] and *Joint general comment No. 4 (2017) of the Committee on the Protection of the Rights of All Migrant Workers and Members of Their Families and No. 23 (2017) of the Committee on the Rights of the Child on State obligations regarding the human rights of children in the context of international migration in countries of origin, transit, destination and return*.[732] These comments are standalone documents, but intended to be complementary and read and implemented together.[733] The General Comments provide greater context for the vulnerabilities of children in migration settings, including the 'double vulnerability' they face 'as children and as children affected by migration who (a) are migrants themselves, either alone or with their families, (b) were born to migrant parents in countries of destination or (c) remain in their country of origin while one or both parents have migrated to another country'.[734] The objective of *General Comment No. 22* is to 'to provide authoritative guidance on legislative, policy and other appropriate measures that should be taken to ensure full compliance with the obligations under the Conventions to fully protect the rights of children in the context of international migration'.[735] *General Comment No. 23* clarifies the 'legal obligations of States parties to protect the rights of children in the context of international migration in their territory' including article 37 (right to liberty); due process guarantees and access to justice (articles 12 and 40);

---

729 Ibid., [1–4].
730 Committee on the Rights of the Child, *Day of General Discussion on 'The Rights of all Children in the Context of International Migration'*. Available at: <https://www.ohchr.org/EN/HRBodies/CRC/Pages/Discussion2012.aspx> (accessed 20 February 2020).
731 CMW/C.GC/3 – CRC/C/GC/22 (16 November 2017).
732 CMW/C/GC/4 – CRC/C/GC/23 (16 November 2017).
733 Ibid., [2].
734 CMW/C.GC/3 – CRC/C/GC/22 (16 November 2017), [3].
735 Ibid., [7].

the right to a name, identity and nationality (articles 7 and 8); right to family life (articles 9, 10, 11, 16, 18, 19, 20 and 27(4)); protection from all forms of violence and abuse, including exploitation, child labour and abduction, and sale or traffic of children (articles 19, 26, and 32–36); the right to protection from economic exploitation (articles 26 and 32); the right to an adequate standard of living (article 27); the right to health (article 23, 24 and 39); and the right to education and professional training (articles 28–31).

The Committee's scrutiny of country reports under this heading provides a wide range of observations, often critical, about the impact of States parties' immigration and asylum-seeking policies. For example, it expressed serious concern over Australia's approach to migrant children in light of the State's intention not to establish an independent guardianship entity for unaccompanied children.[736] While noting that no asylum seeking, migrant or refugee children were being held in Australia's regional 'processing countries' according to the Country Report, the State's Migration Act 1958 'prescribes mandatory detention for irregular migration, including children'.[737] The Committee called on Australia to amend this legislation and adhere to the Convention by prohibiting the detention of asylum seeker, refugee and migrant children.[738] It also further noted that the 'best interests of the child' is not the State's primary consideration leading to 'lengthy assessment and determination procedures'. It referred specifically to the cases of 286 children transferred from Nauru who will not be settled in Australia and instead are being encouraged to 'engage in third country migration options', leaving them in limbo for an indeterminate length of time.[739] A raft of further recommendations was made by the Committee including amendments to existing legislative provisions and enactment of further legislation including for example, 'prohibiting the detention of children and their families in regional processing countries'; in the interim, ensuring that those who are detained in such centres have access to adequate child protection, education and health services; ensuring that the best interests of the child are a primary consideration in decision-making concerning reallocation of children within Australia or to other countries; and 'implement durable solutions' to ensure the early rehabilitation, reintegration and sustainable resettlement' of such children.[740]

In conformity with the Convention which obliges States parties to provide assistance to parents and legal guardians, and entitles children 'temporarily or permanently deprived of his or her family environment' to 'special protection and assistance provided by the State',[741] *General Comment No. 6* makes it clear that States

---

736 CRC/C/AUS/CO/5–6 (30 September 2019) [44].
737 Ibid.
738 Ibid., [45].
739 Ibid., [44].
740 Ibid., [45].
741 CRC, arts 18(2) and 20(1).

are required to 'secure proper representation of an unaccompanied or separated child's best interests' and therefore 'States should appoint a guardian or adviser as soon as the unaccompanied or separated child is identified and maintain such guardianship arrangements until the child has either reached the age of majority or has permanently left the territory and/or jurisdiction of the State'.[742] This is reiterated in both *General Comment No. 22* and *No. 23* (2017).[743] The lack of adherence to this provision was raised by the Committee it its Concluding Observations to several states including Bosnia and Herzegovina, Australia, and Malta.[744]

In the case of Singapore, the Committee urged the State to bring its legislative provisions in line with article 9 of the Convention, 'ensuring that no child is separated from his or her parents'.[745] In the case of Portugal, the Committee highlighted a specific case of the adoption of a bilateral agreement 'aimed at receiving five unaccompanied children from Afghanistan'.[746] However, it also expressed several areas of concern and made a number of recommendations where international treaty obligations were not being met, including those contained within *General Comments No. 22* and *No. 23*, concerning the best interests of the children; detention of children under the age of 18; and registration processes.[747] In the case of Belgium, the Committee raised concerns about the abuse suffered by unaccompanied or separated children, 'including physical violence by local police, unlawful detention for more than 24 hours and a lack of systematic referral to the guardianship service'.[748] It made several recommendations including the effective investigation of cases of abuse of unaccompanied minors.[749]

The Committee acknowledged the positive actions taken by some states to meet their treaty obligations, including Malta where legislative and policy measures taken to improve the safeguards in place for asylum seeking, refugee and migrant children were welcomed.[750] The state put an end to the 'automatic detention of asylum seekers and refugees, including children'; and also granted 'temporary humanitarian protection status to unaccompanied children'.[751] However, despite these positive measures by the state, the positioning of Malta in the Mediterranean at a time of heightened flow of refugees, means acute pressure on its

---

742 Committee on the Rights of the Child, *General Comment No. 6: Treatment of Unaccompanied and Separated Children Outside their Country of Origin*, 39th sess., CRC/GC/2005/6 (1 September 2005) [33].
743 CMW/C.GC/3 – CRC/C/GC/22 (16 November 2017) [17]; CMW/C/GC/4 – CRC/C/GC/23 (16 November 2017) [32].
744 CRC/C/BIH/CO/5-6 (30 September 2019) [43] – [44]; CRC/C/AUS/CO/5-6 (30 September 2019) [44] – [45]; CRC/C/MLT/CO/3-6 ([41] – [42].
745 CRC/C/SGP/CO/4-5 (31 May 2019) [41].
746 CRC/C/PRT/CO/5-6 (27 September 2019) [41].
747 Ibid., [42].
748 CRC/C/BEL/CO/5-6 (28 February 2019) [41].
749 Ibid., [42].
750 CRC/C/MLT/CO/3-6 (26 June 2019) [41]
751 Ibid., [41].

frameworks. The Committee therefore expressed a number of concerns including 'delays in authorizing the disembarkation in the nearest place of safety of rescued migrants and refugees, including children', which often results in them being left stranded at sea.[752] In response to this the Committee recommended that the State review its laws and practices to ensure that they do not 'create, exacerbate or increase the vulnerabilities of asylum-seeking, refugee and migrant children'.[753] A further raft of recommendations was also made to Malta, reflecting the complexity of the state's role in responding to its treaty obligations where such vulnerable children are concerned. These included implementation of a uniform protocol on age determination method that is multidisciplinary and respectful of the child's rights; immediately assigning children with competent guardians free of potential conflicts of interest; processing cases in a positive, humane and expeditious manner, respecting the principles of non-refoulement while facilitating access to asylum procedures; and prioritising the immediate transfer of children and their families from the Initial Reception Facility.[754]

3.7.9.2 Children belonging to a minority or an indigenous group (article 30)

Article 30
In those States in which ethnic, religious or linguistic minorities or persons of indigenous origin exist, a child belonging to such a minority or who is indigenous shall not be denied the right, in community with other members of his or her group, to enjoy his or her own culture, to profess and practise his or her own religion, or to use his or her own language.

This provision is nearly identical to the ICCPR, article 27, but it has the addition to the stated minorities of 'persons of indigenous origin'. The negative formulation of 'a child . . . shall not be denied the right', despite some suggestions during the drafting process that it should be changed to a more positive obligation, 'a child . . . shall have the right . . .', was nevertheless retained in the final text of article 30. In part, this was because the Convention Working Group did not want to pre-empt other international discussions of indigenous rights and how these could be framed in international law (Detrick 1999: 408–14). As noted in the *Implementation Handbook*:

> Article 30 emanated from a proposal by a non-governmental organization called the Four Directions Council, supported by Mexico, to dedicate an article of the Convention to the rights of indigenous children. The drafting

---

752 Ibid.
753 Ibid., [42].
754 Ibid.

Working Group quickly agreed that this should embrace the rights of all minority children and concluded that it would not be helpful to introduce wording which departed from that of the International Covenant on Civil and Political Rights (E/CN.4/1986/39, p. 13; Detrick, p. 408).

(Hodgkin and Newell 2007: 456)

It is therefore instructive to look to *General Comment No. 23*,[755] issued by the Human Rights Committee on this comparable provision, albeit without benefit of the indigeneity element. That *General Comment* provides, *inter alia*, that irrespective of the negative language used in the text of article 27, it nevertheless does recognise the existence of a 'right' and consequently 'a State party is under an obligation to ensure that the existence and the exercise of this right are protected against their denial or violation'.[756]

General Comment No. 11 on indigenous children and their rights under the Convention[757] sets in details the remit of protections for indigenous children in the 'first core human rights treaty to include specific references to indigenous children in a number of provisions'. The Convention provisions acknowledge the 'special measures' required by indigenous children in order to fully enjoy their rights.[758]

> The Committee on the Rights of the Child has consistently taken into account the situation of indigenous children in its reviews of periodic reports of States parties to the Convention. The Committee has observed that indigenous children face significant challenges in exercising their rights and has issued specific recommendations to this effect in its concluding observations. Indigenous children continue to experience serious discrimination contrary to article 2 of the Convention in a range of areas, including in their access to health care and education, which has prompted the need to adopt this general comment.[759]

The *General Comment* followed a *Day of General Discussion* on the rights of indigenous children in 2003 when the Committee reaffirmed its commitment to promote and protect the human rights of indigenous children in its recommendations.[760] A more comprehensive international instrument addressing the rights of *indigenous persons* generally also appeared in the form of the *United Nations Declaration on the Rights of Indigenous Peoples* (2007).[761] The position of indigenous children's rights is given further

---

755 Human Rights Committee, *General Comment No. 23: Article 27 (Rights of Minorities)*, CCPR/C/21/Rev.1/Add. 5 (8 April 1994).
756 Ibid., [6.1].
757 CRC/C/GC/11 (12 February 2009).
758 Ibid., [5].
759 Ibid.
760 Committee on the Rights of the Child, *Day of General Discussion on 'The rights of indigenous children'*, Report on the thirty-fourth session, CRC/C/133 (3 October 2003) [624(2)].
761 General Assembly, *United Nations Declaration on the Rights of Indigenous Peoples* 61st session, UN Doc. A/RES/61/295 (2 October 2007).

detailed treatment in Chapter 10 in this book. Canada made a clear 'statement of understanding' about article 30 on joining the *Convention on the Rights of the Child*.

> It is the understanding of the Government of Canada that, in matters relating to aboriginal peoples of Canada, the fulfilment of its responsibilities under article 4 of the Convention must take into account the provisions of article 30. In particular, in assessing what measures are appropriate to implement the rights recognized in the Convention for aboriginal children, due regard must be paid to not denying their right, in community with other members of their group, to enjoy their own culture, to profess and practice their own religion and to use their own language.[762]

France, however, has made a reservation disapplying article 30 in the light of a provision of the Constitution of the French Republic.[763] However, the Committee took the view that 'equality before the law' may be insufficient to ensure equal enjoyment of rights by minority and indigenous groups in France's overseas departments and territories.[764] Venezuela takes the position, in its interpretative declaration, that article 30 'must be interpreted as a case in which article 2 of the Convention [the principle of non-discrimination] applies'.

The Committee's Concluding Observations comment on children belonging to minority groups under this heading, and also under the non-discrimination principle in article 2 (section 3.7.3.1 above) and other provisions of the Convention. The Committee has referenced, in relation to Singapore for example, the need for the State to 'strengthen its efforts to provide equal opportunities for children of minority groups, in particular the Malay, and that it removes all policies which disadvantage or discriminate against minorities'.[765] The Committee was also concerned that Aboriginal and Torres Strait Islander children and their communities should be more 'meaningfully involved in the planning, implementation and evaluation of policies concerning them'.[766]

3.7.9.3 Children in street situations

Children living and working on the street are obviously in a vulnerable situation and may be prime targets for organised child- and drug-trafficking operations, susceptible to abuse, and may be charged with the crime of vagrancy and generally

---

762 <http://treaties.un.org/Pages/ViewDetails.aspx?src=TREATY&mtdsg_no=IV-11&chapter=4&lang=en> (accessed 20 November 2020).
763 Article 2 of the French Constitution provides a guarantee of 'equality before the law to all citizens without distinction on the basis of origin, race or religion'. The implication was that article 30, by virtue of its selection of minority/indigenous group children was itself discriminatory.
764 CRC/C/FRA/CO/4 (11 June 2009) [101].
765 CRC/C/SGP/CO/4–5 (31 May 2019) [42].
766 CRC/C/AUS/CO/5–6 (30 September 2019) [46].

treated like offenders rather than victims. In some countries, for example in Bosnia and Herzegovina, forced child-begging is a dominant form of child exploitation. There are reports of large numbers of street children in some countries, though the data is often incomplete. The Committee frequently urges States parties to undertake a systematic assessment of the situation of street children in order to obtain a better understanding of root causes.

Children in street situations are not referred to directly in the Convention, and yet they face violations of numerous Convention provisions. The Committee drafted *General Comment No. 21* (2017) on children in street situations[767] following a consultation process where the 327 children and young people from 32 countries were engaged to contribute their views and experiences. The *General Comment* provides authoritative guidance to States 'on developing comprehensive, long-term national strategies on children in street situations using a holistic, child rights approach and addressing both prevention and response in line with the Convention on the Rights of the Child'.[768] *General Comment No. 21* defines these children as:

> (a) children who depend on the streets to live and/or work, whether alone, with peers or with family; and (b) a wider population of children who have formed strong connections with public spaces and for whom the street plays a vital role in their everyday lives and identities. This wider population includes children who periodically, but not always, live and/or work on the streets and children who do not live or work on the streets but who regularly accompany their peers, siblings or family in the streets. Concerning children in street situations, 'being in public spaces' is understood to include spending a significant amount of time on streets or in street markets, public parks, public community spaces, squares and bus and train stations. It does not include public buildings such as schools, hospitals or other comparable institutions.[769]

The *General Comment* calls for a child's rights approach to be taken to children in street situations, who do not share a homogenous group or individual identity across the globe. The Committee's Concluding Observations on these children take a range of approaches. For example, in the case of Syria, the Committee was concerned about increasing numbers of children in street situations who were engaged in begging. They recommended that the State decriminalise begging and prevent the arrest and institutionalisation of these children, instead urging states, with the participation of the children, to 'develop measures for their rehabilitation and social integration'.[770] In the case of Cabo Verde, the Committee welcomed the State's support provided to children in street situations, however, remained

---

767 General Comment No. 21 (2017), CRC/C/GC/21 (21 June 2017).
768 Ibid., [2].
769 Ibid., [4].
770 CRC/C/SYR/CO/5 (6 March 2019) [53].

concerned about their vulnerability to 'exploitation, violence and drug use', recommending that the State provide adequate support for these children, respecting their best interests and giving due weight to their autonomous views 'in accordance with their age and maturity'.[771] In the case of Mozambique, the Committee called on the State to 'conduct a comprehensive study to assess the scope, nature and root causes of the presence of children in street situations in order to develop a national strategy and plan of action, with the participation of children, to support such children'. It also recommended educational opportunities, counselling and family reintegration services to comprehensively respond to the needs of these children.[772]

3.7.9.4 Children in situations of exploitation, including measures for their physical and psychological recovery and social reintegration

(I) ECONOMIC EXPLOITATION, INCLUDING CHILD LABOUR (ART. 32)

Article 32(1)
1. States parties recognize the right of the child to be protected from economic exploitation and from performing any work that is likely to be hazardous or to interfere with the child's education, or to be harmful to the child's health or physical, mental, spiritual, moral or social development.

Article 32(2) further provides a general duty on States parties to take all legislative and other measures to ensure the implementation of these obligations, and in particular: to provide for a minimum age for admission to employment; to provide for the regulation of hours and conditions of employment; and, to provide appropriate penalties or other sanctions to ensure effective enforcement. Exploitative child labour is not only regulated by the Convention, but is also addressed by a number of International Labour Organisation (ILO) Conventions: the *Minimum Age Convention*[773] (1973), the *Elimination of the Worst Forms of Child Labour Convention*[774] (1999), and the *Decent Work for Domestic Workers Convention*[775] (2011). The subject of child labour is dealt with in further detail in Chapter 5 in this book. The Committee

---

771 CRC/C/CPV/CO/2 (27 June 2019) [87] – [88].
772 CRC/C/MOZ/CO/3–4 (1 October 2019) [45].
773 International Labour Organization, *Minimum Age Convention*, ILO Convention No. 138 (26 June 1973).
774 International Labour Organization, *Worst Forms of Child Labour Convention*, ILO Convention No. 182 (17 June 1999).
775 This instrument obliges States parties to commit to 'the effective abolition of child labour': International Labour Organization, *Convention Concerning Decent Work for Domestic Workers*, ILO Convention No. 189 (16 June 2011), PRNo. 15A, art. 3(2)(c).

held a *Day of General Discussion* on the economic exploitation of the child in October 1993.

> The discussion made clear the need for a comprehensive and concerted action for prevention, protection and rehabilitation. The need to strengthen preventive actions was stressed and education was referred to in that regard as an essential tool. Recommendations were also made in the field of the protection of the rights of the child, including the establishment of an ombudsperson who might intervene and assist the child victim of economic exploitation. The important role of recovery and social reintegration of child victims of any form of economic exploitation was recognized. At all levels of action, effective coordination was recognized as an essential aspect to achieve progress, both at the national and the international level.[776]

The Committee adopted the recommendations referred to above at its fifth session in January 1994, including 'the establishment of a national mechanism for coordinating policies and monitoring the implementation of the *Convention on the Rights of the Child*, having specific competence in the area of protection from economic exploitation'.[777] The economic exploitation of children raises many issues in the periodic reports to the Committee, and may involve, for example in Singapore, a conflict between the minimum age for admission to employment (13) and the age for compulsory education (15).[778] In this case, the Committee recommended raising the minimal employment age. In the case of Mozambique, the Committee welcomed the States National Plan of Action to Combat Child Labour 2017–2022, and the raising of the minimum age of employment to 15.[779] It also recommended strengthening the Labour Inspectorate in order to fortify its capacity to monitor employment practices and effectively implement laws and policies on child labour, in particular within the agriculture and mining industries.[780] It further particularly called upon the State to develop programmes which also seek to identify victims of child labour in the informal sector, a setting in which children are least likely to be identified. One of the pervasive difficulties in addressing child labour is that it occurs frequently in the informal sector and in rural areas, often far removed from any official monitoring. As with other areas of Convention rights, the Committee is also concerned that data on child labour is not systematically collected.

The Committee welcomes efforts by States parties to provide legislation consistent with international labour standards and also points out protection gaps in

---

[776] Committee on the Rights of the Child, *Day of General Discussion on 'The Economic Exploitation of the Child'*, Report on the fourth session, CRC/C/20 (25 October 1993) [186–96, at 194].
[777] Committee on the Rights of the Child, *Report on the fifth session*, CRC/C/24 (January 1994) [176–7].
[778] CRC/C/SGP/CO/4–5 (31 May 2019) [43].
[779] CRC/C/MOZ/CO/3–4 (1 October 2019) [44].
[780] Ibid.

domestic legal regimes which may cover paid and unpaid labour. For example, it identified that in the case of Tonga, 'Children are extensively involved in non-economic activities within the household with reduces time for leisure'.[781] The Committee was also seriously concerned that Tonga had failed to adopt an employment relations Bill from 2013 intended to prohibit the worst forms of child labour and establish a minimum age for both hazardous and non-hazardous work.[782] Children in Tonga face severe breaches of Convention provisions and are reported to be involved in the worst forms of child labour, including sexual exploitation. In response, the Committee recommended a raft of measures including adoption of the 2013 Bill into law to protect children from the worst forms of child labour, including the criminalisation of the commercial sexual exploitation of children.[783] The issue of light work was raised by the Committee in the case of Tonga, and regulations including the conditions in which such work can be undertaken without impeding leisure activities and school attendance, was recommended.

(II) USE OF CHILDREN IN THE ILLICIT PRODUCTION AND TRAFFICKING OF NARCOTIC DRUGS AND PSYCHOTROPIC SUBSTANCES (ART. 33)

Article 33
States parties shall take all appropriate measures, including legislative, administrative, social and educational measures, to protect children from the illicit use of narcotic drugs and psychotropic substances as defined in the relevant international treaties, and to prevent the use of children in the illicit production and trafficking of such substances.

The principal international treaties relevant to this provision are: the *Single Convention on Narcotic Drugs* (1961) as amended by a *Protocol* (1972),[784] and the *Convention on Psychotropic Substances* (1971).[785] Alcohol, tobacco and solvents are not controlled by international treaties but their use may be 'illicit'.

> In the post-war decades, children's involvement in illicit drugs was not a significant concern so the issue did not figure in the declarations and conventions of that era. Today, drug abuse by children and young people is causing alarm worldwide because such abuse threatens both the child's development and nations' prosperity and social order.
>
> (Hodgkin and Newell 2007: 504)

---

781 CRC/C/TON/CO/1 (2 July 2019) [59].
782 Ibid.
783 Ibid., [60].
784 *Single Convention on Narcotic Drugs, 1961, as amended by the Protocol amending the Single Convention on Narcotic Drugs, 1961*, 976 UNTS 105 (entered into force 8 August 1975).
785 *Convention on Psychotropic Substances*, opened for signature 21 February 1971, 1019 UNTS 175 (entered into force 16 August 1976).

As the authors of the *Implementation Handbook* make clear: '[t]he problem of drug abuse by children is peculiarly alarming to the adult world because we cannot accurately map it and we do not know how best to tackle it: simply making its production and sale illegal is clearly not enough' (Hodgkin and Newell 2007: 506)

(III) SEXUAL EXPLOITATION AND SEXUAL ABUSE (ART. 34)

Sexual exploitation and abuse (article 34) is discussed in detail in Chapter 8 in this book.

(IV) SALE, TRAFFICKING AND ABDUCTION (ART. 35)

Article 35
States parties shall take all appropriate national, bilateral and multilateral measures to prevent the abduction of, the sale of or traffic in children for any purpose or in any form.

The problem of trafficking and the sale of children has become a global one, and has attracted increasing international attention. Two UN Special Rapporteur mandates have evolved in this area. First, the UNCHR resolved to have a *Special Rapporteur on the sale of children, child prostitution and child pornography* in 1990.[786] Second, a *Special Rapporteur on trafficking in persons, especially in women and children* was established by the UNCHR in 2004[787] and an *Optional Protocol to the Convention on the Rights of the Child on the Sale of Children, Child Prostitution and Child Pornography* (OPSC) entered into force in 2002: see further, Chapter 8 in this book. One example of a 'multilateral measure' referred to in article 35, has been the *Multilateral Cooperation Agreement to Combat Trafficking in Persons* (2005), and the *Joint Plan of Action against Trafficking in Persons, Especially Women and Children*, in the West and Central African region.[788] An earlier draft of article 35 had initially been combined with the text of article 34 (sexual exploitation and abuse), but delegates eventually agreed there should be two separate articles:

> [t]he problem of the sale or traffic of children was wider in scope than that of sexual exploitation and children were subjected to sale or traffic for many reasons: economic exploitation, sexual exploitation and sexual abuse, as well as for reasons of adoption or labour.
>
> (Detrick 1992: 430)

---

786 UN Commission on Human Rights, Resolution 1990/68 (7 March 1990). See also: <www.ohchr.org/en/issues/children/pages/childrenindex.aspx> (accessed 20 February 2020).

787 UN Commission on Human Rights, *Report on the Sixtieth Session*, Supplement No. 3 (23 April 2004), E/CN.4/2004/127; E/2004/23, p 330. See also: <https://www.ohchr.org/EN/Issues/Trafficking/TiP/Pages/Index.aspx> (accessed 20 February 2020).

788 These and other measures can be found in the UN's *Toolkit to Combat Trafficking in Persons*. Available at: <https://www.unodc.org/res/cld/bibliography/toolkit-to-combat-trafficking-in-persons_html/07-89375_Ebook1.pdf> (accessed 20 February 2020).

The *Implementation Handbook* describes article 35 as a 'failsafe' or 'safety net' provision, which is reinforced by OPSC (Hodgkin and Newell 2007: 531). The obvious elements of criminality associated with these activities make it a difficult subject on which to gather reliable data or analysis. The Committee characteristically recommends the establishment of strong monitoring mechanisms and supporting programmes and information campaigns to prevent trafficking. It also refers States to obligations under the SDG Indicator 8.7 which requires states to 'take immediate and effective measures to eradicate forced labour, end modern slavery and human trafficking and secure the prohibition and elimination of the worst forms of child labour, including recruitment and use of child soldiers, and by 2025 end child labour in all its forms'.

The Committee's Concluding Observations make a range of recommendations to states including the improvement of 'mechanisms and procedures for the identification and care of child victims of sale, sex trafficking and forced labour', and adequate training for professionals supporting such child victims.[789] Where prosecution is concerned, the Committee noted the low level of successful prosecutions in the case of Bosnia and Herzegovina and recommended training for judges and prosecutors 'on the strict application of the Criminal Code and the best interest of the child in legal proceedings in cases of trafficking, forced begging and forced marriage of children, so as to ensure that perpetrators of those criminal offences are prosecuted and adequately punished at all levels of jurisdiction'.[790] It also called for stronger training of law enforcement officers at all levels of the investigative processes, and for heightened community awareness of trafficking,[791] a recommendation echoed in the case of Malta, where the Committee called for strengthening of capacity for police officers, border guards and social workers.[792] It is often the most 'vulnerable and marginalized' children including asylum seekers, refugees and migrants who are at a particular risk of being trafficked and the Committee calls on states, for example Malta, to ensure plans to combat trafficking focus in particular on children facing the most vulnerable and marginalised situations.[793]

(V) OTHER FORMS OF EXPLOITATION (ART. 36)

Article 36
States parties shall protect the child against all other forms of exploitation prejudicial to any aspects of the child's welfare.

---

789 Portugal: CRC/C/PRT/CO/5-6 (27 September 2019) [43].
790 CRC/C/BIH/CO/5-6 (30 September 2019) [46].
791 Ibid.
792 CRC/C/MLT/CO/3-6 (26 June 2019) [43].
793 Ibid.

The Implementation Handbook states that 'article 36 was introduced to ensure that the "social" exploitation of children was recognized, along with their sexual and economic exploitation, though examples of what was meant by social exploitation were not provided' (Hodgkin and Newell 2007: 543). They offer several forms of exploitation not addressed under other articles: e.g. the exploitation of gifted children, children used in criminal activities, the exploitation of children in political activities (for example in violent demonstrations), the exploitation of children by the media and the exploitation of children by researchers or for the purposes of medical or scientific experimentation (Hodgkin and Newell 2007: 543–4).

3.7.9.5 Children in conflict with the law, child victims and witnesses of crimes and juvenile justice

The Committee has devoted a *Day General of Discussion*[794] (1995), a *Recommendation*[795] (1999), and *General Comment No. 10*[796] (2007) which was then replaced by *General Comment No. 24*[797] (2019); to the administration of juvenile justice. In the record of the *Day of General Discussion*, it was stated:

> The experience of the Committee has shown that the administration of juvenile justice is of practical concern in all regions of the world and in relation to all legal systems. The challenging and innovative philosophy arising from the Convention on the Rights of the Child and other United Nations standards adopted in the field . . . predicates a child-oriented system that recognises the child as a subject of fundamental rights and freedoms and ensures that all actions concerning him or her are guided by the best interests of the child as a primary consideration.[798]

The *Recommendation* recalls 'that since the beginning of its work, the administration of juvenile justice has received consistent and systematic attention from the Committee' and notes that the Committee's juvenile justice standards 'are in many instances not reflected in national legislation or practice, giving cause for serious concern'.[799] The Committee emphasises in *General Comment No. 24* that its objectives

---

[794] Committee on the Rights of the Child, *Day of General Discussion on 'The administration of juvenile justice'*, Report on the tenth session, CRC/C/46 (18 December 1995) [203–38].
[795] Committee on the Rights of the Child, *Recommendation No. 2: The administration of juvenile justice*, Report on the 22nd session, CRC/C/90 (7 December 1999) pp. 3–4.
[796] Committee on the Rights of the Child, *General Comment No. 10: Children's rights in juvenile justice*, CRC/C/GC/10 (25 April 2007).
[797] Committee on the Rights of the Child, *General Comment No. 24 (2019) on children's rights in the child justice system*, CRC/C/GC/24 (18 September 2019).
[798] Committee on the Rights of the Child, *Day of General Discussion on 'The administration of juvenile justice'*, Report on the tenth session, CRC/C/46 (18 December 1995) [206].
[799] Committee on the Rights of the Child, *Recommendation No. 2: The administration of juvenile justice*, Report on the 22nd session, CRC/C/90 (7 December 1999), pp 3–4.

are to develop and implement a *comprehensive* juvenile justice policy; an approach that should not be limited by the implementation of just articles 37 and 40, but will also take into account the 'general principles' and other relevant provisions of the Convention, in addition to promoting the integration in national juvenile justice policy of a range of existing international standards. Particular examples of these latter 'soft law' instruments were referred to in the *General Comment No. 10*.[800] They are:

- *United Nations Standard Minimum Rules for the Administration of Juvenile Justice*[801] ('the Beijing Rules');
- *United Nations Guidelines for the Prevention of Juvenile Delinquency*[802] (the 'Riyadh Guidelines'); and
- *United Nations Rules for the Protection of Juveniles Deprived of their Liberty*[803] ('the Havana Rules').

The Committee additionally recommends to States parties that they take account of the *Vienna Guidelines for Action on Children in the Criminal Justice System*,[804] and the *United Nations Rules for the Protection of Juveniles Deprived of their Liberty*.[805]

The implementation of *General Comment No. 24* (2019) on children's rights in the child justice system (replacing *General Comment No. 10* (2007)) 'reflects the developments that have occurred since 2007 as a result of the promulgation of international and regional standards, the Committee's jurisprudence, new knowledge about child and adolescent development, and evidence of effective practices, including those relating to restorative justice. It also reflects concerns such as the trends relating to the minimum age of criminal responsibility and the persistent use of deprivation of liberty'.[806] The objectives of the *General Comment* are multiple, and include guiding states towards a holistic implementation of child justice systems; prevention and early intervention; ensuring appropriate treatment of children in criminal proceedings; and expanding the use of non-custodial measures for children.

---

800 Committee on the Rights of the Child, *General Comment No. 10: Children's rights in juvenile justice*, CRC/C/GC/10 (25 April 2007) [4].
801 General Assembly, *United Nations Standard Minimum Rules for the Administration of Juvenile Justice* ('The Beijing Rules'): resolution / adopted by the General Assembly, UN Doc. A/RES/40/33 (29 November 1985).
802 General Assembly, *United Nations Guidelines for the Prevention of Juvenile Delinquency* ('The Riyadh Guidelines'): resolution / adopted by the General Assembly, UN Doc. A/RES/45/112 (14 December 1990).
803 General Assembly, *United Nations Rules for the Protection of Juveniles Deprived of Their Liberty* ('The Havana Rules'): resolution / adopted by the General Assembly, UN Doc. A/RES/45/113 (14 December 1990).
804 Economic and Social Council, *Administration of juvenile justice*, ECOSOC resolution, UN Doc. E/1997/30 (21 July 1997) 85–6.
805 General Assembly, *United Nations Rules for the Protection of Juveniles Deprived of Their Liberty*: resolution / adopted by the General Assembly, UN doc A/RES/45/113 (14 December 1990).
806 CRC/C/GC/24 (18 September 2019), [1].

(I) THE ADMINISTRATION OF JUVENILE JUSTICE (ARTICLE 40), THE EXISTENCE OF SPECIALIZED AND SEPARATE COURTS AND THE APPLICABLE MINIMUM AGE OF CRIMINAL RESPONSIBILITY

Article 40
1. States parties recognize the right of every child alleged as, accused of, or recognized as having infringed the penal law to be treated in a manner consistent with the promotion of the child's sense of dignity and worth, which reinforces the child's respect for the human rights and fundamental freedoms of others and which takes into account the child's age and the desirability of promoting the child's reintegration and the child's assuming a constructive role in society.

Article 40(2) additionally specifies particular guarantees to the child alleged as, or accused of, having infringed the penal law, including the presumption of innocence and the right to be informed promptly and directly of the charges against them. Article 40(3) obliges States parties to promote the establishment of laws, procedures, authorities and institutions 'specifically applicable to children' in conflict with penal law, and in particular to establish a minimum age of criminal responsibility. States are also obliged to seek measures other than judicial proceedings for such children. Article 40(4) stipulates that there should be a variety of dispositions (for example, foster care) as alternatives to 'institutional care'.

The Committee will be concerned where it identifies that a States party is failing to protect children from abuses in the administration of juvenile justice. For example, in the case of the Republic of Korea, the Committee's Concluding Observations included a number of concerns including State proposals to lower the age of criminal responsibility from 14 years to 13 years; the use of pre-emptive detention for 'crime-prone juveniles' under article 4(1)(3) of the Juvenile Act; violations of the rights of children to a fair trial including the exclusion of guardians and lack of due process; inappropriate detention conditions affected by overcrowding, lack of food provisions and less provisions for girls overall; children detained with adults; compulsory DNA and HIV testing; and a lack of non-custodial measures.[807] The Committee made a large number of recommendations, including urging the State to maintain a minimum age of 14 for criminal responsibility; establish a system of specialised child justice courts supported by adequate resources; adhere to article 40 and uphold the right to a fair and closed trial; repeal the 'crime-prone juveniles' provision of the Juvenile Act; promote non-custodial sentences; use detention as a measure of last resort only based on clear grounds; ensure all detention conditions comply with international standards; ensure no child is detained with adults; protect the privacy of children in detention; strengthen non-custodial measures to prevent re-offending; and ensure all children in juvenile justice situations are treated equally.[808]

---

807 CRC/C/KOR/CO/5–6 (27 September 2019) [46].
808 Ibid., [47].

In the case of Mozambique, referring to *General Comment No. 24* shortly after it was published, the Committee called on the state to 'bring its child justice system fully into line with the Convention and other relevant standards'.[809] It called for a number of measures to be implemented including full training for all personnel in the juvenile justice process including prosecutors, the police and other professional groups. It further recommended record-keeping of children in detention, and ensuring that child detention is only a measure of last resort.[810] Concerns were also raised with Japan's administration of juvenile justice, in particular the lowering of the 'minimum age of criminal punishment' from 16 to 14; the right to counsel not being systematically implemented; and as with the Republic of Korea, children designated as 'likely to commit crime' potentially being deprived of their liberty.[811] The Committee's recommendations included the early provision of qualified and independent legal aid for children in juvenile justice situations; the increase in use of non-judicial measures including diversion, probation, mediation and counselling to assist the children, and wherever possible, using non-custodial sentences.[812]

Overall, the Committee has frequently criticised the low age of criminal responsibility existing in some States, and notes with appreciation where the age of criminal responsibility has been raised. The Committee will also be concerned where a States party appears to have no specialised courts, customised to the needs of children, contrary to article 40(3) of the Convention. In some countries, the juvenile justice system may not have been established at all, or be at a very early stage of development. The Committee will also focus their attention on the protection of child victims and witnesses of crime. Finally, the Committee will typically recommend, particularly in relation to States parties whom it considers to have a poor record on juvenile justice standards, that the States party seek technical assistance in this area from the *United Nations Interagency Panel on Juvenile Justice* and its members, including the United Nations Office on Drugs and Crime (UNODC), UNICEF, OHCHR and NGOs and make use of the tools developed by the *Interagency Panel*.

(II) CHILDREN DEPRIVED OF THEIR LIBERTY, AND MEASURES TO ENSURE THAT ANY ARREST, DETENTION OR IMPRISONMENT OF A CHILD SHALL BE USED AS MEASURES OF LAST RESORT AND FOR THE SHORTEST APPROPRIATE TIME AND THAT LEGAL AND OTHER ASSISTANCE IS PROMPTLY PROVIDED (ART. 37 (B)–(D))

Article 37: States Parties shall ensure that:
(b) No child shall be deprived of his or her liberty unlawfully or arbitrarily. The arrest, detention or imprisonment of a child shall be in conformity with the law and shall be used only as a measure of last resort and for the shortest appropriate period of time;

---

809 CRC/C/MOZ/CO/3–4 (1 October 2019) [47].
810 Ibid.
811 CRC/C/JPN/CO/4–5 (5 March 2019) [44].
812 Ibid., [45].

(c) Every child deprived of liberty shall be treated with humanity and respect for the inherent dignity of the human person, and in a manner which takes into account the needs of persons of his or her age. In particular, every child deprived of liberty shall be separated from adults unless it is considered in the child's best interest not to do so and shall have the right to maintain contact with his or her family through correspondence and visits, save in exceptional circumstances;

(d) Every child deprived of his or her liberty shall have the right to prompt access to legal and other appropriate assistance, as well as the right to challenge the legality of the deprivation of his or her liberty before a court or other competent, independent and impartial authority, and to a prompt decision on any such action.

The Committee will be concerned where children are subjected to pre-trial detention without the necessary safeguards. For example, it found in relation to Japan that children designated as 'likely to commit crimes' may be deprived of their liberty, and that children can be sentenced to life imprisonment. The Committee recommended that the State ensures that 'pretrial and post-trial deprivation of liberty are used as a measure of last resort and for the shortest possible period of time and that such deprivation of liberty is reviewed on a regular basis with a view to its withdrawal'.[813] Implementation of these recommendations would bring the State in to compliance with article 37(b).

(III) THE SENTENCING OF CHILDREN, IN PARTICULAR THE PROHIBITION OF CAPITAL PUNISHMENT AND LIFE IMPRISONMENT (ARTICLE 37 (A)) AND THE EXISTENCE OF ALTERNATIVE SANCTIONS BASED ON A RESTORATIVE APPROACH

Article 37: States Parties shall ensure that:
(a) No child shall be subjected to torture or other cruel, inhuman or degrading treatment or punishment. Neither capital punishment nor life imprisonment without possibility of release shall be imposed for offences committed by persons below eighteen years of age

As mentioned above under other categories, the Committee will draw particular attention to each of these provisions within the Convention, and has called for States to '[r]econsider the use of life imprisonment and indeterminate sentences for crimes committed by children and apply the specialized parole system to ensure that detention is used for the shortest appropriate period'.[814]

---

813 CRC/C/JPN/CO/4–5 (5 March 2019) [45].
814 Ibid.

(IV) PHYSICAL AND PSYCHOLOGICAL RECOVERY AND SOCIAL REINTEGRATION (ARTICLE 39)

Article 39
States Parties shall take all appropriate measures to promote physical and psychological recovery and social reintegration of a child victim of: any form of neglect, exploitation, or abuse; torture or any other form of cruel, inhuman or degrading treatment or punishment; or armed conflicts. Such recovery and reintegration shall take place in an environment which fosters the health, self-respect and dignity of the child.

As mentioned above under other categories, the Committee will draw particular attention to each of these provisions within the Convention. For example, in the case of Australia the Committee called on the state to '[a]pply a child-friendly and multisectoral approach to avoid re-traumatization of child victims, and ensure that cases are promptly recorded, investigated and prosecuted, and that perpetrators are duly sanctioned'.[815] Further to this, it called for the national mechanism for the prevention of torture to have access to places where children are placed, in order to provide its services.

(V) THE TRAINING ACTIVITIES DEVELOPED FOR ALL PROFESSIONALS INVOLVED WITH THE SYSTEM OF JUVENILE JUSTICE, INCLUDING JUDGES AND MAGISTRATES, PROSECUTORS, LAWYERS, LAW ENFORCEMENT OFFICIALS, IMMIGRATION OFFICERS AND SOCIAL WORKERS, ON THE PROVISIONS OF THE CONVENTION, THE OPTIONAL PROTOCOLS AS APPLICABLE, AND OTHER RELEVANT INTERNATIONAL INSTRUMENTS IN THE FIELD OF JUVENILE JUSTICE, INCLUDING THE GUIDELINES ON JUSTICE IN MATTERS INVOLVING CHILD VICTIMS AND WITNESSES OF CRIME (ECONOMIC AND SOCIAL COUNCIL RESOLUTION 2005/20, ANNEX)

These steps are outlined in numerous Committee Concluding Observations, as outlined previously.

3.7.9.6 Children in armed conflicts (articles 38 and 39)

Article 38
1. States parties undertake to respect and to ensure respect for rules of international humanitarian law applicable to them in armed conflicts which are relevant to the child.

2. States parties shall take all feasible measures to ensure that persons who have not attained the age of fifteen years do not take a direct part in hostilities.

---

815 CRC/C/AUS/CO/5–6 (30 September 2019).

3. States parties shall refrain from recruiting any person who has not attained the age of fifteen years into their armed forces. In recruiting among those persons who have attained the age of fifteen years but who have not attained the age of eighteen years, States parties shall endeavour to give priority to those who are oldest.

4. In accordance with their obligations under international humanitarian law to protect the civilian population in armed conflicts, States parties shall take all feasible measures to ensure protection and care of children who are affected by an armed conflict.

Article 39
States parties shall take all appropriate measures to promote physical and psychological recovery and social reintegration of a child victim of: any form of neglect, exploitation, or abuse; torture or any other form of cruel, inhuman or degrading treatment or punishment; or armed conflicts. Such recovery and reintegration shall take place in an environment which fosters the health, self-respect and dignity of the child.

The age at which children should be able to participate in armed conflicts was one of the four areas of controversy in the drafting history of the Convention (Cantwell 1992: 26). To an extent and because of the unsatisfactory compromises reached in relation to the drafting of article 38, there remained an appetite within the international community to campaign for an Optional Protocol to raise the age to 18 years and provide more comprehensive protection in this area. Further international recognition of the criminality of conscripting or enlisting children under the age of 15 into national armed forces and non-state militias arrived with the *Rome Statute of the International Criminal Court*[816] (1998). The *Optional Protocol to the Convention on the Rights of the Child on the involvement of children in armed conflict*[817] (OPAC) followed in 2000 (section 3.6.2 above). The subject of children's involvement in armed conflict is given more detailed treatment in Chapter 9 in this book.

The Committee has made some interesting observations in relation to the case of Omar Khadr, a Canadian citizen who was the first person since the Second World War to be prosecuted in a military commission for war crimes committed while still a minor. He was captured by American forces in Afghanistan in 2002 (when he was 15 years and ten months old), and detained at Guantanamo Bay detention camp in Cuba. His father had been a close family friend of the late terrorist leader Osama bin Laden, and had been accused of being a fundraiser for al-Qaida. Omar pleaded guilty in October 2010 in a diplomatic (United States and Canada) plea agreement to murder and providing support for terrorist activities. He accepted an eight-year sentence, with the possibility of a transfer to

---

816 Opened for signature 17 July 1998, 2187 UNTS 90 (entered into force 1 July 2002).
817 25 May 2000, 2173 UNTS 222 (entered into force 12 February 2002).

Canada after at least one year, to serve the remainder of the sentence there. On 29 September 2012 Khadr was repatriated to Canada. Under Canadian law he was eligible for parole in mid-2013. The Committee welcomed his return to the custody of the State party.

> However, the Committee is concerned that as a former child soldier, Omar K[h]adr has not been accorded the rights and appropriate treatment under the Convention. In particular, the Committee is concerned that he experienced grave violations of his human rights, which the Canadian Supreme Court[818] recognized, including his maltreatment during his years of detention in Guantanamo, and that he has not been afforded appropriate redress and remedies for such violations.[819]

The Committee urged the States party, *inter alia*, to 'promptly provide a rehabilitation program for Omar K[h]adr that is consistent with the Paris Principles for the rehabilitation of former child soldiers'.[820] Following several appeals, Khadr was finally released on bail on 9 May 2015, and he subsequently won a lawsuit against the Canadian government where he alleged that they had violated his rights, settling the action for $10.5 million (Canadian) in 2017.

3.8 Concluding remarks

This chapter has provided an in-depth consideration of the provisions of the Convention and its three Optional Protocols. This detailed background on all relevant sources including *General Comments* and Concluding Observations, provides the essential basis for comprehensive considerations of the particular areas of focus in the remainder of this book.

---

818 *Canada (Prime Minister) v Khadr*, 2010 SCC 3, [2010] 1 SCR 44.
819 CRC/C/CAN/CO/3-4 (5 October 2012) [77].
820 CRC/C/CAN/CO/3-4 (5 October 2012) [78].

Chapter 4

Childhood in the digital age

4.1 Introduction

Until recently, analysis of children's experiences, social relations were characterised by face-to-face, physical communication as the primary means through which their everyday lives were constituted (Livingstone and Blum-Ross 2017). The advent of new digital technologies has been marked by a frenzy that often accompanies the advent of new cultural forms. In recent years, as an increasing number of children go online around the world, digital media is radically changing 'childhood' (UNICEF Report 2017).[1] The pace with which networked and online media and information technologies have become embedded in children's lives 'has been overwhelming, triggering a revival of public hyperbole about media-related opportunities and risks, along with a burgeoning of argumentation and experimentation among social researchers keen to explore the significance of "the digital age" for children and childhood'(Livingstone and Blum-Ross 2017: 1). And as the technological landscape changes, childhood and youth, too, transform (Craft 2013: 1). Devices like smartphones and tablets are changing how and where children go online. Mobile phones enable children to access the internet in the privacy of their bedrooms or from a friend's house (Mascheroni and Cuman 2014: 6; Hasebrink et al. 2011: 7). The result is online access that is more personal, more private and less supervised. Children and young people are increasingly connected around the clock, and have a parallel existence in digital space, seamlessly integrated with their actual lives. They are skilful collaborators, capable of knowledge-making as well as information-seeking. They engage in social networks, they navigate digital gaming and they generate and manipulate digital content. They experiment in new ways with forms of their own social face (Craft 2013: 2). The emergence of the 'cyberspace' has ruptured the familial dynamics.

Young children growing up in the digital world of the 21st century have access to a wider range of information communication technologies (ICT) and engage with this technology at a younger age than ever before (Buckingham 2004). In

---

1 UNICEF, *The State of the World's Children – Children in a Digital World* (2017).

fact, technology is becoming a normal part of young children's daily existence. The study on childhood in the digital era has drawn researchers from various disciplines including media and mass communications, psychology and law. It would appear a consensus is emerging that, in different degrees, the digital space is reshaping the 'traditional interests of childhood studies – identity, friendship, learning, family, play, disadvantage, risk and beyond' (Livingstone and Blum-Ross 2017: 2).

This chapter discusses childhood in the digital age. Because of the omnipresence of the internet and increased digital use by children across the world, this is a critical area in the study of childhood studies. The chapter highlights the trends in the usage of the digital space and history of the media consumption by youth. As noted earlier, the recurrent claim by researchers is that digital technology has transformed childhood. The chapter draws on theories of childhood discussed in Chapter 1 as well as introducing other theories related to children and digitalisation. The abiding theme of the chapter is the ambivalence and dialogue between both protective and opportunity-seeking strategies in handling the challenges posed by children's occupation of digital media. The chapter attempts to capture both sides of the debate. A ground-breaking report by UNICEF, *The State of the World's Children – Children in a Digital World* (2017), has been useful in capturing recent research on global usage of the internet by the internet.

4.2 Children and the internet: an overview

The internet has been described as 'the largest experiment involving anarchy in history' (Schmidt and Cohen 2013). Hundreds of millions of people are constantly creating and consuming a large amount of 'digital content in an online world that is not truly bound by terrestrial laws' (Schmidt and Cohen 2013). The origins of the internet lie within the public sector since the mid-to-late 1980s. However, the impetus behind its growth has been the private sector, propelled by the innovation of small start-ups that succeeded by creating a market for new products and services or by disrupting old business models (Leiner et al. 1997: 6). The complexities in the usage of the internet lie in its transnational nature and the fact that it is largely blind to age, treating children and adults equally.

Researchers have observed that the new media exercise an extraordinary power to mould children's consciousness, to determine their identities and to dictate the patterns of their everyday lives (Buckingham 2004; Kardefelt-Winther 2017). Media studies researchers examine the 'media effects' of digital technologies. In this field, debate has emerged on the negative and positive effects of digital usage by children since the internet was established. On the one hand, children's avenues for participation, their resources for education and their circles of connection for friendship and intimacy are all expanded and more accessible (boyd 2008; Dahlgren and Olsson 2008; Willett 2008). Furthermore, access to, and use of, the internet can be a powerful enabler of the realisation of many Sustainable Development Goals (SDGs) that directly impact on children's wellbeing. Access to the internet is closely linked to the ability to receive information and to exercise one's right of freedom of expression, and it can be regarded as a primary precondition for the enabling of the fulfilment of other digital rights, such as participation and provision. Despite suggestions of 'anarchy', ICT has provided benefits to users, including children. ICT forms a valuable learning tool and gives children access to a world they have not previously experienced.

On the other hand, there is growing body of evidence on harmful content and activity that people experience online, resulting in harm. As numerous cases over the years have demonstrated, severe harm can manifest itself as much in mental distress as in real physical injuries, including self-harm and suicide. Major areas of concern in terms of harm include pro-eating disorders and pro-suicide websites as well as cyber bullying and online child sexual abuse and exploitation (UNICEF Report 2017). Digital technology and interactivity pose significant risks to children's safety, privacy and wellbeing, magnifying threats and harms that many children already face offline and making already-vulnerable children even more vulnerable. In fact, it is becoming difficult to separate their online and offline lives. So, even as ICT has made it easier to share knowledge and collaborate, it is acknowledged that it has also made it easier to produce, distribute and share harmful material and other illegal content that exploits and abuses children. A conflict now exists between the child's right to freedom of expression and access to the opportunities it creates and the child's right to be protected from harm.

This poses difficult questions on the relationship between children and the so-called digital space because to manage children's online experiences, policy relating to opportunities must be integrated with, rather than remain entirely separate from that relating to risk and safety (Livingstone 2014a: 2). These realities have divided the discourse on children and the digital space into 'protection' (against risk and harm) on the one hand and 'participation' (or provision and opportunities). These also fit into risk-based and rights-based (or rights first) perspectives which are currently informing internet governance debates. The former premises itself, principally, on protection of children while the latter, the broader rights and encourages children's participation online. These approaches frame the discussion in this chapter.

At the global level, the international policy landscape is characterised by a patchwork of old laws and emerging policies. At domestic level, several countries have promulgated regulatory measures to protect children online. The internet governance approaches to children's use of the internet call on us to reflect on the various theoretical constructs on childhood discussed in Chapter 1. The conception of childhood influences and motivates the reactions and approaches of governments to internet use by children. Policy formulation at domestic level has tended to lean more towards protection than participation. Much of the concern surrounding children's participation online and the 'protectionist' approach is based on an implicit assumption that the child is vulnerable, a mere passive recipient of information and behaviour, and thus deserves protection. Thus, the right to protection has tended to take priority in theory, policy and practice, now online as, traditionally, offline. However, some observers argue that the risked-based approaches are evidence of 'moral panic' (Livingstone 2011; Facer 2012). A moral panic suggests 'a panic or overreaction to forms of deviance or wrong doing believed to be threats to the moral order' (Drislane and Parkinson 2016). Marwick (2008) describes the same as 'technopanics', which pathologise young people's use of digital technology.

There have been propositions of new legal responses to the digital era. The *United Nations Convention on the Rights of the Child* (UNCRC), the centrepiece of the international protective framework, came into force just about the time when the digital age was beginning. Some observers have argued that the Convention has been outpaced by technological development and was no longer fit for purpose. During a Day of General Discussion on 'Digital media and children's rights' called by the Committee on the Rights of the Child (CtRC) in 2014, the possibilities of adopting a General Comment, a new Optional Protocol or even a new Convention on digital media and children's rights were mooted. However, some participants cautioned that new legal instruments may create uncertainties. It may, instead, be better to build upon existing norms and standards and ensure their effective implementation. In the end, the general view appeared to be that, although the UNCRC was formulated in the pre-digital era, 'the rights enshrined in it remained as relevant as ever' (Livingstone 2014b: 4). The Convention places emphasis on children's rights and agency and, therefore, their access to information, participation, freedom of thought and expression, and freedom of association. These are seen to also apply to the digital age. The application of the Convention rights in the digital context is outlined in Table 4.2.

It is, however, recognised that there is still an absence of clarity on a new, overarching international standard for children's rights in a digital era. In light of this, some scholars have argued for the introduction of a General Comment on children and digital rights as 'compelling and urgent' (Livingstone et al. 2017: 3) As a matter of practice, treaty bodies publish their interpretation of the provisions of the respective human rights treaties in the form of 'general comments'. In this case, rather than introduce a new legal instrument on children's rights, the General Comment would interpret provisions of the UNCRC within the context of the digital age. The CtRC has since responded to the call with a 'Concept Note for a General Comment on children's rights in relation to the digital environment', inviting input from interested parties.[2] The Note said the General Comment would clarify how this rapidly evolving environment impacts on the full range of children's rights in positive and negative ways. The purpose of the General Comment would be to strengthen the case for greater action and elaborate what measures are required by States in order to meet their obligations to promote and protect children's rights in and through the digital environment,

---

2 Committee on the Rights of the Child Concept Note for a General Comment on Children's Rights in Relation to the Digital Environment. Available at: <www.ohchr.org/EN/HRBodies/CRC/Pages/GCChildrensRightsRelationDigitalEnvironment.aspx> (last accessed 4 January 2020).

and to ensure that other actors, including business enterprises, meet their responsibilities. Several states and regional organisations had, at the time of publishing, made submissions for the Comment.

As the discussion in this chapter unfolds, it becomes clear that both the risk-based (protection) and rights-based (participation) approaches are not mutually exclusive. There is clear evidence of online harms and undeniable benefits for children's participation in the digital space. The challenge is to formulate interventions which recognise both. Unlike some domestic approaches, international regulatory frameworks like the UNCRC seem to align with a 'mixed approach', which recognises children's own participation in decision-making and a conception of children as having distinct rights that can be asserted, both morally and legally. This approach resonates with the now dominant sociological image of the child as a competent, autonomous and an active social agent. The Convention also emphasises protection and provision. The Council of Europe Strategy for the rights of the child[3] includes a focus on children's rights on the internet, which is now reinforced by the newly adopted Recommendation of the Committee of Ministers to member States on Guidelines to respect, protect and fulfil the rights of the child in the digital environment.[4]

4.3 Children and trends in internet usage

The proposed General Comment by the CtRC reflects the seriousness with which the possible effects, or 'perils', of digital media have been regarded. The intervention demonstrates concerns not only on online harms but also equitable access to the internet by children across the world. Children's internet culture now intersects all dimensions of childhood (Livingstone 2013).

UNICEF's flagship report, *The State of the World's Children – Children in a Digital World* (2017), examines the different ways digital technology is shaping children's lives and life chances, identifying dangers as well as opportunities. Children are now born in homes filled with a panoply of digital devices. Thus, childhood and young people's live are increasingly mediated by these digital technologies. The profile of child user is getting younger with the so-called 'digitods' (Leathers et al. 2013). In the shifting technological landscape, childhood and youth are changing. Connectivity around the clock, with a parallel existence in virtual space, is seamlessly integrated with actual lives (Craft 2013: 1). As children grow, the capacity of digitalisation to shape their life experiences grows with them, offering seemingly limitless opportunities to learn and to socialise, to be counted and to be heard

---

[3] Council of Europe Strategy for the Rights of the Child (2016–2021), Council of Europe, March 2016.
[4] Recommendation CM/Rec(2018)7 of the Committee of Ministers to member States on Guidelines to respect, protect and fulfil the rights of the child in the digital environment (Adopted by the Committee of Ministers on 4 July 2018 at the 1321st meeting of the Ministers' Deputies).

(UNICEF 2017). Organised efforts to encourage, cultivate and channel children's participation using digital tools are varied and growing in scope. While the narrative of 'harm' has been dominant, the internet also creates 'opportunities' for children and young people. To be unconnected in a digital world is to be deprived of new opportunities to learn, communicate and develop skills for the 21st-century workplace (UNICEF 2017: 43).

4.3.1 Digital divide

According to the International Telecommunication Union (ITU)'s 2018 report, 2019 marked the first full year when more than half of the world (51.2%, or 3.9 billion people) had begun to participate in the global digital economy. At a household level, most households in the world now have access to internet at home (57.8% in 2018, up from 18.9% in 2005) (ITU 2018). UNICEF estimates that one-third of internet users globally are children, with the proportion of internet users likely to be higher in lower income countries where the internet is rapidly penetrating all spheres of public life. However, there are concerns over the so-called 'digital divide'. Digital divide refers to the distinction between those who have internet access and are able to make use of new services offered on the world wide web, and those who are excluded from these services.[5] The digital divide can be classified according to criteria that describe the difference in participation according to gender, age, education, income, social groups or geographic location.[6] The definition of the digital divide has expanded beyond differences in access and in ICT investment to include differences in the knowledge and skills required for effective use.

In a world where digital access and digital skills increasingly influence children's futures, UNICEF finds the state of global connectivity troubling. Just over 29% of the world's youth (15–24 years old) – or 346 million – do not use the internet. Africa has the highest share of non-users. The key factors impacting on the divide are socio-economic, gender, educational and geographical. Digital divides reflect prevailing economic gaps, amplifying the advantages of children from wealthier backgrounds and failing to deliver opportunities to the poorest and most disadvantaged children. For children in developing countries, challenges of poor-quality connectivity are likely compounded by high data costs – most of the countries with the least affordable mobile-broadband prices are also among the least developed countries in Africa and Asia and the Pacific.

The digital divide is proving stubbornly persistent in terms of access to broadband internet, including the challenge of extending last-mile access to infrastructure to remote and rural communities. Nearly 9 out of 10 of the young people currently not using the internet live in Africa, Asia or the Pacific. These disparities in access are

---

5 UNESCO-UNEVOC International Centre for Technical and Vocational Education and Training EU (2016) Citing EU Commission (Eurostat) 2016. Available at: <https://unevoc.unesco.org/go.php?q=TVETipedia+Glossary+A-Z&term=Digital+divide> (accessed 4 January 2020).
6 Ibid.

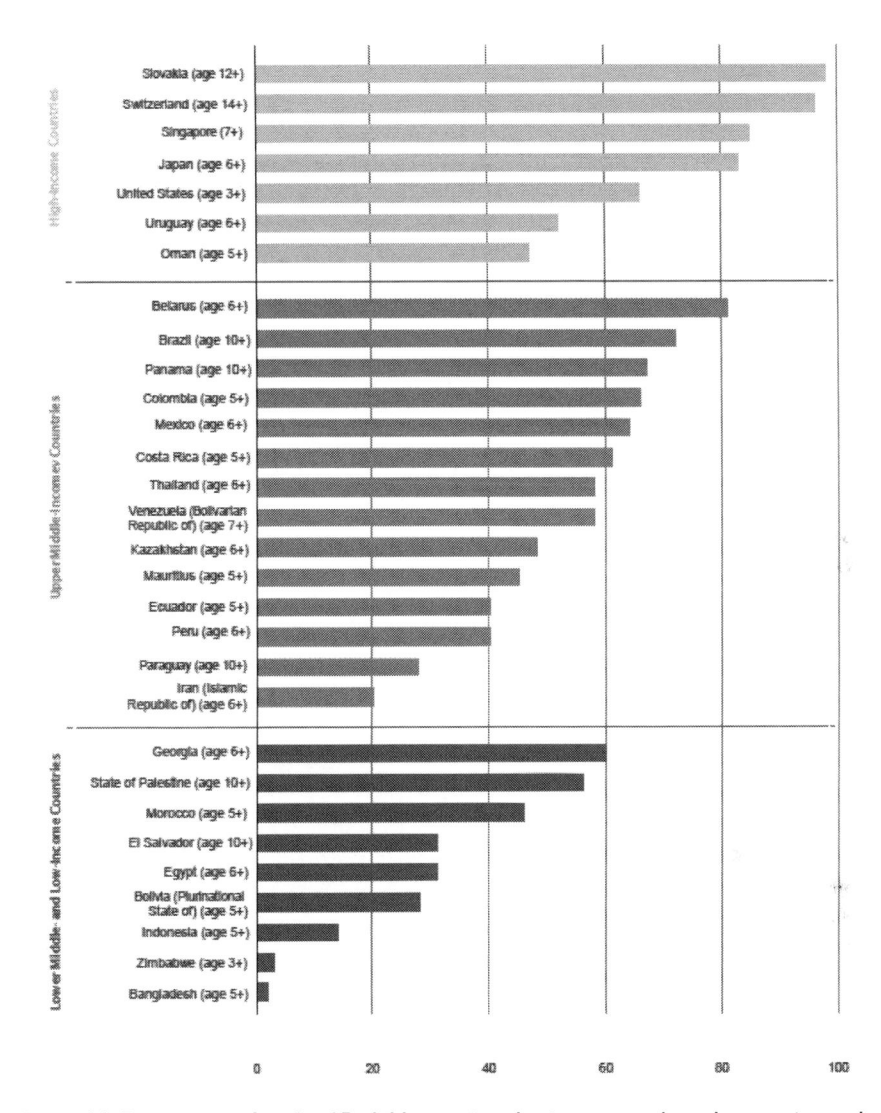

Figure 4.1 Percentage of under-15 children using the internet, selected countries and territories, 2012–2016.

Source: UNICEF 2017: 47.

particularly striking in some low-income countries. In Bangladesh and Zimbabwe, fewer than 1 in 20 children under the age of 15 uses the internet (Figure 4.1).

But it is not only in low-income countries that children face barriers of access. Even in high-connectivity countries, family income does much to determine children's ability to meet their online needs. For example, in the UK, consumers in rural areas continue to be more likely to receive poor broadband speeds: 17% of premises in the UK's rural areas cannot receive decent broadband services, compared to just 2% in urban areas. This urban – rural divide is particularly stark in Northern Ireland and Scotland. In Northern Ireland, less than 1% of urban properties cannot get decent broadband, compared with 23% of rural properties. In Scotland, 2% of urban properties cannot get decent broadband, compared with 27% in rural Scotland. Perhaps, these are more cases of quality of service than availability.

But digital divides do not merely separate the connected and the unconnected. They go deeper, concerning how people – including children – use ICT, as well as the quality of the online experience. Both of these can vary greatly, reflecting factors that include the level of users' skills and education, the types of device they use, family income and the availability of content in their own language. Some children going online for the first time find themselves in a digital space where their language, culture and concerns are notable by their absence.

4.4 Gender gap in digital access

The digital divide is also gendered. The world over, more men than women use the internet; what's more, this gap is not narrowing but widening. Globally, 12% more men than women used the internet in 2017. In India, less than one-third of internet users are female. The Broadband Commission for Digital Development was launched by the ITU and the United Nations Educational, Scientific and Cultural Organization (UNESCO) in response to then UN Secretary-General Ban Ki-moon's call to step up efforts to meet the Millennium Development Goals (MDGs). The 2003 World Summit on the Information Society (WSIS) viewed ICTs as key resources for women's empowerment:

> We are committed to ensuring that the Information Society enables women's empowerment and their full participation on the basis of equality in all spheres of society and in all decision-making processes. To this end, we should mainstream a gender equality perspective and use ICTs as a tool to that end.
> (ITU 2003)

One of the main outcomes of the UN Conference on Sustainable Development (Rio+20), held in Rio de Janeiro in June 2012, was the agreement by Member States to launch a process for developing a set of SDGs, of which Goal 5 refers to gender equality and empowerment of women and involves the use of enabling technologies, in particular ICTs.[7]

---

7 United Nations, 'Outcome document of the United Nations Conference on Sustainable Development Rio de Janeiro', Brazil, 20–22 June 2012.

However, the gender digital divide was proving 'incredibly difficult to overcome, reflecting broader social gender inequalities', according to the Broadband Commission for Digital Development's 2015 report.[8] ITU gender-disaggregated data for 91 economies show an overall wider global gender gap in 2017 than in 2013 (Davaki 2018). A survey by the GSM Association (GSMA) of 22 low- and middle-income countries in 2015 found that various socio-economic and cultural barriers – among them social norms, education levels, lack of technical literacy and lack of confidence – tend to keep girls and women from using mobile phones (GSMA 2015). The Organisation for Economic Co-operation and Development (OECD) noted girls' relatively lower educational enrolment in disciplines that would allow them to perform well in a digital world – such as science, technology, engineering and mathematics, as well as information and communication technologies (OECD 2018). This, coupled with women's and girls' more limited use of digital tools, could lead to widening gaps and greater inequality (OECD 2018). Women used phones less frequently and less intensively than men, especially for higher-level uses such as accessing the internet.

Country-level examples give a sense of the kinds of barriers girls and women confront. In India, for example, where only 29% of all internet users are female, girls in rural areas often face restrictions on their use of ICTs solely because of their gender.[9] One village governing body in rural Rajasthan stated that girls were not to use mobile phones or social media. Another village in Uttar Pradesh banned unmarried girls from using mobile phones (and from wearing jeans and T-shirts).[10] This council believed that mobile phone use would increase crimes against girls and women. In Sri Lanka, a 2015 national study[11] of 11- to 18-year-olds found that girls accounted for only one-third of adolescents using computers and mobile phones to go online. In focus group discussions, parents revealed that they often restricted girls from accessing the internet (UNICEF Sri Lanka 2015).

There are potentially serious consequences for girls excluded from the digital age. They may be unable to access online services and information, including about issues related to their health and sexuality, such as HIV and puberty; they may face barriers to furthering their education and to developing the skills necessary in the global economy of the 21st century; they may not be able to access social and political information that affects them; and they may be excluded from

---

8 ITU and UNESCO, Broadband Commission for Digital Development, Geneva, Switzerland, 2015, p. 9.
9 UNICEF India, *Child Online Protection in India*, UNICEF India, New Delhi, 2016, p. 46; and DNA India, 'Uttar Pradesh: Muslim village panchayat bans jeans, mobile phones for girls', *Daily News & Analysis* (DNA), 20 September 2015.
10 UNICEF India, *Child Online Protection in India*, UNICEF India, New Delhi, 2016, p. 46; and DNA India, 'Uttar Pradesh: Muslim village panchayat bans jeans, mobile phones for girls', *Daily News & Analysis* (DNA), 20 September 2015.
11 UNICEF, *Children in a Digital World*, 2017. The study included a sample of 5,349 children from government, private and international schools.

opportunities to make their voices heard (UNICEF 2017). Unless these gaps in access and skills are identified and closed, rather than being an equaliser of opportunity, connectivity may deepen inequity, reinforcing inter-generational cycles of deprivation. Facilitating access to the internet could empower girls and women.

4.5 Theories of childhood in the digital context

For better or worse, the internet will soon be inseparable from the personal development and social lives of the large majority of children worldwide. The use of digital technology leads to a range of activities that engage children in online practices, but it is also the case that the online domain cannot be separated from the offline domain in these experiences (Burke and Marsh 2014). In high-income contexts, it is becoming difficult to draw the line between the two. In the United States, for example, 92% of 13- to 17-year-olds report going online daily. Mobile devices, particularly smartphones – and 73% of this age group have smartphones – enable some to be online 'almost constantly' (Lenhart 2015: 16). The picture is similar in Europe, where children access the internet from multiple locations and using multiple devices (Mascheroni and Cuman 2014) especially smartphones but also desktop and laptop computers, tablets and game consoles.

Evidence from high-connectivity countries suggests children are going online at ever-younger ages. In Bulgaria, for example, the age at which children first used the internet was commonly ten in 2010 but had dropped to seven by 2016 (Hajdinjak et al. 2016). In China, children under ten made up 2.9% of all internet users in 2016, up from 2.7% in 2015. In Brazil, the proportion of nine- and ten-year-olds using the internet increased from 35% in 2012 to 37% in 2013 (Doneda and Rossini 2015: 230). It is not uncommon for children who are not yet even teenagers to own their own phones. A survey in Algeria, Egypt, Iraq and Saudi Arabia in 2013 found that age ten or 12 was the most common age for receiving a first mobile phone. In 2015, age ten was found to be the common age for a child to first own a mobile phone in the Philippines, while in Honduras it was age 12.

In varying degrees, the digital space is reconfiguring the traditional interests of childhood studies – identity, friendship, learning, family, play, disadvantage, risk and beyond. A significant number of scholars agree that digital technology is increasingly changing childhood (e.g. Livingstone 2013; Craft 2013). The theories of childhood discussed in Chapter 1 are germane to the discussion on children in the digital age. The welfare, authoritarian and laissez-faire models help in interpreting digital use and policy. We shall also discuss and refer to theoretical concepts associated with the digital age such as 'media effects', 'parental mediation' and 'individualism'.

Over the last 30 years, researchers have demonstrated how 'childhood' is produced not only through the practices of family, schooling, medicine and law, but through the management of children's participation in or exclusion from different spaces. Vygotsky (1978) theorised that children became enculturated into the social world as they interacted with their parents and with other significant people in their lives. A dominant feature of Western ideas of childhood since the 19th century has been its association with private rather than public space and the construction of public and adult space as a site of threat to children. The quarantining of children into specific spaces such as homes and schools is central to the production and maintenance of the 'standard model' of adult – child relations. This model produces specific identities for children, as dependent and vulnerable, and also specific identities for adults as protectors and as competent actors in public space (Facer 2012). This perception, in which the parent has a central role, has informed social policy perspectives at domestic level.

The 'welfarist model' is where 'the state intervenes, at least with coercive techniques, when clear dysfunctions are evident'. The welfarist approach aims at protecting children who are seen as vulnerable members of society in need of guidance and control (see Chapter 1). The regulation of access to playgrounds or city streets, to bars or cinemas according to age, all served to construct different ideas of childhood and of adult – child relations (Holloway and Valentine 2000). At the heart of this idea of childhood is the construction of public space as potentially dangerous for children. Children are viewed as passive consumers of a culture already established by adults through socialisation. An 'authoritarian approach' sets out to compel and prohibit certain family behaviour while the laissez-faire model eschews state intervention and regards family life as private not warranting legal intervention.

It is evident, at least at the domestic level, that the welfarist approach, and to some extent, the authoritarian model, have influenced most states' responses to the explosion of the internet and its usage by children. Public policy is built around the child as vulnerable. In the UK, for example, programmes on 'safeguarding' have seen social workers, child protection officers and organisations such as Children and Family Court Advisory and Support Service (Cafcass) intervening with care proceedings in cases of child exploitation, which includes radicalisation. Schools and childcare providers are enjoined 'to be aware of 'the increased risk of online radicalisation, as terrorist organisations such as ISIL seek to radicalise young people through the use of social media and the internet'. The anxieties on the effects of the internet also catalysed the release of a White Paper by the UK government on 'online harms' (4.5.1.1).

The spaces for development have traditionally revolved around schools and homes which have been subjected to institutional and cultural norms and regulatory oversight, are now confronted by socio-technical assemblages 'built on a wholly different foundation' (Coleman 1982: 123). Staksrud argues that the internet has weakened traditional institutions because it was 'intentionally designed to maximise efficiency, with the least possible amount of central control' (2013: 119).

However, the 'moral panic', which brings together media, political, religious and judicial spheres to manage a potential disruption to the status quo, is a familiar and recurring social response to children's use of new leisure technologies (Baker 1989). Whenever the introduction of a new mass medium is defined as a threat to the young, we can expect a campaign by adults to regulate, ban or censor, followed by a lessening of interest until the appearance of a new medium reopens public debate. Each new panic develops as if it were the first time such issues have been debated in public and yet the debates are strikingly similar (Springhall 1998: 7). Postman (1983) traces the changing nature of childhood and youth back the introduction of television which punctured a Western post-Second World War 'institutional cocooning' perspective on childhood (Lee 2001: 155). As children's lives were more confined to the home, the home began to take on protective characteristics which, according to Lee (2001), underpinned its function as a cocoon. Cocooning was, according to Cunningham (1995, 2006), characterised by the home taking precedence as the cradle of childhood, as children moved away from taking on an economic role.

Research on parental mediation of children's use of media, conducted mainly in relation to television, shows that parents tend to combine positive and negative strategies, from the relatively open, non-directional strategy of parent – child co-viewing or sharing the media experience to more restrictive or controlling strategies (Bybee et al. 1982; Dorr et al. 1989; Van Der Bulck and Van Den Bergh 2000). Craft (2013: 2) noted that in the UK,

> the family was increasingly protected by the introduction of the Welfare State following the Beveridge Report (1942) which aimed to provide some support to families in facing five challenges facing society at the time, namely disease, ignorance, want, squalor and idleness.

Cocooning was thus facilitated by such State support and the economic boom which led initially to gendered roles with men earning their living outside the home and women on the whole responsible for making the home and raising children (Craft 2013). In essence, the theory can closely be linked to the 'welfarist' model of childhood. Although, moving into the 21st century, the boundaries of the home are increasingly permeable in many ways, the home continues to be idealised as a place of safety (Harden 2000).

Parental mediation theory posits that parents utilise different interpersonal communication strategies in their attempts to mediate and mitigate the negative effects of the media in their children's lives. Clark (2011: 325).) In the digital age, the so-called 'digital parenting' assumes that interpersonal interactions about media that take place between parents and their children play a role in socialising children into society:

> In a sense, then, although the theory grew out of an interest in the negative effects of the media, it also sought to explore the positive ways in which other factors within a young person's environment – namely, the child's parents and their intentional efforts at mediation – might mitigate the negative effects that television was presumed to have on young people's cognitive development.
> (Clark 2011: 325–6)

The emergence of the internet has unsettled these familial dynamics. In the late 1990s, parents were enticed by special offers to purchase computers (Facer 2012). Soon the internet emerged and the so-called 'digital turn' arrived. Children were repeatedly presented as adept at using new technologies and at risk of being disadvantaged by not having access to the internet. What began as a means of electronic information transmission – room-sized computer to room-sized computer – soon transformed into an omnipresent and endlessly multifaceted outlet for human energy and expression (Schmidt 2013). The shared 'home computer' has been supplanted by mobile technology. New gadgets such as laptops and mobile phones were introduced through which children could explore the digital space without effective governance. Devices like smartphones and tablets are changing how and where children go online. Mobile phones enable children to access the internet in the privacy of their bedrooms or from a friend's house (Mascheroni and Cuman 2014: 6; Hasebrink et al. 2011: 7). The result is online access that is more personal, more private and less supervised. As locations and platforms for internet access diversify, domestic management and regulation of children's internet access and use is increasingly challenging. No longer can parents monitor a single computer in the living room (Livingstone and Bober 2006).

With the growing significance of domestic mass media in the second half of the twentieth century, two distinct trends regarding the home can be identified. These help us understand the difference between childhood in the 1950s when television arrived, and childhood at the turn of the 21st century now that computers and the internet have made similar inroads into the home (Livingstone 2010). The first trend concerns the shifting boundary between the home and outside, altering the balance between life in the community and family privacy, as symbolised by the changing significance of 'the front door' (Livingstone 2010: 2). Extending this spatial framework, the second trend concerns the shifting balance between communal family life and the private life of the child, as symbolised by the growing significance of 'the bedroom door' (Livingstone 2010: 2).

Perhaps a third element can be discerned. Given the dominant narrative in which children are portrayed as technologically competent, parents are seen as the naïve 'digital immigrants', ironically, in an era in which the internet was constructed as a distinctive adult space. In contrast, children are now perceived as the 'digital natives'. This would represent a reversal of perceptions of a 'child' as passive and vulnerable but active agents. The continual multiplication of media goods at home has fostered a shift in media use from that of 'family television' (Morley 1986) to that of individualised media lifestyles (Flichy 2006). Children take the gadgets to bed making it difficult for parents to control 'screen time'.

These patterns of behaviour occasioned by the digital space are often discussed within the broader social dynamics. The works of Giddens, Beck and Beck-Gernsheim, for example, posit that contemporary life in modern or late modern industrial societies is characterised by more choices to be made because people are no longer bound by rules and tradition. Traditional institutions have receded in importance. Beck (1992, 2000) argues that we are witnessing the emergence of a new and unique form of society, which has particular implications for the individual that can no longer be understood through classical sociological models. He conceptualised what he termed 'risk society' in which life pathways are increasingly individualised. Beck and Beck-Gernsheim sum up the emerging state of 'individualisation' by stating thus:

> The ethic of individual self-fulfilment and achievement [becomes] the most powerful current in modern society. The choosing, deciding, shaping human being who aspires to be the author of his or her own life, the creator of an individual identity, is the central character of our time.
> (Beck and Beck-Gernsheim 2002: 22–3)

This theory is connected to the dismantling of the Welfare State from the 1980s, and also to the dominance of liberal and capitalist values in recent decades. As noted earlier, the family was increasingly protected by the introduction of the Welfare State following the Beveridge Report (1942). Now, the nation state has ever less responsibility for the risks in society while the citizens or consumers (and the companies that service them) have ever more responsibility. The individualisation comports with what Maslow (1987) called 'self-actualisation' – that is, creatively making something of one's personal and wider identity and thus pathway through life, which according to Craft (2013) is characteristic of Western 21st-century family life. Giddens (1991: 78) notes that 'self-actualisation is a balance between opportunity and risk'

According to Staksrud (2013), children should indeed be included in the 'risk society' and 'individualisation' thesis, because they 'are individuals in their own right; they can make rational yet often risky decisions and have the ability to act as citizens of a nation-state and human beings with human rights' (155). Tolerance for diversity and respect for individual choices has replaced solidarity and social group cohesion as prime values (Lesthaeghe 2010: 213). The resultant individualisation is often associated with the idea of freedom and choice.

Beck's theory of the 'risk society' and 'individualisation' offers us another useful lens through which we can view the digital age and its effects on children. First, the assumption of the 'risk society' and the disruption of classical social models would align with effects of the digital age on the classical 'welfarist' model of childhood. Second, digital media seem to have resulted in the individualisation of children through the use of gadgets away from the traditional family setting. Perhaps the apt example of individualisation is the so-called 'bedroom culture'. Originally coined by McRobbie and Garber in 1976 to describe the cultural space of girls and young women, the term, in the context of the digital culture, now refers to use of digital technology in the privacy of the bedroom by young people, both male and female. This trend has resulted from the saturation of media goods at home, fostering a shift in media use from that of 'family television' (Morley 1986) to that of individualised media lifestyles (Flichy 2006). The children's media-rich bedrooms not only individualise and privatise media consumption, but also connect children to society at large, surpassing the authority of their parents (Hjarvard 2013: 115). In the second half of the 20th century, growing affluence, changing patterns of family interaction, reduction in family size, the emergence of youth culture and the consumer power of the youth market have all combined to make children's bedrooms increasingly important as sites of leisure and learning (Bovill and Livingstone 2001). The bedroom is where media and identity intersect: in this space, media technology and content are appropriated by young people to sustain and express their sense of who they are (Bovill and Livingstone 2001: 3).

As locations and platforms for internet access diversify, domestic management and regulation of children's internet access and use is increasingly challenging (Livingstone and Bober 2006). Parents are seeking the means to counter the individualising effects of diverse and multiple media so as to sustain some degree of common culture within the home (Livingstone 2004: 14). However,

> The message from historians, then, is that contemporary families must negotiate a rapidly changing society without the traditional resources of hierarchical relations between the generations – with neither guidance based on strong parallels between the parents' childhood and that of their children, nor the moral right of parents to impose rules and sanctions without democratic consultation
>
> (Livingstone 2004: 8)

'Digital parenting' strategies of mediation – open, permissive, supportive, and restrictive or of 'laissez-faire' – rely on numerous interlinked factors like parents' skills, knowledge, attitudes and perceptions towards digital technologies (Chaudron et al. 2018: 13–14). The dilemma is that the internet provides a wealth of opportunities for children. On the one hand, parents are keen to improve their children's educational prospects. On the other, they are also concerned about online dangers (Facer et al. 2003; Livingstone 2002; Turow and Nir 2000). Parents thus share this ambivalence, especially given their children's apparently greater expertise with the internet. Anxiety has been the source of the discourse surrounding children and the internet at the turn of the century, and how it can be managed. Young people growing up in the 'risk society' experience a tension between amplified individualisation of childhood and increased regulation and risk management parents are expected to perform (Harvey 2015).

The theories of childhood discussed in Chapter 1 can be located within the digital contexts. It is apparent that childhood is changing. There are also other theories that can be associated with children in the digital age. The family hierarchical roles have been disrupted (Livingstone 2004), ushering what (Giddens 1992: 184) described as the 'democratisation of the public sphere'. However, the 'bedroom culture' is also individualising. As a consequence, children's view of personal responsibility and risk is shaped accordingly (Carrington 2008). Each is carving out a self-narrative and the individualised pathways and skill sets. The 'risk society' (Beck 1992) has brought about 'anxious parenting' and 'paranoid parenting' (Furedi 2002; Nelson 2010; Stearns 2003). As a result of the fears of the 'risk society', the 'welfarist' and 'authoritarian models' of childhood seem to be re-emerging or continuing to inform national regulatory patterns. The child is viewed as deserving protection while the laissez-faire model has less traction. The 'authoritarian model' of childhood is, perhaps, also notable now in that governments have responded with legislation designed to protect children based on the perception of risk arising from their increasingly individualised digital lifestyles.

4.5.1 Risk-based approach

Evidence is indeed growing that the internet amplifies and intensifies the risk of harm to children (O'Connell and Bryce 2006; Byron 2008). The CtRC in 2011 interpreted Article 19 to include acts committed via ICT, such as mobile phones and the internet. As ICT has made it easier to share knowledge and collaborate, so, too, has it made it easier to produce, distribute and share sexually explicit material and other illegal content that exploits and abuses children. Such technology has opened new channels for the trafficking of children and new means of concealing those transactions from law enforcement. It has become easier for bullies, sex offenders, traffickers and those who harm children to contact potential victims around the world, share images of their abuse and encourage each other to commit further crimes. Digital connectivity has made children more accessible through unprotected social media profiles and online game forums. Certain characteristics of the digital environment magnify the risk that children will be exploited or abused by other users. In particular, online abusers can easily operate anonymously and bypass gatekeepers such as parents or teachers.

There are, indeed, very real and potentially serious risks associated with children's use of digital media, particularly for those children who are most marginalised or vulnerable in their communities. Although there is lack of research on some of the most marginalised communities and groups, existing evidence indicates that the children who are most vulnerable to online harms include girls, children from poor households, children in communities with a limited understanding of different forms of sexual abuse and exploitation of children, children who are out of school, children with disabilities, children who suffer depression or mental health problems and children from marginalised groups. Unguided digital access and a lack of awareness also put children at risk (Burton 2017).

In recent years, bullying through electronic means, specifically mobile phones or the internet, has emerged, often collectively labelled 'cyber bullying'. A corresponding definition of cyber bullying is: 'An aggressive, intentional act carried out by a group or individual, using electronic forms of contact, repeatedly and over time against a victim who cannot easily defend him or herself' (Smith et al. 2008: 376). Whereas in previous generations, children being bullied could escape such abuse or harassment by going home or being alone, no such safe haven exists for children in a digital world. Carrying a mobile phone, laptop or other connected device means that texts, emails, chats and social media posts can arrive anytime, day or night. And online bullying carries on, spreading widely among peers and inflicting reputational harm whether the child is online or off. The links between the online and offline contexts of cyber bullying are particularly striking. A large-scale study in the United Kingdom, involving responses from over 100,000 children, found that very few experienced cyber bullying without also being bullied offline (Przybylski and Bowes 2017).

Studies on cyber bullying have focused primarily on white populations. However, such bullying is ubiquitous given access of digital gadgets globally. In South Africa, for example, almost half (46.8%) of the young people interviewed for a study reported experiencing some form of cyber aggression, including harassment via telephone (Burton and Mutongwizo 2009). Race appeared to be more significant both at home and in the school environment, with black children and youth reporting the highest incidence of cyber aggression, followed by white youths, mixed race youths while Indian/Asian youths reported the lowest incidence. Badenhorst points out that the psychological impact of cyber bullying is often more traumatising than physical bullying. 'Online exposure means that the whole world can witness the victim's humiliation. Since children spend a lot of time on their mobile phones and in cyber space, cyber bullying can happen 24 hours a day' (2011: 3)

Table 4.1 shows the typology of the digital risks and their manifestations. The risks can be classified as *content, contact* and *conduct* risks (Hasebrink et al. 2007). *Content* risks are where a child is exposed to unwelcome and inappropriate content. This can include sexual, pornographic and violent images; some forms of advertising; racist, discriminatory or hate-speech material; and websites advocating unhealthy or dangerous behaviours, such as self-harm, suicide and anorexia (Hasebrink et al. 2007). *Contact* risks result when a child participates in risky communication, such as with an adult seeking inappropriate contact or soliciting a child for sexual purposes, or with individuals attempting to radicalise a child or persuade him or her to take part in unhealthy or dangerous behaviours. *Conduct* risks arise when a child behaves in a way that contributes to risky content or contact. This may include children writing or creating hateful materials about other children, inciting racism or posting or distributing sexual images, including material they have produced themselves (Hasebrink et al. 2007).

In a study of 27 European countries, scholars found that parents are more concerned about contact and content risks than conduct-related ones (Ponte and Alberto 2009). Apart from sexually explicit and self-harm material, content risks include the marketising of childhood, which is now embedded in multiple new digital media (Livingstone 2003), the nature of which enables children not only to consume but also to produce in relation to the marketplace and thus to influence the direction of market growth and change (Craft 2013). Many online services, such as games, require children to provide detailed personal information as a condition of access, such as by logging in using their Facebook credentials. Once

250 Childhood in the digital age

Table 4.1 Typology of ICT-related harms

	Content *Child as recipient*	**Contact** *Child as participant in adult-initiated activity*	**Conduct** *Child as victim/actor*
Aggression and violence	• Self-abuse and self-harm • Suicidal content • Discrimination • Exposure to extremist/violent/gory content	• Radicalisation • Ideological persuasion • Hate speech	• Cyberbullying, stalking and harassment • Hostile and violent peer activity
Sexual abuse	• Unwanted/harmful exposure to pornographic content	• Sexual harassment • Sexual solicitation • Sexual grooming	• Child sexual abuse • Production and consumption of child abuse material • Child-produced indecent images
Commercial exploitation	• Embedded marketing • Online gambling	• Violation and misuse of personal data • Hacking • Fraud and theft • Sexual extortion	• Live streaming of child sexual abuse • Sexual exploitation of children • Trafficking for the purpose of sexual exploitation • Sexual exploitation of children in travel and tourism

Source: Bulger et al. forthcoming

access is granted, providers track online activity in detail, and may entice children to divulge further personal data using personality questionnaires and similar. Dijck et al. (2019) observe that, the 'platform society' is 'entangled in the ecosystem's techno-commercial mechanisms' (134).

Cyber bullying has become a pernicious problem; is not just wilful harm inflicted through the use digital devices. The potential for bullies to hide behind a nameless profile, pose as someone other than themselves and – in a single click – instantly disseminate violent, hurtful or humiliating words or images is unprecedented. Cyber bullying is perpetrated by both adults and young people. For example, in Missouri, US, 13-year-old Megan Meier hung herself in her bedroom in October 2006 after being 'dumped' by someone she thought was a 16-year-old boy on MySpace. The boy, however, turned out to be Lori Drew, the mother of one of her neighbours, who had set up the blog to torment the girl (*Daily Mail*, UK 2008). Testimony showed that they created a teenage boy, 'Josh Evans', as an identity on MySpace to communicate with Megan, who had a history of depression and suicidal impulses. After weeks of online courtship with 'Josh', Megan was distressed one afternoon in October 2006, according to testimony at the trial, when she received an email message from him that said, 'The world would be a better place without you'. Megan wrote back, 'You're the kind of boy a girl would kill herself over'. Megan hanged herself that same afternoon in her bedroom. In 2008, a federal jury convicted Drew of three misdemeanour counts related to the hoax, but a judge threw out the verdict the next year. In May 2008, Missouri lawmakers passed a cyber harassment law called the Megan Meier law.[12]

A 2013 study of 5,907 internet users in the United States aged 13–18 found that those who self-identified as lesbian, gay, bisexual or transgender were disproportionately at risk of online sexual harassment (Mitchell et al. 2014). Most of the risks highlighted above centre on how children may be harmed, but issues of children harming others also arise. In 2011, a 17-year-old high school student in Illinois, US, was arrested for allegedly compiling a Facebook sex list containing the names of approximately 50 fellow students. The list detailed the victims' sexual behaviours, sexual characteristics and physical appearance in explicit and derogatory language. The perpetrator was expelled from school and was arrested on charges of disorderly conduct (qtd. in Badenhorst 2011).

In September 2010, two teenage boys in Canada were charged with sexual assault, and possession and distribution of child pornography after they posted photographs on Facebook of the gang rape of a 16-year-old girl at a private party. In Macclesfield, UK, 15-year-old Megan Gillian a took fatal overdose of painkillers after classmates used the social networking site Bebo to wage a hate campaign against her, an inquest heard. Cheshire Coroner Mr Nicholas Rheinberg said: 'It is unfortunate in this day and age that the tentacles of harassment can reach outside the confines of school walls' (*Manchester Evening News* 2009).

Concern has also been raised on pro-eating disorders and pro-suicide websites. Molly Russell, 14, took her own life in 2017. When her family looked into her Instagram account they found distressing material about depression and suicide. Molly's father said he believed that Instagram was partly responsible for his daughter's death (Crawford 2019).

Child sexual exploitation will be discussed in Chapter 8. However, it is important to note the role of the internet in the perpetration of the crime. To be sure, the online world did not create crimes of child sexual abuse and exploitation. But the online dimension of it has changed the offences in two significant ways. It has facilitated existing 'common' forms and created wholly new forms. The emergence of digital technology has made it easier for child sexual predators to contact potential victims around the world, share images of their abuse and encourage each other to commit further crimes. Digital technology allows offenders to remain anonymous, hide their digital tracks, create false identities, pursue many victims at once and monitor their whereabouts. The increased use of mobile devices and greater access to broadband internet has made children more

---

12 H.R.1966 – Megan Meier Cyberbullying Prevention Act 111th Congress (2009–2010).

accessible than ever through unprotected social media profiles and online game forums. Offenders often begin grooming their victims on these platforms, where they gain a child's attention or trust, before moving the communication to video- and photo-sharing platforms

According to the Internet Watch Foundation (IWF), 57,335 uniform resource locators (URLs) contained child sexual abuse material in 2016. Of these, 60% were hosted in Europe and 37% in North America. Ninety-two per cent of all child sexual abuse URLs identified by the IWF are hosted in five countries: the Netherlands, the United States, Canada, France and the Russian Federation (listed by most to fewest URLs). In response to technological advancements and the ways in which offenders have used ICTs to seek children for abuse, a Special Rapporteur on the sale of children, child prostitution and child pornography, recommended that States 'introduce legislation creating the offence of "internet grooming or luring"' (8.4.1.4 in this book).

A new challenge in the identification of child sexual abuse material is the emergence of self-generated sexually explicit material, which falls under the 'conduct' risks. Sexting – 'texting' and 'sex' – involves the sending of nude or semi-nude photos or videos and/or sexually suggestive messages via mobile phone texting or instant messaging (Cumming 2009). Teenagers have been arrested for this in Canada, Australia and the United Kingdom. For example, a teenage boy in Toronto faced several criminal charges, including the making, possession and distribution of child pornography, for sending nude photos of his girlfriend to her email contacts (Toronto Star 2012).[13] In Australia, teenagers were charged with accessing and distributing child pornography, though most of the teens were cautioned (Bita 2012). However, sexual exploitation can be often conflated with consensual 'sexting'; it can also include material produced non-consensually – for example, through online solicitation and grooming and sexual extortion.[14] Related to 'sexting' is another conducted-related risk, the so-called 'revenge porn': the sharing of private, sexual materials, either photos or videos, of another person without their consent and with the purpose of causing embarrassment or distress. This form of 'revenge' usually occurs after a relationship has broken down. Revenge porn has been criminalised in a number of countries (Citron and Franks 2014).

However, content and conduct risk are not mutually exclusive. Children can consume content which then translates into conduct. An example is radicalisation. Children and young people can be exposed to material that influences them conduct violence. Geeraerts (2012) states that young people are more vulnerable to online radicalisation because they are the heaviest users of the internet, and are more likely to encounter political and civic issues through the medium. This is a fact that extremist groups are exploiting, thus making young people potentially vulnerable to harm and propaganda from Islamic and far-right extremist groups (Twitter confirmed

---

13 The teen also used the nude photos to try to coerce the girl into sending him a nude video of herself, which led to the extortion charges.
14 Europol's European Cybercrime Centre, 'Virtual Global Taskforce Child Sexual Exploitation Environmental Scan 2015', EC3-Europol, October 2015, p. 12.

that between mid-2015 and February 2016 it had suspended over 125,000 accounts globally that were linked to terrorists) (Corb and Grozelle 2014; UK House of Commons 2016; Mughal 2016). Geeraerts (2012: 26) defines radicalisation as:

> a process whereby an individual comes to embrace values and opinions about a certain topic . . . that gradually become more extreme and hence start to deviate more from the normative opinions, while at the same time finding it more difficult to accept opposite opinions.

In recent years, some children have been lured to join terrorist groups abroad. The well-publicised case of Shamima Begum who travelled to join the Islamic State in Syria (ISIS) when she was aged 15 brought this issue to the fore. Shamima was born in England to parents of Bangladeshi heritage. She lived in the London area of Bethnal Green where she attended the Bethnal Green Academy. Together with her friends Amira Abase and Kadiza Sultana (both also 15), she left the UK in February 2015. The trio travelled via Turkey, to join terrorist group ISIS in the war in Syria. In Raqqa, Syria, Shamima married ISIS fighter Yago Riedijk, a Dutch national, and had three children, all of whom died as infants. Her youngest son, Jarrah, was born in a Syrian refugee camp in February 2019. The child also died in the camp. Her companions, Amira and Kadiza, were reportedly killed during the war. Shamima later pleaded to be allowed back to the UK after she was found in a refugee camp. However, she also said she had 'no regrets' about joining ISIS. The UK government stripped her of her citizenship. The lawyer representing Shamima's family wrote to the Home Secretary accusing UK authorities of failing to protect the east London girl from being 'groomed' by ISIS.

Such grooming has been known to take different forms, including consumption of propaganda online. A number of cases have been brought before the courts by care authorities. In *London Borough of Tower Hamlets v B*, *A v London Borough of Enfield*, and *Z, Re*, all three girls involved were subject to influences outside the direct family, and were to a significant degree radicalised on the internet. Two of the girls self-radicalised (Malik 2019). Case Study 4.1 exemplifies the role of the internet in radicalisation of children.

Case study 4.1

London Borough Tower Hamlets v B [2016] EWHC 1707 (Fam)
Abstract: The applicant local authority sought a final care order relating to a 16-year-old girl (B).

The court had earlier granted the local authority's application to remove B from her parents' care following her attempt to travel to Syria and subsequent arrest on suspicion of terrorism-related offences. The court found that she had been exposed to extreme ideology related to the Islamic State while in the family home and that she continued to be at risk of serious emotional harm while in the care of her parents, whose apparent cooperation with the authorities was an elaborate and sophisticated succession of lies. However, B's placement in interim care had proved unsatisfactory. The local authority had encountered resistance from schools when trying to place her. Opportunities for foster care had proved non-existent. The consequence was that she had lived for nine months in very isolated circumstances. It had not been possible for her to be provided with the tuition she required to achieve the AS grades she needed to pursue her chosen career.

The following extracts highlight the role of online radicalisation.

Mr Justice Hayden:

1 'I am concerned here with six children, B, is separately represented, the remaining five children act by their Guardian who, at this hearing, has instructed counsel. This judgment must be read in conjunction with my earlier judgment delivered on the 21st August 2015, *London Borough of Tower Hamlets v B [2015] EWHC 2491 (Fam)*, following an application by the Local Authority to remove all the children into Local Authority care. I do not propose to reprise the reasoning in my earlier judgment other than to observe that the eldest child B was removed from her parents' care, though the other children remained with them.

3 It is convenient here to retrieve my summary of the background from the earlier judgment. Thus:

8 I turn firstly to the background, which I propose to set out summarily. On 6th December 2014, B was reported missing by her mother. Her mother stated that she may have travelled to Syria. This information, it is said, was given to the mother by B's brother. The account was that she, B, had informed her brother of her plans, confidentially, that very morning, i.e. the day she was due to fly. The Metropolitan Police Service Counter Terrorism Command were alerted, and they were able, operating on a narrow time margin, to intercept the flight only minutes before it was due to take off and B was removed. She had therefore very nearly made good her intention to get to Syria. She was, in due course interviewed by the police and, as a minor, questioned in accordance with the Achieving Best Evidence guidelines. During the course of that interview she was frank about her intention to travel to the Islamic State.' [. . .]

9 Professor Andrew Silke and Doctor Catherine Brown prepared detailed reports looking generically at the evolution of radicalisation as well as how it can most effectively be addressed. Their reports have been helpful in bringing context to the circumstances of this particular case. Their research is of wider general interest and, accordingly, it has been agreed that the generic report should be appended to this judgment. Some

of the analysis within the reports requires to be set out extensively for this reason and because I consider the information should be more widely available within the profession and beyond. Before turning to the reports though I would make two observations. Firstly, I have now heard a number of cases concerning allegations of radicalisation of children and I have found that many of the observations within the reports, reinforced as they are by academic research, also resonate with what I have seen for myself in the courtroom. Secondly, I would reiterate that which I have now said in various ways in a number of other cases: the family, as a construct, is infinitely variable and inevitably so too is the route by which children become radicalised within their family.

10 It may be necessary at this stage in our understanding of this new facet of risk to children to look thematically at patterns, traits of behaviour, frequent indicators pointing towards the existence of a radical ideology but it will never be satisfactory to consider these cases paradigmatically. All children are individuals, thus all radicalised children are individuals, arriving at their particular stages of belief through a complex matrix of influences. Silke and Brown articulate this as follows:

'6. There is no single root cause of radicalisation. More than 200 different factors have been identified by research which could play a role in the radicalisation process. Not all factors feature in every case, and there is often very considerable variation.

7. Research has highlighted that radicalisation is the result of the interaction of both personal factors (e.g. individual susceptibility) and environmental factors (e.g. social relationships, community attitudes). Studies have also highlighted that static and dynamic factors both play significant roles in radicalisation. Static elements include, for example, demographic factors such that young people aged 15–24 are most at risk, and males are usually more affected than females.

8. Dynamic factors can include social relationships, which in most cases are probably one of key elements in the radicalisation process. Camaraderie, social support and a sense of belonging can all be powerful incentives for becoming and staying involved with a radical group.

9. Psychological vulnerability can also play a significant role, though this should not be confused with mental illness or psychological problems, which overall are present in relatively few cases of serious radicalisation.'

19 I have read a great deal of material downloaded from the internet, much of it from the 'Dark' net. As is commonly known this enables an individual to search material without trace. Some of the material is, to my mind, extremely sophisticated, particularly that which educates the reader in how best to deceive the agencies of the Western State. The expert report makes this observation:

'The Role of Online Environments'

The issue of community is certainly strongly felt with regard to online environments. Islamic State is a 'young persons' movement and the use of technology is authentic to its members. Online material is highly gendered using particular motifs to exalt behaviours and traits. For women modesty, piety and complementarity with men is emphasised through images of a lion and lioness, or a 'green bird', images of romantic love do emerge, but these are presented as the 'beginning' of a new life rather than an end in itself. Online recruitment frequently relies on existing 'real-world' contacts, but not always. Increasingly non-public platforms are being used — such as telegram, and WhatsApp. Public forums are used for general propaganda and maintaining community and a sense of belonging — having your twitter account suspended is valued and seen as an achievement and celebrated. Islamic State are increasingly suspicious of unsolicited requests, and some reports suggest they require a 'recommendation' from a 'known'/'trusted' individual. Peer-to-Peer recruiters also encourage young women to distrust friends and family or 'traditional' authority figures, arguing 'they don't understand'. Moreover they argue that those in the West, follow an Islam that has been 'perverted' by culture and traditions that are not Islamic, or that those in authority have become corrupted by working for European authorities. On line recruitment is now noticeably female-to-female — in the past some men were actively seeking to recruit women as future wives but this has been noticeably declined.'

20 Following police disclosure Professor Silke and Dr Brown undertook a specific assessment of the material on the family's media devices. The objective was to evaluate the radicalising nature of the material and to provide an assessment of the likely psychological impact. It is agreed between the parties that much of the material here has been downloaded or accessed through the 'Dark Net'. Brown and Silke observe:

31 Whilst the computer records do not themselves establish, conclusively, that a direct search was made by B, I found her denials, in cross examination, to be hollow and unconvincing. Having regard to the breadth of the material that she has viewed, I think it more likely that this search was also intentional. In my judgement B has continued to deny this because she is intelligent enough to appreciate that it points towards the 'attack planning' allegations that the Local Authority has levelled against her. For the reasons set out below, I have not been persuaded of that aspect of the Local Authority's case. The contentious material is more likely to be a manifestation of B's voracious interest in Isis which she has described to me as 'addictive'. There is no evidence to suggest that B was involved in 'attack planning'.

32 B's sense of grievance has plainly been shared by the parents, most conspicuously by the father, who has been indignant at my having traduced

him, as he perceives it, in the earlier judgment. Quite why they contest the legitimacy of the Local Authority's concerns is not easy to follow. Their daughter was prevented from escaping to Syria and was subsequently removed from their household to protect her from the poisonous images which have been described as 'saturating' the family's laptops, smart phones, hard drives and USB sticks. That is an apt description

63 Perhaps the most significant of the concessions made in this statement is that in respect of B's viewing of gruesome killings and torture:

'I saw so much violence that it seemed to lose its effect. Everything merged into one. I can't believe I'm saying that now.'

'In respect of the beheadings of Western people, at the time the message was that they were spies for the West and that's why they had been killed. I thought that Western spies were in the same category as soldiers, which was why they could be executed.'

'I did not really like the fact that they were beheaded but I realized that they did this as a way of trying to grab the West's attention. If they had done that to Syrian soldiers no one would pay attention, but because they were British and American that would mean more publicity.'

64 Concerning the risk that B said she represented to her siblings:

'For about a week after I came back in December 2014, I told H I wished I hadn't been stopped and that I wanted to go there. After that I didn't share with her my up and down feelings about IS. I didn't suggest to her that she ought to go too, but I did say that I should be going, as a good Muslim, so she might have taken that as me suggesting she should go too. I didn't say that with the intention of persuading her to go too, but I accept that might have been the effect on her. H is more likely to follow me than I am to follow her. I accept that if I said things about what I saw as my duty or why it would be right as a Muslim to go, there is a risk the others would have begun to see it that way and may have attempted to go or become involved.'

'I accept therefore that I was "radicalized". I do not accept that I was a risk to the public as I never intended or planned in any way to carry out any attack against others. I did not intend to harm anyone. I completely deny that I was "attack planning" and partly my fear of admitting what I had really been feeling about support for IS was that I thought that everyone would assume that the police theory was true. It wasn't.'

'I accept that I was a risk to myself, and to an extent to my siblings, who might have been influenced by my beliefs.'

65 Confronting obvious credibility issues she tackled them in this way:

'I know it maybe said well how can we believe you now when you've admitted lying? I can only say that I lied to protect myself and because I was too scared and got in so far I couldn't admit that I had been radicalized. I knew if I did everyone would say I was a risk and never believe that I didn't intend to harm anyone. I had hurt my family so much I couldn't admit it to them either. It just got worse and worse as time went on.'

94 The Local Authority has characterised the father's role as 'pivotal'. I agree that it is, though not in the way that the Local Authority initially contended. As I have sought to analyse it, the father's role has been a complex one in which he has, I am satisfied, often failed to appreciate the consequences of his own behaviour and its impact on his daughter. He is, in my evaluation of the evidence, a headstrong man who has a deep suspicion of the press, the courts and to some extent the world generally. He aspires to knowledge and respects learning. I am satisfied that he was simply not prepared to monitor B's use of the computer in the way that he had promised this Court and the CTU that he would. He deceived all the agencies into trusting him to regulate his daughter's use of the internet but, I find, made absolutely no effort to do so. It was anathema to him to curtail B's exploration of ideas however dark or dangerous they may have been. I do not believe that he had ever stopped to reflect on the extent to which his daughter could inflict emotional and psychological damage on herself by what she viewed on the internet. Here, in this particular case, a 16-year-old girl has dehumanised herself by viewing a surfeit of death related images that have left her emotionally numb. It is this that is the most striking feature of the case, more so than her reading the polemics or expressions of radicalised views. Of course, they make their contribution too.

123 Like the father, I am satisfied that the mother made no effort at all to restrict her daughter's use of the internet either before or indeed after her attempted flight to Syria. Accordingly, I find the mother too was party to a deception upon each of the safeguarding authorities involved. They both colluded to create the impression that they were monitoring their daughter's safety. In reality, they were doing nothing of the kind. There is in both parents a deep vein of resistance to authority. I have seen flickers of it during the course of these proceedings, characterised by their combative attitude to the investigation and to those who have been motivated to help them. Nor does either parent, in my view, really engage with the substance of the process. I emphasise, B is not being 'punished' for what she has done, the parents are not being 'punished' either, rather the State is trying to protect their daughter from the damaging consequences of the vile images which she has repeatedly made access to and the corrosive ideology which has beguiled her (see also *London Borough of Tower Hamlets v B [2015] EWHC 2491 (Fam)*).

Case Study 4.1 illustrates the welfarist and authoritarian approaches, the former, as we noticed from Chapter 1, is where 'the state intervenes, at least with coercive techniques, when clear dysfunctions are evident'. An 'authoritarian approach' sets out to compel and prohibit certain family behaviour. While 'online' radicalisation might be new ('physical' radicalisation still occurred), the risks discussed in this section are not entirely new – children have long bullied and been bullied, have often been exposed to, or sought out, violent and sexual material, and have always been at risk from sexual offenders. Bullying could happen on the playground and radicalisation could occur through physical interaction. Most parents probably feel it was easier to protect previous generations from such risks. The front door was once a barrier; now, social media allows them to follow their victims into their homes. It is becoming difficult to separate their online and offline lives.

4.5.1.1 Regulation: internet governance

As an inevitable consequence of this, there is increasing public anxiety about how children's participation in digital spaces might be managed. Risk management measures have been discussed in the context of the concept of 'internet governance'. A working group established after a United Nations-initiated World Summit on the Information Society defined 'internet governance' as: 'the development and application by governments, the private sector and civil society, in their respective roles, of shared principles, norms, rules, decision-making procedures, and programs that shape the evolution and use of the internet'.[15]

Historically, the principal focus of internet governance tended to be on child abuse material or illegal contact by child sex offenders (Livingstone et al. 2015). As noticed earlier, these are important but far from the only issues that concern children; the range of risks is much broader. In public policy regarding children, the right to 'protection' has tended to take priority in theory, policy and practice, now online as, traditionally, offline (Livingtone and Third 2017). Risk mitigation strategies have to take account of the many factors that influence children's experience and activities on the internet: the diffusion of internet technologies or the socio-economic situation of a given country's households (Hasebrink et al. 2009: 21), the locations at which children most often access the internet (e.g. home, school, public places, etc.) and the devices they use (e.g. computer, netbook, mobile phone, game console, etc.)

Most countries' approaches blend legislative, self- and co-regulatory, technical, awareness, and educational measures, as well as positive content provision and child safety zones. However, the degree to which countries rely on each of these policy tools varies. Case Study 4.1 demonstrates the 'welfarist approach' arising from family dysfunction and authoritarian model in which the state intervenes to protect a child from radicalisation. State interventions have now focused on regulating providers of digital services. In a majority of countries, regulation of online content is a cornerstone of their national policy framework. It generally applies to content published on the internet rather than to content passed on via individual data exchange. Content regulation takes a two-pronged approach: a general ban on illegal content and national regulation of child-inappropriate content up to defined age levels (Australia, Korea, Japan,

---

15 Report of the Working Group on Internet Governance, 2005, p. 4. Available at: <www.wgig.org/docs/WGIGREPORT.pdf> (accessed 28 November 2019).

New Zealand and most European countries) (OECD 2011). The definitions of illegal and child-inappropriate content are subject to national interpretation and reflect cultural and societal values. A number of countries have moved towards regulating or otherwise committing internet intermediaries to comply with so-called 'notice and take down procedures' (mandatory in Australia, Italy, Japan, Korea and Turkey; at the time of writing, the UK government had announced that similar powers would be granted to Ofcom) or to introduce mandatory filtering schemes (OECD 2011).

There have been some disparate regional efforts to coordinate internet governance among states. In May 2012, the European Commission set out a European Strategy for a Better Internet for Children (or BIK) to provide children with the digital skills and tools needed to fully and safely benefit from being online.[16] The BIK Map was created to compare and exchange knowledge on policy making and implementation in EU Member States on the themes and recommendations of the BIK strategy first set out by the European Commission in May 2012. The BIK strategy comprises the following five main fields of activity: stimulating quality content online for young people; digital/media literacy in education; stepping up awareness and empowerment; tools and regulation for an online safe environment; and legislation and law enforcement against child sexual abuse and exploitation.

The first BIK report (2014) showed that there was a lack of strong policy framework and a high degree of coordination between the ministries involved was required; there was no common approach to the measurement of online use or risks for children, leading to a lack of comparable or robust data across Europe and that only in a minority of countries were all stakeholder groups involved (O'Neill and Dinh 2018). The 2018 Report reached almost similar conclusions. Most countries confirmed that consultation with children takes place in the design of BIK policies. However, only a third state that there is an opportunity for children to be actively involved in policy design (O'Neill and Dinh 2018: 9–10). In addition, it noted that half of the countries reported that new policy development had been reactive or had been influenced by specific incidents or events related to children's online safety. While this did not happen in Europe, the introduction of the Megan Meier Cyberbullying Prevention Act in the US, mentioned earlier, is one such example.

The EU General Data Protection Regulation (GDPR)[17] includes several provisions aimed at enhancing the protection of children's personal data online, such

---

16 'A European Strategy to Deliver a Better Internet for Our Children'. Available at: <https://ec.europa.eu/digital-single-market/en/european-strategy-deliver-better-internet-our-children> (accessed 28 November 2019).

17 Regulation (EU) 2016/679 of the European Parliament and of the Council of 27 April 2016 on the protection of natural persons with regard to the processing of personal data and on the free movement of such data, and repealing Directive 95/46/EC (General Data Protection Regulation) [2016] OJ L119/1.

as obliging service providers to use a clear and plain language that children can easily understand in all information society services that require personal data processing. For the first time, the GDPR requires parental consent before information society service providers can process the personal data of children under 16 years of age. Although the GDPR's goal is not specifically to protect children from harm, it may have consequences for child protection (Livingstone et al. 2018).

In 2019, the UK government published an 'Online Harms' White Paper (UK WP), which sets out a programme of action to tackle content or activity that harms individual users, particularly children, or threatens the way of life in the UK, either by undermining national security, or by undermining the shared rights, responsibilities and opportunities to foster integration. The range of harms it seeks to combat is indeed quite wide. It includes child sexual exploitation, terrorism and radicalisation, content illegally uploaded from prisons, serious violence online, gang violence, sale of opiods, online harms suffered by children and young people, cyber bullying, self-harms and suicide, underage sharing of sexual imagery (sexting), 'emerging challenge of screentime'; online disinformation (fake news) online manipulation and abuse of public figures (Department of DCMS 2019).

Critically, the government intends to impose a 'duty of care' on the companies. A virtual duty of care would appear to be a first in internet governance. There is currently a range of regulatory and voluntary initiatives aimed at addressing these problems, but these have not gone far or fast enough, or been consistent enough between different companies, to keep UK users safe online. The new statutory duty of care is intended to make companies take more responsibility for the safety of their users and tackle harm caused by content or activity on their services. The UK WP insists that the private sector – especially in the technology and telecommunication industries – has a special responsibility and a unique ability to shape the impact of digital technology on children. Such power and influence should be leveraged to advance industry-wide ethical standards on data and privacy, as well as other practices that benefit and protect children online. Technology and internet companies were expected to take measures to prevent their networks and services from being used by offenders to collect and distribute child sexual abuse images or commit other violations against children.

However, privacy can present unintended difficulties. While measures on privacy can protect children, they can also shield perpetrators. This raises debate on the balance between privacy with public safety. In 2019, Facebook announced it wanted to encrypt messages on all its platforms. The plan raised concern with the UK Home Secretary Priti Patel stating that such a move threatens the 'lives and the safety of our children' (Wakefield 2019). Patel and her counterparts in the US and Australia sent an open letter to Facebook calling on it to rethink its plan. The letter noted that:

> Tech companies like Facebook have a responsibility to balance privacy with the safety of the public. So far nothing we have seen from Facebook reassures

me that their plans for end-to-end encryption will not act as barrier to the identification and pursuit of criminals operating on their platforms.

(Wakefield 2019)

As part of the UK's new duty of care, companies will be expected, where appropriate, to have effective and easy-to-access user complaints functions. Companies will need to respond to users' complaints within an appropriate timeframe and to take action consistent with the expectations set out in the regulatory framework (Department of DCMS 2019: para. 25). All companies in scope of the regulatory framework will need to be able to show that they are fulfilling their duty of care (Department of DCMS 2019: paras 18, 38). The regulator will assess how effectively these terms are enforced as part of any regulatory action. The regulator will have a suite of powers to take effective enforcement action against companies that have breached their statutory duty of care. This may include the powers to issue substantial fines and to impose liability on individual members of senior management (Department of DCMS 2019: para. 20). The regulator will set out how to do this in codes of practice. Compliance with this duty of care will be overseen and enforced by an independent regulator (Department of DCMS 2019: para. 17). However, the UK government acknowledges that this 'novel', 'ambitious' and a 'complex' area for public policy (Department of DCMS 2019: paras 10.2, 40) and it will consult further on the new regulatory framework and non-legislative package. Potential challenges could arise from establishing causality, and the likelihood of disproportionate actions.

4.5.1.2 Moral panic?

Some would argue, with good cause – given the discussions in the previous sections – that these interventionist models are indispensable to the safeguarding of children against the vices of the digital space. A significant weight of evidence has been drawn to illustrate the deleterious effects of the internet. However, other observers note that these practices, which seek to produce a new common sense about childhood in the face of rapidly changing technological environments, are evidence of eruptions of the moral panic (Facer 2012). A moral panic suggests 'a panic or overreaction to forms of deviance or wrong doing believed to be threats to the moral order' (Drislane and Parkinson 2016). Moral panics are usually framed by the media and led by community leaders or groups intent on changing laws or practices. Sociologists are less interested in the validity of the claims made during moral panics than they are in the dynamics of social change and the organisational strategies of moral entrepreneurs. Moral panics gather converts because they touch on people's fears and because they also use specific events or problems as symbols of what many feel to represent 'all that is wrong with the nation' (Drislane and Parkinson 2016). Any moral panic involves a 'heightened level of concern over the behaviour of a certain group or category' (Goode and Ben-Yehuda 2009: 37).

These conceptualisations seem to capture reactions of some states to children's use of digital technology, as reflected by welfarist and authoritarian models. As noted in the European report, some of the regulators measures were 'reactive'. The moral panic framework has, however, been criticised for over-representing the likelihood of harm that children face and distorting the experiences of most children online. In doing so, it, according to Powell, Hills and Nash (2010: 4), obscures and undermines the work of both freedom of expression and child protection advocates.

> It leads to false conclusions about the motives of freedom of expression advocates, and misrepresents the considered actions by many child protection groups to identify and combat actual risks that children face as they access the internet on a daily basis.
>
> (Powell et al. 2010: 4)

Equally, different children can have the same experience online and yet experience very different outcomes (Burton 2017: 1). A review undertaken by UNICEF's Office of Research similarly stressed that 'children's online experiences cannot be studied in isolation from their lives in general' and that 'more control variables need to be included in quantitative studies to ensure that variables that have known effects on child well-being outcomes are not excluded'. These include factors like age, gender, personality, life situation, as well as their social and cultural environment (Kardefelt-Winther 2017: 8).

One 2009 pan-European survey found a range of responses among children to pornographic content. Some children were not concerned about it, some thought it was funny and others wished they had never seen it (Staksrud and Livingstone 2009). When faced with these types of risks, most children in the study responded with strategies that were either positive (seeking help from others) or neutral (ignoring the risk). Others seemed less able to diminish the risk and ended up, in turn, perpetrating other 'conduct' risks themselves. Some commentators even suggest that the 'risk society' provides useful formative ingredients to growing children. For instance, Livingstone and O'Neill (2014: 5) argue that the wholesale elimination of risk is neither feasible nor desirable, asserting that: 'society does not wish to keep children forever in a "walled garden", recognising that they must explore, make mistakes and learn to cope in order to develop into resilient adults and responsible digital citizens'. In other words, this approach insulates children from important socialisation skills. At the same time, we need to understand that some harms are just too grievous to produce any 'educative' outcome.

Coleman and Hagell (2007) also point to research by developmental psychologists suggesting that some exposure to risk is essential for children to learn how to adapt and become resilient. Theory and evidence also make it clear that risk is distinct from harm: not all those who encounter risk are harmed by it, for risk refers only to the probability of harm (Livingstone and O'Neill, 2014: 5).

Assessing the extent to which risks translate into actual harms is, however, extremely difficult. The content-contact-conduct framework used to describe risks, discussed earlier, also provides a way of thinking about the actual harms that children may experience online. While tolerance of risk varies among societies, cultures, communities and individual families, most can agree that some risks are uncomfortably close to the line crossing into harm. Public policy has thus tended to favour protective regulation as noted in the previous section. Such control of spatiality is part of the process of defining the social category of 'youth' itself (Massey 1998). However, critics point out that anxieties over risks serve to maintain the boundaries of the construction of childhood (Livingstone 2009). Critics are concerned about the implicit agenda at stake, suggesting that this is motivated by moral panics about technology and about the mass public and that, in response, it constructs a false ideal of the innocent and vulnerable child which then misleads research and policy (Drotner 2000; Buckingham 2002; Oswell 2002).

4.5.1.3 Benefits of online participation

Research indicates that digital technology seems to, overall, be beneficial for children's social relationships (Kardefelt-Winther 2017). Children create social media profiles and use websites or apps like Facebook, Twitter, Instagram, Tumblr, Snapchat, WhatsApp and some activities on YouTube. Children go online to strengthen friendships and seek new friends. Some may share photos and videos with families and friends through social networking sites such as Instagram or Facebook, while others distribute to a wider public through wikis, blogs, vlogs, and so on (Davies and Merchant 2009). The role of social networking in expanding friendships can be seen in countries as diverse as Egypt, India, Indonesia, Iraq and Saudi Arabia, where more than 90% of children using mobiles reported that social networking strengthens relationships with close friends.[18]

An international group of scientists described the concept of screen-time as 'simplistic and arguably meaningless'. Focusing on the amount of screen-use was similarly deemed 'unhelpful'. What was missing from the evidence base, they argued, was an examination of the 'context of screen use, and the content that children encounter when using digital technologies', both of which may 'have a much greater impact than sheer quantity alone'.

Children also go online to access information and learning: Using the internet to do homework is increasingly common in high income countries but it is also a primary online practice in some middle-income countries. In Brazil in 2013, schoolwork ranked first among children's main activities on the internet (Doneda and Rossini 2015). In Argentina, around 80% of adolescents reported searching on Wikipedia or Google, and using video tutorials on subjects such as

18 Lenhart et al. 2015.

mathematics and history (UNICEF 2017). Children value the information they can access online, including information on a wide range of recreational activities and health issues. For young people, using social media for social activism is practically second nature. From the Ice Bucket Challenge in 2014 – where a stunt by young people trying to raise money for a terminally ill friend unleashed a global movement that raised millions of dollars for disease research – to pre-teens using the internet to launch local campaigns around personal concerns, digital technology has enabled a new age of digital participation (UNICEF 2017).

The impact of social media has also been felt in political issues. In Brazil in 2013, for example, thousands of mostly young people used social media platforms to coordinate a protest against corruption and demand better public policies. In Kenya, for example, since 2009, a community mapping initiative called Map Kibera – which uses digital open-mapping techniques and GPS devices, along with digital information-sharing – has helped young people in a Nairobi slum identify hazards in their communities and advocate for solutions to specific concerns. This information, in turn, is being shared with and used by policy-makers, helping drive real change (UNICEF 2017). The General Assembly High Level Meeting, which reviewed the implementation of the WSIS outcomes, makes a specific link to the 2030 Agenda and recognises internet access as a development indicator and aspiration in and of itself.[19] Although there are increasingly more examples of child-centred initiatives that embed children's insights and experiences at their core, current debates in many parts of the world continue to focus almost exclusively on the risks associated with children's digital media engagements, and debate results in an overwhelmingly protection-oriented approach to children's use of technology.

4.5.2 Rights-based approach

In human rights, 'will' theorists focus on 'autonomy', asserting that the purpose of human rights was to protect the choices made by an individual in respect of her own life. On the other hand, 'interest' theorists, by contrast, focus on welfare, arguing that rights existed to protect the interests of the holders by placing duties on others to respect those interests. A central critique of interest theory, which has carried particular weight in matters relating to children, relates to how the protected interests are identified (McCarthy 2018).

Eekelaar's model of children's rights, which he termed 'dynamic self-determinism' attempted to merge protection of welfare and promotion of autonomy within a single justification for children's rights. In Eekelaar's model, children's rights in general are designed to protect their basic, developmental and autonomy interests (Eekelaar 1986). However, these interests may be in conflict.

---

19 On the occasion of the UNGA review heads of the UN Agencies decided that beyond 2015 WSIS Forum can serve as a key forum for discussing the role of ICTs as a means of implementation of the Sustainable Development Goals and targets, with due regard to the global mechanism for follow-up and review of the implementation of the 2030 Agenda for Sustainable Development, as set out in General Assembly resolution A/70/1.

For instance, allowing a child the autonomy to engage in dangerous activity may harm her developmental interests (McCarthy 2018). According to Eekelaar, this can be resolved by ordering the three categories of interests in a hierarchy. 'We may therefore rank the autonomy interest subordinate to the basic and developmental interests. However, where they may be exercised without threatening these two interests, the claim for their satisfaction must be high' (Eekelaar 1986: 171).

The 'will' and 'interest' theories aptly capture the discourses around the digital space. Eekelaar's attempt to reconcile both welfare and protection illustrates the dilemmas in internet governance. The 'rights-based' or 'rights first' approach, which gives precedence to the rights of children, prioritises autonomy. Most international guidelines, special reports and recommendations that deal with human rights, child rights and the internet, however, emphasise the importance of striking a balance between opportunities and risks, freedom of expression and the right to privacy, children's rights to special protection measures as well as online and offline dimensions of children's experiences (Livingstone 2014b). They urge that enabling these benefits while also minimising the internet-facilitated abuse of children requires a coordinated international-level action and global policy framework (Livingstone et al. 2015).

A 'rights first' approach maximises children's enjoyment of all of their rights online equitably, including children who currently have little or no access to the internet. It is designed to support children's own participation in decision-making and is based on a conception of children having distinct rights that can be asserted, both morally and legally. This approach resonates with the dominant sociological image of the child as a competent, autonomous and active social agent. At the core of the rights approach is the notion of freedom of expression. The right to freedom of opinion and expression is enshrined in Articles 19 of the *Universal Declaration of Human Rights* (UDHR) and the *International Covenant on Civil and Political Rights* (ICCPR). Article 19 ICCPR states that:

> Everyone shall have the right to hold opinions without interference. Everyone shall have the right to freedom of expression; this right shall include freedom to seek, receive and impart information and ideas of all kinds, regardless of frontiers, either orally, in writing or in print, in the form of art, or through any other media of his choice. The exercise of the rights provided for in paragraph 2 of this article carries with it special duties and responsibilities. It may therefore be subject to certain restrictions, but these shall only be such as are provided by law and are necessary: (a) For respect of the rights or reputations of others; (b) For the protection of national security or of public order (ordre public), or of public health or morals.

The *African Charter on Human and Peoples' Rights* also enshrined freedom of opinion and expression. It includes the freedom to express and impart information and ideas of all kinds that can be transmitted to others, in whatever form, and regardless of media. Expression can take forms such as spoken, written and sign language as well as nonverbal expression such as images and objects of art, all of which are protected. Means of expression can include books, newspapers, pamphlets, posters and banners as well as all forms of audio-visual, electronic and internet-based modes of expression.

The *African Charter on the Rights and Welfare of the Child* (ACRWC) provides express protections for the rights of freedom of expression and privacy of children. In this regard, Article 7 of the ACRWC provides that:

> Every child who is capable of communicating his or her own views shall be assured the rights to express his opinions freely in all matters and to disseminate his opinions subject to such restrictions as are prescribed by laws'; and Article 10 provides that: 'No child shall be subject to arbitrary or unlawful interference with his privacy, family home or correspondence, or to the attacks upon his honour or reputation, provided that parents or legal guardians shall have the right to exercise reasonable supervision over the conduct of their children. The child has the right to the protection of the law against such interference or attacks.

Frank La Rue, the former UN Special Rapporteur on Freedom of Expression has criticised overly protectionist policies that focus exclusively on risks and neglect the potential of the internet to empower and benefit children. The internet is 'an important vehicle for children to exercise their right to freedom of expression and can serve as a tool to help children claim their other rights, including the right to education, freedom of association and full participation in social, cultural and political life. It is also essential for the evolution of an open and democratic society, which requires the engagement of all citizens, including children' (La Rue 2014: 16). A narrow lens positions children solely as vulnerable victims, neglecting their agency and rights to access, information, privacy and participation (Mueller 2010; DeNardis 2014; Decherney and Pickard 2015). The problematic consequence is that highly protectionist or restrictive policies are advocated for children in ways that may undermine their freedom of expression or that trade children's particular needs off against adult freedoms online (Livingstone 2011; Siebert 2007).

The free expression right intersects with other rights of children. The adoption of the UNCRC in 1989 marked a very important milestone in the development of an international framework of rights for children and young people. The UNCRC recognises children as independent bearers of human rights. It became and remains the broadest and most rapidly adopted multilateral treaty in history. Child rights advocates generally agree that the UNCRC's

> greatest contribution has been in transforming the public perception of children. Whereas children previously tended to be seen as passive objects of charity, the Convention identified them as independent holders of rights. States parties are no longer just given the option to pursue policies and practices that are beneficial to children – they are required to do so as a legal obligation.
> (UNICEF 2014: 40)

The UNCRC places emphasis on children's agency and, therefore, their access to information, participation, freedom of thought and expression, and freedom of association.

The complex interrelation between the media, children and their rights has regularly been the subject of attention and debate about the UNCRC.

4.5.3 UNCRC in the digital era

The UNCRC encompasses a broader range of rights than any other human rights treaty, from humanitarian to economic and socio-cultural to civil and political rights. The heavy involvement of non-governmental organisations in both the drafting and the implementation of the UNCRC sets it apart from other international treaties. It is also unique in that it specifies the obligations of State Parties in implementing children's rights, and provides the CtRC with tools to monitor compliance. The international child rights community has increasingly recognised children's capacity to make independent decisions about their day-to-day lives, and has recognised these capacities at ever lower ages. Granting children rights to make decisions about contraception and about medical treatment are cases in point. Articles of the UNCRC also delineate the responsibilities of parents and carers, the community, the media, and other agencies and organisations in promoting and protecting children's rights. While the UNCRC is not the first international treaty to protect children's rights, it stands apart from previous declarations in that it enshrines the idea of children as rights-holding individuals. Previous debates and declarations mostly focused on protection and provision rights, addressing children's 'vulnerability' by asserting their developmental needs for health and social care, education, and protection from harm. By contrast, the UNCRC constructs children as people with the right to express their opinion in matters that concern them, thus adding participation rights to those of protection and provision. Participation rights imply a degree of self-determination, albeit in accordance with the child's age and maturity, which is much closer to the notion of civil and political rights previously reserved for adults. Article 12 – the right to be heard – is recognised as one of the four guiding principles underpinning the implementation of the UNCRC. Part 1 of the UNCRC (Articles 1–41) concerns substantive rights, while Part 2 (Articles 42–54) concerns their implementation.

Some observers have contended that the UNCRC was now outmoded in light of the rapid advancement in digital technology. Livingstone (2014b: 4), however, argued that although the Convention had been formulated in the pre-digital era, the rights enshrined therein remained as relevant as ever. During the Day of General Discussion on 'the child and the media', she provided an overview of key articles of the Convention relevant to children's rights in the digital age; she pointed out that the emphasis should be on the right to protection from harm, the right to provision to meet needs and the right to participation as an agent, or citizen. While they should be understood as part of a holistic framework, the substantive rights are commonly divided into the three 'Ps'.

Table 4.2 Selected articles of the UNCRC of particular relevance to the digital age

Provision:
- To the resources necessary for life, survival and development. (Article 6)
- To preserve his or her name, identity, nationality and family relations. (Article 8)
- Which recognizes 'the important function performed by the mass media' and so encourages provision of diverse information and material of social and cultural benefit to the child (including minorities) to promote children's wellbeing. (Article 17a – d)
- Of an education to facilitate the development of their full potential. (Article 28)
- Of an education that will facilitate 'the development of the child's personality, talents and mental and physical abilities to their fullest potential' and prepare them 'for responsible life in a free society'. (Article 29)
- For rest, play, recreation and leisure as appropriate to their age, including the provision necessary to 'promote the right of the child to participate fully in cultural and artistic life'. (Article 31)
- Of 'all appropriate measures to promote physical and psychological recovery and social reintegration of a child victim of any form of neglect, exploitation, or abuse [so as to foster] the health, self-respect and dignity of the child'. (Article 39)
- 'A child belonging to such a [ethnic, religious or linguistic] minority or who is indigenous shall not be denied the right, in community with other members of his or her group, to enjoy his or her own culture', religion and language. (Article 30)

Protection against:
- Any kind of discrimination. (Article 2)
- 'Arbitrary or unlawful interference with his or her privacy, family, or correspondence, nor to unlawful attacks on his or her honour and reputation'. (Article 16)
- 'Information and material injurious to the child's well-being'. (Article 17e)
- 'All forms of physical or mental violence, injury or abuse, neglect or negligent treatment, maltreatment or exploitation, including sexual abuse'. (Article 19)[20]
- All forms of sexual exploitation and sexual abuse, including '(a) The inducement or coercion of a child to engage in any unlawful sexual activity; (b) The exploitative use of children in prostitution or other unlawful sexual practices; (c) The exploitative use of children in pornographic performances and materials'.(Article 34)
- 'The sale of or traffic in children for any purpose or in any form'. (Article 35)
- 'All other forms of exploitation prejudicial to any aspects of the child's welfare'. (Article 36)
- 'Torture or other cruel, inhuman or degrading treatment or punishment'. (Article 37)

(Continued)

---

20 The second part of this Article is particularly pertinent for internet governance institutions: 'Such protective measures should, as appropriate, include effective procedures for the establishment of social programmes to provide necessary support for the child and for those who have the care of the child, as well as for other forms of prevention and for identification, reporting, referral, investigation, treatment and follow-up of instances of child maltreatment described heretofore, and, as appropriate, for judicial involvement' (*United Nations Convention on the Rights of the Child* 1989).

Table 4.2 (Continued)

Participation rights:
- The right of children to be consulted in all matters affecting them. (Article 12)[21]
- Freedom of expression. (Article 13)[22]
- Freedom of thought. (Article 14)
- Freedom of association and peaceful assembly. (Article 15)
- Access to information. (Article 17)
- The right to participate freely in cultural life and the arts. (Article 31)

Extracted from Livingstone et al. 2015

Third et al.'s (2014) consultation with children living in 16 countries concluded that children now regard access to digital media as a fundamental right and, further, they recognise that digital media are fast becoming the means through which they exercise their rights to information, education and participation. In recent years, various UN agencies and related bodies concerned with children's wellbeing have addressed the importance of the internet in relation to children's rights. The link to the right to freedom to receive and impart information (article 17) of the UNCRC is outlined by the CtRC as follows:

> Fulfilment of the child's right to information, consistent with article 17 is, to a large degree, a prerequisite for the effective realisation of the right to express views. Children need access to information in formats appropriate to their age and capacities on all issues of concern to them. This applies to information, for example, relating to their rights, any proceedings affecting them, national legislation, regulations and policies, local services, and appeals and complaints procedures.

In 1996, the Committee recognised the essential role of the media in the implementation and promotion of the UNCRC during a Day of General Discussion on 'the child and the media' focusing on child participation, protection against harmful influences, and respect for the integrity of the child. A working group was subsequently set up to further explore the relationship between media and young people, with a particular focus on how child participation in the media might

---

21 This is a qualified right, contingent on a judgment of the child's maturity: 'States Parties shall assure to the child who is capable of forming his or her own views the right to express those views freely in all matters affecting the child, the views of the child being given due weight in accordance with the age and maturity of the child' (ibid.).

22 Note that this right is not qualified according to the child's maturity, although, as for adult freedom of expression, it is qualified in order to respect the rights or reputations of others, national security, public order or public health or morals.

contribute to the better implementation of the UNCRC. Article 19 of the CRC deals with the protection of children from all forms of abuse, neglect, violence and maltreatment, whether inflicted by care-givers or parents or others having responsibility for the child. The broad sweep of article 19 is complemented by specific protection against sexual exploitation contained in article 34 of the CRC, and by the *Optional Protocol to the CRC on the Sale of Children, Child Prostitution and Child Pornography (2000)*. The UNCRC has three Optional Protocols: on the sale of children, child prostitution and child pornography, the involvement of children in armed conflict, and on a communications procedure. The third Optional Protocol on Communications Procedure allows individual children to submit complaints regarding specific violations of their rights under the Convention. This procedure could also apply to the digital space.

4.5.4 Digital space and the 'best interests' principle

As can be noticed from the discussion in this chapter, divergent views exist on approaches to children's usage of the digital space. On the one hand, some favour greater protection while for others, 'participation' should be given priority. Ultimately, commentators seek to defer to the 'best interests' principle, discussed in the previous chapter (see section 3.7.3.2) as the determinant. The interpretation of the 'best interests' principle remains controversial. The General Comment on the principle exhorts a rights-based approach when considering matters relating to children (*General Comment No. 14*, para. 5). With regards to the digital space, does the blurring of public and private spaces for a child's development require us to re-think, revise or reconceptualise the 'best interests of the child' principle? At its core, the precept of the 'best interests' is that in all decisions, the child's best interests have been a primary consideration. General Comment 14 makes an attempt to clarify the concept, suggesting that it is 'flexible and adaptable'.

However, it also notes that such an interpretation could be susceptible to manipulation by governments, state authorities and parents. Those arguing for increased protectionism on the digital space would argue that such an approach is the best interests of children. Contrarily, proponents of 'participation' as the guiding principle, would also contend such a stance is in the best interests of children.

It would seem, however, that both the risk-based (protection) and rights-based (participation) approaches are not mutually exclusive. After all, 'protection' is also a right children should enjoy. The rights would also include 'provision' of the necessary resources for enjoyment of rights. In the final analysis, the UNCRC seems to provide a balance between the three: protection, provision and participation rights. As Livingtone et al. (2019) argue, all children's rights should be supported, valued, and developed in both online and offline spheres of engagement.

4.5.4.1 Proposal for 'General Comment' on children's digital rights

The ground-breaking UNICEF Report (2017: 29) observed that:

> There is no shortage of international instruments, guidelines, agreements and principles that deal with issues such as internet freedom, openness, net neutrality, accessibility and respect for human rights. What is needed are not more guidelines, per se, but agreed-upon principles and priority actions that recognize the responsibility we share to protect children from the perils of a digital world and to help all children benefit from the promise of connectivity.

In September 2014, the CtRC devoted a special Day of General Discussion to children's rights and the digital media in order to 'develop rights-based strategies to maximise the online opportunities for children while protecting them from risks and possible harm without restricting any benefits'.

Their recommendations reinforced the imperative to re-examine each article of the UNCRC in the digital age. Not only did the committee recommend that national laws and policies dealing with children need to incorporate ICT-specific provisions while ICT-related legislation needs to assess the impact on children, but also that children's equal and safe access to the internet should be part of the post-2015 development agenda.

In 2018, the CtRC decided to develop a General Comment on children's rights in relation to the digital environment. Under public international law, Article 31 of the 1965 Vienna Convention on Law of Treaties, stipulates that treaties need continuous contextual interpretation. Furthermore, with their initial ratification of the treaty states accept that the treaty bodies play a key role in the interpretation of human rights treaties. A treaty body may adopt General Comments or Recommendations, which are official statements adopted by the Committee that elaborate on the meaning of treaty obligations. The CtRC's Concept Note observed that the digital environment posed broad-ranging opportunities and challenges for States, businesses and non-governmental organisations in respect of all the rights embodied in the UNCRC. The Committee was responding to calls by governments, businesses, child rights organisations and civil society for principled, evidence-based guidance to shape the interpretation and implementation of the Convention in a digital age.

Some General Comments or Recommendations may be procedural in nature, others may address substantive provisions of the treaty and provide the Committee's interpretation of treaty rights. It would appear the Comment will address the substantive content. According to the CtRC, the proposed General Comment:

will clarify how this rapidly evolving environment impacts on the full range of children's rights in positive and negative ways. The purpose of the General Comment will be to strengthen the case for greater action and elaborate what measures are required by States in order to meet their obligations to promote and protect children's rights in and through the digital environment, and to ensure that other actors, including business enterprises, meet their responsibilities.

Since the rights of the child are universal, indivisible and interdependent, the General Comment would provide an overarching framework. Cross-cutting general principles important in the digital environment include: non-discrimination; the best interests of the child; the right to life, survival and development; and the child's right to be heard in matters which affect them.

In March 2019, the CtRC invited all interested parties to comment on the concept note of the General Comment.[23] By the deadline for submissions (15 May 2019), the Committee had received 132 submissions from States (26), regional organisations (3), United Nations agencies (2), national human rights institutions and children's Commissioners (6), children's and adolescent groups (5), civil society organisations (52), academics (19), the private sector (7), and other entities and individuals (12). Conspicuously, the list does not include any country or regional representation from Africa. The Concept Note proposed the following areas of focus for the contributions: access to information and freedom of expression and thought, right to education and digital literacy, freedom of assembly, right to culture, leisure and play, protection of privacy, identity and data processing, protection from violence, sexual exploitation and other harm, family environment, parenting and alternative care and health and wellbeing.[24]

4.6 Concluding remarks

Children's media landscape has changed dramatically over the past few decades. The rapid growth of the internet and digital media platforms has given rise to a new digital media culture. It would appear that the new culture has brought a sense of individualism among children and reconfigured familial dynamics. It is plausible to conclude that childhood is changing. The parent – child relationships have been disrupted, raising fears around the 'perils'

---

23 Committee on the Rights of the Child Concept Note for a General Comment on Children's Rights in Relation to the Digital Environment. Available at: <www.ohchr.org/EN/HRBodies/CRC/Pages/GCChildrensRightsRelationDigitalEnvironment.aspx> (last accessed 4 January 2020).
24 Ibid.

on the digital space. On the other hand, such reaction has been regarded by some as unwarranted 'moral panic'. Evidently, internet governance has been informed by competing constructions of childhood. Children are still regarded as vulnerable to online harms while at the same time they are increasingly considered as rights-holders with individual agency. Evidence shows that children do face risks in the digital space while the internet also presents opportunities for them. Fears around digital harms may result in disproportionate responses aimed at protecting children while potentially undermining their digital participation. Ultimately, the risk-based and the rights-based or rights first approaches are not mutually exclusive. The 'new childhood' needs to be accommodated. Navigating risks and opportunities, so that children enjoy the benefits of the digital age while also being protected is the challenge for policy-makers and international child law.

Chapter 5

Child labour

5.1 The phenomenon of child labour

The complexity of the phenomenon of child labour is widely acknowledged. It can be viewed as an economic, structural, governmental, moral and ethical issue, including human rights concerns (Abernethie 1998: 83). Business enterprises increasingly operate on a global scale through complex networks of subsidiaries, contractors, suppliers and joint ventures.[1] The pervasive process of globalisation has enabled a more intense international focus on the problem, and has also added to the complexities in debates surrounding it (Fyfe 2007; Muntarbhorn 1998: 255). The elimination of child labour by 2025 is the subject of Target 8.7 of Sustainable Development Goals (SDGs).

Child labour involves not only concerns about children's welfare and development but also considerations of effects on macroeconomic and labour markets. Furthermore, the different economic, developmental, humanitarian and moral grounds that might justify the elimination of child labour sometimes conflict with each other. For example, the elimination of child labour from factories could lead to an increase in adult employment and wage rates, but might also negatively affect children's welfare if there are no adequate schools available and the children's only remaining option is to undertake more hazardous work in the 'informal sector' of the economy (Anker 2000: 264). Furthermore, the image of child labour is too often portrayed as a phenomenon principally relevant to the *developing* countries, whereas there is evidence of child labour in industrialised Europe, the United States and other *developed* nations (Selby 2008; Kilkelly 2003). In the field of child labour, one needs particularly to be aware of the different perceptions of childhood in Northern and Southern countries respectively. Arguably, the ethnocentrism of industrialised countries inappropriately dominates the international discourse on children's rights (Boyden 1997). This chapter discusses the phenomenon of child labour, the trends and its sociological conceptions. The Chapter also captures the contrasting

---

1 *Convention on the Rights of the Child* General comment No. 16 (2013) on State obligations regarding the impact of the business sector on children's rights CRC/C/GC/16, 17 April 2013.

views on the 'harms' and 'benefits' of child work as well as the legal framework for child labour.

5.1.1 Difficulties of definition and types of child labour

The concept of 'child labour' tends to conjure up several stereotypes which are not always helpful in properly identifying the nature of the problem. One such image is of children working in terrible conditions in sweatshops in India in the carpet or garment industries, or in the firecracker or matches industries in China. Another such image focuses on exploitation in export-related jobs and sex tourism. However, the reality is that most child labourers in the world are employed in the agriculture sector. The International Labour Organization (ILO) estimates that there are 152 million children who are child labourers globally (ILO 2017a: 11). The agriculture sector accounts for 71% of all those in child labour and for 108 million children in absolute terms. This includes fishing, forestry, livestock herding and aquaculture, and comprises both subsistence and commercial farming (ILO 2017a: 12).

It has been estimated that exploitation in export-related jobs accounts for a quite small proportion of the total number of child labourers, and that commercial sexual exploitation of children is dominated by local rather than foreign customers. There are also believed to be a large number of children working in the 'informal economy', in other words, children doing work outside a country's formal employment sector. Such work may be exploitative, for example, where children are working long hours under bad conditions in family-run enterprises or in illegal activities within an organised crime environment.

But work in the informal sector may also be beneficial to an individual child, depending on the context; for example, work delivering newspapers, babysitting or gardening (Selby 2008: 170; Morrow and Boyden 2018: 39). Some studies have identified quite positive attitudes by children themselves towards 'light work' and helping out in the family and home environment (Bourdillon 2017; Ochaíta et al. 2000: 31). Therefore, some tasks thus prohibited are traditionally part of acceptable child-rearing practice.

It should be clear that, for the purposes of imposing a legal regime to reduce child labour or eliminate it entirely, we need to define more precisely what 'child labour' should mean for these purposes. The task of defining child labour has been much discussed and contested precisely because there are many different views about what type of work or work characteristics are consistent with a child's welfare and development and what types do not, or indeed may have deleterious consequences. It is now generally accepted, and also reflected in the international legal regime, that a distinction must be drawn between work that children do, either at home within the family or for an external employer, which may be *beneficial* and contribute to their development and wellbeing, and 'child labour' that can be said to be *exploitative*. This begs the question of what practices can be regarded as 'exploitative' for these purposes. Exploitation is a somewhat value-laden term that is difficult to define objectively (Anker 2000: 260–61). But of course not all forms of child labour are exploitative, and in some settings child work may be an 'integral part of the socialization process' (Bourdillon et al. 2006; Alston 1989: 36). There is clearly a need to view the work that children do as lying on a continuum between dangerous and exploitative work on the one hand and beneficial work on the other.

> We can speak of dangerous and exploitative work when it has the following characteristics: it is carried out full-time at too early an age; the working day is excessively long; it is carried out in inadequate conditions; it is not sufficiently well-paid; it involves excessive responsibility; it undermines the child's dignity and self-esteem. On the other hand, beneficial work is defined as that which promotes or stimulates the child's integral development – physical, cognitive and social – without interfering in his/her scholastic or recreational activity or rest. This type of work contributes to children's socialisation, offering them the opportunity to carry out certain tasks that provide them with feelings of competence and independence that are fundamental to the proper development of their self-concept and self-esteem.
>
> (Ochaíta et al. 2000:19–20)

It is now widely accepted that the dividing line between exploitative/dangerous and beneficial child work is identified by an examination of how such work impacts on a child's development. The United Nations *Convention on the Rights of the Child*[2] obliges States parties to 'recognize the right of the child to be protected from economic exploitation and from performing any work that is likely to be hazardous or to interfere with the child's education (see Case Study 5.1), or to be harmful to the child's health or physical, mental, spiritual, moral or social development'[3] (section 3.7.7 in this book). Governments and economists responsible for collecting national statistics may have a rather narrower definition of child labour where they define it initially as 'employment'. This might capture those with a 'contract of employment' and also those recognised as 'self-employed', but could miss a range of others engaged in exploitative work. The definition of 'economic' used by the UN's System of National Accounts (SNA) is formulated in broader terms relating to the content and productive nature of the work; so gathering fuel for household use would come within the SNA definition, even though it often occurs outside a market context, and such children would be classed as child labourers. On the other hand, burning fuel in the process of cooking a meal would not be classified as economic and many would say this was a case of a child being engaged in household 'chores', a delineation that typically has gender consequences (Dorman 2008).

---

2 *United Nations Convention on the Rights of the Child*, opened for signature 20 November 1989, 1577 UNTS 3 (entered into force 2 September 1990) ('CRC' or 'UNCRC').
3 CRC, art. 32.

ILO (section 2.4.1.4 in this book) currently uses four categories for children in: 'employment', 'child labour' 'worst forms of child labour', with the subset of 'hazardous work', and 'light work'. The ILO definitions are reproduced below:

> *Children in employment* are those working in any form of market production and certain types of non-market production (principally, the production of goods such as agricultural produce for own use). This group includes children in forms of work in both the formal and informal economy; inside and outside family settings; for pay or profit (in cash or in kind, part-time or full-time); and domestic work outside the child's own household for an employer (paid or unpaid).
>
> *Children in child labour* are a subset of *children in employment*. They include those in the worst forms of child labour and children in employment below the minimum age, excluding children in permissible light work, if applicable. Child labour is therefore a narrower concept than 'children in employment'; child labour excludes those children who are working only a few hours a week in permitted light work and those above the minimum age whose work is not classified as a worst form of child labour, including 'hazardous work' in particular.
>
> *Children in the worst forms of child labour* are those in the categories of child labour set out in Article 3 of ILO Convention No. 182. These categories comprise: (a) all forms of slavery or practices similar to slavery, such as the sale and trafficking of children, debt bondage and serfdom, and forced or compulsory labour, including forced or compulsory recruitment of children for use in armed conflict; (b) the use, procuring or offering of a child for prostitution, for the production of pornography or for pornographic performances; (c) the use, procuring or offering of a child for illicit activities, in particular for the production and trafficking of drugs as defined in the relevant international treaties; and (d) work which, by its nature or the circumstances in which it is carried out, is likely to harm the health, safety, or morals of children.
>
> 'Children in hazardous work' are those involved in any activity or occupation that, by its nature or the circumstances in which it is carried out, is likely to harm their health, safety, or morals. In general, hazardous work may include night work and long hours of work, exposure to physical, psychological, or sexual abuse; work underground, under water, at dangerous heights or in confined spaces; work with dangerous machinery, equipment, and tools, or which involves the manual handling or transport of heavy loads; and work in an unhealthy environment which may, for example, expose children to hazardous substances, agents, or processes, or to temperatures, noise levels, or vibrations damaging their health. Hazardous work by children is often treated as a proxy category for the worst forms of child labour. This is for two reasons. First, reliable national data on the worst forms of child labour other than hazardous work, such as children in bonded and forced labour or in commercial

sexual exploitation, are still difficult to come by. Second, children in hazardous work account for the overwhelming majority of those in the worst forms of child labour.

Children in light work are persons from 13 years of age (or 12 years in countries that have specified the general minimum working age as 14 years) in work which is: (a) not likely to be harmful to their health or development; and (b) not such as to prejudice their attendance at school, their participation in vocational orientation or training programmes approved by the competent authority or their capacity to benefit from the instruction received. Children performing household chores refer to those performing domestic and personal services for consumption within their own households. Household chores include caring for household members; cleaning and minor household repairs; cooking and serving meals; washing and ironing clothes; and transporting or accompanying family members to and from work and school. In more technical terms, these tasks constitute a 'non-economic' form of production.

(ILO 2017a: 21)

SDGs, also known as the Global Goals,[4] were adopted by United Nations Member States in 2015 as a universal call to action to end poverty, protect the planet and ensure that all people enjoy peace and prosperity by 2030. The SDGs include a renewed global commitment to ending child labour. Specifically, target 8.7 of the SDGs calls on the global community to:

> Take immediate and effective measures to eradicate forced labour, end modern slavery and human trafficking and secure the prohibition and elimination of the worst forms of child labour, including recruitment and use of child soldiers, and by 2025 end child labour in all its forms.

The ILO definitions are useful in understanding the nuances of children and work. However, there is no universally accepted definition of 'child labour'. The phrase is used in public discourse to refer to 'child time in activities that are somehow harmful to the child' (Edmonds 2008). Economists think in terms of 'opportunity costs' to determine what might be 'harmful', that is, what activities would the child participate in if s/he was *not* working, and on balance would these be more beneficial? In other words, 'harmful' could be understood as implying the child would be made better off by not participating in the activity. However, according to Edmonds, who reviewed a large number of academic papers and reports on this problem, this definition of child labour creates 'the problem of the counterfactual',

---

4 The Sustainable Development Goals (SDGs) are a collection of 17 global goals. Under child labour, the discussion has also included SDG Goal 4 to: Ensure inclusive and equitable quality education and promote lifelong learning opportunities for all.

that is, it is impossible to know what such children would be doing in the absence of work (2008: 1). He argues that this problem is implicitly recognised in the *ILO Convention concerning the Prohibition and Immediate Action for the Elimination of the Worst Forms of Child Labour*[5] (1999) (hereafter '*The Worst Forms of Child Labour Convention*'), where hazardous work and other *worst forms* of child labour are identified on the basis of job characteristics. He concludes that the international definition of child labour needs to be based on the key *ILO Conventions* and defined on the basis of a list of job attributes and work characteristics that can be tracked; for example, total hours worked, numbers of children working in certain industries (manufacturing, mining and quarrying, hotels and restaurants, private residences other than child's family), and certain working conditions (streets, at night or predawn, low lighting, lack of ventilation, operating machinery or powered tools) (2008: 38).

A further problem with efforts to define child labour is that the pattern of child labour is frequently *intermittent*; for example, it may occur intensely in rural communities around harvest time. Many children may move from school into work and back again several times; some children attend school and also work and these patterns may vary considerably over time. In one study, using longitudinal data from Brazil, where the authors tracked the employment patterns of thousands of children aged 10–16 during four months of their lives in the 1980s and 1990s, it was concluded that 'intermittent employment is a crucial characteristic of child labour which must be recognised to capture levels of child employment adequately and identify child workers (Levison et al. 2007: 245). Such problems of definition also pose difficulties in attempting to construct credible measurements of the extent of child labour (see section 5.1.9 below).

5.1.2 Identifying the causes of child labour

The complexity of the phenomenon of child labour is particularly apparent in analyses of its *causes*. Some commentators have attempted to produce typologies of causation deploying categories which range from the dynamics of the family unit, through to the school system, the labour situation of adults and finally macrosystemic elements such as prevailing cultural attitudes towards childhood, economic and social policies and existing legislation (Ochaíta et al. 2000: 16–17). The income from child labour may reflect a family's strategy to simply subsist. Children's labour in many countries fills the income gap.

ILO has estimated the incidence of child labour against different levels of national income, grouping countries into four categories according to their national income per capita (GNI). In low-income countries, child labour tends to decline with increases in gross per capita domestic product (GDP) (Betcherman et al. 2004: 12–13). As Table 5.1 shows, the lesser the national income,

---

5 International Labour Organization, *Worst Forms of Child Labour Convention*, ILO Convention No. 182 (17 June 1999).

Table 5.1 Number and percentage of children in child labour and hazardous work, by national income grouping, 2016

	Children in child labour		Children in hazardous work	
	Number ('000s)	%	Number ('000s)	%
Low-income	65203	19.4	29664	8.8
Lower-middle-income	58184	8.5	33465	4.9
Upper-middle-income	26209	6.6	7751	2.0
High-income	2025	1.2	1645	1.0

Source: ILO 2017a: Table 3, p. 32.

the higher the incidence of child labour and hazardous work. A key feature of child labour is that it is not only caused by structural economic, educational and social disadvantage, but it also contributes to the maintenance of such inequalities (Crivello and van der Gaag 2016: 19). Child labour is often regarded as a consequence of poverty. By depriving the child of education and an opportunity for development to her or his full potential, child labour is also a cause of perpetuating poverty to the next generation. It is necessary to break the vicious cycle with a strong political will and comprehensive set of practical measures, supported by solid legal framework (Noguchi 2010: 533).

The research literature (Dorman 2008) is replete with discussion of the linkage with poverty and the lack of education and health services. The ILO asserts that: 'Education helps break intergenerational cycles of poverty and provides a worthwhile alternative to child labour' (2017a: 52). This is known as the 'human capital' theory. The next section explores the nexus between poverty and education.

5.1.3 The 'poverty and education' thesis

The increasing recognition of child labour located within a poverty matrix indicates much about the remedial strategies to tackle the problem, that is, strategies which integrate anti-poverty and wider development goals (Cooper 1997: 429). The way in which the matrix of poverty, educational disadvantage and child labour are linked by both cause and effect prompted ILO to announce a decade ago that:

> We have surely reached a moment in history where the absolute number of child labourers, and the proportion of a country's children who are subject to child labour, particularly to its worst forms, should become key indicators of economic and social development.
>
> (ILO 2002a: para. 63)

Policy contribution to mitigating child labour and improving income-earning outcomes have to be seen in the larger context of an enabling structural change, aided and abetted by appropriate public policies and supported by strong fiscal and monetary measures (ILO 2017a: 33).

The role of education is a key component in any discussion about the causes of child labour; '[c]hild labour can be defined as a form of denial of the right to education' (Humbert 2009: 33; Rosati et al. 2015b: 32). There is, perhaps unsurprisingly, a lot of evidence confirming the adverse impact of child labour on educational attainment (Betcherman et al. 2004: 13) There is wider evidence that working children lag behind their non-working peers in terms of educational outcomes and progression (Guarcello et al. 2015: 18; UNESCO 2015: 65;[6] Quattri and Watkins 2016: 16). The hard physical labour that often characterises children's work alongside the high costs and inflexibility displayed by the school system combine to create difficulties for working children who also wish to attend school (Morrow 2015: 17). Exhaustion resulting from long working hours can hamper children's concentration in the classroom and subsequent learning (UNESCO 2015: 65). Many poor children faced difficulties when trying to re-enrol in school, even after short periods of absence (Boyden et al. 2016: 22). Children trying to balance both work and schooling often have inadequate support to do so (Aufseeser 2014: 114).

In a study on Bangladesh, it was observed that children from poorer households who had little access to secondary education became engaged in a range of economic activity some of which was hazardous (Masum 2002: 266). Abolishing school fees and providing support for additional costs, such as books, school uniforms and transport can encourage working children to attend school (ILO 2017a: 52) Tetteh (2011: 230) argues, in relation to child domestic workers in Ghana, that '[i]f governments can ensure that all children have access to a free compulsory universal basic education . . . , the problem of girl child labour will be drastically reduced'. Children also drop out of school often because of poor teaching and learning conditions and they are predominantly poor, rural and disproportionately female (Betcherman et al. 2004: 17; Morrow 2015; Boyden et al. 2016: 22; Singh and Khan 2016: 11; Quattri and Watkins 2016: 19). Research by Boyden et al. (2016: 22) found that in Ethiopia poor quality education was a stronger determinant of the interruption of children's schooling than work. If the States parties' obligations under the *Convention on the Rights of the Child* to make primary education compulsory and available free for all (section 3.7.8 in this book),[7] and the SDG[8] goal to strengthen universal primary education are to be achieved, then it follows that child labour will necessarily diminish.

The persistence of child labour in any country is clearly a significant obstacle to achieving universal education (Betcherman et al. 2004: 2). Despite the considerable

---

6 UNESCO Institute for Statistics and UNICEF (2015) *Fixing the broken promise of education for all: Findings from the global initiative on out-of-school children*. Montreal: UNESCO Institute for Statistics.
7 CRC, art. 28(1)(a).
8 SDG Goal 4 aims to: Ensure inclusive and equitable quality education and promote lifelong learning opportunities for all.

progress on education access and participation over the past years, 262 million children and youth aged 6–17 were still out of school in 2017.[9] It is thought that school attendance will both prevent child labour from occurring and have the potential to rehabilitate rescued child labourers and ensure their social reintegration.

However, it should not be thought that the causative factors underlying child labour follow the same pattern in every country. A reasonable assumption in relation to the United Kingdom, the first industrialised nation, might be that child labour is intimately linked with the process of industrialisation. However, that assertion is belied by the widespread incidence of child labour in India, where the majority of child labourers are employed in small-scale enterprises and in agriculture (Weiner 1994: 122). The pervasiveness and durability of the causative mix of factors leading to child labour in any one country is explained better by detailed investigation of the national profile. This, at least, should enable the disposal of several myths that have grown up around the child labour issue, for example, that children's 'nimble fingers' enable them to handle more efficiently tasks such as producing knots in the weaving of carpets, picking tea leaves and packing matches. A detailed study surveying the gem, brassware, glass, pottery and lock industries in India refutes a number of these claims (Burra 1995).

In their large-scale study of the relationship between child labour and education in poor households in Dhaka's slums, Quattri and Watkins (2016: 9) found that parents were often compelled to send their children to work to meet minimum income requirements – what the authors term a 'distress choice'. Unaffordable, inaccessible and/ or irrelevant education, results in a lack of perceived returns to education in poor households, particularly in rural areas (Krauss 2016). This can make sending children to work seem a more useful option than sending them to school (Brown 2012; Pereznieto et al. 2016: 13). The extra household income from working may actually facilitate the child's schooling by relieving all or part of the associated financial burden to the household (Maconachie and Hilson 2016).

Given the causative significance of poverty to the existence and extent of child labour, it is tempting to conclude that any remedial strategy should prioritise the eradication of poverty. The problem is that such policies take many years, sometimes several generations, to make significant development gains. The UN Commission on Human Rights[10] (UNCHR) stated long ago that '[p]overty is often the main cause of child labour, but generations of children should not be condemned, until poverty is overcome, to exploitation' (UNCHR 1993: para. 2). Human rights advocates are in agreement with this point: 'To argue that the enormous problem of poverty must be solved first and that the problem of child labor should be addressed gradually is antithetical to the inherent logic of human rights' (Silk and Makonnen 2003: 368).

It would seem that '[a]dvances in the right to education therefore cannot but go hand in hand with the elimination of child labour' (Noguchi 2002: 362). However,

---

9 See UN Sustainable Development Goal 4 https://sustainabledevelopment.un.org/sdg4
10 Replaced in 2006 by the United Nations Human Rights Council (UNHRC). See section 2.5.1.1 in this book.

developing nations have often been reluctant to invest in universal education on the basis of the large costs involved, and that poor families rely upon their children's income. Such arguments appear unsatisfactory when one considers the historical evidence which suggests a range of factors contributing to the introduction of universal education. Japan introduced compulsory education in 1872 and North and South Korea, Taiwan and China introduced compulsory education shortly after the Second World War; all at a time when per capita incomes in those countries were low and poverty widespread. Nevertheless, in one country after another the phased extension of the age of compulsory education accompanied further restrictions on the employment of children (Weiner 1994: 128).

While poverty is understood to push many poor children out of the classroom into work, child labour is a complex phenomenon, affected by many factors (Dammert et al. 2017: 2). The reduction of educational disadvantage and poverty cannot be a complete answer to the problem of child labour. There have been significant efforts in India, for example, to reduce poverty and strengthen education. However, one study observes that '[n]otwithstanding these economic successes, the number of children working in India has not decreased significantly and may have even increased', and that it is important that the Indian government stops thinking in terms of child labour being a problem simply associated with poverty (Agarwal 2004: 665, 713). Some empirical research shows that the relationship between poverty and child labour is weaker than is often believed (Betcherman et al. 2004: 3). Indeed, the causative strength of poverty and lack of education weakens when we consider the persistence of child labour within the developed nations. In Europe, it seems likely that a significant number of children, rather than being motivated by family survival strategies typical in developing nations, are more motivated by the desire to obtain 'supplementary income necessary to meet their consumer desires and the demands of peer pressure' (Kilkelly 2003: 347). Others causes of child labour include inequality (Pereznieto et al. 2016: 16), economic uncertainty, created or intensified, by droughts, floods, rising food prices and/ or family illness or deaths (Brown 2012: 10; Chuta 2014; Dammert et al. 2017: 3).

5.1.4 TWAIL, cultural relativism and child labour

An often-underused tool for analysis is the so-called Third World Approaches to International Law (TWAIL). Chimni asserts that the international legal system 'represents a culture that constitutes the matrix in which global problems are approached, analysed, and resolved. This culture is shaped and framed by the dominant ideas of the time' (Chimni 2006: 15). TWAIL scholarship is considered as an intellectual resistance closely linked to decolonisation movement and postcolonial experiences of Third World nations in international law (Anghie 2007; Gathii 2011; Haskell 2014; Mutua 2000).

However, TWAIL seems to have been marginalised in international legal scholarship (Sunter 2007; Chimni 2006). TWAIL can offer an alternative perspective in the analysis of international law. It would appear quite useful in, but not limited to, analysis of child labour and associated laws. Anghie (2007) has argued that international law is driven, in part, by a dynamic of cultural difference.

Social and cultural norms can play a part in child labour; in many countries, labour is seen as a productive, valuable and normal use of a child's time (Pereznieto et al. 2016: 13). The issue of 'cultural relativism' and 'childhood' has been explored in Chapter 1. The conceptions of childhood may be culturally dependent. On the one hand, there is a general agreement that childhood is the period of a human being characterised by their physical and mental growth stages (Myers 2001). On the other, 'cultural relativism' asserts that the construction of childhood depends upon the social mores that highly draw on cultural variations. Some commentators have argued that the ethnocentrism of industrialised countries inappropriately dominates the international discourse on children's rights (Edwards 2015; Boyden 1997).Thus the campaigns against 'child labour' targeted primarily the work of deprived children and communities in low-income countries, largely ignoring many jobs undertaken by children in high-income countries. Campaigns focused on activities that contrasted with Western, middle-class, largely urban, perceptions of 'childhood' (Bourdillon et al. 2006).

A criticism of international law is that the body of law places a priority on civil and political rights over social, economic, and cultural rights.[11] Some of the earlier policy thinking about child labour was dominated by the idea that the ultimate goal should be to remove all children from work completely and that children's 'best interests' would be served by freeing them to enjoy a childhood in caring family environments. Yet this approach ignored important variances in global social, cultural and economic orders. Such perceptions have led to the growing calls for the 'decolonisation of international law', and indeed curricula. TWAIL scholars rationalise international law only in the context of the lived history of the peoples of the Third World. The experience of colonialism and neo-colonialism has made Third World peoples acutely sensitive to power relations among states (Anghie and Chimni 2003: 185–6). The wholesale ban on child labour became discredited on the basis that it depended on a Northern-country ideal of childhood and led to caution by Southern countries to open dialogue with Northern donors and development agencies on the issue of child labour (Crawford 2000).

To some societies, the distinction between childhood and adulthood seems to be less categorical and therefore the idea of child labour is not as outrageous as it is universally presented today. In Southern countries, children's work is more likely to be considered an acceptable element of family survival strategy. The number of children and the amount of human capital in a household is contingent upon legal restrictions on child labour. The basic differences in the underlining perceptions of childhood in Northern/developed/industrialised on the one hand, and Southern/developing/non-industrialised countries on the other, has provided ongoing obstacles to the reception of the international legal regime. Thus, a 'TWAIL analysis helps scholars to critique the oft-proclaimed high moral ground occupied by the West and mainstream international law' (Badaru 2008: 383)

---

11 UN GAOR, 3rd Sess., 183rd plen. mtg, UN Doc. A/PV. 183 (10 Dec. 1948) [hereinafter 183rd Plenary Meeting].

Recent scholarship shows a more nuanced perspective on child labour. Several studies highlight both benefits and risks related child labour (Tafere and Pankhurst 2015; Morrow 2015). Although children's work can negatively affect children's educational achievement (Woldehanna and Gebremedhin 2015), working can enable children to pursue education (Aufseeser 2014: 114; Tafere and Pankhurst 2015: 20). Many children engage in both school and work; in some cases this is not only necessary, but useful (Tafere and Pankhurst 2015: 4). The notion of educational linear progression may be irrelevant for working children in many contexts. Tafere and Pankhurst (2015: 24) argue that while banning children's work 'may seem logical at face value', such initiatives may be unrealistic in some social settings; some children need to work, either to support their families or to be able to afford schooling. Boyden et al. (2016: 24) found in that in rural Ethiopia, children did not attend school continuously; instead, they attended school when possible, balancing this with their economic and household responsibilities. In some studies, it is argued that the reality and need for children to work should be acknowledged, and therefore the design of education systems should try to accommodate the working child (Tafere and Pankhurst 2015 13; Bourdillon 2017). Morrow and Boyden (2018: 38) note that schools that have adjusted school timetables to the 'subsistence cycle' – allowing children breaks to help with harvesting – have helped prevent working children from dropping out of formal education.

In such contexts, education is regarded as an activity to fit around other aspects of life, especially work (Crivello and van der Gaag 2016: 19). In such cases, policy concern should be with supporting children who combine working and education, rather than with abolishing children's work (Bourdillon 2017; Morrow and Boyden 2018). Disregarding socio-economic and cultural diversity, globalised notions of childhood and child work would be odds with children's interests (Khair 2010). 'Reimagining' child labour would leave room for children to be seen as 'economic actors'.

However, although there may be credible arguments that minimum age rules are driven by the ethnocentric concerns of the developed nations, it is less easy to maintain such criticisms in relation to the desire to eliminate the *worst forms* of child labour. As one commentator notes, 'it is important not to confuse the argument that some types of employment may be acceptable with cultural relativist arguments that exploitative or harmful child labour may be tolerable because of cultural differences' (Selby 2008: 171). It is also is important to recognise that some regard for the differing perspectives of developing, non-industrialised countries has been built into the ILO Constitution.[12] This will be discussed later (see section 5.2.3 below).

5.1.5 The extent and location of exploitative child labour

ILO's global report on child labour announced optimistically in 2006 that 'a future without child labour is at last within reach' (ILO 2006: 1). The claim was principally based on the identification of a significant fall (11.2%) in the number

---

12 International Labour Organization, *Constitution of the International Labour Organisation (ILO)*, 1 April 1919, art. 19(3).

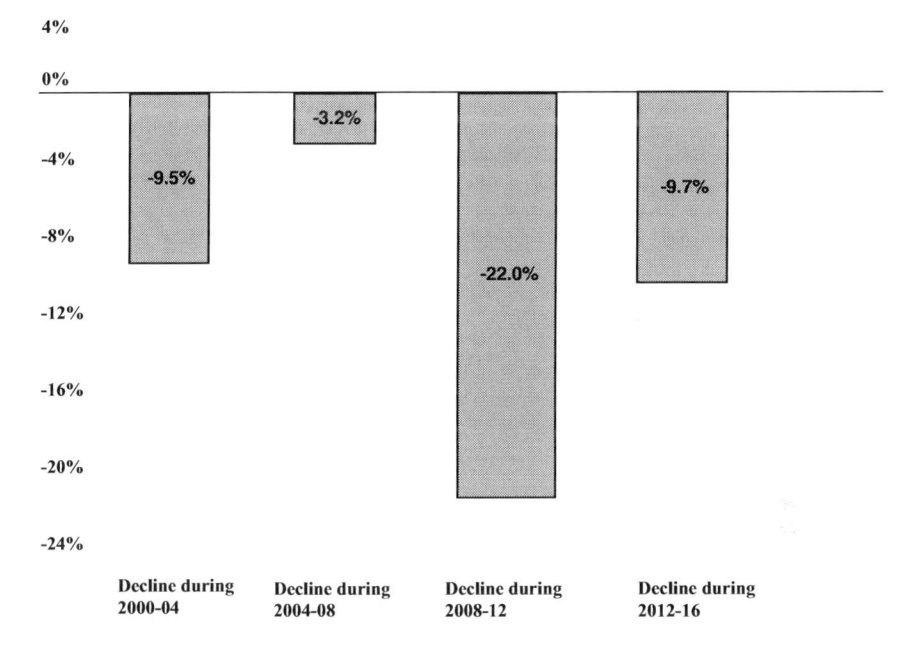

Figure 5.1 Changes in rates of progress against child labour since 2000.

Source: ILO 2017a: 26.

of children in child labour from 245.5 million in 2000 to 218 million in 2004. Furthermore, within this figure the number of children in 'hazardous work' had fallen even more steeply (26.1%) from 170.5 million in 2000 to 126 million in 2004.[13] Improvements in these figures have continued in recent years. Child labour declined during the period from 2012 to 2016, continuing a trend seen since the publication of the ILO's first global estimates of child labour in 2000. The 16-year period starting in 2000 saw a net reduction of 94 million in children in child labour (ILO 2017a). There were almost 134 million fewer children in employment in 2016 than in 2000. The downward trend has been remarkable. The comparable figures show a fall from 215 million children in child labour in 2008 to 168 million in 2012 – a reduction by 22% (Table 5.1), and a fall from 115 million to 85 million in the same period in relation to hazardous work.

Nonetheless, in actuality, progress slowed during 2012 to 2016. A narrower focus on the most recent four-year period indicates a significant slowing down of progress. The reduction in the number of children in child labour amounted to 16 million for the 2012 to 2016 period (9.7%), compared to the 22% between 2008 and 2012. The decline in hazardous work slowed in a similar fashion (ILO 2017a).

13 See the second edition of this book, Table 4.2, p. 173.

288 Child labour

The latest estimates suggest that a total of 152 million children – 64 million girls and 88 million boys – are in child labour globally, accounting for almost one in ten of all children worldwide (ILO 2017a: 11). The number of children in hazardous work has plummeted from 170, 5 million in 2000 to 72, 5 million in 2016 (Figure 5.2). The incidence of child labour across the five regions in Table 5.2 below shows that Africa ranks highest both in the percentage of children in child labour – one-fifth – and the absolute number of children in child labour – 72 million. Asia

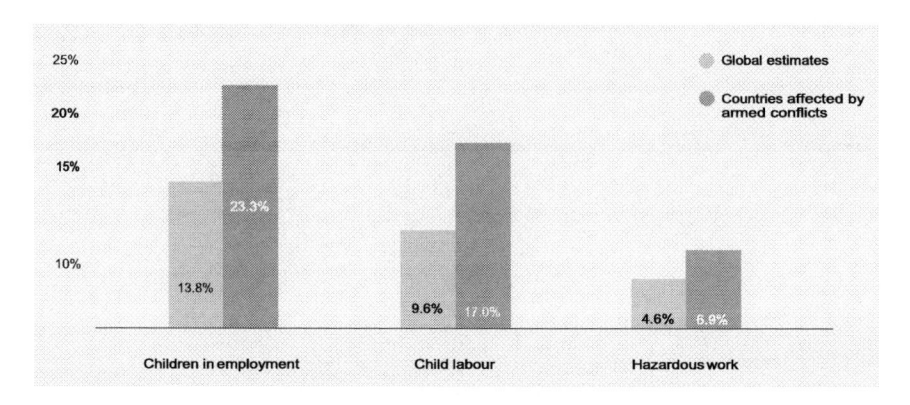

Figure 5.2 Percentage of children in employment, child labour and hazardous work, 5–17 years age range, globally and in countries affected by armed conflict, 2016.

Source: ILO 2017a: Fig. 7, p. 31. Countries classified as 'affected by armed conflict' are taken from the Report of the Secretary General on children and armed conflict, submitted to the UN Security Council in 2015.

Table 5.2 Number and percentage of children in child labour and hazardous work, by region, 2016

		Children in child labour		Children in hazardous work	
		Number ('000s)	%	Number ('000s)	%
World (5–17 years)		151622	9.6	72525	4.6
Region	Africa	72113	19.6	31538	8.6
	Arab States	1162	2.9	616	1.5
	Asia and the Pacific	62077	7.4	28469	3.4
	Americas	10735	5.3	6553	3.2
	Europe and Central Asia	5534	4.1	5349	4.0

Source: ILO 2017a: Table 2, p. 28.

and the Pacific ranks second highest in both these measures – 7% of all children, 62 million in absolute terms, are in child labour in this region.

The Africa and Asia and Pacific regions together account for almost nine out of every ten children in child labour worldwide. The remaining child labour population is divided among the Americas (11 million), Europe and Central Asia (6 million), and the Arab States (1 million). The 2016 estimates suggest that sub-Saharan Africa witnessed a rise in child labour during the 2012 to 2016 period – despite the number of targeted policies implemented by African governments to combat child labour – in contrast to the other major regions, where child labour continued to decline. ILO attributes the spike to have been 'driven in important part by broader economic and demographic forces acting against governmental efforts, although this is a matter requiring further research' (ILO 2017a: 29).

The sectoral distribution of child labour is usually presented by ILO in terms of three generic sectors: agriculture; industry; and services. Agriculture consists primarily of work on smallholder family farms, although it also extends to activities such as livestock production, fishing and aquaculture. The service sub-sectors of most relevance for child labour include hotels and restaurant, wholesale and retail trade (commerce); maintenance and repair of motor vehicle; transport; other community, social and personal service activities; and domestic work. The industry sub-sectors of most relevance for child labour include construction, mining and manufacturing (ILO 2017a). Globally, child labour is concentrated in agriculture (Table 5.3 below). The sector accounts for 71% of all those in child labour and for 108 million.

Although the widely held assumption that exploitative child labour occurs mostly in the developing world is borne out by the ILO estimates, it should not be thought that the occurrence of child labour in developed countries is insignificant (Avis 2017; Dorman 2001). A General Comment on International Convention on

Table 5.3 Child labour by sector

		Agriculture % share	Industry % share	Services % share	Total % share
World		70.9	11.9	17.2	100
Region	Africa	85.1	3.7	11.2	100
	Arab States	60.3	12.4	27.4	100
	Americas	51.5	13.2	35.3	100
	Asia and the Pacific	57.5	21.4	21.1	100
	Europe and Central Asia	76.7	9.7	13.6	100
Sex	Male	71.5	12.4	16.1	100
	Female	70.3	11.1	18.6	100
Age range	5–14	78.0	7.4	14.5	100
	15–17	49.3	25.6	25.1	100

Source: ILO 2017a: 34.

the Protection of the Rights of All Migrant Workers and Members of their Families (2017) noted that: 'Unaccompanied and separated children may face further vulnerabilities and can be more exposed to risks, such as gender-based, sexual and other forms of violence and trafficking for sexual or labour exploitation'.[14] The involvement of migrant children in commercial agriculture is prevalent in developed countries. For example, in the United States, children of migrant agricultural workers and workers resident in the US numbered an estimated 800,000, according to an ILO report of 2006.[15] Indeed, even where the employment of children is lawful, such work may be injurious (O'Donnell and White 1999). The *General Comment* on business and children's rights enjoins states to put in place measures to ensure that business activities take place within appropriate legal and institutional frameworks in all circumstances regardless of size or sector of the economy so that children's rights can be clearly recognised and protected.[16] However, relatively effective labour regulatory systems in the developed countries are unlikely to identify or exert much influence over children who are involved in informal or illegal work, outside the scope of health and safety legislation and hidden from national monitoring systems (Kilkelly 2003: 347).

The ILO has observed that in Europe, there have always been a relatively large number of children working for pay, in seasonal activities, street trades, small workshops or in a home work setting. There is a similar pattern in the United States, where 'the growth of the service sector, the rapid increase in the supply of part-time jobs and the search for a more flexible workforce have contributed to the expansion of the child labour market' (ILO 1996: para. 13). The global headline estimates and profiles of child labour produced by ILO and other international institutions can also mask the nature of child labour experienced in individual countries. In a study of Bangladesh, for example, it was found that 63.5% of child labourers worked unpaid in family enterprises and that wage employment accounted for only 8.5% of total child employment (Masum 2002: 237). In a study in the United States, a high proportion of children, often from ethnic minorities and immigrant groups, were identified as working in agriculture (Davidson 2001: 206–7). Unfortunately, the variety of studies using different methodologies and statistical categories does not make the task of comparing one country's performance with another any easier.

---

14 Committee on the Protection of the Rights of All Committee on the Rights of the Child Migrant Workers and Members of Their Families and Committee on the Rights of the Child: Joint General Comment No. 3 (2017) of the Committee on the Protection of the Rights of All Migrant Workers and Members of Their Families and No. 22 (2017) of the Committee on the Rights of the Child on the general principles regarding the human rights of children in the context of international migration CMW/C/GC/3-CRC/C/GC/22 16 November 2017.
15 ILO 2006. ILCCR: Examination of individual case concerning Convention No. 182, Worst Forms of Child Labour, 1999 United States (ratification: 1999).
16 *Convention on the Rights of the Child* General comment No. 16 (2013) on State obligations regarding the impact of the business sector on children's rights CRC/C/GC/16, 17 April 2013.

A *General Comment* on children in street situations (2017)[17] noted that data are not systematically collected or disaggregated, so it is not known how many children are in these circumstances. Estimates fluctuate according to definitions used that reflect socio-economic, political, cultural and other conditions. The CtRC stated:

> The criminalization of begging or unlicensed trading can result in worse forms of survival behaviours, such as commercial sexual exploitation. Savings schemes to develop budgeting skills and safeguard earnings for children in street situations are beneficial.[18]

5.1.6 Forced labour and marriage

The ILO also publishes global estimates of modern slavery, focusing on: forced labour and forced marriage (ILO 2017b).[19] Forced labour is defined as 'all work or service that is exacted from any person under the menace of any penalty and for which the said person has not offered himself voluntarily'.[20] With regards to children, forced labour is work performed by a child under coercion applied by a third party (other than his or her parents) either to the child or to the child's parents, or work performed by a child as a direct consequence of his or her parent or parents being engaged in forced labour.

The ILO estimate of forced labour comprises coercive labour in the private economy (forms of forced labour imposed by private individuals, groups, or companies in all sectors except the commercial sex industry), forced sexual exploitation of adults and commercial sexual exploitation of children, and state-imposed forced labour.

An estimated 40.3 million people were victims of modern slavery in 2016. In other words, on any given day in 2016, there were likely to be more than 40 million men, women and children who were being forced to work against their will under threat or who were living in a forced marriage that they had not agreed to. Of these 40.3 million victims, 24.9 million people were in forced labour (see also 8.1.2 in this book). That is, they were being forced to work under threat or coercion (ILO 2017b).

Women and girls are disproportionately affected by modern slavery, accounting for 28.7 million, or 71% of the overall total. More precisely, women and girls represent 99% of victims of forced labour in the commercial sex industry and 58% in other sectors, 40% of victims of forced labour imposed by state authorities, and 84% of victims of forced marriages.

---

17 *Committee on the Rights of the Child* General comment No. 21 (2017) on children in street situations CRC/C/GC/21, 21 June 2017.
18 Ibid., para. 59.
19 See ILO 2017b.
20 International Labour Organization, Forced Labour Convention, 1930 (No. 29).

Forced marriage refers to situations where persons, regardless of their age, have been forced to marry without their consent. A person might be forced to marry through physical, emotional, or financial duress, deception by family members, the spouse, or others, or the use of force, threats, or severe pressure. About 15.4 million people were living in a forced marriage to which they had not consented. That is, they were enduring a situation that involved having lost their sexual autonomy and often involved providing labour under the guise of 'marriage'. While men and boys can also be victims of forced marriage, most victims (88%) were women and girls, with more than a third (37%) of victims under 18 years of age at the time of the marriage. Among child victims, 44% were forced to marry before the age of 15 years.

Child marriage is generally considered to be forced marriage, given that one and/or both parties by definition has not expressed full, free and informed consent. According to the Committee on the Discrimination against Women and the CtRC:

> A child marriage is considered to be a form of forced marriage, given that one and/or both parties have not expressed full, free and informed consent. As a matter of respecting the child's evolving capacities and autonomy in making decisions that affect her or his life, a marriage of a mature, capable child below 18 years of age may be allowed in exceptional circumstances, provided that the child is at least 16 years of age and that such decisions are made by a judge based on legitimate exceptional grounds defined by law and on the evidence of maturity, without deference to culture and tradition.[21]

It is clear that the notion of 'labour' and the remit of the ILO has now been expanded to include, as noted above, forced and child marriages and as shall be discussed in section 5.2.3, children who participate in armed conflict.

5.1.7 Child labour and armed conflict

There is also a strong correlation between child labour and situations of conflict and disaster (ILO 2017a: 12). The Africa region has been among those most affected by situations of conflict and disaster, which in turn heighten the risk of child labour.

The *Report of the Secretary-General on Children and Armed Conflict* (S/2015/409), submitted to the UN Security Council in 2015, indicates that the share of children in employment, child labour, and hazardous work is significantly higher in countries affected by armed conflict than global averages. The incidence

---

21 Joint general recommendation No. 31 of the Committee on the Elimination of Discrimination against Women/general comment No. 18 of the Committee on the Rights of the Child on harmful practices, 14 November 2014 (CEDAW/C/ GC/31-CRC/C/GC/18).

of child labour in countries affected by armed conflict is 77% higher than the global average, while the incidence of hazardous work is 50% higher in countries affected by armed conflict than in the world as a whole. The CtRC also noted possibilities of greater risk of child labour being used by business enterprises (including within supply chains and subsidiaries) in times of conflict.[22] An ILO study of Syrian refugees in Jordan shows poor Syrian children are much more exposed to child labour than their Jordanian peers (Blanco et al. 2017). Other studies also suggest that the Syria crisis is associated with an alarming rise in child labour (UNICEF/Save the Children Foundation 2015; Terre de Hommes International Federation 2016). This situation underscores the importance of prioritizing child labour within humanitarian responses and during reconstruction and recovery (ILO 2017a: 12).

5.1.8 Covert nature of child labour

It is widely accepted that a dominant and characteristic feature of child labour is that it frequently occurs covertly and in the so-called 'informal sector', for example, family-based enterprises outside of State regulatory regimes. In some countries the proportion of children in the informal economy is very high. In Bangladesh it has been reported that the informal segment within the private sector accounted for 94% of total child employment (Masum 2002: 237; Quattri and Watkins 2016). This has now been exacerbated by the movement of about 700,000 members of the Rohingya ethnic minority in 2017, who were fleeing from attacks in Burma.[23] Of these, nearly 400,000 of those displaced are children, some of whom are subjected to trafficking and labour exploitation (IOM 2017). There are reports that Rohingya children are exploited in bonded labour in the fish drying industry. Girls typically work in domestic service, in the homes of Bangladeshi families living up to 150 kilometres from the Rohingya refugee camps (UNICEF 2018; IOM 2018). In one study on Africa, it was noted that less than 10% of the population were employed by the formal sector (Bonnet 1993: 381). In Pakistan, labour participation in the informal economy vastly outstrips that in the formal economy: 72.6% of all labour participation is informal.[24] With the exception of embroidery, most tasks done by home-based workers were relatively low-skilled.

Of the workers surveyed for one research, 145 reported that they had helpers aged under 18 who spent an average of 3.6 hours on home-based work per day

---

22 *Convention on the Rights of the Child* General comment No. 16 (2013) on State obligations regarding the impact of the business sector on children's rights CRC/C/GC/16, 17 April 2013.
23 Child Labour and Forced Labor Reports: Bangladesh: 2017 Findings on the Worst Forms of Child Labour Bureau of International Labor Affairs, US Department of Labour.
24 Pakistan Bureau of Statistics: Labour Force Survey 2014–15 (Islamabad, 2014). Available at: www.pbs.gov.pk/sites/default/files//Annual%20Report%20of%20LFS%202014-15.pdf (accessed 29 November 2019).

(Zhou 2017). Cropping and zip work in particular were often done by children in the household. In one study, it was observed that most child labourers work unpaid in the home and the government had no way to keep track of them; less than half of all children attend school, and there is no way to monitor the children (Johnson 1999: 170). The covert forms of child labour in the informal sector will often be outside the remit and/or practical reach of regulatory labour inspectorates. For example, in Lesotho's and Portugal's thriving shoe industries and in the Philippine garment industry 'entire families work at home, making inspection nearly impossible' (Davidson 2001: 220). In the Philippines, for example, while labour inspectors have a mandate to monitor informal settings where the vast majority of child labourers are found, their capacity rarely lets them do so effectively (Rosati et al. 2015a: 79).

It is difficult to collect reliable data on child labour which is carried out covertly and/or in the informal sector of an economy. It does seem likely, however, that gender is an important element to help explain national child labour profiles. For example, in a study relating to Turkey it is reported that it is traditionally expected that a young woman remains chaste if she is unmarried, and consequently it is thought best to keep young females within the domestic setting to protect her and the honour of the family (Boyden et al. 2013; Bakirci 2002: 56). These kinds of societal attitudes will often be responsible for a disproportionate number of girls being engaged in home-based, domestic settings for a range of child labour activities.

5.1.9 Measuring the extent of child labour

The definitional difficulties discussed in section 5.1.1 and the clandestine nature of much of the informal economy discussed in section 5.1.8 make the task of measuring its incidence much harder. However, despite the conceptual, technical and infrastructural obstacles to establishing reliable statistical profiles of child labour, the estimates do at least prompt attention to the size of the problem as a legitimate concern for the international community. The literature reviewing statistical work shows that the scale of the problem is often *underestimated* because of the covert nature of child labour (Felicini 2013). Nevertheless, international organisations, national governments and non-governmental organisations (NGOs) all have their own agendas and no doubt headline figures are often deployed for 'advocacy' purposes (Invernizzi and Milne 2002). In addition, national efforts to collect relevant data in the formal sector are variable and use different methodologies. The landscape of child labour is often fast-moving and 'intermittent' (Levison et al. 2007) and difficult to capture. While human rights advocates may have an interest in *overestimation* to focus public discussion, national governments may have an interest in *underestimating* the extent of the problem; consequently it is unsurprising that official statistics may be underestimating the real size of the problem (IREWOC 2010: 7; Bakirci 2002: 55). In *developing* countries there may be the additional problem of a lack of governmental infrastructure to support accurate statistical survey activity. But it should not be assumed that there are no significant defects in the data relating to *developed* countries. It has been observed that many of the European States have insufficiently effective systems of data collection and there remains an overwhelming lack of such data in Europe (Kilkelly 2003: 326, 346).

ILO and the CtRC have been aware for some time of the need for more reliable and appropriately calibrated statistical estimates in order better to inform the policy-making process at the global, regional, national and local levels. Indeed, there is a requirement in the *Worst Forms of Child Labour Recommendation No. 190*[25] (1999) on ILO Member States to compile and maintain detailed statistical data.[26] There have been attempts, since the 'International Year of the Child' in 1979, to collate reliable global statistics on the extent of child labour disaggregated by age, gender, region, formal/informal economy, economic sector, type of work and other criteria. The different estimates made by ILO, other international bodies and NGOs prompted one commentator to observe that '[t]hese divergences reflect the difficulty of obtaining any sort of precise figures in relation to a practice which is generally ignored by official statistics' (Alston 1989: 36). In 1998, a unit within ILO's 'International Programme on the Elimination of Child Labour' (IPEC) – the 'Statistical Information and Monitoring Programme on Child Labour' (SIMPOC) – was established to provide more sophisticated estimates. It has been argued by one observer that several estimates are needed to represent the different types of work and their location along the exploitative/beneficial continuum of child labour (Anker 2000: 265).

The first integrated study of the economic costs and benefits of eliminating child labour throughout the developing and transitional countries was undertaken by ILO in 2004 (ILO/UNICEF 2004). A general programme of action was developed and (hypothetically) applied in each country under examination, estimations being made of the costs and benefits from eliminating child labour. Estimates were made of the two principal benefits: first, the benefits of improved productivity and earning capacity resulting from greater education; and second, the benefits of reduced illness and injuries, due to the elimination of the worst forms of child labour. The study found that the total economic benefits, resulting from the elimination of child labour over the period 2000–2020, would be $5,106.3 billion, whereas the total economic costs would be $760.3 billion. In other words, there would be a total net economic benefit of $4,346.1 billion. The study concluded that the 'single most import result is that the elimination of child labour and its

---

25 *R190 – Worst Forms of Child Labour Recommendation*, 1999 (No. 190), Recommendation concerning the prohibition and immediate action for the elimination of the worst forms of child labour. Adoption: Geneva, 87th ILC session (17 June 1999). *ILO Recommendations* are not binding in international law, 'but are frequently found by governments, by national parliaments, by employers' and workers' organisations and other interested groups to be a useful checklist of actions that may be taken to give effect to the obligations entered into by ratification of a Convention' (ILO 2002a: 35).

26 *R190 Worst Forms of Child Labour Recommendation*, para. 5(1).

replacement by universal education is estimated to yield enormous economic benefits (ILO/UNICEF 2004: 4).

5.2 International legal protection of child labour

Child labour, a term that was first coined in Britain during the nineteenth century (Humbert 2009: 27), became increasingly a matter of concern as the Industrial Revolution in Europe advanced. Legislation regulating safety and other labour standards in factories and elsewhere arose as a result of these developments and were prompted by the pressures brought to bear by vigorous trade union movements. The *ILO Conventions*, discussed in the following paragraphs, first made their appearance in 1919. International concern was focused on child labour by a major international campaign run by the Anti-Slavery Society for the Protection of Human Rights in 1975, and in 1980 the United Nations appointed a Special Rapporteur, Abdelwahab Bouhdiba, whose report provided further impetus for international action (Bouhdiba 1982).[27]

There are three main international instruments to consider which in combination form the core of international legal standards in this area:

(1) the *Minimum Age Convention of 1973*;[28]
(2) various articles of the *Convention on the Rights of the Child* (1989);[29]
(3) the *Worst Forms of Child Labour Convention of 1999*.[30]

Arguably, these three Conventions reflect competing notions of childhood and the role of children's work. It is argued that the *Minimum Age Convention* reflects traditional and Northern-country ethnocentric ideas about children and work, and that it treats children as helpless victims needing adults to intervene on their behalf and does not give children any participation rights. The *Convention on the Rights of the Child*, on the other hand, reflects albeit a Euro-American view of more active children requiring adult partnership rather than imposed supervision. Finally, the *Worst Forms of Child Labour Convention* reflects 'a more democratic model better structured to accommodate diversity while focusing on a realistic social objective against which progress can be monitored' (Myers 2001: 45–53; Gamlin and Pastor 2009).

---

27 The Committee on the Rights of the Child noted that this report needed to be updated. Committee on the Rights of the Child, *Day of General Discussion on 'The Economic Exploitation of the Child'*, Report on the fourth session, CRC/C/20 (25 October 1993) [186–96, at 190].
28 International Labour Organization, *Minimum Age Convention, ILO Convention No. 138* (26 June 1973).
29 UN General Assembly, *Convention on the Rights of the Child*, opened for signature 20 November 1989, 1577 UNTS 3 (entered into force 2 September 1990).
30 International Labour Organization, *Worst Forms of Child Labour Convention*, ILO Convention No. 182 (17 June 1999).

One commentator identifies *four stages* in the development of the international legal protection of child labour (Smolin 2000: 943). First, there were five specific areas of work identified for minimum age regulation between 1919 and 1932 in ILO Conventions.[31] The standards of these old Conventions were low compared with contemporary ones. There were broad exemptions for work in a family business and domestic work within a family performed by family members. The abolition of child labour was not specifically identified as an ultimate goal, and the minimum age set for admission to employment was generally 14 years (but with younger ages permitted for India and Japan). However, these Conventions began a process of recognition, in an increasingly competitive and industrialised world, that nations had to all move in the same direction in reducing child labour. This was seen as necessary because, putting aside any humanitarian or welfare argument, countries needed to maintain fair and economic positions in the context of an increasingly competitive and global economy. A second wave of ILO Conventions raised the minimum age from 14 to 15 years.[32] There were also attempts to regulate certain hazardous forms of employment.[33] However, the absence of any principle to *abolish* child labour remained. A third stage saw a process of consolidation of the existing Conventions in the form of the *Minimum Age Convention*, which would gradually replace the ten previous, more specific ILO Conventions. Smolin's fourth stage of development starts in the 1990s and continues to the present (Smolin 2000: 945). This period is characterised by efforts to *mainstream* the issue of child labour within the core business of ILO and other international institutions.

The following sections deal with the three principal international instruments in addition to a further section on 'other international instruments'. The broader roles of the *Convention on the Rights of the Child* and the CtRC have been dealt with in Chapter 3, but in this Chapter we also look at the wider role of ILO (section 5.2.5 in this book) as a key international actor in formulating, establishing and monitoring international labour standards.

5.2.1 The Minimum Age Convention of 1973

The *Minimum Age Convention*[34] was adopted by the International Labour Conference on 26 June 1973 and entered into force on 19 June 1976. The overall aim of the *Minimum Age Convention* was expressed in terms of the *abolition* of child labour

---

31 *Minimum Age (Industry) Convention of 1919 (No. 5); Minimum Age (Sea) Convention, of 1920 (No. 7); Minimum Age (Agriculture) Convention of 1921 (No. 10); Minimum Age (Trimmers and Stokers) Convention of 1921 (No. 15);* and, *Minimum Age (Non-Industrial Employment) Convention of 1932 (No. 33).*
32 *Minimum Age (Sea) Convention (Revised) of 1936 (No. 58); Minimum Age (Industry) Convention (Revised) of 1937 (No. 59);* and *Minimum Age (Non-Industrial Employment) Convention (Revised) of 1937 (No. 60).*
33 *Minimum Age (Fishermen) Convention of 1959 (No. 112),* and, *Minimum Age (Underground Work) Convention, 1965 (No. 123).*
34 International Labour Organization, *Minimum Age Convention, ILO Convention No. 138* (26 June 1973). This Convention had 166 parties (1 November 2013).

and each of ILO's Member States[35] is under an obligation 'to pursue a national policy designed to ensure the effective abolition of child labour and to raise progressively the minimum age for admission to employment or work to a level with the fullest physical and mental development of young persons'.[36] Some commentators argue that this Convention reflects ethnocentric, Northern-country ideas about children and work (Khair 2010; Gamlin and Pastor 2009: 119; Myers 2001: 47). Indeed, it has been argued that one of the effects of the *Minimum Age Convention*, in relation to the developing countries, has been that child work below a certain age is not regulated and may be criminalised, with the consequence that such children are subsequently pressurised into the worst forms of child labour (Calitz 2013). The overall intention was that it should apply throughout all spheres of economic activity, replacing the previous *ILO Conventions* applicable to limited economic sectors. However, the Convention did not supply much guidance as to the contents of such 'national policy'.[37] The phrase 'employment or work' is significant in that it encompasses child labour performed irrespective of whether there is a contract of employment; it will include the self-employed working under contracts for services in addition to those working in family arrangements without any formal legal status (Creighton 1997: 372).

The core obligation placed on each Member State is to declare upon ratification a minimum age for admission to employment.[38] Further declarations may raise the specified age. The general rule is that the minimum age must not be less than that for completion of compulsory education, and in any event not less than 15 years, though there is a concession for developing countries to specify a minimum age of 14 years.[39]

Although it is necessary to achieve a suitable nexus between compulsory education and the minimum permissible age for work, compliance with this provision, according to ILO's Committee of Experts on the Application of Conventions and Recommendations (CEACR), further requires appropriate restrictions on work undertaken outside school hours. In order to provide States with some flexibility according to their national profiles, the *Minimum Age Convention* contains a number of permissible departures from the declared minimum age contained in articles 4 to 7. One of the criticisms levelled against the Convention has been its lack of flexibility. To an extent, this criticism has been strengthened by a lack of awareness and low take-up of the various departures from the prescribed obligations contained in it.

---

35 There were 185 Member States of ILO as at 1 November 2013.
36 *Minimum Age Convention of 1973*, art. 1.
37 There is some guidance on 'national policy' in: *R146 – Minimum Age Recommendation*, 1973 (No. 146), Recommendation concerning Minimum Age for Admission to Employment. Adoption: Geneva, 58th ILC session (26 June 1973), para. 5.
38 *Minimum Age Convention of 1973*, art. 2(1).
39 *Minimum Age Convention of 1973*, arts 2(3) and (4). See also, *R146 – Minimum Age Recommendation*, 1973 (No. 146), para. 7.

First, article 4 allows the State's 'competent authority', after consultation with employers and workers, to exclude from the application of the Convention 'limited categories of employment or work in respect of which special and substantial problems of application arise'. There is no specification within the Convention as to which 'categories' might be excluded. The omission was deliberate, in order to allow national authorities a wide measure of discretion to apply the Convention appropriately to its own national profile; possible exclusions discussed during the Convention's preparatory stages included employment in family undertakings, domestic service in private households, homework, and other work outside the supervision and control of employers (Creighton 1997: 374). Each Member State ratifying the Convention must list such excepted categories in its first report to ILO and give reasons for such exclusions.[40] Implicitly, the range of exclusions cannot be extended subsequently to the submission of the first report. There was some concern that this prescription might be too rigid and/or might lead countries to produce an expanded list of exclusions in the first report (Creighton 1997: 375). However, this does not appear to have occurred. Indeed, it would appear that Member States' lack of awareness about this and other 'flexibility' clauses contributed to the slow pace of its ratification (Creighton 1997: 375).

Second, under article 5, there is also a generic concession to Member States 'whose economy and administrative facilities are insufficiently developed' (i.e. developing countries) which are 'initially' allowed to 'limit the scope of application' of the Convention. Where a Member State does so limit its application, it must append a declaration to its ratification specifying 'the branches of economic activity or types of undertakings' to which it will apply the Convention.[41] However, as a minimum protective requirement the Convention will always be applicable to the following activities:

> mining and quarrying; manufacturing; construction; electricity, gas and water; sanitary services; transport, storage and communication; and plantations and other agricultural undertakings mainly producing for commercial purposes, but excluding family and small-scale holdings producing for local consumption and not regularly employing hired workers.
> (Minimum Age Convention, article 5(3))

Third, article 6 provides that the Convention does not apply to work done by children and young persons in schools or in other training institutions where this is an integral part of a course of education or training for which a school or training institution is responsible, or a training programme in an undertaking approved by the competent authority, or a programme of guidance to facilitate occupation choice or training. It is also inapplicable to work done in undertakings by persons

---

40 *Minimum Age Convention of 1973*, art. 4(2).
41 *Minimum Age Convention of 1973*, art. 5(2).

of 14 years or more as part of an apprenticeship or similar arrangement. Care must be taken that a 'training' relationship should not be used as a subterfuge to enable an employer to put children to work before the legal minimum age. The *ILO Recommendation* therefore provides that measures should be taken 'to safeguard and supervise the conditions in which children and young persons undergo vocational orientation and training within undertakings, training institutions and schools for vocational or technical education and to formulate standards for their protection and development'.[42]

Fourthly, article 7 provides that 'light work' may be authorised by national laws in relation to children aged 13–15 years on two conditions: first, it must be 'not likely to be harmful to their health or development'; and second, it must be 'not such as to prejudice their attendance at school, their participation in vocational orientation or training programmes . . . or their capacity to benefit from the instruction received'. National laws may also permit the employment of persons who are at least 15 years old but have not completed their compulsory schooling. Developing countries are given further concessions to the general rule on light work by allowing them to specify 12 instead of 13 years and 14 instead of 15 years.[43] Where national laws or regulations do permit light work, the competent authority must prescribe 'the number of hours during which and the conditions in which such employment or work may be undertaken'.[44]

In 2009, the CEACR issued a 'general observation' on the concept of 'light work' contained in the *Minimum Age Convention* on the basis that 'the need to determine the types of light work that are authorised and the related conditions are often poorly understood by States parties and therefore likely to give rise to abuse'.[45] The general observation[46] notes that the Convention's 'preparatory work'[47] showed that differences of views had emerged during the drafting process, but the drafting committee did adopt article 7 on the basis that it 'attempts to combine the measure of flexibility necessary to permit the wide application of the Convention (especially in view of its general scope) with the restrictions necessary to ensure adequate protection'.[48] It is noted that a large number of countries have determined the age of admission to light work and, in particular,

---

42 *R146 – Minimum Age Recommendation*, 1973 (No. 146), Recommendation concerning Minimum Age for Admission to Employment. Adoption: Geneva, 58th ILC session (26 June 1973), para. 12(2).
43 *Minimum Age Convention of 1973*, art. 7(4).
44 *Minimum Age Convention of 1973*, art. 7(3).
45 Committee of Experts on the Application of Conventions and Recommendations (CEACR), *General Report of the Committee of Experts on the Application of Conventions and Recommendations 2009*, International Labour Conference, 98th session, Geneva: International Labour Office, p. 34.
46 CEACR, *General Observation concerning Convention No 138*, International Labour Conference, ILO-LEX document no. 052009138, 2009, Geneva: International Labour Office.
47 International Labour Conference (ILC), 57th Session, 1972, Report IV(2), pp. 39–43; and ILC, 58th Session, 1973, Report IV(2), pp. 19–21.
48 CEACR, *General Observation concerning Convention No. 138*, International Labour Conference, ILO-LEX document no. 052009138, 2009, Geneva: International Labour Office.

that in countries that have specified a minimum age for admission to employment or work of 15 or 16 years, the age from which employment on light work may be authorised has been set at 13 years, while in those countries which have determined a minimum age for admission to employment of 14 years, the age for admission to light work is 12 years. Furthermore, in respect of certain countries that had not determined an age of admission, it was observed that 'in the great majority of these cases, this is because they have not regulated employment in these types of work'. As regards article 7(3), it was observed that only a few countries had determined the types of light work and established the hours of work and other conditions that could be undertaken. The general observation notes that the types of light work most frequently determined by Member States were as follows.

(1) agricultural work, such as the preparation of seeds and crops, the maintenance of crops without the use of insecticides or herbicides, the harvesting of fruit, vegetables or flowers, picking and sorting in farms and herding;
(2) forestry work and landscaping, including the planting of bushes and the maintenance of public gardens, without the use of insecticides or herbicides;
(3) domestic work, such as kitchen help, household help or looking after children; and
(4) the distribution of mail, newspapers, periodicals or publicity.[49]

The Committee further noted that some countries had laid down the hours of work for light work, that is, between two and four-and-a-half hours a day and between ten and 25 hours a week. Certain countries have established that the time spent in school and on light work shall not exceed seven hours a day, while others prohibit light work during school term time. Furthermore, certain countries prohibit night work (between 8 p.m. and 6 a.m.) and work on Sundays and public holidays, while others provide for annual leave of up to four weeks a year.

Article 8 of the *Minimum Age Convention* provides a general concession to the prohibition of work for children below the declared minimum age under article 2, which the competent authority can grant by permit 'in individual cases' and 'for such purposes as participation in artistic performances'. Such permits will limit 'the number of hours during which and prescribe the conditions in which employment or work is allowed'.[50] The five 'flexibility' clauses (articles 4–8) discussed earlier all provide for concessions to the general rule of a minimum age of not less than the age of completion of compulsory education, or in any event 15 years (or 14 years for developing countries). However, article 3 provides that the minimum age for admission to employment or work 'which by its nature or the circumstances in which it is carried out is likely to jeopardise health, safety or

---

49 Ibid.
50 *Minimum Age Convention of 1973*, art. 8(2).

morals of young persons' must not be less than 18 years.[51] Although this appears to establish a prescriptive standard more demanding than the general obligation in article 2, the types of employment or work which are referred to in article 3 must be determined again 'by national laws or regulations or by the competent authority' after consultation.[52] In determining the types of employment or work to which article 3 applies, 'full account should be taken of relevant international labour standards, such as those concerning dangerous substances, agents or processes (including ionising radiations), the lifting of heavy weights and underground work' and the list of types of such employment or work 'should be re-examined periodically and revised as necessary'.[53] Furthermore, such national laws may authorise employment from the age of 16 years, 'on condition that the health, safety and morals of the young persons concerned are fully protected'.[54] As regards enforcement, article 9 provides that 'all necessary measures, including the provision of appropriate penalties' must be taken by the competent authority to ensure the 'effective enforcement' of the Convention. National laws or regulations or the competent authority shall define 'the persons responsible for compliance with the provisions giving effect to the Convention',[55] and they will also prescribe the 'registers or other documents' that must be kept and made available by employers of persons whom he employs and who are less than 18 years.[56] The guidance on enforcement given in the Minimum Age *Recommendation* emphasises the strengthening of labour inspection, and the inspectors' close coordination and cooperation with the services responsible for the education, training, welfare and guidance of children and young persons. It also states that special attention should be paid to the enforcement of provisions concerning employment in hazardous types of employment or work; and to the prevention of the employment or work of children and young persons during the hours when instruction is available. Measures to facilitate the verification of ages should include the maintenance of an effective system of birth registration,[57] and a requirement that employers keep and make available registers or other documents not only of children and young persons employed by them but also of those receiving vocational

---

51 *Minimum Age Convention of 1973*, art. 3(1). Furthermore, 'Where the minimum age for admission to types of employment or work which are likely to jeopardise the health, safety or morals of young persons is still below 18 years, immediate steps should be taken to raise it to that level': *R146 – Minimum Age Recommendation*, 1973 (No. 146), Recommendation concerning Minimum Age for Admission to Employment. Adoption: Geneva, 58th ILC session (26 June 1973), para. 9.
52 *Minimum Age Convention of 1973*, art. 3(2).
53 *R146 – Minimum Age Recommendation*, 1973 (No. 146), Recommendation concerning Minimum Age for Admission to Employment. Adoption: Geneva, 58th ILC session (26 June 1973), para. 10.
54 *Minimum Age Convention of 1973*, art. 3(3).
55 *Minimum Age Convention of 1973*, art. 9(2).
56 *Minimum Age Convention of 1973*, art. 9(3).
57 For birth registration and identity rights in the *Convention on the Rights of the Child*, see section 3.7.4.1 in this book.

orientation or training in their undertakings.[58] Finally, article 10 provides for the revision of the ten previous *ILO Conventions* on minimum age-setting in various industries.

Despite the merits of the *Minimum Age Convention*, some commentators have concluded that it did not 'constitute an adequate response' to the problem of abusive child labour (Creighton 1997: 386). Creighton identified a number of problems, for example, a lack of flexibility:

> [A]rticle 7 proceeds on the assumption that employment or work for children under thirteen is to be impermissible in all circumstances. This means that it is not acceptable in terms of the Convention for a twelve-year-old to work on a morning or evening newspaper route, or for an eleven-year-old to wash cars or weed a neighbour's garden on a Saturday afternoon. Furthermore, since the Convention applies to employment or work, it would be necessary to regulate unpaid work by children or young people on a family farm or in a family restaurant.
>
> (Creighton 1997: 387)

Developing countries have had difficulties in complying with the Convention as it is premised on the assumption that child labour should be entirely eliminated, which is simply not a practical proposition for many countries (Bourdillon et al. 2006). The Convention also fails to articulate clear national priorities. Much is left to the discretion of Member States without sufficient guidance on setting priorities for national action. There has developed a growing awareness that the process of eliminating child labour must be an *incremental* one and strategies should be fully integrated with other measures to promote economic and educational development and protect employment standards (Creighton 1997: 396). It is not just the developing countries that had have difficulty with the *Minimum Age Convention*; the United States and New Zealand have not ratified this Convention. As regards New Zealand, one commentator observes that there is little hard information available about child labour and the national census no longer collects information about the employment of children and children are invisible to the tax system (Roth 2010).

The *Minimum Age Convention of 1973* was a significant advance over previous efforts, but it failed in its first two decades of existence to attract sufficient ratifications to truly deliver the intended reforms. Indeed, it is difficult to say that there was any real coherence in international standards on child labour prior to the late 1990s. By 1996, only 49 of the Member States had ratified it. The Asian countries and other developing nations were conspicuously absent from the list of ratifying countries during this period. At the time of the adoption of the *Worst Forms of Child*

---

58 *R146 – Minimum Age Recommendation*, 1973 (No. 146), Recommendation concerning Minimum Age for Admission to Employment. Adoption: Geneva, 58th ILC session (26 Jun 1973), paras 14–16.

Labour Convention of 1999, the *Minimum Age Convention of 1973* had attracted only 76 ratifications. The success of the *Worst Forms of Child Labour Convention* prompted further ratifications to the *Minimum Age Convention*. Two years after the coming into force of the former (in November 2002), the ratifications to the *Minimum Age Convention* rose to 121. As at 1 February 2020 there were 172 parties to this Convention.

An important contributory factor to the increasing international attention to child labour, following the *Minimum Age Convention*, has been the combination of ILO's focus on international labour standards with the recognition of their importance within the post-war human rights and children's rights agendas. The arrival of the rights-based approach of the *Convention on the Rights of the Child* (1989) has reinforced and helped to transform ILO's older approaches to labour standards, first commenced in 1919.

5.2.2 The UN Convention on the Rights of the Child and Child Labour

In the 1980s and 1990s there was further recognition of the rights of children at the international level, reflected in particular by the introduction of the *Convention on the Rights of the Child* in 1989 (see generally, Chapter 3 in this book). There are a number of provisions of this Convention[59] that, it can be claimed, provide a framework of rights relevant to child labour. The *Convention on the Rights of the Child* has tended to produce standards of a broad general nature, as compared to those adopted by ILO which contain a more detailed and precise set of standards (Alston 1989: 37). In particular, article 32 (protection from economic exploitation and child labour) contains some core obligations in this area, and indeed was the subject of one of the CtRC's first *Days of General Discussion*.[60] The original proposal of the text of article 32 during the drafting process of the Convention specifically placed duties on States parties to set a minimum age for admission to employment of 15 years, comparable to article 2 of the *Minimum Age Convention of 1973*. However, that proposal was not adopted and instead the phrase 'work' was used in the text to cover both work within the employment relationship and work falling outside of that relationship (Detrick 1992: 418–19). The CtRC has generally been reticent about expressing an opinion about the merits or otherwise of the linkage between international trade and labour standards. It had often referred to the *ILO Conventions* as the key framework in assessing national situations of child labour (Doek 2003: 243). However, in its Concluding Observations for the Republic of Korea,[61] the CtRC

---

59 CRC, arts 11, 34, 35 and 38.
60 Committee on the Rights of the Child, *Day of General Discussion on 'The Economic Exploitation of the Child'*, Report on the fourth session, CRC/C/20 (25 October 1993) [186–96].
61 CRC, Consideration of Reports Submitted by States Parties under Art. 44 of the Convention. Concluding Observations: Republic of Korea, UN Doc. CRC/C/KOR/CO/3–4 (2011), paras 26–7.

made a direct comment, suggesting that import restrictions might be required with regard to products from third states that are investigated by the ILO for using child labour.

It is tempting also to draw comparisons between the effectiveness of the reporting processes undertaken by the CtRC and by ILO in the field of child labour. Some commentators take the view that the UN supervisory regime is 'less rigorous and comprehensive than that of the ILO' (Creighton 1997: 369). Kilkelly (2003: 324) notes that many of the reports submitted to the CtRC 'fail to address the issue of economic exploitation of children under Article 32 in a complete manner, or at all'. Others view the *Convention on the Rights of the Child* and ILO Conventions, and their respective monitoring procedures, as increasingly operating in a more helpful complementary manner to each other (Noguchi 2002: 357, 368). However, in the 1990s there was an increasing urgency within the international community around child labour issues. This was prompted to some extent by the recognition that the process of globalisation was exposing more intense competitive behaviour which, it was feared, could generate more child labour rather than reduce it. Governments attending the ILO Conference in Geneva in June 1996 agreed that there was a pressing need to proceed immediately with the prohibition of the most intolerable features of child labour. The CtRC also lent its support to ILO's new project to establish a Convention aimed at the *worst forms* of child labour, and made observations on the drafts of the new *ILO Convention* (Noguchi 2002: 365) discussed in the next section.

5.2.3 Elimination of the Worst Forms of Child Labour Convention of 1999

The decision of ILO's Governing Body in March 1996 to place 'intolerable' forms of child labour on the Conference agenda for 1998 reflected the frustrations with the apparent failures of ILO efforts to gather support for the *Minimum Age Convention of 1973* (section 5.2.1 in this book). The disappointment with the slow ratification rate in relation to this Convention encouraged the international community to design a new Convention that was more narrowly focused in order that it could match the areas of concern where there was more obviously an emerging global consensus (Davidson 2001: 203). ILO also adopted in June 1998 a landmark 'soft law' instrument, the *Declaration on Fundamental Principles and Rights at Work and its Follow-up*,[62] in which the International Labour Conference declared that all Member States should respect principles concerning four 'fundamental rights', including the elimination of child labour. The *Worst Forms of Child Labour Convention of 1999*[63]

---

62 See: www.ilo.org/declaration/lang-en/index.htm (2 November 2013).
63 International Labour Organization, *Prohibition and Immediate Action for the Elimination of the Worst Forms of Child Labour Convention, ILO Convention No. 182*, (17 Jun 1999). This Convention had 177 parties as at November 2013.

came into force on 19 November 2000. Since 2002, the UN's 'World Day against Child Labour' has been celebrated on 12 June of each year, marking the date of adoption in 1999 of this landmark *ILO Convention*. Each year a different theme is selected for the World Day.[64] The *Worst Forms of Child Labour Convention* is distinctive in that it was the only *ILO Convention* to have been unanimously adopted by the tripartite representation of Member States, and it has had the best record in ILO history for rapid ratification. At the time of writing, the Convention had 186 ratifications. It should be noted that the *Worst Forms of Child Labour Convention* does not revise or replace the *Minimum Age Convention*. The latter remains the foundation for international action to abolish child labour, whereas the *Worst Forms of Child Labour Convention* supplements and highlights this underlying aim by setting out standards to eliminate and prohibit the *worst forms* of child labour. However, the policy aims of the *Worst Forms of Child Labour Convention* were not to produce just another *ILO Convention* to fill gaps in protection. There was a more ambitious aim to adopt an instrument that would 'pack a real punch and be capable of encouraging real impact' (Crawford 2000: 5). The adoption of the *Worst Forms of Child Labour Convention* can also be seen as a part of the process of mainstreaming child labour in ILO's activities (Smolin 2000: 945; Noguchi 2002: 362).

A key innovative feature of the *Worst Forms of Child Labour Convention* was to focus on areas where there clearly existed strong international agreement, that is, the elimination of the worst forms of child labour that had been generally recognised as intolerable. This has had the effect of extending the policy areas of concern through the explicit inclusion of such (criminal) matters as prostitution, pornography and drug trafficking. These distinctive features of the *Worst Forms of Child Labour Convention* have resulted in its iconic presence in the international legal regime to eliminate child labour. Much of the commentary reflects the optimism that this Convention is both more analytically sound and has a better chance of making a real difference (Betcherman et al. 2004: 29).

The preambular paragraphs of the *Worst Forms of Child Labour Convention* make it clear that the intention was to *complement* the *Minimum Age Convention*, not only by ensuring the elimination of the worst forms of child labour but also by providing for children's 'rehabilitation and social integration', a duty resonant with article 39 of the *Convention on the Rights of the Child*. It is also interesting to note the clear recognition of poverty as the root cause of child labour and that, according to the text, the solution indicated lies in 'sustained economic growth'. The preambular paragraphs also 'recall' the text of the *Convention on the Rights of the Child* and the ILO's landmark *Declaration on Fundamental Principles and Rights at Work and its Follow-up* (see section 5.2.5 in this book), adopted by the International Labour

---

64 For example, the exploitation of girls in child labour (2009); the goal of ending child labour (2010); children in hazardous work (2011); and, child labourers in domestic work (2013). See: <www.ilo.org/ipec/Campaignandadvocacy/wdacl/lang--en/index.htm> (accessed 2 November 2013).

Conference in June 1998. ILO's Governing Body identified the *Worst Forms of Child Labour Convention* as one of eight Conventions[65] that it regards as being *fundamental* to people's rights at work, irrespective of the level of development of individual States.

The core duty contained in the *Worst Forms of Child Labour Convention* is stark. Nothing less than 'immediate and effective measures' are required from Member States to secure the results of both the 'prohibition' and 'elimination' of the worst forms of child labour 'as a matter of urgency'.[66] This does not mean that a State is violating the Convention if the worst forms are not immediately erased. The duty requires immediate 'measures', not necessarily 'results'. For example, this may mean the adoption of appropriate legislation and regulation that will, in the future, ensure the prohibition and elimination of child labour. The definition of a child is taken as applying to all persons under the age of 18 years.[67] This does not imply, however, a comprehensive ban on work for all persons less than 18 years of age. The general minimum age for work is usually lower than 18 and such work is legitimate provided it does not fall foul of the criteria defining the worst forms of child labour. It should be noted that the *Worst Forms of Child Labour Convention* does not make any exception to the 18 years limit. However, it should be remembered that not all countries have an adequate system of birth registration (section 3.7.4.1 in this book).

The international community found some difficulty in arriving at a definition of the 'worst forms of child labour'. There was the need to identify the common denominator of what a majority of States would find to be intolerable. There was also a need for a formulation that would provide a reasonable fit with national laws, in particular in relation to prostitution and the armed forces. Article 3 of the *Worst Forms of Child Labour Convention* defines the meaning of 'worst forms of child labour', which comprises the following.

(a) all forms of slavery or practices similar to slavery, such as the sale and trafficking of children, debt bondage and serfdom and forced or compulsory labour, including forced or compulsory recruitment of children for use in armed conflict;
(b) the use, procuring or offering of a child for prostitution, for the production of pornography or for pornographic performances;

---

65 The eight 'fundamental' Conventions are: *Forced Labour Convention of 1930* (No. 29) (177 parties); *Freedom of Association and Protection of the Right to Organise Convention of 1948* (No. 87) (152 parties); *Right to Organise and Collective Bargaining Convention of 1949* (No. 98) (163 parties); *Equal Remuneration Convention of 1951* (No. 100) (171 parties); *Abolition of Forced Labour Convention of 1957* (No. 105) (174 parties); *Discrimination (Employment and Occupation) Convention of 1958* (No. 111) (172 parties); *Minimum Age Convention of 1973* (No. 138) (166 parties); and, the *Worst Forms of Child Labour Convention of 1999* (No 182) (177 parties). As at 2 November 2013.
66 *Worst Forms of Child Labour Convention of 1999*, art. 1.
67 *Worst Forms of Child Labour Convention of 1999*, art. 2.

(c) the use, procuring or offering of a child for illicit activities, in particular for the production and trafficking of drugs as defined in the relevant international treaties;
(d) work which, by its nature or the circumstances in which it is carried out, is likely to harm the health, safety or morals of children.

The first three categories provide unqualified protection, while the last (d) is necessarily more elusive and is left for further definition by the national authorities. The first three categories are often referred to as the 'intolerable forms of child labour' and the more elusive category (d) as 'hazardous work'. It should be noted that category (a) conspicuously falls short of an outright ban on the use of children as soldiers in armed conflict; it only applies where recruitment is 'forced or compulsory'. It has been said that this was one of the most controversial aspects of the drafting negotiations and that the United States blocked a proposal that would have produced broader prohibition of child soldiers (Davidson 2001: 217). Controversy about this provision was perhaps unsurprising given the similar controversy experienced in relation to the drafting of article 38 of the *Convention on the Rights of the Child* (section 3.7.9.5 in this book). This category includes a list of forbidden practices, such as 'debt bondage'.

> Bonded labour is considered to be a temporary form of slavery, where an individual pays off a debt with his or her own work, and where he or she is not free to leave the work place or change the employer. Half of these bonded labourers, approximately 5.7 million, are estimated to be children.
> (Molfenter 2011: 261)

A further difficult issue in the drafting negotiations was the approach to be taken to 'hazardous work'. Worker representatives at ILO wanted a specific list of hazardous work conditions (e.g. work underground, at dangerous heights, or in confined spaces), thus removing discretion from governments to regulate such work. Most government representatives preferred a more flexible approach which permitted them to take into account circumstances in their countries that would make work more or less hazardous. A compromise was reached, allowing the discretion of Member States to determine what constitutes hazardous work, and there was an understanding between employer and worker members that article 3(d) did not encompass situations where children work on their parents' family farms (Dennis 1999: 945). The repeated use of the word 'work' (rather than 'employment') in articles 2 and 3 ensures that the definition of the worst forms of child labour does not have any link with the existence of a contractual employment relationship or production for commercial or trading purposes (Noguchi 2002: 360). The *Worst Forms of Child Labour Convention* can therefore be applied to employment and work in both the formal and the informal sectors and in family settings where there is no commercial/trading product. The wording of article 3 differs from that of article 3(1) of *Minimum Age Convention*, which only deals with employment or work which 'is likely to jeopardise the health, safety or morals of young persons'. A State that has ratified the *Minimum Age Convention* will still have to determine a list of hazardous work for the purposes of the *Worst Forms of Child Labour Convention*. In practice, the lists may be identical but they need not be so, given the different aims of these two Conventions. In earlier *ILO Conventions*, 'domestic' work had been expressly excluded from the protected areas. However, it is thought that domestic work is implicitly included in all categories contained in article 3.

The literature on child labour consistently cites domestic work and the informal economy as areas where child labour is prevalent (Scullion 2013). Yet there are difficult distinctions between child labour that ought to be prohibited and that which ought to be regarded as legitimate precisely in this area. There is a qualitative difference between situations where children 'give a 'helping hand' in their own home and "child domestic labour' where children perform domestic tasks in the home of a third party or 'employer' under exploitative conditions' (IPEC 2004: 1). Crawford observes that there are a number of 'hidden' forms of child labour that have not been fully drawn out in the text of article 3 (2000: 12–13).

The precise boundaries of meaning in the 'hazardous work' category in article 3(d) are left to be determined at the national level after consultation, and in particular taking into account the guidance on hazardous work laid down in an *ILO Recommendation*.[68] The *Recommendation* provides some detailed criteria for identifying the types of work referred to in category (d).[69] It specifically provides that this category of work should be positively authorised by a State in respect of children aged 16 years or more, but only after due consultation with workers and employers and subject to the safeguards regarding children's health, safety, morals and sufficient training. The requirement for competent authorities to identify such work[70] was added in an amendment and was intended to ensure that countries positively investigated the existence of such practices rather than merely going through a hypothetical definitional exercise. The duties to identify the various categories of child labour are also to be periodically reviewed and monitored by States.[71] This will enable them to retain some flexibility in updating their lists of prohibited child labour in a changing industrial environment.

Each Member State is under a duty to take all necessary measures to ensure the effective implementation of the *Worst Forms of Child Labour Convention*.[72] The *Recommendation* provides, in particular, that Member States should compile '[d]etailed information and statistical data on the nature and extent of child labour' as 'a

---

68 *R190 – Worst Forms of Child Labour Recommendation*, 1999 (No. 190), Recommendation concerning the prohibition and immediate action for the elimination of the worst forms of child labour. Adoption: Geneva, 87th ILC session (17 June 1999).
69 Ibid., para. 4.
70 *Worst Forms of Child Labour Convention of 1999*, art. 4(2).
71 *Worst Forms of Child Labour Convention of 1999*, art. 4(3).
72 *Worst Forms of Child Labour Convention of 1999*, art. 7(1).

basis for determining priorities for national action'.[73] In addition, each Member State must, after consultation with employers' and workers' organisations, 'establish or designate appropriate mechanisms to monitor the implementation' of the Convention.[74]

This is again reinforced by the *Recommendation*, which urges Member States to ensure coordination between the national competent authorities, to cooperate with any international efforts and to identify responsible persons in the event of non-compliance with national provisions.[75] Most importantly, Member States 'shall design and implement programmes of action to eliminate as a priority the worst forms of child labour'.[76] This is given some practical substance in the *Recommendation*, which states that such programmes should aim at the identification and prevention of the worst forms of child labour, giving due attention to vulnerable groups of children.[77]

Each Member State has a mandatory duty to take all necessary measures to ensure the effective implementation of the *Worst Forms of Child Labour Convention*, including penal or other sanctions.[78] The guidance provided by the *Recommendation* indicates that Member States should designate three categories as criminal offences (practices similar to slavery, child prostitution and other illicit activities).[79] This list is in fact identical to the wording of the first three categories of the *Worst Forms of Child Labour Convention* (articles 3(a) to (c)) with the addition of the regulation of 'firearms'. Additionally, the *Recommendation* advises that, where appropriate, Member States should provide criminal penalties for violations of any national provisions prohibiting and eliminating the hazardous work referred to in article 3(d). It also suggests the 'special supervision of enterprises which have used the worst forms of child labour, and, in cases of persistent violation, consideration of temporary or permanent revoking of permits to operate'.[80] If a Member State has additionally ratified the *Forced Labour Convention of 1930*,[81] then the protection offered there against illegal compulsory labour would already be punishable as a criminal offence.[82] The *Recommendation* reinforces the provisions of the *Worst Forms of Child Labour Convention* and urges

---

73 *R190 – Worst Forms of Child Labour Recommendation, 1999 (No. 190)*, para. 5(1).
74 *Worst Forms of Child Labour Convention of 1999*, art. 5.
75 *R190 – Worst Forms of Child Labour Recommendation, 1999 (No. 190)*, paras 8–11.
76 *Worst Forms of Child Labour Convention of 1999*, art. 6(1).
77 *R190 – Worst Forms of Child Labour Recommendation, 1999 (No. 190)*, para. 2.
78 *Worst Forms of Child Labour Convention of 1999*, art. 7(1).
79 *R190 – Worst Forms of Child Labour Recommendation, 1999 (No. 190)*, para. 12.
80 *R190 – Worst Forms of Child Labour Recommendation, 1999 (No. 190)*, paras 13 and 14.
81 *C029 – Forced Labour Convention of 1930 (No. 29)*, Convention concerning Forced or Compulsory Labour (entered into force 1 May 1932). Adoption: Geneva, 14th ILC session (28 June 1930).
82 'The illegal exaction of forced or compulsory labour shall be punishable as a penal offence, and it shall be an obligation on any Member ratifying this Convention to ensure that the penalties imposed by law are really adequate and are strictly enforced': *Forced Labour Convention of 1930*, art. 29.

cooperation with international efforts by exchanging information concerning such criminal offences.[83]

The centrality of education in any strategy to eliminate child labour is confirmed in article 7(2) which obliges Member States, in taking effective and time-bound measures, to take into account 'the importance of education in eliminating child labour'. IPEC has developed a number of 'time-bound' programmes to reflect the commitment contained in article 7(2). One of the listed measures under this provision is to 'ensure access to free basic education, and, wherever possible and appropriate, vocational training, for all children removed from the worst forms of child labour'.[84] The relationship between exploitative labour and education was another key issue in the drafting negotiations.

> Some governments, including the United States, as well as all worker members, wanted the Convention to cover work that systematically prevents a child from taking advantage of available or compulsory education. Other delegations opposed this formulation, asserting that lack of access to education was fundamentally different from the other abuses targeted by the Convention and that its inclusion would harm the prospects for ratification.
> (Dennis 1999: 946)

There were also some discussions about the meaning of 'basic education'; some interpretations in other international instruments correlate this phrase with primary education. Dennis notes that the worker and employer members clarified the record with their understanding that a broader meaning should be given, that is, 'basic education means primary education plus one year (i.e. eight or nine years of schooling), such education being based on curriculum and not age' (1999: 946). It should be noted that the aim of article 7(2)(c) is to provide rehabilitation and reintegration of children who have been 'removed' from the worst forms of child labour; a provision that resonates with the general duty in the *Convention on the Rights of the Child* (article 39) on States parties to achieve the recovery and social reintegration of a child victim of any form of neglect, exploitation or abuse. The *Recommendation* further encourages 'adopting appropriate measures to improve the educational infrastructure and the training of teachers to meet the needs of boys and girls'.[85]

The growing acknowledgment that the problem of child labour was indeed a global one requiring action at the international level, is reflected in the text of article 8 that obliges Member States to 'take appropriate steps to assist one another' in giving effect to the Convention 'through enhanced international co-operation and/or assistance including support for social and economic development, poverty

---

83 *R190 – Worst Forms of Child Labour Recommendation, 1999 (No. 190)*, para. 11.
84 *Worst Forms of Child Labour Convention of 1999*, art. 7(2)(c).
85 *R190 – Worst Forms of Child Labour Recommendation, 1999 (No. 190)*, para. 15(j).

eradication programmes and universal education'. The *Recommendation* indicates various measures on which States may cooperate, such as mutual legal assistance and technical assistance, including the exchange of information.[86]

In the drafting negotiations, the worker and employer members, together with governments of most developing countries, had sought an amendment that would have committed governments to 'enhanced international cooperation and assistance, including support for social and economic development'. Some governments, however, felt this might create a legal obligation to increase financial contributions to other States or ILO child labour programmes. The ILO Deputy Legal Adviser confirmed that the final text did not create any legal obligations concerning the nature or amount of any cooperation or assistance (Dennis 1999: 947).

There seems little doubt that the arrival of the *Worst Forms of Child Labour Convention of 1999* marked a new confidence in the growing coherence and influence of a worldwide movement to progress international labour standards.[87] Commentators note the attempt by the Convention to address the conflicting conceptions of childhood. The Convention establishes international guidelines and standards that ratifying countries commit to follow through in national policy. It neither specifies the specific 'worst form' of employment (aside from work that is already illegal in most countries) nor imposes programmes and policies. Instead, it attempts to draw the difficult balance between relativism and universalism by asserting that the worst forms of child labour shall be 'determined by national laws or regulations . . . ' (Gamlin and Pastor 2009: 122). As such, it enables different societies to work towards the implementation of the tool within their own realities and limitations, and by concentrating resources on children in the most pressing need of attention it sets an achievable aim. In this sense, it is more in tune with both theory and praxis, being structured to accommodate diversity while focussing on both immediate and overarching objectives (Myers 2001).

The campaign work of ILO and NGOs that occurred before, during and after the adoption of the *Worst Forms of Child Labour Convention* has been very successful, certainly if success is measured by the fast rate of ratification. The optimistic environment that appears to have existed around the introduction of this Convention has also been significant in terms of providing international donors with some assurance about the strength of international support which has helped to increase funding for ILO campaigns against child labour. One commentator has observed that this shows 'a recognition that, for an issue like child labour, changing

---

86 *R190 – Worst Forms of Child Labour Recommendation, 1999 (No. 190)*, para. 16(b) and (c).
87 One commentator remarked: 'Before it had even arrived, the U.S. Senate had taken the unusual step of adopting, by a 98–1 roll-call vote, a sense-of-the-Senate amendment to the Foreign Relations Authorization Act that commended the ILO Member States for negotiating this "historic convention" and "called for the U.S. to continue to work with all foreign nations and international organizations to put an end to abusive and exploitative child labour". Early ratification by the United States should encourage other states to follow suit' (Dennis 1999: 948).

people's perception and way of thinking is not an auxiliary action of public information but itself a substantive measure to tackle the phenomenon effectively and from its roots' (Noguchi 2002: 365).

More recently, a Global Child Labour Conference was held in The Hague in May 2010, organised by the Ministry of Social Affairs and Employment of the Netherlands in close collaboration with ILO.[88] More than 500 representatives from 97 countries around the world participated. The Conference adopted a 'roadmap' (ILO 2010a) for achieving the elimination of the worst forms of child labour by 2016. A further Global Child Labour Conference was hosted by Brazil with ILO in October 2013 in order to measure the progress made towards the goal of 2016.[89]

5.2.4 Other international instruments relating to child labour

A further *ILO Convention* on domestic workers was adopted in 2011.[90] The *Domestic Workers Convention of 2011* requires that States parties commit to, *inter alia*, 'the elimination of all forms of forced or compulsory labour' and 'the effective abolition of child labour'.[91] In addition, Member States must set a minimum age for domestic workers consistent with the *Minimum Age Convention* and the *Worst Forms of Child Labour Convention*, which must be 'not lower than that established by national laws and regulations for workers generally'. Member States are further obliged to take measures 'to ensure that work performed by domestic workers who are under the age of 18 and above the minimum age of employment does not deprive them of compulsory education, or interfere with opportunities to participate in further education or vocational training'.[92]

There are a number of UN international instruments relevant to eliminating child labour. The *Supplementary Convention on the Abolition of Slavery, the Slave Trade and Institutions and Practices Similar to Slavery of 1956*[93] provides that States parties 'shall

---

88 See, The Hague Global Child Labour Conference, Towards a World without Child Labour – Mapping the Road to 2016 (10–11 May 2010, The Hague, The Netherlands). See: <www.ilo.org/ipec/Campaignandadvocacy/GlobalChildLabourConference/lang–en/index.htm> (accessed 13 October 2013).
89 III Global Conference on Child Labour – Brasilia, 8–10 October 2013, Towards a Child Labour-Free World. See website: <www.ilo.org/ipec/Campaignandadvocacy/BrasiliaConference/lang–en/index.htm> (accessed 13 October 2013).
90 *C189 – Domestic Workers Convention of 2011 (No. 189)*, Convention concerning decent work for domestic workers (entered into force 5 September 2013). Adoption: Geneva, 100th ILC session (16 June 2011). This Convention had ten parties as at 2 November 2013.
91 *Domestic Workers Convention of 2011*, art. 3(2)(b) and (c).
92 *Domestic Workers Convention of 2011*, art. 4(1) and (2).
93 *Supplementary Convention on the Abolition of Slavery, the Slave Trade and Institutions and Practices Similar to Slavery of 1956*, opened for signature 7 September 1956, 266 UNTS 3 (entered into force 20 April 1957).

take all practicable and necessary legislative and other measures to bring about progressively and as soon as possible the complete abolition or abandonment' of a number of listed institutions and practices, 'whether or not they are covered by the definition of slavery contained in article 1 of the Slavery Convention [of 1926]'. The four types of servile statuses are: (a) debt bondage, (b) serfdom, (c) forced marriage and (d) child exploitation.

> Any institution or practice whereby a child or young person under the age of 18 years, is delivered by either or both of his natural parents or by his guardian to another person, whether for reward or not, with a view to the exploitation of the child or young person or of his labour.[94]

The kind of practice which the drafting committee had in mind underlying this provision is well illustrated by the following extract from the proceedings of an ad hoc committee on slavery in 1951:

> The Committee next turned to the practice, particularly prevalent in the Far East, which in some localities is known as 'mui tsai'. This involves the sale of a child's working capacity and usually takes the form of the transfer of a small child, usually a girl, for employment as a domestic servant by means of an adoption procedure, sometimes fraudulent. The custom has been known to exist under other names in other regions of the world, including parts of Africa. The Committee recognised that in many cases an element of servitude may not be involved. Often the parents of the child affect such a transfer in what they believe to be the best interests of the child. The Committee therefore felt that a status or condition of servitude existed only when the conditions of the transfer were such as to permit the exploitation of the child regardless of its welfare.[95]

A few years later, the following 'principle' was drafted in the (non-binding) *Declaration of the Rights of the Child* (1959):

> The child shall be protected against all forms of neglect, cruelty and exploitation. He shall not be the subject of traffic, in any form.
>
> The child shall not be admitted to employment before an appropriate minimum age; he shall in no case be caused or permitted to engage in any occupation or employment which would prejudice his health or education, or interfere with his physical, mental or moral development.[96]

---

94 Ibid, art. 1(d).
95 Economic and Social Council, *Report of the Ad Hoc Committee on Slavery* (second session), UN Doc. E/1988, E/AC33/13, 4 May 1951, p. 2. Cited in Allain (2008: 305).
96 General Assembly, *Declaration of the Rights of the Child*, 14th session, UN Doc. A/RES/1386 (XIV), (20 November 1959), principle 9.

The *International Covenant on Civil and Political Rights* (ICCPR) (1966) carries the following provision:

> 1. Every child shall have, without any discrimination as to race, colour, sex, language, religion, national or social origin, property or birth, the right to such measures of protection as are required by his status as a minor, on the part of his family, society and the State.[97]

And the *International Covenant on Economic, Social and Cultural Rights* (ICESCR) 1966 carries the following provision:

> Special measures of protection and assistance should be taken on behalf of all children and young persons without any discrimination for reasons of parentage or other conditions. Children and young persons should be protected from economic and social exploitation. Their employment in work harmful to their morals or health or dangerous to life or likely to hamper their normal development should be punishable by law. States should also set age limits below which the paid employment of child labour should be prohibited and punishable by law.[98]

These various provisions, combined with the relevant provisions of the *Convention on the Rights of the Child*, the *Minimum Age Convention* and the *Worst Forms of Child Labour Convention*, comprise a fairly comprehensive international legal regime addressing the economic exploitation of children in the employment/work context. ILO's role as a leader within the international community in this field is explored further in the next section.

The Minamata Convention on Mercury[99] was prompted by a strange and un-diagnosable disease in the fishing village of Minamata, Japan in 1956. For many years the cause of a mysterious disease was unknown. It was not until 25 years after the first outbreak that the Japanese government finally acknowledged that releases of an unwanted by product of chemicals manufacturing offshore into the ocean were the source of the ailment.

In many developing countries, small-scale mining is primarily a poverty-driven activity which plays an important economic role. Artisanal mining has experienced explosive growth in recent years due to the rising value of mineral prices and the increasing difficulty of earning a living from agriculture and other rural activities. An estimated 40.5 million people were directly engaged in small-scale

---

97 *International Covenant on Civil and Political Rights*, opened for signature 16 December 1966, 999 UNTS 171 (entered into force 23 March 1976), art. 24(1). At the time of writing it had 167 parties.
98 *International Covenant on Economic, Social and Cultural Rights*, opened for signature 16 December 1966, 993 UNTS 3 (entered into force 3 January 1976), art. 10(3). At the time of writing it had 160 parties.
99 The Minamata Convention on Mercury. The Convention was adopted on 10 October 2013 (entered into force 16 August 2017).

mining in (Fritz et al. 2017). Most artisanal gold miners include both adults and children. These miners use mercury to extract gold from the ore as it is easy to obtain and the cheapest and easiest method available. Mercury is toxic, damaging to the brain and nervous system, particularly in young children and infants, as well as to the heart and kidneys. Annexure C 1(i) of the Minamata Convention on Mercury enjoins the implementation of strategies to prevent the exposure of vulnerable populations, particularly children and women of child-bearing age, especially pregnant women, to mercury used in artisanal and small-scale gold mining. At time of publication, the international treaty had been signed by 128 of the 193 UN member states and ratified by 113 countries, which are now legally obliged to comply with its provisions. However, like most treaties, the Convention would also encounter challenges in monitoring.

5.2.5 The wider role of the International Labour Organization (ILO)

ILO has been the most important and longstanding inter-governmental organisation in the field of international labour standards generally and child labour in particular. The International Labour Conference adopted the *Minimum Age (Industry) Convention of 1919*[100] at its very first session. The current 185 Member States of ILO includes the membership of the United States of America with which ILO has had an erratic relationship. The USA did not join ILO until 1934; it withdrew its membership in 1934 and rejoined in 1980. ILO's structure, and the way in which its standards are formulated and monitored, are grounded in *tripartism*, that is, the involvement of Government, Worker and Employer representation (aka 'social partners'). This provides several advantages, in particular ILO is uniquely positioned to monitor and report on child labour violations; the workers' groups provide access to data on current labour conditions and the employers' and government representatives 'lend it legitimacy with both private and public actors' (Ho 2006: 342). ILO has also forged partnerships with other international organisations better to facilitate its work of establishing international labour standards and meeting the challenges of child labour, for example, with the international human rights treaty bodies, including the CtRC, with UNICEF, and with the World Bank (Betcherman et al. 2004: 30). Although other international organisations and NGOs have taken an interest in child labour issues – for example, the UNHRC,[101] UNICEF (1997), the International Organization of Employers, the Anti-Slavery Society and the International Confederation of Free Trade

---

100 *C005 – Minimum Age (Industry) Convention of 1919 (No. 5)*, Convention Fixing the Minimum Age for Admission of Children to Industrial Employment (entered into force 13 June 1921). Adoption: Washington, first ILC session (28 November 1919).
101 See, for example, UN Commission on Human Rights (UNCHR) *Programme of Action for the Elimination of the Exploitation of Child Labour*, E/CN.4/RES/1993/79, Geneva: Office of the United Nations High Commissioner for Human Rights.

Unions – ILO 'has always considered itself to have a special mandate in this area' (Creighton 1997: 366). ILO has played a central role in producing international standards of protection. NGOs do not have a formal role in the preparation of new ILO standards, but 'in practice NGOs do have opportunities to make a contribution' (Blagbrough 1997: 126).

In many ways the policy trends that have informed ILO's activities are punctuated by three 'soft law' instruments (section 2.2.6 in this book). First, there was the *Declaration of Philadelphia* concerning the aims and purposes of the International Labour Organization, issued on 10 May 1944. This reaffirms the fundamental principles on which the organisation is based, in particular, that:

(a) labour is not a commodity;
(b) freedom of expression and of association are essential to sustained progress;
(c) poverty anywhere constitutes a danger to prosperity everywhere;
(d) the war against want requires to be carried on with unrelenting vigor within each nation, and by continuous and concerted international effort in which the representatives of workers and employers, enjoying equal status with those of governments, join with them in free discussion and democratic decision with a view to the promotion of the common welfare.[102]

The *Declaration of Philadelphia* also observes that 'lasting peace can be established only if it is based on social justice' and affirms that 'all human beings, irrespective of race, creed or sex, have the right to pursue both their material well-being and their spiritual development in conditions of freedom and dignity, of economic security and equal opportunity'.[103] However, there is little in the way of specific provision relating to children, and it is certainly not couched in the language of children's rights. Among the world programmes to which ILO declares its commitment is the 'provision for child welfare and maternity protection'.[104] ILO continued to produce a number of Conventions in the post-war period through to the 1960s and 1970s. There was a shift away from 'standard-setting' in the international community in the early 1980s to public awareness campaigns (Cordova 1993) and, at the beginning of the 1990s, an emphasis on 'technical assistance' to Member States (ILO 1996: para. 99). The appropriate balance between 'hard' and 'soft' law in international legal protection and their integration with practical programmes of assistance became an issue attracting greater attention.

---

102 The General Conference of the International Labour Organization, *Declaration concerning the aims and purposes of the International Labour Organisation* ('*Declaration of Philadelphia*'), 26th session, 10 May 1944, Philadelphia, § I.

The *Declaration of Philadelphia* has now been annexed to ILO's Constitution. See: International Labour Organization, *Constitution of the International Labour Organisation* (ILO), 1 April 1919. Adopted by the Peace Conference in April 1919, the ILO Constitution became Part XIII of the *Treaty of Versailles* (1919).

103 The *Declaration of Philadelphia of 1944*, § II(a).
104 The *Declaration of Philadelphia of 1944*, § III(h).

Second, in June 1998, ILO adopted the soft law instrument, the *Declaration on Fundamental Principles and Rights at Work and its Follow-up*,[105] and instrument which, *inter alia*:

> Declares that all Members, even if they have not ratified the Conventions in question, have an obligation arising from the very fact of membership in the Organization to respect, to promote and to realize, in good faith and in accordance with the Constitution, the principles concerning the fundamental rights which are the subject of those Conventions, namely:
>
> (a) freedom of association and the effective recognition of the right to collective bargaining;
> (b) the elimination of all forms of forced or compulsory labour;
> (c) the effective abolition of child labour; and
> (d) the elimination of discrimination in respect of employment and occupation.[106]

ILO's Director-General annually prepares a 'global report' on one of these fundamental rights, thus providing a four-year periodic cycle of reporting on each. There have been three global reports on child labour at the time of writing (ILO 2002b, 2006, 2010b).

The *Declaration on Fundamental Principles and Rights at Work and its Follow-up of 1998* has been an important landmark in the history of ILO. Although it is a 'soft law' instrument, its authority is enhanced by the fact that it was unanimously agreed by ILO Member States. Arguably, the *Declaration* provided the necessary flexibility required in an increasingly globalised world. Such core labour rights could be better universalised and reach further afield through the development of such principles. Alston (2004: 518–21) provides a robust critique of this approach, noting that the *Declaration* marks a new normative hierarchy whereby the four core labour standards are privileged at the expense of ILO's careful construction of 'rights' in the various *ILO Conventions* over many years. Replying to these criticisms, Langille (2005) argues that these core labour standards are conceptually coherent and in fact *support* the existing international labour regime rather than undermine it. ILO's first global report on child labour concluded with an action plan resting on three 'pillars':

- The first pillar is to reinforce the work of IPEC.
- The second pillar is to mainstream the abolition of child labour more actively across other ILO programmes and strengthen cross-sectoral collaboration and policy integration to this end.

---

105 *ILO Declaration on Fundamental Principles and Rights at Work and its Follow-up*. Adopted by the International Labour Conference at its 86th session, Geneva, 18 June 1998 (Annex revised 15 June 2010).
106 Ibid., art. 3.

- The third pillar is to forge closer partnerships with employers' and workers' organizations, as well as with other institutions and groups that share the goal of abolishing child labour.

(ILO 2002b: 118–19)

ILO's second global report in 2006 set out an action plan that is built upon the three-pillar approach, and it concluded optimistically that the elimination of the worst forms of child labour was within reach and set a goal to achieve this by 2016 (ILO 2006: 83–90). In its third quadrennial global report in 2010, ILO observed more cautiously that the goal to eliminate the worst forms of child labour by 2016 appeared to be slipping away:

> There are clear signs of progress but also disconcerting gaps in the global response. As things are today, the pace of progress is not fast enough to achieve the 2016 target. A flagging in the worldwide movement, a certain 'child labour fatigue', must be prevented.

(ILO 2010b: xiii)

The report identified that 'the critical fight against child labour has to be won in South Asia, where the greatest numbers of child labourers are to be found' (ILO 2010b: xv).

5.2.6 ILO reporting, representation and complaints procedures

ILO has a unique supervisory mechanism that provides two types of international monitoring: regular supervision and ad hoc procedures (Noguchi 2002: 366). The system is based on the *ILO Constitution*,[107] so separate Conventions do not contain dedicated provisions on reporting and monitoring as they do in relation to, for example, the *Convention on the Rights of the Child* (section 3.5 in this book). ILO relies (usually) on public shaming through documentation in ILO reports, together with technical expertise and financial assistance to promote compliance (Ho 2006: 341).

5.2.6.1 Regular supervision and reporting

Regular supervision is provided under article 22 of the *ILO Constitution*. Each Member State ratifying an *ILO Convention* agrees to make an annual report to the International Labour Office on the measures it has taken to give effect to

---

107 International Labour Organization, *Constitution of the International Labour Organisation* (ILO), 1 April 1919. Adopted by the Peace Conference in April 1919, Constitution became Part XIII of the *Treaty of Versailles* (1919).

the Conventions it has ratified. The Governing Body decides the form and content of such reports. They are then examined by the Committee of Experts on the Application of Conventions and Recommendations (CEACR). The Director-General must present summaries of the reports so received before the next Conference.[108] The reports, when submitted to the conference, are then discussed by a tripartite committee. In practice, reports are submitted every two years for the so-called 'fundamental'[109] and 'priority' Conventions,[110] and every five years for other Conventions, unless the CEACR requests them sooner. Since 2003, reports have been submitted according to Conventions grouped by subject matter. Governments are required to provide relevant legislation, statistics and documentation necessary for the full examination of their reports. Where a government has not satisfactorily provided such information, CEACR will write requesting it.

Although, in certain respects, there are distinct merits to the system of reporting under the *Convention on the Rights of the Child* (section 3.5 in this book), the ILO reporting procedures can be seen to have some advantages. There is, for example, an opportunity for a technical analysis by independent experts (the CEACR) in addition to an examination by the tripartite bodies of ILO (that is, governments, workers and employer representatives). Like the *Convention on the Rights of the Child* system, there is regular monitoring on the basis of country reports and responses to reports, but there is also the opportunity under the ILO machinery for the use of ad hoc procedures in cases of severe violations. The *Declaration on Fundamental Principles and Rights at Work and its Follow-up of 1998* provides for a system for gathering information from countries that have not yet ratified the relevant fundamental Conventions through annual reports.[111]

The CEACR produces two types of commentary on the application of the Conventions: *observations* and *direct requests*. 'Individual observations' contain comments on fundamental questions raised by the application of a particular

---

108 International Labour Organization, *Constitution of the International Labour Organisation (ILO)*, 1 April 1919, arts 22 and 23.
109 See n. 65 above, for the eight 'fundamental' *ILO Conventions*.
110 ILO's Governing Body designated four Conventions as 'priority' instruments. Since 2008, these Conventions are now referred to as 'Governance Conventions'. They are: *C081 – Labour Inspection Convention of 1947 (No. 81)*, Convention concerning Labour Inspection in Industry and Commerce (entered into force 7 Apr 1950) Adoption: Geneva, 30th ILC session (11 July 1947); *C122 – Employment Policy Convention of 1964 (No. 122)*, Convention concerning Employment Policy (entered into force 15 July 1966) Adoption: Geneva, 48th ILC session (9 July 1964); *C129 – Labour Inspection (Agriculture) Convention of 1969 (No. 129)*, Convention concerning Labour Inspection in Agriculture (entered into force 19 January 1972) Adoption: Geneva, 53rd ILC session (25 June 1969); *C144 – Tripartite Consultation (International Labour Standards) Convention of 1976 (No. 144)*, Convention concerning Tripartite Consultations to Promote the Implementation of International Labour Standards (entered into force 16 May 1978) Adoption: Geneva, 61st ILC session (21 June 1976).
111 *ILO Declaration on Fundamental Principles and Rights at Work and its Follow-up*. Adopted by the International Labour Conference at its 86th session, Geneva, 18 June 1998 (Annex revised 15 June 2010), § IIA(1) and (2).

Convention by a particular government, and these are reproduced in the Committee's annual report[112] (e.g. International Labour Conference 2009). Occasionally, it also produces a 'general observation' on one of the Conventions. For example, in 2009 the CEACR issued a 'general observation'[113] on the concept of 'light work' in the *Minimum Age Convention* (section 5.2.1 in this book). 'Direct requests' usually relate to more technical questions or questions of lesser importance and are not published in the report, but are communicated directly to the governments concerned.

5.2.6.2 Ad hoc procedures

Where there are acute problems or persistent non-observance of a ratified Convention, the *ILO Constitution* provides for ad hoc procedures.[114] As ILO depends heavily on a principle of voluntarism by Member States, these procedures are not invoked routinely. There are two types of procedure to consider: 'representation' and 'complaints' procedures. There are two 'representation' procedures available. First, representations can be made, by either an industrial association of employers or workers, that any of the Member States 'has failed to secure in any respect the effective observance within its jurisdiction of any Convention to which it is a party'. The Governing Body may then communicate this representation to the government concerned and invite it to make a statement. If either the government fails to make a statement in response, or the Governing Body does not deem its response satisfactory, then the latter may publish the representation and the statement, if any, made in reply to it.[115] Second, there is a 'reference' procedure[116] available for Member States where another Member has failed to respond to ILO standard-setting. A Member State, when ratifying a Convention or a Recommendation, is under an obligation[117] to bring the measure 'before the authority or authorities within whose competence the matter lies, for the enactment of legislation or other action' within one year from the adoption of the measure or, in exceptional circumstances, 18 months. There is, additionally, a 'complaint' procedure[118] available. Member States have a right to file a complaint with the International Labour Office if they are

---

112 E.g. International Labour Conference, *General Report of the Committee of Experts on the Application of Conventions and Recommendations 2009*, 98th session, Geneva: International Labour Office.
113 International Labour Conference, *General Observation concerning Convention No. 138*, 98th session, Committee of Experts on the Application of Conventions and Recommendations, Geneva: International Labour Office.
114 International Labour Organization, *Constitution of the International Labour Organisation* (ILO), 1 April 1919, arts 24 and 26.
115 Ibid., arts 24 and 25.
116 Ibid., art. 30.
117 Ibid., arts 19(5)(b) and (6)(b).
118 Ibid., arts 26–8.

not satisfied that any other Member is securing the effective observance of any Convention which both have ratified. The Governing Body has a discretion to request a statement from the government in question. If there is no satisfactory reply, or the Governing Body does not think it necessary to request one, it may appoint a Commission of Inquiry to consider the complaint and report. After full consideration of the complaint, the Commission must prepare a report setting out its findings of facts and such recommendations it may have as to the steps to be taken to meet the complaint and their timing. The Director-General must then communicate the report to the Governing Body and to each of the governments concerned in the complaint and arrange for its publication. Each of the governments must respond within three months, stating to the Director-General whether it accepts the recommendations contained in the Commission's report. If not, the governments may indicate that they propose to refer the complaint on to the International Court of Justice (ICJ) (section 2.4.1.1 in this book). The ICJ's decisions with regard to a complaint shall be final and 'may affirm, vary or reverse any of the findings or recommendations of the Commission of Inquiry, if any'.[119] ILO has reserved the use of Commissions of Inquiry for really grave and persistent violations of the international labour standards.[120] For example, the Commission's report on Myanmar in 1998[121] detailed the widespread and systematic use of forced labour in that country and a broad pattern of violation of fundamental human rights by the military government. The ruling military regime had used the civilian population (including women and children) as an unlimited pool of labourers to build and maintain a number of projects in construction, agriculture, and in hotels and other infrastructure projects (Sarkin and Pietschmann 2003). A Member State failing to carry out the recommendations of a Commission of Inquiry or a decision of the ICJ[122] will be vulnerable to the Governing Body recommending 'such action as it may deem wise and expedient to secure compliance therewith' to the Conference.

---

119 International Labour Organization, *Constitution of the International Labour Organisation* (ILO), 1 April 1919, arts 29, 31 and 32.
120 An example is the Commission of Inquiry set up in March 1997 following a complaint lodged by 25 worker delegates to the 83rd Session of the International Labour Conference in June 1996, to examine the application of the Forced Labour Convention of 1930 in Myanmar: see ILO (1998). This situation also resulted in the unprecedented invocation of article 33 of the ILO Constitution which provides certain enforcement powers.
121 ILO Commission of Inquiry, *Forced Labour in Myanmar (Burma)*, report of the Commission of Inquiry under article 26 of the Constitution of the International Labour Organization to examine the observance by Myanmar of the Forced Labour Convention, 1930 (No. 29), 2 July 1998, Geneva: International Labour Office. Available at:
<www.ilo.org/public/english/standards/relm/gb/docs/gb273/myanmar.htm#Part I> (accessed 13 October 2013).
122 International Labour Organization, *Constitution of the International Labour Organisation* (ILO), 1 April 1919, arts 33 and 34.

The involvement of ILO's 'social partners' in initiating ad hoc procedures and examining a case of representation is significant:

> They [the social partners] have a power to channel concerns of civil society into the mechanism of international standards. In the above-mentioned regular supervision, workers and employers organizations are very much encouraged to submit their comments and observations on the government's reports.
> (Noguchi 2002: 367)

5.3 Progressing the elimination of exploitative child labour

This section discusses how best the global movement to eliminate child labour can move forward. The rapid ratification of the *Worst Forms of Child Labour Convention of 1999* and the substantial amounts of donor funding that have supported IPEC are encouraging developments, though there remain a few conspicuous omissions to the ratification list of this Convention and the *Minimum Age Convention of 1973*.[123] It has been recognised that a holistic approach to the elimination of child labour is required to address the multifaceted nature of the problem; its complexity is certainly no excuse for inaction. As one commentator remarked: 'The indivisibility and interdependence of all human rights, which is the lynchpin of the United Nations approach, is perhaps nowhere more evident tha[n] in the quest for solutions to the problem of the exploitation of child labour' (Alston 1989: 39).

Most commentators prefer an integrated strategy to tackle the elimination of child labour (Masum 2002). Earlier commentaries have remarked on the unwillingness of governments to acknowledge the existence or at least the extent of child labour within jurisdictions, and indeed official acknowledgment is a prerequisite in seeking international, technical or financial assistance (Alston 1989: 38). However, there are no uniform, pre-packaged solutions in this field. CEACR noted long ago that the uneven incidence of child labour within countries required detailed investigation followed by pilot programmes to determine the most effective measures.[124] It is clear that the elimination of child labour will involve legislative, judicial and administrative interventions, but these are only one element of measures taken at the national level. Equally, the adoption of inappropriately tough legislation may make such practices go underground. Furthermore, a prerequisite for any credible programme to tackle child labour requires detailed and specific information; there

---

123 At the time of writing there were 19 States (including the USA) that had *not* ratified the *Minimum Age Convention of 1973*, and eight States that had *not* ratified the *Worst Forms of Child Labour Convention of 1999*. Six parties had not ratified *either* Convention: India, Marshall Islands, Myanmar, Palau, Somalia and Tuvalu.
124 CEACR, *General Survey by the Committee of Experts on the Application of Conventions and Recommendations: Minimum Age*, International Labour Conference, 67th session, Report III, pt 4B, 1981, Geneva: International Labour Office, p. 407.

is a continuing need for studies to provide robust analysis and policy prescriptions (Alston 1989: 40–6).

5.3.1 Child labour in international law: assessing the role of law and the enforceability problem

Much of public international law is vulnerable to the criticism that it lacks 'teeth', but that is often because inappropriate expectations are made of the extent to which it can deliver progress, particularly in relation to complex social, economic and cultural problems such as child labour. It should not be thought that the existence of law to eliminate child labour is *necessarily* the best form of intervention. The decline in child labour in the industrialised countries between 1880 and 1920 'is thought to be due to both economic and legal reasons, with the former predominating' (Betcherman et al. 2004: 25). It should also be remembered that international law has evolved alongside a deep history that supports the autonomy and equality of State sovereignty which has comprised 'the basic constitutional doctrine of the law of nations' (Crawford 2012: 289). The principles of the sovereign equality of all State Members of the UN and non-intervention in domestic jurisdictions are enshrined in the *Charter of the United Nations*.[125]

It has been said that the lack of enforceability of Conventions often reflects concern in the drafting process about the preservation of State sovereignty (Silk and Makonnen 2003: 363; Selby 2008: 175). Furthermore, international human rights instruments are the result of political consensus within the international community; they 'reflect what governments and interest groups could agree on, not necessarily what experts believe should be done' (Betcherman et al. 2004: 5). However, despite such limitations, these instruments do provide important standards from which national policy and benchmarks to assess policy interventions can be derived. In considering the *enforceability* dimension to the three key international instruments discussed in this chapter, it should not be forgotten that ultimately they rely heavily on national efforts. For example, it is particularly important that appropriate national systems of labour inspection are established given children's powerlessness in many work situations (Alston 1989: 44).

As we have seen in section 5.1.4 above, the dilemma between universal standard-setting and cultural relativity is a poignant one in relation to child labour. Northern countries tend to articulate children's rights against a background idea of childhood as a biologically driven natural phenomenon 'characterized by physical and mental growth stages that are everywhere roughly the same' (Myers 2001: 40). This dominant view of childhood tends to keep children separated off from adulthood and discourages participation in adult concerns, particularly the economic maintenance of the family. On the other hand, Southern societies stress

---

125 *Charter of the United Nations and Statute of the International Court of Justice*, concluded 26 June 1945, 1 UNTS XVI, (entered into force 23 October 1945), art. 2(1) & (7).

collective family unity and solidarity and accept a much greater degree of participation and contribution to the economic maintenance of the family (Stalford 2013: 883–4; Okyere 2012; Khair 2010).

The problem of delay in the reporting processes of many international mechanisms appears also in the ILO machinery. Some commentators have observed that the dilemma in this area is that there are (now) strong legal norms but weak enforcement mechanisms, a process which has in turn contributed to a rise in private action to prevent child labour (Silk and Makonnen 2003: 359). Silk and Makonnen offer a useful model of the evolution of human rights enforcement to consider. The identification of human rights abuses leads to the setting of strong international legal standards, but with weak institutions and processes of enforcement; this in turn leads to a range of NGO and IGO interventions of a non-law enforcement character aiming to achieve compliance with the established normative standards. Finally, aspects of these private initiatives may in turn be incorporated into effective, enforceable national and international law (Silk and Makonnen 2003: 369).

5.3.2 Partnership and coordination

It is widely accepted that the implementation of human rights standards generally will benefit greatly from well-planned partnerships between governments and NGOs. It has been said that NGOs may be able to be more robustly abolitionist in their stance towards child labour than official international institutions which are always dependent on political compromise and diplomacy (Fyfe 2017; Tobin 2019; Silk and Makonnen 2003: 369). They have certainly undertaken some very successful anti-sweatshop campaigns in the 1990s, for example. NGOs are often able to strike clearer, principled aims and objectives. The increasing focus on the NGO contribution is derived, to an extent, from the growing recognition of the limitations of standard-setting. Most commentators agree that the complexity and multifaceted nature of child labour in particular requires national governments to strike such constructive partnerships. The development of NGO action around child labour issues has involved the emergence of, for example, voluntary codes of corporate conduct. Indeed, some of the independent monitoring schemes evolved in this way have been criticised by organised labour as a 'privatisation of law enforcement', undermining the traditional protections for workers of collective bargaining (Silk and Makonnen 2003: 365). The increasing need for partnerships with NGOs and IGOs also assumes there will be successful coordination between these bodies to achieve the desired synergies. In the past, there have certainly been criticisms that ILO has carried 'virtually singlehandedly' the burden of international efforts in relation to the elimination of child labour (Alston 1989: 48). There is greater coordination now, and other bodies such as UNICEF, the UN Development Program (UNDP) and the Food and Agriculture Organization (FAO) have more input in this field than they used to. But it is not only coordination between the relevant international and other bodies concerned that is required. There is also a need to coordinate the policy approaches taken, particularly in relation to education at the national level. The role of education (see section 5.1.3 above) is central to debates about child labour, both causatively and consequentially. With regard to developing countries, where it seems likely that the worst forms of child labour will persist for longer, it is important to construct an approach that is integrated with wider development policies available to improve social conditions (Selby 2008: 178).

The research literature relating to child labour raises interesting questions about the potential role of, and partnership with, the business community in assisting with efforts to eliminate child labour. The Social Dialogue Section of ILO-IPEC supports businesses' efforts to reduce child labour and to increase compliance with the ILO's child labour standards: Convention No. 138 on Minimum Age and Convention No. 182 on Worst Forms of Child Labour. Hassel (2008) argues that in the last decade, and prompted by the *ILO Declaration on Fundamental Principles and Rights at Work and its Follow-up* of 1998, there has been a fundamental change of approach by business and governments towards global labour and social issues (section corporate social responsibility). The Child Labour Platform, a thematic membership-based workstream under the supervision and oversight of the UN Global Compact Labour Working Group (LWG), aims to identify the obstacles to the implementation of the ILO Conventions in supply chains and surrounding communities, identify practical ways of overcoming these obstacles, and catalyse collective action.

International labour law has moved away from *ILO Conventions* towards the principles of 'core labour standards'. This has in effect led to an indirect pattern of self-regulation. Indeed, it is argued that the proliferation of corporate codes and a variety of company-based independent monitoring schemes indicate 'an apparent shift from reliance on public international measures to private action' (Silk and Makonnen 2003: 363). Furthermore, the adoption by ILO of this 'soft law' approach fits better into the wider debate of linking trade with labour standards (Hassel 2008: 237).

5.3.3 Linking trade and labour standards

The frustrations with the defects in the international legal regime have opened up another front for action at the international level, the linkage of the issue of child labour with international trade regulation (Chaudhuri and Dwibedi 2016: Cooper 1997: 420). Debates over the design of an appropriate trade policy response to the employment of child labor in export industries have ranged from the inclusion of a 'social clause' in the World Trade Organization (WTO), to calls for import bans to be imposed on products made with child labour. Supporters of the trade – labour linkage have relied on competition and human rights arguments. The competition-based argument is that countries with lower labour standards generally have lower production costs which offer them a competitive trade advantage. Consequently, there may be a 'race to the bottom', that is, a lowering of labour standards to remain competitive. The human rights argument is simply that by imposing the linkage the international community is protecting individuals against the violation of core labour standards (including the abolition of child labour). In 2011, the UN launched the 'Guiding Principles on Business and Human Rights: Implementing the United Nations "Protect, Respect and Remedy" Framework',[126] which were developed by the Special Representative of the Secretary-General on the issue of human rights and transnational corporations and other business enterprises. The Guiding Principles provide companies with a practical framework for meeting this responsibility.

The counter-argument to the human rights approach relies on the theory of protectionism: in effect, that trade – labour linkage would allow developed countries to protect their interests by preventing less developed nations from exploiting their lower wage cost advantages and that would slow economic growth, further worsening the child labour problem (Chaudhuri and Dwibedi 2016; Ho 2006: 343). However, the protectionist argument is not as credible if applied to the worst forms of child labour. Nevertheless, there are those that do not see trade sanctions as a primary remedy for eliminating child labour. As one commentator observes, '[c]ountries with large, affluent populations of consumers will always have more leverage both in adopting sanctions against countries and deflecting them against themselves' (Cullen 1999: 25). Trade – labour linkage supporters have argued either for a stronger enforcement mechanism within ILO, such as trade sanctions, or the addition of a labour clause in the World Trade Organization (WTO) agreements. Some argue the need to integrate child labour elimination into national economic regulation. Various organisations have advocated the need to link trade and labour standards. For example, the International Confederation of Free Trade Unions has advocated the prohibition of imports of any goods produced with exploitative child labour. In essence, the proposition to have a 'social clause' inserted into WTO and other trade agreements, will involve an obligation by parties to the agreement to respect labour standards, including the elimination of child labour, and recognition that the obligation can be enforced with trade sanctions.

The advocacy to establish trade – labour linkages has met with fierce resistance, mainly on the basis that such a linkage could be seen as a disguised form of protectionism and an attempt to undermine the competitive advantage of developing countries (Cooper 1997: 421). National trade boycotts have had a mixed reception When a Bill that would ban entry of any goods into the United States manufactured with the use of child labour was introduced into Congress by Senator Harkin in 1993 (see also section 5.3.4 in this book), employers in Bangladesh laid off tens of thousands of children. Subsequent UNICEF studies showed that none of these children returned to school (Cooper 1997: 423), though in

---

126 The Human Rights Council endorsed the Guiding Principles in its resolution 17/4 of 16 June 2011.

the aftermath of international pressure there were a number of improvements achieved (English 1997: 439). Child labour legislation in India prescribed fines for employers and made the employment of children more costly, but this caused the wages of children to drop, 'causing either more children in the household to work or those already working to work more hours' (Betcherman et al. 2004: 27). Simplistic measures such as dismissal of child labourers without any effort to rehabilitate and reintegrate them into the community should be avoided (Muntarbhorn 1998: 305).

WTO rejected in principle the formulation of a trade – labour link at the Singapore Ministerial Conference in 1997.[127] WTO has in effect moved the discussion back to ILO and has since refused to consider any sort of trade – labour linkage (Ho 2006: 344). It would seem, for the present at least, that the option of persuading the WTO to embrace a social clause is not available.

Equally, ILO has been averse to pursuing the trade – labour link as it 'is concerned to protect its institutional legitimacy which is founded on tripartism and voluntarism' (Cullen 1999: 29). As the options that might have been possible via WTO and ILO action appear to be closing, Ho argues that a *nationalised* trade – labour linkage would better provide enforcement against child labour violations than trying to create a strong *international* system (Ho 2006: 349). The argument is that the system of child labour regulation could be best accommodated by focusing on ILO facilitating a nationalisation of the international movement to abolish child labour (Ho 2006: 338). The basic idea is that developed countries, such as the United States, could create unilateral or bilateral trade agreements through which trade benefits or sanctions are not determined by individual countries but by ILO findings. Humbert (2009: 375) argues forcefully that 'trade measures should complement the existing ILO and UN implementation systems for the prohibition of child labour'.

5.3.4 Corporate social responsibility

Major international brands and retailers adopt vertically integrated models of production and source directly from formal manufacturers that adhere to both international and national labour standards (Zhou 2017: x). Other brands, without direct supply arrangements, source from intermediaries, whose involvement in the supply chain increases the likelihood of outsourcing to Pakistan's informal sector manufacturers. As a result, there is evidence that some textiles and garments made by workers in the informal economy under conditions that violate international labour standards and national wage legislation are exported to destinations such as the US, the EU as well as elsewhere (Zhou 2017: x).

---

127 Ministerial Conference of the World Trade Organization, *Singapore Ministerial Declaration*, adopted 13 December 1996, 36 I.L.M. 218 (1997).

As noted earlier, in its Concluding Observations for the Republic of Korea,[128] the CtRC suggested that import restrictions might be required with regard to products from third states that are investigated by the ILO) for using child labour. In a General Comment on the business sector and children's rights (2013),[129] the Committee pointed out that States should encourage a business culture that understands and fully respects children's rights. To this end, States should include the issue of children's rights and business in the overall context of the national policy framework for implementation of the Convention.

Non-governmental organisations and pressure groups have been active in efforts to reduce child labour (Fyfe 2007; Haufler 2001; Tobin 2019). Some of the corporations have recognised that the sale of goods associated with child labour has catalysed initiatives such as 'labelling' and consumer boycotts (Di Maio and Fabbri 2013). Labelling campaigns can also be useful to assure consumers that products have been manufactured without child labour.[130] If consumers decide to boycott products that are produced by child labour, then firms will realise that the use of child labour will lower the price of their product. Hence, the existence of a boycott will make child labour a less attractive input than it would have been otherwise. For instance, the threat of a US boycott of goods produced by children under 14 years in led to the mass lay-off of adolescent girls employed in garment factories (ILO/UNICEF 2004).[131]

However, some researchers suggest that the use of product boycotts by consumers could, in fact, lead to increased child labour, especially in poor households (Tobin 2019; Basu and Zarghamee 2009). This could be the result of the 'displacement effect', whereby children simply move to activities where there is no boycott. Labelling could also suffer from lack of credibility and trustworthiness (Ballet et al. 2011).

There has, however, been some imaginative collaboration between multinational corporations and their local suppliers, in combination with international organisations, to eliminate child labour in a specific industrial sector. For example, international concerns over the widespread use of children to hand-stitch footballs persuaded the Sialkot region in Pakistan to sign a memorandum of understanding with ILO, UNICEF and Save the Children – UK in Atlanta in 1997 (Johnson 1999). This started a unique programme in Pakistan, coordinated by IPEC. The

---

128 CRC, Consideration of Reports submitted by States Parties under Art. 44 of the Convention. Concluding Observations: Republic of Korea, UN Doc. CRC/C/KOR/CO/3–4 (2011), paras 26–7.
129 *Convention on the Rights of the Child* General comment No. 16 (2013) on State obligations regarding the impact of the business sector on children's rights CRC/C/GC/16, 17 April 2013.
130 For example, the Rugmark system established in 1994. Rugmark International is an international NGO working to end illegal child labour in the handmade rug industry and to offer educational opportunities to children in India and Nepal. Rugmark was replaced by Good Weave on all rugs certified as from August 2009.
131 ILO/UNICEF report of the MOU project, *Addressing Child Labour in the Bangladesh Garment Industry 1995–2001: A Synthesis of UNICEF and ILO Evaluation Studies of the Bangladesh Garment Sector Projects* (Geneva/New York, August, 2004).

number and range of IPEC's partners have expanded over the years and now include employers' and workers' organisations, other international and government agencies, private businesses, community-based organisations. The Social Dialogue Section of ILO-IPEC and the Child Labour Platform, overseen by the International Organisation of Employers (IOE) and the International Trade Union Confederation (ITUC) have been vehicles for broad engagement. The 'Accelerating action for the elimination of child labour in supply chains in Africa' (ACCEL Africa, 2018) is a regional project with particular focus on the specific supply chains, namely cocoa, coffee, cotton, gold and tea.

For most companies, the major influence for cooperation and action has been the idea of corporate social responsibility (SCR). This concept entails business' commitment to embrace ethical practices, legal standards, international norms and respect for the greater public interest. It thus involves taking proactive measures by adopting responsible corporate practices (Carroll and Shabana 2010) point out that the concept of CSR represents an encompassing framework of different concepts that study the relationship of companies and the community in which the company operates, regardless of whether the community is local, national or global (Carroll and Shabana 2010). The concept, without doubt, possesses a clear strategic determinant and represents an integral part of the business model of modern global corporations throughout the world today (Nielsen and Thomson 2009). Some research suggests a correlation between consumers' CSR perceptions and a positive impact on their consumer attitudes (Hoffmann and Hutter 2012; Neilson 2010). In other words, consumers 'reward' companies which are CSR-oriented.

An example of a CSR imitative is the Harkin – Engel Protocol.[132] The Protocol was signed in September 2001 by the Chocolate Manufacturers Association (CMA) and the World Cocoa Foundation (WCF). It was prompted by media exposés about the existence of child slavery on Ivory Coast cocoa farms, triggering an avalanche of criticism. Two members of the US Congress, Senator Tom Harkin and Representative Eliot Engel proposed a rider to an agricultural Bill that a federal system certifies and labels chocolate products as 'slave free' (Global Exchange 2005). The Protocol was intended to be an effort led by the chocolate industry to develop a framework for the cocoa industry to eliminate the worst forms of child and slave labour in the growing and processing of cocoa beans and their derived products (IPEC 2007: 12). In addition, the signatories agreed to implement, by July 2005, an industry-wide certification scheme informing consumers that the WFCL were not employed in the production of cocoa used in their chocolate products.

However, the companies were accused of failing to meet the commitment. On 14 July 2005, three individuals from Mali and Global Exchange (a human rights organisation) filed a class action lawsuit in California federal court against Nestlé,

---

132 Sometimes also known as the 'Harkin Protocol'. The official name of the protocol is the 'Protocol for the growing and processing of cocoa beans and their derivative products in a manner that complies with ILO Convention 182 concerning the prohibition and immediate action for the elimination of the worst forms of child labor',, although this is rarely used.

Archer Daniels Midland and Cargill.[133] The individuals (known, in the case, by the pseudonym 'John Doe') alleged they had been trafficked from Mali as child slaves and forced to work harvesting and/or cultivating cocoa beans on farms in Côte d'Ivoire. The plaintiffs were between 12 and 14 years old at the time they first began working at the farms The plaintiffs alleged that they were forced to work 'cutting, gathering, and drying' cocoa beans for 12–14 hours a day, six days a week, kept in locked rooms when not working and suffered severe physical abuse by those guarding them. Thus, they alleged that the companies aided, abetted or failed to prevent the torture, forced labour and arbitrary detention that they had suffered as child slaves. The lawsuit alleged violations of the Alien Tort Claims Act,[134] Torture Victim Protection Act, US Constitution and California state law. The plaintiffs further claimed that the companies' economic benefit from the labour of children violates international labour conventions, the law of nations and customary international law.

The case has been running for more than ten years with a number of twists and turns. In the first Court action in 2010, the court concluded there was no support in the relevant sources of international law for the proposition that corporations were legally responsible for international law violations. Further, international law was silent on this question: no relevant treaties, international practice, or international case law provide for corporate liability. Instead, all of the available international law materials applied only to states or natural persons. However, in a subsequent appeal in 2018, the court reached a different decision

The following is a summary of the case.

Case study 5.1

John Doe, I; John Doe, II; John Doe, III; John Doe, IV; John Doe, V; and John Doe, VI, each individually and on behalf of proposed class members, *Plaintiffs-Appellants*,
v.
Nestlé, S.A.; Nestlé USA, INC.; Nestlé Ivory Coast; Cargill Incorporated Company; Cargill Cocoa; Cargill West Africa, S. A.; Archer Daniels Midland

---

133 *John Doe, I; John Doe, II; John Doe, III; John Doe, IV; John Doe, V; and John Doe, VI, each individually and on behalf of proposed class members v. Nestlé, S.A.; Nestlé USA, inc.; Nestlé Ivory Coast; Cargill Incorporated Company; Cargill Cocoa; Cargill West Africa, S. A.; Archer Daniels Midland Company*, No. 17–55435 D.C. no. 2:05-cv-05133-svw-mrw.

134 The Alien Tort Statute (ATS) is a US federal law first adopted in 1789 that gives the federal courts jurisdiction to hear lawsuits filed by non-US citizens for torts committed in violation of international law.

Company,
Defendants-Appellees
Appeal from the United States District Court or the Central District of California
Stephen V. Wilson, District Judge, Presiding
Argued and Submitted June 7, 2018
Pasadena, California
No. 17–55435 D.C. No. 2:05-cv-05133-SVW-MRW
Filed October 23, 2018
Amended July 5, 2019

On 14 July 2005, three individuals from Mali and Global Exchange (a human rights organisation) filed a class action lawsuit in California federal court against Nestlé, Archer Daniels Midland and Cargill. The individuals alleged they had been trafficked from Mali as child slaves and forced to work harvesting and/or cultivating cocoa beans on farms in Côte d'Ivoire.

In August 2005, Nestlé filed a motion to force the disclosure of the names of the former child slave plaintiffs, which was opposed by the plaintiffs. In addition, the defendants filed a motion to dismiss the case. On 27 July 2006, the court ordered further briefings to be filed on various issues related to 'aiding and abetting' standards. On 8 September 2010, the court dismissed the case finding that the case could not be brought under the Alien Tort Claims Act. The court concluded that existing authorities did not demonstrate that corporate liability was sufficiently well established and universal to satisfy a claim under the Alien Tort Claims Act. The plaintiffs appealed the dismissal.

In December 2013, a federal appeals court overturned the 2010 ruling and allowed the plaintiffs to refile the lawsuit. In September 2014, the federal appeals court replaced its December 2013 opinion with an expanded one reversing and vacating the lower court's dismissal of the case. The new opinion sets forth expanded reasoning for allowing the plaintiffs to amend their complaint to show the connection their claims have to the United States. The court found that the plaintiffs have standing to bring their Alien Tort case because of the universal prohibition against slavery. In September 2015, the defendants petitioned the Supreme Court to throw out the federal appeals court's ruling and decide if companies were subject to liability under the Alien Tort Claims Act. In January 2016, the Supreme Court declined to hear the companies' appeal.

In July 2016, the plaintiffs submitted an amended complaint. In March 2017, a judge dismissed the lawsuit, finding that the plaintiffs could not sue over forced labour in Côte d'Ivoire when they could not prove that there was conduct by the companies in the US linked to the wrongdoing overseas. On 30 March 2017, the plaintiffs filed an appeal, arguing that Nestlé's and Cargill's decisions to give the cocoa farmers money and technical support were made at the companies' US headquarters and, therefore, the lawsuit had a sufficient link to the US. On 23 October 2018, the 9th Circuit Court of Appeal allowed the lawsuit against Nestlé and Cargill under the Alien Tort Statute to proceed. In the 2019 action, the court had to decide if the plaintiffs could be allowed to amend their complaint. The Court ruled that:

> 'Defendants do not dispute that plaintiffs suffered concrete injury by being abused and held as child slaves. In addition, plaintiffs' injuries are redressable because when 'one private party is injured by another, the injury can be redressed in at least two ways: by awarding compensatory damages or by imposing a sanction on the wrongdoer that will minimize the risk that the harm-causing conduct will be repeated'. *Steel Co. v. Citizens for a Better Env't, 523 U.S. 83, 127 (1998)*. Plaintiffs also satisfy the traceability requirement as to Cargill because they raise sufficiently specific allegations regarding Cargill's involvement in farms that rely on child slavery'.
>
> Plaintiffs' allegations against Nestlé are far less clear, though part of the difficulty is plaintiffs' reliance on collective allegations against all or at least multiple defendants. Notwithstanding this deficiency, the allegations are sufficient to at least allow plaintiffs a final opportunity to replead. On remand, plaintiffs must eliminate the allegations against foreign defendants and specifically identify the culpable conduct attributable to individual domestic defendants'.
>
> After detailing all the reasons, the Court decided to 'reverse the district court and remand to allow plaintiffs to amend their complaint to specify whether aiding and abetting conduct that took place in the United States is attributable to the domestic corporations in this case.

> Supplementary information from: **Business and Human Rights Resource Centre**
> They originally sued Nestlé USA, Archer-Daniels-Midland Co and Cargill Inc [CARG.UL] in 2005. Archer-Daniels-Midland was dismissed from the lawsuit in 2016, according to court records. The case has since made its way to the U.S. Supreme Court, which in 2016 rejected the companies' bid to have the lawsuit thrown out.

Other cases have been initiated by US citizens. For instance, in *Dana v. The Hershey Company et al*[135] (2016), Laura Dana and Californian consumers alleged that the worst forms of child labour were used in Côte d'Ivoire to produce Hershey's chocolate products, and that the company's failure to disclose this information to consumers at the time of sale violates the state's consumer protection laws.

---

135 *Dana v. The Hershey Company et al.* U S District Court Northern District of California Case No.15-cv-04453 JCS.

Hershey is one of the largest chocolate companies in the United States and was a signatory to the Harkin Protocol in 2001. The court stated:

> The Issue before this Court, however, is whether California law requires corporations to inform customers of that fact on their product packaging and point of sale advertising', the court noted. 'Every court to consider the issue has held that it does not. This Court agrees.[136]

California's consumer protection laws do not create any obligation to make such disclosures. Like the Hersey Company, Nestlé has also launched a CSR initiative. The 'Nestlé Responsible Sourcing Standard' (2018) enjoins its suppliers 'to behave transparently and to commit to continuous improvement in their operations to reach this Standard exhaustively'.[137] Failure to continuously improve upon this can impact the ability of our supply chain to deliver to Nestlé, which could lead to, for example, delisting. The company states:

> If the Supplier employs young workers, defined as between the ages of 15 and 18, it shall demonstrate that the employment of young people contributes to their personal education and does not expose them to undue physical risks that can harm physical, mental or emotional development.[138]

5.4 Concluding remarks

Child labour is a pervasive issue globally, especially in developing countries. Children work for different reasons, particularly as a result of poverty. However, as we have noticed from this chapter the notion of 'child labour' is far more nuanced. There are different types of work – some of which are hazardous, while others are permissible. When it comes to international law, it is important to take a sociological examination, given the different cultures to which law will be applied. A conception of 'child labour' may not be universal across all societies. In some parts of the world, some work which might cause disapprobation may not necessarily be a source of outrage in those communities. The challenge for international labour law is on either accommodating socio-economic and cultural differences or ignoring them. As this chapter has noted, some children have to work to contribute to family incomes. A corpus of anti-child labour has evolved over the years, with early instruments intolerant of all forms of child labour. Over time, it would appear that, as the legal framework for child labour developed, some concessions were made, particularly concerning 'hazardous work'. Notably, the number of children in child labour seems to declining but perhaps not fast enough. However, implementing the anti-child labour laws remains a teething problem.

---

136 *Dana v. The Hershey Company et al.* U S District Court Northern District of California Case No.15-cv-04453 JCS, p. 1.
137 Nestlé Responsible Sourcing Standard, Nestec Ltd, 2018, p. 3.
138 Nestlé Responsible Sourcing Standard, Nestec Ltd, 2018, para. 4.2.1.

Chapter 6

International parental child abduction

6.1 International parental child abduction

The act of removing children from their usual abode to another country and in the context of a parental dispute will almost inevitably be damaging to the welfare of those children.[1] A child is likely to feel uprooted from a familiar environment, especially in circumstances where the child loses contact with friends and relatives. The move may disrupt not only the child's relationships but also their education and general sense of security, particularly if such a move is conducted in the context of a parental dispute. The year 2020 marks the 37th anniversary of the entry into force of the *Hague Convention on the Civil Aspects of International Child Abduction of 1980*[2] (hereafter, the 'Hague Convention'). The treaty provisions are intended to reduce the traumatic impact of separation on the child(ren) and left-behind parent, by providing a framework for rapid return where abduction takes place. Its preamble sets out the states' parties' intent: 'to protect children internationally from the harmful effects of their wrongful removal or retention and to establish procedures to ensure their prompt return to the State of their habitual residence'.

In a study undertaken in the United Kingdom, involving interviews with 30 adults and ten children, it was found that 'abduction and its effects linger for many years after the ending of the abduction' and 'the lack of contact between parents and children during the period of the abduction is a source of immense continuing anxiety for those concerned, many years after the abduction' (Freeman 2006: 46). Further research on the long-term effectiveness of mediation (section 6.5 below) in cases of international parental child abduction informed by interviews with 52 adults and involving 46 children also revealed evidence of severe health effects in relation to both the *left-behind* and *taking parents* involved (Buck 2012: 65, 70).

In many national jurisdictions child abduction is regarded as a sufficiently serious matter to require the protection of the criminal law. For example, the English common law developed a criminal law offence of 'kidnapping', defined by the House of

---

1 See generally, Lowe et al. (2004, 2017) and Shuz (2013).
2 Hague Conference on Private International Law, concluded 25 October 1980 (entered into force 1 December 1983).

Lords as the taking or carrying away of one person by another, by force or by fraud, without the consent of the person taken or carried away and without lawful excuse.[3] Furthermore, the Child Abduction Act 1984 provides that 'a person connected with a child under the age of 16 commits an offence if he takes or sends the child out of the United Kingdom without the appropriate consent'. The maximum penalty for a conviction is seven years' imprisonment.[4] Parental child abduction convictions are not numerous in the UK because, unlike the offence of child abduction by strangers, no prosecution for this offence can be instituted except by or with the consent of the Director of Public Prosecutions.[5] Furthermore, criminal proceedings against a parent for child abduction will not result in the child being returned and therefore serves little purpose. Child abductions by strangers will usually be covered by the national criminal code relevant to the country in which the abduction took place (Newiss and Fairbrother 2004). There are also various provisions in the *UN Convention on the Rights of the Child*[6] (1989) and the *Optional Protocol on the Rights of the Child on the Sale of Children, Child Prostitution and Child Pornography*[7] (2000) (OPSC) relevant to those scenarios. OPSC, for example, is intended to both strengthen the international criminalisation of such practices and provide welfare protection for child victims (Buck 2008). Some national jurisdictions also provide civil regulation of child abduction carried out within their own borders. In the United Kingdom, for example, the Family Law Act 1986 provides for common jurisdictional rules to apply and a set of rules for the mutual recognition and enforcement of custody orders in each territory of the United Kingdom. However, once a child has been removed from the United Kingdom, parental abduction is usually treated as a civil matter.[8]

The focus of this chapter is on the private international law aspects of the parental/carer abduction of the child and, in particular, the operation of the Hague Convention. However, before analysing this set of rules, it is worth considering for a moment the social phenomenon of international parental child abduction. What are the underlying causes? Are there any distinctive characteristics of those parents who abduct children? What kind of dysfunctional family scenario is likely to result in abduction? Are men more likely to abduct children than women? Are babies and infants more likely to be abducted than older children? There is some empirical evidence available to address these questions, but it is a changing and incomplete picture.

When the Hague Convention was being prepared in the 1970s, the paradigm case was that of the father taking the child abroad and possibly attempting to conceal his own and the child's whereabouts from the left-behind mother. He may have been motivated by bitter feelings generated by a deteriorating relationship with the mother,

---

3 *R v. D* [1984] AC 778, 800.
4 Child Abduction Act 1984, ss. 1, 2 and 4(1).
5 Child Abduction Act 1984, s. 4(2).
6 Opened for signature 20 November 1989, 1577 UNTS 3 (entered into force 2 September 1990).
7 Opened for signature 25 May 2000, 2171 UNTS 227 (entered into force 18 January 2002).
8 In the UK, the International Child Abduction and Contact Unit (ICACU) deals with applications for the return of abducted children. See: <www.gov.uk/government/publications/international-child-abduction-and-contact-unit-application-form> (accessed 27 September 2019).

and he may have been frustrated by restrictions on his access. He may have lost legal custody of the child(ren). However, even the few surveys that were available in the 1990s challenged this stereotype (Beaumont and McEleavy 1999: 9–10). The statistical evidence on international parental abduction has not yet been fully developed, although the work of Lowe (2011a,b,c) and Lowe et al. (1999, 2006) has influenced the Hague Conference to develop its own statistical database.[9] Lowe (2011a: paras 27–30) estimated that (in 2008) there was a maximum of 2,460 Hague applications globally comprising 2,080 return (85%) and 380 access (15%) applications. Combining both incoming and outgoing applications, some Central Authorities of the States parties had higher workloads than others. The USA handled the most (598 applications), followed by England & Wales (466), Germany (383), Mexico (272) and Italy (238), and some Central Authorities handled no applications at all in 2008.

With regard to return applications, it is at least now clear that the stereotype of a non-custodial father removing or retaining his children does not reflect the reality of proceedings made under the Hague Convention. Lowe estimated that in 2008, 69% of taking persons were the mothers of the children involved, 28% were fathers, and the remaining 3% involved grandparents, institutions or other relatives (Lowe 2011a: para. 42). Overall, 72% of taking persons were the child's primary or joint primary carer (Lowe 2011a: para. 47). It should not be assumed that the taking person will necessarily take the child to his or her own country, though most did. In 2008, 60% of taking persons took the children to a State of which they were a national (Lowe 2011a: para. 50).

Statistical analysis of Hague Convention applications in 2015 (Lowe and Stephens 2017) took account of country statistics collected in 1999, 2003, 2008 and 2015, enabling an analysis of trends over a period of 16 years. The authors received responses from the Central Authorities of 72 Contracting States, with an estimate of capture of 94% of all applications. The statistics revealed that mothers were still consistently most likely to be the taking person. In 2015, 73% of the taking person were mothers, and this figure was 69% in 1999, 86% in 2003 and 69% in 2008. In 2015, fathers were the taking persons in 24% of cases, with 2% of cases involving grandparents or others. In 83% of cases, the taking person was the primary caregiver or joint primary caregiver; with this proportionately being 92% where the mother was the taking person and 60% where the father was the taking person. In 58% of the cases, the taking person travelled to a state of which they were a national. In 2015, at least 2,904 children were the victims of international child abduction, and there were 2,191 return applications in total. The average age of the children was 6.8 years, and the children were almost evenly divided between genders, with 53% being boys and 47% being girls.

The following table details the outcome of return applications between 1999 and 2015.

---

9 On 28 September 2007 an electronic statistical database, INCASTAT, was launched, which generates the annual statistical forms covering return and access applications relating to the Hague Convention of 1980; it also produces statistical charts. INCASTAT is available only to the central authorities designated under the 1980 Child Abduction Convention.

Table 6.1 Outcome of return applications 1999–2015

	1999	2003	2008	2015
Return rate	50%	51%	46%	46%
Access agreed	–	3%	3%	3%
Judicial refusal	11%	13%	15%	12%
Withdrawal of application	14%	15%	18%	14%
Pending	9%	9%	8%	5%
Rejection by central authority	11%	6%	5%	3%

For those applications decided in court (42% in 2015), 238 cases resulted in a judicial refusal to order the return of the children. The reasons for refusal varied, including 'grave risk' to the child, the child not being habitually resident in the Requested State, and the child's objections. The time period for resolving a case varied according to the outcome, with an average of 158 days for a judicial return decision and 244 days for a judicial refusal decision.

The emerging picture of international parental abduction is that although the absolute number of abductions remains relatively modest, there has been a steady increase in the 37 years since the Hague Convention was concluded. It would appear that the number is rising as the process of globalisation provides more opportunities for international marriages or partnerships to take place. Motivations to abduct vary from parents wanting to force reconciliation with the left-behind parent, to having a desire to blame or punish the left-behind parent, or to protect the child from a parent who is perceived to abuse or neglect the child (Chiancone 2001). One possible explanation for parental child abduction lies in the impact of reformed custody laws. The international legal recognition of the child's right to contact with both parents under the *Convention on the Rights of the Child*[10] has increasingly been observed (section 3.7.5 in this book). Part of the explanation may also lie in the increasing number of persons who marry or cohabit with a person of a different nationality. When the relationship fails there may well be pressures on the couple to return to their respective countries of habitual residence. It may appear to be the obvious course of action for the primary carer to return home with their children. However, this often proves to be a complex multi-jurisdictional predicament.

6.2 Introduction to the international legal instruments

There are four international instruments considered here in relation to international parental child abduction: the *Convention on the Rights of the Child* (articles 9–11); the *European Convention on Recognition and Enforcement of Decisions Concerning*

---

10 CRC, art. 9(1) and (3).

Custody of Children and on Restoration of Custody of Children[11] (1980) (hereafter, the 'European Convention of 1980'); *Council Regulation (EC) No 2201/2003*[12] (hereafter the 'Revised Brussels II Regulation'); and the *Hague Convention on Child Abduction of 1980*. The first three are dealt with, in outline only, in the following three sections. This Chapter is focused mainly on the *Hague Convention on Child Abduction of 1980*, which is dealt with in more depth in section 6.3 below.

6.2.1 UN Convention on the Rights of the Child

Article 9(1) of the *Convention on the Rights of the Child* provides that:

> States Parties shall ensure that a child shall not be separated from his or her parents against their will, except when competent authorities subject to judicial review determine, in accordance with applicable law and procedures, that such separation is necessary for the best interests of the child.

Furthermore, States parties are obliged to 'respect the right of the child who is separated from one or both parents to maintain personal relations and direct contact with both parents on a regular basis, except if it is contrary to the child's best interests'.[13] This latter provision resonates with, and was in part based upon, the recognition given in the *Hague Convention on Child Abduction* to the maintenance of relations between children and both parents, in particular where the parents are of different nationalities (Detrick 1999: 194). Article 10(2) provides that '[a] child whose parents reside in different States shall have the right to maintain on a regular basis, save in exceptional circumstances personal relations and direct contacts with both parents'.

Article 11 of the *Convention on the Rights of the Child* is, according to Hodgkin and Newell (2007: 143), 'primarily concerned with parental abductions or retentions'. It further obliges States parties to 'take measures to combat the illicit transfer and non-return of children abroad' and to this end they must promote the conclusion of bilateral or multilateral agreements,[14] which is taken to be principally a reference to the *Hague Convention on Child Abduction*. The reference to the 'illicit transfer and non-return of children abroad' is, according to Detrick (1999: 201), a reference to international child abduction by a parent; '[i]t is to be distinguished from the specific form of exploitation of children which is referred to in article 35 as the

---

11 *European Convention on Recognition and Enforcement of Decisions concerning Custody of Children and on Restoration of Custody of Children*, opened for signature 20 May 1980, CETS No. 105 (entered into force 1 September 1983).
12 *Council Regulation (EC) No. 2201/2003 of 27 November 2003 concerning jurisdiction and the recognition and enforcement of judgments in matrimonial matters and the matters of parental responsibility*, repealing Regulation (EC) No. 1347/2000, [2003] OJ L 338/1–29.
13 CRC, art. 9(3).
14 CRC, art. 11(1) and (2).

"abduction of children'". In summary, articles 9 to 11 of the *Convention on the Rights of the Child* provide a legal framework that emphasises the child's right to maintain personal relations with his or her parents in circumstances including where a parental abduction or retention has occurred. States are obliged to combat the problem of international parental child abduction, mainly by ratifying and implementing relevant international instruments such as the *Hague Convention on Child Abduction*. However, as will be seen, the *Hague Convention* does little to maintain the child-centred focus of articles 9 to 11.

It should also be noted that the *Convention on the Rights of the Child* has started to have a more pervasive influence over the way in which *Hague Convention* cases are dealt with; a process that has been advanced in particular by the case law emanating from the European Court of Human Rights (ECtHR) (Schuz 2003, Jacobsen 2016). ECtHR cases[15] have emphasised that the *European Convention on Human Rights* (ECHR) cannot be interpreted in a vacuum. According to article 31(3)(c) of the *Vienna Convention on the Law of Treaties* (1969), any relevant rules of international law applicable to the contracting States parties must be taken into account. Furthermore, the positive obligations that article 8 of the ECHR impose on States with respect to reuniting parents with their children must therefore be interpreted in the light of the *Convention on the Rights of the Child* and the *Hague Convention of 1980*.

6.2.2 European Convention on Recognition and Enforcement of Decisions Concerning Custody of Children and on Restoration of Custody of Children of 1980

The *European Convention of 1980*,[16] as its name suggests, is concerned with the enforcement and recognition of custody orders and decisions relating to access. Consequently, and in contrast to the *Hague Convention of 1980*, it requires that there is a custody or access 'order' in existence as a necessary pre-condition for invoking its jurisdiction. The *European Convention of 1980* requires that each contracting State must establish an administrative body, the 'Central Authority', which will collate and send information to the appropriate agencies and, if necessary, initiate legal proceedings. For example, the Central Authority for England & Wales under both the *European Convention of 1980* and the *Hague Convention of 1980* is the Lord Chancellor, who delegates the duties of the Central Authority to the International Child Abduction and Contact Unit (ICACU) which is based in the Office

---

15 E.g. *Neulinger and Shuruk v. Switzerland (Application No. 41615/07)*, Grand Chamber, 6 July 2010; (2012) 54 E.H.R.R. 31, HC/E/ 1323; and, *Šneersone and Kampanella v. Italy (Application no. 14737/09)*, 12 July 2011; *Vladimir Ushakov v. Russia (Application No. 15122/17)*, Third Section, 18 June 2019.
16 *European Convention on Recognition and Enforcement of Decisions concerning Custody of Children and on Restoration of Custody of Children*, opened for signature 20 May 1980, CETS No. 105 (entered into force 1 September 1983). 37 of the 47 Member States of the Council of Europe had ratified or acceded to this Convention (as at 22 February 2020).

of the Official Solicitor and Public Trustee. ICACU is also the designated Central Authority under the *Revised Brussels II Regulation* (section 6.2.3 in this book).

The underlying assumption behind each Convention is that a peremptory return of the child to the *status quo ante* will ultimately be in the child's best interests. The *European Convention of 1980* can be used to assist in finding the whereabouts of a child and/or securing the recognition or enforcement of a custody order. If an application is made within six months of abduction, it is likely that the restoration of custody will be immediate on establishing the facts of an unlawful removal. An application outside of this time limit, however, will have to satisfy further conditions.

6.2.3 *The* Revised Brussels II Regulation of 2003

Under the *Revised Brussels II Regulation*[17] since 1 March 2005, abductions and the enforcement of orders for contact or access within the European Union (other than Denmark) have been governed by the *Hague Convention of 1980* as modified by the EU instrument with regard to intra-EU parental child abductions. The *Regulation* has introduced a more streamlined process for dealing with parental abductions within Europe. The details of how this Regulation interacts with the Hague Convention are quite complex.[28]

As will be discussed in the next section, the *Hague Convention of 1980* in essence establishes a peremptory return order procedure whereby an abducted or retained child under the age of 16 will be returned by the court in the country to which the child has been removed (the 'requested State', or the 'State of refuge') to the country of the child's habitual residence (the 'requesting State'). The underlying policy presumption is that most child welfare and custody or access issues will be determined in the requesting State following an order of return from the State of refuge. There are some limited discretionary 'exceptions' or 'defences' (section 6.3.3 below) built into Hague proceedings to resist the usual outcome of a return order. If one or more of those exceptions are made out in the proceedings, then as a matter of discretion the court is at liberty to make a 'non-return order', i.e. authorising the child to *remain* in the country of refuge (the 'requested State'). The original proposal of the European Commission for an *EU Regulation* in this area would have replaced entirely the Hague machinery and provided a new legal regime for intra-EU child abductions that would have reduced the courts' jurisdiction in the country of refuge to an even more limited facility to make provisional holding orders only, without any possibility to make a permanent 'non-return order'. In the negotiations leading up to the making of the Regulation, this proposal was very controversial and it was eventually agreed in essence to retain the Hague Convention machinery, subject to more minor adjustments.

---

17 *Council Regulation (EC) No. 2201/2003 of 27 November 2003 concerning jurisdiction and the recognition and enforcement of judgments in matrimonial matters and the matters of parental responsibility*, repealing Regulation (EC) No. 1347/2000 , [2003] OJ L 338/1–29.

The overriding policy of the legal regime under the *Regulation* is to strengthen the existing machinery of peremptory return orders under the Hague Convention. There are four key points to note.

1   Preservation of jurisdiction of the courts of the country of the child's habitual residence (the 'requesting State').
2   Presumption of child's right to be heard in proceedings .
3   Court in the country of refuge (the 'requested State') cannot make a non-return order on basis of 'grave risk of harm' where there would exist adequate protective arrangements for the child after return.
4   Where a non-return order has been made in the country of refuge, the left-behind parent may still litigate the issue of residence/custody on its merits in the requesting State, and this will override the decision of the court in the country of refuge.

First, the *Regulation* does aim to prevent the jurisdiction of the child's country of habitual residence being changed by an abduction event. Article 10 of the Regulations provides that the courts of the child's country of habitual residence shall retain their jurisdiction until the child has acquired habitual residence in another Member State. This protects the right of the court of country of the child's habitual residence to hear any custody dispute except in specified circumstances.

Second, article 11(2) of the Regulation establishes a presumption supporting the child's participation rights in proceedings. Where a court in the country of refuge is considering making either a return order or a non-return order under the Hague Convention, 'it shall be ensured that the child is given the opportunity to be heard during the proceedings unless this appears inappropriate having regard to his or her age or degree of maturity'. The House of Lords determined in *Re D (A Child) (Abduction: Rights of Custody)*[18] that this provision will apply, not only when one or more of the 'defences' is raised but in every Hague return application reaching the court. Baroness Hale observed that the introduction of the Regulation would lead to children being heard more frequently in Hague Convention proceedings than before. Interestingly, in the same case, the court held that the obligation to hear the child would also apply in non-intra-EU Hague Convention cases because of the developing influence of the participation rights contained in article 12 of the *Convention on the Rights of the Child*.[19] Also, the Regulation provides the parent requesting a return (the 'left-behind parent') to be given an opportunity to be heard in non-return order cases. The details of how these rights are secured in national courts is left to national law and consequently the procedures

---

18   [2006] UKHL 51; [2007] 1 A.C. 619.
19   The Court of Appeal approved the seeking of the views of children of sufficient age and maturity as a principle of universal application in *Re M. (A Child) (Abduction: Child#s Objections to Return)* [2007] EWCA Civ 260, [2007] 2 FLR 72.

for hearing the child will vary between Member States. In some jurisdictions the judge will hear the child directly in others there may be exclusive reliance on written documentation. In England & Wales, the Court of Appeal has made it clear that the child must be heard in return proceedings under the Regulation.[20] Since the drafting of the Hague Convention of 1980 there has been an increased recognition of children's 'agency' which has led to increased European support for the further development of children's legal procedural rights (Lamont 2008). This can be seen in recital 33 of the Preamble to the Regulation which references article 24 (rights of the child) of the *Charter of Fundamental Rights of the European Union*.[21] To some extent this strengthening of children's participation rights in this context may conflict with the dominant theme of the Regulation to reinforce the Hague Convention return order machinery.

Third, the *Regulation* provides that '[a] court cannot refuse to return a child on the basis of Article 13b [the 'grave risk of harm' defence] of the 1980 Hague Convention if it is established that adequate arrangements have been made to secure the protection of the child after his or her return.'[22] This provision in effect constrains the court's discretion to make a non-return order on the basis of a perceived grave risk of harm to the child if returned to the requesting State in circumstances where adequate protective arrangements are available in that State. All the other 'defences' in the *Hague Convention* machinery are left untouched by the *Regulation*.

Fourth, even where a non-return order has been made[23] in the requested State, or where the removal or retention has not been found to be 'wrongful', the left-behind parent may still litigate the issue of residence on its merits in the requesting State. In other words, the requesting State in such circumstances retains control over custody issues and the children's ultimate return to that State. The court in the country of refuge that made a non-return order will, in effect, be overridden by the court in the requesting State if it chooses to issue a return order following a merits review.[24]

In summary, although the *Regulation* enhances the procedure for hearing the child's views, it also reinforces the policy of peremptory return of the child to the country of the child's habitual residence, by supporting the preservation of jurisdiction by requesting States and their ability to override the requested State's non-return order(s). Arguably, the interaction of these two elements has not been well thought out. Further strengthening of the return policy may result in the tendency that a child's views are accorded little weight. For example, in *JPC v.*

---

20 *Re F (Abduction: Child's Wishes)* [2007] EWCA Civ 468.
21 Council of the European Union, *Charter of Fundamental Rights of the European Union (2007/C 303/01)*, 14 December 2007.
22 *Council Regulation (EC) No. 2201/2003*, art. 11(4).
23 The 'non-return order' or 'refusal order' must be made under one of the limbs of article 13 of the Hague Convention (but not under articles 12(2) or 20).
24 *Council Regulation (EC) No. 2201/2003*, art. 11(6) – (8). See generally, the first reported English case on the *Regulation*: *Re A (Custody Decision after Maltese Non-Return Order)* [2006] EWHC 3397 (Fam), [2007] 1 FLR 1923.

SLW and SMW (Abduction) [2007] EWHC 1349 (Fam); [2007] 2 FLR 900, a 14-year-old's cogent objection was not enough to prevent the operation of the return mechanism. A number of commentators have questioned the value and purpose and effectiveness of article 11(2) of the *Regulation* (McEleavy 2005; Lowe 2007; Lamont 2008; Schulz 2008; Loo 2016). Indeed, given the predominance of female taking parents, and the EU policy of 'gender mainstreaming', i.e. including gender concerns into the formation of EU law, it has been argued that the gendered nature of child abduction was insufficiently addressed in the development of the *Regulation* (Lamont 2011).

6.2.3.1 The impact of Brexit

On 31 January 2020, the UK left the European Union. The impact of Brexit will be felt across all spheres of life, not least of all by the state's family law institutions. In 2015, 'abductions to and from other EU Member States (except Denmark) accounted for 67% and 68% respectively of all return applications made and received by England and Wales' under the Hague Convention (Lowe 2017: 254). The *Revised Brussels II Regulation* is a significant instrument in such abduction cases, yet its future applicability is under question. Lowe outlines three potential approaches post-Brexit:

1. The UK could abandon BIIa, which would be the consequence if the European Communities Act 1972 was simply repealed.
2. The UK could enact BIIa domestically, that is, the 1972 Act could be repealed but specific European legislation, such as BIIa, could be enacted by domestic legislation. This is sometimes referred to as the 'unilateral option'.
3. The UK could seek to continue to be bound by BIIa either entirely or with some modifications.

(Lowe 2017: 255)

It is yet to be seen which option shall be pursued, if any, and the resultant impact on the integrity of families in the UK.

6.3 The *Hague Convention on the civil aspects of international child abduction* (1980)

The *Hague Convention of 1980*[25] puts contracting States under an obligation to take appropriate measures to implement the Convention's primary objectives: to secure the prompt return of children 'wrongfully removed to or retained in any

---

25 Hague Conference on Private International Law, *Convention on the civil aspects of international child abduction*, concluded 25 October 1980 (entered into force 1 December 1983).

contracting state' and to ensure that rights of custody and access are respected.[26] States must use 'the most expeditious procedures available'[27] to achieve these objectives. The assumption is that the main remedy in the Convention of a speedy return order will be appropriate to all the main participants involved in international child abduction. It will act as a deterrent to would-be abductors. It will reduce the harm done to the children and it will protect the rights of the left-behind parent. The Supreme Court of Canada commented on the aims of the Convention.

> The automatic return procedure implemented by the Act [in Canada implementing the Hague Convention] is ultimately intended to deter the abduction of children by depriving fugitive parents of any possibility of having their custody of the children recognized in the country of refuge and thereby legitimizing the situation for which they are responsible. To that end, the Act favours the restoration of the status quo as soon as possible after the removal of the child by enabling one party to force the other to submit to the jurisdiction of the court of the child's habitual place of residence for the purpose of arguing the merits of any custody issue. The Act, like the Convention, presumes that the interests of children who have been wrongfully removed are ordinarily better served by immediately repatriating them to their original jurisdiction, where the merits of custody should have been determined before their removal. Once that determination has been made, the Convention and the Act give full effect thereto by protecting custody rights through the mandatory return process. [. . .]
>
> Thus, the Convention and the Act represent a compromise between the flexibility derived from reviewing each situation on its merits and the effectiveness needed to deter international child abduction, which depends in particular on the rapidity of the return procedure.[28]

It should be noted that a Convention application can be activated only in relation to a child that has not attained the age of 16 years.[29]

Delay in a child abduction situation can, of course, have very serious and permanent consequences for the relationship between the child and the left-behind parent (Freeman 2003, 2006). Speed is therefore an important element to the structure of the Convention,[30] and this is reinforced by an implicit duty[31] on the relevant judicial or administrative authorities of each contracting State to reach a

---

26 *Convention on the civil aspects of international child abduction*, art. 1.
27 *Convention on the civil aspects of international child abduction*, art. 2.
28 *W.(V.) v. S.(D).*, (1996) 2 SCR 108, (1996) 134 DLR 4th 481m, HC/E/CA 17.
29 *Convention on the civil aspects of international child abduction*, art. 4.
30 *Convention on the civil aspects of international child abduction*, art. 11.
31 *Convention on the civil aspects of international child abduction*, art. 11(2). There is a concrete obligation to reach a decision under the *Revised Brussels II Regulation*, art. 11(3).

decision within six weeks of the date of commencement of proceedings. The reality of expedition in Hague proceedings is different. In *Chafin v. Chafin* the Supreme Court of the United States of America observed that:

> Cases in American courts often take over two years from filing to resolution; for a six-year-old such as E. C., that is one-third of her lifetime. Expedition will help minimize the extent to which uncertainty adds to the challenges confronting both parents and child.[32]

It should also be noted that, in keeping with the practice of the Hague Conference on Private International Law, an explanatory report was produced on the *Hague Convention of 1980* (Pérez-Vera 1980). Such explanatory reports have an especially persuasive status when the courts are trying to interpret the Convention's provisions (section 2.2.1 in this book). Indeed, the essential aims of the explanatory report relating to the *Hague Convention of 1980* are described as follows.

> On the one hand, it must throw into relief, as accurately as possible, the principles which form the basis of the Convention and, wherever necessary, the development of those ideas which led to such principles being chosen from amongst existing options. [. . .] This final Report must also fulfil another purpose, viz to supply those who have to apply the Convention with a detailed commentary on its provision.
>
> (Pérez-Vera 1980, paras 5–6)

Thus, the Pérez-Vera report on this Convention remains an authoritative source of interpretative material. For example, the following extract indicates that an implicit aim of the Convention is to ensure that consideration of any issue around the custody of the children should occur in the State where the children had their habitual residence prior to the removal or retention.

> In a final attempt to clarify the objects of the Convention, it would be advisable to underline the fact that, as is shown particularly in the provisions of article 1, the Convention does not seek to regulate the problem of the award of custody rights. On this matter, the Convention rests implicitly upon the principle that any debate on the merits of the question, *i.e.* of custody rights, should take place before the competent authorities in the State where the child had its habitual residence prior to its removal; this applies as much to a removal which occurred prior to any decision on custody being taken – as to a removal in breach of a pre-existing custody decision.
>
> (Pérez-Vera 1980, para. 19)

---

32 *Chafin v. Chafin*, 133 S. Ct. 1017, 185 L. Ed. 2d 1 (2013); HC/E/US 1206.

The task of establishing place of habitual residence is not always straightforward, as demonstrated by the case of *In the Matter of C (Children)*[33] appealed to the UK Supreme Court in 2018 (see Case Study 6.2).

The structure of the *Hague Convention of 1980* (see Figure 6.1) can be summarised as follows. First, it defines what is meant by a 'wrongful' removal or retention. Second, if the facts fit this definition then an immediate duty arises for the court in the country of refuge to make a return order. The child is returned to the country from which he or she has been removed to uphold the position as it was before the removal or retention. Further disputes about the child will then have to be addressed in domestic proceedings in the child's country of habitual residence. The full force of the duty to order a peremptory return will last for 12 months from the date of removal or retention.[34] Third, after the 12-month period has elapsed there is a proviso which permits the court to refuse to order a return if it considers that the child is sufficiently settled in its new environment to justify a departure from the underlying duty to return. Fourth, the duty to return may also be refused if one or more of the 'exceptions', sometimes referred to as 'defences' applies.

Finally, even if one or more of these exceptions/defences are made out, the court will still have *discretion* to make the return order if it sees fit. It can choose to exercise its discretion in favour of the taking parent and refuse to make a return order (aka a 'non-return order'), or in favour of the left-behind parent by making the return order. The following sections examine these elements in further detail.

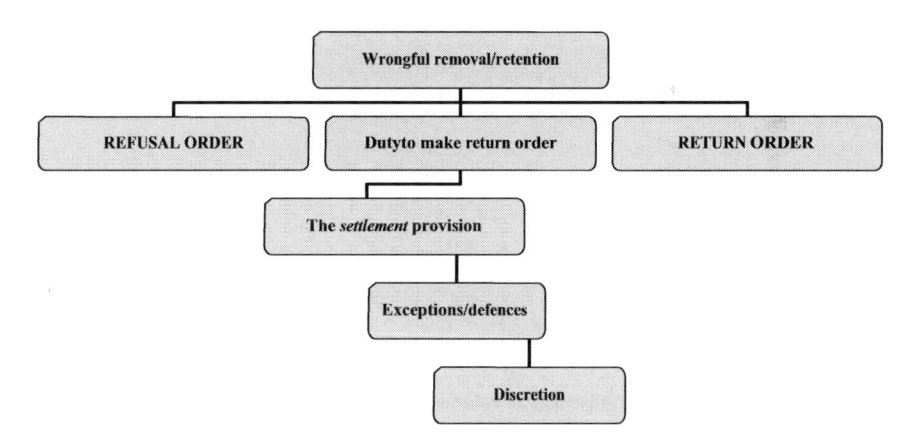

Figure 6.1 The structure of the Hague Convention of 1980.

---

33 [2018] UKSC 8, (on appeal from: [2017] EWCA Civ 980).
34 This is one of the reasons why the Hague Convention of 1980 is preferred over the *European Convention of 1980* where the active time period is only six months.

Finally, it should be noted that there is now a considerable case law in many jurisdictions of the States that are parties to the *Hague Convention of 1980*. In order to encourage a consistent interpretation of the Convention, the Permanent Bureau of the Hague Conference established in 1999 the International Child Abduction Database (INCADAT), which contains all the leading decisions.[35] The cases cited in this chapter end with the INCADAT citation where available.

6.3.1 Wrongful removal or retention

The *Hague Convention of 1980* defines what is to be considered a wrongful removal or retention.

> *Article 3*
> The removal or the retention of a child is to be considered wrongful where –
>
> a) it is in breach of rights of custody attributed to a person, an institution or any other body, either jointly or alone, under the law of the State in which the child was habitually resident immediately before the removal or retention; and
> b) at the time of removal or retention those rights were actually exercised, either jointly or alone, or would have been so exercised but for the removal or retention.
>
> The rights of custody mentioned in sub-paragraph a) above, may arise in particular by operation of law or by reason of a judicial or administrative decision, or by reason of an agreement having legal effect under the law of that State.[36]

The applicant who is seeking a return order under the *Hague Convention* has the evidential burden of showing that there has been a wrongful removal or retention. It should be noted that the inclusion of the notion of a wrongful *retention* ensures that a much wider number of situations are covered than would otherwise be the case. A typical retention might involve a child leaving his or her country of habitual residence with the agreement of person(s) having custody rights for a defined period of time (e.g. for a holiday or visitation period). Where a child is not returned on the expiry of an agreed period and in breach of the left-behind parent's custody rights, there is a wrongful retention, and this may occur earlier than the agreed period if the abducting parent has formed such an intention at an earlier time. Consequently, the *Hague Convention* is sufficiently broad to cover cases where the wrongful retention is identified as occurring sometime after an initial (and lawful) *removal* takes place. It can be seen from the text of article 3 that whether a removal

---

35 See: <www.incadat.com/en> (accessed 28 September 2019).
36 *Hague Convention of 1980*, art. 3.

or retention is 'wrongful' will depend largely upon the consideration of two key legal concepts: 'rights of custody' and 'habitual residence', which are discussed in the following sections.

6.3.1.1 Rights of custody

'Rights of custody' are defined non-exhaustively in article 5(a) of the Convention to include 'rights relating to the care of the person of the child and, in particular, the right to determine the child's place of residence'.[37] The relevant law to determine whether rights of custody exist will be the law of the country of the child's habitual residence immediately before the removal/retention.[38] The final paragraph of article 3 (above) indicates three ways in which rights of custody *may* arise. The concept of 'operation of law' includes rights of custody that are recognised in the internal law of the relevant domestic jurisdiction.[39] Custody rights arising 'by reason of a judicial or administrative decision', according to Pérez-Vera requires a wide interpretation and 'embraces any decision or part of a decision (judicial or administrative) on a child's custody and, on the other hand, that these decisions may have been issued by the courts of the State of the child's habitual residence as well as by the courts of a third country' (Pérez-Vera 1980: para. 69). Finally, rights of custody may arise 'by reason of an agreement having legal effect under the law of that State'. This includes '[i]n principle, the agreements in question may be simple private transactions between the parties concerning the custody of their children' (Pérez-Vera 1980: para. 70). It is again a broad category that in principle will include all custody arrangements that are not specifically prohibited by law.

Even if rights of custody cannot be identified as belonging in either of the above three categories, the notion of 'inchoate' rights of custody has been developed. This provides a way in which persons who have been actual carers of the children in question but who lack formally recognised forms of legal custody may nevertheless be able to be regarded as having rights of custody for Convention purposes. Such 'inchoate' rights of custody were first identified in an English decision in 1994,[40] and have been followed subsequently in that jurisdiction.[41] In some jurisdictions the concept has attracted support; for example, in New Zealand.[42] However, the notion was rejected by the Irish Supreme Court in *H.I. v. M.G.*,[43] a

---

37 *Hague Convention of 1980*, art. 5(a).
38 *Hague Convention of 1980*, art. 3(a).
39 '[C]ustody *ex lege* can be based either on the internal law of the State of the child's habitual residence, or on the law designated by the conflict rules of that State' (Pérez-Vera 1980: para. 68).
40 Re B. (A Minor) (Abduction) [1994] 2 FLR 249; HC/E/UKe 4.
41 E.g. Re G. (Child Abduction) (Unmarried Father: Rights of Custody) [2002] EWHC 2219 (Fam); [2002] ALL ER (D) 79 (Nov); [2003] 1 FLR 252; HC/E/UKe 506.
42 Anderson v. Paterson [2002] NZFLR 641; HC/E/NZ 471.
43 H.I. v. M.G. [1999] 2 ILRM 1; [2000] 1 IR 110; HC/E/IE 284.

position that was upheld by the Court of Justice of the European Union.[44] Several jurisdictions have accepted that the doctrine of *patria potestas* ('power of a father'), which exists still in many Spanish-speaking jurisdictions, may also give rise to Convention rights of custody.[45]

It is perhaps unsurprising that the developing interpretation of 'rights of custody' under the Convention has been generally broadened. The adoption of a narrower, formalist approach would have excluded many meritorious applications for a return order. Indeed, most contracting States have now accepted that a person's mere right of veto over the removal of the child amounts to a right of custody for Convention purposes.[46] There was some division of opinion in the Federal Courts of Appeal in the USA until the Supreme Court decision of *Abbott v. Abbott*,[47] which endorsed the international standard. This position has also been confirmed by the European Court of Human Rights in *Neulinger & Shuruk v. Switzerland*.[48] However, where a person merely has a right to object to a removal and apply to a court to prevent such removal, several jurisdictions have held that this falls short of a right of veto and does not rank as a right of custody for Convention purposes.[49] This position has also been confirmed by the Court of Justice of the European Union.[50]

A further element of the definition of 'wrongful removal or retention' is the requirement contained in article 3(b) (see section 6.3.1 above). The purpose of this provision is to ensure that applications for return orders cannot be initiated by persons whose custody rights have gone 'stale', for example, where a person has in effect abandoned all responsibility in relation to a child. This will generally occur through a failure to actively engage with the child over a significant period of time. There needs to be at least some evidence of the actual exercise of the custody rights in question to fulfil the legal requirements of a 'wrongful removal or retention'. In practice, however, it is unusual for this element of the definition to be a live issue in the overwhelming majority of cases. The desire on the part of the left-behind parent to make an application in the first place is generally prompted by having some form of active participation in the child's life prior to the occurrence of a removal or retention.

> This condition, by defining the scope of the Convention, requires that the applicant provide only some preliminary evidence that he actually took

---

44 Case C-400/10 PPU J. McB. v. L.E.; HC/E/ 1104, 5 October 2010.
45 Whallon v. Lynn, 230 F.3d 450 (1st Cir. October 27, 2000); HC/E/USf 388.
46 E.g. *Re D (A Child) (Abduction: Rights of Custody)* [2006] UKHL 51, [2007] 1 AC 619, HC/E/UKe 880.
47 *Abbot v. Abbott*, 130 S. Ct. 1983 (2010), HC/E/USf 1029.
48 Neulinger & Shuruk v. Switzerland, No. 41615/07, 6 July 2010, HC/E/ 1323.
49 Canada: W.(V.) v. S.(D.), 134 DLR 4th 481 (1996), HC/E/CA17; Ireland: W.P.P. v. S.R.W. [2001] ILRM 371, HC/E/IE 271; UK: Re V.-B. (Abduction: Custody Rights) [1999] 2 FLR 192, HC/E/UKe 261.
50 Case C-400/10 PPU J. McB. v. L.E., HC/E/ 1104, 5 October 2010.

physical care of the child, a fact which normally will be relatively easy to demonstrate. Besides, the informal nature of this requirement is highlighted in article 8 which simply includes, in sub-paragraph c, 'the grounds on which the applicant's claim for return of the child is based', amongst the facts which it requires to be contained in applications to the Central Authorities.

(Pérez-Vera 1980: para. 73)

It should also be noted that the rights of custody contained in article 3(a) (see section 6.3.1 above) must be 'attributed to a person, an institution or any other body'. Article 8 repeats this formula to identify eligible applicants for a return order under the Convention. Parents seek the majority of return applications, but the drafting is wide enough to enable applications from public law bodies that have 'rights of custody' to apply; two examples drawn from the case law include a licensed adoption agency in Texas[51] and an Irish court.[52]

6.3.1.2 Article 15 declarations

Article 15

The judicial or administrative authorities of a Contracting State may, prior to the making of an order for the return of the child, request that the applicant obtain from the authorities of the State of the habitual residence of the child a decision or other determination that the removal or retention was wrongful within the meaning of Article 3 of the Convention, where such a decision or determination may be obtained in that State. The Central Authorities of the Contracting States shall so far as practicable assist applicants to obtain such a decision or determination.

This article allows, as a matter of discretion, a request by the court or administrative authority of the country of refuge that the applicant (the left-behind parent) obtain a determination from the authorities of the State of the habitual residence of the child on the question whether the removal or retention was 'wrongful'. The House of Lords (United Kingdom: England & Wales) held[53] that where such a declaration was sought, then the ruling of the foreign court as to the content of the rights held by the applicant must be treated as conclusive, save in exceptional cases; for example, where the ruling has been obtained by fraud or in breach of the rules of natural justice. It was also noted that recourse to an article 15 declaration would lead to delay and therefore the procedure should be used selectively; a

---

51 *Re JS (Private International Adoption)* [2000] 2 FLR 638.
52 *Re H (A Minor) (Abduction: Rights of Custody)* [2002] 2 AC 291.
53 *Re D. (A Child) (Abduction: Rights of Custody)* [2006] UKHL 51; [2007] 1 A.C. 619; HC/E/UKe 880.

balance had to be struck between acting on too little information and over-zealous examination. The underlying problem with article 15 declarations would appear to be that they tend to trespass on the development of a number of 'autonomous' Convention concepts.

> Common law jurisdictions are divided as to the role to be played by the Article 15 mechanism, in particular whether the court in the child's State of habitual residence should make a finding as to the wrongfulness of the removal or retention, or, whether it should limit its decision to the extent to which the applicant possesses custody rights under its own law. This division cannot be dissociated from the autonomous nature of custody rights for Convention purposes as well as that of 'wrongfulness' i.e. when rights of custody are to be deemed to have been breached.
>
> (McEleavy and Fiorini n.d.)

In some jurisdictions the view is that the court in the country of the child's habitual residence should constrain its consideration to matters of national law but not move into the consideration of whether a removal was 'wrongful' or not. The courts in the State of refuge should undertake that function using its assessment of the autonomous law of the Convention.[54]

6.3.1.3 Habitual residence

'Habitual residence' is a key concept within the definition of a wrongful removal or retention contained in article 3 (see section 6.3.1 above). The identification of the country in which a child was habitually resident prior to a removal or retention is important in two respects. First, it locates the relevant jurisdiction to be examined in order to determine whether the left-behind parent has any 'rights of custody' (or can rely on the rights of custody vested in a court or other body) in the relevant domestic law. Second, the jurisdiction of the *Hague Convention of 1980* will apply only 'to any child who was habitually resident in a Contracting State immediately before any breach of custody or access rights'.[55] The underlying notion of habitual residence is that a child should be returned to the country where he or she has the most obvious connection prior to a wrongful removal or retention. This reflects the philosophy of the Convention to place the parties back into the position they were in prior to the alleged wrongful removal or retention (*status quo ante*) and to prevent and deter parents from taking the unilateral action implied by a removal or retention. The

---

54 *Fairfax v. Ireton* [2009] NZFLR 433 (NZ CA), HC/E/NZ 1018.
55 *Hague Convention of 1980*, art. 4.

country of the child's habitual residence is a logical and practical starting point. It is certainly a more appropriate and practical connecting factor between a child and a sovereign State than the abstract legal concepts of 'domicile' or 'nationality'.

The concept of habitual residence is not defined in the Convention; it is left to be determined as a question of fact. This allows some flexibility for the courts and Central Authorities to come to practical solutions across the range of cases presented. However, such flexibility has also brought difficulties in arriving at consistent interpretations across the diverse jurisdictions of the contracting States. There has been an increasing volume of case law emerging from many of these domestic jurisdictions (Beaumont and McEleavy 1999: 88–113; Schuz 2001a, 2001b). This is perhaps unsurprising as if a taking parent can establish that the country of refuge has in fact become the country of the child's 'habitual residence', then the left-behind parent will not be able to access the Convention's jurisdiction at all.[56] One of the problems is that some jurisdictions have favoured the decision on habitual residence being led by a *factual* enquiry; how long had the child lived in the country in question? Others have placed more emphasis on the identification of an *intentionality* element; is there a settled purpose to habitually reside in the country in question? It is beyond the remit of this book to provide a comprehensive coverage of the voluminous case law across many jurisdictions in this area, but the following commentary provided on the Hague Conference INCADAT case analysis website pages provides a useful and authoritative signpost to the underlying difficulties of interpretation.

> The interpretation of the central concept of habitual residence (Preamble, Art. 3, Art. 4) has proved increasingly problematic in recent years with divergent interpretations emerging in different jurisdictions. There is a lack of uniformity as to whether in determining habitual residence the emphasis should be exclusively on the child, with regard paid to the intentions of the child's care givers, or primarily on the intentions of the care givers. At least partly as a result, habitual residence may appear a very flexible connecting factor in some Contracting States yet much more rigid and reflective of long term residence in others.
>
> (McEleavy and Fiorini n.d.)

A situation involving 'a more tentative' move, at least in the first instance was addressed in a case from the High Court of New Zealand.

---

56 *Hague Convention of 1980*, art. 4.

Case study 6.1

High Court of New Zealand
***RCL v. APBL* [2012] NZHC 1292; HC/E/NZ 1231, per J W Gendall J**
Judgment 11 June 2012

Facts:
[1] This is an appeal against a decision of District Court Judge S J Coyle in the Family Court at Queenstown (heard at Alexandra) ordering that the two children of the appellant and respondent be returned to the United Kingdom pursuant to s 105 of the Care of Children Act 2004 (the Act) and the Hague Convention.

Background

[2] The parties (to be described as mother and father) are the parents of two boys born in the United Kingdom on 31 May 2006 and 4 November 2007. They were aged five and four at the time of the hearing in the Family Court. The parents were originally from New Zealand and moved to live in the United Kingdom in mid 2001, and were married in August 2002. The marriage broke down and the parties were divorced on 23 March 2010.

[3] On 14 May 2010, the parents, in the course of mediation, reached an agreement relating to custody and care of the children in the United Kingdom, but as part of which agreed that the mother could make a trip to New Zealand via South Africa from August 2010, to return to the United Kingdom in March 2011. It was agreed that then the children would be in the care of each of the parents on a shared and equal basis. Consequently on 28 August 2010, the mother left the United Kingdom with the children and arrived in New Zealand.

[4] Within three weeks, the mother advised the father that she would not be returning to the United Kingdom. The father did not agree to the children staying in New Zealand. The mother naturally wished the children to remain with her, but she indicated to the father that he could come to New Zealand and collect the children to return to the United Kingdom. She believed it was unlikely that he would come (although this was not actually stated until the proceedings were well in train). So although there was a wish the children remain in New Zealand, the mother did not say that she would refuse to yield them up and appeared to accept that the children could be collected by their father in March 2011.

[5] The father's position was that, through emails and other communications, the mother had led him to believe that he could travel to New Zealand to collect the children in March 2011 as had been agreed. The father, on 1 December 2010, said:

I still struggle to come to grips with the fact that you were taking the boys to NZ for a 6 month holiday and within a month of getting to NZ you decided to stay, even though the agreement at mediation was for this not to happen. Whilst not legally binding, I took your word on the fact that you would be back and also that we had set up co-parenting arrangements which we both wanted and you seemed genuinely happy with.

[6] And on 2 December 2010:

Clearly very upset and angry that you have in effect abducted my children away from me . . .

[7] Later, on 9 January 2011, the mother and father had a further electronic communication in which they agreed that the children could remain in New Zealand until the youngest boy was due to start school – he turns five on 4 November 2012. So the father's understanding was that the children would remain living in New Zealand for some time until November 2012. Thereafter they would live and go to school in the United Kingdom and practical childcare arrangements would be looked at or 'revisited'. The father and his partner travelled to New Zealand in late February/early March 2011 to see the children.

[8] On 29 May 2011, the mother and the children went from New Zealand to the United Kingdom for an 18-day holiday, intended to be until 16 June 2011. In his judgment, the subject of appeal, Judge Coyle said:

What is unclear is why [the father] did not, with the children in the jurisdiction of United Kingdom Courts, apply for an order preventing [the boys] being removed from the United Kingdom at that point in time. The reality however is that he did not.

[9] One explanation might be that the father believed there was an agreement that the children would be returned to the United Kingdom in November 2012.

[10] At about 4pm on Sunday, 12 June 2011, the mother and father met at a café and she then informed him that she would not be returning the children to the United Kingdom in November 2012, or ever, and the children would live with her thereafter in New Zealand. The mother left the United Kingdom with the children on their return flight to New Zealand on Thursday, 16 June 2011. The father sought legal advice and made an application to the United Kingdom Central Authority for return of the children on 31 August 2011.

[11] On 14 November 2011, the father's application for return of the children to the United Kingdom was filed in the Family Court in Queenstown.

Held:
Conclusion

[122] For the foregoing reasons, the appeal fails. I agree with Judge Coyle that the children must be returned. In summary:

The children's habitual residence is in the United Kingdom and this has not changed.

The parents agreed that the children could be removed to New Zealand for a limited period from August 2010 to March 2011.

That agreement was varied to extend the period in New Zealand until November 2012.

The mother, when in the United Kingdom on holiday with the children, unequivocally repudiated the agreement.

The father never accepted that repudiation.

The anticipatory breach of the agreement by the mother entitled the father to cancel it.

The removal of the children on 16 June 2011 after they had been temporarily in the United Kingdom was wrongful removal given the mother's anticipatory breach.

The father did not thereafter consent to, or acquiesce in, the children's continued residence in New Zealand.

Judge Coyle was correct in his decision on the basis of the case as argued in the Family Court. Although the case as argued on appeal differs, it nevertheless fails upon full reconsideration.

[123] The appeal is dismissed. The children are to be returned to the United Kingdom as directed by Judge Coyle.

[124] The father is entitled to costs if the mother is not legally aided. Counsel may submit memoranda as to that fact, and quantum.

The analysis of the 'habitual residence' issue in the same case is instructive.

> The unilateral purpose of one parent cannot change the habitual residence of a child, because to hold otherwise will go against the policy of the Hague Convention and provide encouragement for abduction and retention. But a very lengthy period of residence, even in such a situation, might eventually

change a child's habitual residence. A length of stay in the country to which a child is taken is a factor to take into account, but only one factor, with the purpose of the stay and strength of ties to the existing state also to be taken into account. Even in cases where residence in another state is intended to be for a limited, defined period, followed by return to an existing habitual residence, that will not automatically lead to a finding that habitual residence remains in the old state. . . . [I]t will depend on the circumstances of the particular case.[57]

The Court made it clear 'that the enquiry into habitual residence had to be a broad factual enquiry, with the notion being free from technical rules which might produce rigidity and inconsistencies'.[58]

Similar complexities can be seen at work in *A v. A (Children) (Habitual Residence)* from the Supreme Court (United Kingdom: England & Wales).[59] In this case, there was a thorough review of the case law on habitual residence and the court concluded with eight key points.

1 '[H]abitual residence is a question of fact and not a legal concept such as domicile. There is no legal rule akin to that whereby a child automatically takes the domicile of his parents.;
2 Habitual residence for the purpose of the Brussels IIa Regulation must be interpreted consistently with the concept in the 1980 Hague Child Abduction Convention and the Family Law Act 1986.
3 The test adopted by the European Court is 'the place which reflects some degree of integration by the child in a social and family environment' in the country concerned.
4 'It is now unlikely that the latter test would produce any different results from that hitherto adopted in the English courts under the 1986 Act and the Hague Child Abduction Convention.'
5 '[T]he test adopted by the European Court is preferable to that earlier adopted by the English courts, being focussed on the situation of the child, with the purposes and intentions of the parents being merely one of the relevant factors. The test derived from R v. Barnet London Borough Council, ex p Shah should be abandoned when deciding the habitual residence of a child.'
6 'The social and family environment of an infant or young child is shared with those (whether parents or others) upon whom [the child] is dependent. Hence it is necessary to assess the integration of that person or persons in the social and family environment of the country concerned.'
7 'The essentially factual and individual nature of the inquiry into habitual residence should not be glossed with legal concepts which would produce a different result from that which the factual inquiry would produce.'
8 '[I]t is possible that a child may have no country of habitual residence at a particular point in time.'

57 *RCL v. APBL* [2012] NZHC 1292; HC/E/NZ 1231 [95].
58 *RCL v. APBL* [2012] NZHC 1292; HC/E/NZ 1231 [99].
59 *A v. A (Children) (Habitual Residence)* [2013] UKSC 60; HC/E/UKe 1233.

Case study 6.2

Supreme Court UK
Judgement In the matter of C (Children) [2018] UKSC 8[60]
14 February 2018

Supreme Court judgment determining that (i) the 1980 Abduction Convention cannot be invoked if by the time of the alleged wrongful act, whether by removal or retention, the child is habitually resident in the state where the request for return is lodged; and (ii) repudiatory retention is possible in law. The Supreme Court was unanimous on the principles but Lords Kerr and Wilson gave dissenting judgments on the outcome of the case on its facts. Appeal by mother allowed; cross-appeal by father dismissed.

This matter centres around a married man and woman who, until 2015, had been living together in Australia with their two children. By the end of 2014 the marriage was in difficulties. The mother, who holds British citizenship, wanted to make a trip to England with the children before returning to work from maternity leave. The father agreed to an eight-week stay. The mother and the children came to England on 4 May 2015 where they have since remained. Discussions between the mother and father resulted in the father agreeing to an extension of the eight-week visit up to a year. Based on the extension, the mother gave notice to her employer and looked for work in England.

In September 2015, the mother enrolled the older child at a local preschool. Without telling the father, on 2 November 2015, she applied for British citizenship for both children who had entered England on six-month visitor visas. Her solicitors wrote a letter to the immigration authorities on her behalf indicating that she and the children could not return to Australia for fear of domestic abuse.

In continuing correspondence, the father pressed the mother on the children's expected date of return. The mother indicated that she did not know what her plans were but made clear that she would not be returning in May 2016. In June 2016, she expressed her intention to remain in the UK.

The father made an application in the High Court under the Convention of 25 October 1980 on the Civil Aspects of International Child Abduction (the 'Abduction Convention'). The issue of when the mother had decided not to return to Australia was in contention. The mother's own case was

---

60 Supreme Court Press Summary.

that by April 2016 she had felt she and the children would not be returning. The arguments before the Court meant that, on any view, there was a decision not to return to Australia before the expiry of the agreed year. The judge held that the children were habitually resident in England and Wales by the end of June 2016 so that mandatory summary return was unavailable under the Abduction Convention. But he accepted mother's evidence that she did not have the intention, in November 2015, or before April 2016, not to return to Australia.

The mother now appeals against the Court of Appeal's decision. The issues in the appeal are: (1) what is the effect on an application under the Abduction Convention if a child has become habitually resident in the destination state before the act relied on as a wrongful removal or retention occurs; and (2) if a child has been removed from their home state by agreement with the left-behind parent for a limited period can there be a wrongful retention before the agreed period of absence expires (so-called 'repudiatory retention')? The father cross-appeals on the issue of habitual residence.

Judgment

The Supreme Court allows the appeal and dismisses the cross appeal. Lord Hughes gives the lead judgment with whom Lady Hale and Lord Carnwath agree. Lord Kerr and Lord Wilson each give judgments concurring on the two points of principle but dissenting on the outcome of this case on its facts.

Reasons for the judgment:

Issue 1

When considering the general scheme of the Abduction Convention, the construction that summary return is available if, by the time of the act relied on as a wrongful removal or retention, a child is habitually resident in the state where the application for return is made is unpersuasive. That construction is inconsistent with the operation of the Abduction Convention since 1980 and its treatment by subsequent international legal instruments. [19]

The Abduction Convention is designed to provide a summary remedy which negates the pre-emptive force of wrongful removal or retention and to defeat forum-shopping. [21] The point of the scheme adopted by the Abduction Convention was to leave the merits to be decided by the courts of the place of the child's habitual residence. If the forum state is the habitual residence of the child, there can be no place for a summary return to somewhere else, without a merits-based decision. This understanding of the scheme of the Abduction Convention is reflected in the provisions of both the Revised Brussels II Regulation and the 1996 Hague Convention on Recognition, Enforcement and Cooperation in respect of Parental Responsibility and Measures for the Protection of Children. [23]

The Abduction Convention cannot be invoked if by the time of the alleged wrongful act, whether by removal or retention, the child is habitually resident in the state where the request for return is lodged. In such a case, that state has primary jurisdiction to decide on the merits, based on the child's habitual residence, and there is no room for a mandatory summary decision. [34]

Issue 2

Repudiatory retention has been recognised in some jurisdictions, but no generally accepted international practice or authority exists on the point. [39] The desirability of inducing a prompt change of mind in the retaining parent is an argument for recognising a repudiatory retention when and if it occurs. The 12 month time limit for seeking mandatory summary return runs from the point a repudiatory retention occurs and that period may pass before an applicant is aware of the repudiatory retention. However, it is not a limitation period but a provision in the child's interest to limit mandatory summary return. Once elapsed it renders a summary return discretionary. The concern that repudiatory retention would make Abduction Convention applications longer and more complicated is a point well made. However, Family Division judges are used to managing applications actively and controlling any tendency to spill outside the relevant issues. Further, if repudiatory retention requires an overt act or statement, this lessens the danger of speculative applications. [46–48]

Repudiatory retention is possible in law. The objections to it are insubstantial, whereas the arguments in favour are convincing and conform to the scheme of the Abduction Convention. It would be unwise to attempt an exhaustive definition of proof or evidence. An objectively identifiable act of repudiation is required, but it need not be communicated to the left-behind parent nor does an exact date need to be identifiable. [50–51]

On the present facts there could not have been a wrongful retention in April 2016 as the mother's internal thinking could not by itself amount to such. If she had such an intention in November 2015, the application to the immigration authorities could have amounted to a repudiatory retention. But it was open to the judge to believe the mother's evidence that she did not possess this intention in November. [55] There is no basis in law for criticising the judge's decision as to habitual residence. [57]

Lord Kerr dissents on the outcome of this case on its facts. He expresses misgivings about repudiatory retention requiring an overt act by the travelling parent. [63] The judge's finding that wrongful retention did not arise in this case could not be reconciled with his statement that the mother had concluded by April 2016 that she and the children should remain in England. [68] Moreover, the judge's conclusion that the mother had not formed any intention to retain the children in England in November 2015 is insupportable as he failed to address the question of what bearing the letter of November 2015 had on her intention. [72]

Lord Wilson also dissents on the outcome of this case on its facts. The solicitor's letter to the immigration authorities in November 2015 represented a major obstacle to any finding that the mother had not by then intended to keep the children in the UK indefinitely. The judge's finding as to the mother's intention in November 2015 was flawed and the Court of Appeal were correct to order a fresh inquiry into her intention. [91–92]

The complex facts in this case brought to fore the question of 'anticipatory retention', and the court held that the *Hague Convention* could not be invoked where the child has become a habitual resident in the state from which a return order is sought, by the time the alleged wrongful act (retention or removal) has occurred. The core issue was the lack of requisite intent on the part of the mother, and therefore no actual wrongful retention in April 2016.

6.3.2 The duty to make a return order

Once the applicant (left-behind person) has met the evidential burden of showing that there was a 'wrongful removal or retention' within the meaning of article 3, a duty to return the child arises.

Article 12
- Where a child has been wrongfully removed or retained in terms of Article 3 and, at the date of the commencement of the proceedings before the judicial or administrative authority of the Contracting State where the child is, a period of less than 1 year has elapsed from the date of the wrongful removal or retention, the authority concerned shall order the return of the child forthwith.
- The judicial or administrative authority, even where the proceedings have been commenced after the expiration of the period of 1 year referred to in

the preceding paragraph, shall also order the return of the child, unless it is demonstrated that the child is now settled in its new environment.
- Where the judicial or administrative authority in the requested State has reason to believe that the child has been taken to another State, it may stay the proceedings or dismiss the application for the return of the child.

This article 'forms an essential part of the Convention, specifying as it does those situations in which the judicial or administrative authorities of the State where the child is located are obliged to order its return' (Pérez-Vera 1980: para. 106). There are two cases to consider: where a period of less than one year has elapsed since the wrongful removal/retention and up to the commencement of proceedings; and where a period of one year or more has elapsed within this timeframe. It can be noted that the duty set out in the first case in article 12§1 emphasises the peremptory nature of the return order procedure; the return must be made 'forthwith'. In the second case article 12§2 ensures that the duty to return still remains where the taking person and child have been in the country of refuge for a period of one year or more, subject to a finding that the child 'is now settled in its new environment'. The evidential burden to demonstrate such settlement will rest on the taking person to resist a return order. For ease of reference this route to avoid a return avoid is referred to in this Chapter as the 'settlement exception'. There are also other exceptions to the underlying duty to return. Most of these appear in article 13 and there is also an exception contained in article 20. These are explained in the following sections and by way of introduction Table 6.2 below

Table 6.2 Reasons for judicial refusal in 2015

Reasons for refusal	Frequency	Percentage
Child not habitually resident in requesting State	36	19%
Applicant no rights of custody	11	6%
Art. 12	21	11%
Art. 13(1) a) not exercising rights of custody	4	2%
Art. 13(1) a) consent	21	11%
Art. 13(1) a) acquiescence	9	5%
Art. 13(1) b) grave risk	33	18%
Child's objections	18	10%
Art. 20	2	1%
Other	30	16%
Total	185	100%

Source: Lowe and Stephens 2017: 15.[61]

61 Lowe and Stephens point out that 'the statistics do not reveal how often the exceptions were argued unsuccessfully nor do they include those cases where an exception was made out but the court nevertheless exercised its discretion to make a return order. (2017: 15).

indicates the proportion of cases that have relied on one or more of the various exceptions in litigation across all the contracting States. In addition this Table includes cases where there was no wrongful removal/retention on the basis of either a finding that the child was not habitually resident in the requesting State or that the applicant left-behind parent had no rights of custody. The data is derived from Lowe and Stephen's statistical survey in respect of 285 applications in 2015 which received judicial refusal and for which the reasons for refusal were available.

6.3.3 Exceptions from the duty to make a return order

The following sub-sections include an outline of the various 'exceptions' to the underlying duty to make a return order. These are:

- the 'settlement' exception – article 12, §2
- not exercising custody rights at time of removal/retention – article 13, §1(a)
- consent to removal/retention – article 13, §1(a)
- acquiescence to removal/retention – article 13, §1(a)
- grave risk of harm to child – article 13, §1(b)
- child objects to return – article 13, §2
- not permitted by human rights protection of the requested State – article 20

The exceptions founded on article 13 are sometimes also referred to in the case law as 'defences'.

6.3.3.1 The settlement exception

Article 12, §2 (see section 6.3.2 above) provides a limited exception to the return order in circumstances where the applicant left-behind person can demonstrate 'the child is now settled in its new environment'. As with several other areas of case law in respect of the *Hague Convention of 1980*, there have been divergent approaches to this provision across the contracting States:

> A uniform interpretation has not emerged with regard to the concept of settlement; in particular whether it should be construed literally or rather in accordance with the policy objectives of the Convention. In jurisdictions favouring the latter approach the burden of proof on the abducting parent is clearly greater and the exception is more difficult to establish.
>
> (McEleavy and Fiorini n.d.)

In earlier cases there had been some debate whether settlement prompted an obligation not to return, or simply provided a discretion not to order a return. This matter was resolved in favour of the latter position by the House of Lords (United Kingdom: England & Wales) in *Re M. (Children) (Abduction: Rights of Custody)*.[62] It can

---

62 [2007] UKHL 55, [2008] 1 AC 1288, HC/E/UKe 937.

also be seen that where a taking person has deliberately concealed the whereabouts of the child, it would be inequitable if that provided an unjustified advantage in terms of the expiry of the one year period. On the other hand, an automatic deduction of any period of time during which there was deliberate concealment might not provide the required flexibility for the court. The Court of Appeal (United Kingdom: England & Wales) approached the matter in *Cannon v. Cannon*[63] by examining more intensely the necessary elements of settlement in concealment cases. Lord Justice Thorpe concluded:

> 61. I would unhesitatingly uphold the well-recognised construction of the concept of settlement in Article 12(2): it is not enough to regard only the physical characteristics of settlement. Equal regard must be paid to the emotional and psychological elements. In cases of concealment and subterfuge the burden of demonstrating the necessary elements of emotional and psychological settlement is much increased. The judges in the Family Division should not apply a rigid rule of disregard but they should look critically at any alleged settlement that is built on concealment and deceit especially if the defendant is a fugitive from criminal justice.
>
> 62. Even if settlement is established on the facts the court retains a residual discretion to order a return under the Convention. The discretion is specifically conferred by Article 18. But for Article 18 I would have been inclined to have infer the existence of a discretion under Article 12, although I recognise the power of the contrary arguments.[64]

6.3.3.2 Approach to article 13 exceptions/defences

Article 13

- Notwithstanding the provisions of the preceding Article, the judicial or administrative authority of the requested State is not bound to order the return of the child if the person, institution or other body which opposes its return establishes that –

    a) the person, institution or other body having the care of the person of the child was not actually exercising the custody rights at the time of removal or retention, or had consented to or subsequently acquiesced in the removal or retention; or

    b) there is a grave risk that his or her return would expose the child to physical or psychological harm or otherwise place the child in an intolerable situation.

---

63 [2004] EWCA Civ 1330, [2005] 1 FLR 169, [2005] 1 W.L.R. 32.
64 *Cannon v. Cannon* [2004] EWCA Civ 1330; [2005] 1 FLR 169; HC/E/UKe 598, [61–2].

- The judicial or administrative authority may also refuse to order the return of the child if it finds that the child objects to being returned and has attained an age and degree of maturity at which it is appropriate to take account of its views.
- In considering the circumstances referred to in this Article, the judicial and administrative authorities shall take into account the information relating to the social background of the child provided by the Central Authority or other competent authority of the child's habitual residence.

The drafters of the Convention envisaged that any routes to mitigate the inevitability of a return order should be narrowly construed; 'they are to be interpreted in a restrictive fashion if the Convention is not to become a dead letter', and furthermore, 'a systematic invocation of the said exceptions, . . . would lead to the collapse of the whole structure of the Convention by depriving it of the spirit of mutual confidence which is its inspiration' (Pérez-Vera 1980: para. 34). However, as authoritative commentators on the case law have previously observed, 'a desire to give effect to the primary goal of promoting return and thereby preventing an over-exploitation of the exceptions, had led to an additional test of exceptionality being added to the exceptions' (McEleavy and Fiorini n.d.). This additional test of *exceptionality* was laid to rest by the House of Lords (United Kingdom: England & Wales) in *Re M. (Children) (Abduction: Rights of Custody)* by Baroness Hale:

> I have no doubt at all that it is wrong to import any test of exceptionality into the exercise of discretion under the Hague Convention. The circumstances in which return may be refused are themselves exceptions to the general rule. That in itself is sufficient exceptionality. It is neither necessary nor desirable to import an additional gloss into the Convention.[65]

As with the 'settlement exception' (section 6.3.3.1 above), the evidential burden of proof to establish one or more of the article 13 exceptions to achieve a non-return order rests with the person opposing the return order, i.e. the taking person. Even if one or more of the exceptions in article 13 has been made out, the court will still need to consider whether it nevertheless has available an overriding discretion to go ahead with a return order rather than a non-return order. Again, there are differences of approach by various contracting States on this issue and it is dealt with in further detail in section 6.3.4 below.

6.3.3.3 Failure to exercise custody rights

One of the objectives of the Convention is that a person should not be able to rely on a breach of rights of custody that have, in fact, been overtaken by subsequent

---

65 *Re M. (Children) (Abduction: Rights of Custody)* [2007] UKHL 55, [2008] 1 AC 1288, HC/E/UKe 937, [40].

events, or have gone stale. As can be seen from Table 6.2 above, judicial refusals are rarely based on this exception.

> The Convention includes no definition of 'actual exercise' of custody, but this provision expressly refers to the care of the child. Thus, if the text of this provision is compared with that of article 5 which contains a definition of custody rights, it can be seen that custody is exercised effectively when the custodian is concerned with the care of the child's person, even if, for perfectly valid reasons (illness, education, etc.) in a particular case, the child and its guardian do not live together. It follows from this that the question of whether custody is actually exercised or not must be determined by the individual judge, according to the circumstances of each particular case.
>
> (Pérez-Vera 1980: para. 115)

It will be recalled that the failure to exercise custody rights is also an integral element to the way in which the Convention defines a wrongful removal or retention within the meaning of article 3 (section 6.3.1.1 above). A distinction in the meaning of the failure to actually exercise rights of custody as it appears in articles 3 and 12 was made in a High Court (Family Division) case (United Kingdom: England & Wales).

> Article 13(a) refers to rights of custody which are not being actually exercised by the person who has the care of the person of the child: this contrasts with Art 3 which refers to rights of custody generally. The Art 13(a) defence in this context is thus limited to the situation in which the child's actual caretaker is not actually taking care of him. This is a much narrower situation, and plainly does not apply in the instant case.[66]

It is perhaps unsurprising, given the underlying central policy theme to support the return order procedure, that in many jurisdictions there has been some generosity in viewing even the applicant's limited engagement with a child as sufficient to rank as an exercise of rights of custody for the purpose of article 13(a). The Supreme Court of Ireland has held[67] that a father's imprisonment did not divest him of his rights of custody under the Convention. The court referred to other situations where a parent might have a low-level input to the routine care of a child: for example, where a parent was disabled, incapacitated, or in a job which necessitated long absences from home. On the facts, his children had visited him in prison and he had taken a sufficient interest to obtain a prohibited steps order. However, there are remaining differences in approach across the contracting States. Some have made it clear that what is required is quite clear and unequivocal evidence of abandonment in order to establish a failure to exercise custody rights; others set the threshold somewhat lower.[68]

---

66 *Re W (Abduction: Procedure)* [1995] 1 FLR 878; HC/E/UKe 37.
67 [2000] 3 IR 390.
68 Compare the cases of O. v. O. 2002 SC 430; HC/E/UKs 507, and S. v. S., 2003 SLT 344; HC/E/UKs 577.

6.3.3.4 The consent exception

Earlier case law had considered whether the issue of consent was better understood in terms of the concept of wrongful removal/retention as defined in article 3 rather than in article 13(a). However, it would appear that the majority view now is that it can be better understood exclusively within article 13(a).[69] Equally, previous case law that determined only clear and compelling evidence of consent in writing[70] would suffice, appears to have been overtaken with a more practical and fact-specific understanding of consent.[71] For example, the Austrian Supreme Court[72] has observed that consent may be implicit but it must refer to a permanent change of residence and can be evidenced by a statement or derived from a set of circumstances. The key point was the nature of the taking person's understanding of the left-behind person. It would appear that both consent and acquiescence are ultimately questions of fact to be determined on their merits in each case.

6.3.3.5 Acquiescence

It would seem that the practical distinction between *consent* and *acquiescence* is one of timing (Ranton 2009: 20). Consent will generally pre-date the removal or retention, whereas acquiescence occurs after such removal or retention. Earlier case law identified different approaches for 'active' and 'passive' acquiescence, but the House of Lords (United Kingdom: England & Wales) in *Re H (Abduction: Acquiescence)*[73] stressed that the key question was whether the subjective state of mind of the left-behind parent constituted acquiescence. The only departure from this would be where any words or actions of the left-behind parent unequivocally showed, and led the abducting parent to believe, that the left-behind parent would not assert their right to summary return; then the court would be likely to hold that the left-behind parent had acquiesced.

The cases also indicate that where the parties are merely undertaking negotiations with each other about where the child is to live, such negotiations will not amount to 'acquiescence'.[74] To take the opposite view would have undermined the support provided by the *Hague Convention of 1980* to achieving voluntary settlement where possible.[75]

---

69 For example in Australia, see: Director-General, Department of Child Safety v. Stratford [2005] Fam CA 1115, HC/E/UKe 830.
70 Re W. (Abduction: Procedure) [1995] 1 FLR 878; HC/E/UKe 37.
71 See, for example: Re K. (Abduction: Consent) [1997] 2 FLR 212; HC/E/UKe 55.
72 1Ob256/09t, Oberster Gerichtshof, HC/E/AT 1049.
73 [1998] AC 72
74 E.g. *Re I (Abduction: Acquiescence)* [1999] 1 FLR 778.
75 *Hague Convention of 1980*, art. 7(c).

6.3.3.6 Grave risk of harm/intolerable situation

As can be seen from Table 6.2 above, this exception/defence is one of the most frequently litigated exception in Hague proceedings. It is therefore important that the scope of behaviours it may cover appropriately reflects the underlying philosophy of the *Hague Convention of 1980* and achieves an appropriate balance between the provision of a robust return order procedure while taking into account children's interests in individual cases that might justify a departure from the standard process. Inevitably, different contracting States have taken differing approaches to identifying the precise nature and scope of the exception. The statistical surveys undertaken under the auspices of the Hague Conference have indicated, in respect of the last survey of data relating to 2015, that globally, 'the large majority (80%) of taking persons were the "primary carer" or "joint-primary carer" of the child (Lowe and Stephens 2017: 3). In such cases there are likely to be stronger child welfare justifications for a non-return order than cases where the taking person has not had a primary carer role.

Some contracting States will only accept the grave risk defence in genuinely atypical situations. In other States, there are indications of a more liberal approach. For example, in the United States, one commentator found from a study of 47 published US state and federal court opinions involving the Convention and allegations of domestic violence perpetrated by the left-behind parent that US courts were reluctant to employ the provisions under the Convention that could prevent children from being returned to the mother's batterer (Vesneski, Lindhorst and Edleson **2011**).

The European Court of Human Rights has moved from the former to the latter position in its analysis of the issue. The most cited position is represented in the more child-centric case of *Neulinger & Shuruk v. Switzerland*. This case concerned a child born in Israel in 2003 to a Swiss mother and Israeli father. The father had joined a religious sect and the custody of the child had been withdrawn from him on account of the atmosphere of fear that he had created at the family home. The mother secretly took the child to Switzerland in June 2005 and the father filed his return petition a year later. The first instance court in Switzerland found a grave risk of harm and refused to order a return of the child to Israel. This was confirmed on appeal, but in August 2007 the Swiss Federal Court ordered a return, finding no basis for the grave risk exception to be upheld. The mother and child petitioned the ECtHR in September 2007. Interim measures were applied not to return the child. On 8 January 2009, the ECtHR ruled by a 4 to 3 majority, that there had not been a breach of the mother and child's right to family life under Article 8 of the *European Convention on Human Rights* (ECHR).[76]

The applicants requested in March 2009 that the case be referred to the Grand Chamber of the ECtHR. The Grand Chamber gave judgment on 6 July

---

76 Neulinger and Shuruk v. Switzerland, No. 41615/07; HC/E/ 1001.

2010,[77] holding by 16 to 1 that, if the return order were enforced there would be a violation of the mother and child's right to family life under article 8 of the ECHR. The ECtHR held, *inter alia*, that article 8 of the ECHR required that a child's return could not be ordered mechanically whenever the *Hague Convention of 1980* was applicable, and that what was in the child's best interest had to be assessed in each case. The Court held that:

> [138] It follows from art.8 [ECHR] that a child's return cannot be ordered automatically or mechanically when the Hague Convention is applicable. The child's best interests, from a personal development perspective, will depend on a variety of individual circumstances, in particular his age and level of maturity, the presence or absence of his parents and his environment and experiences. For that reason, those best interests must be assessed in each individual case. That task is primarily one for the domestic authorities, which often have the benefit of direct contact with the persons concerned. To that end they enjoy a certain margin of appreciation, which remains subject, however, to a European supervision whereby the Court reviews under the Convention the decisions that those authorities have taken in the exercise of that power.
>
> [139] In addition, the Court must ensure that the decision-making process leading to the adoption of the impugned measures by the domestic court was fair and allowed those concerned to present their case fully. To that end the Court must ascertain whether the domestic courts conducted an in-depth examination of the entire family situation and of a whole series of factors, in particular of a factual, emotional, psychological, material and medical nature, and made a balanced and reasonable assessment of the respective interests of each person, with a constant concern for determining what the best solution would be for the abducted child in the context of an application for his return to his country of origin.[78]

The judgement has prompted some controversy as the notion of a full scale welfare inquiry to be applied when the exception is raised in the courts of the country of refuge arguably conflicts with the underlying policy of the *Hague Convention of 1980* to have such issues debated in the courts of the *requesting* States. The apparent implication of *Neulinger* was that national courts should abandon their traditionally restrictive approach to the interpretation of the exceptions and instead should carry out an in-depth examination of the best interest of the child (Walker 2010; Paton 2012). Chamberland (2012) argues that the return of the child under the *Hague Convention of 1980* should not be subordinate to a consideration of the

---

77 *Neulinger and Shuruk v. Switzerland (Application No. 41615/07)*, Grand Chamber, 6 July 2010; (2012) 54 E.H.R.R. 31, HC/E/ 1323.
78 *Neulinger & Shuruk v. Switzerland, (Application No. 41615/07)*, Grand Chamber, 6 July 2010; (2012) 54 E.H.R.R. 31, paras 138–39; HC/E/1323.

best interests of the child. Equally, it is important that the jurisdictions of the ECtHR and the ECJ are reasonably aligned in this field and do not travel along contrasting pathways (Walker and Beaumont 2011). The Supreme Court (United Kingdom: England & Wales) has also doubted the recommendation in *Neulinger* to conduct an extensive welfare enquiry. See Case Study 6.3.

Case study 6.3

***In re S (A Child) (Abduction: Rights of Custody)* [2012] UKSC 10, [2012] 2 A.C. 257**

Facts: The Australian father and the British mother, who also had Australian citizenship, lived together unmarried in Australia. Their son was born and habitually resident there. In 2011 the mother returned to live in England, taking the son with her without the father's consent or the permission of an Australian court. The removal of the son was thus in breach of the father's custody rights under Australian law and was therefore wrongful for the purposes of article 3 of the Hague Convention on the Civil Aspects of International Child Abduction (1980). The father issued proceedings in England under section 1(2) of the Child Abduction and Custody Act 1985 and article 12 of the Convention for the immediate return of the son to Australia. The mother resisted the application in reliance on article 13(b) of the Convention on the grounds that to order the son's immediate return would put him at grave risk of being placed in an intolerable situation. She did not give oral evidence before the judge but adduced written evidence, including e-mails and texts, to explain why her life with the father in Australia had become so intolerable that she had returned with the son to England. In doing so she made serious allegations against the father which she linked with medical evidence about the state of her psychological health while she had been in Australia. The father put forward by undertakings measures to protect the mother and the son if they returned to Australia. The judge concluded that the mother was genuinely convinced that she had been the victim of domestic abuse, that her anxieties were based on objective reality and that the protective measures offered by the father would not obviate the grave risk that, if returned to Australia, the son would be placed in an intolerable situation, and he accordingly refused to order the son's return. The Court of Appeal, holding that the crucial question for the judge was whether the mother's asserted risk, insecurities and anxieties were realistically and reasonably held in the face of the package of protective measures which could be put in place and declining to accept that the mother's subjective perception of risks on return leading to an intolerable situation for the child was a permissible ground for refusing a return order, allowed the father's appeal and ordered the son's return.

On the mother's appeal –

Held: Allowing the appeal, that the terms of article 13(b) of the Hague Convention were plain, needing neither elaboration nor gloss; that the critical question, where on an application under article 12 a defence under article 13(b) was raised, was what would happen if, with the parent who had wrongfully removed him, the child were returned; that if the court concluded that, on return, that parent would suffer such anxieties that their effect on her mental health would create a situation which was intolerable for the child, the child should not be returned, and it mattered not whether those anxieties would be reasonable or unreasonable, although the extent to which there would, objectively, be good cause for such anxieties would nevertheless be relevant to the court's assessment of her mental state if the child were returned; that it was for the trial judge, whether or not he had received oral evidence, to make the judgment about the level of risk which article 13(b) required, and an appellate court should not overturn his judgment unless, whether by reference to the law or to the evidence, it had not been open to the judge to make it; that, although the judge had not heard oral evidence, he had carefully studied the written evidence which revealed that several of the allegations made by the mother against the father were admitted or could not realistically be denied; that it had been open to the judge to decide that in the light of all the evidence the interim protective measures offered by the father did not obviate the grave risk to the son if he were returned to Australia; and that, accordingly, it had not been open to the Court of Appeal to substitute its contrary view for that of the judge (post, paras 6, 7, 27, 29, 31–32, 34, 35, 36).

In re J (A Child) (Custody Rights: Jurisdiction) [2006] 1 AC 80, HL(E) applied.

In re E (Children) (Abduction: Custody Appeal) [2012] 1 AC 144, SC(E) explained.

Per curiam: In the determination of an application under the Hague Convention for a summary order for a child's return to the state of his habitual residence it would be entirely inappropriate for the court to conduct an in-depth examination of the entire family situation and of factors of a factual, emotional, psychological, material and medical nature (post, paras 37, 38).

Dictum in Neulinger and Shuruk v. Switzerland [2011] 1 FLR 122, para. 39, GC doubted.

Decision of the Court of Appeal sub nom S v. C [2011] EWCA Civ 1385; [2012] 1 FCR 172 reversed.

It can be appreciated that, in general, some level of psychological harm is almost inevitable in the context of parental child abduction. However, something more than the expected level of harm is required, after all there must be a 'grave' risk, in other words, something very serious. One factor that may take a case into this higher level of risk is where the court is satisfied that an established pattern of domestic violence may have induced the removal or retention in the first place.[79] However, it must be remembered that the wording of article 13(1)(b) requires the exposure of the *child* to physical or psychological harm. Domestic violence aimed at a *parent* will only be relevant to the extent that such action can be shown to be damaging to the child.

One category of case concerns allegations of a grave risk of harm due to the security situation pertaining in the country of the child's habitual residence. It would seem that it does not matter whether it is actually a state of war or terrorist activity, or some other civil commotion. What is important is to assess the actual level of risk of harm to the child from the available evidence. The argument was not accepted in an English Court of Appeal case[80] relating to an Israeli mother who had removed her child to England and argued that a return to Israel would expose her child to the difficult security situation there: see further (Schuz 2003). The House of Lords (United Kingdom: England & Wales) in *Re M. (Children) (Abduction: Rights of Custody)* also rejected the argument that the moral and political climate in Zimbabwe meant that children generally would be at grave risk of psychological harm, or should not be expected to tolerate living there.[81]

One factor which could heighten the risk of harm is where the court is not satisfied that there are sufficient institutional protective arrangements in the country of the child's habitual residence.[82] As we have seen the *Revised Brussels II Regulation* (section 6.2.3 above) provides that, in intra-EU cases (other than ones involving Denmark), a court *cannot* refuse to return a child on the basis of the grave risk of harm exception if it is established that adequate arrangements have been made to secure the protection of the child after return. Equally, in other Hague Convention cases it would appear that the discretion that is available to make a non-return order in the face of the exception having been established is also quite constrained (see section 6.3.4 below).

6.3.3.7 The child's objections

This exception is of particular interest in international child law as it touches upon the extent to which a child's 'autonomy rights' will be respected (see section 1.2.1.2 in this book). The requirement is not only that a child 'objects' but also that the child 'has attained an age and degree of maturity at which it is

---

79 See *Sonderup v. Tondelli* 2001 (1) SA 1171 (CC) (Constitutional Court of South Africa); *Walsh v. Walsh No. 99–1747* (1st Cir July 25, 2000) (US Court of Appeals for the First Circuit).
80 See *Re S (A Child) (Abduction: Grave Risk of Harm)* [2002] EWCA Civ 908, [2002] 3 FCR 43; HC/E/UKe 469.
81 *Re M. (Children) (Abduction: Rights of Custody)* [2007] UKHL 55, [2008] 1 AC 1288, HC/E/UKe 937.
82 For example, see *TB v. JB (formerly JH) (Abduction: Grave Risk of Harm)* [2001] 2 FLR 515; *W v. W* [2004] 2 FLR 499.

appropriate to take account of its views'. The question of a child's maturity is a matter of fact in which the court is required to exercise its judgment on the basis of the available evidence. The key question is about maturity rather than merely chronological age.

Some of the cases have shown the practical difficulty of ordering a return in the face of a child who persistently objects to it.[83] The older the child, the more likely that greater weight will be given to his/her views. Pérez-Vera (1980: para. 30) concluded that 'it would be very difficult to accept that a child of, for example, 15 years of age, should be returned against its will'. However, the courts will be wary to exercise their discretion to refuse a return order where the evidence shows that a parent has heavily influenced and/or coached the child to adopt those objections.[84]

Although there are differences of approach across the contracting States in approaching this exception (McEleavy 2008), the majority do appear to accept that a mere preference for the State of refuge will not be sufficient. For example, in the Ontario Superior Court of Justice (Canada) in *Crnkovich v. Hortensius* the judge held, *inter alia*, that:

> [34] There has been considerable jurisprudence defining and commenting on the meaning and breadth of the verb 'objects'. In *R(A Minor) (Abduction), Re* [1992] 1 F.L.R. 105 (Eng. C.A.), Bracewell J. said, 'The word "objects" imports a strength of feeling which goes far beyond the usual ascertainment of the wishes of the child in a custody dispute.' The passage is oft quoted in cases dealing with this Article 13 issue.
>
> [35] To meet the 'objects' criteria, it must be shown that the child displayed a strong sense of disagreement to returning to the jurisdiction of his habitual residence. He must be adamant in expressing his objection. The objection cannot be ascertained by simply weighing the pros and cons of the two competing jurisdictions, such as in a best interests analysis. It must be something stronger than a mere expression of preference.[85]

The Japanese case of 2017 *(Ju) No. 2015*[86] evidences an added complexity of a child's objections evaluated in light of the behaviour of the taking parent, and the latter's perceived influence over the child's free will. In this case, the child was removed from the US where he lived for his entire life up to age 11 years and three months. His parents were both dual nationals of the US and Japan.

---

83 For example, in *Re HB (Abduction: Child's Objections) (No. 2)* [1998] 1 FLR 564.
84 See *AQ v. JQ* Outer House of the Court of Session (Scotland), 12 December 2001, HC/E/UK 415.
85 *Crnkovich v. Hortensius* [2009] W.D.F.L. 337, 62 R.F.L. (6th) 351, 2008; HC/E/CA1028. [34–5] per O'Connor J.
86 Case of a request for Habeas Corpus relief. March 15, 2018, Judgment of the First Petty Bench.

The mother wrongfully removed the child to Japan and despite a return order being granted within nine months, the execution of the order failed when both mother and child physically resisted by wrapping themselves in a duvet bedcover when the court execution officer attempted to remove the child from the home. However, in this case, despite the child objecting to return, due to the behaviour of the mother and the lack of contact with the father, and the child's previous life in the US, it was held that in certain circumstances a mature child (aged 13 at the time), is not exercising free will in choosing to stay with the taking parent. In particular, the removing parent's strong resistance to the child being returned to the US, and this occurring in front of the child was held to put the child in a difficult position. Further, a restriction on the child's ability to obtain varied and objective information in order for him to make an informed decision about where he wishes to live, impacted on the way in which his objections to returning to the US are to be viewed. In this particular case, post-return order being granted and custody being given to the father by the US courts, it was held that 'there are special circumstances in which the restrained child cannot be seen as staying with the appellee based on his free will.'[87] Thus, despite the child's objections, the failed repatriation was deemed to be due to the taking parent unlawfully restraining the child.

As we have seen, article 11(2) of the *Revised Brussels II Regulation* (section 6.2.3 above) establishes a presumption supporting the child's participation rights in proceedings. The House of Lords (United Kingdom: England &Wales) determined in *Re D (A Child) (Abduction: Rights of Custody)*[88] that this provision will apply in every Hague return application reaching the court, and Baroness Hale observed that this would lead generally to children being heard more frequently in Hague proceedings. This would require more than the taking person presenting the child's views; separate representation of the child may also be required. In a subsequent House of Lords case, *Re M (Abduction: Zimbabwe)*,[89] it was pointed out that child objection and settlement cases (section 6.3.3.1 above) were very likely to be combined and the court must consider at the outset how best to hear the child's views. Ordering separate representation would not be automatic, even in all child objections cases, but this might be more routinely ordered in settlement cases. The question for the directions judge would be 'whether separate representation of the child will add enough to the court's understanding of the issues that arise under the Hague Convention to justify the intrusion, the expense and the delay that may result'.[90] This exception also raises the issue of the extent to which the separate representation of children who object should be arranged (Boezaart 2013).

---

87 Ibid., 6.
88 [2006] UKHL 51; [2007] 1 A.C. 619.
89 [2007] UKHL 55; [2008] 1 FLR 251.
90 Per Baroness Hale, [2008] 1 FLR 251.

6.3.3.8 Article 20

Article 20
The return of the child under the provisions of Article 12 may be refused if this would not be permitted by the fundamental principles of the requested State relating to the protection of human rights and fundamental freedoms.[91]

This article provides the court with an additional, but little-used, discretion (see Table 6.2 above) to refuse a return order on the basis that otherwise the return of the child would breach the fundamental principles of human rights of the country of refuge. In the United Kingdom, article 20 was not expressly incorporated in its domestic legislation, the Child Abduction and Custody Act 1985. It was thought that the violation of primary human rights was likely to be a breach of article 13(1)(b) and therefore this article would have been otiose. Baroness Hale observed in *Re D (A Child) (Abduction: Rights of Custody)*[92] that article 20 had in essence been given effect through the adoption of the Human Rights Act 1998.

The trend appears to be that this provision will be used only where there is an *obvious* conflict with fundamental principles of human rights. For example, article 20 was considered by the full Court of the Family Court of Australia in *Director-General, Department of Families, Youth and Community Care v. Rhonda May Bennett*,[93] which noted that the regulation giving effect to article 20 was extremely narrow and should only be invoked exceptionally where the return of a child would utterly 'shock the conscience' of the court or offend all notions of due process. It was held that the return of a child of Aboriginal or Torres Strait Islander heritage to a foreign country would not *per se* breach any fundamental principle in Australia relating to the protection of human rights and fundamental freedoms.

The few reported English cases that refer to article 20 suggest a reluctance to use this provision to refuse a return order. In *N.J.C. v. N.P.C.*,[94] the Inner House of the Court of Session (United Kingdom: Scotland) rejected a father's argument that the Convention proceedings had breached his right to a fair trial under article 6 of the ECHR; he may not have been able to focus his submissions as a professional lawyer would, but he had had every opportunity to address the relevant issues. In *Re M (Children) (Abduction: Rights of Custody)*[95] Baroness Hale declined to accept arguments based on article 20 and the ECHR. She held that

---

91 *Hague Convention of 1980*, art. 20.
92 [2007] UKHL 55 [19]; [2008] 1 AC 1288; HC/E/UKe 937.
93 [2000] Fam CA 253, HC/E/AU 275.
94 [2008] CSIH 34, 2008 S.C. 571.
95 [2007] UKHL 55 [19]; [2008] 1 AC 1288; HC/E/UKe 937.

returning the children against their will would be a graver interference with their rights than failing to do so would be with the rights of the father. Calculating the proportionality of interfering with his rights against the proportionality of interfering with the rights of the mother and the children would lead to the same result.

In the *Nottinghamshire County Council v. K.B. and K.B.*, a case from the Supreme Court of Ireland,[96] an interesting distinction is made between the article 13 exceptions and article 20. The latter, in its view, 'does not so much create an exception as recognise one'.[97] The Court's analysis of article 20 is instructive:

> Article 20 does not ask whether the law, or even the constitutional law, of the requested state *differs* from that of the requesting State. If it did, it would be difficult to see how the Convention could function effectively. In such circumstances Article 20 might not merely prevent the return of children *from* Ireland, but might just as effectively inhibit the return of children *to* Ireland. The text of the Convention makes it clear however that this is not the test. The focus of Article 20 is not upon what occurs or may occur in the requesting State (in this case England). On the contrary it is what occurs in the requested State (the return) which is the focus for the Court of the requested State (in this case Ireland). The concept of 'return' directs attention to at least two relevant matters. First, that the child has a prior connection with the State requesting the return (defined under the Convention as the State of habitual residence) to which he or she may be going back. Second, that a difference in the legal regime, and even a constitutional difference, will not itself suffice to trigger Article 20. The test is rather whether what is proposed or contemplated in the requesting State is something which departs so markedly from the essential scheme and order envisaged by the Constitution and is such a direct consequence of the Court's order that return is not permitted by the Constitution.[98]

6.3.4 Exercising discretion

Even if the taking person can demonstrate that one or more of the exceptions discussed in the previous sections applies on the facts, a non-return order will *not* be given *automatically*, but relies on the court's further consideration of whether to make a return order or not as a matter of its exercise of discretion. As with other areas of the Convention, different approaches to determining the nature of this discretion and the particular factors that may be taken into account and the

---

96 *Nottinghamshire County Council v. K.B. and K.B.* [2011] IESC 48, HC/E/IE 1139.
97 Ibid. [21], per O'Donnell J.
98 *Nottinghamshire County Council v. K.B. and K.B.* [2011] IESC 48, HC/E/IE 1139, para. 54, per O'Donnell J.

extent to which they can be relied upon have varied across the contracting States. For example, the High Court of Australia has arguably undertaken a departure at times from the international consensus in its approach to some of the exceptions/ defences and a tendency for the Court to refuse to make return orders appeared (Kirby 2010).

There have been some differences in approach concerning the nature of the discretion applicable to the exceptions according to where the various discretions are located in the legal framework of the Convention. The settlement exception in article 12(2) can be contrasted with the exceptions in article 13. The latter article *expressly* provides the competent authorities with discretion to make a return order, whereas the former does not. The permissive language used in the article 20 exception also expressly provides discretion. Furthermore, article 18 appears as arguably a general discretionary default power available where other claims to appeal to an authoritative source of discretionary power run out. Article 18 provides that '[t]he provisions of this Chapter do not limit the power of a judicial or administrative authority to order the return of the child at any time'.

> This provision [. . .] underlines the non-exhaustive and complementary nature of the Convention. In fact, it authorizes the competent authorities to order the return of the child by invoking other provisions more favourable to the attainment of this end. This may happen particularly in the situations envisaged in the [settlement exception].
> (Pérez-Vera 1980: para. 112)

Although earlier cases had based the discretion stage of determination on the text of article 18, this approach was expressly rejected in *Re M. (Children) (Abduction: Rights of Custody)*,[99] where it was pointed out that article 18 did not confer any new power to order the return of a child under the Convention, it merely contemplated powers conferred by domestic law. The court retains its discretion to make a return order.

What has remained controversial in the developing case law and across the contracting States is the *approach* that may be taken towards applying these categories of discretion. In earlier cases there had been some debate whether settlement exception prompted an obligation not to return, or simply provided discretion not to order a return. This matter was resolved in favour of the latter position by the House of Lords (United Kingdom – England & Wales) in *Re M. (Children) (Abduction: Rights of Custody)*. This case provided a comprehensive review of the exercise of discretion with regard to the exceptions to a return order.

---

99 [2007] UKHL 55, [2008] 1 AC 1288, HC/E/UKe 937.

Case study 6.4

Re M. (Children) (Abduction: Rights of Custody) [2007] UKHL 55, [2008] 1 AC 1288, HC/E/UKe 937

Facts: Two girls who were born in Zimbabwe to Zimbabwean parents lived there with their father after their parents separated early in 2001. In March 2005 they were brought secretly to England by their mother who claimed asylum. The asylum claim was refused in April 2005 but she and the children remained in England because of a moratorium on the return of failed asylum seekers to Zimbabwe. The girls were not happy in England at first and in September 2005 they contacted their father asking him to come and take them home. However, it was not until a year later that the father commenced proceedings under the Hague Convention on the Civil Aspects of International Child Abduction 1980, as scheduled to the Child Abduction and Custody Act 1985, for their return. The English central authority did not receive notification from the Zimbabwean central authority until January 2007 and proceedings were finally issued in May 2007, more than two years after the children had been removed. By that time the girls, who were then 13 and 10 years old, felt settled in their new home and did not want to return. The judge found that the children were indeed settled in England, and so he was under no duty to order their return under article 12 of the Convention; that they genuinely objected to being returned to Zimbabwe; and that they were of an age and maturity which made it appropriate for him to take account of their views under article 13. However, he decided that the case was not exceptional and he thus declined to exercise his discretion to refuse to order the girls' immediate return. The Court of Appeal upheld his decision.

On appeal by the mother, with the girls intervening –

Held: (1) (Lord Rodger of Earlsferry dissenting) that once a child had become settled for the purposes of article 12 the court still had a discretion to return him within the Convention procedures (post, paras 1–5, 30–31, 59).

(2) That when exercising the discretion under the Convention there were general policy considerations, such as the swift return of abducted children, comity between contracting states and the deterrence of abduction, which might be weighed against the interests of the child in the individual case; that the Convention discretion was at large and the court was entitled to take into account the various aspects of the Convention policy alongside the circumstances which gave the court a discretion in the first place, and

the wider considerations of the child's rights and welfare; that the weight to be given to the Convention considerations and to the interests of the child would vary enormously, as would the extent to which it would be appropriate to investigate such other welfare considerations; that it did not necessarily follow that the Convention objectives should always be given any more weight than any other consideration; and that the further away one got from the speedy return envisaged by the Convention the less weighty those general Convention objectives must be, since the major objective of the Convention could not be met (post, paras 1–2, 7–8, 31–32, 38–39, 41–44, 47–48, 59).

In re J (A Child) (Custody Rights: Jurisdiction) [2006] 1 AC 80, HL(E) considered.

(3) That the circumstances in which the Convention itself provided that return might be refused were themselves exceptions to the general rule which amounted to sufficient exceptionality; that it was neither necessary nor desirable to import an additional gloss into the Convention; and that, accordingly, a judge did not need to find something exceptional in a case before he could refuse to order return under the Convention (post, paras 1–2, 8, 34–37, 40, 59).

Zaffino v. Zaffino (Abduction: Children's Views) [2006] 1 FLR 410, CA and *Vigreux v. Michel* [2006] 2 FLR 1180, CA disapproved.

(4) That in cases where the child objected to being returned the range of considerations might be even wider than those under the other exceptions to ordering immediate return; that taking account of a child's views did not mean that those views would always be determinative or even presumptively so, but that was far from saying that a child's objections should only prevail in the most exceptional circumstances; and that the older the child was the greater the weight her objections were likely to carry (post, paras 1–2, 8, 46–47, 57, 59).

(5) Allowing the appeal, that, since the trial judge had erroneously regarded the case as needing to be exceptional before he should exercise his discretion to refuse return, it was open to the House to reach its own conclusion; that, having considered the facts and that the children felt fully settled in England and wanted to stay, the policy of the Convention could carry little weight; that the children should not be made to suffer for the sake of general deterrence of the evil of child abduction worldwide; and that, accordingly, the father's proceedings would be dismissed (post, paras 1–2, 8, 34–36, 49, 52, 54–56, 58–59).

Decision of the Court of Appeal [2007] EWCA Civ 992 reversed

As regards the grave risk/intolerable exception, the Supreme Court (United Kingdom: England & Wales)[100] has held (see Case Study 6.3) that although technically the establishment by a respondent of this exception confers upon the court only a discretion not to order the child's return, '[i]n reality, however, it is impossible to conceive of circumstances in which, once such a risk is found to exist, it would be a legitimate exercise of the discretion nevertheless to order the child's return'.

6.4 International parental abduction and non-convention countries

The *Hague Convention of 1980* has been successful in many respects in securing the prompt return of children to the country of habitual residence prior to removal. An increasing number of States have ratified the Convention.[101] The level of judicial and administrative cooperation has grown and become more sophisticated with the advent, for example, of international judicial seminars where the details of the Convention's mechanics can be fully aired. However, there remains the very significant problem of resolving international parental abductions where the taking person chooses to go to a country that has not ratified the Convention. One commentator divides the States that have not become parties to the Hague Convention into two categories: those with a principled objection to the Convention such as some of the Islamic States; and those that do not have such a principled objection but have not yet ratified it such as India (Sharma and Viswanathan 2011).

Where a taking person does remove a child to a country that has not ratified the *Hague Convention of 1980* and/or where there is no relevant regional instrument, the court will need to consider and balance the interests of the child alongside the general international policy in this area, for example, the requirement under the *Convention on the Rights of the Child* to prevent the illicit transfer and non-return of children abroad[102] (section 6.2.1 above). In the absence of any amicable, voluntary solution between the taking and left-behind person, the latter must attempt to commence proceedings in the domestic courts of the country of refuge.

The Scottish Government's website contains the following caution.

> In some Islamic countries, non-Muslim mothers have very little chance of winning custody and return of your child may not be an option. The Foreign and Commonwealth Office can provide advice on the options available to you and practical information about the customs and laws of the foreign country.[103]

---

100 *In re S (A Child) (Abduction: Rights of Custody)* [2012] UKSC 10, [2012] 2 A.C. 257, para. 5.
101 At the time of writing there were 101 Contracting Parties to the *Hague Convention of 1980*.
102 CRC, art. 11(2).
103 Scottish Government website: <www.scotland.gov.uk/Topics/Justice/law/17867/fm-children-root/18533/13579/13588> (accessed 22 February 2020).

For countries that have already ratified the *Hague Convention of 1980* the choice of approach has been between favouring a focus on the child's individual welfare or applying Convention case law analogously to non-convention countries. In *Re J. (A Child) (Return to Foreign Jurisdiction: Convention Rights)*,[104] the House of Lords (United Kingdom: England & Wales) favoured a child-centric approach. See Case Study 6.5.

Case study 6.5

***Re J. (A child) (Return to foreign jurisdiction: convention rights),* [2005] UKHL 40, [2006] 1 AC 80, HC/E/UKe 801**

Facts: The mother was born in the United Kingdom and had dual British and Saudi Arabian citizenship. She was raised largely in Saudi Arabia until the age of 16 when she was educated in Britain. After completing her education she returned to Saudi Arabia and married the father, a Saudi national, in accordance with Shariah law. Their child spent his early years in Saudi Arabia. In mid-2002 mother and child came to the United Kingdom and, with the father's consent, arranged to stay for a year while the mother studied for a master's degree. During the course of the year the marriage failed and the mother decided that she did not wish to return to Saudi Arabia. In May 2003 she presented a divorce petition in England and also applied to the British Muslim authorities for a divorce under Shariah law. The father applied for a stay of the divorce proceedings so that the matter could be dealt with in Saudi Arabia according to Shariah law and a specific issue order, pursuant to section 8 of the Children Act 1989, that the child be summarily returned to Saudi Arabia. The judge refused to make the order. The decisive factor in his reasoning was that the father had raised, and then withdrawn, allegations against the mother which would, if raised before a Shariah court, have disastrous consequences for the mother and thereby seriously damage the child's interests. The Court of Appeal reversed the judge's decision on the ground that he had given that particular concern more weight than the evidence justified.

On appeal by the mother –

Held:

(1) allowing the appeal, that whether the father was likely to resurrect his allegations against the mother was a matter which depended on the judge's evaluation of the father's oral evidence, involving findings of credibility and primary fact with which an appeal court was not entitled to

---

104 [2005] UKHL 40, [2006] 1 AC 80, HC/E/UKe 801.

interfere; that once those findings had been made they became factors to be weighed in the balance in the exercise of the judge's discretion; that an appellate court was not entitled to interfere with the judge's discretion unless his decision was plainly wrong; that the Court of Appeal had not found that the judge's decision had been based on error; and that, accordingly, on that ground alone the appeal should be allowed (post paras 1–4, 10–12, 46–8).

Piglowska v. Piglowski [1999] 1 WLR 1360, HL(E) and *G v. G (Minors: Custody Appeal) [1985] 1 WLR 647, HL(E) applied.*

(2) That any court which was determining any question with respect to the upbringing of a child had a statutory duty to regard the welfare of the child as its paramount consideration; that the application of the welfare principle might be specifically excluded by statute as, for example, by the Child Abduction and Custody Act 1985 which gave effect in domestic law to the Hague Convention on the Civil Aspects of International Child Abduction; that a court did have power, in accordance with the welfare principle, to order the immediate return of a child to a foreign jurisdiction without conducting a full investigation of the merits; that, however, there was no warrant, either in statute or authority, for the principles of the Hague Convention to be extended or applied by analogy to countries which were not parties to it; that, where non-Convention countries were involved, a trial judge had to focus on the individual child in the particular circumstances of the case; that, if there was a genuine issue between the parents as to whether it was in the best interests of the child to live in the United Kingdom or elsewhere, it was a relevant factor that the courts of the non-Convention country to which he was to be returned had no choice but to do as the father wished so that the mother could not ask them to decide, with an open mind, in which country the child would be better off living; that in such circumstances an English court would have to take into account whether it would be in the interests of the child to enable that dispute to be heard; and that, accordingly, in some cases, the absence of a jurisdiction to allow a child to be relocated against his father's wishes from the non-Convention country might be a decisive factor in refusing to order his summary return to that country (post paras 1–4, 18, 20, 22, 25–6, 28–9, 39, 46–8).

In re B's Settlement [1940] Ch 54, *McKee v. McKee [1951] AC 352, PC, J v. C [1970] AC 668, HL(E)* and *In re JA (Child Abduction: Non-Convention Country) [1998] 1 FLR 231, CA applied.*

Osman v. Elasha [2000] Fam 62, CA disapproved.

Decision of the Court of Appeal [2004] EWCA Civ 417; [2004] 2 FLR 85 reversed.

There have also been attempts to provide 'soft law' solutions (see section 2.2.6 in this book) to bridge the gap in international mechanisms. For example, both Pakistan and Egypt have not ratified the Hague Convention. A *UK – Pakistan Protocol*[105] was agreed between the President of the Family Division and the Hon Chief Justice of Pakistan in 2003 (see Freeman 2009). In essence, in a spirit of international judicial cooperation and assisted by a system of liaison judges, it was agreed in the *Protocol* that '[i]n normal circumstances the welfare of a child is best determined by the courts of the country of the child's habitual/ordinary residence' and that 'the judge of the court of the country to which the child has been removed shall not ordinarily exercise jurisdiction over the child, save in so far as it is necessary for the court to order the return of the child to the country of the child's habitual/ordinary residence'.[106] Similarly, a (non-binding) arrangement between the UK and Egypt, known as the *Cairo Declaration*,[107] was concluded in 2005, comprising a number of agreed principles applying to cross-border cases. However, the *Cairo Declaration* does not appear to have been as successful as the *UK – Pakistan Protocol*.

6.5 The use of mediation in international parental child abduction

The profile of the international regulation of parental child abduction would not be complete without some mention of the role that mediation is having on the process. Both the *Hague Convention of 1980* and the *Revised Brussels II Regulation* contain strong messages for the parties to family disputes and professionals to facilitate agreement rather than solely relying on litigation to reach a resolution. The former instrument provides that:

Article 7
Central Authorities shall co-operate with each other and promote co-operation amongst the competent authorities in their respective States to secure the prompt return of children and to achieve the other objects of this Convention. In particular, either directly or through any intermediary, they shall take all appropriate measures –
[. . .]
c) to secure the voluntary return of the child or to bring about an amicable resolution of the issues;
[. . .]

---

105 Available from Reunite's website: <www.reunite.org/edit/files/Library%20-%20International%20Regulations/UK-Pakistan%20Protocol.pdf> (accessed 27 September 2019).
106 Ibid., paras 1 and 2.
107 Available at: <www.reunite.org/edit/files/Library%20-%20International%20Regulations/Cairo%20Declaration.pdf> (accessed 27 September 2019).

The latter instrument provides that:

> *Article 55*
> *Cooperation on cases specific to parental responsibility*
> The central authorities shall, upon request from a central authority of another Member State or from a holder of parental responsibility, cooperate on specific cases to achieve the purposes of this Regulation. To this end, they shall, acting directly or through public authorities or other bodies, take all appropriate steps in accordance with the law of that Member State in matters of personal data protection to:
> [...]
> (e) facilitate agreement between holders of parental responsibility through mediation or other means, and facilitate cross-border cooperation to this end.

'Mediation' provides *one* process to facilitate agreement/amicable resolution as required in both instruments. Some States, for example, seek to encourage dispute resolution either before initiating court process or as a first step and such efforts can be effective too. Vigers identifies three broad models of mediation:

- a process within the State of refuge, designed by the State and using mediators trained in that State;
- a bi-national co-mediation process where the scheme is constructed and operated across both States and usually one mediator trained or connected to each State; and
- a 'mediation-based' approach whereby all relevant professionals view the application against the backdrop of mediation.

(Vigers 2011: 36, 38)

Vigers strongly prefers the first model (similar to the *Reunite* scheme in the UK) and argues that the ethos of the bi-national approach is 'flawed' and 'can be unduly onerous' though it may be 'a useful first-step as States experiment with developing Convention mediation', while the third model misses the point that mediation should be viewed as a discrete element of the general procedure for handling Convention applications and that some cases will not be suitable for mediation and will require court resolution.

In her examination of the additional added value to be had from Convention mediation, she notes that 'the demographic of child abduction has [...] undergone a well-documented paradigm shift' (Vigers 2011: 63) from mainly taking fathers, to taking mothers. This has meant that the benefits of some of the practical outcomes of the Convention have been lost: a return to the country of the child's habitual residence will not generally be a return to the primary carer – more often it will be a return to the left-behind (and secondary carer) father. Furthermore, subsequent litigation on the merits is likely to result in residence awarded to the taking (primary carer) mother who will then relocate with the child, thus 'subjecting the child to the disruption of three locations' (Vigers 2011: 63). Return orders may well lead to the separation from the primary carer. On the issue of whether mediation might add to the problem of delay, she argues that the evidence so far shows that a discrete specialist mediation scheme within the Convention framework can operate expeditiously and need not result in any undue delay.

Some empirical research has also been conducted to examine the long-term effectiveness of mediation in international parental child abduction in the *Reunite*[108] scheme in Leicester (UK) (Buck 2012). The study population consisted of those parents who had participated in mediation with *Reunite* between December 2003 and December 2009. In total, 52 individual parents agreed to be interviewed, and comprised 22 taking parents and 30 left-behind parents. These all concerned (except one case) 'incoming cases', i.e. a taking parent coming from another country into the UK. The resulting analysis divided the cases into (29) 'resolved cases', i.e. where the Memorandum of Understanding drafted following mediation had been reached quickly followed by a consent order in the courts; and (23) 'unresolved cases', where the dispute was not agreed in mediation and had to be further referred back to the courts for an authoritative decision. The overall message from the research was that mediation does have a significant role to play in the context of the legal process of Hague proceedings, but it needs to be used proportionately and with care, particularly with regard to devising a robust mechanism to select cases that might be suitable for mediation in the first place. The research found that the effects are durable in the sense that, at least for 'resolved cases' so defined, the agreed MoUs provided broadly a framework or template that shaped future family arrangements. But in 'unresolved' cases the mediation attempt had very little or no impact on alleviating the families' difficulties and they opted for what often turned out to be lengthy repeated court appearances before their family arrangements could find a more settled resting point.

The Hague Conference has been proactive in supporting mediation schemes across the contracting States, and currently encourages these developments through 'soft law' techniques rather than advocating a new legally binding instrument to integrate mediation into Hague proceedings. It has produced a comprehensive *Guide to Good Practice on Mediation*[109] in consultation with Contracting States. It emphasises friendly settlements, invoking the principles in articles 7 and 10 of the Hague Convention (Gonzalez Martin 2015: 368).

---

108 *Reunite: International Child Abduction Centre*, is the principal NGO in the UK. See Reunite's website: <www.reunite.org/> (accessed 28 September 2019).
109 *Guide to Good Practice: Mediation*, Permanent Bureau of the Hague Conference on Private International Law, June 2012. Available at: <www.hcch.net/upload/guide28mediation_en.pdf> (accessed 28 October 2019).

6.6 Concluding remarks

A fundamental tension present in the *Hague Convention of 1980* is that there is a persistent conflict between *collective* and *individual* rights. One can see that, in general, it will be in children's best interests collectively to have a decision on their future made by courts located in their countries of habitual residence. However, the children's rights agenda, considerably strengthened by the appearance of the *Convention on the Rights of the Child* in 1989, also prompts a focus on the best interests of the individual child. To an extent, the availability of the settlement exception (section 6.3.3.1 above), and the additional exceptions/defences in article 13 (sections 6.3.3.2–6.3.3.7 above) and the possibility of an article 20 (section 6.3.3.8 above) argument, all provide possible routes whereby the centre of gravity of a Convention case can be steered away from the underlying aim of peremptory return to the country of habitual residence and focus instead on the individual child's welfare interests in the country of refuge. Nevertheless, the process of increasing international judicial cooperation and the holding of Special Commissions on the Convention has developed a recognisable way of dealing with these cases. The position of abductions to non-convention countries (section 6.4 above) remains a worrying concern, though the production of bilateral agreements such as the *UK–Pakistan Protocol* appears to be a beneficial development.

Chapter 7

Intercountry adoption

7.1 Introduction

Intercountry adoption is a subject that has seized much popular attention, and on occasion has attracted news headlines about celebrity adoptions. A storm of protest occurred when Madonna attempted to adopt an infant from an orphanage in Malawi (Mezmur 2008, 2009), and Angelina Jolie's adoption of an infant from Ethiopia has been said to have had a role to play in the increased number of adoptions from that country (Mezmur 2012: 51). In one respect, intercountry adoption is seen as an act which provides a loving and secure home to a child who faces an otherwise bleak future. As such, intercountry adoption has been considered to be in the 'best interests' of the child (Bartholet 2017). On the other hand, depictions of intercountry adoption include reports of child-trafficking, children being kidnapped, mothers relinquishing their children under dubious circumstances, and comments that intercountry adoption is an exploitation of poor countries and impoverished inhabitants of those States by wealthier and more powerful nations. Intercountry adoption remains a controversial area that generates different views about its utility and necessity. There are complexities too around the question of what motivates States to engage with intercountry adoption and the effect of these motivations on the approach taken to the 'best interests' standard (Sargent 2009). Cases of failed adoptions resulting from a variety of reasons, including cultural problems, have arisen. Some adoptive parents have eventually reneged on adoptions citing intractable personal conflicts with adoptees as highlighted in the documentary *Unwanted in America: The Shameful Side of International Adoption* (2014).

Intercountry adoption, or *international adoption*, as it is sometimes known, has occurred historically alongside various causes of population displacement and migration. For example, in the United Kingdom child migration was used for a number of policy aims unconnected with child welfare. It has been estimated that some 130,000 children were 'exported' to various parts of the former British Empire between around 1860 and 1930 in order to provide a cheap method to populate the colonies. Many were subjected to abuse and cruelty and brought up to believe they were orphans. After the Second World War, there were around 10,000 children who were sent off to Canada, Australia, New Zealand and

Southern Rhodesia (now Zimbabwe),[1] the last batch, in 1967 (Bean and Melville 1989). In post-war Australia, the catchphrase of 'populate or perish' drove the country's immigration policy. From evidence available to the *Child Migration Programmes Investigation Report* (2018), there was a sense in which these children were treated by some of the sending institutions as 'commodities' with one institution even referring to its 'requisition' for a specific number of children to be sent to Australia. Many of the later cohorts of children were never placed in families and some found themselves in harsh conditions. The placements were arranged by reputable childcare agencies and the view at the time was that arranging for their migration was in their best interests. There was evidence, however, of exploitation and abuse in respect of these children. Many of the voluntary organisations involved failed in their duty to exercise proper monitoring or aftercare, having dispatched children, in some cases as young as five. Some witnesses described 'care' regimes which included physical, emotional and sexual abuse as well as neglect (Child Migration Programmes 2018: vii).

Given this background, a House of Commons committee urged 'extreme caution' when considering applications for intercountry adoption.

> Child migration was a bad and, in human terms, costly mistake [. . .] We have met many former child migrants who continue to suffer from emotional and psychological problems arising directly from this misguided social policy [. . .] Many child migrants were separated from siblings and lived in profound geographical and social isolation, which left them unable to prepare themselves effectively for integration into adult life and society at large.[2]

Warfare too has had its influence on child migration patterns. The United States, the biggest 'receiving State' of children for adoption from other countries, is reckoned to have experienced its first wave of such adoptions at the end of the Second World War, with children being adopted from war torn Europe and Japan. A second wave began with the Korean War in the 1950s where children who were orphaned, or born as a result of liaisons with United States military personnel, were adopted. The appearance of intercountry adoption, at least in its modern form, is said to have started during and following the end of the Korean War in the 1950s (Hubinette 2006: 139). In the United States, private, and often religious-based, agencies promoted the adoption of Korean children. The rules on how intercountry adoption was to occur were

---

1 *Child Migration Programmes Investigation Report*, March 2018: 2; see also *Report of the Historical Institutional Abuse Inquiry* (delivered to the First Minister of Northern Ireland on 6 January 2017), Module 2, Chapter 6.
2 Select Committee on Health, *The Welfare of Former British Child Migrants*, Third Report, Select Committee on Health, 1997–98 session, 23 July 1998, London: The Stationery Office, p. 98.

only those that were made by the agencies, with very little oversight from either the South Korean or the American governments. Agencies worked in tandem with the governments, but the privileging of private agencies has to an extent been introduced into the *Hague Convention on Protection of Children and Co-operation in respect of Intercountry Adoption*[3] (hereafter the '*Hague Convention of 1993*'). One scholar comments on the occurrence of intercountry adoption in South Korea, the role of the agencies and government and the children who were sent to other countries:

> Of the many needy children, mixed-race children were most likely to be considered for homes abroad by the Korean government and private adoption agencies. Most mixed-race children were born to Korean women and U.S. soldiers stationed at U.S. bases in Korea during and after the war. The women who gave birth to mixed-race children were regarded as military prostitutes. Thus, those children bearing the stigma of their mothers' occupation are identified as a group of children who needed homes outside of Korea. In 1954, the South Korean government established the Child Placement Service . . . to place biracial children in foreign adoption, particularly to their father's country, the United States.
>
> (Kim 2007: 136)

A third wave occurred similarly as a result of the Vietnam War in the 1970s. A mass evacuation of children ('Operation Babylift') from South Vietnam to the USA and other countries was organised at the end of the Vietnam War from 3 to 6 April 1975 and many of these children were adopted. It is estimated that a total of 2,547 orphans were processed under Operation Babylift and of these 602 went on to other countries, leaving a total of 1,945 adopted in the United States.[4] From the 1990s, substantial numbers of children started to be adopted internationally from countries such as Romania, the former Soviet Union and China, and the children displaced most recently by the wars in Afghanistan and Iraq continue to present challenges to the process of intercountry adoption (Richards 2013).

Finally, intercountry adoption is often appealed to as a solution to children orphaned as a result of natural disasters. For example, calls for such action followed the devastation caused by an earthquake in Haiti in early 2010, though some would caution against taking children away from their homeland, especially in times of crisis (Selman 2011).

---

3 Hague Conference on Private International Law, concluded 29 May 1993 (entered into force 1 May 1995).
4 United States Agency for International Development, *Operation Babylift Report* (Emergency Movement of Vietnamese and Cambodian Orphans for Intercountry Adoption, April–June 1975), Washington, DC, pp. 1–2, 5, 6, 9–10, 11–12, 13–14.

7.1.1 Intercountry adoption: the statistics

As intercountry adoption operates across many countries and their respective family law and official statistics regimes are diverse, there have been difficulties in determining the global number of children involved in intercountry adoption. Selman's work on the statistics of intercountry adoption is the most authoritative. He estimates that there has been a global total of around 970,000 intercountry adoptions since 1948. In the most recent decade (2000 to 2010) there have been around 410,000 children adopted by citizens of 27 countries: 'the highest number for any decade' (Selman 2012: 4). See Figure 7.1 below.

Figure 7.1 shows the successive increases in intercountry adoptions in the decades following the Second World War. Tables 7.2, 7.3 and 7.4 below provide a more detailed profile of intercountry adoptions by continent, receiving States and sending States respectively in the period 2004–2017.

Table 7.1 shows that Africa no longer holds the status as the dominant sending continent. A report from the African Child Policy Forum entitled *Africa: The New*

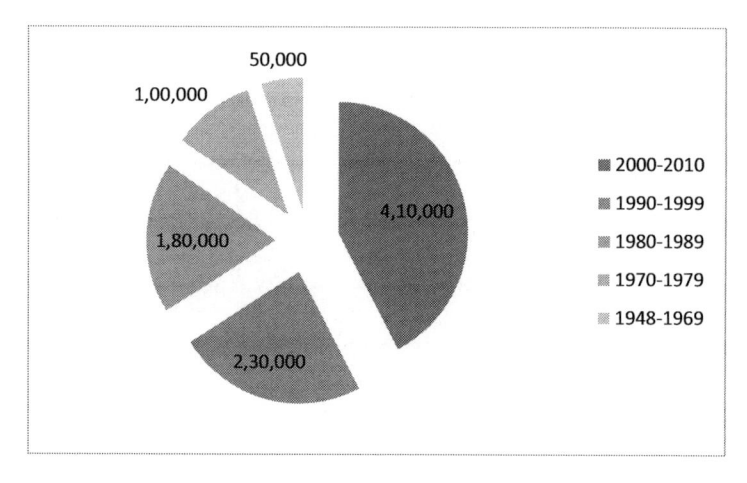

Figure 7.1 Estimated numbers of children adopted via intercountry adoption 1948–2010 – total 970,000 adoptions.

Source: Derived from Selman (2012: 4).

Table 7.1 International adoption by continent

	2004	2007	2008	2010	2012	2014	2015	2016	2017	2004–17
Africa	7%	13%	17%	22%	27%	21%	20%	19%	16%	16%
Asia	42%	40%	35%	36%	35%	40%	43%	45%	48%	40%
Europe	31%	21%	21%	20%	24%	22%	22%	21%	18%	24%
Latin America	17%	23%	24%	19%	12%	14%	12%	14%	16%	18%
Other	3.0%	3.0%	3.4%	2.6%	1.5%	2.3%	2.3%	2.2%	1.7%	2.5%

Table 7.2 Top 5 states of origin 2004–2017

	2004	2005	2006	2007	2008	2009	2010	2011	2012	2013	2014	2015	2016	2017	2004–17
China	13.412	14.484	10.765	8.749	5.882	5.011	5.429	4.373	4.136	3.406	2.948	3.055	2.671	2.212	86.533
Russia	9.440	7.569	6.837	4.926	4.174	4.058	3.426	3.424	2.683	1.838	1.057	779	481	343	51.035
Ethiopia	1.534	1.799	2.184	3.041	3.911	4.551	4.369	3.455	2.786	2.009	1.088	684	321	470	32.202
Guatemala	3.425	3.870	4.230	4.852	4.175	784	58	36	11	26	32	13	7	4	21.523
Colombia	1.749	1.500	1.681	1.643	1.613	1.403	1.828	1.599	933	575	536	523	485	550	16.618
TOP FIVE	**29.560**	**29.222**	**25.697**	**23.211**	**19.755**	**15.807**	**15.110**	**12.887**	**10.549**	**7.854**	**5.661**	**5.054**	**3.965**	**3.579**	**207.911**

Selman (2018).

Table 7.3 Top 5 receiving countries

	2004	2005	2006	2007	2008	2009	2010	2011	2012	2013	2014	2015	2016	2017	2004–17
Country															
USA	22.989	22.726	20.675	19.601	17.449	12.744	12.149	9.320	8.668	7.094	6.441	5.648	5.372	4.714	175.590
Italy	3.402	2.874	3.188	3.420	3.977	3.964	4.130	4.022	3.106	2.825	2.206	2.216	1.872	1.439	42.641
Spain	5.541	5.423	4.472	3.648	3.156	3.006	2.891	2.573	1.669	1.191	824	799	567	531	36.291
France	4.079	4.136	3.977	3.162	3.270	3.017	3.508	2.003	1.569	1.343	1.069	815	956	685	33.589
Canada	1.949	1.858	1.568	1.715	1.614	1.695	1.660	1.513	1.162	1.243	905	895	790	621	19.188
TOP FIVE	**37.960**	**37.017**	**33.880**	**31.546**	**29.466**	**24.426**	**24.338**	**19.431**	**16.174**	**13.696**	**11.445**	**10.373**	**9.557**	**7.990**	**307.299**

Frontier for Intercountry Adoption described the continent as a growing source of adoptions (ACPF 2012). However, the statistics above show that Africa is in third place as source of international adoptions. At the time of publishing, Selman had released new figures (2005–2018) showing similar trends.

Table 7.2 above shows that China sent the most children for intercountry adoption (86,533), followed by Russia (51,035), Ethiopia (32,2002), and Guatemala (21,523). The lowest number of the 15 top sending countries were sent by Poland (4,631). Although the global figures since 1948 (Figure 7.1 above) suggest an ever-increasing trend upwards in the number of intercountry adoptions, this is not necessarily so. Selman comments on the trends:

> The global number of intercountry adoptions peaked in 2004 after a steady rise in annual numbers from the early 1990s. Since then, annual numbers have decreased to the point that by 2008 the total was lower than it had been in 2001 [. . .] and by 2009 lower than it was in 1998 [. . .] During this time, the rise and fall was evident in most regions and countries. In 2009, however, things began to change, with more children going to European countries than to the United States – which had, until that time, accounted for about half of all international adoptions since the mid-1980s.
>
> (Selman 2012: 2)

The United States received the highest number of intercountry adoptions in the period (175,590), followed by Italy (42,641), Spain (36, 291) France (33,589), and Canada (19,188). The lowest was Andorra (48). In total there were 364,693 intercountry adoptions in the period 2004 to 2017 (Selman 2018).

7.1.2 The sending and receiving countries

As Tables 7.2 and 7.3 above suggest, there are a number of countries that can be viewed as 'sending' States and others that can be characterised as 'receiving' States. However, over time these patterns do change and the bilateral relationships between a pair of sending and receiving States, e.g. the US and South Korea, France and Vietnam, come and go. Studies of intercountry adoption have tended to focus on the conditions prevalent in the *sending countries* that have generated the *supply* side of the adoption equation. There is less research about the *demand* for intercountry adoptions from the *receiving countries*. 'Consequently, current scholarship in this area tends to perpetuate the understanding of intercountry adoption as a symptom of what is wrong with source [sending] countries' (Chen 2003). There is much controversy surrounding the practice of intercountry adoption, not least the impression that it is an act of international charity or 'rescue'. The perspective of children's rights, on the other hand, emphasises the 'best interests' of the child principle, now concretised in the *Convention on the Rights of the Child* (1989)[5] (section 3.7.3.2 in this book).

---

5 Opened for signature 20 November 1989, 1577 UNTS 3 (entered into force 2 September 1990).

The power balance between the generally poorer sending countries and the richer receiving countries tends to emphasise the practice of intercountry adoption as primarily a means of addressing the interests and needs of the prospective adoptive parents in the receiving States and also reflects on the weaknesses of family care options within the sending States rather than maintaining the focus on the needs of the child. The attraction of relatively high adoption fees in sending States, for example in China, can sustain the intercountry adoption market for much longer and out of proportion with the original demographic factors triggering these practices. The prospect of profit has created an incentive for intermediaries.

However, intercountry adoptions may have a negative impact on domestic children's services. The history of intercountry adoptions from South Korea is a good example. The original factors of war-related disruption to the population, giving rise to intercountry adoptions in the 1950s, are no longer relevant today. South Korea is now a relatively prosperous country with a low birth rate. It is a plausible argument, as in the Romanian case, that the continuation of intercountry adoption has, in fact, discouraged the proper development of internal children's services in South Korea (Sarri, Baik and Bombyk, 1998).

7.2 The need for international legal regulation

7.2.1 *The* Hague Convention of 1965

International legal regulation of intercountry adoptions started with the appearance of the *Hague Convention on Jurisdiction, Applicable Law and Recognition of Decrees Relating to Adoptions*[6] (1965). The purpose of that Convention was seen by one contemporary commentator as

> mainly concerned with recognition [of decrees relating to adoption] and its key provision is found in Article 8 under which every adoption governed by this Convention and granted by an authority competent under it shall be recognised without further formality in all contracting states.
>
> (Unger 1965: 463)

That there should be a Convention that dealt solely with international adoptions was found to need explanation:

> its scope is severely limited since, under Article 2(b), it will not apply in the ordinarily case where these parties are all nationals of the same state and are habitually resident in it. The machinery and conditions of recognition

---

6 Hague Conference on Private International Law, concluded 15 November 1965 (entered into force: 23 October 1978; denounced and *ceased to have effect on 23 October 2008*).

established by the Convention will therefore operate only in cases of what Article 6 describes as 'inter-country adoption'.

(Unger 1965: 464)

This Convention was based on the European situation in the 1960s: that is, 'international adoptions spanning relatively short geographical distances and between countries with more or less comparable socio-economic, cultural and legal systems' (Van Loon 1995; Jäntera-Jareborg 1994). The Convention met with limited success and did not enter into force until 1978, by which time the social reality had changed with larger numbers of children from developing countries being adopted by families in the industrialised countries. The Convention was only ratified by three States (Austria, Switzerland and the United Kingdom) though it was subsequently denounced and ceased to have effect from 23 October 2008.

7.2.2 Adoption and the UN Convention on the Rights of the Child

A Special Commission (section 2.4.2 in this book) of the Hague Conference appointed by the Permanent Bureau in January 1988 again took up the subject of legal cooperation in relation to intercountry adoption. The emerging global phenomenon of intercountry adoption required a different approach 'with more emphasis on the need to define substantive safeguards and procedures for courts, administrative authorities and private intermediaries than on traditional rules of conflict of jurisdiction and of applicable law' (Van Loon 1995: 463). The *Hague Convention on the Civil Aspects of International Child Abduction*[7] (1980) had set a useful precedent in moving away from legal standards that were constrained to sorting out rules of jurisdiction and choice of applicable law, to establishing standards that advanced practical measures for judicial and administrative cooperation. In addition, the *UN Convention on the Rights of the Child* acted as a source of inspiration during the negotiations for a new Hague Convention to regulate intercountry adoptions.

Article 21 of the *Convention on the Rights of the Child* had included, for the first time in international human rights law, principles of good adoption practice (Detrick 1999: 343). The text of article 21 and some detailed commentary can be found in section 3.7.5.2 in this book. The duties in this article only apply to States that 'recognise and/or permit the system of adoption', thus providing an escape clause for a number of Islamic countries that did not recognise the institution of adoption. Arguably, countries that did not recognise adoption but permitted children to leave and be adopted abroad come within the ambit of article 21 (Van Bueren 1994b: 102). If the wording left any doubt about the matter, a State could always

---

7 Hague Conference on Private International Law, concluded 25 October 1980 (entered into force 1 December 1983).

lodge a reservation.[8] Where the article does apply, the standard required of States is to ensure that the best interests of the child shall be the *paramount* consideration. This article recognises the principle that intercountry adoption may be considered as an alternative means of care for children, if the child cannot be cared for in the child's country of origin (the 'subsidiarity principle' – section 3.7.5.2 in this book) (Tobin 2019: 795–6). The *travaux préparatoires* reveal that intercountry adoption will only be regarded as a subsidiary means of care when all other possibilities are exhausted (Tobin 2019: 801; Detrick 1999: 351). Furthermore, the safeguards and standards should be 'equivalent' to those existing in domestic adoptions and States should take all appropriate measures to prevent 'improper financial gain' from intercountry adoptions. The *Hague Convention of 1993* specifies clearly that 'only costs and expenses including reasonable professional fees' may be charged or paid.[9] Finally, article 21 of the *Convention on the Rights of the Child* provides that these principles and standards should be promoted by 'concluding bilateral or multi-lateral arrangements or agreements' (such as the *Hague Convention of 1993*). This latter paragraph 'particularly reflects the concern of the drafters of the *Convention on the Rights of the Child* over the sale and trafficking of children for the purposes of intercountry adoption' (Detrick 1999: 354).

7.2.3 The Special Commission and the Hague Convention of 1993

A Hague Conference Special Commission (section 2.4.2 in this book) recommended that non-Member States participate in the preparatory work on drafting a new Convention. The principle of participation by non-Member States had been accepted by the 14th session of the Hague Conference in 1980. Around 70 States and 20 international organisations participated in the negotiations. The Hague Conference viewed the involvement of non-Member States as indispensable, given that many children subject to intercountry adoption arrangements originated from these 'sending' States. There was a general acknowledgement of the inadequacy of existing international legal instruments to meet the perceived problems of intercountry adoption. In particular, it was recognised that there was a need to establish legally binding standards and a system of supervision to ensure observance. There was also a need to establish channels of communication and cooperation between authorities in countries of origin and in receiving States. In short, there was:

> [a] clear practical need for a multilateral instrument which would not, or not only, be a convention unifying private international law rules. As a matter of fact, it was felt that actual protection of children required the definition of

---

8 Reservations lodged by Islamic countries in respect of CRC, art. 21: Bangladesh, Brunei Darussalam, Jordan, Kuwait, Maldives, Oman, and the United Arab Emirates. Egypt withdrew its reservation on 31 July 2003, and the Syrian Arab Republic partially withdrew its reservation on 13 June 2012.

9 *Hague Convention of 1993*, art. 32(2).

certain substantive principles and the establishment of a legal framework of co-operation between authorities in the States of origin and in the receiving States.

(Parra-Aranguren 1994: para. 8)

Several meetings of the Special Commission took place from 1990 to 1992. Its report and a draft of the Convention were considered by the 17th session of the Hague Conference in May 1993. *The Hague Convention on Protection of Children and Co-operation in respect of Intercountry Adoption*[10] of 1993 was unanimously approved and concluded at the end of May 1993. The *Hague Convention of 1993* was intended to provide solutions in a difficult and complex area in relation to both jurisdictional and substantive points of legal regulations:

> Intercountry adoption is legally complex. Rules of private substantive law governing adoption vary significantly from one country to another, which gives rise to problems of private international law such as questions of jurisdiction, applicable law and recognition of foreign adoptions. In many countries intercountry adoption is, in addition, subject to various provisions which override those rules of private international law, including laws requiring preliminary permission to adopt a child in intercountry cases, immigration laws and nationality laws. The Hague Convention on Intercountry Adoption aims to solve many of these problems. It is not a typical private international law convention. It does provide for a framework to solve problems of conflicts of jurisdiction and of applicable law. However, it also provides for substantive safeguards and procedures in respect of intercountry adoption, and judicial and administrative co-operation in matters of private law.
>
> (Detrick 1999: 355)

The development of the Hague Convention was an outgrowth of globalisation and the necessity to encourage global societal interests in protecting children (Schmit 2008). Because of the increased interdependency of countries with regards to adoption, it 'meant to create rules and guidelines for countries to follow when processing intercountry adoptions, so that there can be global uniformity and consistency' (Dillon 2003). The Convention places a duty on the Secretary-General of the Hague Conference to 'convene a Special Commission' at regular intervals 'in order to review the practical operation of the Convention'.[11]

---

10 Hague Conference on Private International Law, concluded 29 May 1993 (entered into force 1 May 1995).
11 *Hague Convention of 1993*, art. 42. Subsequent Hague Conventions have contained a similar provision. See: Hague Conference on Private International Law, *Convention on Jurisdiction, Applicable Law, Recognition, Enforcement and Co-operation in respect of Parental Responsibility and Measures for the Protection of Children, concluded 19 October 1996 (entered into force 1 January 2002);* Hague Conference on Private International Law, *Convention on the International Recovery of Child Support and Other Forms of Family Maintenance*, concluded 23 November 2007 (entered into force 1 January 2013); and Hague Conference on Private International Law, *Protocol on the Law Applicable to Maintenance Obligations, concluded 23 November 2007 (entered into force* 1 August 2013).

This codifies the practice, evolved under other Hague Conventions requiring judicial and administrative cooperation, of holding periodic meetings of Special Commissions to undertake the review work:

> Article 42 [. . .] takes into account the remarkable experience of other Hague Conventions, in particular the Child Abduction Convention, to express the idea that the Convention on intercountry adoption should not be an end in itself, but rather lay the groundwork for an ongoing review and amelioration of its application. Therefore, the Secretary-General of the Hague Conference on Private International Law shall, after the Convention enters into force, convene Special Commissions, at regular intervals, to review its operation – meetings that may be attended by all States Parties, together with Member States and other non-Member States that participated in the Seventeenth Session, as well as by international organisations, public and private, invited to participate.
>
> (Parra-Aranguren 1994: para. 586)

There have been four Special Commissions examining the *Hague Convention of 1993*, in 1994, 2001, 2005 and 2010 respectively.[12] For example, the Special Commission of 2010 gave its general endorsement to a draft of the *Guide to Good Practice No. 2*[13] concerning accredited bodies and authorised the Permanent Bureau to progress work on the drawing up of accreditation criteria. The Special Commission also made the following recommendations relating to intercountry adoptions in the wake of disasters.

Response to disaster situations
38. The Special Commission recognised that, in a disaster situation, efforts to reunite a displaced child with his or her parents or family members must take priority. Premature and unregulated attempts to organise the adoption of such a child abroad should be avoided and resisted.

39. No new adoption applications should be considered in the period after the disaster or before the authorities in that State are in a position to apply the necessary safeguards.

40. The Special Commission also recognised the need for a common approach on the part of Central Authorities in dealing with such situations and for Central Authorities to discuss and review actions taken in response to, and lessons learned from, disaster situations.[14]

---

12 See HCCH website: <www.hcch.net/index_en.php?act=conventions.publications&dtid=2&cid=69> (accessed 10 November 2013).
13 Permanent Bureau of the Hague Conference on Private International Law, *Guide to Good Practice No. 2: Accreditation and Adoption Accredited Bodies, Bristol: Family Law*. Available at: <www.hcch.net/upload/adoguide2en.pdf> (accessed 12 November 2013).
14 Permanent Bureau of the Hague Conference on Private International Law, *Conclusions and Recommendations and Report of the Special Commission on the practical operation of the 1993 Hague intercountry adoption convention (17–25 June 2010)*, March 2011.

7.2.4 UNICEF's position

The United Nations Children's Fund (UNICEF) (section 2.4.1.2 in this book) released statements in October 2007, July 2010 and June 2015 to clarify its position on the priority that should be accorded to intercountry adoption. The latter statement is reproduced below.

> **UNICEF's position on Intercountry adoption**
> From: <www.unicef.org/media/intercountry-adoption> (accessed 5 September 2019)
>
> Since the 1960s, there has been an increase in the number of intercountry adoptions. Concurrent with this trend, there have been growing international efforts to ensure that adoptions are carried out in a transparent, non-exploitative, legal manner to the benefit of the children and families concerned. In some cases, however, adoptions have not been carried out in ways that served the best interest of the children – when the requirements and procedures in place were insufficient to prevent unethical practices, such the sale and abduction of children, coercion or manipulation of birth parents, falsification of documents and bribery.
>
> The Convention on the Rights of the Child, which guides UNICEF's work, clearly states that every child has the right to grow up in a family environment, to know and be cared for by her or his own family, whenever possible. Recognising this, and the value and importance of families in children's lives, families needing assistance to care for their children have a right to receive it. When, despite this assistance, a child's family is unavailable, unable or unwilling to care for her/him, then appropriate and stable family-based solutions should be sought to enable the child to grow up in a loving, caring and supportive environment.
>
> Intercountry adoption is among the range of stable care options. For individual children who cannot be cared for in a family setting in their country of origin, intercountry adoption may be the best permanent solution.
>
> UNICEF supports intercountry adoption, when pursued in conformity with the standards and principles of the 1993 Hague Convention on Protection of Children and Co-operation in Respect of intercountry Adoptions – currently ratified by 95 countries. This Convention is an important development for children, birth families and prospective foreign adopters. It sets out obligations for the authorities of countries from which children leave for adoption, and those that are receiving these children. The Convention is designed to ensure ethical and transparent processes. This international legislation gives paramount consideration to the best interests of the child and provides the framework for the practical

application of the principles regarding inter-country adoption contained in the Convention on the Rights of the Child. These include ensuring that adoptions are authorised only by competent authorities, guided by informed consent of all concerned, that intercountry adoption enjoys the same safeguards and standards which apply in national adoptions, and that intercountry adoption does not result in improper financial gain for those involved in it. These provisions are meant first and foremost to protect children, but also have the positive effect of safeguarding the rights of their birth parents and providing assurance to prospective adoptive parents that their child has not been the subject of illegal practices.

The case of children separated from their families and communities during war or natural disasters merits special mention. Family tracing should be the first priority and intercountry adoption should only be envisaged for a child once these tracing efforts have proved fruitless, and stable in-country solutions are not available. This position is shared by UNICEF, UNHCR, the UN Committee on the Rights of the Child, the Hague Conference on Private International Law, the International Committee of the Red Cross, and international NGOs such as the Save the Children Alliance and International Social Service.

UNICEF offices around the world support the strengthening of child protection systems. We work with governments, UN partners and civil society to protect vulnerable families, to ensure that robust legal and policy frameworks are in place and to build capacity of the social welfare, justice and law enforcement sectors.

Most importantly, UNICEF focuses on preventing the underlying causes of child abuse, exploitation and violence.

New York
26 June 2015

7.3 The *Hague Convention on Intercountry Adoption of 1993*

There are, at the time of writing, 98 States[15] that have ratified or acceded to the *Hague Convention of 1993*.[16] The Special Commission also drew up a (non-binding) *Recommendation* on the general principles to be applied when implementing the Convention specifically to refugee and other internationally displaced children.

---

15 See: Hague Conference on Private International Law '1993–2018 25th Anniversary of the 1993 Hague Convention on Protection of Children and Co-operation in Respect of Intercountry Adoption' Brochure 'Celebrating 25 Years of Protecting Children in Intercountry Adoption'.
16 Hague Conference on Private International Law, concluded 29 May 1993 (entered into force 1 May 1995).

HAGUE RECOMMENDATION ON REFUGEE CHILDREN
(ADOPTED ON 21 OCTOBER 1994)

From: <www.hcch.net/upload/recomm33refugee_en.pdf> (accessed 9 November 2013)

Pursuant to the Decision of the Seventeenth Session of the Hague Conference on Private International Law, held at The Hague from 10 to 29 May 1993, to convene a Special Commission to study the specific questions concerning the application to refugee children and other internationally displaced children of the *Hague Convention of 29 May 1993* on *Protection of Children and Co-operation in Respect of Intercountry Adoption*.

The Special Commission gathering at The Hague from 17 to 21 October 1994, in consultation with the Office of the United Nations High Commissioner for Refugees,

Adopts the following Recommendation –

RECOMMENDATION

Whereas the *Hague Convention on Protection of Children and Co-operation in Respect of Intercountry Adoption* was concluded at The Hague on 29 May 1993,

Considering that in the application of the Convention to refugee children and to children who are, as a result of disturbances in their countries, internationally displaced, account should be taken of their particularly vulnerable situation,

Recalling that according to the Preamble of the Convention each State should take as a matter of priority appropriate measures to enable the child to remain in the care of his or her family of origin, and that intercountry adoption may offer the advantage of a permanent family to a child for whom a suitable family cannot be found in his or her State,

The Hague Conference on Private International Law recommends to the States which are, or become, Parties to the Convention that they take into consideration the following principles in applying the Convention with respect to refugee children and to children who are, as a result of disturbances in their countries, internationally displaced –

1 – For the application of Article 2, paragraph 1, of the Convention, a State shall not discriminate in any way in respect of these children in determining whether they are habitually resident in that State.

With respect to these children, the State of origin referred to in Article 2, paragraph 1, of the Convention, is the State where the child is residing after being displaced.

2 – The competent authorities of the State to which the child has been displaced shall take particular care to ensure that –

a) before any intercountry adoption procedure is initiated,
- all reasonable measures have been taken in order to trace and reunite the child with his or her parents or family members where the child is separated from them; and
- the repatriation of the child to his or her country, for purposes of such reunion, would not be feasible or desirable, because of the fact that the child cannot receive appropriate care, or benefit from satisfactory protection, in that country;

b) an intercountry adoption only takes place if
- the consents referred to in Article 4 c) of the Convention have been obtained; and
- the information about his or her identity, adoptability, background, social environment, family history, medical history including that of the child's family, the child's upbringing, his or her ethnic, religious and cultural origins, and any special needs of the child, has been collected in so far as is possible under the circumstances.

In carrying out the requirements of sub-paragraphs a and b, these authorities will seek information from the international and national bodies, in particular the Office of the United Nations High Commissioner for Refugees, and will request their co-operation as needed.

3 – The competent authorities shall take particular care not to harm the well-being of persons still within the child's country, especially the child's family members, in obtaining and preserving the information collected in connection with paragraph 2, as well as to preserve the confidentiality of that information according to the Convention.

4 – The States shall facilitate the fulfilment, in respect to children referred to in this Recommendation, of the protection mandate of the United Nations High Commissioner for Refugees.

The Hague Conference also recommends that each State take these principles and those of the Convention into account for adoptions creating a permanent parent – child relationship between, on the one hand, spouses or a person habitually resident in that State and, on the other hand, a refugee or internationally displaced child in the same State.

As regards the practical operation of the Hague Convention, the reader may want to consult the detail contained in the *Guide to Good Practice No. 1* issued by the Permanent Bureau of the Hague Conference in 2008.

1. *The Implementation and Operation of the 1993 Hague Intercountry Adoption Convention: A Guide to Good Practice* is a project of post-Convention support initiated

by the Permanent Bureau for the purpose of assisting States (whether or not already Contracting States) with the practical implementation of the Convention, in a manner which achieves the objects of the Convention, namely, the protection of children who are adopted internationally. It is the first such Guide for the 1993 Convention, and it identifies important matters related to planning, establishing and operating the legal and administrative framework to implement the Convention. It does not always claim to be a guide for best practices because some practices are necessarily different in different Contracting States.[17]

The following sub-sections outline the principal features of the *Hague Convention of 1993*.

7.3.1 The best interests of the child are paramount

The *Hague Convention of 1993*, as we have seen, was inspired by the *UN Convention on the Rights of the Child* (1989), and to an extent was conceived to build upon article 21 of the earlier Convention (section 7.2.2 above) which prescribes that 'the best interests of the child shall be the *paramount* consideration' (my emphasis) for States parties' development and the operation of their adoption systems. The debate on whether the intercountry adoptions are in the best interests of the child or not will be captured later. Suffice to say at this stage that, where intercountry adoption is developed as an option within a national child care system, it should be ethical and child-centred. Consequently, the *Hague Convention of 1993* provides certain rules to ensure that adoptions take place in the best interests of the child. It contains the best interests principle explicitly in relation to two key determinations made by the State of origin. First, the sending State must determine, after possibilities for placement of the child have been given due consideration, that an intercountry adoption is in the child's best interests.[18] Second, the sending State must determine on the basis of the evaluation reports relating to the child and the prospective adoptive parents whether the envisaged match is in the best interests of the child.[19] Clearly, there may often be ambiguities around the process of identifying what is in an individual child's best interests, a dilemma that is arguably exemplified by perceptions of intercountry adoption as a form of 'rescue' (Davies 2011).

More broadly, the best interests principle is further supported by State obligations to:

- ensure the child is adoptable;
- preserve information about the child and his/her parents;

---

17 Permanent Bureau of the Hague Conference on Private International Law, *Guide to Good Practice No. 1: The Implementation and Operation of the 1993 Hague Intercountry Adoption Convention*, 2008, Bristol: Family Law, [1]. Available at: <www.hcch.net/upload/adoguide_e.pdf> (accessed 12 November 2013).
18 *Hague Convention of 1993*, art. 4(b).
19 *Hague Convention of 1993*, art. 16(1)(d).

- evaluate thoroughly the prospective adoptive parents;
- match the child with a suitable family;
- impose additional safeguards where needed; and
- implement the principle of subsidiarity (section 7.3.2 in this book);

A Hague Convention adoption will only apply in relation to persons under the age of 18 years at the time the agreements required are granted.[20] The age of 18 is consistent with the definition of the child to be found in the *Convention on the Rights of the Child*,[21] but the *Hague Convention of 1993* is silent as to the age limit relevant to the question of whether a child is 'adoptable'. This is left to the applicable law determined by the conflict rules of each State. For example, if the applicable law only permits adoption under a lower age, for example, 12 years old, then this must be respected (Parra-Aranguren 1994: para. 96). The competent authorities of the State of origin must establish that the child is adoptable (under the relevant applicable law); it must determine that an intercountry adoption is 'in the child's best interests' after due consideration has been given to possibilities of placement within its own State.[22] The competent authorities of the receiving State must determine that the child is or will be authorised to enter and reside permanently in that State.[23]

Central authorities (or their delegate bodies) in both States of origin and receiving States are obliged to 'collect, preserve, and exchange information about the situation of the child and the prospective adoptive parents, so far as is necessary to complete the adoption'.[24]

The competent authorities of contracting States are further obliged to 'ensure that information held by them concerning the child's origin, in particular information concerning the identity of his or her parents, as well as the medical history, is preserved' and that children or their representatives have access to such information under appropriate guidance.[25] In one study, the authors argue that 'preservation of a child's background is perceived to be in conflict with other interests of the child, such as gaining a position in her/his adoptive family equal to that of a biological child and being loved unconditionally (Lind and Johansson 2009: 235).

Prospective adoptive parents must apply to the central authority of their own State if they wish to adopt a child habitually resident in another contracting State.[26] The evaluation of prospective adoptive parents is undertaken by the competent authorities of the receiving State. They must be satisfied that 'the prospective adoptive parents are eligible and suited to adopt' and must have ensured that the prospective adoptive parents 'have been counselled as may be necessary'.[27]

20 *Hague Convention of 1993*, art. 3.
21 CRC, art. 1.
22 *Hague Convention of 1993*, art. 4(a).
23 *Hague Convention of 1993*, art. 5(c).
24 *Hague Convention of 1993*, art. 9(a).
25 *Hague Convention of 1993*, art. 30.
26 *Hague Convention of 1993*, art. 14.
27 *Hague Convention of 1993*, art. 5(a) and (b).

The matching of the child with prospective adoptive parents is undertaken following an exchange of reports by the receiving State and the State of origin. Once the receiving State is satisfied that the applicants are eligible and suited to adopt, it is obliged to 'prepare a report including information about their identity, eligibility and suitability to adopt, background, family and medical history, social environment, reasons for adoption, ability to undertake an intercountry adoption, as well as the characteristics of the children for whom they would be qualified to care'.[28] Once the State of origin is satisfied that the child is adoptable, it is also under a duty to 'prepare a report including information about his or her identity, adoptability, background, social environment, family history, medical history including that of the child's family, and any special needs of the child'.[29] In addition to this, it must ensure that due consideration has been given to 'the child's upbringing and to his or her ethnic, religious and cultural background' and ensure that the necessary consents have been obtained.[30] Then it will determine on the basis of the reports relating to the child and the prospective adoptive parents 'whether the envisaged placement is in the best interests of the child'.[31] The central authority of the State of origin will transmit its report on the child back to the central authority of the receiving State along with proof of any necessary consents and the reasons for the placement, 'taking care not to reveal the identity of the mother and father if, in the state of origin, these identities may not be disclosed'.[32] The necessary pre-conditions for a placement decision to occur in the State of origin are set out in article 17. These are:

- that the prospective adoptive parents agree;
- that the central authority of the receiving State has approved such a decision (where such approval is required under the law of that State or by the central authority of the State of origin);
- that the central authorities of both States have agreed that the adoption may proceed; and it has been determined that the prospective adoptive parents are 'eligible and suited to adopt'; and
- that the child is or will be authorised to enter and reside permanently in the receiving State under article 5.

Both the State of origin and the receiving State are obliged to ensure that all necessary steps are taken to obtain permission for the child to leave the State of origin and enter and reside permanently in the receiving State.[33]

The transfer of the child should take place 'in secure and appropriate circumstances' and if possible in the company of the adopters.[34] The central authorities

---

28 *Hague Convention of 1993*, art. 15(1).
29 *Hague Convention of 1993*, art. 16(1)(a).
30 *Hague Convention of 1993*, art. 16(1)(b) and (c).
31 *Hague Convention of 1993*, art. 16(1)(d).
32 *Hague Convention of 1993*, art. 16(2).
33 *Hague Convention of 1993*, art. 18.
34 *Hague Convention of 1993*, art. 19(2).

are put under a continuing duty to monitor the progress of the transferred child, particularly where there is a probationary placement in the receiving State.[35] If the placement does not work out, it is provided that the central authority of the receiving State will take measures necessary to protect the child. This can include arranging for the return of the child to the sending State, withdrawal from the prospective adopters, and placement in temporary care. It can also involve an arrangement of a new placement or alternative long-term care, after consultation with the sending State.[36]

In short, the sending State must verify compliance with four main conditions:

- the adoptability of the child;
- respect for the subsidiarity principle;
- the necessary consents of other persons than the child; and
- the wishes, opinions or consent of the child.

Similarly, the receiving State has responsibility to verify that:

- the prospective adoptive parents are eligible and suited to adopt;
- the prospective adoptive parents have been counselled as may be necessary; and
- the child is or will be authorised to enter and reside permanently within its territory

To be 'eligible' to adopt means to fulfil all the legal conditions, according to the applicable law. To be 'suited' to adopt means to satisfy the necessary socio-psychological qualifications (Parra-Aranguren 1994: para. 180).

7.3.2 Subsidiarity principle

This principle, as we have seen, was first recognised in relation to intercountry adoption by the *Convention on the Rights of the Child*[37] (section 3.7.5.2 in this book). In the context of the *Hague Convention of 1993*, the principle of subsidiarity means that States recognise that generally children should be raised by their parents or extended family where possible. If that is not possible other options of permanent care in the State of origin should be explored.[38] It is only where the national solutions have been considered and found wanting should intercountry adoption be explored, and then only if it is in the individual child's best interests.[39] In general, institutional care should be considered as a last resort. Whether intercountry

---

35 *Hague Convention of 1993*, art. 20.
36 *Hague Convention of 1993*, art. 21.
37 CRC, art. 21(b).
38 *Hague Convention of 1993*, Preamble §2.
39 *Hague Convention of 1993*, art. 4(b).

adoption does in fact reduce the number of children remaining in institutional care remains contentious. Chou and Browne (2008a: 45–7) concluded 'that countries with high proportions of outgoing international adoptions also had high numbers of young children in institutional care' and the evidence did not support the proposition that intercountry adoption reduced the number of children remaining in institutional care.[40]

7.3.3 Safeguards to protect children from abduction, sale and trafficking

One of the overall objectives of the Hague Convention is to establish safeguards and thereby to 'prevent the abduction, the sale of, or traffic in children'[41] by:

- protecting birth families from exploitation and undue pressure;
- ensuring only children in need of a family are adoptable and adopted;
- preventing improper financial gain and corruption; and
- regulating agencies and individuals involved in adoptions by accrediting them in accordance with Convention standards.

The protection of birth families from exploitation and undue pressure is achieved principally by the requirements that States of origin must meet to ensure that the necessary consents[42] have been given. The persons whose consent is necessary for adoption must have been

> counselled as may be necessary and duly informed of the effects of their consent, in particular whether or not an adoption will result in the termination of the legal relationship between the child and his or her family of origin.[43]

Such consents must be given: 'freely, in the required legal form, and expressed or evidenced in writing'; must not have been 'induced by payment or compensation of any kind'; and, the mother's consent (where required) must have been given *after* the birth of the child.[44] Similarly, the competent authorities of the State of origin must ensure that, having regard to the child's age and degree of maturity, the *child* is counselled and informed of the effects of the adoption, consideration

---

40 See also Gay y Blasco et al. (2008) and Browne and Chou (2008).
41 *Hague Convention of 1993*, art. 1(b).
42 The draft version of the Convention additionally required that consents would be 'unconditional'. However, that would have precluded adoptions where consent had been conditional on placing a child in a family of the same religion. It was thought that there might be circumstances where the imposition of some conditions by the biological parents would be appropriate and permitted by the State of origin (Parra-Aranguren 1994: para. 143).
43 *Hague Convention of 1993*, art. 4(c)(i).
44 *Hague Convention of 1993*, art. 4(c)(ii) – (iv).

is given to the child's wishes and feelings, and the child gives freely in the required legal form, his or her own consent (where required) to the prospective adoption.[45]

In addition, the Convention lays down that there shall be no contact between the prospective adopters and the child's parents or any other person who has care of the child until the requirements of Arts 4(a) – (c) and 5(a) have been met, unless the adoption takes place within a family or is in compliance with the conditions established by the competent authority of the State of origin.[46] The aim of this provision is:

> to prevent trafficking and any other kind of practices that may be contrary to the purposes of the Convention, in particular, to avoid the result whereby consents required for the granting of the adoption are induced by payment or compensation, which is expressly forbidden by Article 4, sub-paragraph c (3).
> (Parra-Aranguren 1994: para. 495)

Such practices occurred in Romania and were known to have occurred in Latin America and Asia (Van Loon 1995: 467).

The Convention contains two articles preventing improper financial gain and corruption:

Article 8
Central Authorities shall take, directly or through public authorities, all appropriate measures to prevent improper financial or other gain in connection with an adoption and to deter all practices contrary to the objects of the Convention.

Article 32
(1) No one shall derive improper financial or other gain from an activity related to an intercountry adoption.
(2) Only costs and expenses, including reasonable professional fees of persons involved in the adoption, may be charged or paid.
(3) The directors, administrators and employees of bodies involved in an adoption shall not receive remuneration which is unreasonably high in relation to services rendered.

Article 32 is designed to prevent anyone from deriving improper financial or other gain from an activity related to intercountry adoption. This also reflects the principle that has been established in the *Convention on the Rights of the Child*:[47]

> The importance of the matter had been strongly stressed in the Special Commission, where it was recalled 'the existing situation reveals that it is not

---

45 *Hague Convention of 1993*, art. 4(d).
46 *Hague Convention of 1993*, art. 29.
47 CRC, art. 21(d).

only the intermediary bodies that are attracted by improper financial gain', because 'as it has sometimes happened, lawyers, notaries, public servants, even judges and university professors, have either requested or accepted excessive amounts of money or lavish gifts from prospective adoptive parents' (Report of the Special Commission, No. 310).

(Parra-Aranguren 1994: para. 527)

The extent to which these provisions have been successful remains controversial.

[I]n some ways a Hague-based intercountry adoption system could be even more vulnerable to child laundering schemes than the pre-Hague system. The Hague regime can appear to allocate the tasks of ensuring that children are truly orphans eligible for adoption to the sending country, despite the fact that many sending countries have significant problems with corruption, large-scale document fraud and inadequate legal, administrative, or governmental processes.

(Smolin 2007: 54)

One of the safeguards provided by the Convention is the system of accreditation of agencies and individuals involved in intercountry adoptions. The Convention provides that '[a]ccreditation shall only be granted to and maintained by bodies demonstrating their competence to carry out properly the tasks with which they may be entrusted'.[48] The Convention further provides certain minimum standards for accredited bodies.

Article 11
An accredited body shall –

a) pursue only non-profit objectives according to such conditions and within such limits as may be established by the competent authorities of the State of accreditation;
b) be directed and staffed by persons qualified by their ethical standards and by training or experience to work in the field of intercountry adoption; and
c) be subject to supervision by competent authorities of that State as to its composition, operation and financial situation.

Furthermore, a body accredited in one contracting State may act in another State 'only if the competent authorities of both States have authorised it to do so', and the names and addresses of the accredited bodies must be communicated by each State to the Permanent Bureau of the Hague Conference.[49]

---

48 *Hague Convention of 1993*, art. 10.
49 *Hague Convention of 1993*, arts 12 and 13.

7.3.4 Cooperation between States and within States

In order to ensure that the safeguards, discussed above, are respected, the one of the Convention's overall objectives is 'to establish a system of cooperation among Contracting States'.[50] Article 7(1) confers a duty on central authorities to 'co-operate with each other and promote co-operation amongst the competent authorities in their States to protect children and to achieve the other objects of the Convention'. The central authorities must take directly all appropriate measures to: (a) provide information about their State laws and other general information; and (b) keep each other informed about the operation of the Convention.[51] Finally, a competent authority that detects any abuse, or serious risk of abuse, of the Convention is put under a duty to immediately inform the central authority of its State, and the latter is placed in a position of responsibility for ensuring appropriate measures are taken.

The cooperative framework is established by means of an agreed division of responsibilities. The Convention provides that both the State of origin[52] and the receiving State[53] must ensure that a number of pre-conditions are met before a Convention adoption can occur. These conditions therefore establish a set of minimum standards that must be adhered to. However, it remains open to each contracting State to impose additional (and higher) conditions. The general approach behind the Convention is that it 'should restrict itself to only regulating the essential issues of substantive law in relation to intercountry adoption, leaving all others to the applicable law' (Parra-Aranguren 1994: para. 165).

7.3.5 Automatic recognition of adoption decisions

One of the overall objectives of the Convention is 'to secure the recognition in Contracting States of adoptions made in accordance with the Convention'.[54] A key achievement of the *Hague Convention of 1993* has been its establishment of a system of automatic recognition of adoptions. The adoptions covered in the *Hague Convention of 1993* are those 'which create a permanent parent – child relationship'.[55] A tighter definition of 'adoption' was rejected on the basis that many States have systems of 'simple' or 'limited' adoption, that is, adoption that will not entirely *terminate* the legal relationship with the birth family and transfer *all* parental rights to the adoptive family. As a result, both simple and full adoptions that have been certified and made in accordance with Convention procedures, are recognised 'by operation of law' in all other contracting States.[56] Consequently, the

---

50 *Hague Convention of 1993*, art1(b).
51 *Hague Convention of 1993*, art. 7(2).
52 *Hague Convention of 1993*, art. 4.
53 *Hague Convention of 1993*, art. 5.
54 *Hague Convention of 1993*, art. 1(c).
55 *Hague Convention of 1993*, art. 2(2).
56 *Hague Convention of 1993*, art. 23.

status of the child is made more certain and it precludes the need for a procedure for recognition of orders, or re-adoption in the receiving State. This procedure therefore superseded:

> the [then] existing practice that an adoption already granted in the State of origin is to be made anew in the receiving State only in order to produce such effects, and also prevents a revision of the contents of the foreign adoption. For these reasons, it only requires a certification, made by the competent authorities of the State where the adoption took place, attesting that the Convention's rules were complied with and that the agreements under sub-paragraph (c) of Article 17 were given, specifying when and by whom.
> (Parra-Aranguren 1994: para. 402)

Recognition of an adoption may be refused exceptionally by a contracting State on the grounds that the 'adoption is manifestly contrary to its public policy, taking into account the best interests of the child'.[57] It is understood that this exception is to be construed restrictively; otherwise the overall objective to secure recognition in contracting States would be undermined (Parra-Aranguren 1994: para. 426).

The concept of 'recognition' of a Convention adoption is given finer focus by article 26. This proved to be a difficult issue in the drafting process of the Convention. However, most participants were of the view that it would not be desirable to restrict the scope of the Convention to the type of adoption that terminates the legal relationship between the child and his or her birth family ('full' adoptions). All kinds of intercountry adoption ought to be covered.

The Convention defines (non-exhaustively) what such recognition will include.

Article 26(1)
The recognition of an adoption includes recognition of –

(a) the legal parent – child relationship between the child and his or her adoptive parents;
(b) parental responsibility of the adoptive parents for the child;
(c) the termination of a pre-existing legal relationship between the child and his or her mother and father, if the adoption has this effect in the Contracting State where it was made.

Where an adoption has had the (usual) effect in (c) above, article 26(2) provides that the adopted child shall enjoy, in the receiving State, equivalent rights to persons adopted under the purely internal law of the contracting State. Article 26(3) safeguards the application of any provision 'more favourable' to the child in force in the contracting State that recognises the adoption. Where an adoption granted in the State of origin does *not* have the effect of terminating completely a pre-existing

---

57 *Hague Convention of 1993*, art. 25.

legal parent – child relationship, for example, in the case of a 'simple' or 'limited' adoption, there is available a 'conversion' procedure,[58] if the law of the receiving State so permits and subject to the grant of the necessary consents.[59]

7.3.6 Competent authorities, Central Authorities and accredited bodies

The Convention requires that only 'competent authorities' should perform Convention functions. Competent authorities may be:

- Central Authorities;
- public authorities, including judicial or administrative authorities;
- accredited bodies.

The Convention provides for a system of Central Authorities in all Contracting States and imposes certain general obligations on them, such as:

- cooperation with one another, for example, through the exchange of general information concerning intercountry adoption;
- the elimination of any obstacles to the application of the Convention (art. 7(2) b));
- a responsibility to deter all practices contrary to the objects of the Convention (art. 8).

The Convention requires that contracting States 'designate a Central Authority' to discharge the duties imposed by the Convention.[60] The Convention provides that some functions need to be performed directly by the central authorities; for example, the duty to cooperate with each other and promote cooperation internally, and to provide certain types of information about the laws of the State and statistical information.[61] However, other functions could be delegated; for example, the duty to prevent improper financial gain and other practices, and certain measures to preserve and exchange information, facilitate proceedings, promote adoption counselling, and provide general evaluation reports.[62] Consequently, the responsibilities assigned to the central authorities may be discharged, depending on the function in question, by other public authorities, accredited bodies, or even by non-accredited bodies or persons.

---

58 *Hague Convention of 1993*, art. 27.
59 However, it should be noted that the conversion procedure does not cover the case where the adoption is granted in the *receiving State*: see Parra-Aranguren (1994, para. 477).
60 *Hague Convention of 1993*, art. 6. See also the comparable provision in the *Hague Convention on International Child Abduction of 1980*, art. 6.
61 *Hague Convention of 1993*, art. 7.
62 *Hague Convention of 1993*, arts 8 and 9.

The appearance of 'accredited bodies' was a novelty and probably driven by the history of the US, the largest receiving State, that had privileged private agencies as intermediaries for intercountry adoption arrangements:

> It reflects the present reality that private organisations play an important role as intermediaries in the intercountry adoption process. Their role is recognised, but also defined and regulated by the Convention, in particular as to their competence, non-profit objectives and the need for supervision.
> (Van Loon 1995: 466)

Therefore, the central authorities are not the sole operators of the Convention. Cooperation may be obtained through other channels, as permitted by the law of each contracting State:

> This feature makes the present Convention different from the Hague Child Abduction Convention, where the Central Authority remains the unique institution responsible for compliance with the obligations imposed by the Convention. For this reason, it is more flexible and may bring about a factual decentralisation of the functions assigned to the Central Authority.
> (Parra-Aranguren 1994: para. 225)

The Permanent Bureau of the Hague Conference has produced an extensive *Guide to Good Practice* on accreditation issues.[63] Indeed, one of the most contentious points about the *Hague Convention of 1993* has been the provision in article 22 permitting private persons and bodies to act as intermediaries in international adoptions. Article 22 deals with the difficult area of 'independent' or 'private' adoptions, that is, adoptions carried out by bodies other than 'accredited' ones. Although all applications have to be made to a central authority, another public authority or an accredited body, other bodies and persons may act as intermediaries, but only under certain conditions:

> [F]irstly, the Contracting State must have made a specific declaration to that effect; secondly, they must meet the requirements fixed by the Convention; thirdly, the names and addresses of these bodies and persons must be made known to the Secretariat of the Hague Conference; fourthly, the reports on the child and prospective adoptive parents should in all cases be prepared under the responsibility of the central authority or an accredited body; and finally, any State of origin may veto the activities of such other bodies or persons in the adoption process concerning its children.
> (Van Loon 1995: 467)

---

63 Permanent Bureau of the Hague Conference on Private International Law, *Guide to Good Practice No. 2: Accreditation and Adoption Accredited Bodies*, Bristol: Family Law. Available at: <www.hcch.net/upload/adoguide2en.pdf> (accessed 12 November 2013).

It is thought that this does provide scope for the intrusion of trafficking and sale of children into the intercountry adoption system, and there are concerns that this provision, potentially allowing untrained and possibly unsuitable persons a key role, cannot possibly promote the best interests of children (Sachlier 1993). Arguably, the safeguarding role of the Convention is compromised by the 'Convention's implicit toleration of the involvement of so-called 'approved (non-accredited) persons' at critical stages in the ICA [intercountry adoption] process' (Watkins 2012: 390). However, this matter remains contentious. One commentator argues that 'the Convention was designed to scrutinise independent adoptions, not to get rid of them' and that the Convention, in fact, strikes a fair balance between authoritative State regulation and a liberal environment for civil society and individuals (Hayes 2011: 316).

7.4 Hague Conference International Centre for Judicial Studies and Technical Assistance

The Hague Conference International Centre for Judicial Studies and Technical Assistance was established in 2006 at the Academy Building on the premises of the Peace Palace, as an integral part of the Permanent Bureau of the Hague Conference on Private International Law.[64] The Centre has been developed in response to the increase in cross-border movement of people: 'As an increasing number of States become Party to the Conventions, the need for implementation assistance expands in parallel'.[65] The Centre provides administrative and logistical support to Convention-specific projects, as well as regional and other initiatives being undertaken and developed by the Permanent Bureau in consultation with its Member States. There are three major themes of action:

a) identifying weaknesses or needs in States/regions or where a Hague Convention is about to come into operation;
b) considering what the Hague Conference is able to offer itself and in co-operation with others (States Parties, Regional Bodies or NGOs) in the way of training and technical assistance; and
c) examining how to access any necessary funding.[66]

From time to time, the Centre has been instrumental in arranging fact-finding missions to places of particular interest in terms of intercountry adoption practice.

---

64 Hague Conference of Private International Law, *The Hague Conference International Centre for Judicial Studies and Technical Assistance: the intercountry adoption technical assistance programme*, November 2009, Permanent Bureau: The Hague, Netherlands.
65 Ibid., [1].
66 Ibid., [4].

Fact-finding missions have been undertaken in relation to: Guatemala (2007),[67] Nepal (2009)[68] and Kazakhstan (2011).[69]

Case Study 7.1 below provides an extract from the report of the Kazakhstan mission and illustrates a number of contemporary issues concerning the operation of the *Hague Convention of 1993*. By way of background, it should be noted that Kazakhstan acceded to the Convention on 9 July 2010 and the Convention entered into force on 1 November 2011 in respect of this State. The 'Children Rights Protection Committee' of the Ministry of Education and Science (MOES) was designated as the Central Authority. Kazakhstan had had a system of private, independent adoptions in the past, and as a consequence there had been serious problems with its intercountry adoption system, which had been assessed as quite unsafe by the International Social Service. That report (Boéchat and Cantwell 2007) identified various problems, in particular the money required by different intermediaries in Kazakhstan, and the (false) categorisation of children as having special needs for the purposes of getting them into the intercountry adoption stream.

The Government of Kazakhstan requested UNICEF to help it achieve compliance with the Convention while setting up a new system to implement it. UNICEF then sent a request for technical assistance to the Permanent Bureau. The main objective of the Hague mission was to provide technical assistance to the Government of Kazakhstan (in particular to the Children Rights Protection Committee) by sharing the international experience from the States who are parties to the Convention and advising on development of policies, structures and capacities for the implementation of the Convention.

Case study 7.1

Extract from:
Hague Conference of Private International Law, *Report of Mission to Kazakhstan (9–12 May 2011)*, Jennifer Degeling and Laura Martínez-Mora, July 2011, Permanent Bureau: The Hague, Netherlands.

5. GENERAL OBSERVATIONS

We were very pleased to see that the Central Authority leaders have good knowledge and understanding of 1993 Hague Adoption Convention and its

---

67 Hague Conference of Private International Law, *Report of a Fact-Finding Mission to Guatemala in Relation to Intercountry Adoption 26 February – 9 March 2007*, prepared by Ignacio Goicoechea, Liaison Legal Officer for Latin America with the assistance of Jennifer Degeling, Principal Legal Officer, May 2007, Permanent Bureau: The Hague, Netherlands.
68 Hague Conference of Private International Law, *Report of Mission to Nepal (23–27 November 2009)*, Jennifer Degeling, 4 February 2010, Permanent Bureau: The Hague, Netherlands.
69 Hague Conference of Private International Law, *Report of Mission to Kazakhstan (9–12 May 2011)*, Jennifer Degeling and Laura Martínez-Mora, July 2011, Permanent Bureau: The Hague, Netherlands.

requirements and have been using the *Guide to Good Practice No 1 on the Implementation and Operation of the 1993 Hague Adoption Convention (Guide to Good Practice No 1)* which has been translated into Russian. The Government seems committed to preparing for the effective implementation of the 1993 Hague Adoption Convention.

In addition they have a good understanding of the subsidiarity principle. This is reflected in the practice, as national adoptions are very developed and are reported as very high i.e. almost 80% of all adoptions.

However, there seems to be fragmented approach to child protection. The responsibilities are spread over a number of ministries and it seems that there is a lack of effective co-ordination as ministries are protecting their own territory and may not wish to be directed by a body at the level of the Committee.

It has to be noted that it was not possible to get any view of how things are working in the regions, and Astana is not representative of the rest of the country.

6. RECOMMENDATIONS

a. Elements of a safe system: Recommendation No 1 of 2010 Special Commission on the practical operation of the 1993 Hague Adoption Convention

We would like to draw the attention of the Government of Kazakhstan to the recommendations made during the 2010 Special Commission regarding the elements of a safe system of adoption. The following are essential features of a well regulated system:

a) effective application of Hague Convention procedures and safeguards including, as far as practicable, in relation to non-Convention adoptions;
b) independent and transparent procedures for determining adoptability and for making decisions on the placement of a child for adoption;
c) strict adherence to the requirements of free and informed consent to adoption;
d) strict accreditation and authorisation of agencies, and in accordance with criteria focussing on child protection;
e) adequate penalties and effective prosecution, through the appropriate public authorities, to suppress illegal activities;
f) properly trained judges, officials and other relevant actors;
g) prohibition on private and independent adoptions;
h) clear separation of intercountry adoption from contributions, donations and development aid;
i) regulated, reasonable and transparent fees and charges;

j) effective co-operation and communication between relevant authorities both nationally and internationally;
k) implementation of other relevant international instruments to which States are parties;
l) public awareness of the issues.

b. Revisions to the chapters on adoption of the Family Code

The Permanent Bureau recalls its offer of assistance to revise the amended version of the chapters related to adoption of the Family Code if it is translated into English.

c. Address the issue of fragmentation of functions and responsibilities

It is not easy to understand who is responsible for what in the child protection system. This fragmentation of functions and responsibilities can be very problematic. It is therefore recommended to address this issue and to try to concentrate functions and responsibilities more effectively.

d. Ensure effective co-ordination between national authorities and bodies – a Central Authority responsibility under Art. 7

The Central Authority has to promote co-operation amongst the competent authorities in Kazakhstan to protect children and to achieve the objectives of the 1993 Hague Adoption Convention (art. 7). According to the 2007 ISS Report, regional authorities may have different approaches and the rate of intercountry adoptions may vary tremendously from region to region. As mentioned in the report, a co-ordinated national policy and assurance of good co-operation is needed.

e. Ensure all authorities and bodies are aware of the obligation of the protection of the best interests of child as the guiding principle in decision making

The protection of the best interest of the child should always be the primary consideration in all matters related to adoption. An adoption should only be made when it is in the child's best interests to do so. This has to be clear for all authorities and bodies involved.

f. Matching must be done by professionals

We understood that the modifications to the Family Code include a major and very important change: prospective adoptive parents will no longer be allowed to choose a child personally.

As it is said in the Guide to Good Practice No 1, the matching should not be done by the prospective adoptive parents, for example, parents should not visit an institution to pick out an appealing child or choose a child from photo lists. The matching should be assigned to a team and not be left to the responsibility of an individual; the team should be composed of child protection professionals trained in adoption policies and practices. They should preferably be specialists in psycho-social fields. Matching should not be done by computer alone even if an initial screening is made on criteria such as age, gender or special needs of the child. The final match should always be made by professionals and take into account the child's wishes and best interest.

g. Training and supervision for regional authorities and persons involved in child homes

All regional authorities and bodies involved in the adoption procedure should be trained on how to properly implement the 1993 Hague Adoption Convention and on the new legal framework when it will be approved. This should also include the personnel of children's homes.

New responsibilities should be explained properly and procedural manuals to implement the new legal framework properly should be written for staff of the Central Authority and others.

h. Proper regulation for the authorisation of foreign adoption bodies and limits on the number of foreign adoption accredited bodies in Kazakhstan

Kazakhstan should include in its new legislation proper regulation for the authorisation of foreign adoption bodies to work in the country. We understood that this is the intention and therefore some of our presentations during the mission focussed on this aspect.

It is also recommended that Kazakhstan limits the number of foreign adoption accredited bodies that it authorises to work in the country. This will help to prevent pressure. The number of adoption accredited bodies should be proportionate to the number of intercountry adoptions. In addition special attention should be given to selecting the best ones using ethical criteria (see *Draft Guide to Good Practice No. 2 on Accreditation and Adoption Accredited Bodies*).[8]

i. Foreign adoption accredited bodies' representatives in Kazakhstan

It is recommended that foreign adoption accredited bodies have their own representatives in Kazakhstan who they will support, train, monitor and for whom they will be responsible. Therefore, it will no longer be needed to have "independent facilitators", as this task should be assumed by the adoption accredited bodies and their respective representatives. This will make it easier to ensure that adoption accredited bodies and their representatives follow the same standards (see Draft Guide to Good Practice No. 2, chapter 7).

j. Financial issues

The ISS Report makes quite worrying statements regarding financial issues surrounding intercountry adoption in Kazakhstan, in particular the costs associated with agencies and facilitators. This issue was not raised in our public meetings. However, some interlocutors were also very concerned and told us that it was a widespread problem.

Contracting States and their respective Central Authority have a particular responsibility to regulate the cost of intercountry adoption by taking measures to prevent improper financial gain. It is reasonable to expect that payments will be necessary for both government and non-government services connected with intercountry adoptions. Both receiving States and States of origin are permitted to charge reasonable fees for services provided. The 1993 Hague Adoption Convention is concerned with achieving transparency in costs and fees as a means of preventing improper financial gain.

Regarding this point we recommend following all the recommendations set out in Chapter 5 of the Guide to Good Practice No. 1. The modifications to the Family Code should include regulation of adoption financial issues. Costs and fees should be very transparent, accountable and clear. We also recommend that as a requirement for authorisation to work in Kazakhstan, all adoption accredited bodies publish their costs and charges on their website and on the website of the Central Authority of Kazakhstan.

k. Special Needs Children

Special needs children are usually not adopted domestically. Therefore, special campaigns should be carried out in order to promote their adoption in Kazakhstan. For instance, good campaigns have improved the rate of adoption of siblings and older children in States of origin.

The problem of categorising children as special needs children when they are not special needs, in order to put them in the intercountry adoptable stream more quickly, should be addressed. It is recommended that authorities ensure that medical reports are accurate.

7.5 Decline in intercountry adoptions

The numbers of international adoptions have dropped drastically over the years. By 2017, intercountry adoptions from 20 states of origin had dropped remarkably to 9, 386 in total, with only 3,579 from the top five sending countries (see Table 7.2). Many countries have closed or severely restricted their international adoption programmes (Montgomery and Powell 2018). Overall trends in adoption in the European Union (EU) also indicate this fall in numbers of intercountry adoptions. Domestic adoptions now far outnumber intercountry adoptions, and that there has been a decline in the number of children being adopted into the EU from third countries (European Parliament Briefing 2016[70]).While there is consensus on the fall in the number of children available for adoption, this has not been the result of the decline in the number of couples or individuals wishing to adopt (Rotabi and Bromfield 2016).

Several reasons have been cited for the decline, factors such as national esteem, stringent regulations and the ban on private intermediaries. Sending countries with high rates of international adoptions cite 'abuse' as one of the reasons for putting an end to the practice. The policy change is seen in those countries as in the 'best interest of the child' (Montgomery and Powell 2018). Ethiopia, for example, passed legislation in early 2018 restricting adoption of children by foreign parents. It followed the death of a 13-year-old girl adopted by an American couple in 2011. The adoptive parents were convicted of homicide and manslaughter. South Korea, Romania, Guatemala, China, Kazakhstan and Russia have also banned or cut back on international custody transfers. In 2012, the Russian parliament voted to ban adoptions by Americans after two-year-old Dima Yakovlev died in 2008 after being locked in a hot car by his adoptive father. There have been some 19 confirmed cases of death of Russian adoptees in the United States (Compton 2016).

Many countries in South and Central America have since banned private intermediaries, and have as a result largely eliminated international adoption (Bartholet 2010). These include Bolivia, Chile, Ecuador, El Salvador, Honduras, Paraguay and Peru. Guatemala has enacted legislation eliminating private intermediaries in any future international adoption system. The fall in the number of children available may be connected with increasing regulation and growing sentiment in some countries of origin against sending children abroad for adoption (European Parliament 2016).

If numbers continue to decline, it seems likely that childless couples might have to turn to the new reproductive technologies for solutions to infertility and in particular to international surrogacy (Cahn 2009). Rotabi and Bromfield (2016) note that global surrogacy has gained in popularity owing, in part, to improved assisted reproductive technology methods and the ease with which people can make global surrogacy arrangements.

7.6 Conflicting perceptions on intercountry adoption

As has been noted in the discussion, intercountry adoption has been regarded as in the 'best interests' of the child while another school of thought opposes such adoptions by banning or imposing strict regulations. Bartholet (2010: 92) claims that UNICEF and other international children's organisations have promoted the idea that unparented children should where possible be kept in their country of origin. However, UNICEF noted in its 2015 statement that: 'Intercountry

---

70 European Parliament Adoption of Children in the European Union Briefing June 2016.

adoption is among the range of stable care options. For individual children who cannot be cared for in a family setting in their country of origin, intercountry adoption may be the best permanent solution.'[71] One of the proponents of the 'liberal approach' to intercountry adoption, Bartholet, asserts that regulation prohibiting private intermediaries has been the death knell for international adoption in many countries. The ban on intermediaries, such as attorneys, and other organisations, had taken away 'the lifeblood of adoption' (2010: 93). She argues that intercountry adoption fulfils the 'best interests' precepts articulated in Article 21 of the UNCRC and Article 1 of Hague Convention (Bartholet 2010). She also cites jurisprudence from the Madonna case and judgements in South African and India courts as examples of judicial endorsements of the practice.[72] If not adopted, she argues, almost all are destined to live either in orphanages or on the streets. She asserts that: 'The extreme contrast between the homes international adoption offers and orphanage or street life should make unnecessary any debate as to what best serves children' (Bartholet 2010:95). To Bartholet, stays in orphanages are 'damaging' (2010: 93, 94).

According to Isanga (2012) opponents of intercountry adoptions took note of a growing trend of celebrity intercountry adoptions from Africa and argue that the promise of a materially better life is not necessarily in the best interest of the child. Opponents also argue that prospective adoptive parents primarily seek to satisfy their self-interest and not necessarily the best interest of the adoptable child (Isanga, 2012: 245). In many 'sending countries' national pride has prompted calls to stop selling, or giving away, 'our most precious resources', and to claims that the country should 'take care of our own'. 'Receiving countries' have been responsive to these attacks (Bartholet 2007: 167).

There is little agreement on whether the liberal approach, on the one hand, or the restrictive approach, on the other, to intercountry adoption serves the child's 'best interests'. The 'best interests' of the child was central to court decision in the adoption of two children from Malawi by Madonna. Her first adoption with then husband Guy Ritchie, of David Banda[73] concluded without difficulty. The judge noted that Malawi's Adoption of Children Act, stated in Section 3(5):

> An adoption order shall not be made in favour of any applicant who is not resident in Malawi or in respect of any infant (child) who is not so resident.'

---

71 UNICEF Statement, 'Intercountry adoption' New York 2015. Available at www.unicef.org/media/intercountry-adoption (accessed 11 December 2019).
72 *A. D. & Another v. D. W. & Others* 2008 (3) SA 183 (CC) (S. Afr.); *Lakshmi Kant Pandey v. Union* of India, A. I. R. 1984 (S. C.) 469; in Re: CJ A Female Infant of C/o PO Box 30871, Chichiri, Blantyre 3 (Msca Adoption Appeal No. 28 of 2009) [2009] MWSC 1 (12 June 2009); Adoption case No. 2 of 2006 in the matter of the Adoption of Children Act (CAP.26:01) and in the matter of David Banda (a male infant) (Malawi High Court 243t) (28 May 2008).
73 In Re: Adoption of Children Act (Cap.26:01); In Re: David Banda (Adoption Cause No. 2 of 2006) (of) [2008] MWHC 243 (27 May 2008);

The Court noted that 'the bare fact is that the petitioners are not resident in Malawi and therefore that this is clearly a case of inter-country adoption. The question for consideration is whether the whole matter then collapses at that and the Court should not at all proceed to any other consideration.'[74] The Court proceeded to recognise that Malawi had ratified UNCRC in 1991 and was also a party to the African Charter on the Rights and Welfare of the Child (ACRWC).[75]

> It is therefore our solemn duty to comply with the provisions of the Conventions. If for a moment the argument that the Conventions are not part of our law found favour, then at least on part of the Court the duty is to interpret and apply our statutory law, so far as the spirit of the statute could allow, so that it is in conformity and not in conflict with our established obligation under these Conventions. And therefore that unless the statute, by its words and spirit compels our Courts to ignore international laws that is binding on us, the practice of our Courts is to avoid a clash and the way is to construe the domestic statute in such a way as to avoid breaching the obligation.[76]

The court observed that both the UNCRC and ACRWC recognised the 'best interests' of the child. David's father had given informed consent to the adoption. The requirement as to residence, be it important, was merely a means to an end. The judge stated he had no doubt in his mind that the 'end' is the best interest of the child.[77] Thus far it could safely be said the requirement of residence had served its purpose and that in its absence there were much more 'weighty considerations in the welfare of our needy children which in themselves would suffice and compel a decision in favour of an adoption by those that are not resident in this country.'[78]

However, reappearing as Madonna Louise Ciccone, her adoption of her second child from Malawi did not proceed as smoothly. She had applied to adopt a three-year-old girl, CJ (Chifundo Mercy James). CJ's mother had died shortly after giving birth, and the identity of the father was unknown.[79] CJ's relatives had placed her in an orphanage, but no family had applied to adopt her. However, the judge in this case took a different approach on requirement of residence. Madonna had jetted into the country during the weekend just days prior to the hearing of her application. The last time that she had been in the country was in 2008 at the time of the final adoption order for David Banda. The judge ruled that this would completely remove Madonna from the definition of a 'resident'. He also noted

---

74 Ibid., 15.
75 Ibid., 10.
76 Ibid., 10–11.
77 Ibid., 18
78 Iibid, 19
79 In Re: Adoption of Children Act CAP. 26:01; In Re: CJ (A Female Infant) of C/o Mr. Peter Baneti, Zomba (Adoption Case No. 1 of 2009) ((A Female Infant)) [2009] MWHC 3 (02 April 2009);

that intercountry adoptions should only be granted as a last resort, in accordance with article 24 of the UNCRC. He therefore declined to grant the application for the adoption. The judge noted:

> Clearly inter-country adoption is supposed to be the last resort alternative. In my internal struggle to come to some sane conclusion I asked myself a number of questions. Can CJ be placed in a foster or adoptive family? Incidentally the Act does not define what 'a foster or adoptive family' is. The answer therefore is neither here nor there. It is evident however, that CJ no longer is subject to the conditions of poverty of her place of birth as described by the Probation Officer since her admission at Kondanani Orphanage. In the circumstances can it be said that CJ cannot in any suitable manner be cared for in her country of origin? The answers to my questions are negative. In my view 'in any suitable manner' refers to the style of life of the indigenous or as close a life to the one that the child has been leading since birth. Presently CJ is in the care of Kondanani Orphanage and no evidence to the contrary has been brought as to the inability or unwillingness of Kondanani Orphanage to continue looking after CJ. This situation must be distinguished from the case of David who, according to facts on record, was to be returned to his biological father within a period of six months from the time that Mchinji Orphanage had admitted him.[80]

Madonna appealed. The Supreme Court of Malawi granted her application, noting that any person had a right to adopt under national legislation, that the Adoption of Children Act did not limit intercountry adoptions to instances of last resort, and that there was no conflict between the Malawi Adoption of Children Act, or the Constitution with either the UNCRC or the African Charter on the Rights and Welfare of the Child. In this case, Ms Ciccone (Madonna) was the only person who had sought to adopt CJ, and it was in the best interests of CJ to be adopted by a foreign parent rather than to be raised in an orphanage.[81]

> This is not to say, however, that our own Act is not adequate or comprehensive in dealing with adoption issues, far from it. All we are saying here is that when we look at our Constitution and the Act there is no clash or conflict whatsoever between what is provided for in our own laws and what is provided for in the various conventions that have been referred to us.[82]

However, a children's rights organisation, Child Rights International Network, commented that the decision was inconsistent with the UNCRC to the extent

---

80 Ibid., unnumbered.
81 Ibid.
82 Ibid.

that, despite the Court's finding to the contrary, Article 21 of the Convention *does* indeed specify that intercountry adoption should be considered only as a last resort 'if the child cannot be placed in a foster or an adoptive family or cannot in any suitable manner be cared for in the child's country of origin.' Nevertheless, CRIN noted, an intercountry adoption may be in the best interests of the child, and the Court was correct to assert the paramountcy of the child's best interest in such cases.[83]

Isanga (2012) notes that, strictly speaking, David was not an orphan. His father, a potato farmer, brought him to the orphanage because he was too poor to take care of him any more. Even with the consent of David's father, consideration of the best interests of the child demands that the Courts must first consider that a father's love is paramount and trumps the prospect of a baby being taken away to be raised in splendour (Isanga 2012)

Critics of intercountry adoptions point to reasons such as the lack of self-esteem of sending countries, sending off future generations, failed cultural adjustments, abuse and death of adoptees. Indeed, some transnational adoptions have been successful and ended in tragedy. A documentary, *Unwanted in America: The Shameful Side of International Adoption*, captures some of the poignant incidences of failed adoptions in the United States and the consequences. These had left both the children and parents in deep distress. In the event of the 'disruptions', the adopting parents would then 'advertise' the children for 'rehoming', resulting in the dissolution of the adoption.

The case of Hana Williams, the Ethiopian adoptee who died in the US in 2011 – about three years after the death of the Russian toddler, Dima – raised a lot of debate. US citizens Larry and Carri Williams adopted Hana together with her brother, Immanuel. The Williams's had seven biological children. Investigators discovered that Carri Williams had forced Hana out into the rain as punishment shortly before she died. While outside, hypothermia-induced confusion drove Hana to shed her clothes in the cold. She lost consciousness soon after, and died naked and face down in mud.

The courts concluded that Carri and Larry engaged in systematic punishment, deprivation and humiliation of the two children. Hana died of hypothermia brought on by malnutrition and being forced to remain outside on a cold rainy night after being accused of stealing food.[84] In the *State of Washington v. Larry Williams*, the court of appeal summarised the events of Hana's death as follows:

> On May 11, 2011, (Hanna Williams) H.W. was outside of the home for most of the day and night. Carrie told C.W. (H.W.'s sister who was fourteen at trial)

---

83 Child Rights International Network, case summary and comment: <https://archive.crin.org/en/library/legal-database/matter-adoption-children-act-chapter-2601-laws-malawi-and-matter-chifundo.html> (accessed 11 December 2019).

84 *State of Washington v. Carri Darlene Williams*, Court of Appeals-State of Washington Division One No. 71193-81-26 February 2015.

that H.W. had stolen food earlier in the day. The weather was rainy and cold. H. W. got cold so Carri ordered her to do jumping jacks and standing and sitting exercises to keep warm. When H.W. stopped, Carri had two of the boys go outside and hit H.W. on the legs to force her to do them. C.W. looked out the window to keep an eye on H.W. C.W. saw Carrie hit H.W. on the back of her legs with the switch. Later H.W. began to either throw herself, or fall, to the ground outside on multiple occasions. After that H.W. removed her clothing, and was nude, outside.

C.W. saw H.W. naked, lying face down near the patio and told Carri. HW (Hana's sister who was thirteen at trial) looked out the window and saw H.W. lying face down on the ground. C.W. and Carri went out to check on H.W.

They went in the house to get a sheet to cover her nudity then told the older brothers to go carry her in. Carri spoke with Larry while on his way home from work saying H.W. was acting up. Five to ten minutes later, Carri called Larry saying that H.W. was unresponsive and not breathing. Larry told Carri to call 911. Carri called 911 and started CPR. When H. W. arrived at the hospital she had an abnormal heart rhythm called ventricular fibrillation.

A normal heart rhythm was never restored. Contributing causes to her death by hypothermia included malnourishment. At death H.W. was abnormally thin. She was 78 pounds and 5 feet tall. She had marks to her body consistent with being beaten with implements.[85]

Carri Williams was convicted by a jury of homicide and sentenced to 37 years. She was also sentenced to 123 months for the assault of Hana's brother, Immanuel. Larry was convicted of first-degree manslaughter. He was jailed for 28 years. This case is considered to have influenced the Ethiopian government to revise its adoption law. The Russians also later introduced the Federal law of Russian Federation no. 272-FZ of 2012-12-28, which, among other things, banned adoptions of Russian children by US citizens, amid reports of deaths of other Russian adoptees.

In another case, US citizen Torry Hansen adopted seven-year-old Artem Vladimirovich Saveliev, from Russia, whom she had renamed Justin Hansen. A few months later, after experiencing difficulties with the child, she placed the child on a one-way flight to Russia and sought to annul the adoption. The adoption agency that brokered the adoption filed this lawsuit against the respondent in juvenile court, seeking child support and alleging that the child was dependent and neglected. Lower courts had ruled that she was responsible for child support payments to her adopted son.[86] However, Hansen disagreed and appealed. Case Study 7.2 provides extracts from the appeal decision. The case shows the role of adoption agencies and, more importantly, some of the problems that might arise from intercountry adoption.

85 *State of Washington v. Larry Williams*, Court of Appeals-State of Washington Division One No. 71112-1-I 6 August 2015.
86 See *Hansen v. Hansen*, No. 12062 (17th Jud. Dist. Tenn. May 17, 2012).

Case study 7.2

No. M2013–02517-COA-R3-JV
Court of Appeals of Tennessee at Nashville
In re Justin H.
Decided May 29, 2015

The child at issue in this lawsuit, Petitioner/Appellee Justin A. H., was born in Russia in April 2002. In 2009, Defendant/Appellant Torry Hansen sought to adopt Justin through Russian adoption procedures. The World Association for Children and Parents ("WACAP"), based in the State of Washington, was the adoption and placement agency that processed Justin's adoption. As part of the adoption process, WACAP and Ms. Hansen entered into a 'Child Acceptance and Placement & Post-Placement Agreement' ("Placement Agreement"). In the Placement Agreement, WACAP agreed to provide Ms. Hansen with all of the information it had about the child, but it did not 'guarantee the present or future mental or physical health of the child(ren)' In turn, Ms. Hansen agreed to "remain financially responsible for all costs of care for the child(ren)" if the child were removed from Ms. Hansen's home. Ms. Hansen agreed to 'reimburse WACAP for any and all costs incurred by WACAP for the care of the child after removal from [Ms. Hansen's] home.' On September 18, 2009, Ms. Hansen officially adopted Justin in proceedings before the Primorsky Krai Court of the Russian Federation. By virtue of the adoption, Justin became a United States citizen. Ms. Hansen then returned to the United States with the child to live in Bedford County, Tennessee.

Not long after Ms. Hansen returned to Tennessee with Justin, she began experiencing behavioral difficulties with the child. In April 2010, Ms. Hansen placed the child on a one-way flight back to Russia. On the transnational flight, the child was unaccompanied and had no provisions and no luggage besides a backpack. Ms. Hansen pinned a note to the child's backpack addressed to the Ministry of Education in Moscow. The note described Justin as "mentally unstable" and asserted that Ms. Hansen was "misled by the Russian Orphanage workers and director regarding his mental stability and other issues."

For those reasons, Ms. Hansen said, she no longer wanted to parent the child. In the note, Ms. Hansen indicated that she was "returning [the child] to [the Ministry of Education's] guardianship and would like the adoption disannulled [*sic*]." After the child was delivered to the Ministry of Education, he was placed in a Russian children's home/orphanage.

On May 11, 2010, WACAP, the adoption agency that brokered the adoption, filed this lawsuit against Ms. Hansen in the circuit court of Bedford County, alleging that the child was dependent and neglected and seeking the appointment of a guardian and a guardian ad litem for the purposes of seeking child support. The lawsuit generated widespread media attention, and Ms. Hansen in particular was vilified. On May 19, 2010, shortly after she was served with process in the circuit court lawsuit, Ms. Hansen relocated from Tennessee to an undisclosed location in California.

The trial court found that Ms. Hansen was $8,000 in arrears as of September 2013. Therefore, it appears that she was current in her child support obligation only through January 2013. The record on appeal does contain an affidavit from the court clerk's office indicating that the clerk received checks (cheques)in February and April 2013 from Ms. Hansen's mother. The checks contained lengthy diatribes covering the front and back of the checks, alleging that the child support order was obtained by fraud, illegal and void. The clerk forwarded the first check to counsel for the petitioners but returned the second check to Ms. Hansen's mother. The clerk's letters instructed her to reissue a check without lengthy writings that could cause delays in processing and also noted that the February 2013 order required child support checks to be mailed to counsel for the petitioners rather than the court clerk. According to the clerk's affidavit, she did not receive any more checks from Ms. Hansen. This limited evidence does not lead us to conclude that the trial court erred in finding that Ms. Hansen willfully violated the court's orders regarding the payment of child support.

CONCLUSION
[. . .] the decision of the chancery court is hereby affirmed and remanded for further proceedings. Costs of this appeal are taxed to the appellant, Torry Hansen, and her surety, for which execution may issue if necessary.

However, these incidences need to be counterbalanced with successful adoptions (Compton 2016). It is undeniable that intercountry adoption retains the potential to serve the best interests of children in certain circumstances (Isanga 2012). Emphasising the abuses rather than the benefits of intercountry adoption amounts to scapegoating for lack of effort on the regulatory plane. A total ban or suspension of intercountry adoptions amounts to an abdication that would negatively impact the best interests of otherwise adoptable children. Bartholet observed that international adoption provided homes for roughly 40,000 children annually, including more than 20,000 homes in the United States (2011). Compton cautions on the difference between anecdotes and systematic research. She asserts: 'In my experience, only one stereotype about adoptive parents holds true, and that is that they are tenacious fighters for the rights of "their" children' (2016: 10).

7.7 Concluding remarks

Despite the attempts to provide better international legal regulation of intercountry adoption there are remaining concerns about the success of the overall project of international adoptions. Smolin comments:

> The Hague Convention was a response to the chaotic, corrupt, and abusive practices endemic to pre-Hague intercountry adoptions. The purpose of the Convention was to engender an orderly, ethical, intercountry adoption system free of child trafficking. Adoption advocates also saw the Hague Convention as providing a greater measure of legitimacy for intercountry adoption than exists under the Convention on the Rights of the Child. Seventeen years after the creation of the Hague Convention, the Convention thus far has failed to meet its goals. Child laundering scandals have continued to arise in the Hague era in sending countries such as Cambodia, Chad, China, Guatemala, Haiti, India, Liberia, Nepal, Samoa, and Vietnam. Many potential sending countries, particularly in Africa and Latin America, have decided to close themselves to all or almost all intercountry adoptions, in significant part based on concern over abusive practices. Years of determined cheerleading by the adoption community have failed to cleanse intercountry adoption from its associations with scandal, corruption, trafficking, and profiteering. The boom in intercountry adoption that accompanied the initial decade after the creation of the Hague Convention is now abating, with further declines anticipated. The legitimacy that intercountry adoption sought has been diminished by a sense of lawlessness, despite the extensive regulation and bureaucratic procedures which often accompany it.
>
> (Smolin 2010: 493)

At the core of the debate on intercountry adoption is the 'best interests' principle. There are no easy answers to how such interests can be served as this chapter has shown. Some adoptions have ended in tragedy while some adoptees have failed to adapt to new families and cultural environments. Yet, it would be painting a false picture to suggest all adoptions end in failure. Some children have been plucked from orphanages to experience better lives with adopted parents. While there is consensus on the need to uphold the principle of the 'best interests' of the child, there is a lack of consensus on how, precisely, those best interests are to be decided. It would appear that the best interests of the child in intercountry adoption can only be decided on a case-by-case basis through scrupulous assessments of the benefits and disadvantages.

Chapter 8

Child sexual exploitation

8.1 Introduction

It has been remarked that an outside observer would believe that the issue of child sexual abuse and exploitation is a modern concept (Phoenix and Oerton 2005: 52), yet we know this is not true. The sexual abuse and exploitation of children has occurred throughout human history. However, it was not until the latter years of the 20th century that the issue of child sexual exploitation began to be taken seriously at a policy level in many countries, and certainly not until the 1990s that it began to feature notably at an international level. The emergence of the Internet (Chapter 4) has exacerbated concerns on the use of the digital space to facilitate sex crimes against children. This chapter analyses how international law seeks to prevent the sexual exploitation and abuse of children.

8.1.1 What is child sexual exploitation?

The first issue is to identify what sexual exploitation is. A variety of terms can be used in this area, but the two most often used are 'sexual abuse' and 'sexual exploitation'. There is disagreement as to what these terms mean and whether they are interchangeable. Historically, some authors believe that each term is the equivalent of the other (Kempe 1978: 382) and it will be seen later that the *UN Convention on the Rights of the Child*[1] does not differentiate between the terms: see the text of article 34 in section 3.7.6.3 in this book. However, some believe that a distinction can, and arguably should, be drawn. Van Bueren argues that abuse is the wider term and that 'all forms of exploitation are intrinsically abusive', although she then purports to draw a distinction between them by stating 'the distinguishing feature of sexual exploitation is that it generally involves notions of commercial gain' (Van Bueren 1994a: 52). Others would undoubtedly contest the argument that exploitation necessarily involves commercialisation, and Ost suggests that a more appropriate definition is 'a situation or context in which an individual takes unfair advantage of someone else for his own ends' (Ost 2009: 139). At the heart of this concept is Ost's belief, in the context of child pornography and child solicitation (and it is submitted that this applies equally to child prostitution and child trafficking), that

---

1 Opened for signature 20 November 1989, 1577 UNTS 3 (entered into force 2 September 1990).

exploitation involves an imbalance of power or abuse of a position of vulnerability (Ost 2009: 130). If Ost is correct, and it is submitted she is, then the commercial element sought by Van Bueren is unnecessary. There has undoubtedly been an expansion of the discourse since the turn of the 21st century and this has largely rendered any definition of 'child sexual exploitation' as vague and ambiguous (Asquith and Turner 2008; Melrose 2012). This has led to a certain elasticity, which means that a variety of situations and behaviours can be interpreted as 'child sexual exploitation' (Melrose 2012).

The natural meanings of the words 'exploitation' and 'abuse' would appear to confirm that there is a distinction between them and that exploitation is the wider term. A dictionary definition of 'exploit' is 'make use unfairly; benefit unjustly from the work or actions of' something.[2] This supports the definition adopted by Ost, and it is submitted that reference to unfairness and unjustness also implicitly support the notion of vulnerability, something particularly important in the context of the sexual exploitation of a child. Abuse is defined, *inter alia*, as 'treat with cruelty or violence; assault sexually; cruel and violent treatment'. While there is undoubtedly some overlap, it would seem that sexual abuse could be considered to be the direct inappropriate sexual assault on a child, whereas exploitation includes those who do not directly assault the child but use the child sexually for their own (material) benefit.

Child sexual abuse and exploitation remain inherently secretive phenomena and this causes significant difficulties in estimating their prevalence in society (Johnson 2004: 462). This is particularly true at the international level. As will be seen, international law commonly tackles the commercial sexual exploitation of children and indeed it has been noted that prior to the appearance of the *Convention on the Rights of the Child*[3] in 1989 sexual abuse rather than exploitation of a child never featured in international law (Van Bueren 1994: 46). Arguably, the actions of the international legal order during the era of the League of Nations challenges this assertion. The activities of the League in relation to children have been discussed in sections 1.2.1 and 3.2 in this book; however, it is worth briefly mentioning the *International Convention for the Suppression of Traffic in Women and Children 1921*. The significance of the 1921 Convention with regards to children has been noted, adopting a broad and inclusive approach to 'child trafficking'. Although, sexual abuse does not feature explicitly, it is implied through the activities of the League, which closely associated the 'exploitation for immoral purposes', legal age of marriage and the production of 'obscene publications', with the trafficking of children (Faulkner 2019b).

Although international law does not offer a distinct definition of the sexual exploitation of children, some commentators have asserted that the discourse of child sexual exploitation 'is produced by and reproduced by the dominant discourse of childhood in the West, and more specifically, a discourse of female childhood in which female sexuality is constructed from within a sexual double

---

2 *Concise Oxford English Dictionary*.
3 Opened for signature 20 November 1989, 1577 UNTS 3 (entered into force 2 September 1990).

standard' (Melrose and Pearce 2013). In spite of what Melrose terms the 'pretentions to gender neutrality' the imagined child of the discourse of commercial sexual exploitation is invariably female and therefore young men/boys are largely rendered invisible by it[4] (Dennis 2008; Melrose 2010).

The focus on commercial sexual exploitation in international law is perhaps understandable, as it has become a lucrative and global enterprise. In the early 2000s, a single child pornography website – 'Landslide Productions' – had receipts of $1.4 million per month (Taylor and Quayle 2003: 5) and this was by no means the only commercial child pornography website. The global crackdown on such illicit activity has resulted in it becoming more difficult to trace, due to use of the dark web and cryptocurrency payments. In October 2019, reports emerged of a US/Korean 'bust' breaking up 'the world's largest markets of child pornography, a crime that is proliferating at the furious pace with the rise of crypto currency and encrypted online content.'[5] As part of this single operation, 377 people were arrested in 38 countries around the world, including site users in the UK, Germany, Brazil, Saudi Arabia, the UAE and the US. 23 child victims were also rescued.[6] The available details of this global bust demonstrate the emergence of a globalised phenomena in which the use of the dark web renders state borders meaningless. In the last decade, a number of initiatives[7] have been implemented to tackle the emergence of the online and/or virtual commercial sexual exploitation of children, with the current Special Rapporteur (Maud de Boer-Buquicchio) prioritising the issue of sexual exploitation of children and Information and Communication Technologies (ICTs) since her appointment in 2014.[8]

8.1.2 Emerging issues: the trafficking of children and 'modern slavery'

Human trafficking has a lengthy legal and political history which distinguishes it from many contemporary international legal issues (Gallagher 2011: 13). The term 'trafficking' in relation to human beings first appeared in the early

---

4 For an example of the invisible status of boys in the discourse see initiatives such as the 'Together for Girls Iniative to End Sexual Violence <www.togetherforgirls.org/> (accessed 9 September 2019).
5 Bloomberg: David Voreacos (2019) 'U.S., South Korea Bust Giant Child Porn Site by Following a Bitcoin Trail', Bloomberg, 16 October 2019, <www.bloomberg.com/news/articles/2019-10-16/giant-child-porn-site-is-busted-as-u-s-follows-bitcoin-trail> (accessed 29 October 2019).
6 Ibid.
7 See further the Virtual Global Taskforce (VGT) <https://virtualglobaltaskforce.com> (accessed 9 September 2019); Global Alliance against Child Sexual Abuse Online (launched 5 December 2012) by the European Commission and the US – aiming to raise global standards and unify efforts to effectively combat online sexual crimes against children <https://ec.europa.eu/home-affairs/what-we-do/policies/organized-crime-and-human-trafficking/global-alliance-against-child-abuse_en> (accessed 9 September 2019); #WePROTECT Children Online Initiative <www.weprotect.org/> (accessed 9 September 2019).
8 See further Report of the Special Rapporteur on the sale of children, child prostitution and child pornography, Maud de Boer-Buquicchio, Human Rights council, 28th session, A/HRC/28/56 (22 December 2014).

20th century[9] and was connected to the prevalent issue of the time – 'white slavery'.[10] A full critical analysis of trafficking[11] and an in-depth view of the historical evolution of trafficking under international law both fall outside of the parameters of this chapter.[12] It is, however, important to acknowledge that the historical evolution of the international legal definition provides a unique insight into how ideas, beliefs and assumptions have shaped and informed the way that individuals, states and the international community have perceived and responded to trafficking (Gallagher 2011: 13).

Human trafficking is as profitable as child pornography, with the suggestion that the trafficking of persons is now worth more than the smuggling of drugs and arms (Kelly 2002: 13), and the ILO estimating in its last report that $150 billion in illegal profits are generated annually from this (2014). Trafficking is perpetually presented and often 'discussed as a problem of epic proportions that requires urgent attention, however the prevalence of trafficking is notoriously difficult to verify' (Kotiswaran 2017). While it has been acknowledged that, given the nature of the deed, it is difficult to be precise as to the number of persons trafficked for the purposes of sexual exploitation (Riiskjær and Gallagher 2008: 5), the United Nations Office on Drugs and Crime (UNODC) *Trafficking in Persons Report* 2018 indicated that the vast majority of detected victims of trafficking have suffered sexual exploitation.[13] Savona and Stefanizzi observed that the available information on trafficking is 'fragmentary, heterogeneous, difficult to acquire, uncorrelated and often outdated' (Savona and Stefanizzi 2007), providing an insight into the contested space surrounding the quantification of human trafficking.[14] However, in tackling the issue, quantification becomes integral to the development of safeguards and solutions. The International Labour Organization (ILO) estimated in 2016 that approximately 29.4 million people were in forced labour, of whom up to a quarter were children[15] (see also 5.1.6 in this book). It is unclear what this estimate accounts for, as the subversive nature of trafficking and sexual exploitation makes accurate quantification almost impossible. A report from the Special Rapporteur further stressed that 'exploitation through

---

9 The first Convention against White slavery was adopted in 1904 and sought to suppress the 'criminal traffic' of women and girls compulsively procured for 'immoral purposes'. See further Doezema 2010.
10 The terms 'white slavery' and 'white slave traffic' are frequently placed in quotation marks to reflect disquiet among scholars. The term 'White Slave Traffic' was considered troublesome during the early 20th century, today it is offensive and is clearly objectionable on a number of grounds, most obviously its overt racism. For further discussion on this, see Allain 2012.
11 See, for example, Doezema 2010; Sanghera 2012.
12 For an overview of the historical evolution of human trafficking, see Gallagher 2011, chapter 1. For an introduction to the development of a legal response to child trafficking, see Faulkner 2019a.
13 United Nations Publications, Sales No. E.19.IV.2, (2018) Preface 3.
14 See further: Kerry 2017; Kotiswaran 2017.
15 Forced Labour, Modern Slavery and Human Trafficking: Facts and Figures <www.ilo.org/global/topics/forced-labour/lang--en/index.htm> (accessed 29 October 2019).

new technologies and in particular through the 'dark web' has further complicated the collection of data'.[16]

The previous edition of this text asserted, '[t]rafficking is similarly lucrative and has become a modern-day slave trade' (Buck 2014: 354). The conflation between trafficking and slavery has continued to gain traction, with a vast metropolis of international, regional and national initiatives to address the 'modern slavery' (Segrave et al. 2018). However, the critical modern slavery discourse challenges the dominant rhetoric of human trafficking and modern slavery as a contemporary scourge.[17]

Chuang has argued that;

> Each of modern-day slavery's purported component practices – slavery, trafficking and forced labour – is separately defined under international law, subject to separate legal frameworks and overseen by separate international institutions. Conflating trafficking and forced labour with the far more narrowly defined (and extreme) practice of 'slavery' – however rhetorically effective – is not only legally inaccurate, but it also risks undermining effective application of the relevant legal regimes.
>
> (Chuang 2014: 146)

Moreover, Weitzer (2014) and Chuang (2014) have observed that the conflation between slavery and trafficking has occured in order to acknowledge other forms of exploitation that have been missed or excluded in existing international legal frameworks and international anti-trafficking policy regimes (Segrave et al. 2018: 5). The competition between the category of human trafficking and the emerging catch all term 'modern slavery' (O'Connell Davidson 2015; Chuang 2014) has been described as a 'distraction' (Segrave et al. 2018: 9).

A child subject to sexual exploitation is not able to exercise free control over its activities. An adult can, in some situations, exercise a degree of choice over the activities that they participate in. While the common perception of trafficking is based on coercion, trickery, or abduction it is clear that this is not necessarily always the case, with some women choosing to migrate to work in the sex industry (Melrose and Barrett 2006: 114; Kempadoo et al. 2012). Similarly, it can be said that some adults make the choice to enter the sex industry as a sex worker[18] or choose to be involved in pornography. However, while some argue that adult women have the ability to make this choice – although it should be noted that those who argue that the sex industry is about the subjugation of women

---

16 United Nations Special Rapporteur on the Sale of Children, Child Prostitution and Child Pornography (2016) '25 years fighting the sale and sexual exploitation of children: addressing new challenges': 2.
17 See further: O'Connell Davidson (2015); Kotiswaran (2017); Bunting and Quirk (2017).
18 Collectives such as the International Union of Sex Workers (<www.iusw.org>) campaign for the right of adults to join a legalised sex work industry.

fiercely resist such an argument – a child does not have this choice, nor is he or she equipped to make the choice (Pearce 2013). So what about children? The paradigm of human trafficking assumes that no parent would choose or allow a child to migrate for work. Moreover, that no minor is capable of making such a choice independently. Poverty, ignorance, trickery and 'the corruption of tradition' are frequently identified as the agency-denying dominant cause factors that drive trafficking (Howard 2017). Under the Trafficking Protocol, the legal definition of child trafficking is different from adult trafficking. It is not necessary to show that the child was deceived or coerced, the trafficking of children omits the requirement of the means element and child trafficking therefore only requires that the action and purpose (of the three elements of the definition) are present.

A child has the right not to be sexually exploited. At the first 'World Congress against Commercial Sexual Exploitation of Children'[19] in Stockholm it was stated: 'The commercial sexual exploitation of children can result in serious, lifelong, even life threatening consequences for the physical, psychological, spiritual, moral and social development of children' (First World Congress 1996: 9).

The consequences for trafficking and prostitution include threats of violence (including threats to kill), pregnancy (including forcible terminations) and the contracting of sexually transmitted diseases including AIDS. A premium can be charged for children and for not using condoms, the latter meaning that the risks are greater. The consequences of being involved in child pornography are similar. Where penetrative activity is being filmed the same risks above are present but, regardless of what type of pornography is filmed, it becomes a permanent record of the activity. The impact of the digital age has been discussed comprehensively in Chapter 4. Research suggests that once an image has been placed on the internet it is almost impossible for it to be recovered as it is quickly downloaded, mirrored and disseminated (Taylor and Quayle 2003: 24). The impact on the child of this is that they fear, for the rest of their lives, that the photograph will be seen by someone known to them who may believe that they were willingly involved in the activity rather than being exploited (Palmer 2005), potentially leading to psychological difficulties. It has been cogently argued that child pornography can amount to the revictimisation of a child who has been sexually assaulted (Taylor and Quayle 2003: 31).

There is an inherent power imbalance between the adult photographer and the child (Taylor and Quayle 2003: 4), and the status of a child as a 'minor' makes this exploitative. The same logic can be found with the other forms of commercial

---

19 This event as heralded as 'ground-breaking' by the current Special Rapporteur (Maud de Boer-Buquicchio) and was followed by two more congresses in Yokohama in 2001 and Rio de Janeiro in 2008. However, the Special Rapporteur has also asserted that 'the numerous political commitments made by participating States have remained mostly unfulfilled. There is an urgent need for a common strong political will to move forward towards implementation through effective and sustained allocation of the necessary resources', United Nations Special Rapporteur on the Sale of Children, Child Prostitution and Child Pornography (2016): V.

child sexual exploitation and it is this, together with the negative consequences of involvement, which requires action to be taken.

8.2 International action

The Special Rapporteur has asserted that at the 'international level, there is potential for concrete action with the multiplication of cooperation initiatives'. She further stated that '[o]ngoing initiatives and alliances at the international level, such as the Virtual Global Taskforce, the Global Alliance against child sexual abuse online and the *WePROTECT* initiative need to be more inclusive and ensure further coordination and cooperation amongst themselves.'[20] Therefore, before turning to examine the principal international legislation that exists in this area it is worth pausing to note the bodies that have a mandate to combat child sexual exploitation.

8.2.1 Global bodies

The final decade of the 20th century led to the issue of child sexual abuse and exploitation beginning to feature at the international level. In the broader policy context, the United Nations and its agencies began to take seriously the issue of child sexual exploitation and they began to assist non-governmental organisations (NGOs) who sought to work directly with victims and agencies trying to combat the sexual exploitation of children. Perhaps the most notable NGO to be set up was ECPAT ('Ending Child Prostitution and Trafficking'[21]), an international organisation that was established in 1990 by a series of researchers. Quickly ECPAT began to formalise and by 1996 it was acting in partnership with the United Nations. It remains an independent organisation (with its headquarters based in Bangkok, Thailand) but it has a close relationship with global, regional and local governments. At governmental level there are two bodies of particular note: the G7 and the United Nations.

8.2.1.1 The Group of 7

The G7 (formerly G8) owes its origins to an economic summit in 1975 attended by the then five richest countries (France, Germany, Japan, the United Kingdom and the United States of America). By the end of the decade the group became the G7 with the addition of Italy and Canada, but during the 1980s and 1990s the Soviet Union (and then Russia after the dissolution of the USSR) was invited to

---

20 31st session of the Human Rights Council, 8 March 2016, <www.ohchr.org/EN/NewsEvents/Pages/DisplayNews.aspx?NewsID=19975&LangID=E> (accessed 9 September 2019).
21 Originally ECPAT meant 'Ending Child Prostitution in the Asian Territories': see <www.ecpat.net/> (accessed 29 September 2019).

attend the meetings, which had begun to stray beyond mere economics and into more geopolitical issues. In 1998 the group formally changed its name from the G7 to the G8 until the suspension of Russia over the illegal annexation of Crimea in March 2014, the influential bloc has reverted to its pre-1980s membership.[22]

In 2001 the G8 established the Lyon/Roma group that was designed to tackle international crime. A sub-group of the Lyon/Roma group was specifically tasked to examine the issue of sexual exploitation, and by 2003 a strategy was created (G8 2003: paras 15–17). In 2009, following a global symposium on the issue of child pornography, the G8 issued a ministerial declaration on 30 May in Rome. This declaration reaffirmed their commitment to tackling child pornography, and stated: 'Effective international cooperation would be achieved through a wider membership in multilateral task forces, sharing specialised software and closely coordinating on-line undercover investigations and other international law enforcement operations' (G8 2009: 6).

This was followed in 2013 by a ministerial declaration on combating child sexual abuse during conflicts, including the use of rape as a weapon and the use of children as sex slaves. The G8 reaffirmed that sexual violence in armed conflict could amount to a war crime and that the G8 accepted responsibility, in part, for ensuring that such crimes were prosecuted. They also committed to assisting victims of armed conflict and working to provide more long-term support (G8 2013: 2).

These statements demonstrate how the G7 previously evolved a policy role on tackling child sexual exploitation and, while it has not yet produced any treaties, its declaration arguably reaffirms the action that it has committed to in the various international instruments discussed in the following sections. However it is important that these are not mere words. The G7 includes the three permanent members of the UN Security Council and so they have influence that should be used to tackle child sexual exploitation at an international policy level. It is also important that they themselves show a lead, something that does not always seem to occur (see the comments below in respect of the UN Special Rapporteur).

8.2.1.2 United Nations

The principal global player in this area is the United Nations. The final decades of the 20th century led to the issue of child sexual abuse and exploitation beginning to feature on the United Nations global agenda, particularly through the

---

22 Russia was one of the four permanent UN Security Council members and has recently announced its intention to leave permanently and prioritise the G20. The influence or prominence of the bloc has recently come under scrutiny; arguably with the exclusion of Russia the group has become more homogenous. However, any organisation that excludes China needs to reflect upon its relevance to the global stage.

United Nations Children's Fund (UNICEF) (see section 2.4.1.2 in this book), the United Nations Human Rights Council (UNHRC) (section 2.5.1.1) and the UN Economic and Social Council (ECOSOC) (section 2.4.1). The United Nations also works closely with national governments, regional groupings and NGOs to fund and operate programmes that are designed to provide real assistance to victims of child sexual exploitation. The continued focus upon sexual exploitation and abuse is evidenced within the UN Secretary-General's report in 2017 on Special measures for protection from sexual exploitation and abuse, which called for new efforts to end abuses and 'bring this scourge to a heel'. The strategy placed an emphasis upon a system-wide approach that puts victims first, ends impunity, engages civil society and other external partners and finally raises awareness of the issue.[23]

What are arguably the four most notable initiatives of the United Nations will all be discussed in this chapter. Three are legislative: the first is the *Convention on the Rights of the Child* of 1989, which is discussed throughout this book but is considered later in the specific context of the sexual exploitation of children; the second instrument is the *Optional Protocol to the Convention on the Rights of the Child on the Sale of Children, Child Prostitution and Child Pornography of 2000*[24] (OPSC) (section 3.6.1). This has quickly established itself as the leading instrument specifically designed to tackle forms of child sexual exploitation, and it will also be discussed further below. The third instrument is the *Optional Protocol to the Convention against Transnational Organized Crime to Prevent, Suppress and Punish Trafficking in Persons Especially Women and Children*.[25] The near universal acceptance of the first international legal definition of trafficking as established by the Trafficking Protocol has not seen a decline in debates over what constitutes trafficking, nor has it proven sufficient to assure a uniform understanding of where the boundaries lie, particularly in regards to criminal justice practice (Gallagher 2017: 85).

The fourth initiative is the establishment of the *Special Rapporteur on the sale of children, child prostitution and child pornography*.[26] Established in 1990, following a

---

23 UN General Assembly, Report of the Secretary-General 2017, *Special Measures for Protection from Sexual Exploitation and Abuse: a new approach*, 71st session (28 February 2017).
24 25 May 2000, 2171 UNTS 227 (entered into force 18 January 2002).
25 The Protocol was adopted by resolution A/RES/55/25, 15 November 2000, 55th session of the General Assembly (entered into force 25 December 2003)
26 See the website of the Special Rapporteur at: <www.ohchr.org/en/issues/children/pages/childrenindex.aspx> (accessed 29 October 2019). Previous mandate holders are Mr Vitit Muntarbhorn (1991–4), Ms Ofelia Calcetas-Santos (1994–2001), Mr Juan Miguel Petit (2001–8), Ms Najat M'jid Maalla (Morocco 2008–14) and Ms Maud de Boer-Buquicchio was appointed Special Rapporteur in May 2014, with her mandate renewed for an additional three-year term in March 2017.

resolution of the UN Commission on Human Rights,[27] the mandate has been continuously renewed. The mandate[28] includes:

- To consider matters relating to the sale of children, child prostitution and child pornography;
- To continue, through continuous and constructive dialogue with Governments, intergovernmental organisations and civil society . . . the analysis of the root causes of the sale of children, child prostitution and child pornography; addressing all the contributing factors, especially the demand factor;
- To identify and make concrete recommendations on preventing and combating new patterns of sale of children, child prostitution and child pornography;
- To continue . . . to promote comprehensive strategies and measures on the prevention of sale of children, child prostitution and child pornography.[29]

In order to discharge her mandate, the Special Rapporteur will visit a number of countries (Buck 2008: 169) in order to have policy-level discussions and consider how the States parties are discharging their obligations under OPSC. The Special Rapporteur produces an annual report to the Human Rights Council (e.g. Boer-Buquicchio 2019),[30] which in turn reports to the UN General Assembly.

Buck, while observing the valuable work that the Special Rapporteur performs, notes that a difficulty is that the office is under-resourced (2008: 170). The mandate of the Special Rapporteur has been underfunded since its creation, and has operated without a specific budget from the Human Rights Council.[31] This is despite the fact that the mandate passed by the Human Rights Council requests the Secretary-General of the United Nations and the High Commissioner for Human Rights to 'provide all the human, technical and financial assistance' needed by the Special Rapporteur.[32] The under-resourcing of the office means that the Special Rapporteur is limited in the amount of research that can be commissioned and visits conducted. Ideally it would be beneficial for there to be an 'Office of the Special Rapporteur' that would employ a (small) number of staff to also conduct visits, commission and interpret research. Instead, a single mandate

---

27 UN Commission on Human Rights, resolution 1990/68 (7 March 1990). The mandate was renewed by: UN Human Rights Council, *Rights of the Child: a holistic approach to the protection and promotion of the rights of children working and/or living on the street*: Resolution 16/12, UN Doc. A/HRC/RES/16/12 (3 May 2011).
28 Human Rights Council, *Mandate of the Special Rapporteur on the sale of children, child prostitution and child pornography*, Resolution 7/13, 40th meeting (27 March 2008).
29 Ibid., para. 2.
30 Report of the Special Rapporteur on the Sale of Children, Child Prostitution and Child Pornography (2019) A/HRC/40/51, *Sale and Sexual Exploitation of Children in the Context of Sports*.
31 United Nations Special Rapporteur on the Sale of Children, Child Prostitution and Child Pornography (2016) *25 Years Fighting the Sale and Sexual Exploitation of Children: addressing new challenges*: V.
32 Human Rights Council, *Mandate of the Special Rapporteur on the sale of children, child prostitution and child pornography*, Resolution 7/13, 40th meeting (27 March 2008), para. 5.

holder is in place and, while her role is invaluable, it does mean that its use is somewhat limited.

Another problem with the Special Rapporteur is the extent to which it can be said that countries cooperate with her office. Despite States being requested to cooperate with the Special Rapporteur it does not appear that this always occurs. For example, two reports from the former Special Rapporteur Maalla have examined two important themes (child sexual exploitation following national disasters (Maalla 2011) and child sex tourism (Maalla 2012). Both thematic reports involved evidence gathering. The Special Rapporteur sent a questionnaire to all (193) member States of the UN and yet only 23 States responded to the 2011 request (Maalla 2011:4) and 35 for the 2012 report (Maalla 2012:4). Of this latter report – which concerned an issue of child sexual exploitation where citizens of developed countries are responsible for the majority of the abuse – it is notable that only two members of the former G8 (Germany and Russia) responded, the other six members did not. This perhaps demonstrates a lack of support by leading countries in supporting the work of the Special Rapporteur in discharging her mandate, something that is to be regretted. Developed countries, especially leading ones such as those belonging to the G7 or G20, should be setting an example and dismissing requests from the Special Rapporteur to identify an evidence base does not do this.

8.2.1.3 Global Sustainable Development Goals

In 2015, the adoption of the 17 Sustainable Development Goals (SDGs) set a renewed development framework, the 2030 Agenda for Sustainable Development. Improving capacity to deliver reliable data and statistics plays a major role in this context. Each Goal includes indicators to measure improvements towards the agreed targets. SDG goal 5 aims to eliminate all forms of violence against all women and girls in the public and private spheres, including trafficking and sexual and other types of exploitation, as well as to eliminate all harmful practices, such as child, early and forced marriage and female genital mutilation.[33] Goal 8 calls for immediate and effective measures to eradicate forced labour, end modern slavery and human trafficking and secure the prohibition and elimination of the worst forms of child labour, including recruitment and use of child soldiers, and by 2025 end child labour in all its forms. Goal 16 aims to end abuse, exploitation, trafficking and all forms of violence against and torture of children. SDG indicator 16.2 specifically calls upon Member States to end abuse, exploitation, trafficking and all forms of violence and torture against children. Moreover, indicator 16.2.2 requires Member States to measure the number of victims of human trafficking

---

33 The Special Rapporteur reports on combating and preventing the sale and sexual exploitation of children through the implementation of the Sustainable Development Goals from a child rights perspective to the General Assembly (A/73/174 and Corr.1) (17 July 2018).

per 100,000 population, by sex, age and form of exploitation. In order to report on this indicator, Member States must gather trafficking data using defined methodologies to estimate the total number of trafficking victims.

8.2.2 Regional bodies

It is not only global bodies that have a mandate to combat child sexual exploitation; some regional groupings also operate in this area. Regional mandates exist in part as a method of strengthening the work undertaken at global level but also to demonstrate a regional commitment to tackling this problem. The key difference between the global and regional mandates is that the regional ones, as their name suggests, ordinarily involve localised action. The mandate does demonstrate the political will to work towards combating child sexual exploitation. Examples of regional instruments include the Organisation of African Unity's (OAU) *African Charter on the Rights and Welfare of the Child*[34] and the South Asian Association for Regional Co-operation (SAARC[35]) *Convention on Preventing and Combating Trafficking in Women and Children for Prostitution*[36] of 2002 which attempted to address one particular form of commercial sexual exploitation.

Perhaps the most active geopolitical region in seeking to combat child sexual exploitation is Europe. As is well known, there are two principal groupings within Europe; the Council of Europe (which consists of 47 member States) and the European Union (EU) (which has 27 member States). There are other groupings (e.g. the 'Council of Baltic Sea States'[37]), but these tend to work in conjunction with both of the other bodies.

The Council of Europe is best known for its work in human rights, particularly the *European Convention on Human Rights*[38] (ECHR), but it has, in recent years, been active in seeking to combat exploitative actions against individuals, including the

---

34 OAU, *African Charter on the Rights and Welfare of the Child*, 11 July 1990, CAB/LEG/24.9/49 (1990), entered into force 29 November 1999. 49 of the 55 African States had ratified/acceded to this treaty as at 29 October 2019. Article 16, requires States parties to protect children against abuse, including sexual abuse.
35 SAARC is comprised of seven States: Bangladesh, Bhutan, India, Maldives, Nepal, Pakistan and Sri Lanka.
36 *SAARC Convention on Preventing and Combating Trafficking in Women and Children for Prostitution*, Kathmandu, Nepal, 5 January 2002. Available at: <http://saarc-sec.org/digital_library/detail_menu/saarc-convention-on-preventing-and-combating-trafficking-in-women-and-children-for-prostitution> (accessed 15 October 2019).
37 The Council of the Baltic Sea States (<www.cbss.org>) is a political forum for regional intergovernmental cooperation. The Members of the Council are the 11 states of the Baltic Sea Region and the European Commission. The States are: Denmark, Estonia, Finland, Germany, Iceland, Latvia, Lithuania, Norway, Poland, Russia, Sweden.
38 *European Convention for the Protection of Human Rights and Fundamental Freedoms*, opened for signature 4 November 1950, ETS No. 5, 213 UNTS 221 (entered into force 3 September 1953).

sexual exploitation of children.[39] Most of its work has been on a legislative basis, although it does fund projects that seek to tackle these areas. Some of its legislation relates specifically to the exploitation of vulnerable persons (most notably the *Convention on Action against Trafficking in Human Beings*[40] and the *Convention on the Protection of Children against Sexual Exploitation and Sexual Abuse*),[41] but at other times the legislative action is found within more general provisions. Perhaps the most notable example of this is the *Convention on Cybercrime*,[42] which includes a provision that defines and mandates action against child pornography.[43]

The European Union has become involved in this area only comparatively recently, although this is perhaps unsurprising since prior to the *Treaty of Maastricht*[44] of 1992 the European Community (as it was then known) was simply an economics vehicle. However, by the mid-1990s there was increased interest in child sexual exploitation (Gillespie 2011: 299), eventually culminating in a number of legislative instruments including a Council Decision on combating child pornography,[45] a Council Framework Decision[46] on combating the sexual exploitation of children and child pornography and ultimately a (legally binding) Directive.[47] The main purpose of the Directive is to ensure that the laws on child sexual exploitation are harmonised across the Union and it includes minimum levels of punishment. The Directive requires States to act in an extraterritorial manner (explained in the following discussion) and provide programmes of assistance to victims of sexual exploitation.

---

39 See further: The Council of Europe Convention on Protection of Children against Sexual Exploitation and Sexual Abuse, also known as 'the Lanzarote Convention', which requires criminalisation of all kinds of sexual offences against children. It was open for signature on 25 October 2007. It has been signed by all 47 CoE states and ratified by 44: <www.coe.int/en/web/children/lanzarote-convention> (accessed 19 September 2019); End Online Child sexual Exploitation and Abuse (EndOCSEA@Europe) project implemented by the Children's Rights Division of the Council of Europe, in cooperation with the Cybercrime Office (C-PROC) in Bucharest, Romania: <www.coe.int/en/web/cybercrime/endocsea-europe> (accessed 9 September 2019); European Day on the protection of children against sexual violence which aims to raise public awareness of the issues.
40 Opened for signature 16 May 2005, CETS No. 197, (entered into force 1 February 2008).
41 Opened for signature 25 October 2007, CETS No. 201, (entered into force 1 July 2010).
42 Opened for signature 23 November 2001, CETS No. 185, (entered into force 1 July 2004).
43 Council of Europe, *Convention on Cybercrime*, CETS No. 185, article 9.
44 European Union, *Treaty on European Union (Consolidated Version), Treaty of Maastricht*, 7 February 1992, *Official Journal of the European Communities* C 325/5; 24 December 2002.
45 Council Decision 2000/375/JHA of 29 May 2000 to Combat Child Pornography on the Internet, [2000] *Official Journal of the European Communities* L 138/1.
46 Council Framework Decision 2004/68/JHA of 22 December 2003 on Combating the Sexual Exploitation of Children and Child Pornography, [2004] *Official Journal of the European Communities* L 13/44.
47 Directive 2011/92/EU of the European Parliament and of the Council of 13 December 2011 on Combating the sexual abuse and sexual exploitation of children and child pornography, and replacing Council Framework Decision 2004/68/JHA [2011] *Official Journal of the European Communities* L 335/1.

The European Union's greatest impact, however, has probably been in its non-legislative action. The Treaty of Maastricht of 1992 established a European Law Enforcement Agency, 'Europol',[48] which is designed, *inter alia*, to facilitate cooperation between the law enforcement agencies of each member State. Europol came into existence in 1998 and as early as 2000 it had participated in international operations against child sexual exploitation (Europol 2009: 21), something it continues to this day. Its 'Internet Safety Programme and Internet Safety Plus' programme – Akdeniz (2008) provides a useful summary of these initiatives – has led to significant funding becoming available to ensure the safety of children from, for example, child pornography and grooming. Funding has also been used to establish Inhope[49] and Insafe,[50] both of which have been successful in safeguarding children from abuse.

8.2.3 Industry

While we would tend to think of governments as being the key actors of international action, it is not limited to them. In the context of child sexual exploitation it is clear that other actors can become involved and this includes 'industry'. For example, individual companies have sometimes spent considerable resources to combat child pornography. For example both Google and Microsoft have developed software that provides assistance to law enforcement in the identification and detection of child pornography images (Westlake et al. 2012). Microsoft, for example, has created 'PhotoDNA' that allows images to be tracked around the internet and identifies whether they are new but also, perhaps importantly, whether the child is already identified as vulnerable or whether other images exist (Farid 2018). The latter is important because it could tell investigators that images they are looking at of a child aged five is that of a child in other known images where the child is aged 12, for example. This would save the police wasting time searching for a five-year-old when the child is, in fact, much older.

While individual companies may contribute, it is perhaps more interesting when industry as a whole cooperates because they then truly become a form of international action. Perhaps one of the best examples of this is in relation to child sex tourism (see section 8.6.1 below). Child sex tourism can be best summarised as where an adult travels abroad and engages in sexual activity with children.[51] In many instances the purpose of the travel will be to abuse a child but in other instances it may be that an opportunity arises while the traveller is in a particular country (the hotel, for example, arranges for a child prostitute or a person attends a sexual massage parlour). Some cases such as *United States v. William Irey* involve the trafficking of children for the purposes of sexual exploitation. In this case William Irey engaged in sex acts

---

48 Europol's website is available at: <www.europol.europa.eu/> (accessed 14 October 2019).
49 See <http://www.inhope.org> This is an international network of hotlines that allows members of the public to report websites they suspect of hosting child pornography or other exploitative material.
50 See <http://www.saferinternet.org> This is a network of contact centres that provide assistance and educational initiatives to the public and educators to safeguard children and young persons online.
51 See further: O'Connell Davidson (2005).

with girls between the ages of four and 16, with some of those girls flown to him in China from Cambodia. Irey photographed and videotaped the abuse and torture of the girls, using the material for his own gratification and as a means to gain access to child pornography websites. This case illustrates both the international nature of abuse, but also the developing role of technology in facilitating the abuse and allowing federal agents to detect it through incriminating emails.[52]

Child sex tourism is a largely hidden form of abuse (Svensson 2006: 643), partly because there are concerns that in some instances the families of the children are complicit within it, partly for financial reasons (Montgomery 2008: 909). However the travel industry is perhaps one of the biggest and most lucrative forms of international commerce. There is a realisation that the tourism industry itself could assist in the combating of child sexual exploitation. The industry created the *Task Force to Protect Children from Sexual Exploitation in Tourism*, which was highlighted by the Special Rapporteur.[53] The *Task Force* is a mixture of government agencies, NGOs and industry representatives that seek to gather information on the main trends of child sex tourism.[54]

Perhaps the more notable action by industry was its development of two codes. The first is the *Global Code of Ethics for Tourism*, which was developed by the *World Tourism* Organisation (WTO) and adopted by the WTO General Assembly.[55] This is a global umbrella group for tourist providers and the global code of ethics sets out a series of principles for corporate social responsibility, including making reference to child sex tourism (Tepelus 2008: 107). The difficulty with it, as the Special Rapporteur has noted, is that it is not binding and there are no sanctions if organisations simply turn a blind eye to it (Maalla 2012: 17). Child sex tourism is also included within a long list of other factors rather than it being the target of specific action. In 2015, the World Committee on Tourism Ethics submitted to the General Assembly of the UNWTO a proposal to convert the Global Code of Ethics for Tourism into an international convention to reinforce its effectiveness. This Convention became the first International Convention to be adopted under the aegis of the UNWTO, with Article 5(3) explicitly addressing the issue of child sex tourism:[56] 'The exploitation of human beings in

---

52 *United States v. William Irey*, UNODC No.: USA062 <https://sherloc.unodc.org/cld/case-law-doc/traffickingpersonscrimetype/usa/2007/united_statesv.william_irey.html?tmpl=old> (accessed 9 September 2019).
53 Human Rights Council, *Report submitted by the Special Rapporteur on the sale of children, child prostitution and child pornography, Juan Miguel Petit*, seventh session, UN Doc. A/HRC/7/8, 9 January 2008, para. 14.
54 United Nations Special Rapporteur on the Sale of Children (2017) 'Tackling the Demand for the Sexual Exploitation of Children', A/HRC/31/58; Committee on the Rights of the Child 'An important aspect underlying these offences lies in the demand that exists, both among sex offenders and economic profiteers, of children for purposes of sexual exploitation and abuse', 2019 Draft Guidelines on the implementation of the *Optional Protocol to the Convention on the Rights of the Child* on the sale of children, child prostitution and child pornography.
55 A/RES/406(XIII) (Santiago, Chile, 27 September – 1 October 1999). Available at: <http://ethics.unwto.org/en/content/full-text-global-code-ethics-tourism> (accessed 29 October 2019).
56 UNWTO Convention on Tourism Ethics, Article 5(3), approved by A/RES/707(XXII) during the 22nd General Assembly (September 2017).

any form, particularly sexual, especially when applied to children, conflicts with the fundamental aims of tourism and is the negation of tourism'.

The more pertinent code is that created by the *Sexual Exploitation in Travel and Tourism* initiative, which is specifically created by the industry to combat sexually exploitative behaviour. Its *Code of Conduct for the Protection of Children in Travel and Tourism*[57] addresses these issues in more detail and commits the industry to ensuring that it takes positive action to combat child sexual exploitation. These are very practical initiatives, including the provision of training to hotel employees and the distribution of literature by air carriers. Of course, the difficulty with it is that it relies on cooperation as there are few sanctions, but it is a major step forward from what existed before and it has led to the situation where, for example, major hotel companies are no longer considered 'safe' places to conduct child sex tourism from (Maalla 2012: 8).

More can be done, however. There is a strong link between poverty and child sex tourism (Maalla 2012: 10) and it is incumbent on large players, e.g. tour operators, to use their financial muscle to implement the Code. For example, an independent hotelier in a tourist resort may be heavily reliant on the business from a tour operator (who will block-book the hotel). The Code could, and should, be incorporated into the contract between them. However the tourism industry also has to look at paying a living wage to employees of hotels, etc. It is perhaps unsurprising that an employee who is paid a poverty-level wage will find it an attractive proposition to procure a child for a Western tourist when the rewards for doing so could be many months' wages.

It is not only the tourist industry that is seeking to tackle child sexual exploitation. Another good example is the finance industry. There is still a considerable amount of commercially available child pornography; in other words, material that is purchased. In 2006 the Special Rapporteur was concerned about the fact that some financial bodies had created anonymous payment systems, which could cause problems in tracing those who purchase exploitative images of children.[58] While some anonymous forms do still exist – and indeed are marketed as being a source of evading law enforcement – the financial industry has taken steps to try and tackle child pornography. In North America, the *Financial Coalition against Child Pornography* involves many of the major banks, credit card companies and e-commerce bodies (e.g. PayPal). An equivalent exists in Europe, the *European Financial Coalition against Commercial Sexual Exploitation of Children Online*.[59] Both coalitions work closely with law enforcement to identify individuals who use their services to, *inter alia*, purchase child pornography but they also use intelligence to

---

57 Available at: <www.osce.org/cea/41835> (accessed 29 October 2019).
58 Commission on Human Rights, *Report of the Special Rapporteur on the sale of children, child prostitution and child pornography*, Economic and Social Council, 62nd session, UN Doc. E/CN.4/2006/67, 12 January 2006, para. 5.
59 See: <www.europeanfinancialcoalition.eu/> (accessed 29 October 2019).

deny banking services to those who market child pornography, in essence making it difficult to trade such material.

These examples show that industry can have an important part to play in combating child sexual exploitation and it is for this reason that governments and governmental bodies are increasingly trying to work with industry. This, as will be seen, is reflected in some international instruments that widen the meaning of cooperation to include all forms of agencies.

Case study 8.1

Child sex tourism

The issue of child sex tourism has been discussed briefly already in this chapter. It is an example of a particular type of child sexual exploitation that requires international cooperation to combat.

Child sex tourism is now recognised as covering a broad range of behaviours. The archetypal view of child sex tourism continues to be the traditional notion involving a (usually) male offender travelling from a developed (usually Western) country to a poorer country where he engages in sexual activity with a child. Asian countries, particularly Thailand and Sri Lanka, were some of the earliest countries in which child sex tourism developed.

The difference in economic wealth means that access to children can be relatively easy. Early research noted, for example, that many communities 'survived through the prostitution of children' (Montgomery 2008: 908) and that families would not consider their children to be abused but rather considered the offender as a 'friend' or 'sponsor' to the family (Montgomery 2008: 909). This reflected a particular type of child sex tourism where the abuse and exploitation was not an isolated incident but rather the offender would return to the family on a number of occasions, befriending them.

As understanding of the behaviour developed, it was discovered that the issue of child sex tourism was more complicated than previously thought. Two types of child sex tourism have been identified; 'core sex tourists' and 'opportunistic sex tourists'. Core sex tourists are sometimes also called 'preferential offenders' and are those that travel to a specific country with the intention of abusing or exploiting a child. An opportunistic sex tourist is someone that goes to a country for a legitimate reason (e.g. a business trip) but who will take the opportunity to abuse a child if it arises (for example, in a massage parlour or if approached in a hotel bar) (O'Connell Davidson 2000). Of course the reality is that an offender could be both: they will travel to specific countries with the intention of abusing a child but will take opportunities that arise while travelling legitimately. The fact that there are different types of child sex tourism is important in considering how to tackle it. For example, focusing attention on preferential abusers by, for example, tracking those sex offenders who travel or even preventing travel will not stop those who have travelled for legitimate reasons. Neither would, for example, warning people when booking travel to a certain country that child sex tourism is illegal.

When considering the States involved, it is common to also divide countries into two; those that are 'sending' States (i.e. those countries the perpetrator originates from) and 'receiving' States (i.e. those countries the offender visited and where the victim is based). However, this binary division is not always appropriate, as some countries may be both, for example, South Africa (Vrancken and Chetly 2009).

Responding to child sex tourism

The response to child sex tourism is perhaps a good example of how international law and policy can target a particular area. ECPAT,[60] probably one of the most famous international NGOs working in the area of child sexual exploitation, was created specifically to tackle child sex tourism, particularly in Asia.[61] The charity sought to raise awareness of the issue both domestically, in both sending and receiving countries, and at a global level. Its campaign led to the First World Congress against Commercial Sexual Exploitation in 1996, which was one of the first attempts to bring together a global coalition of public and private agencies committed to identifying how to tackle child sexual exploitation.

One of the key elements of the drive against child sexual tourism was the recognition that there needed to be legislation at both the domestic and international level. Many destination countries were targeted because child protection was largely ignored by these countries (Fredette 2009: 13). In many instances, no domestic legislation was put in place that specifically tackled child sex abuse, or if it did exist it was widely ignored.

A difficulty in concentrating legal efforts on destination countries, however, is that it may be ineffective. Legislation is only of use if there are appropriate strategies to detect, investigate and prosecute offenders. Most destination countries do not have the expertise to do this or face problems with corruption which impedes officials and prosecutors from taking action (in return for bribes) (Fredette 2009: 15). Even if the police were able to detect the crime, it was not unusual in many instances for the victims of the offence to deny that there had been any crime, partly because the offender was seen as being the benefactor of the family (Montgomery 2008: 909). Once again, this militated against prosecutions occurring.

---

60 Ending Child Prostitution and Trafficking.
61 While it is still based in Asia, its sphere of influence is now global.

Extraterritorial legislation
Sending States began to realise that they had a responsibility to protect children from the actions of their own citizens (Montgomery 2010). Sending States began to consider the use of extraterritorial jurisdiction, i.e. the right to prosecute their own citizens for conduct outside their territorial borders. The advantage of extraterritorial jurisdiction was that it could bypass many of the difficulties that existed with prosecution in destination countries. However extraterritorial legislation is far from being a perfect solution, as in many situations there will still be a need for local law enforcement to become involved. For example, the victim and witnesses are likely to be in the destination countries and so either local police forces would need to gather the evidence or, in many countries, facilitate the gathering of evidence by foreign police forces. Of course not every crime would require local evidence. Where, for example, a person filmed himself abusing a child and that footage was found when he returned to his country of origin; extraterritorial jurisdiction would allow an offender to be prosecuted for the sexual acts on the evidence from that footage.

While some countries did exercise extraterritorial jurisdiction, many did not. A major barrier in some countries however is the requirement for 'dual criminality'. This is the principle that requires an action to be criminalised in both the prosecuting State and the State in which the crime took place. So, for example, if D (a citizen of England) went to Thailand where he sexually exploited four children, it would be necessary that child sexual exploitation was a crime in *both* England and Thailand. As noted above, many destination countries do not have effective child protection laws which has led to the Special Rapporteur calling for its abolition (Maalla 2012: 11). However, many countries had already abolished this provision independently due to the difficulty that this caused to prosecutions (Svensson 2006: 655).

International instruments
The fact that extraterritorial jurisdiction could be an effective method of tackling child sex tourism has been recognised in international instruments. The OPSC expressly includes a call for States to consider using extraterritorial jurisdiction (article 4) and similar provisions can be found in, for example, the Lanzarote Convention (article 25). However the fact that only 44 States have implemented extraterritorial jurisdiction does demonstrate a lack of willingness on the part of some countries. 166 states have ratified the OPSC, and therefore clearly not all countries are adhering to the provisions they committed themselves too.

Police cooperation
The adoption of extraterritorial legislation is only one part of the solution that can be offered by sending States. Ideally extraterritorial legislation

need not be used but instead the local police in destination countries would identify and prosecute abuse. A considerable amount of effort is therefore placed on cooperation between police forces. This is sometimes in respect of evidence-gathering or part of the extradition process (which the OPSC specifically mentions in articles 6 and 10), but it is also frequently beyond this and involves, for example, the sharing of best practice, training events etc. A good example of this is the work undertaken by INTERPOL which has a specific training and capacity-building programme. Much of this work involves demonstrating to destination countries how to detect child sexual exploitation, how to interview children, and training on other relevant areas, etc. This is vitally important as it means that destination countries begin to take responsibility for tackling child sexual exploitation and send out a signal that such activities will not be tolerated within their borders.

Industry
In section 7.2.3 above it was noted that the tourism industry has become involved in the fight against child sex tourism. This was welcomed by the Special Rapporteur (Maalla 2012: 17). The tourism industry has a particular responsibility in prevention, as it in essence can be said to facilitate child sex tourism. While in many instances the activity occurs without their knowledge, this is not always the case, with examples of instances where active marketing of child sex tourism occurs (Fredette 2009: 6).

A shifting problem
The Special Rapporteur has noted that it is important for countries to harmonise their laws in accordance with the basic international instruments (Maalla 2012: 12). It is envisaged that mirror laws in multiple states will mean there are fewer places to hide. Without such international consensus, one issue of concern is that child sex tourism becomes a *reactive* phenomenon. In other words, as countries begin to develop strategies against it, there is concern that it simply displaces the activity to other states (Maalla 2012: 7). So, for example, when Thailand began to actively prosecute child sex tourists and created specialist police units to disrupt the behaviour, there was a subsequent increase in neighbouring countries such as Cambodia and Vietnam.

It is incumbent on the international community therefore to act *proactively*. While encouragement should be given to those who are destination countries to introduce new laws, considerable effort needs to be placed in predicting vulnerable states. Early intervention in those countries could help ensure that there is an appropriate framework in place (including international agreements) to combat this.

While enacting laws sends a strong signal to offenders, these are only useful when implemented effectively. However, it is also crucial to understand and recognise the root causes of child sex tourism. Almost one-third of child sex tourists convicted in the USA committed their offences in Mexico (Maalla 2012: 6). Mexico is a country that is generally thought to have a well-established system of governance and laws against such crimes. However it is also a country that has considerable poverty in areas. Laws to combat child sex tourism will only be effective where the conduct is detected, including by the victim reporting the sexual assault. Where a family is paid the equivalent of a year's salary to gain access to the child, it is unlikely that the offence will be reported and indeed the family may put pressure on the victim not to do so (Montgomery 2008). It is for this reason that work must be done to support victims (expressly stated in article 8 of the OPSC), and also address the root causes, including poverty. This may be in very localised pockets; for example, Fredette (2009: 11) notes that where local economies collapse as a result of internationalisation (rural areas) or outsourcing, there is a rise in commercial child sexual exploitation.

8.3 International instruments

Having outlined the international action that is being undertaken to combat the sexual exploitation of children, it is now necessary to consider the international legal instruments that exist to tackle this phenomenon.

8.3.1 UN Convention on the Rights of the Child

As has been noted already in other parts of this book (sections 1.2.1 and 3.1), the *Convention on the Rights of the Child*[62] is perhaps the most important international instrument relating to children's rights. It is a wide-ranging treaty that governs the social, civil and political rights of the child. Many of the provisions within the Convention are not directly relevant to the issue of sexual exploitation, but there are two articles that are specifically relevant to this issue. The first, and perhaps most significant, is article 34, although article 35 is also of relevance in this context. The Special Rapporteur has said of this that, 'the [Convention] promotes a comprehensive system for protecting children from violence and from sexual and other forms of exploitation' (Maalla 2011: 9).

Article 34 is the wider provision of the two:

> *States Parties undertake to protect the child from all forms of sexual exploitation and sexual abuse. For these purposes, States Parties shall in particular take all appropriate national, bilateral and multilateral measures to prevent:*
>
> *(a) The inducement or coercion of a child to engage in any unlawful sexual activity;*
> *(b) The exploitative use of children in prostitution or other unlawful sexual practices;*
> *(c) The exploitative use of children in pornographic performances and materials.*

---

62 Opened for signature 20 November 1989, 1577 UNTS 3 (entered into force 2 September 1990).

At first sight this appears useful: it provides a clear statement that countries shall protect a child from both sexual abuse and sexual exploitation. While this is a worthy statement, there is, however, difficulty in terms of how it is expressed. Article 34 does not make clear how a State should protect a child from sexual exploitation. Does it mean take civil steps? Criminal steps? Presumably both, but the article does not set this out clearly. This simply means that state parties undertake to protect all children (regardless of class, gender or race) from all forms of sexual exploitation and abuse (Faulkner 2019a).

Article 34 seeks to define sexual exploitation in paragraphs (a) to (c), but again the specific terms used are not defined and this can lead to questions being raised as to what precisely article 34 seeks to protect. Moreover, Article 34 fails to explicitly reference the traffic of children, which in light of the former Special Rapporteur's comments noted above constrains the scope of the article to effectively tackle trafficking. Some have argued that article 34 was a fudge and a compromise between the desire to protect children from exploitative practices and, at the same time, ensuring that adolescent experimentation was not the subject of mandatory intervention (Alexander et al. 2000: 482). The difficulty with compromised wording is that it allows debates to occur as to what its objectives are. For example, paragraph (a) refers to coercion or inducement but these can be said to be opposite ends of the same scale. What of situations where sexual activity takes place without coercion (which suggests pressure or force) or inducement (which suggests grooming or reward)? In paragraph (b) there is reference to 'child prostitution' but it is not clear what this covers. The term 'prostitute' covers a wide range of behaviour and indeed many argue the term is inappropriate (Pearce 2006). Without a clear understanding of what the term means, is article 34 seeking to protect only against, for example, the payment of money to a child for sex or does it cover other parts of the sex industry (e.g. online chatrooms, telephone sex lines etc.)? Does it cover situations where an adolescent has sex with someone in return for being given food or shelter?[63] Is this prostitution for the purposes of article 34?

It may seem unreasonable to concentrate on the wording of the article when it could be argued that, like many of the other articles within the Convention, it was drafted deliberately widely to allow flexibility.[64] However the first Special Rapporteur noted that vague terminology can cause difficulties in assessing legal frameworks.[65] This in turn makes the task of protecting children more difficult. If article 34 suffers from a lack of precision, article 35 is perhaps even more problematic: 'States Parties

---

63 Research suggests that this is not uncommon: see, for example, Chase and Statham (2005) and Pearce et al. (2002).
64 See Chapter 3, section 3.2 in this book for an account of the *Convention on the Rights of the Child*'s provenance.
65 Commission on Human Rights, *Report of the Special Rapporteur on the sale of children, child prostitution and child pornography*, Economic and Social Council, 63rd meeting, UN Doc. E/CN.4/1991/51, 6 March 1991.

shall take all appropriate national, bilateral and multilateral measures to prevent the abduction of, the sale of or traffic in children for any purpose or in any form.'

A major flaw of the CRC is its failure to provide authoritative definitions of the terms 'abduction', 'sale' or the 'traffic in children'. Subsequently the exact scope and applicability of Article 35 is brought under scrutiny, despite the relatively clear incorporation of obligations upon state parties (Faulkner 2019a). The obligations have a horizontal effect, meaning that they require state parties to go beyond punishing the perpetrators of trafficking and prevent trafficking from occurring (Humbert 2009). UNICEF has advocated that one of the major strengths of the CRC is its ability to be used as a framework for both measuring and understanding trafficking and the related commercial sexual exploitation of children in the broadest context.[66] However, article 35 does not expressly mention the sexual exploitation of children, but it is undoubtedly covered since the provision refers to 'for any purpose or in any form'. Is the lack of explicit reference problematic? Arguably, it is, because the abduction of a child by a parent is considerably different to the trafficking of children for sex, and yet article 35 appears to cover both situations. A provision as wide as this raises the same issues as before. How can States be held to account for failures if the benchmark they are being measured against – in this case, article 35 – is not sufficiently defined?

8.3.2 Convention on the Worst Forms of Child Labour (1999)

In 1999 the International Labour Organization (ILO) (see section 2.4.1.4 in this book), a specialist agency of the United Nations charged with developing and enforcing labour standards, passed the *Convention on the Worst Forms of Child Labour*[67] (see generally, section 5.2.3 above). At the time this Convention appeared, the ILO estimated that 250 million children were at work, with some 80 million involved in what it refers to as 'the worst forms of labour' (NGO Group 2001: 5). The *Convention on the Worst Forms of Child Labour* defines a child as a person under the age of 18.[68] This can be contrasted immediately with the *Convention on the Rights of the Child*, which, while suggesting that the age of majority should be 18, allows that it can be lowered by domestic legislation.[69] Article 3 defines the 'worst forms of child labour' and paragraph (b) includes 'the use of children for prostitution and pornography'. Paragraph (d) may also be of relevance as it refers to work that 'is likely to endanger the health, safety or morals of children'. The use of the term

---

66 *Children and Prostitution: How can we measure the Commercial Sexual Exploitation of Children? A literature review and annotated bibliography* (UNICEF, 2nd edn, 1996).
67 International Labour Organization, *Prohibition and Immediate Action for the Elimination of the Worst Forms of Child Labour Convention*, ILO Convention No. 182, (17 Jun 1999). This Convention had 177 parties as at November 2013.
68 *Convention on the Worst Forms of Child Labour*, article 2.
69 *Convention on the Rights of the Child*, article 1.

'morals' may be of assistance in terms of dealing with some forms of commercial sexual exploitation that do not come within either prostitution or pornography.

Article 7 of the *Convention on the Worst Forms of Child Labour* commits States parties, *inter alia*, to take measures to prevent a child's involvement in the worst forms of child labour and to provide assistance to those children who are working. Accompanying the Convention is a recommendation that provides guidance to signatory States on how to implement the Convention. The Recommendation includes, for example, the suggestion that criminal offences should be invoked to tackle those who employ children in the worst forms of labour,[70] and also protocols on how information should be fed back to the ILO.

The ILO Convention does, at least, recognise that the commercial sexual exploitation of children is unacceptable and should be tackled. An advantage of the *Convention on the Worst Forms of Child Labour* is that it brings together not just governments but also employers, NGOs and trade unions. Their diverse membership means that the issue of commercial sexual exploitation is raised at different levels: see further section 5.3 in this book. That said, however, it is focused on very narrow areas, is restricted to commercial forms of child sexual exploitation (since otherwise they would not be 'labour') and does not provide appropriate definitions of the various terms. To an extent, therefore, it can be said to be an additional recognition of the issue but it does not, by itself, take matters much further than the standards as formulated in the *Convention on the Rights of the Child*.

8.3.3 Optional Protocol to the Convention on the Rights of the Child on the sale of children, child prostitution and child pornography of 2000 (OPSC)

As noted already, shortly after the drafting of the *Convention on the Rights of the Child* the issue of child sexual exploitation, particularly sex tourism, became of great concern and the United Nations appointed its first *Special Rapporteur on the sale of children, child prostitution and child pornography*. The Special Rapporteur was concerned about whether the *Convention on the Rights of the Child* was sufficient to tackle child sexual exploitation, and by 1994 the UN Commission on Human Rights[71] had created a working group to examine the possibility of an Optional Protocol to the *Convention on the Rights of the Child* specifically related to the issue of (commercial) sexual exploitation.[72] Pressure to change increased with the holding

---

70 *R190 – Worst Forms of Child Labour Recommendation*, 1999 (No. 190), Recommendation concerning the prohibition and immediate action for the elimination of the worst forms of child labour. Adoption: Geneva, 87th ILC session (17 June 1999), para. 12.
71 The UN Commission on Human Rights (UNCHR) was replaced by the UN Human Rights Council (UNHRC) in 2006: see section 2.5.1.1 in this book.
72 UN Commission for Human Rights, *Need to adopt effective international measures for the prevention and eradication of the sale of children, child prostitution and child pornography*, resolution 1994/90, 66th meeting (9 March 1994).

of the first World Congress against the Commercial Sexual Exploitation of Children ('the Stockholm Conference').[73] An important outcome of this Congress was support for strengthening the international rules relating to commercial sexual exploitation, including the possibility of drafting a new legal instrument. Part of this pressure arose from the unsatisfactory wording of article 34, and it has been suggested that this was a major reason for the development of the Optional Protocol so soon after the *Convention on the Rights of the Child* had come into force (Alexander et al. 2000: 482).

Ultimately the demand for change led to the drafting of OPSC.[74] The Optional Protocol[75] differs from the *Convention on the Rights of the Child* in that it is more specific in terms of its definitions and its obligations on signatory States. The OPSC goes beyond the CRC in several important respects, in particular adopting an explicitly criminal justice approach and in detailing obligations accordingly (Gallagher 2011: 67). A former Special Rapporteur has noted that the wording of OPSC is sufficient to allow her to 'implement her mandate within a clear legal framework and yet take into consideration endemic situations and emerging problems' (Maalla 2008: 6). That is not to say, however, that OPSC is perfect as, like any international instrument, it contains the negotiated wording resulting from the discussions and diplomatic compromises made by various States parties. Perhaps the most significant issue is that, unlike article 34 of the *Convention on the Rights of the Child*, the Optional Protocol is arguably too narrow. OPSC does not refer to the sexual abuse or sexual exploitation of children (unlike, e.g., the Council of Europe's *Convention on the Protection of Children against Sexual Exploitation and Sexual Abuse*,[76] which does seek to cover most forms), but rather it is focused specifically on commercial sexual exploitation. Indeed, it is clear from article 1 that it is restricted to three forms:

- child trafficking (the sale of children);
- child prostitution;
- child pornography.

If the sexual behaviour is not within these three heads then it is outside the scope of OPSC. It is notable that OPSC is clearer than the *Convention on the Rights of the Child* in terms of how it defines child prostitution. The wording of article 2 makes clear that it applies to sexual activity 'for remuneration or any other form of consideration' and, accordingly, the comments made earlier about youths providing sex in return for gifts or a place to stay overnight, would come within this definition.

---

73 First World Congress against Commercial Sexual Exploitation of Children, Stockholm (1996). There have subsequently been two more world congresses: in 2001, held in Yokohama, Japan; and in 2008, held in Rio de Janeiro.
74 25 May 2000, 2171 UNTS 227 (entered into force 18 January 2002).
75 OPSC had 121 signatories and 176 ratifications as at 8 October 2019.
76 Opened for signature 25 October 2007, CETS No. 201, (entered into force 1 July 2010).

454   Child sexual exploitation

The technological revolution has, in recent years, arguably placed great strain on OPSC as there is evidence of exploitation which is not within these headings, most notably the issue of sexual solicitation or grooming.[77] This will be discussed further later in respect of the criminalisation of the commercial sexual exploitation of the child.

8.3.4   Optional Protocol to Prevent, Suppress and Punish Trafficking in Persons Especially Women and Children 2000

The international legal framework protecting children exists to both empower and protect children. This includes the *Optional Protocol to the UN Convention against Transnational Organised Crime*; The Protocol to Prevent, Suppress and Punish Trafficking in Persons, especially Women and Children.[78] The Trafficking Protocol was adopted in 2000, and although not exclusively linked to the issue of child sexual exploitation it remains an important instrument that contributes to the international legal framework implemented to address the sexual exploitation of children.[79] The Trafficking Protocol (through article 3) created the first international legal definition of human trafficking.[80] This is noteworthy in light of the inclusion of the phrase 'trafficking' in numerous legal instruments since the turn of the 20th century.[81] The adoption of an agreed upon definition of trafficking within the context of a legally binding treaty was a critical step forward, as it demonstrated a common understanding of the issue of trafficking and thereby established some level of consensus around the necessary responses.[82]

---

77 See: UN Commission on Human Rights, *Rights of the Child: report submitted by the Special Rapporteur on the sale of children, child prostitution and child pornography*, Economic and Social Council, 61st session, UN Doc. E/CN.4/2005/78, (23 December 2004), 7. For a discussion on the meaning of such terms, see Gillespie (2002); Craven et al. (2006).
78 The Protocol was adopted by resolution A/RES/55/25, 15 November 2000. It entered into force on 25 December 2003. It currently has 117 signatories and 173 parties (January 2019). Hereinafter 'the Trafficking Protocol'.
79 See further: Faulkner 2019a.
80 Gallagher 2010.
81 See further: International Agreement for the Suppression of White Slave Traffic 1904; International Convention for the Suppression of the White Slave Traffic 1910; International Convention for the Suppression of Traffic in Women and Children 1921 and International Convention for the Suppression of the Traffic in Women of Full Age 1933; 1949 Convention for the Suppression of Traffic in Persons and the Exploitation of the Prostitution of Others; Convention on the Elimination of All Forms of Discrimination against Women (CEDAW) 1979; *Convention on the Rights of the Child* 1989 and its two Optional Protocols (OPSC and OPAC); and was finally addressed in the *2000 Optional Protocol to Suppress and Punish Trafficking in Persons* especially women and children.
82 See further: Gallagher 2017.

Article 3 defines human trafficking thus:

(a) 'Trafficking in persons' shall mean the recruitment, transportation, transfer, harbouring or receipt of persons, by means of the threat or use of force or other forms of coercion, of abduction, of fraud, of deception, of the abuse of power or of a position of vulnerability or of the giving or receiving of payments or benefits to achieve the consent of a person having control over another person, for the purpose of exploitation. Exploitation shall include, at a minimum, the exploitation of the prostitution of others or other forms of sexual exploitation, forced labour or services, slavery or practices similar to slavery, servitude or the removal of organs;
(b) The consent of a victim of trafficking in persons to the intended exploitation set forth in subparagraph (a) of this article shall be irrelevant where any of the means set forth in subparagraph (a) have been used;
(c) The recruitment, transportation, transfer, harbouring or receipt of a child for the purpose of exploitation shall be considered 'trafficking in persons' even if this does not involve any of the means set forth in subparagraph (a) of this article;
(d) 'Child' shall mean any person under eighteen years of age.

Article 3 (a) establishes three separate elements to the definition, namely (i) the action, (ii) the means and the (iii) purpose or exploitation. All three of the listed elements must be present for a situation of 'trafficking in persons' to be recognised, the only exception to this relates to the trafficking of children, in relation to whom the means element is waived.[83] What does this mean for children? Essentially, that trafficking will exist in situations where the child has been subject to an act such as recruitment, transportation, or receipt – the purpose of which is the exploitation of that child. It is therefore unnecessary to show that force, deception or any other means were used for trafficking in children, which according to Gallagher (2011: 29) infers that 'the identification of victims and the identification of their exploiters can be expected to be easier for child victims as compared to adults'.

It is worth noting that despite the fact the Trafficking Protocol has been widely embraced by the international community and states (in terms of level of law and formal policy) the integration into national law and practice since its adoption has proven 'messy and complicated' (Gallagher 2017: 83). Over time, questions have arisen relating to certain aspects of the definition and in relation to children for example a question that arises is under what circumstances, if any, will the exploitation of a child for profit not be trafficking? It is worth looking briefly to

---

83 Trafficking Protocol, at Art. 3(c). The distinction between adults and children in relation to trafficking is not new. The 1910 International Convention for the Suppression of the White Slave Traffic established the distinction between adults and children though the omission of the means element. This distinction between young victims ('in relation to whom the 'means' by which they were procured were irrelevant') and adult victims (in relation to whom some evidence of compulsion as required.) has survived through the omission of the means element in relation to children under the Trafficking Protocol of 2000.

the United Kingdom, which has sought to position itself as a world leader in the fight against 'modern slavery'.

8.4 States' responsibilities

The international instruments discussed earlier place a number of responsibilities onto State parties. For ease of analysis, these responsibilities will be considered as key themes. The themes are:

- criminalisation of child sexual exploitation;
- establishing jurisdiction over child sexual exploitation;
- international cooperation and support in tackling child sexual exploitation;
- measures to assist victims of child sexual exploitation.

8.4.1 Criminalisation

Perhaps the most significant part of OPSC is the requirement in article 3 to ensure that 'as a minimum' a series of acts and activities are subject to the criminal law. The acts and activities are, *inter alia*:

(a) offering, delivering or accepting, by whatever means, a child for the purposes of its sexual exploitation,
(b) offering, obtaining, procuring or providing a child for child prostitution,
(c) producing, distributing, disseminating, importing, exporting, offering, selling or possessing for those purposes child pornography.

(OPSC, article 3(1))

Article 3(2) requires States to ensure that an attempt to commit an offence in article 3(1) is also an offence. The Optional Protocol does not define what an attempt is but rather leaves this to each domestic legal system to identify.

Article 3(3) requires States to 'make these offences punishable by appropriate penalties that take into account their grave nature'. This is somewhat vague but could, in a positive sense, be read as meaning that there must be recognition that the crimes set out in article 3(1) are serious and should be reflected by strong punishments. However, in the more negative sense it is notable that the Convention has not, for example, suggested that they should ordinarily be punishable by imprisonment, or set minimum punishments. The reasoning behind this approach is that it is most unusual for treaties to set out minimum punishments,[84] in part

---

84 Council Framework Decision 2004/68/JHA of 22 December 2003 on Combating the Sexual Exploitation of Children and Child Pornography, [2004] *Official Journal of the European Communities* L 13/44, does provide minimum standards but this is not a treaty *per se*, rather, a legal instrument of the European Union.

because each jurisdiction will have its own system of punishments and agreeing a coherent approach could be difficult to negotiate. It was noted earlier that the *Convention on the Rights of the Child* has been almost universally ratified and 166 countries have ratified OPSC to date. The drafters of OPSC were no doubt careful to ensure that there was nothing in this instrument that would restrict the likelihood of ratification.

8.4.1.1 Sale of children

Article 3(1) tackles the sale of children. The demarcation between this and child prostitution is open to debate but it is likely that this heading is designed to tackle those who treat children as a commodity, to be bought and sold. While the term 'trafficking' is not used expressly, the language of OPSC which refers to 'offering, delivering or accepting, by whatever means, a child' means it is likely that this is what was meant (UNICEF 2009: 9). That said, however, it has been noted that trafficking does not need to involve a child being physically sold (UNICEF 2009: 10), and this demonstrates a potential lacuna in the Optional Protocol in that in the absence of a sale, or if it does not come within the definition of child prostitution, the trafficking of a child may not be included. However, as noted by Gallagher (2011) the provided definition of the 'sale of children' is sufficiently broad to encompass most situations within which children are trafficked. Article 2 of the OPSC defines it as 'any act or transaction whereby a child is transferred by any person or group of persons to another for remuneration or any other consideration'. The link is subsequently confirmed by the practice of the CRC Committee, which reveals a marked tendency to associate trafficking with the sale of children.[85] The Committee has however been careful to maintain a distinction between the two concepts, for example noting that some cases of the sale of children may not involve the element of exploitation that is essential to the definition of trafficking. In this regard, Cedrangolo (2009) concludes that while the sale of children and trafficking will coincide when the sale is made for any consideration and involving an exploitative purpose, not all cases of trafficking involving children constitute acts of sale of children.

It is notable that the wording of article 3(1) includes 'offering', 'delivering' and 'accepting' and thus it tackles not only the person who sells the child but also an intermediary who 'receives' the child for another. 'Delivering' would seem to include those who are responsible for the actual movement of the child irrespective of whether they are necessarily involved in the sale itself. So, for example, X asks Y to smuggle V into country A. X is to be paid $5,000 for V. X is the one who

---

85 See, for example, UN Committee on the Rights of the Child, *General Comment No. 6:* Treatment of Unaccompanied and Separated Children Outside Their Country of Origin, UN Doc. CRC/GC/2005/6, 3 June 2005, at para. 2, where conversely the sale of children by parents is listed as an example of trafficking.

has 'sold' V, but Y is undoubtedly delivering her and accordingly would be covered in this Protocol. 'Offering' would seem to imply that the actual transaction need not take place, and advertising the sale of the child may be covered also. As will be seen, it is somewhat regrettable that the same is not true for either child prostitution or child pornography.

8.4.1.2 Child prostitution

It was noted in the first section of this chapter that 'child prostitution' is a controversial label and doubt exists over what precisely is covered. Article 3(1)(b) criminalises the 'offering, obtaining, procuring or providing' of a child for the purposes of child prostitution. The emphasis of the article would appear to be on those who control the child ('offering', 'procuring' and 'providing' must relate to the person who 'supplies' the child). What of the person who actually pays to have sexual contact with a child? It could be argued that the term 'obtains' covers this behaviour, although in the context of Article 3(1)(b) the term 'obtains' may be more apposite to describe a person who receives the child in order to control him or her. That said, the Special Rapporteur indicated his belief that OPSC did mandate the criminalisation of the clients of child prostitutes[86] and, while it may have been preferable for the language of OPSC to be clearer, it is to be hoped States adopt that reasoning.

UNICEF (2009: 12) has noted that the issue of sex tourism is only mentioned in passing by OPSC but argues that sex tourism could be considered child prostitution. Presumably UNICEF means by this the fact that many sex tourists will seek to pay either a child or an agency for sexual activity with a child. Where this is the case, it should be possible to read article 3 in such a way that covers this activity. Certainly this argument is supported by the Special Rapporteur who, in her latest report which specifically examined the issue of child sex tourism, considered that it fell within OPSC through child prostitution and possibly child pornography (Maalla 2012:10). While this is true it is perhaps a matter of regret that it is not expressly mentioned as a form of abuse and exploitation in its own right.

The implicit inclusion of child sex tourism in child prostitution does raise an issue in terms of how child prostitution is defined and criminalised. The definition in article 2 appears to be focused quite specifically on the individual who supplies the child, but what of the person who controls the activities, or some of the activities, of a child prostitute? In the context of sex tourism this could involve the travel agent who knowingly sends a person to a particular country and, indeed, a particular villa or hotel. Can it really be said that this person has

---

86 Commission on Human Rights, *Report of the Special Rapporteur on the sale of children, child prostitution and child pornography*, Economic and Social Council, 62nd session, UN Doc. E/CN.4/2006/67, 12 January 2006, 13.

offered, procured or provided a child? The only possibility would be to suggest that he has procured child prostitution, but realistically it may still be one step away. Had OPSC referred to 'facilitates', then the issue would have been put beyond doubt.

8.4.1.3 Child pornography

Child pornography is something that continues to defy a precise definition (Gillespie 2010), but OPSC does, at least, define what it considers the term to mean. In article 2(c) it states child pornography is 'any representation, of whatever means, of a child engaged in real or simulated explicit sexual activities or any representation of the sexual parts of a child for primarily sexual purposes'. It is not the place of this chapter to critique this definition,[87] but it should be noted that the OPSC definition is arguably one of the widest and would include all forms of representation, including text, drawings and photographs.

Article 3(1)(c) requires a number of actions relating to child pornography to be criminalised. The first set of offences is concerned with the creation and dissemination of child pornography. The language of article 3 is deliberate and ensures that, for example, there is no doubt that the creation (production) of child pornography should be criminalised as should any form of the dissemination of child pornography. So, for example, the article is careful to ensure that dissemination includes not only distribution, but also the importing and exporting of material. The advent of communication technologies has meant that the clear majority of child pornography is hosted online (Taylor and Quayle 2003), which does raise issues about whether information is 'imported' or 'exported' when it is merely accessed on the internet as those terms are traditionally understood to mean the physical moving of an item into or out of the country.

An interesting issue in the wording of article 3(1) is whether the simple possession of child pornography is criminalised. The wording of article 3(1) suggests it is not, but that possession with the intention of disseminating the images is criminalised. This can be contrasted with, for example, article 9 of the *Convention on Cybercrime*[88] which states that simple possession of child pornography may[89] be a criminal activity, or article 20 of the *Convention on the Protection of Children against Sexual Exploitation and Sexual Abuse*.[90] UNICEF has noted the potential lacuna in the wording of OPSC, although it suggests that the Committee on the Rights of the Child has attempted to fill this lacuna by making comments in national

---

87 See Gillespie (2010) for further discussion.
88 Council of Europe, *Convention on Cybercrime*, CETS No. 185.
89 Although article 9(1)(c) is not equivocal, article 9(4) provides that States may reserve, in whole or in part, the right not to apply that provision.
90 Opened for signature 25 October 2007, CETS No. 201, (entered into force 1 July 2010).

reports (Cedrangolo 2009: 9–10). In his first thematic report on child pornography, the then Special Rapporteur also noted this omission and recommended that simple possession be criminalised so as to tackle the 'participant chain' in the production and dissemination of child pornography.[91] This has recently been reinforced by the current Special Rapporteur who, along with calling for simple possession to be criminalised, has argued that liability should additionally be extended to those who knowingly access or watch material online (Maalla 2009: 23).

8.4.1.4 Missing activities

It was noted previously that OPSC does not seek to criminalise all forms of child sexual abuse but is restricted to commercial forms of sexual abuse, as is the *Convention on the Worst Forms of Child Labour*. It will be remembered that the *Convention on the Rights of the Child* itself does not provide expressly for the criminalisation of any specific forms of behaviour, although article 34 does, at least, suggest that, *inter alia*, all forms of sexual abuse should be criminalised.

In response to technological advancements and the ways in which offenders have used information and communication technologies to seek children for abuse, the then Special Rapporteur recommended that States 'introduce legislation creating the offence of "internet grooming or luring"'.[92] This was an interesting call, since it would seem to fall outside the definitions put forward in OPSC (as grooming rarely involves any commercial aspect). The call could be taken as evidence of a desire to move OPSC beyond commercial sexual exploitation into a wider instrument to address the sexual abuse and exploitation of children. In the absence of a change to the text of the instrument, however, the Special Rapporteur can only make recommendations rather than ensuring that they form part of the obligations of a State. The effect of this is perhaps evident from the fact that a report of the current Special Rapporteur made the same point about grooming (Maalla 2009: 23). Despite this, few countries appear to have introduced legislation to tackle grooming (Maalla 2009: 12) and there is no indication that the position has changed in recent years.

8.4.1.5 Victims as criminals

It was noted in the preceding discussion that article 34 of the *Convention on the Rights of the Child* was considered to be a compromise because of concerns that alternative wording may have led to adolescent sexual experimentation being criminalised.

---

91 UN Commission on Human Rights, *Rights of the Child: report submitted by the Special Rapporteur on the sale of children, child prostitution and child pornography*, Economic and Social Council, 61st session, UN Doc. E/CN.4/2005/78, (23 December 2004), 23.
92 Ibid.

A more difficult problem is that in some countries it would appear that the victim of child sexual exploitation could be criminalised. It may be thought that this was only in less developed countries, but it should be noted that, theoretically at least, under English law a child involved in prostitution continues to be subject to the criminal law through, for example, soliciting (Gillespie 2007; Phoenix 2003). The Special Rapporteur has previously denounced the criminalisation of victims of sexual exploitation[93] and the current Special Rapporteur has announced an advocacy programme with the intention of urging countries to decriminalise victims (Maalla 2008: 11).

A difficulty, however, is that international instruments are somewhat vague on this issue. The *Convention on the Rights of the Child* merely states in general that non-judicial alternatives should be adopted where possible,[94] and OPSC requires only that 'the best interests of the child shall be a primary consideration'.[95] It is notable that OPSC says it should be *a* primary consideration and not *the* primary consideration. The absence of a definitive statement[96] is undoubtedly causing difficulties for some children – who may not report the fact that they are being exploited for fear of prosecution – and it is to be hoped that the Special Rapporteur is able to develop a presumption against the criminalisation of victims.

Case study 8.2

Aziz & Others v Secretary of State for the Home Department [2018]

In the United Kingdom, cases of wide scale exploitation of girls were reported in the towns of Rotherham, Telford, Rochdale and Huddersfield, among others. Shabir Ahmed, 66, Qari Abdul Rauf, 50, Abdul Aziz, 48 and Adil Khan, 49, were among nine men convicted in 2012 of a series of serious sex offences against vulnerable victims in Rochdale. They were sentenced to a total of 77 years. Apart from stiff jail sentences, the Home Secretary took further punitive action and revoked their British citizenship. The men unsuccessfully appealed against the decision.

---

93 Commission on Human Rights, *Report of the Special Rapporteur on the sale of children, child prostitution and child pornography*, Economic and Social Council, 62nd session, UN Doc. E/CN.4/2006/67, 12 January 2006, 21.
94 *Convention on the Rights of the Child*, art. 40(3)(b).
95 OPSC, art. 8(3).
96 It was originally intended that a definitive clause would be present, but several States objected to this (Cedrangolo 2009: 13).

Aziz & Others v Secretary of State for the Home Department [2018] EWCA Civ 1884

1. The appellants are naturalised British citizens. At the time of the relevant decisions of the Secretary of State, the First-tier Tribunal ('FTT') and the Upper Tribunal (UT), the appellants had dual nationality, being citizens of Pakistan. This appeal concerns the proposal of the Secretary of State to make an order to deprive the appellants of their British citizenship pursuant to section 40 of the British Nationality Act 1981.

2. The appellants are part of a group of men convicted in 2012 of a range of offences involving the grooming, sexual abuse and trafficking of girls in Rochdale in a case which attracted national attention and notoriety. The steps to deprive the appellants of British nationality are a prelude to possible deportation to Pakistan. Each of the appellants has children in the UK and an established private life in the UK. They maintain that deportation to Pakistan would violate their right to respect for family and private life as set out in Article 8 of the *European Convention on Human Rights*, as given effect in domestic law by the *Human Rights Act 1998*. They also maintain that deportation would be in breach of the obligation of the Secretary of State and the tribunals to have regard to the interests of their children as a primary consideration, pursuant to section 55 of the Borders, Citizenship and Immigration Act 2009 ('section 55').

6. In 2012, the appellants were part of a group of nine men convicted at the Crown Court in Liverpool in respect of the grooming and sexual exploitation of several girls aged in their early teens in Rochdale. The men were sentenced on 9 May 2012. The sentencing judge described how in some cases the girls were raped callously, viciously and violently; and in some cases they were driven round Rochdale and Oldham to be made to have sex with paying customers. All the men treated the girls as though they were worthless and beyond all respect. They were motivated by lust and greed.

8. In July 2015, the Secretary of State gave notice to each of the appellants pursuant to section 40(5) of the 1981 Act that she proposed to make an order to deprive him of citizenship, acting under section 40(2), on the grounds that it would be conducive to the public good to do so. Representations were made on behalf of each appellant to complain that the Secretary of State had not given adequate consideration to the interests of the appellants' children when deciding to give such notice. In the light of those representations the Secretary of State withdrew those notices.

9. By further notices dated 2 December 2015 sent to each of the appellants, the Secretary of State again gave notice under section 40(5) that she proposed making an order to deprive him of citizenship, again in reliance on section 40(2). These notices stated in each case that the Secretary of State took the view that the offences of which the appellant had been convicted were 'serious and organised offences, involving collusion with others as is evident from the length of your sentence'. In each notice the Secretary of State stated that she was aware that the appellant had children aged under 18, but took the view that 'Deprivation of [his] citizenship (as distinct from deportation) will not, in itself, have a significant effect on the best interests of [his] children'. She referred in that regard to her duty under section 55, and stated that she considered 'that the public interest in depriving [the relevant appellant] of citizenship clearly outweighs any interest your children might have in [his] remaining a British citizen.'

17. The appellants appealed against these decisions to the Upper Tribunal. Each of the appellants was represented at the hearing in the Upper Tribunal. The Upper Tribunal dismissed their appeals.

18. The appellants now appeal to this court on the two limited grounds of appeal in respect of which the Upper Tribunal granted them permission to appeal.

Appeals dismissed.

Held: 36 . . . The Secretary of State and the FTT both considered that the offending by the appellants amounted to participation in serious organised crime. They were lawfully entitled to make that evaluative assessment in the circumstances of these cases. The crimes were plainly very serious and there was a sufficient element of organisation in the way they were committed to justify characterising the offending as participation in serious organised crime within the meaning of that expression in para. 55.4.4 of the Nationality Instructions. Accordingly, the Secretary of State and the FTT were entitled to find that the deprivation of citizenship in the case of each appellant would be compliant with the policy set out in that paragraph.

Twenty members of the grooming gang were also later convicted of a catalogue of rape and abuse against girls as young as 11 in Huddersfield. The men were convicted of more than 120 offences against 15 girls. Throughout the three trials, jurors were told how the men had plied their victims with drink and drugs before sexually abusing them (Evans 2018). The abuse took place between 2004 and 2011 and involved victims aged between 11 and 17.

The majority of theories on sexual deviance suggest that sexual offenders specialise in types of victims and or offences (Simon 1997). Indeed, the cases discussed above seemed to hold similar characteristics. Police were accused of refraining from investigating the crimes out of political correctness. While the perpetrators were portrayed as 'Asian grooming gangs', generally, caution needs to be taken on the racialisation or ethnicisation of crimes. Such approaches could result in inequality of outcomes in the criminal justice system. Further, a narrow focus on a few unique incidents could lend it itself to false generalisations and create a distorted picture of the demographics of child sex offenders. Research has demonstrated that the consistent finding in child abuse cases is that the majority of perpetrators are male (Walker et al. 2018); this comports with previous prevalence and agency data, where males are disproportionately found to be perpetrators of sexual abuse (Vandiver and Walker 2002; Alexy et al. 2005; Berelowitz 2012). Such offenders were found across the whole racial spectrum.

8.4.2 Establishing jurisdiction

Article 4 of OPSC highlights the issue of jurisdiction. Article 4(1) requires States to ensure that their domestic laws establish jurisdiction of the criminal offences discussed earlier when committed in its territory, on board a ship or on an aircraft registered in that State. This can be said to be the traditional approach to jurisdiction (Hirst 2003) and it is relatively uncontroversial. However, OPSC goes further and suggests that jurisdiction should be extended in certain circumstances.

Article 4(2) requires States parties to ensure that jurisdiction over the offences referred to in article 3(1) (those discussed in section 7.4.1) should also be secured where the alleged perpetrator is a national or habitual resident of that State or where the victim is a national of that State.[97] Many countries have now adopted so-called 'sex tourism' legislation that seeks to tackle those who commit sexual offences abroad,[98] but few countries secure jurisdiction by reference to victims. Despite this provision in OPSC, it would seem that some countries continue to refuse to adopt the principle of extraterritoriality and many apply the principle of double jeopardy (Maalla 2009: 13). In this context, the rule of double jeopardy prevents somebody from being tried twice for the same offence. Accordingly, if D is prosecuted for crime X and is acquitted, then he cannot be prosecuted again.

In the context of extraterritorial jurisdiction this would mean that if D is prosecuted in country X, where the crime took place, he could not then be prosecuted in country Y (the country of his residence). Some are concerned that the principle of double jeopardy can be misused in countries where sexual exploitation of a child will attract a very low penalty (Beaulieu 2008: 12). The Special Rapporteur has urged that double jeopardy should not apply to cases involving

---

97 See OPSC, article 4(2)(a) and (b) respectively.
98 A useful history of this can be found in Hirst (2003: 268–9).

the sexual exploitation of children (Maalla 2009: 23) but, while some countries may agree to try individuals who have been prosecuted but not convicted, many countries would baulk at the notion that someone will be punished twice for the same conduct.

Even where countries adopt extraterritorial jurisdiction, some challenges remain. For example, in some jurisdictions there is the requirement of 'dual criminality'. Put at its most basic, this means that the crime must be illegal in both the country that is to try the offence (i.e. the State exercising extraterritorial jurisdiction) and the country where the act took place. In many instances this may well be appropriate, but in the context of commercial sexual exploitation, particularly in respect of sex tourism, this can be problematic. In some countries the age of consent remains extremely low and the principle of dual criminality would therefore permit a sex tourist the right to go to this country for the sole purpose of sexually exploiting a child. Abolishing the principle of dual criminality would mean that the same standard is expected of a country's citizens wherever they may go, but it does mean that a citizen of country X but resident in country Y may be prevented from doing something that is perfectly lawful in country Y. This can be particularly problematic where, for example, a person is a citizen of more than one country. Where dual criminality is no longer recognised, then it is presumably reliant on prosecutors to use their extraterritorial powers only where there is clear evidence of abuse or exploitation.

The far greater challenge for extraterritorial jurisdiction is the evidence. While legislating for extraterritorial jurisdiction is relatively easy to do, securing its practical use is more challenging. In many countries the standard of evidence gathering may be poorer than that which is expected by the courts of the country exercising jurisdiction. There is also the difficulty of securing witness testimony. That said, it can sometimes be a useful provision; an example could be:

> D is a citizen of country X. He went on holiday to country Y where he recorded himself having sexual activity with a child. Upon his return to country X he is arrested for an unconnected matter and his camera is analysed. The images show him sexually abusing the child in country Y. Applying extraterritorial jurisdiction, D could be tried in country X for the crimes committed in country Y, the photographs serving as the principal evidence.

Also, in the context of sex tourism, many would argue that it serves as a deterrent in that offenders know that they are not necessarily safe from prosecution when they return to their country of residence.

8.4.2.1 Refusal to extradite

Article 5 of OPSC, discussed in the following section, provides for rules relating to extradition. However some countries adopt an approach of not extraditing their citizens. Article 4(3) states that where an alleged offender is within State borders and the State refuses to extradite him, then domestic legislation should be sufficient to ensure that the person can be prosecuted in that State. It has been noted that although article 4(3) is silent as to nationality, it is likely that it means a citizen of that State (UNICEF 2009: 13). That said, there is no reason why it should be restricted to this and where, for example, domestic or international rules on extradition would prevent the extradition of non-citizens,[99] article 3(4) could ensure that they do not escape justice.

8.4.2.2 Extradition

Article 5 raises the issue of extradition.[100] It is recognised that international travel makes it relatively easy for an offender to leave the State where a crime was committed or a State that seeks to prosecute him for the offence. The rules of extradition have existed for some time and allow for a country to remove a person from its State borders and deliver him to the requesting country. Extradition operates on a bilateral basis, with countries agreeing treaties among themselves as to how the extradition process operates (see section 2.2.1 in this book). Article 5(1) requires the extradition treaties to be amended (and new treaties to be drafted) so as to include the offences contained within article 3.

Where an extradition treaty does not exist between parties, then article 5(2) requires the State to treat OPSC as a treaty authorising extradition between signatory parties. Obviously this is limited to the offences contained within article 3(1) but, if State courts take this into account, it will allow for the extradition of an offender. Article 5(3) is related to this issue as it states that where a country is prepared to extradite in the absence of a treaty, it should recognise the offences within article 3(1) as extraditable offences. This is required because in the absence of such provision it is quite possible that only certain offences would be subject to extradition without a treaty.

Article 5(4) is an important provision in that it requires States to recognise the extension of jurisdiction in article 4. Extradition ordinarily applies in respect of offences that are deemed to have been committed in the requesting country's territory. As noted in the previous discussion, article 4(2) asks countries to extend jurisdiction to include situations where a citizen of their country is alleged to have committed, or been the victim of, an offence. Article 5(4) requires countries to recognise this extended jurisdiction, meaning that country X could request country Y to extradite a citizen of country X where it is alleged that he committed an offence within Article 3(1) in country Z.

---

99 For example, some instruments prevent extradition to countries where the perpetrator could be tortured or subject to capital punishment (see, most notably, the *European Convention on Human Rights* as set out in *Soering v. United Kingdom* (1989) 11 EHRR 439 and *Ahmed v. Turkey* (1997) 24 EHRR 278.
100 Note that Article 4 (3) includes a requirement of *aut dedere aut juidacre* (extradite or prosecute).

8.4.3 International cooperation and support

Article 6 of OPSC requires States to 'afford one another the greatest measure of assistance in connection with investigations or criminal or extradition proceedings . . . including assistance in obtaining evidence at their disposal necessary for the proceedings'. It was noted earlier that a difficulty with extending jurisdiction is that the evidence may not be immediately available, and article 6 seeks to address this in part. Article 6 is reinforced by article 7, which requires, *inter alia*, States to take prompt measure to seize and confiscate goods, materials and proceeds of sexual exploitation,[101] including requests from other States.[102] The mischief of article 7 is obviously to ensure that those who are involved in commercial sexual exploitation do not profit from their activities. OPSC does not, however, say what should happen to the monies realised. It would have been useful if, at the very least, the Optional Protocol had recommended that the monies were placed in a fund to assist victims.

International cooperation and support is not restricted to government agencies. Considerable cooperation exists at other levels, something hinted at by article 10(1) which, along with obliging States to cooperate internationally, requires States to work with international organisations and NGOs. It was noted earlier (see section 7.2.3) that this can include cooperation with industry and this has become increasingly important in recent years.

A good example of cooperation can be found from the 2009 annual report of the current Special Rapporteur, which highlights the work of the 'Virtual Global Taskforce' (VGT) (Maalla 2009: 21). The VGT was established in 2003 and

> comprises the Australian Federal Police as Chair, the Child Exploitation and Online Protection Centre in the UK, the Royal Canadian Mounted Police, the US Department of Homeland Security, INTERPOL, the Italian Postal and Communication Police Service, the Ministry of Interior for the United Arab Emirates, the New Zealand Police and Europol.[103]

In recognition of the need for multi-party cooperation, the VGT's aims are to make the internet a safer place by identifying, locating and helping children at risk and holding perpetrators to account.

8.4.4 Assisting victims

A difficulty with the global nature of child sexual exploitation is that it makes the identification of victims somewhat difficult. A (local) police unit may receive, for example, a pornographic picture of a child or an advertisement for sex with a

---

101 OPSC, art. 7(1).
102 OPSC, art. 7(2).
103 See <www.afp.gov.au/what-we-do/crime-types/child-protection/virtual-global-taskforce> (accessed 29 October 2019).

child but they may not know who that child is. If they recover children from trafficking or prostitution it may not necessarily be easy to identify where they came from. One commentator has noted that cooperation at the international level is necessary to safeguard children (Palmer 2005: 66), and this is reflected within the text of OPSC.

Article 10(2) requires States parties to cooperate 'to assist child victims in their physical and psychological recovery, social reintegration and repatriation'. OPSC goes further and notes that social and economic deprivation could be a causal link to sexual exploitation and that these matters must be addressed too (article 10(3)), including by the provision of 'financial, technical or other assistance' at a multilateral, regional or bilateral level (article 10(4)).

The principal provision that deals with assistance to victims is contained within article 8 of OPSC. Article 8(1) requires a series of measures to be adopted 'at all levels of the criminal justice system'. The measures are:

(a) adapting the court proceedings to recognise the vulnerability of victims as witnesses,
(b) informing the child of their rights, their role and the timing and progress of the proceedings,
(c) allowing the views, needs and concerns of the child victim to be raised,
(d) providing appropriate support services to child victims throughout the process,
(e) protecting the privacy and identity of the child victim,
(f) providing, in appropriate cases, for the safety of the child victim and their family,
(g) avoiding unnecessary delay in the disposition of the case.

These are challenging measures for most judicial systems, including developed countries. It is an area that both the Special Rapporteur and the Committee on the Rights of the Child pay particular attention to, although an annual report of the Special Rapporteur suggests that the broad picture is that there is still inadequate provision of assistance to victims (Maalla 2009: 16).

Article 8(2) of OPSC states that where there is doubt as to the age of the child this should not prevent the initiation of criminal investigation. It should be noted that this provision does not state that criminal proceedings cannot be initiated – since in many jurisdictions identifying the age of the child would be critical to a prosecution – but it does require an investigation to occur as this may allow the age of the child to be ascertained.

Article 8(6) makes clear that the provisions of the article are not designed to prevent the accused from receiving a fair trial. This is an important point as other international instruments will uphold the right of a suspect to be treated fairly. The essence of article 8(6) is to ensure that the various States consider how to best balance the needs of the victim and the rights of the defendant.

8.4.4.1 States obligation to 'trafficked children'?

It is important to note that 'children' are not a homogenous group, with differences in age and maturity giving rise to different needs, expectations and vulnerabilities. Girls and boys can be similarly disaggregated (Gallagher 2011: 427). States have a specific obligation to address the special vulnerabilities of the child, however little clarity with regards to the substantive content of that obligation exists (Gallagher 2011). In accordance with Article 35 of the CRC, the Committee and the Special Rapporteur have called upon States Parties to take appropriate measures to prevent trafficking, including identifying unaccompanied and separated children,[104] the appointment of guardians, regularly inquiring as to their whereabouts, and 'conducting information campaigns that are age appropriate, gender-sensitive and in a language and medium that is understandable to the child'.[105]

8.5 Reporting mechanisms

The reporting mechanism of the *Convention on the Rights of the Child* is discussed elsewhere in this book (section 3.5) and, obviously, States parties are obliged to follow this in respect of article 34 (sections 3.7.6.3 and 3.7.9.3). However, in the wider field of commercial sexual exploitation there are additional reporting mechanisms. There are two of primary relevance here; the Special Rapporteur and the mechanism provided in OPSC.

The office of the Special Rapporteur was outlined earlier (section 7.2.1.1), but part of her work is to visit countries to assess their approach to tackling the behaviour under her remit: see the former Special Rapporteur Maalla (2008: 9), who discusses the role of visits in the context of her mandate. These visits are summarised in each annual report and cross-references are also made to the reports submitted by countries under either the *Convention on the Rights of the Child* or OPSC. The ability to visit and comment on countries should allow for an additional check to be made on the monitoring process, although it was noted earlier (section 7.2.1.2) that there are concerns about whether the office of the Special Rapporteur is adequately funded.

Article 13(1) of OPSC requires a State that has ratified the Optional Protocol to provide a report to the Committee on the Rights of the Child giving comprehensive information about the measures taken to implement the Optional Protocol in domestic law. After this initial report, States are required to report every five years.[106] Where a States party has also ratified the *Convention on the Rights of the Child*,

---

104 Report of the Special Rapporteur on Sale of Children, Child Prostitution and Child Pornography, Juan Miguel Petit, Addendum: Mission to Greece (UN Doc. E/CN.4/2006/67/Add.3), 27 March 2006; and CRC General Comment No. 6.
105 CRC General Comment No. 6, Treatment of unaccompanied and separated children outside their country of origin (CRC/GC/2005/6), 1 September 2005.
106 OPSC, art. 12(2).

its report on OPSC should form a discrete part of its wider five-yearly report on the *Convention on the Rights of the Child*. Where a State has not ratified the *Convention on the Rights of the Child* but has ratified OPSC (e.g. the United States), then its report will focus solely on the Optional Protocol.

It has already been observed that the reporting process of the *Convention on the Rights of the Child* has suffered from delays, both in terms of the delay of the Committee on the Rights of the Child in processing reports and in the willingness of States to submit their country reports on time (see section 3.5, Table 3.3). This has been a pervasive problem both in the *Convention on the Rights of the Child* mechanisms and for other human rights treaty bodies, but there appears some evidence to suggest that this has improved in respect of the reports relating to the Optional Protocol. It is obviously crucial to the integrity of the process that the reports are considered promptly but also carefully. A 'rubber stamp' is of no assistance, but neither are delays of several years.

8.6 Concluding remarks

The issue of child sexual exploitation will undoubtedly continue to be a prevalent issue requiring increasingly sophisticated legal and political solutions. The advent of the internet has heralded an era of borderless crimes of which child sexual exploitation is fast becoming among the most profitable. This necessitates cooperation between states in order to bring perpetrators to justice, and such collaboration has been crucial in bringing down the world's largest markets of child pornography in 2019. Interstate legal responses will no doubt be a marked feature of future criminal prosecutions for child sexual exploitation.

Chapter 9

Children in armed conflict

9.1 Children and armed conflict: the international law framework

This chapter discusses the international framework relating to children's involvement and association with armed conflict. This takes a number of forms: the treatment of child civilians in armed conflicts; the damaging impact of armed conflicts on children; the recruitment and use of children by State and non-State armed forces; the reintegration of child soldiers into society; and the international criminal justice available for those (including child soldiers themselves) who may have committed 'crimes against humanity' and 'war crimes'. This involves a consideration of 'international humanitarian law', 'international human rights law' and 'international criminal law.'

There are some important contextual points to note before we examine the relevant international law. First, the international legal framework has had to respond to the changing patterns of armed conflicts over the past 60 years; *inter*-State wars are now significantly eclipsed by the proliferation of *intra*-State conflicts. The former could involve two or more states in armed conflict while the latter could involve non-state armed groups ('rebels') against state armed forces or rebels in warfare with each other. There has also been in recent years an increase in the number of intra-State conflicts that are internationalized, that is where another State supports one side or another and this 'often has the effect of increasing casualty rates and prolonging conflicts' (SIPRI 2013: 2). The protracted conflicts in Syria and Yemen come to mind. Second, the proportion of civilian casualties has greatly increased over the same period and the largest proportion of these has been women and children. Third, the ground-breaking 'Machel Report'[1] in 1996 on the impact of armed conflict on children galvanised a unique confluence of humanitarian concern with the growing presence of the children's rights agenda on the international stage (see section 9.2.3 below). Finally, the United Nations

---

1 General Assembly, *Impact of Armed Conflict on Children: report of the expert of the Secretary-General, Ms. Graça Machel*, submitted pursuant to General Assembly resolution 48/157 (the 'Machel Report'), UN Doc. A/51/306 (26 August 1996). Available at: <www.un.org/documents/ga/docs/51/plenary/a51-306.htm> (accessed 15 November 2013).

has, following a series of Security Council resolutions (section 9.2.1), attempted to mainstream issues around children and armed conflict within its primary mission to maintain global peace and security.

This section examines the influences of international humanitarian law, principally the *Geneva Conventions of 1949*[2] along with the *Additional Protocols of 1977*,[3] followed by consideration of the main international human rights instruments relevant to this area, that is, the *UN Convention on the Rights of the Child*[4] along with the *Optional Protocol to the Convention on the Rights of the Child on the involvement of children in Armed Conflict*[5] (OPAC), the *African Charter on the Rights and Welfare of the Child*[6] and the *Worst Forms of Child Labour Convention*.[7]

9.1.1 Child soldiering

One of the manifestations of modern armed conflict is the increased use of child soldiers. International law now has to grapple with the scourge of children recruited by state and non-state groups perhaps at a scale, hitherto, unseen. As Fox notes,

> it is important to stress that the contemporary child soldiers phenomenon is very new indeed, for in the post-cold war era it has reached proportions – both in terms of scope and extremes – that stretch far beyond any previous occurrences in human history. It is simply unprecedented.
>
> (2005: 28)

---

2 International Committee of the Red Cross (ICRC), *Geneva Convention for the Amelioration of the Condition of the Wounded and Sick in Armed Forces in the Field (First Geneva Convention)*, adopted 12 August 1949, 75 UNTS 31 (entered into force 21 October 1950).

ICRC, *Geneva Convention for the Amelioration of the Condition of Wounded, Sick and Shipwrecked Members of Armed Forces at Sea (Second Geneva Convention)*, adopted 12 August 1949, 75 UNTS 85 (entered into force 21 October 1950). ICRC, *Geneva Convention Relative to the Treatment of Prisoners of War (Third Geneva Convention)*, 12 August 1949, 75 UNTS 135 (entered into force 21 October 1950).

ICRC, *Geneva Convention Relative to the Protection of Civilian Persons in Time of War (Fourth Geneva Convention)*, 12 August 1949, 75 UNTS 287 (entered into force 21 October 1950). At the time of writing 195 States parties had ratified/acceded to each of the four *Geneva Conventions of 1949*.

3 ICRC, *Protocol Additional to the Geneva Conventions of 12 August 1949, and relating to the Protection of Victims of International Armed Conflicts (Protocol I)*, 8 June 1977, 1125 UNTS 3 (entered into force 7 December 1979). ICRC, *Protocol Additional to the Geneva Conventions of 12 August 1949, and relating to the Protection of Victims of Non-International Armed Conflicts (Protocol II)*, 8 June 1977, 1125 UNTS 609 (entered into force 7 December 1978).

4 Opened for signature 20 November 1989, 1577 UNTS 3 (entered into force 2 September 1990).

5 Opened for signature 25 May 2000, 2173 UNTS 222 (entered into force 12 February 2002). OPAC had 129 signatories and 152 ratifications as at 16 November 2013.

6 OAU, *African Charter on the Rights and Welfare of the Child*, 11 July 1990, CAB/LEG/24.9/49 (1990), entered into force 29 November 1999; 47 of the 54 African States had ratified/acceded to this treaty as at 21 February 2013. Article 16 requires States parties to protect children against abuse, including sexual abuse.

7 International Labour Organization, *Prohibition and Immediate Action for the Elimination of the Worst Forms of Child Labour Convention*, ILO Convention No 182 (17 Jun 1999). This Convention had 177 parties as at 18 November 2013.

With the changing nature and proliferation of conflicts, children have increasingly become victims of recruitment into warfare. Recent wars in places such as Syria and Yemen have witnessed the recruitment of children.

There are a variety of reasons for the involvement of children in armed conflicts. State armies and armed group find children as a resource from which armies and non-state armed groups can boost their troops and replenish their diminishing fighting forces. Groups such as the so-called Islamic State of Iraq and Syria (ISIS) regarded minors as an essential component of the continued existence of the 'caliphate' (AIVD and NCTV 2017).

Children are considered easy to manipulate and without a sense of danger. Commercial and illegal trafficking in small arms has replaced transfers of heavier, high maintenance weapons, which had once kept children in support roles when participating in armed conflict. Now, children can participate on the battlefront. Light weapons such as AK-47s, which are cheap in some countries, easy to carry and widely available are easy to use and maintain. Recruitment of children can also be considered in the context of poverty and ethnic affiliations. Many children, particularly in eastern DRC have joined militias in defence of their ethnic group, with the tacit consent of elders and parents, or under the powerful influence of militia leaders of their own ethnic group (Redress Trust 2006). Many others have been driven to enlist as a result of abject poverty, after suffering terrible losses in conflict, or as a means of putting food on their family's table or defending their family or communities' livelihood from continuous attack by other groups.

9.1.1.1 *International humanitarian law*

This is the body of law that comprises 'all those rules of international law which are designed to regulate the treatment of the individual – civilian or military, wounded or active – in international armed conflicts' (Fleck 2013: 11). It famously includes the *Geneva Conventions of 1949* and two *Additional Protocols* to these Conventions in 1977, though the term 'international humanitarian law' does not appear in any of these instruments.

9.1.1.1.1 THE GENEVA CONVENTIONS OF 1949

Most of the content of the Geneva Conventions[8] is now considered to be declaratory of customary international law (Fleck 2013: 28). The various Conventions adopted prior to 1949, the so-called 'Hague Law' focused on weapons and combatants, not civilians. Protections for civilians were annexed to the *Hague*

---

8 See n. 2 above. The full text of the *Geneva Conventions of 1949* and the *Additional Protocols of 1977*, along with commentaries, can be found on the International Committee of the Red Cross (ICRC) website. Available at: <www.icrc.org/ihl> (accessed 16 November 2013).

Conventions of 1899 and 1907 as regulations.[9] However, the *Geneva Convention IV: Relative to the Protection of Civilian Persons in Time of War of 1949* ('Geneva Convention IV')[10] was the first treaty to focus on the protection of civilians during armed conflict, though it is principally concerned with their treatment while 'in the hands of an opposing party or who are the victims of war, rather than with regulating the conduct of parties to a conflict in order to protect civilians' (Harvey 2003: 7). The Geneva Conventions of 1949 reflected people's experiences of the Second World War.

> Recent wars have emphasized in tragic fashion how necessary it is to have treaty rules for the protection of children. During the last World War, in particular, the mass migrations, bombing raids and deportations separated thousands of children from their parents. The absence of any means of identifying these children, some of whom were even too young to vouch for their own identity, had disastrous consequences. Thousands of them are irretrievably lost to their own families and thousands of fathers and mothers will always suffer the grief of their loss. It is therefore to be hoped that effective measures can be taken to avoid such harrowing experiences in the future.[11]

Geneva Convention IV contains a brief section[12] concerning the general protection of the civilian population against certain consequences of war. Most of Geneva Convention IV[13] addresses the status and treatment of protected persons, of which children form one category. One provision of Geneva Convention IV allows that the parties to a conflict may establish 'hospital and safety zones' in order to protect from the effects of war, the 'wounded, sick and aged persons, children under fifteen, expectant mothers and mothers of children under seven'.[14] Another provision mandates parties to the conflict to 'endeavour to conclude local

---

9 International Conferences (The Hague), *Convention (II) with Respect to the Laws and Customs of War on Land and Its Annex: Regulations Concerning the Laws and Customs of War on Land*, 29 July 1899 (entered into force 4 September 1900). International Conferences (The Hague), *Hague Convention (IV) Respecting the Laws and Customs of War on Land and Its Annex: Regulations Concerning the Laws and Customs of War on Land*, 18 October 1907 (entered into force 26 January 1910).
10 ICRC, *Geneva Convention Relative to the Protection of Civilian Persons in Time of War (Fourth Geneva Convention)*, 12 August 1949, 75 UNTS 287 (entered into force 21 October 1950).
11 ICRC, *Commentaries on the Geneva Conventions of 1949*, Conv. IV, art. 24, 185. Available at: <www.icrc.org/ihl> (accessed 16 November 2013).
12 *Geneva Convention IV*, Part II, arts 13–26.
13 *Geneva Convention IV*, Part III, arts 27–141.
14 'Certain definite categories – children under fifteen and mothers of children under seven – were nevertheless chosen because the Conference considered that they were appropriate, reasonable and generally in accord with the requirements of the physical and mental development of children.' *ICRC Commentaries*, Conv. IV, art. 14, p. 126.

agreements for the removal from besieged or encircled areas' of a number of vulnerable groups including children.[15]

Subject to certain conditions, there is also a provision that prescribes that States parties to the Convention must allow 'the free passage of all consignments of medical and hospital stores and objects necessary for religious worship', and this requires the free passage of 'essential foodstuffs, clothing and tonics intended for children under fifteen, expectant mothers and maternity cases'.[16] As will be noticed later, the indication of 'under fifteen' as the prominent protective threshold for children, was later to influence the development of the international legal architecture on children during armed conflict in a problematic way. The Geneva Conventions do not specifically reference child soldiers or define childhood. Geneva Convention IV also contains a *general* child welfare protective clause:

- The Parties to the conflict shall take the necessary measures to ensure that children under fifteen, who are orphaned or are separated from their families as a result of the war, are not left to their own resources, and that their maintenance, the exercise of their religion and their education are facilitated in all circumstances. Their education shall, as far as possible, be entrusted to persons of a similar cultural tradition.
- The Parties to the conflict shall facilitate the reception of such children in a neutral country for the duration of the conflict with the consent of the Protecting Power, if any, and under due safeguards for the observance of the principles stated in the first paragraph.
- They shall, furthermore, endeavour to arrange for all children under twelve to be identified by the wearing of identity discs, or by some other means.[17]

The International Committee of the Red Cross (ICRC) comments that the principles set out in this article 'apply to all the children in question who are living in the territory of a Party to the conflict, whether they are nationals of that country or aliens'.[18] The provision regarding accommodating children in a neutral country is based on the belief that '[h]owever well organised child welfare measures may be, they will never be able to protect the children completely from all the various privations suffered by the population of a belligerent country'.[19] Given the consistent use of the age of 15 years elsewhere in Geneva Convention IV, it is perhaps

---

15 'Unlike Article 14 (Hospital and Safety Zones), the present Article does not fix an age limit up to which children are to be evacuated. The belligerents concerned are free to come to an agreement on the ... subject; the upper limit of 15 years of age, which applies to admission to a safety zone, seems reasonable and would appear to merit adoption in the present instance.' *ICRC Commentaries*, Conv. IV, art. 17, pp. 138–9.
16 *Geneva Convention IV*, art. 23.
17 *Geneva Convention IV*, art. 24.
18 ICRC Commentaries, Conv. IV, art. 24, p. 187.
19 ICRC Commentaries, Conv. IV, art. 24, p. 188.

surprising to see the reference to an age limit of 12 years in relation to the third paragraph of article 24. This was chosen at an earlier international conference of the ICRC on the basis that 'it was considered that children over 12 were generally capable of stating their own identity'.[20] It would seem that there was some contention over this provision at the Diplomatic Conference in 1949.[21]

There are also provisions that mandate the 'occupying power', with the cooperation of the national or local authorities, to 'facilitate the proper working of all institutions devoted to the care and education of children'. The occupying power is also obliged to 'take all necessary steps to facilitate the identification of children and the registration of their parentage' and cannot change their personal status 'nor enlist them in formations or organizations subordinate to it'. For children whose identity is in doubt, there is provision for a special section of the 'official information Bureau'[22] to take responsibility for them. The occupying power is also obliged not to hinder any preferential measures regarding food, medical care and protection against the effects of war that were in place before an occupation 'in favour of children under 15 years, expectant mothers, and mothers of children under 7 years.'[23]

With regard to detainment, it is provided that members of the same family 'and in particular parents and children' must be accommodated in the same place of internment, subject to certain exceptions, and internees 'may request that their children who are left at liberty without parental care shall be interned with them'.[24] Furthermore, internees who are expectant and nursing mothers and children under 15 years 'shall be given additional food, in proportion to their physiological needs'.[25] There is also an obligation on the 'detaining power' to 'encourage intellectual, educational and recreational pursuits, sports and games amongst internees', and specifically the education of children and young people is protected; 'they shall be allowed to attend schools either within the place of internment or outside' and 'special playgrounds shall be reserved for children and

---

20 *ICRC Commentaries*, Conv. IV, art. 24, p 189.
21 'The idea of identity discs was treated with scepticism by many delegates, who pointed out for instance how mistakes could arise from children losing or exchanging their identity discs. That danger certainly exists and although experience of this method of identification in the armed forces has been generally satisfactory, that does not necessarily prove anything in regard to children'. *ICRC Commentaries*, Conv. IV, art. 24, p. 189.
22 This must be set up under the terms of article 136 on the outbreak of hostilities or in case of occupation. 'The primary function of these Bureaux is . . . to transmit to the State of origin all available information concerning measures taken in regard to its subjects by the Power in whose hands they are. The official Bureau which the Occupying Power is thus bound to open in occupied territory is a valuable source of information of all kinds. It is in a position to render useful service, particularly in the case of children whose identity has not been established by the local services concerned'. *ICRC Commentaries*, Conv. IV, art. 50, p. 289.
23 *Geneva Convention IV*, art. 50.
24 *Geneva Convention IV*, art. 82.
25 *Geneva Convention IV*, art. 89.

young people'.[26] Finally, the rules regarding the release of interned persons by the detaining power privilege 'in particular children, pregnant women and mothers with infants and young children, wounded and sick, and internees who have been detained for a long time'.[27]

However, a significant weakness of the Geneva Conventions is that they apply only to international conflicts and not to the non-international/internal conflicts which, as already noted, have become the predominant mode of armed conflict in recent decades. Understandably, the framework was developed after the Second World War, a conflict which involved war between states rather than internal warfare. The exception to this is found in an article which appears in all four Geneva Conventions and is known as 'common article 3'.

Article 3
In the case of armed conflict not of an international character occurring in the territory of one of the High Contracting Parties, each Party to the conflict shall be bound to apply, as a minimum, the following provisions:

(1) Persons taking no active part in the hostilities, including members of armed forces who have laid down their arms and those placed 'hors de combat' by sickness, wounds, detention, or any other cause, shall in all circumstances be treated humanely, without any adverse distinction founded on race, colour, religion or faith, sex, birth or wealth, or any other similar criteria. To this end, the following acts are and shall remain prohibited at any time and in any place whatsoever with respect to the above-mentioned persons:

   (a) violence to life and person, in particular murder of all kinds, mutilation, cruel treatment and torture;
   (b) taking of hostages;
   (c) outrages upon personal dignity, in particular humiliating and degrading treatment;
   (d) the passing of sentences and the carrying out of executions without previous judgment pronounced by a regularly constituted court, affording all the judicial guarantees which are recognized as indispensable by civilized peoples.

(2) The wounded and sick shall be collected and cared for. An impartial humanitarian body, such as the International Committee of the Red Cross, may offer its services to the Parties to the conflict.

---

26 *Geneva Convention IV*, art. 94. 'This provision is one more proof of the interest shown by the Geneva Conventions in child welfare. It represents a most useful addition to the provisions contained in Article 50, which is one of the Articles (14, 17, 24, 26 etc.) laying down exceptions to the ordinary regulations in favour of children and contains special provisions dealing with their care and education.'. *ICRC Commentaries*, Conv. IV, art. 94, p. 412.

27 *Geneva Convention IV*, art. 132.

> The Parties to the conflict should further endeavour to bring into force, by means of special agreements, all or part of the other provisions of the present Convention.
>
> The application of the preceding provisions shall not affect the legal status of the Parties to the conflict.[28]

Article 3
applies to non-international conflicts only, and will be the only Article applicable to them until such time as a special agreement between the Parties has brought into force between them all or part of the other provisions of the Convention.[29]

This article ensures that a set of minimum standards are recognised and

> provides a legal basis for charitable interventions by the International Committee of the Red Cross or any other impartial humanitarian organization – interventions which in the past were all too often refused on the ground that they represented unfriendly interference in the internal affairs of a State.[30]

As can be observed, the Geneva Conventions provided protection for children *not* involved in war but not to those who *participated* in armed conflict, commonly known as 'child soldiers." This is despite indications that children did take part in the Second World War.

9.1.1.2 UN Declaration on the Protection of Women and Children in Emergency and Armed Conflict of 1974

This (non-binding) Declaration was adopted by the General Assembly in 1974.[31] It condemns and prohibits attacks and bombings on the civilian population, recognising that these inflict incalculable suffering, 'especially on women and children, who are the most vulnerable members of the population'.[32] It severely condemns the use of chemical and bacteriological weapons, recognising that this will inflict heavy civilian losses 'including defenceless women and children'.[33] States must make 'all efforts' in armed conflicts and military operations 'to spare women and

---

28 *Geneva Convention I*, art. 3; *Geneva Convention II*, art. 3; *Geneva Convention III*, art. 3; and, *Geneva Convention IV*, art. 3.
29 *ICRC Commentaries*, Conv. IV, art. 3, p 34
30 Ibid.
31 General Assembly, *Declaration on the Protection of Women and Children in Emergency and Armed Conflict*, 29th session, UN Doc. A/RES/29/3318 (14 December 1974).
32 *Declaration of 1974*, art. 1.
33 *Declaration of 1974*, art. 2.

children from the ravages of war' and '[a]ll the necessary steps shall be taken to ensure the prohibition of measures such as persecution, torture, punitive measures, degrading treatment and violence, particularly against that part of the civilian population that consists of women and children'.[34] The *Declaration of 1974* also indicates the criminal nature of violations of humanitarian law:

> All forms of repression and cruel and inhuman treatment of women and children, including imprisonment, torture, shooting, mass arrests, collective punishment, destruction of dwellings and forcible eviction, committed by belligerents in the course of military operations or in occupied territories shall be considered criminal.[35]

Finally, the Declaration asserts that (civilian) women and children 'shall not be deprived of shelter, food, medical aid or other inalienable rights.'[36] Again, the declaration did not make any pronouncements on the protection of 'child soldiers'.

9.1.1.3 The Additional Protocols of 1977 to the Geneva Conventions of 1949

Protocol I[37] extended the protection of persons affected by international conflicts by, among other things, upgrading the standards relating to the conduct of hostilities. It also offered further protection for children in international conflicts, and contains a general child protection clause as follows.

> 1. Children shall be the object of special respect and shall be protected against any form of indecent assault. The Parties to the conflict shall provide them with the care and aid they require, whether because of their age or for any other reason.
>
> 2. The Parties to the conflict shall take all feasible measures in order that children who have not attained the age of fifteen years do not take a direct part in hostilities and, in particular, they shall refrain from recruiting them into their armed forces. In recruiting among those persons who have attained the age of fifteen years but who have not attained the age of eighteen years the Parties to the conflict shall endeavour to give priority to those who are oldest. . . . [paras 3, 4 and 5 omitted][38]

---

34 *Declaration of 1974*, art. 4.
35 *Declaration of 1974*, art. 5.
36 *Declaration of 1974*, art. 6.
37 ICRC, *Protocol Additional to the Geneva Conventions of 12 August 1949, and relating to the Protection of Victims of International Armed Conflicts (Protocol I)*, 8 June 1977, 1125 UNTS 3 (entered into force 7 December 1979).
38 *Protocol I*, art. 77(1) and (2)).

And for the first time, international humanitarian law made direct reference to child soldiering. The remaining paragraphs of article 77 above: continue the protection offered by this article for children under 15 years who have taken a direct part in hostilities and have fallen into the hands of an adverse party;[39] prescribe that children who are arrested, detained or interned have separate quarters from adults;[40] and prohibit the death penalty for a child less than 18 years for offences related to the armed conflict.[41] A criticism of *Protocol 1* is that it restricted its protection to children who took '*direct* part in hostilities'. Further, *Protocol I*[42] provides some ground rules regulating the parties to a conflict in arranging the evacuation of children other than their own nationals to a foreign country.[43] This is only permitted for a temporary period 'where compelling reasons of the health or medical treatment of the children or, except in occupied territory, their safety, so require' and parental consent must be obtained. Article 78 of *Protocol I*, attempts to ensure that 'each child's education, including his religious and moral education as his parents desire, shall be provided while he is away with the greatest possible continuity'. Finally, with a view to returning the children, the party arranging the evacuation and the authorities of the receiving country must establish a prescribed list of identity details for each child, which they shall send to the Central Tracing Agency of the ICRC.

Protocol II[44] was, significantly, the first binding international instrument to deal with the parties' conduct in *non-international* armed conflicts. It develops the basic guarantees of 'common article 3' of the *Geneva Conventions of 1949* (see text in section 9.1.1.1) and contains an abbreviated version of the child protection provisions contained in *Protocol I*.

Article 4(3)
Children shall be provided with the care and aid they require, and in particular:

(a) they shall receive an education, including religious and moral education, in keeping with the wishes of their parents, or in the absence of parents, of those responsible for their care;

---

39 *Protocol I*, art. 77(3).
40 *Protocol I*, art. 77(4).
41 *Protocol I*, art. 77(5). *Protocol I*, art. 68 also prohibits pronouncing the death penalty on persons under 18 years of age, a provision also adopted in the ICCPR, art. 6(5).
42 *Protocol I*, art. 78.
43 'This is to avoid the risk of removal for the purposes of ethnic cleansing and unnecessary removal of children, representing a major change in practice from World War II when mass evacuation of children took place' (Harvey 2003: 10).
44 ICRC, *Protocol Additional to the Geneva Conventions of 12 August 1949, and relating to the Protection of Victims of Non-International Armed Conflicts (Protocol II)*, 8 June 1977, 1125 UNTS 609 (entered into force 7 December 1978).

(b) all appropriate steps shall be taken to facilitate the reunion of families temporarily separated;
(c) children who have not attained the age of 15 years shall neither be recruited in the armed forces or groups nor allowed to take part in hostilities;
(d) the special protection provided by this article to children who have not attained the age of 15 years shall remain applicable to them if they take a direct part in hostilities despite the provisions of subparagraph (c) and are captured;
(e) measures shall be taken, if necessary, and whenever possible with the consent of their parents or persons who by law or custom are primarily responsible for their care, to remove children temporarily from the area in which hostilities are taking place to a safer area within the country and ensure that they are accompanied by persons responsible for their safety and well-being.[45]

Protocol II provided stronger protection. Article 4(3)(c) states that 'children who have not attained the age of 15 years shall neither be recruited in the armed forces or groups nor allowed to take part in hostilities.' It includes 'groups' and implies that *indirect* participation of children is also impermissible. Unfortunately, *Protocol II* is expressly not applicable to 'situations of internal disturbances and tensions, such as riots, isolated and sporadic acts of violence and other acts of a similar nature, as not being armed conflict'.[46] Consequently, it is applicable to a smaller range of internal conflicts than that covered by common article 3 of the *Geneva Conventions of 1949*.

9.1.2 International human rights law

In addition to the body of international humanitarian law outlined above, this section considers the principal international human rights instruments impacting on children and armed conflict. It deals, in particular, with the *Convention on the Rights of the Child* (1989) and the *Optional Protocol to the Convention on the Rights of the Child on the Involvement of Children in Armed Conflict* (OPAC). It should be remembered that international concern for the plight of children in armed conflicts is not new. Indeed, it is clear that one of the main motivating factors underlying the adoption of the *Declaration of the Rights of the Child* in 1924 by the League of Nations (the 'Jebb Declaration') (see section 3.2 in this book) had been the disastrous impact that the war in the Balkans had had on children (Marshall 1999: 106).

---

45 *Protocol II*, art. 4(3).
46 *Protocol II*, art. 1(2).

9.1.2.1 UN Convention on the Rights of the Child of 1989

From the outset, the issue of children and armed conflict was of particular concern to the drafters of the *Convention on the Rights of the Child*[47] (UNCRC) and to the Committee on the Rights of the Child.

> During the drafting of article 38, there was a strong move not only to ensure that its provisions did not in any way undermine existing standards in international humanitarian law but also to go beyond existing international standards so that children were protected up to the age of 18, in order to secure consistency with the rest of the Convention. The final version of article 38 was a compromise.
>
> (Hodgkin and Newell 2007: 574)

Indeed, this topic formed the subject of the Committee's first *Day of General Discussion* in 1992.[48] The UNCRC contains two significant articles relating to children and armed conflict. The first – article 38 – proved to be one of the most controversial issues dealt with by the drafters of the Convention: see the text of article 38 in section 3.7.9.5 in this book.

The first paragraph of this article ties in States parties' obligations to respect (and *ensure* respect for) the rules of international humanitarian law (section 9.1.1.1), though it does not appear to raise in any way these (minimum) standards of humanitarian law. The second paragraph obliges States parties to take 'all feasible measures', a formulation allowing States a certain amount of discretion, 'to ensure that persons who have not attained the age of fifteen years do not take a direct part in hostilities.' The Convention was a reversal of the protection offered by *Protocol II* by referring to the limited protection of children not to take *direct* part in hostilities.

As we have seen in the discussion above, the age of 15 years is frequently adverted to in the *Geneva Conventions of 1949* and the *Additional Protocols of 1977*, and was therefore a natural age limit for the drafters of the *Convention on the Rights of the Child* to alight upon and to do so consistently with the existing body of international humanitarian law and customary international law. However, there was substantial discomfort about the 15-year age limit. These are the only provisions of the UNCRC that do not apply to all children under 18 years. The third paragraph mandates States parties to refrain from recruiting under-15-year-old persons into the armed forces, and, in recruiting 15-to-17-year-olds, States parties should endeavour to prioritise the recruitment of the oldest. By contrast, the comparable article appearing in the *African Charter on the Rights*

---

47 Opened for signature 20 November 1989, 1577 UNTS 3 (entered into force 2 September 1990).
48 Committee on the Rights of the Child, *Day of General Discussion on 'Children in armed conflicts'*, Report on the second session, CRC/C/10, (19 October 1992) [75(e)].

and Welfare of the Child[49] does not carry the 15-year limit and is more explicit in its application to internal armed conflicts.[50]

The fourth paragraph of article 38, for the avoidance of any doubt, makes it expressly clear that States parties must observe their obligations in international humanitarian law to protect children from the impact of armed conflict. There was some general dissatisfaction by human rights groups and States parties about the 15-year threshold. Several States parties registered declarations or reservations in respect of article 38, disagreeing with the provisions in paragraphs 2 and 3 of this article concerning the participation and recruitment of children from the age of 15 years.[51] Others likewise rejected the 15-year threshold on the basis that this was, in any event, inconsistent with article 3(1) of the *Convention on the Rights of the Child* which determines that the best interests of the child is a primary consideration.[52] Others expressly declared that 'it would have been preferable to fix that age at 18 years in accordance with the principles and norms prevailing in various regions and countries'.[53] In the UK, 16- and 17-year-olds can join the British Army as soldiers, with consent from their parents. However, soldiers cannot be deployed to the frontline until they are aged 18.

The second key provision of the UNCRC is article 39, which deals with the recovery and reintegration of the child following armed conflict: see the text of article 39 in section 3.7.9.5.

This provision recognises, *inter alia*, the serious and potentially long-lasting effects of armed conflict on children and reflects some aspects of international humanitarian standards. The Committee commented in its *Day of General Discussion*:

> Consideration was particularly given to article 39 of the Convention: different experiences and programmes were brought to the attention of the Committee, underlying the need for resources and goods (namely, food and medicine). Moreover, emphasis was put on the need to consider a coherent plan for recovery and reintegration, to be planned and implemented in a combined effort by United Nations bodies and non-governmental organizations. Attention should be paid to (a) the implementation and monitoring of

---

49 OAU, *African Charter on the Rights and Welfare of the Child*, 11 July 1990, CAB/LEG/24.9/49 (1990) (entered into force 29 November 1999).
50 Ibid., art. 22: '1. States Parties to this Charter shall undertake to respect and ensure respect for rules of international humanitarian law applicable in armed conflicts which affect the child. 2. States Parties to the present Charter shall take all necessary measures to ensure that no child shall take a direct part in hostilities and refrain in particular, from recruiting any child. 3. States Parties to the present Charter shall, in accordance with their obligations under international humanitarian law, protect the civilian population in armed conflicts and shall take all feasible measures to ensure the protection and care of children who are affected by armed conflicts. Such rules shall also apply to children in situations of internal armed conflicts, tension and strife'.
51 For example, the declarations of Andorra, Argentina, The Netherlands and Spain.
52 See the declarations of Austria and Germany.
53 See the reservations of Colombia and Uruguay.

adequate strategies and (b) the need to reinforce the involvement of the family and the local community in this process.[54]

The Committee further highlighted the need to provide rehabilitative care in relation to children who were unaccompanied and separated from their parents outside their country of origin in a *General Comment* in 2005.

> 48. The obligation under article 39 of the Convention sets out the duty of States to provide rehabilitation services to children who have been victims of any form of abuse, neglect, exploitation, torture, cruel, inhuman and degrading treatment or armed conflicts. In order to facilitate such recovery and reintegration, culturally appropriate and gender-sensitive mental health care should be developed and qualified psychosocial counselling provided.
>
> 49. States shall, in particular where government capacity is limited, accept and facilitate assistance offered by UNICEF, the World Health Organization (WHO), United Nations Joint Programme on HIV/AIDS (UNAIDS), UNHCR and other agencies (art. 22 (2)) within their respective mandates, as well as, where appropriate, other competent intergovernmental organizations or non-governmental organizations in order to meet the health and healthcare needs of unaccompanied and separated children.[55]

The *General Comment* focuses on States parties' obligations towards former child soldiers in the following extract:

> *Former child soldiers*
> 56. Child soldiers should be considered primarily as victims of armed conflict. Former child soldiers, who often find themselves unaccompanied or separated at the cessation of the conflict or following defection, shall be given all the necessary support services to enable reintegration into normal life, including necessary psychosocial counselling. Such children shall be identified and demobilized on a priority basis during any identification and separation operation. Child soldiers, in particular, those who are unaccompanied or separated, should not normally be interned, but rather, benefit from special protection and assistance measures, in particular as regards their demobilization and rehabilitation. Particular efforts must be made to provide support and facilitate the reintegration of girls who have been associated with the military, either as combatants or in any other capacity.

---

54 Committee on the Rights of the Child, *Day of General Discussion on 'Children in armed conflicts'*, Report on the second session, CRC/C/10 (19 October 1992), [74].

55 Committee on the Rights of the Child, General Comment No. 6, Treatment of unaccompanied and separated children outside their country of origin, 39th session (CRC/GC/2005/6) 1 September 2005, [48–9].

57. If, under certain circumstances, exceptional internment of a child soldier over the age of 15 years is unavoidable and in compliance with international human rights and humanitarian law, for example, where she or he poses a serious security threat, the conditions of such internment should be in conformity with international standards, including article 37 of the Convention and those pertaining to juvenile justice, and should not preclude any tracing efforts and priority participation in rehabilitation programmes.[56]

The identification of the importance of achieving the recovery and reintegration into society of child soldiers and child victims of armed conflicts increasingly resonated with the more sophisticated analyses given to the impact of armed conflict on children in the debates appearing in the UN institutions, as reflected in the ground-breaking Machel report: see section 9.2.3 below.

9.1.2.2 The Worst Forms of Child Labour Convention of 1999

As we have seen (section 5.2.3), the definition of the *worst forms* of child labour according to the Convention[57] includes, *inter alia*, the 'forced or compulsory recruitment of children for use in armed conflict',[58] a definition that controversially fell short of a much broader prohibition on the use of children as soldiers in armed conflicts by some of the delegates to that negotiation (Davidson 2001: 217). The associated *Recommendation* to the *Worst Forms of Child Labour Convention* also notes that States parties should provide that forced or compulsory recruitment of children for use in armed conflict is made a criminal offence.[59]

9.1.2.3 Optional Protocol to the Convention on the Rights of the Child on the involvement of children in armed conflict of 2000 *(OPAC)*

In part, precisely because of the unsatisfactory compromises reached in relation to the drafting of article 38 of the UNCRC, there was sufficient support to establish *Optional Protocol to the Convention on the Rights of the Child on the involvement of children in armed conflict of 2000* (OPAC).[60] The appearance of a landmark

---

56 Ibid. [56–7].
57 International Labour Organization, ILO Convention concerning the Prohibition and Immediate Action for the Elimination of the Worst Forms of Child Labour, ILO Convention No. 182 (17 June 1999).
58 *The Worst Forms of Child Labour Convention of 1999*, art. 3(a).
59 *R190 – Worst Forms of Child Labour Recommendation*, 1999 (No. 190), Recommendation concerning the prohibition and immediate action for the elimination of the worst forms of child labour. Adoption: Geneva, 87th ILC session (17 June 1999), [12(a)].
60 Opened for signature 25 May 2000, 2173 UNTS 222 (entered into force 12 February 2002). OPAC had 129 signatories and 152 ratifications as at 16 November 2013.

report[61] by the expert, Mme Graça Machel, appointed by the Secretary-General, which had followed two years of consultation, extensive research and field visits, was also a key influence in the production of OPAC. The UN Commission on Human Rights (UNCHR)[62] established a working group to draft OPAC in 1994. In 1996 the General Assembly recommended, in response to the Machel report, that the Secretary-General appoint for a period of three years a *Special Representative on the impact of armed conflict on children*: see section 9.2.3 below. There were delays in the drafting process, not least because of the need to deal with a number of difficult issues: the minimum age of persons participating in hostilities; the issue of direct or indirect involvement in hostilities; the age of recruitment (voluntary or compulsory) into the armed forces; and whether or not a clause should be included to prevent child recruitment by non-governmental armed groups. The Committee issued *Recommendation No 1*[63] in 1998 on the subject of children and armed conflict, following its *Day of General Discussion* on the topic. The *Recommendation* expressed concerns about the delays in drafting OPAC. It also reaffirmed the belief that 'this new legal instrument is urgently needed in order to strengthen the levels of protection ensured by the Convention' and referred to its previous suggestion 'on the fundamental importance of raising the age of all forms of recruitment of children into the armed forces to 18 years and the prohibition of their involvement in hostilities'.[64]

In the meantime, another landmark international instrument was gaining attention, the *Rome Statute of the International Criminal Court* of 1998 (see section 9.3.1 below) which provided a mechanism of accountability for war crimes, crimes against humanity and other serious violations of humanitarian law. The Rome Statute came into force on 1 July 2002. At the time of publication, 138 states were signatories but only 123 are considered parties to the treaty.Read More The United States is a signatory to the treaty, but not a party.

OPAC entered into force on 12 February 2002. It attempts to lay down a higher standard than the UNCRC to prevent the direct participation of under-18-year-olds in armed combat or their compulsory recruitment:

> *Article 1*
> States Parties shall take all feasible measures to ensure that members of their armed forces who have not attained the age of 18 years do not take a direct part in hostilities.[65]

---

61 General Assembly, *Impact of Armed Conflict on Children: report of the expert of the Secretary-General, Ms. Graça Machel*, submitted pursuant to General Assembly resolution 48/157 (the 'Machel Report'), UN Doc. A/51/306 (26 August 1996).
62 The UNCHR was reconstituted as the UN Human Rights Council (UNHRC) in 2006: see section 2.5.1.1 in this book.
63 Committee on the Rights of the Child, *Recommendation No 1: Children in Armed Conflict*, 19th session, CRC/C/80, September 1998.
64 Ibid. [1, 3 and 5].
65 OPAC, art. 1.

Article 2
States Parties shall ensure that persons who have not attained the age of 18 years are not compulsorily recruited into their armed forces.[66]

This 18-year threshold is a leap from Article 38 of the UNCRC, which prohibits those under the age of 15 from taking a direct part in hostilities. This is a substantial step towards eliminating the long-existent trend of a two-tiered age division within the under-18 age group. Article 2 prohibits the compulsory recruitment of under-18-year-olds into a state's armed forces, also a step beyond the CRC, which does not specifically mention compulsory recruitment restrictions. However, the 'direct part' proviso is maintained. OPAC also falls short of achieving an absolute threshold of 18 years for participation and recruitment in armed conflict '. . . due to the reluctance of certain States, most notably the USA' (Harvey 2003: 13). It allows voluntary recruitment. Article 3 of OPAC provides a mechanism whereby each State party must raise in years the minimum age for voluntary recruitment from that set out in article 38(3) of the UNCRC.[67] However, it does not specify what it must be raised to, only that it must be raised. States parties must deposit a binding declaration upon ratification of, or accession to, OPAC that sets out the minimum age at which it will permit voluntary recruitment into its national armed forces and a description of safeguards it has adopted to ensure that such recruitment is not forced or coerced.[68] OPAC provides that States that do permit voluntary recruitment under the age of 18 years must maintain certain safeguards:

Article 3(3)
3. States Parties that permit voluntary recruitment into their national armed forces under the age of 18 years shall maintain safeguards to ensure, as a minimum, that:

(a) Such recruitment is genuinely voluntary;
(b) Such recruitment is carried out with the informed consent of the person's parents or legal guardians;
(c) Such persons are fully informed of the duties involved in such military service;
(d) Such persons provide reliable proof of age prior to acceptance into national military service.

It would appear then that states like the UK, which allow voluntary recruitment of those under 18, would be seen to be in compliance if provisions of Article 3 are met.

---

66 OPAC, art. 2.
67 The requirement to raise the minimum age for voluntary recruitment does not apply, however, 'to schools operated by or under the control of the armed forces' that are in keeping with the education standards set out in the *Convention on the Rights of the Child:* see OPAC, art. 3(5).
68 OPAC, art. 3(2).

A significant advance achieved in OPAC is the explicit recognition that 'armed groups', as distinct from the 'armed forces' of a State, have comparable impacts on children. The Preamble of OPAC states:

> § Condemning with the gravest concern the recruitment, training and use within and across national borders of children in hostilities by armed groups distinct from the armed forces of a State, and recognizing the responsibility of those who recruit, train and use children in this regard.[69]

Under article 4(1) of OPAC, such (non-State) armed militias or groups are absolutely prohibited from recruiting, or using in hostilities, under-18-year-olds. This different standard has not escaped observation. One commentator has noted that '[p]redictably, States have bound potential opponents with stronger obligations than they are prepared to accept for themselves, agreeing to stricter recruitment and deployment standards for rebel groups' (Harvey 2003: 28). However, the rationale appears to be based on the difficulties in monitoring the practices on non-state armed groups. States parties are encouraged to prevent any recruitment and use of children in hostilities, including the adoption of 'legal measures necessary to prohibit and criminalise such practices'.[70] This article also carefully notes that its application 'shall not affect the legal status of any party to an armed conflict'.[71] Nothing in OPAC shall be construed as 'precluding provisions in the law of a State Party or in international instruments and international humanitarian law that are more conducive to the realization of the rights of the child'.[72] States parties are under a duty, comparable to that contained in article 4 of the *Convention on the Rights of the Child* (see section 3.7.1 in this book) to take all necessary measures to ensure OPAC's effective implementation and enforcement within their own jurisdictions and to disseminate its principles and provisions widely.[73] States parties are also under a duty to take 'all feasible measures' to ensure the demobilisation of children who are recruited or used in hostilities in contravention of OPAC, and must 'when necessary' offer such persons appropriate assistance for their 'physical and psychological recovery and their social reintegration'.[74]

Article 7 of OPAC mandates States parties to cooperate in the implementation of the Optional Protocol, including the prevention of activity violating the Optional Protocol, and in the rehabilitation and social reintegration of victims. Technical cooperation and financial assistance is undertaken by the States parties and relevant international organisations.[75] States parties that are, 'in a position

---

69 OPAC, Preamble §11.
70 OPAC, art. 4(2).
71 OPAC, art. 4(3).
72 OPAC, art. 5.
73 OPAC, art. 6(1) and (2).
74 OPAC, art. 6(3).
75 OPAC, art. 7(1).

to do so', must provide assistance through existing multilateral, bilateral or other programmes, 'or, inter alia, through a voluntary fund established in accordance with the rules of the General Assembly'.[76]

OPAC also contains its own reporting procedure: see section 3.5 in this book for further details of the reporting procedures under the two substantive Optional Protocols. By way of illustrating how OPAC may be applied in practice, Case Study 9.1 contains some extracts from the Committee's Concluding Observations on China's initial report submitted under OPAC.

Case study 9.1

[Extract from:]
Concluding observations on the initial report of China submitted under article 8 of the Optional Protocol to the Convention on the Rights of the Child on the involvement of children in armed conflict, adopted by the Committee at its sixty-fourth session (16 September – 4 October 2013), CRC/C/OPAC/CHN/CO/1 (29 October 2013).

... [paras 1–3 omitted]

II. General observations
Positive aspects
4. The Committee welcomes the revision of the Law of the People's Republic of China on the Protection of Minors in December 2006 and in October 2012.
5. The Committee further welcomes the progress achieved in the adoption of national plans and programmes to facilitate the implementation of the Optional Protocol, including the adoption in July 2011 of the National Programme for Child Development (2011–2020) for mainland China.

III. General measures of implementation
Legislation
6. The Committee regrets that the Law of the People's Republic of China on National Defence does not explicitly criminalize recruitment of children up to 18 years.
7. The Committee recommends that the State party consider amending the Law on National Defence to criminalize recruitment and involvement of children under the age of 18 years in the Armed Forces.

---

76 OPAC, art. 7(2).

Independent monitoring
8. The Committee is concerned about the absence of an independent national human rights institution in line with the principles relating to the status of national institutions (the Paris Principles) to regularly monitor progress in the fulfilment of child rights under the Optional Protocol and to receive and address complaints from children.
9. In the light of its general comment No. 2 (2002) on the role of independent national human rights institutions in the promotion and protection of the rights of the child and of the recommendations made by several United Nations human rights bodies on the necessary establishment of an independent national human rights institution in line with the Paris Principles, the Committee urges the State party to establish an independent mechanism to monitor the fulfilment of rights under the Optional Protocol and to deal with children's complaints in a child-friendly and expeditious manner.

Dissemination and awareness-raising
10. The Committee recommends that the State party ensure that the principles and provisions of the Optional Protocol are widely disseminated among the general public, children and their families.

Training
11. The Committee regrets that the training programmes for members of the Armed Forces and relevant professional groups dealing with children do not fully cover the provisions of the Optional Protocol.
12. The Committee encourages the State party to provide training on the Optional Protocol to all members of its Armed Forces, in particular personnel dealing with children, authorities working for and with asylum-seeking and refugee children, the police, lawyers, judges, military judges, medical professionals, social workers and journalists.

Data
13. The Committee regrets the absence of information on the measures taken to establish a central data collection system in the State party – mainland China, Hong Kong, China, and Macao, China – to register all children within its jurisdiction who may have been recruited or used in hostilities.
14. The Committee recommends that the State party establish central data collection systems in mainland China, Hong Kong, China, and Macao, China, to identify and register all children within its jurisdiction

who may have been recruited or used in hostilities abroad, or detained or maimed. The Committee also recommends that the State party ensure that data on refugee and asylum-seeking children who have been victims of such practices are properly collected. All data should be disaggregated by, inter alia, sex, age, nationality, ethnic origin and socioeconomic background.

IV. Prevention
Voluntary recruitment

15. The Committee expresses concern that the Military Service Law of the People's Republic of China allows voluntary recruitment of children below the age of 18 years into the active military service. It regrets that the State party does not intend to raise the age of voluntary recruitment to 18 years. In addition, while the minimum voluntary enlistment age in the State Party is reported to be 17 years, its binding declaration in respect of the Optional Protocol, made at the time of accession, appears to contain a contradictory statement that citizens who have not yet reached 17 years by 31 December of a given year may be recruited for active service.

16. The Committee is also concerned about:

(a) The high number of total recruits under 18 years enrolled in the Armed Forces; and
(b) The absence of policy and practice to ensure that children under 18 years are not involved in participation in hostilities.

17. The Committee recommends that the State party review and raise the age for voluntary recruitment into the Armed Forces to 18 years in order to promote and strengthen the protection of children through an overall higher legal standard. It further recommends that the State party:

(a) Provide in its next periodic report information on the number and percentage of recruits under 18 years of age, if any, to the Armed Forces, as well as on the reported cases of recruitment irregularities, the nature of the complaints received and sanctions undertaken; and
(b) Explicitly prohibit the deployment of children under 18 years to areas where they may be at risk of indirect or direct participation in hostilities. The Committee further recommends that until such policy reform is undertaken, the State party put in place effective safeguards, including policies to ensure that children under 18 years are effectively screened before deployment to situations of armed conflict.

Age verification procedures

18. While noting that the State party has established procedures to verify the ages of incoming recruits, the Committee remains concerned at the low level of birth registration, especially among migrant children, in the State party, which may impact on the effectiveness of these procedures.

19. The Committee underlines the importance of birth registration as a measure to prevent recruitment of underage children, and recommends that the State party continue and strengthen its efforts to establish a free national birth registration system for all children, including migrant children.

Military training

20. The Committee is concerned that military training is included in the mainstream education curriculum and schools provide compulsory military education and training activities, including various levels of exposure to the handling of firearms, for all children under 18 years.

21. The Committee recommends that the State party exclude military training from the general education curriculum and take measures to ban military training with the use of firearms for children under the age of 18 in the mainstream education curriculum and schools.

Military schools

22. The Committee notes that the State Council and the Central Military Commission are allowed to recruit 17-year-old students graduating from ordinary high schools on a voluntary basis. The Committee is, however, concerned that:

(a) Although the enrolment plans, specifically aimed at enrolling young students in military colleges and schools, are approved by the Ministry of Education and the General Political Department of the People's Liberation Army, each military college or school sets up its own educational curriculum and military training programmes;

(b) No concrete information on the curriculum and military training activities – in particular regarding the handling of firearms – in military schools is provided;

(c) Children in military colleges and schools lack access to an independent complaints mechanism.

23. The Committee recommends that the State party:

(a) Ban military-type training – including on the use of firearms – for children and ensure that any military training for children takes into account human

rights principles, and that the educational content is approved and periodically monitored by the Ministry of Education;
(b) Provide in its next periodic report data, disaggregated by sex, age, nationality, ethnicity and socioeconomic background, on children enrolled in military colleges, vocational colleges and schools, as well as on the types of activities they carry out; and
(c) Set up independent and gender-sensitive mechanisms for complaints and investigation that are accessible to children in military colleges and schools, in order to monitor the welfare of and investigate complaints by children in such programmes.

Human rights and peace education
24. The Committee regrets that human rights and peace education, as well as knowledge on the Optional Protocol, is not specifically incorporated as a mandatory part of the primary and secondary school curricula and in teacher training programmes.
25. With reference to its general comment No. 1 (2001) on the aims of education, the Committee recommends that the State party, in the context of its education reform, consider including peace education in school curricula at all levels, with special reference to the crimes covered by the Optional Protocol.
... [paras 26–38 omitted]

9.2 The United Nations and children associated with armed forces or armed groups

9.2.1 Security Council resolutions

In the late 1990s, the UN Security Council (see section 2.4.1 in this book) started to express its commitment to address the widespread impact of armed conflict on children in the context of its primary responsibility for the maintenance of international peace and security. On an unprecedented occasion during the Security Council's new annual debate on children and armed conflict, a 14-year-old former child soldier from Sierra Leone addressed the Council.[77] A Security Council resolution in 1999,[78] reflecting the first Security Council debate on this issue,

---
77 'Child soldier asks United Nations for help', *BBC News* (21 November 2001). Available at: <http://news.bbc.co.uk/1/hi/world/africa/1667683.stm> (accessed 17 November 2013).
78 UNSC Res. 1261 (25 August 1999) UN Doc. S/RES/1261.

expressed 'grave concern at the harmful and widespread impact of armed conflict on children and the long-term consequences this has for durable peace, security and development' and strongly condemned the targeting of children in situations of armed conflict, 'including killing and maiming, sexual violence, abduction and forced displacement, recruitment and use of children in armed conflict in violation of international law', and called upon parties to comply strictly with their obligations under international law. A further resolution in 2000[79] welcomed the appearance of OPAC and reaffirmed its strong condemnation of the deliberate targeting of children in armed conflicts and the damaging impact such conflicts had on children and the long-term consequences for durable peace, security and development. It extended its list of concerns by, for example, also emphasising 'the responsibility of all States to put an end to impunity and to prosecute those responsible for genocide, crimes against humanity and war crimes, and, in this regard, stresses the need to exclude these, where feasible, from amnesty provisions and relevant legislation'.[80]

Another resolution in 2001[81] expressed readiness to include provisions for the protection of children when considering the mandates of peacekeeping operations and reaffirmed its readiness to include, where appropriate, child protection advisers in peacekeeping operations. It also committed itself to intensifying, monitoring and reporting activities on the situation of children in armed conflicts. This resolution built on previous ones with a list of concerns, for example; the need to pay attention to the rehabilitation of children affected by armed conflict in order to reintegrate them into society, and to develop and expand regional initiatives. Furthermore, the resolution requested the *Special Representative of the Secretary-General for children and armed conflict* (see section 9.2.3 below) to annex to her annual report a list of parties that recruit and use children. There are in fact two lists: one lists the parties that recruit or use children in situations of armed conflict which are on the Security Council's agenda;[82] and the second list includes parties that recruit or use children in situations of armed conflict which are not on the Security Council's agenda.[83]

A subsequent Security Council resolution in 2004[84] expressed deep concern 'over the lack of overall progress on the ground, where parties to conflict continue

---

79 UNSC Res. 1314 (11 August 2000) UN Doc. S/RES/1314.
80 UNSC Res. 1314 (11 August 2000) UN Doc. S/RES/1314, para. 2.
81 UNSC Res. 1379 (20 November 2001) UN Doc. S/RES/1379.
82 As at May 2013, there were various parties in this category in the following States: Afghanistan, Central African Republic, Chad, Democratic Republic of Congo, Iraq, Mali, Myanmar, Somalia, South Sudan, Sudan, Syrian Arab Republic, Uganda and Yemen. General Assembly, *Children and armed conflict: Report of the Secretary-General*, 67th session, UN Doc. A/67/845 – S/2013/245 (15 May 2013), Annex I.
83 As at May 2013, there were various parties in this category in the following States: Colombia, Philippines. General Assembly, *Children and armed conflict: Report of the Secretary-General*, 67th session, UN Doc. A/67/845 – S/2013/245 (15 May 2013), Annex II.
84 UNSC Res. 1539 (22 April 2004) UN Doc. S/RES/1539.

to violate with impunity the relevant provisions of applicable international law'. Significantly, it also requested the Secretary-General to devise urgently 'an action plan for a systematic and comprehensive monitoring and reporting mechanism', including timebound measures, that would utilise United Nations, national, regional and NGO expertise to provide reliable information on 'the recruitment and use of child soldiers in violation of applicable international law and on other violations and abuses committed against children affected by armed conflict'. The resolution also expressed the Security Council's intention to consider sanctions on parties failing to develop such action plans, for example, a ban on the export or supply of small arms and of other military equipment. In a further resolution in 2005,[85] the plans to devise monitoring and reporting mechanisms were strengthened. A working group of the Security Council[86] was established to review reports from the monitoring mechanisms and to review progress in the development of action plans. The Security Council also expressed grave concern about

> the documented links between the use of child soldiers in violation of applicable international law and the illicit trafficking of small arms and light weapons and stressing the need for all States to take measures to prevent and to put an end to such trafficking.[87]

In a later Security Council resolution on children and armed conflict,[88] the success in bringing to justice some persons alleged to have committed crimes against children in situations of armed conflict was welcomed. The resolution also expressed a conviction that 'the protection of children in armed conflict should be an important aspect of any comprehensive strategy to resolve conflict'. It reaffirmed the intention to take action against persistent perpetrators of crimes against children in armed conflict, and expressed deep concern that children continue to account for a considerable number of casualties resulting from killing and maiming in armed conflicts 'including as a result of deliberate targeting, indiscriminate and excessive use of force, indiscriminate use of landmines, cluster munitions and other weapons and use of children as human shields'.[89]

In the Security Council's recent resolution in 2011 on children and armed conflict, it stated, *inter alia*:

> *Noting* that Article 28 of the Convention on the Rights of the Child recognizes the right of the child to education and sets forth obligations for State parties

---

85 UNSC Res. 1612 (26 July 2005) UN Doc. S/RES/1612.
86 The UN Security Council's Working Group's documents are available at: <www.un.org/children/conflict/english/securitycouncilwgroupdoc.html> (accessed 14 November 2019). See the group's latest annual report: SCWG (2009).
87 UNSC Res. 1612 (26 July 2005) UN Doc. S/RES/1612 (preamble, p. 1).
88 UNSC Res. 1882 (4 August 2009) UN Doc. S/RES/1882.
89 UNSC Res. 1882 (4 August 2009) UN Doc. S/RES/1882.

to the Convention, with a view to progressively achieving this right on the basis of equal opportunity;

1 Strongly *condemns* all violations of applicable international law involving the recruitment and use of children by parties to armed conflict, as well as their re-recruitment, killing and maiming, rape and other sexual violence, abductions, attacks against schools or hospitals and denial of humanitarian access by parties to armed conflict and all other violations of international law committed against children in situations of armed conflict;

2 *Reaffirms* that the monitoring and reporting mechanism will continue to be implemented in situations listed in annex I and annex II ('the annexes') to the reports of the Secretary-General on children and armed conflict, in line with the principles set out in paragraph 2 of its resolution 1612 (2005), and that its establishment and implementation shall not prejudge or imply a decision by the Security Council as to whether or not to include a situation on its agenda;

3 *Recalls* paragraph 16 of its resolution 1379 (2001) and requests the Secretary-General to also include in the annexes to his reports on children and armed conflict those parties to armed conflict that engage, in contravention of applicable international law;

   (a) in recurrent attacks on schools and/or hospitals
   (b) in recurrent attacks or threats of attacks against protected persons in relation to schools and/or hospitals in situations of armed conflict, bearing in mind all other violations and abuses committed against children, and notes that the present paragraph will apply to situations in accordance with the conditions set out in paragraph 16 of its resolution 1379 (2001);[90]

A further resolution in 2012[91] indicates the Security Council's increasing resolve to impose increasing pressures on persistent perpetrators of violations and abuses committed against children in situations of armed conflict. Indeed, some commentators argue that the Security Council should further develop sanctions against governments and other groups who breach their international obligations by using children in armed conflict, rather than focusing on enforcement through the prosecution in international courts and tribunals (see section 9.3 below) of those who recruit and enlist child soldiers (Happold 2005).

The Secretary-General's now annual report on armed conflict[92] includes information on compliance with the relevant international law relating to the recruitment and use of children in armed conflict and other grave violations committed

---

90 UNSC Res. 1998 (12 July 2011) UN Doc. S/RES/1998.
91 UNSC Res. 2068 (19 September 2012) S/RES/2068.
92 For example, General Assembly, *Children and armed conflict: Report of the Secretary-General*, 67th session, UN Doc. A/67/845 – S/2013/245 (15 May 2013).

against children affected by armed conflict. It also reports progress on the implementation of the monitoring and reporting mechanism and action plans mandated in the resolutions discussed above, and provides summaries of the situations on the two lists referred to above.

The report of 2017[93] (SG Report 2017) notes 1,340 child casualties verified by the UN in Yemen. The cross-border activities of ISIS, coupled with responses to that group, also led to significant child casualties, with over 2,000 children documented as killed or maimed in Iraq and Syria. The number of child casualties in the Democratic Republic of the Congo (DRC) was also the highest recorded since 2012 (ibid.: 2). In the Lake Chad basin, Boko Haram activities continued to expand from Nigeria into neighbouring countries. Sexual violence against girls was prevalent as well as in other country situations, such as the DRC, the Sudan, Somalia, South Sudan and Syria (ibid.).

The report notes that recruitment and use of children increased sharply in Syria: the number of verified cases more than doubled compared with 2015 (SG Report 2017: 25) In Yemen, United Nations verified 517 cases of the recruitment and use of boys as young as eleven. In 69 verified cases, boys were used in combat: two boys were killed and five injured at checkpoints or on the battlefield. Recruits for the Popular Resistance were often motivated by a desire to secure income for their families (SG Report 2017: 27). In South Sudan, 1,022 children were recruited and used (ibid.: 2)

Pursuant to Security Council resolutions 1379 (2001), 1882 (2009), 1998 (2011) and 2225 (2015), parties that commit grave violations affecting children in situations of armed conflict on the agenda of the Security Council, the report proceeds to list parties that have not put in place measures during the reporting period to improve the protection of children.

The Report of the Special Representative of the Secretary-General for Children and Armed Conflict (SG Report 2017: 4)[94] indicates that 28 action plans had been signed with parties to conflict to end violations against children and establish mechanisms to prevent them. Indiscriminate attacks, including attacks carried out by air, shelling and crossfire, as well as the use of imprecise weaponry resulting in the killing of students and educational personnel, damage to schools and school closures continued to be a serious concern. With more than 245 million children estimated to be living in conflict zones, the issue of children missing out on education owing to the effects of conflict deserved urgent attention (SG Report 2017: 4). In recent years, the denial of humanitarian access to children in armed conflict had become a more prevalent violation and, in 2016, 994 incidents were verified by the United Nations. The SRSG empathises that it is essential to engage

---

93 General Assembly, *Children and armed conflict: Report of the Secretary-General* 71st session, UN Doc. A/72/361 – S/2017/821 (24 August 2017).
94 General Assembly, *Report of the Special Representative of the Secretary-General for Children and Armed Conflict*, 72nd session, UN Doc. A/72/276 (2 August 2017).

'additional actors' partnerships, such as regional and subregional organisations, in pursuit of greater protection of children (SG Report 2017: 3).

9.2.2 The 'Paris Principles'

UNICEF's 'Cape Town Principles and Best Practices' defines child soldiers as 'any person under 18" that is part of any "regular or irregular armed force or group in any capacity.'[95] These were modifies slightly at by the 'Paris commitments and principles'. At a Conference held in Paris, 'Free Children from War', organised jointly by the French Ministry of Foreign Affairs and UNICEF on 5–6 February 2007, 59 States supported the adoption of the *Paris Commitments to Protect Children Unlawfully Recruited or Used by Armed Forces or Armed Groups*[96] and the *Paris Principles and Guidelines on Children associated with Armed Forces or Armed Groups*'[97] (hereafter the 'Paris Commitments' and 'Paris Principles' respectively).[98] Such international documents are a good example of 'soft law' (see section 2.2.6 in this book). The Paris Commitments are intended to strengthen political action to prevent association of children with armed conflict and to ensure their reintegration with society. States commit themselves to uphold and apply the Paris Principles, a set of operational guidelines. The language used in these documents had broadened out from referring to 'child soldiers' to a definition of 'a child associated with an armed force or armed group'.[99] Generally, when people speak of 'child soldiers', the popular image is that of boys rather than the thousands of girls who recruited into armed forces and groups. The extract below, concerning the specific situation of girls, provides an illustration of the detail that has been provided in the Paris Principles.

> 4.0 There are almost always a significant number of girls amongst children associated with armed forces or armed groups. For a range of reasons, however, these girls are rarely provided with assistance. While there are

---

95 UNICEF (1997) *Cape Town Principles and Best Practices*, adopted at the Symposium on the Prevention of Recruitment of Children into the Armed Forces and on Demobilization and Social Reintegration of Child Soldiers in Africa, New York: UNICEF.
96 Available at: <www.icrc.org/eng/assets/files/other/pariscommitments_en.pdf> (accessed 18 November 2013).
97 UNICEF, *The Paris Principles. Principles and Guidelines on Children Associated with Armed Forces or Armed Groups*, February 2007. Available at: <www.refworld.org/docid/465198442.html> (accessed 18 November 2013).
98 The last ministerial follow-up forum on the Paris Commitments and the Paris Principles and Guidelines was held at UNHQ in New York on 29 September 2009. Further countries endorsed the Paris Commitments, bringing the total number of country endorsements to 84. Available at: <http://childrenandarmedconflict.un.org/our-work/paris-principles/> (accessed 18 November 2013).
99 ' . . . any person below 18 years of age who is or who has been recruited or used by an armed force or armed group in any capacity, including but not limited to children, boys, and girls used as fighters, cooks, porters, messengers, spies or for sexual purposes. It does not only refer to a child who is taking or has taken a direct part in hostilities' (Paris Principles, para. 2.1).

commonalities between the circumstances and experiences of girls and boys, the situation for girls can be very different in relation to the reasons and manner in which they join the armed forces or armed groups; the potential for their release; the effects that the experience of being in the armed force or armed group has on their physical, social and emotional well being; and the consequences this may have for their ability to successfully adapt to civilian life or reintegrate into family and community life after their release.

4.1 From the planning stage onwards, through the design of eligibility criteria and screening procedures for inclusion in release and reintegration programmes and informal release processes through to programming for reintegration, monitoring and follow-up, actors should recognise that girls are at risk of being 'invisible' and take measures to ensure that girls are included and relevant issues addressed at all stages. It is important that the differences between girls' and boys' experiences are understood and taken into account by all actors and that programming for children who are or have been associated with armed forces or armed groups explicitly reflects the particular situation of both girls and boys.

4.2 Actors should establish the means to share and learn from one another's experience and expertise including findings on research and outcomes of pilot programmes for girls associated with armed forces or armed groups.

4.3 Issues relating particularly or specifically to girls are considered throughout the Principles.[100]

9.2.3 The Special Representative of the Secretary-General for children and armed conflict

A significant landmark in the international attention paid to children and armed conflict was the appearance of the UN commissioned report 'Impact of armed conflict on children' in 1996. The report was authored by Graça Machel, an expert designated by the Secretary-General to undertake the study, and has become known as the 'Machel report'.[101] It set out a comprehensive and detailed analysis of the problem:

> In 1995, 30 major armed conflicts raged in different locations around the world. All of them took place within States, between factions split along ethnic, religious or cultural lines. The conflicts destroyed crops, places of worship and schools. Nothing was spared, held sacred or protected – not children, families or communities. In the past decade, an estimated two million

---

100 UNICEF, *The Paris Principles. Principles and Guidelines on Children Associated with Armed Forces or Armed Groups*, February 2007, [4.0–4.3].
101 General Assembly, *Impact of Armed Conflict on Children: report of the expert of the Secretary-General, Ms. Graça Machel*, submitted pursuant to General Assembly resolution 48/157 (the 'Machel Report'), UN Doc. A/51/306 (26 August 1996). Available at: <www.un.org/documents/ga/docs/51/plenary/a51-306.htm> (accessed 15 November 2013).

children have been killed in armed conflict. Three times as many have been seriously injured or permanently disabled, many of them maimed by landmines. Countless others have been forced to witness or even to take part in horrifying acts of violence.[102]

The report observed, for example, that 'the proportion of war victims who are civilians has leaped dramatically from 5 per cent to over 90 per cent'.[103] Furthermore, it noted that children were rarely mentioned in reconstruction plans and advised that 'the seeds of reconstruction should be sown even during conflict'.[104] The report was a powerful call to action and the General Assembly unanimously welcomed the report in a resolution in which it also established the mandate of the *Special Representative of the Secretary-General for Children and Armed Conflict*.[105] The General Assembly has since extended the mandate several times and there have to date been four successive holders of the mandate.[106] The website of the Special Representative announces its mission thus:

'To promote and protect the rights of all children affected by armed conflict'.

- The Special Representative serves as a moral voice and independent advocate for the protection and well-being of boys and girls affected by armed conflict.
- The Special Representative works with partners to propose ideas and approaches to enhance the protection of children and armed conflict and to promote a more concerted protection response.
- The Special Representative and her Office advocate, build awareness and give prominence to the rights and protection of children and armed conflict.
- The Special Representative is a facilitator, undertaking humanitarian and diplomatic initiatives to facilitate the work of operational actors on the ground with regard to children and armed conflict.

The Office of the Special Representative does not have a field presence but promotes and supports the efforts of operational partners.[107]

---

102 Ibid. [2].
103 Ibid. [24].
104 Ibid. 243.
105 Office of the General Assembly, *The rights of the child*, UN Doc. A/RES/51/77 (20 February 1997) [35–7].
106 Mr Olara A. Otunnu (1998 to 2005); Ms Karin Sham Poo, Interim Special Representative in the Fall of 2005; Ms Radhika Coomaraswamy (April 2006 – August 2012); Ms Leila Zerrougui (September 2012 to present).
107 Office of the Special Representative of the Secretary-General for Children and Armed Conflict website. Available at: <http://childrenandarmedconflict.un.org/about-us/> (accessed 18 November 2013).

The Special Representative makes annual reports to the UN Human Rights Council (UNHRC).[108] In September 2000, at the *World Summit for Children*, Canada hosted the International Conference on War-Affected Children in Winnipeg. In preparation for the conference, Canada commissioned the 'Machel Review 1996–2000', to review progress in protecting war-affected children and to serve as principal background document for the Conference. This review[109] concluded that there had been some progress; for example, children were now more central to the UN's peace and security agenda and that war crimes against children had started to be prosecuted and violations against children were being documented more systematically, and that more is now known about how small arms and light weapons are damaging children's lives. However, the damaging impact on children by armed conflicts continues:

> In spite of this progress the assaults against children continue. An estimated 300,000 children are still participating in armed combat . Children in 87 countries live amid the contamination of more than 60 million landmines. At least 20 million children have been uprooted from their homes. Girls and women continue to be marginalised from mainstream humanitarian assistance and protection. Humanitarian personnel continue to be targeted and killed. Millions of children are abandoned to cope with the multiple and compounded effects of armed conflict and HIV/AIDS. Hundreds of thousands of children continue to die from disease and malnutrition in flight from conflict or in camps for displaced persons. Small arms and light weapons continue to proliferate excessively. Millions of children are scarred physically and psychologically.[110]

To mark the tenth anniversary of the landmark Graça Machel study of 1996, UNICEF and the Special Representative of the Secretary-General (SRSG) reviewed the current situation faced by children in armed conflict. The 'Machel Strategic Review'[111] (SRSG 2007) identifies emerging challenges and priorities and the responses required for the next decade. It concludes with 15 recommendations: for example, urging the end of impunity for violations against children; strengthening the monitoring and reporting mechanisms; supporting inclusive reintegration strategies; operationalising the engagement of regional bodies; and integrating

---

108 For example, Human Rights Council, *Annual Report of the Special Representative of the Secretary-General for Children and Armed Conflict, Radhika Coomaraswamy*, 21st session, UN Doc. A/HRC/21/38 (28 June 2012).
109 General Assembly, *The Machel Review 1996–2000: A Critical Analysis of Progress Made and Obstacles Encountered in Increasing Protection for War-Affected Children*, 55th session, UN Doc. A/55/749 (26 January 2001).
110 Ibid., 61.
111 General Assembly, *Report of the Special Representative of the Secretary-General for Children and Armed Conflict*, 62nd session, UN Doc. A/62/228 (13 August 2007).

children's rights in peacemaking, peacebuilding and preventive actions.[112] The main objectives of the current Special Representative's strategic plan are:

> (1) to support global initiatives to end grave violations; (2) to promote rights-based protection for children affected by armed conflict; (3) to make children and armed conflict concerns an integral aspect of peacekeeping and peace-building; (4) to identify new trends and strategies for the protection of children through research; (5) to secure political and diplomatic engagement on CAAC [Children And Armed Conflict] initiatives and (6) to raise global awareness with regard to all issues relating to children and armed conflict.[113]

The Office of the Special Representative has also instituted a series of working papers 'to assist the community of practice working on the protection of children affected by armed conflict'. The first of these working papers (Kolieb 2009) identifies the legal foundations of 'six grave violations' against children during armed conflict. The normative standards which are examined and clarified in the paper and which address these six grave violations are headlined as follows.

- Parties to a conflict must protect children from being killed or seriously injured;
- Parties to a conflict must not recruit or deploy children as soldiers, and must prevent children from participating in hostilities;
- Parties to a conflict must not rape or otherwise abuse children;
- Parties to a conflict must not abduct children;
- Parties to a conflict must not attack schools or hospitals, other education or medical facilities ordinarily used by children; and
- Parties to a conflict must not deny humanitarian access for children even in a conflict zone.

Subsequent Working Papers explored the rights and guarantees of internally displaced children in armed conflict (Mooney and Paul 2010) and the ways in which children who have suffered grave violations during armed conflicts can access justice (Hamilton and Dutordoir 2011).

9.3 International courts and tribunals

Over the past two decades, there have been important developments in international efforts to prosecute crimes against humanity, war crimes and other serious violations against international humanitarian law, including ending impunity for crimes against children. The arrest and trial of individuals in leadership positions

---

112 Ibid. [103–17].
113 Special Representative for Children and Armed Conflict website. Available at <http://childrenandarmedconflict.un.org/our-work/strategic-plan/> (accessed 20 November 2013).

alleged to have committed such crimes has been seen to send a powerful message that such behaviour may not be tolerated in the future. Combined with the various initiatives of the United Nations discussed earlier, these international justice mechanisms hold out some hope that relevant parties will be brought into compliance with international law standards in this field. The sections to follow essentially discuss *international criminal law* relating to child soldiers, focusing on the International Criminal Court (2.4.3 in this book), the International Criminal Tribunal for the former Yugoslavia (ICTY), the International Criminal Tribunal for Rwanda (ICTR) and the Special Court of Sierra Leone. The international justice system, such as it is, remains challenged by the difficulties of dealing with child soldiers who have themselves been accused of war crimes, a problem that 'illustrates the complexity of balancing culpability, a community's sense of justice and the "best interests of the child"' (United Nations 1996: para. 250). It would appear, however, that a consensus is emerging from the practice of the ICC and other international tribunals that children below the age of 18 years should not be prosecuted for such crimes by international courts and tribunals. However, the exemption children on account of lack of agency does not appear to be a settled matter and will be discussed in more detail later in this chapter. There is also the political difficulty of whether the particular international court or tribunal is dispensing, or is seen as dispensing, 'victors' justice', a problem that undoubtedly impacts on the long-term legitimacy of such bodies. The various international courts/tribunals are discussed below in the chronological order of their establishment.

9.3.1 The International Criminal Tribunal for the former Yugoslavia (ICTY)

In May 1993, the International Criminal Tribunal for the former Yugoslavia (ICTY) was established by the United Nations in response to mass atrocities taking place in Croatia and Bosnia and Herzegovina. The ICTY is situated in The Hague, the Netherlands. The ICTY was the first war crimes court created by the United Nations and the first international war crimes tribunal since the Nuremberg and Tokyo tribunals. It was established as an ad hoc court by the Security Council in accordance with Chapter VII of the *UN Charter*. The Tribunal laid the foundations for what is now the accepted norm for conflict resolution and post-conflict development globally, namely, that leaders suspected of crimes against humanity, war crimes and other serious violations of international humanitarian law will be exposed to face justice. The ICTY was empowered to prosecute persons responsible for serious violations of international humanitarian law committed in the territory of the former Yugoslavia since 1991, genocide and crimes against humanity.[114] Several leaders, including Momcilo Krajišnik, president of

---

114 *UN Security Council, Statute of the International Criminal Tribunal for the Former Yugoslavia (as amended on 17 May 2002)*, adopted by UN Doc. S/RES/827/93 (25 May 1993), arts 1–5.

the Bosnian Serb Assembly during the 1992–5 war, Slobodan Miloševic, former president of the Federal Republic of Yugoslavia and, and Karadžić were charged with these crimes. The work of the Tribunal showed that the mass murder at Srebrenica, where it is estimated that around 8,000 Bosnian Muslims were murdered, was indeed 'genocide'. Most of the key cases heard at the Tribunal have dealt with alleged crimes committed by Serbs and Bosnian Serbs, but the Tribunal has also investigated and brought charges against persons from every ethnic background. Its indictments address crimes committed from 1991 to 2001 against members of various ethnic groups in Croatia, Bosnia and Herzegovina, Serbia, Kosovo and the Former Yugoslav Republic of Macedonia. As of May 2013, 69 individuals have been convicted and currently 25 people are in different stages of proceedings before the Tribunal.[115] Under the *Statute of the International Criminal Tribunal for the Former Yugoslavia*,[116] there is no mention of the crime of child soldiery although children were used in the conflict. The number of children involved in the 1992–5 Balkan wars is difficult to identify accurately, but is variously estimated as between around 3,000[117] to 20,000.[118]

9.3.2 International Criminal Tribunal for Rwanda (ICTR)

On 6 April 1994, a plane carrying the Rwandan President Habyarimana, a Hutu, was shot down. Violence began almost immediately after that. Hutu extremists launched their plans to destroy the entire Tutsi civilian population. In the weeks after 6 April 1994, 800,000 men, women, and children perished in the Rwandan genocide. Acting again under Chapter VII of the *United Nations Charter*, the Security Council resolved in 1994 to create the International Criminal Tribunal for Rwanda (ICTR)[119] in response to the recognition of the serious violations of humanitarian law committed in Rwanda between 1 January and 31 December 1994. The Tribunal is located in Arusha, United Republic of Tanzania. The purpose was to contribute to the process of national reconciliation in Rwanda and to the maintenance of peace in the region. ICTR was established for the prosecution of persons responsible for genocide and other serious violations of international humanitarian law, including violations of 'common article 3' of the *Geneva Conventions of 1949* (section 9.1.1.1), committed in the territory of Rwanda. It also has jurisdiction to deal with the prosecution of Rwandan citizens responsible for

---

115 See ICTY website: <www.icty.org/sections/AbouttheICTY> (accessed 18 November 2013).
116 *UN Security Council, Statute of the International Criminal Tribunal for the Former Yugoslavia (as amended on 17 May 2002)*, adopted by UN Doc. S/RES/827/93 (25 May 1993), art. 3.
117 'Child Soldiers of the Balkans', Radio Free Europe. Available at: <www.rferl.org/content/Child_Soldiers_Of_The_Balkans/1349516.html> (accessed 18 November 2013).
118 See Child Soldiers International, *Child Soldiers Global Report 2001 – Bosnia-Herzegovina, 2001*, n. 263. Available at: <www.refworld.org/docid/4988060e28.html> (accessed 18 November 2013).
119 UNSC Res. 955 (8 November 1994) UN Doc. S/RES/955.

genocide and other such violations of international law committed in the territory of neighbouring States during the same period. However, ICTR Statute is silent on the conscription or enlistment of child soldiers.

The ICTR is governed by its Statute, which is annexed to Security Council Resolution 955 of 1994. The Tribunal consists of three organs: the Chambers and the Appeals Chamber; the Office of the Prosecutor, in charge of investigations and prosecutions; and the Registry, responsible for providing overall judicial and administrative support to the Chambers and the Prosecutor.

On 2 September 1998, the ICTR issued the first conviction for the crime of genocide in *Prosecutor v. Akayesu*.[120] The decision in *Prosecutor v. Kambanda* denoted genocide as the 'crime of crimes'.[121] Child combatants were involved in the conflict. In 1994, the Rwandan Ministry of Defence agreed to demobilise all child soldiers – commonly referred to as *kadogo* or 'little ones' in Kswahili. Estimations of children's involvement is again difficult to state with precision but it would appear both government forces and the guerilla forces used child soldiers possibly around 15,000 to 20,000 individuals were involved.[122] It would appear, however, that the genocide in Rwanda, branded the 'crime of crimes', eclipsed any other crimes such as the recruitment and enlistment of child soldiers that occurred during the conflict. The ICTR has convicted 63 persons, 16 of whom are awaiting further appeal. A further 12 have been acquitted.[123]

9.3.3 Special Court for Sierra Leone (SCSL)

In response to some of the perceived disadvantages of the ICTY and ICTR the international community developed a further model of international justice with the appearance of 'hybrid' or 'experimental' courts/tribunals, involving a blend of international and domestic law (Dickinson 2003). The SCSL was established jointly by the Government of Sierra Leone and the United Nations. It is now located at The Hague, in the Netherlands. It is mandated to try those who bear the "greatest responsibility" for serious violations of international humanitarian law and Sierra Leonean law committed in the territory of Sierra Leone since 30 November 1996.[124]

---

120 *The Prosecutor v. Akayesu (Judgement)*, (International Criminal Tribunal for Rwanda, Trial Chamber I, Case No. ICTR-96-4-T, 2 September 1998.
121 *The Prosecutor v. Kambanda (Judgement and Sentence)*, (International Criminal Tribunal for Rwanda, Trial Chamber I, Case No. ICTR-97-23-S, 2 September 1998 [16].
122 See Child Soldiers International, *Child Soldiers Global Report 2001 – Rwanda, 2001*, n. 1618. Available at: <www.refworld.org/docid/498805d326.html> (accessed 18 November 2013).
123 See ICTR website: <www.unictr.org/Cases/tabid/204/Default.aspx> (accessed 18 November 2013).
124 UN Security Council, *Statute of the Special Court of Sierra Leone*, 16 January 2002, as established pursuant to UNSC Res. 1315 (14 August 2000) UN Doc. S/RES/1315, art. 1(1).

Thirteen indictments were issued by the Prosecutor in 2003. Two of those indictments were subsequently withdrawn in December 2003 due to the deaths of the accused. The trials of three former leaders of the Armed Forces Revolutionary Council (AFRC) in *The Prosecutor vs. Brima, Kamara and Kanu*[125] *(AFRC Case)* have resulted in convictions and sentences. There have also been completed trials of two members of the Civil Defence Forces (CDF)[126] and of three former leaders of the Revolutionary United Front (RUF),[127] including appeals.

In the case of Sam Hinga Norman (AFRC),[128] the Special Court Prosecutor charged Sierra Leonean politician Norman with war crimes and crimes against humanity, including the recruitment of child soldiers. The Norman Defence argued that 'child soldiering' was not a crime under international law, at the times relevant to the indictment (before 1996), which meant that there can be no offence without a crime. The Appeals Chamber found that a prohibition on child recruitment had become international custom and law even before 1996, citing the CRC, the Geneva Convention, and the African Charter on the Rights and Welfare of the Child, among other legal instruments.[129] The court stated that 'rules of customary international law are not contingent on domestic practice in one given country'.[130]

The *AFRC Case* was something of a breakthrough when in 2007 the SCSL convicted three rebel leaders for the crime of using child soldiers. The Appeals Chamber, on 22 February 2008,[131] upheld sentences in the *AFRC Case* of 50 years for Brima, 45 years for Kamara and 50 years for Kanu. (Norman had died). For the first time, international law proscribed child soldiering as a crime under customary international law in definitive terms. An interesting defence was advanced by Kanu's defence team, based on cultural relativism. As noticed in the theoretical constructs on childhood in Chapter 1 in this book, cultural relativism is premised on the notion that cultural beliefs and behaviours are most appropriately seen as relative to each other. Therefore, an act is right or wrong in so far as it is right or wrong for a particular culture, and not for a universal domain. Along these lines, the Kanu defence submitted before the Trial Chamber that:

---

125 *The Prosecutor vs. Brima, Kamara and Kanu ('AFRC Case') (Sentencing Judgement)*, (Special Court for Sierra Leone, Trial Chamber II, Case No. SCSL-04-16-T, 19 July 2007.
126 *Prosecutor v. Fofana and Kondewa ('CDF Case') (Sentencing Judgement)*, (Special Court for Sierra Leone, Trial Chamber I, Case No. SCSL-04-14-T, 9 October 2007).
127 *Prosecutor v. Sesay, Kallon and Gbao ('RUF' Case) (Judgement)*, (Special Court for Sierra Leone, Trial Chamber I, Case No. SCSL-04-15-T, 2 March 2009).
128 *Prosecutor v. Sam Hinga Norman* – Decision on Preliminary Motion Based on Lack of Jurisdiction (Child Recruitment), Case No. SCSL-2004-14-AR72(E), Special Court for Sierra Leone, 31 May 2004. Available at: <www.refworld.org/cases, SCSL, 49abc0a22.html> (accessed 7 April 2019).
129 'Prosecutor v. Norman' (Archive.crin.org, 2004). Available at: <https://archive.crin.org/en/library/legal-database/prosecutor-v-norman.html> (accessed 7 April 2019).
130 AFRC Trial Judgement, para. 732.
131 *The Prosecutor vs. Brima, Kamara and Kanu ('AFRC Case') (Appeal Judgement)*, (Special Court for Sierra Leone, Trial Chamber II, Case No. SCSL-2004-16-A, 22 February 2008).

the age of 15 years is 'arbitrary' as 'the ending of childhood' [in the traditional African setting] has little to do with achieving a particular age and more to do with physical capacity to perform acts reserved for adults.[132]

The Prosecution observed that the Appeals Chamber had already ruled that conscripting or enlisting children under the age of 15 years into armed forces or groups or using them to participate actively in hostilities was a crime entailing individual criminal responsibility at the time of the acts alleged in the Indictment. In its judgement, the Appeals Chamber referred to its dictum that:

> The rejection of the use of child soldiers by the international community was widespread by 1994 . . . Citizens of Sierra Leone, and even less, persons in leadership roles, cannot possibly argue that they did not know that recruiting children was a criminal act in violation of international humanitarian law. Child recruitment was criminalized before it was explicitly set out as a criminal prohibition in treaty law and certainly by November 1996, the starting point of the time frame relevant to the indictments. As set out above, the principle of legality and the principle of specificity are both upheld.[133]

The trial chamber followed the decision of Appeals, rejecting the defence on the distinction of childhood. Further, in the *CDF Case (Appeals Chamber)* the Court similarly held:

> 139. The Appeals Chamber affirms that the crime of recruitment by way of conscripting or enlisting children under the age of 15 years into an armed force or group and/or using them participate actively in hostilities constitutes a crime under customary international law entailing individual criminal responsibility. Pursuant to Article 4.c of the State, the crime of conscripting or enlisting children or using them to participate actively in hostilities, constitutes an other serious violation of international humanitarian law. The *actus reus* requires that the accused recruited children by way of conscripting or enlisting them or that the accused used children to participate actively in hostilities. These modes of recruiting children are distinct from each other and liability for one form does not necessarily preclude liability for the other.[134]

Former Liberian President Charles Taylor was indicted on 7 March 2003 for his role in the Sierra Leone conflict. He was convicted of, among other charges, using

---

132 AFRC Trial Judgement, para. 730.
133 Special Court for Sierra Leone, *Prosecutor v. Sam Hinga Norman*, Decision on Preliminary Motion Based on Lack of Jurisdiction, 31 May 2004 [para. 295].
134 *Prosecutor v. Fofana and Kondewa ('CDF Case') (Appeal Judgement)*, (Special Court for Sierra Leone, Appeals Chamber, Case No. SCSL-04-14-A, 28 May 2008) [139].

children in armed conflict, and sentenced in 2012 to 50 years in prison, a sentence that was confirmed on appeal on 26 September 2013.[135] The UN, which convened the SCSL, issued an appeal for a country to host him after his conviction, and the UK volunteered. He was detained at a maximum security prison in Durham (Webber 2017).

9.3.4 International Criminal Court (ICC)

An outline of the origins, establishment and jurisdiction of the International Criminal Court (ICC) has been given in section 2.4.3 in this book. The *Rome Statute of the International Criminal Court*[136] (1998) provides a definition of 'war crimes' that includes, *inter alia*, '[c]onscripting or enlisting children under the age of 15 years into the national armed forces or using them to participate actively in hostilities'.[137] It also defines as a 'war crime' other serious violations of the laws and customs applicable in 'armed conflicts not of an international character', within the established framework of international law, including the conscription or enlisting of children under 15 years into 'armed forces or groups or using them to participate actively in hostilities'.[138] The death penalty is prohibited under ICC rules. A unique feature of the ICC is the establishment is the participation of victims of atrocities during the legal proceedings. The Victims Participation and Reparations Section (VPRS) of the Registry is responsible for assisting victims in the process of applying for participation in proceedings, and reparations in case of a conviction. It also assists victims and the Chamber in finding an appropriate legal representation of victims during the proceedings. Victims may include individuals, but also organisations or institutions that have sustained direct harm to any of their property which is dedicated to religion, education, art or science or charitable purposes, and to their historic monuments, hospitals and other places and objects for humanitarian purposes. If there is a conviction at the end of the trial, the Trial Chamber may order a convicted person to pay reparations to the victims of the crimes of which the person was found guilty. The Court may order such reparations to be paid through the Trust Fund for Victims.

The ICC's first trial of Congolese rebel militia leader Thomas Lubanga Dyilo, began on 26 January 2009, following an application for arrest made on 12 January

---

135 *Prosecutor v. Charles Ghankay Taylor (Trial Judgement)* (Special Court for Sierra Leone, Case No. SCSL-03–01-T-1283, 18 May 2012); *Prosecutor v. Charles Ghankay Taylor (Sentencing Judgement)* (Special Court for Sierra Leone, Case No. SCSL-03–01-T-1285, 30 May 2012); *Prosecutor v. Charles Ghankay Taylor (Appeal Judgement)* (Special Court for Sierra Leone, Appeals Chamber, Case No. SCSL-03–01-A, 26 September 2013).
136 *Rome Statute of the International Criminal Court*, opened for signature 17 July 1998, 2187 UNTS 90 (entered into force 1 July 2002).
137 *Rome Statute of the International Criminal Court*, art. 8(2)(b)(xxvi).
138 *Rome Statute of the International Criminal Court*, art. 8(2)(e)(vii).

2006.[139] Lubanga was indicted for war crimes consisting of both of the offences referred to above. The number of children involved in fighting forces in the Democratic Republic of the Congo (DRC) conflict was estimated by the United Nations to be around 30,000. Lubanga was the President of the 'Union of Congolese Patriots' and is alleged to have served as commander-in-chief of the former military wing of the Union, namely the 'Patriotic Forces for the Liberation of Congo'. The Union of Congolese Patriots aimed to establish dominance of the Hema ethnic group through violence against mainly Lendu militias and civilians. Lubanga was originally arrested in 2005 and transferred from the DRC to the ICC a year later, in March 2006. After long delays, his trial started at the ICC on 26 January 2009.

On 14 March 2012, Lubanga was convicted of committing, as co-perpetrator, war crimes under article 8(2)(e)(vii) of the Rome Statute, consisting of 'enlisting' and 'conscripting' of children under the age of 15 years into the Force patriotique pour la libération du Congo [Patriotic Forces for the Liberation of Congo] (FPLC) and 'using them to participate actively in hostilities' in the context of an armed conflict not of an international character from 1 September 2002 to 13 August 2003

The elements of 'enlistment', 'conscription' and use 'to participate actively in hostilities' are key to the commission of the crime: these are explained later. The court noted that these 'offences are continuous in nature. They end only when the child reaches 15 years of age or leaves the force or group.'[140] This is a particularly interesting conclusion given the case of Dominic Ongwen (see Case Study 9.2) also at the ICC, who was abducted by a Ugandan rebel group as a child, and left as an adult. He was arrested for a raft of charges, including the recruitment of children for the group, a crime he was once a victim of. Was he still a victim of the 'continuous' child soldiering crimes during all his time with the rebel group until he left as an adult and, if so, should he be prosecuted? With regards to Lubanga, there was some disappointment that he was charged only with child conscription/enlistment offences and not with additional offences of murder and sexual violence. As this was the first trial in the ICC brought to completion, it has naturally attracted much academic and other commentary assessing its significance and contribution to the development of the law in this field (e.g. Catani 2012; Graf 2012; Lieflãnder 2012; Roberts 2012; Steffen 2012). One point of interest in the Lubanga judgment is the endorsement of the persuasive value of the judgments of the SCSL within ICC's development of jurisprudence.

> 603. The jurisprudence of the SCSL has been considered by the Trial Chamber. Although the decisions of other international courts and tribunals are

---

139 *The Prosecutor v. Thomas Lubanga Dyilo (Warrant of Arrest)*, (International Criminal Court, Pre-Trial Chamber I, Case No. ICC-01/04–01/06, 10 February 2006).

140 *Prosecutor v. Thomas Lubanga Dyilo*, Summary of the 'Judgment pursuant to Article 74 of the Statute' ICC-01/04–01/06 (14 March 2012) para. 23.

not part of the directly applicable law under Article 21 of the Statute, the wording of the provision criminalising the conscription, enlistment and use of children under the age of 15 within the Statute of the SCSL is identical to Article 8(e)(vii) of the Rome Statute, and they were self-evidently directed at the same objective. The SCSL's case law therefore potentially assists in the interpretation of the relevant provisions of the Rome Statute.[141]

The jurisprudence of the SCSL was instrumental in interpreting the Rome Statute's core elements of the crime: conscription and enlistment. In the case against former Liberia president Charles Taylor, the SCSL Trial Chamber held that conscription and enlistment are both types of recruitment, and while conscription involved an element of express compulsion or *coercion*, this element was absent in enlistment.[142] Enlistment entailed accepting and enrolling individuals when they *volunteer* to join an armed force or group.[143] The Lubanga case followed the same interpretations:

> The Rome Statute prefers the terms 'conscripting' and 'enlisting' to 'recruitment' . . . the Chamber holds the view that 'conscripting' and 'enlisting' are two forms of recruitment, 'conscripting' being forcible recruitment, while 'enlisting' pertains more to voluntary recruitment.[144]

The Lubanga Trial Judgment then went on to state that 'the consent of a child to his or her recruitment does not provide an accused with a valid defence.'[145] However, as we will see later, removing the ability of children to join armed forces or groups voluntarily has been a source of debate. It has to be noted that 'conscription' 'enlistment' and using them to 'participate actively in hostilities' are three separate crimes. On what constitutes participating actively in hostilities, the Trial Chamber held that:

> [t]he extent of the potential danger faced by a child soldier will often be unrelated to the precise nature of the role he or she is given. Those who participate actively in hostilities include a wide range of individuals, from those on the front line (who participate directly) through to the boys or girls who are involved in a myriad of roles that support the combatants. All of these

---

141 *Prosecutor v. Thomas Lubanga Dyilo (Judgement)*, (International Criminal Court, Trial Chamber I, Case No ICC-01/04–01/06, 14 March 2012), [603].
142 SCSL, Taylor Trial Judgment 18 May 2012, para. 442 citing SCSL, *Brima* et al. Trial Judgment 20 June 2007, para. 734–735; SCSL, *Fofana* and *Kondewa* Trial Judgment 2 August 2007, para. 140, 144; and SCSL, *Sesay* et al. Trial Judgment 2 March 2009, para. 184; supported by the ICC, Lubanga Trial Judgment 14 March 2012, para. 607 (emphasis added).
143 Ibid. (emphasis added).
144 ICC, Lubanga Confirmation Decision, 29 January 2007, para. 246.
145 Lubanga Trial Judgment 14 March 2012, para. 617.

activities, which cover either direct or indirect participation, have an underlying common feature: the child concerned is, at the very least, a potential target. The decisive factor, therefore, in deciding if an "indirect" role is to be treated as active participation in hostilities is whether the support provided by the child to the combatants exposed him or her to real danger as a potential target.[146]

Lubanga's deputy, Bosco Ntaganda, was also charged with enlisting, conscripting and using child soldiers in armed conflict in the first warrant of arrest issued in January 2006, and following a second warrant of arrest for additional charges in July 2012,[147] voluntarily surrendered to ICC custody on 22 March 2013. On 8 July 2019, Ntaganda was found guilty of 18 counts of war crimes and crimes against humanity committed in Ituri, DRC. On 7 November 2019, he was sentenced to 30 years imprisonment, subject to appeal. The Appeals Chamber unanimously confirmed the jurisdiction of the ICC over the war crimes of rape and sexual slavery committed by members of an armed group against members of that same armed group. International courts such as the ICC, due to limited resources and other reasons, focus on the prosecution of only those 'bearing the greatest responsibility' Of course, the strategy of the ICC and other international courts and tribunals to prosecute what must inevitably be a very small number of commanders remains contentious. As can be imagined, the 'mass crimes' of recruiting hundreds of child soldiers would involve a significant number of people. Lower-ranking members may escape justice creating yet again an 'impunity gap' because of the focus on those bearing the greatest responsibility, the high-ranking members and leaders. As Drumbl (2012: 207) comments; '[t]he current preference to criminally prosecute a handful of adult commanders for unlawful recruitment of children yields only faint print of justice.' Some scholars have concluded that the role of international criminal courts is only limited to the 'expressive function of law' (expressivism) rather than achieving, among other traditional penal goals, deterrence and retribution (Amann 2002; Drumbl 2007; Sloane 2007; deGuzman 2012; Nyamutata 2015). Such trials can only reinforce law. While the ICC can make only a very small impact in terms of such goals as retribution and deterrence, the Court can effectively promote global norms with a limited number of illustrative prosecutions (deGuzman 2012: 270).

At the time of writing, 27 *cases* in 11 *situations* had been brought before the ICC. Cases are either instigated by the prosecutor (*proprio motu*), referred by the United Nations Security Council or states refer themselves to the court. Four States parties to the *Rome Statute* – Uganda, the Democratic Republic of the Congo, the Central African Republic and Mali – had referred situations occurring on their territories to the Court. However, a common accusation is that states only refer themselves to

---

146 Lubanga Trial Judgment 14 March 2012, para. 628.
147 *Prosecutor v. Bosco Ntaganda, (Decision on the Prosecutor's Application under Article 58)*, (International Criminal Court, Pre-Trial Chamber II, Case No. ICC-01/04–02/06, 13 July 2012).

the court with the expectation to precipitate proceedings against their 'rivals', for example, rebel groups, when states themselves might be guilty of crimes during those conflicts.

In addition, the Security Council has referred the situation in Darfur, Sudan, and the situation in Libya – both non-States parties. It therefore means, not being a party to the Rome Statute, might not prevent investigation by the ICC.

Pre-Trial Chamber II, on 31 March 2010, granted the Prosecution authorisation to open an investigation *proprio motu* in the situation of Kenya. In addition, on 3 October 2011, Pre-Trial Chamber III granted the Prosecutor's request for authorisation to open investigations *proprio motu* into the situation in Côte d'Ivoire.[148] A significant inclusion is the investigation of the UK. It comes against the background of threats by African leaders to withdraw from the ICC because, according to them, the court targeted African countries.

9.3.5 Child soldiers: victims or perpetrators?

One of the enduring dilemmas of armed conflicts is the treatment of child soldiers in terms of their criminal responsibility for war crimes. There is ample evidence that child soldiers commit crimes during armed conflicts. Ishmael Beah, who was a child soldier in Sierra Leone, recounts a scene when he saw young rebels with blood-stained clothes laughing and boasting and holding a man's head by the hair.[149] The issue becomes more poignant considering that child soldiers might return to live within the communities in which they perpetrated atrocities. At the same time, a common perception of child soldiers is that they are only victims and lack any agency to make to decisions on joining conflicts and crimes they commit. Generally, humanitarian discourse disfavours the prosecution of child soldiers. This has often been premised on the idea that, as discussed in Chapter 1 in this book on the theories of childhood, children are vulnerable and thus lack agency to join armed conflict. The Machel Report supported this conception while evidence to this effect was adduced in the Lubanga case.[150] The contention, to this end, remains that rehabilitation and reintegration are the more appropriate approaches to children who have participated in war.

It would appear, however, that some international legal instruments do presuppose the prosecution of children. Article 14(3)(d) of the International Covenant on Civil and Political Rights grants children the right to legal assistance in the preparation of their defence. Article 40 of the UNCRC alludes to child accused or guilty of breaking the law being treated with dignity and respect. The child has the right to

---

148 ICC website. Available at: <www.icc-cpi.int/en_menus/icc/situations%20and%20cases/Pages/situations%20and%20cases.aspx> (accessed 20 November 2018).
149 See Beah (2008).
150 ICC-01/04–01/06–1729-Anx1, Annex 1 to: Report of Ms. Elisabeth Schauer following the 6 February 2009 'Instructions to the Court's expert on child soldiers and trauma'.

legal assistance and a fair trial that takes account of their age. UNCRC General Comment No. 10 encourages states parties to continue to increase the age of criminal responsibility higher than 12 years.[151] UNCRC considers that designated systems of youth justice should apply to all young people until they reach 18 years.

Some argue that child soldiers should be prosecuted, for the sake of restorative justice, because they have the competence or agency to make decisions. So far, international criminal law has been inconsistent on this subject. These debates played out in the formation of the Special Court of Sierra Leone. The Statute of SCSL gave the court jurisdiction not to prosecute children from age 15 but strictly regulated prosecution of minors between the age of 15 and 18.[152] The UN Secretary-General stated at the time that:

> Within the meaning attributed to it in the present Statute, the term 'most responsible' would not necessarily exclude children between 15 and 18 years of age. [. . .] the gravity and seriousness of the crimes they have allegedly committed would allow for their inclusion within the jurisdiction of the Court.[153]

The report noted that the government of Sierra Leone and representatives of Sierra Leone civil society clearly wished to see a process of judicial accountability for child combatants presumed responsible for the crimes falling within the jurisdiction of the Court. It is said that the people of Sierra Leone would not look kindly upon a court which failed to bring to justice children who committed crimes of that nature and spared them the judicial process of accountability.[154] However, international non-governmental organisations responsible for childcare and rehabilitation programmes, together with some of their national counterparts, were unanimous in their objections to any kind of judicial accountability for children below 18 years of age for fear that such a process would place at risk the entire rehabilitation programme so painstakingly achieved.[155]

Regardless of the provision of SCSL Statute, the chief prosecutor, David Crane, stated that he would not prosecute children:

> The Prosecution decided early in developing a prosecutorial plan that no child between 15 and 18 had the sufficiently blameworthy state of mind to commit war crimes in a conflict setting. Aware of the clear legal standard

---

151 Committee on the Rights of the Child: General Comment No. 10 (2007) – Children's rights in Juvenile Justice.
152 Statute of the Special Court for Sierra Leone 2002 s (4)(c).
153 Report of the Secretary-General on the Establishment of a Special Court for Sierra Leone, UN Doc. S/2000/915 (4 October 2000) para. 30.
154 Ibid., paras 34–5.
155 Ibid., paras 34–5.

highlighted in international humanitarian law, the intent in choosing not to prosecute was to rehabilitate and reintegrate this lost generation back into society. It would have been impractical to prosecute even particularly violent children because there were so many.

(Crane 2008: 15).

The ICC began its prosecutions after the SCSL. Article 26 of the Rome Statute, which established the ICC, states that: 'The Court shall have no jurisdiction over any person who was under the age of 18 at the time of the alleged commission of a crime.'[156] Unlike the SCSL Statute, the Rome Statute effectively rules out the prosecution of child soldiers.

A few problems emerge. As noted earlier, under Article 8 of the Statute, war crimes against child soldiers include conscripting or enlisting children under the age of 15 years, or using them to participate actively in hostilities. This then creates an 'impunity gap' in respect of child soldiers between the ages of 15 and 18. In other words, children older than 15 are not considered 'child' soldiers in terms of being the subject of the crimes of conscription, enlistment, and use of child soldiers in hostilities. Yet, also, the children aged 15 to 18 cannot be prosecuted as Article 26 prohibits prosecution of persons who commit crimes when they are under the age of 18. A legal vacuum is created whereby, for instance, a 16-year-old soldier who commits mass atrocities is neither a victim nor a perpetrator of war crimes.

However, the exemption of children has been contested. Drumbl (2012), for instance, notes that the international community has tended to uncritically 'replay the same narratives and circulate the same assumptions' about child soldiers (vii). The 'international legal imagination' has thus become unduly saturated by the image of a child soldier as a 'faultless passive victim.' This image, he argues, results in a 'legal fiction' (101), because it fails to account for the under-explored and under-appreciated notion of youth volunteerism, itself connected to the idea that children are capable of being social navigators who understand, especially when adolescents, more than the international legal imagination wishes to acknowledge. According to Drumbl, child soldiers should not be 'cocooned' from the reality of their possible involvement in mass violence by over-emphasising the 'faultless passive victim' image (Drumbl 2012: 22). Ascribing faultlessness and an absence of responsibility may be seen to legitimise irresponsibility and also obscure the child soldier's possible agency (2012: 40, 42). Drumbl concludes that the reasons for enlistment (voluntary recruitment) are multifaceted and incapable of generalisation (2012: 79). Some research concluded that when child soldiers took part in hostilities 'they did not feel like innocent victims . . . they would discuss among themselves the feeling

---

156 Rome Statute, 1998, art. 26.

of acting independently . . . do not feel traumatized . . . but perpetrators of war crimes' (Akello et al. 2006: 236). Child soldiers may go beyond what is asked of them (Honwana 2006: 71) showing an element of their own will when committing atrocities. Such acts have raised questions on how, without any measures of justice, former child soldiers can settle in the communities against which such atrocities were committed.

Drumbl notes that criminal trials may be undesirable as they tend to prioritise incarceration over rehabilitation and reintegration. He points out that the accountability of child soldiers should not be ignored but can take different forms such as inquiries and community involvement of questions of reintegration and restoration (2012: 99). The victims' quest for justice cannot be secondary to the rehabilitation and forgiveness of a child soldier (Lafayette 2013: 298). This delicate balance is difficult to accommodate and certain nonjudicial mechanisms, such as truth and reconciliation commissions and cultural cleansing rites, have provided some relief for both the victims and perpetrators (Lafayette 2013: 298).

9.3.5.1 Dominic Ongwen

The question of accountability characterised one of the most complex cases to be handled by the ICC. Dominic Ongwen allegedly held the rank of Brigadier General in the Ugandan rebel group, the Lord's Resistance Army (LRA), when he surrendered himself to United States forces in the Central African Republic in January 2015. He had been the subject of an ICC warrant of arrest issued in 2005, along with the elusive leader of the ICC, Joseph Kony and others. Ongwen (Case Study 9.2) was handed over to the ICC and charged with, among other crimes, a crime of which he was once a victim – recruiting children for armed conflict. The case was intriguing as Ongwen himself was abducted by the LRA in 1988 when, according to the ICC, he was 14 years old (some give a different age, but most under 15). This case required the court to confront the difficult question of how to hold to account a high-ranking member of the LRA who was also a victim of the group's abductions and forced to become a soldier. Most of the rank and file members of the LRA are or were children who had been abducted and forced to join the group. At the time of his surrender and arrest, Ongwen was in his late thirties. Against the backdrop of what Drumbl describes as the 'international legal imagination', which exonerates child soldiers as victims of adult malevolence, a debate emerged in scholarly circles and the court on whether Ongwen deserved to be prosecuted even if he was now an adult. How should 'victims who victimise' be treated? How much weight should be given to Ongwen's abduction as minor? As will be noticed in the Case Study (9.2), ICC Chief Prosecutor Fatou Bensouda argued that his conscription should only amount to mitigation.

Case study 9.2

Dominic Ongwen Case

***Prosecutor v. Dominic Ongwen* ICC-02/04–01/15**
The case of Dominic Ongwen, a former commander of the Lord's Resistance Army (LRA), before the International Criminal Court (ICC) is one of many firsts; the first member of the LRA to appear before the ICC. He is the first former child soldier to be prosecuted before an international tribunal, and the first person to be charged by an international tribunal for committing some of the same crimes of which he is also a victim, namely the conscription and use of child soldiers and enslavement. Joseph Kony, the wanted leader of the LRA is surrounded by mystique. He is said to lead the LRA through prayer and the orders/commands of the Spirits. His 'War Council' consisted of him and several Spirits. When being possessed by the Spirits, Kony would go into a trance, changing his demeanour and sometimes speaking in tongues.[157] This was a powerful tool in his ability to control people from children to adults.

As a former child soldier himself, Ongwen's case raises a critical issue for a Court that has shed light on the problem of child soldiers and their illegal recruitment. This complex situation raises the dilemma of whether the ICC should take consideration of Ongwen's status as a victim of the crimes he is alleged to have committed himself.

In July 2005, the ICC issued warrants of arrest against the leader of the LRA, Joseph Kony, and four of his commanders, including Dominic Ongwen, the only one of the five indicted who was a former child soldier, for numerous counts of crimes against humanity and war crimes. Almost ten years after the ICC indicted him, Dominic Ongwen made his first appearance before the Court in The Hague on 26 January 2015 for his initial appearance hearing after surrendering himself at an American military base in CAR. On 21 December 2015, the Prosecutor charged Ongwen with additional crimes to the seven counts of war crimes and crimes against humanity listed in the original arrest warrant. Ongwen is charged with a total of 70 counts of various acts, alleged to have been committed between 2002 and 2005.

The confirmation of charges hearing took place on 21 to 27 January 2016 and on 23 March 2016, the Pre-Trial Chamber of the ICC issued its decision confirming the 70 charges against Ongwen and committed him to trial. *Prosecutor v. Dominic Ongwen* Pre-trial Chamber II No. ICC-02/04–01/15, 23 March 2016.

The charges are divided into six categories. Ongwen faces a total of 49 counts of *crimes against humanity* and *war crimes* for attacks on four camps against people who were displaced from their homes in northern Uganda

---

157 *Prosecutor v. Dominic Ongwen* 'Third Public Redacted Version of "Defence Brief for the Confirmation of Charges Hearing", filed on 18 January 2016 as ICC-02/04–01/15–404-Conf 25 May 2016, para. 20 (footnotes removed from excerpt).

between 2002 and 2005. The camps of internally displaced persons (IDPs) that were attacked are Abok, Lukodi, Odek and Pajule. Ongwen is also facing charges for sexual and gender-based crimes. Under this category he is charged with 19 counts of crimes against humanity and war crimes. Additionally, he faced two counts of war crimes for the conscription and use of child soldiers, a crime of which he was once a victim.

Below are some extracted paragraphs from the decision on the confirmation of charges:

3. In the late 1980s, the Lord's Resistance Army (LRA), an armed group originating from northern Uganda, began an insurgency against the government of Uganda, with the stated objective to overthrow the government of Yoweri Museveni, who had taken power in 1986 at the head of the National Resistance Army. Until the present day, there has been armed fighting at varying levels of intensity, mostly in northern Uganda, but also in the neighbouring areas of Uganda, Sudan/South Sudan, the Democratic Republic of Congo and the Central African Republic, between the LRA fighters under the command of Joseph Kony, on the one hand, and the Ugandan government, on the other hand, which in the course of the years launched different military offensives against the LRA. Deliberate targeting of civilians and grave civilian suffering are notorious traits of this long conflict.

54. Before addressing in sequence the 70 charges presented by the Prosecutor, the Chamber lays out briefly its conclusions as concerns the nature and structure of the LRA and Dominic Ongwen's status in the organisation at the time relevant for the charges, namely between 1 July 2002 and 31 December 2005 . . .

58. As concerns Dominic Ongwen, the evidence demonstrates that at all times relevant to the charges, he was a commander in position to direct the conduct of the significant operational force subordinate to him. In August 2002, he is reported to have been the commander of Oka battalion. In September 2003, he progressed to the position of second in command of the Sinia brigade, and in March 2004, he became the brigade's commander. It is also notable that the evidence indicates that Dominic Ongwen's performance as commander was valued highly by Joseph Kony, and it is indeed telling that his appointments to more powerful command positions and his rise in rank followed and were associated with his operational performance, which included the direction of attacks against civilians as discussed below.

59. As commander, Dominic Ongwen was aware of the powers he held, and he took sustained action to assert his commanding position, including by the maintenance of a ruthless disciplinary system, abduction of children to replenish his forces, and the distribution of female abductees to his subordinates as so-called 'wives'.

Trial began on 6 December 2016. The Prosecution completed its presentation of evidence, and the Legal Representatives of Victims also called witnesses to appear before the Chamber

Ongwen's defence argued against his prosecution on the ground of 'duress', stating that he was a victim. Because of Ongwen's abduction at a young age, it was argued he lost any sense of childhood and made decisions out of duress and fear for his life. He lived his life like many child soldiers who are fighting on front lines. In light of the many child soldiers around the globe, the defence appealed to the court to pay credence to the 'very special and significant issue' of his victimisation.[158] In its opening statement, the defence told the court:

> The most pertinent issue you must resolve, and, we propose very strongly, that you should resolve it in favour of the accused: What was the impact of indoctrination, of spiritualism, of the coercive environment, of the injuries, of everything that happened to Dominic Ongwen in 27 years, what was the impact on his mind?[159]

The defence referred to the protections granted to children in the *Additional Protocols I and II, United Nations Convention on the Rights of the Child, Optional Protocol on the Involvement of Children in Armed Conflict* (2000), African Charter on the Rights and Welfare of the Child, Cape Town Principles, and Paris Principles, arguing that the law which was meant to protect Ongwen was being used against him. According to the defence:

> Society forgives and rehabilitates young people who had the good fortune of leaving an armed group, but questions are raised in relation to adults who were abducted at childhood and who did not have the same opportunity or assistance to do so.[160]

Bensouda, acknowledged that people following the case against Ongwen may do so with 'mixed emotions'. They would, one the one hand, feel horror and revulsion at his crimes, and on the other, a sense of sympathy because he was a victim of abduction by the LRA. One Prosecution witness had told the Court that, generally, Ongwen was a good man, who would play and joke with the boys under his command and was loved by everyone. However, Bensouda argued that Ongwen committed brutalities for which deserved to be prosecuted. Having suffered victimisation in the past was not a justification, nor an excuse to victimise others. She argued the focus of the ICC's criminal process was not on the goodness or badness of the accused person, but on the criminal acts which he or she had committed.[161]

---

158 *Prosecutor v. Dominic Ongwen* Pre-Trial Chamber II ICC-02/04–01/15 Defence for Dominic Ongwen Third Public Redacted Version of 'Defence Brief for the Confirmation of Charges Hearing, filed on 18 January 2016 as ICC-02/04–01/15–404-Conf', 25 May 2016, para. 36.
159 *Prosecutor v. Dominic Ongwen* Trial hearing Opening Session: Defence Opening Statements Criminal Court ICC-02/04–01/15 18 September 2018, para. 41.
160 The *Prosecutor v. Dominic Ongwen* Pre-Trial Chamber II ICC-02/04–01/15 Defence for Dominic Ongwen Third Public Redacted Version of 'Defence Brief for the Confirmation of Charges Hearing, filed on 18 January 2016 as ICC-02/04–01/15–404-Conf', 25 May 2016, para. 38.
161 Statement of the Prosecutor of the International Criminal Court, Fatou Bensouda, at the opening of Trial in the case against Dominic Ongwen.

Bensouda pointed out that Ongwen could have deserted well before his surrender and arrest. Between July 2002 and December 2005, the Amnesty Commission records show that over 9,000 LRA members surrendered and received amnesty. But Ongwen, Bensouda argued, did not take that course. Instead, he accepted the power and authority which came with his rank and his appointment.

Those sympathetic to Ongwen note, however, that LRA leader Kony is a somewhat mystical figure believed to have powers of mind control. He has been described as 'an all-seeing and all-knowing individual, making it unthinkable for a recruit/abductee to escape.'[162] Absolute obedience to the spiritual rules was therefore the only way to survive life with the LRA. The defence argued:

> This type of indoctrination was not without consequence. This was a powerful tool in Kony's arsenal and in his ability to control people from children to adults who were trained to believe that he was a prophet and in the vengeance of the Spirits. This is no insignificant given that many of the children in the LRA came from societies where spiritual beliefs are important. From this indoctrination, Kony ruled with complete and unfettered power. His orders were final and meant to be followed. Disobeying orders of the prophet resulted in torture, death or even worse.[163]

Ongwen committed egregious acts. The question which arises from this case is on the weight to be given to Ongwen's forced recruitment (conscription) into the LRA, an offence by his abductors itself. According to Bensouda:

> The circumstances in which he himself was abducted and conscripted into the LRA many years before may perhaps amount to some mitigation of sentence in the event that he is convicted of these crimes. They cannot begin to amount to a defence, or a reason not to hold him to account for the choice that he made; the choice to embrace the murderous violence used by the LRA and to make it the hallmark of operations carried out by his soldiers.

However, Ongwen's defence insisted that the fact that one was forcibly conscripted as a child soldier and lived in that environment of ruthlessness and duress

---

162 *Prosecutor v. Dominic Ongwen* 'Third Public Redacted Version of "Defence Brief for the Confirmation of Charges Hearing", filed on 18 January 2016 as ICC-02/04-01/15-404-Conf ICC-02/04-01/15', 25 May 2016.

163 *Prosecutor v. Dominic Ongwen* 'Third Public Redacted Version of "Defence Brief for the Confirmation of Charges Hearing", filed on 18 January 2016 as ICC-02/04-01/15-404-Conf ICC-02/04-01/15', 25 May 2016 para. 18 (footnotes removed).

throughout one's life cannot simply be regarded as a matter to be resolved during the sentencing phase at trial when addressing mitigation.[164]

Drumbl (2016) observes that, irrespective of his ascension, Ongwen's point of entry remained fixed as a young, kidnapped, orphaned, and abused child. The Lubanga case had cast the linkage between the past as a child soldier and the present as a former child soldier as linear and continuous. The child soldiering experience

> was constructed as ongoing and assured: it rendered the children as victims damaged for life, with their reality today as derivative of their previous suffering. Once a child soldier in fact, always a child soldier in mind, body, and soul.

In Ongwen, however, the linkage between the accused's past as a child soldier and his present as a former child soldier was seen as discontinuous and contingent (Drumbl 2016). Here, Drumbl does not necessarily argue that child soldiers should be treated as victims only, but that international criminal law should proceed in consistent and predictable ways. The Pre-Trial Chamber in Ongwen case's understanding of the agency of actual and former child soldiers departed from the understanding previously deployed by the Lubanga Trial and Appeals Chambers, in particular in the sentencing judgements.

9.4 Concluding remarks

As has been noticed in this chapter, child soldiering remains a troubling phenomenon of modern armed conflicts. Thousands of children are still recruited for purposes of war. It might be argued that the law was rather slow in catching up with the practice. As a result, the framework on children and armed conflict developed as a patchwork, with gaps. However, international courts have prosecuted cases for recruitment of child combatants. A number of people have appeared in court for recruiting child soldiers, with the jurisprudence offering some degree of clarity on the nature of the war crime. However, the debate on the culpability of child soldiers – whether they are victims or perpetrators – continues.

While not a child at the time of his trial, the case of Ongwen, a former child soldier, is one of the most momentous since the creation of the ICC, and raises difficult questions of responsibility and blame. The debate on whether he was a victim or a perpetrator has also been associated with this case. The case divided the prosecution and the defence as it did among scholars of international criminal law. The binary of 'victim or perpetrator' might not be helpful. Perhaps the appropriate approach would be to treat child soldiers as victims of armed conflict but also perpetrators of serious crimes. Ongwen's trial was ongoing at the time of publication.

---

164 *Prosecutor v. Dominic Ongwen* Pre-Trial Chamber II ICC-02/04–01/15 'Defence for Dominic Ongwen Third Public Redacted Version of "Defence Brief for the Confirmation of Charges Hearing", filed on 18 January 2016 as ICC-02/04–01/15–404-Conf', 25 May 2016, para. 36.

Chapter 10

Indigenous children

10.1 Introduction

There has been an emerging interest in indigenous *peoples*' rights over the past 30 years. It is estimated that there are more than 370 million indigenous people in some 90 countries worldwide.[1] The United Nations human rights system has contributed greatly to the heightened focus in international law and policy on the human rights protection of indigenous peoples. However, there does not exist yet a dedicated international instrument that addresses exclusively the rights of indigenous *children*. There are some provisions in the *Convention on the Rights of the Child* that directly address the rights of indigenous children.[2] In addition, there is an *ILO Convention concerning Indigenous and Tribal Peoples in Independent Countries*.[3] A landmark achievement has been the General Assembly's adoption of the *United Nations Declaration on the Rights of Indigenous Peoples*[4] (the *Declaration of 2007*).

10.1.1 Who are indigenous peoples?

The definition of who are *indigenous* peoples remains a contested question. The *Declaration of 2007* does not define 'indigenous'.[5] The key criterion would appear to be:

- self-identification;
- historical continuity with pre-invasion and/or pre-colonial societies that developed on their territories;
- distinctiveness;

---

1 United Nations Permanent Forum on Indigenous Issues website, available at: <http://undesadspd.org/IndigenousPeoples/AboutUsMembers/History.aspx> (accessed 24 November 2013).
2 *Convention on the Rights of the Child*, arts 17(d), 30.
3 International Labour Organization, *Indigenous and Tribal Peoples Convention*, ILO Convention No. 169 (27 June 1989), entered into force 5 September 1991.
4 General Assembly, *United Nations Declaration on the Rights of Indigenous Peoples*, resolution / adopted by the General Assembly, 61st session, UN Doc. A/RES/61/295 (2 October 2007).
5 See *Declaration of 2007*, arts 9 and 33.

- non-dominance;
- determination to preserve, develop and transmit to future generations their ancestral territories and identity as peoples in accordance with their own cultural patterns, social institutions and legal system;[6]
- a strong link to territories and surrounding natural resources;
- distinct social, economic or political systems; and
- distinct language, culture and beliefs.[7]

Two-thirds of the world's indigenous peoples are estimated to live in Asia, in other words, approximately 260 million people representing 2,000 distinct civilisations and languages. The different terms used to refer to them at the national level, ranges from 'hill tribes' and 'indigenous nationalities', to 'tribal peoples', 'ethnic minorities', and 'natives', and testify to the variety of their experiences in the region (Errico 2017: 1).[8] Many indigenous peoples retain some autonomy in relation to their political and legal structures and a strong connection to their lands, territories and resources; some practise nomadic lifestyles. Indigenous peoples' relationships with their land and resources are frequently a defining feature. The Inter-American Court of Human Rights stated:

> The close ties of indigenous people with the land must be recognized and understood as the fundamental basis of their cultures, their spiritual life, their integrity, and their economic survival. For indigenous communities, relations to the land are not merely a matter of possession and production but a material and spiritual element which they must fully enjoy, even to preserve their cultural legacy and transmit it to future generations.[9]

The legal status of indigenous peoples is distinct from that of *minorities*, '[but] they are often, though not always, in the minority in the States in which they reside'.[10] Many of the human rights challenges for indigenous peoples are rooted in pressures on their lands, territories and resources often arising from more dominant non-indigenous groups in their countries. The impacts of climate change were serious and life-threatening. Indigenous peoples continue to be 'overrepresented

---

6 See Office of the UN High Commissioner for Human Rights, *Fact Sheet No. 9/Rev. 2*, 'Indigenous Peoples and the United Nations Human Rights System', August 2013, New York and Geneva: OHCHR. Available at: <www.ohchr.org/Documents/Publications/fs9Rev.2.pdf> (accessed 22 November 2013). And the influential report by José Martínez Cobo, *Study of the problem of discrimination against indigenous populations*. Available at: <http://undesadspd.org/IndigenousPeoples/LibraryDocuments/Mart%C3%ADnezCoboStudy.aspx> (accessed 24 November 2013).
7 United Nations Permanent Forum on Indigenous Peoples has stressed these latter elements.
8 Errico (2017).
9 *Case of the Mayagna (Sumo) Awas Tingni Community v. Nicaragua*, Judgement of 31 August 2001, Series C, No. 79, para. 149.
10 Office of the UN High Commissioner for Human Rights, *Fact Sheet No. 9/Rev. 2*, 'Indigenous Peoples and the United Nations Human Rights System', August 2013, New York and Geneva: OHCHR, 3.

amongst the poorest and most marginalised, representing a shocking 33% of the people living in extreme rural poverty, and therefore having fewer resources and resilience to cope with climate change'.[11] There is growing recognition of the contribution of indigenous peoples' traditional knowledge to sustainable development and ecosystem management, biodiversity conservation, and climate change adaptation. Making progress in implementing the 2030 Agenda for Sustainable Development and the Paris Agreement on climate change thus requires renewed efforts in addressing the rights of indigenous and tribal peoples (Errico 2017: 5).

The historical background of the relationship between an indigenous people and the modern sovereign State will often shape and perpetuate discriminatory perceptions and practices. It is perhaps, above all, in the area of discrimination that issues relating specifically to indigenous children have arisen. Scholars of the TWAIL persuasion (see section 5.1.4 in this book) have argued in favour of expanding the subject of TWAIL scholarship to include themes such as indigenous peoples and hierarchical caste systems (Gathii 2019). TWAIL proponents argue that discrimination against indigenous people was maintained under international law based on differences on scale of civilisation (Shrinkhal 2019). The Special Rapporteur on the Rights of Indigenous Peoples reported in 2018 'the dismal state of protection of the collective rights of indigenous peoples to their lands, territories and resources.'[12] Regarding the education system, many States have considered the provision of mother tongue-based bilingual education, the teaching of indigenous languages and the adoption of special measures to ensure equal opportunities to access education for indigenous girls and boys. Some progress has indeed been made towards improving indigenous children's enrolment in school.

In the report on Asia, Errico (2017: 54) concludes nonetheless:

> Illiteracy and drop-out rates, however, particularly after primary education level, for indigenous girls and boys remain higher than national averages owing to a range of different factors, including, among others, discrimination, language barriers, lack of facilities and teachers, the content of school curricula, distances and costs. Only in a few countries, such as Nepal and the Philippines, does the national legislation recognize the right of indigenous peoples to establish and manage educational institutions.

In her report to the Human Rights Council on Timor-Leste (2019),[13] Victoria Tauli-Corpuz, Special Rapporteur on the Rights of Indigenous Peoples, noted

---

11 Statement of Ms Victoria Tauli-Corpuz, Special Rapporteur on the Rights of Indigenous Peoples, 17th Session of the United Nations Permanent Forum on Indigenous Issues Agenda Item 10, New York, 18 April 2018, p. 5.
12 Ibid., p. 3.
13 Report of Rapporteur on the rights of indigenous peoples, Victoria Tauli-Corpuz, on Timor-Leste from the visit of 8–16 April 2019. Human Rights Council 42nd session, 9–27 September 2019; 2 August 2019 A/HRC/42/37/Add.2, para. 68.

that primary school children who struggled to understand their teachers become disengaged, which resulted in high dropout rates, putting them at a disadvantage in continuing their education. In practice, this had impacted Timorese children whose mother tongue is a local language other than Tetum.[14] In her Ecuador report (2019),[15] she noted that the National Directorate for Bilingual Intercultural Education had been dismantled, and the educational system was centralised around schools known as 'Millennium school'. These schools, which were set up with the stated aim of ensuring educational excellence, entailed closing down the community schools, causing major displacements for indigenous children, risks to their security and increased expenses for their families.

10.2 Indigenous peoples: international law and policy

Although there does not yet exist one discrete international instrument dedicated to protecting specifically indigenous *children's* rights, rather than indigenous *peoples'* rights, there has evolved a body of relevant international law relevant to all indigenous people. This is explored in the sections below.

10.2.1 United Nations Human Rights Treaties

In addition to the *Convention on the Rights of the Child* (see section 9.2.2 in this book), there are four other UN human rights treaties that address indigeneity issues. Many of the provisions discussed below derive from article 27(1) of the *Universal Declaration of Human Rights*,[16] which states that 'everyone has the right freely to participate in the cultural life of the community'.

The *International Covenant on Civil and Political Rights* (ICCPR) contains a right to self-determination[17] and the rights of persons belonging to minorities to enjoy their own culture, to profess and practise their own religion or to use their own language (article 27). The Human Rights Committee has elaborated on indigenous peoples' rights during the course of its periodic reporting and individual complaints procedures. For example, Francis Hopu and Tepoaitu Bessert, both ethnic Polynesians and inhabitants of Tahiti, French Polynesia claimed to be victims of violations of various articles of the ICCPR by France in relation to a

---

14 Tetum speakers, accounting for about 25 per cent of the population, are the largest indigenous group; other groups include the Mambae, Kemak, Bunak and Fataluku. The Tetum and Portuguese languages have been given official status in the country.
15 Report of the Special Rapporteur on the rights of indigenous peoples, Victoria Tauli-Corpuz, on Ecuador from the visit of 19–29 November 2018. Human Rights Council 42nd session, 9–27 September; 4 July 2019 A/HRC/42/37/Add.1.
16 UN General Assembly, *Universal Declaration of Human Rights*, 10 December 1948, 217 A (III).
17 *International Covenant on Civil and Political Rights*, opened for signature 16 December 1966, 999 UNTS 171 (entered into force 23 March 1976), art. 1.

land tract in Tahiti which they argued they were dispossessed of in 1961 and on which the landowners wanted to construct a luxury hotel complex on the site in 1990. The applicants ('authors') in an individual communication addressed to the Human Rights Committee asserted that the land encompassed the site of a pre-European ancestral burial ground and that the lagoon remained a traditional fishing ground and provided the means of subsistence for some thirty families living next to it. The Human Rights Committee determined, *inter alia*, that there had been a violation of the applicants' right to respect for family life by interpreting 'family' to include the relationship between the applicants and their ancestral burial grounds.

> The Committee observes that the objectives of the Covenant require that the term 'family' be given a broad interpretation so as to include all those comprising the family as understood in the society in question. It follows that cultural traditions should be taken into account when defining the term 'family' in a specific situation. It transpires from the authors' claims that they consider the relationship to their ancestors to be an essential element of their identity and to play an important role in their family life.[18]

The Human Rights Committee has also indicated, in a concluding observation of a United States periodic report, the need to consider the right to self-determination when interpreting article 27.

> The State party should review its policy towards indigenous peoples as regards the extinguishment of aboriginal rights on the basis of the plenary power of Congress regarding Indian affairs and grant them the same degree of judicial protection that is available to the non-indigenous population. The State party should take further steps to secure the rights of all indigenous peoples, under articles 1 and 27 of the Covenant, so as to give them greater influence in decision-making affecting their natural environment and their means of subsistence as well as their own culture.[19]

A right to self-determination is also included in the *International Covenant on Economic, Social and Cultural Rights*[20] (ICESCR) and has been applied similarly to indigenous peoples. The Committee on Economic, Social and Cultural Rights refers to indigeneity issues in three General Comments. In *General Comment No. 7*, it observed that '[w]omen, children, youth, older persons, indigenous people, ethnic and other minorities, and other vulnerable individuals and groups all suffer

---

18 Communication No. 549/1993, *Hopu and Bessert v. France*, views of 29 July 1997, [10.3].
19 CCPR/C/USA/CO/3 (15 September 2006) [37].
20 Opened for signature 16 December 1966, 993 UNTS 3 (entered into force 3 January 1976), art. 1.

disproportionately from the practice of forced evictions'.[21] In *General Comment No. 17*, the Committee asserted that 'States parties should adopt measures to ensure the effective protection of the interests of indigenous peoples relating to their productions, which are often expressions of their cultural heritage and traditional knowledge' and should therefore adopt measures to protect scientific, literary and artistic productions of indigenous peoples.[22] Finally, in *General Comment No. 21*,[23] the Committee observed, *inter alia*, that:

> The strong communal dimension of indigenous peoples' cultural life is indispensable to their existence, well-being and full development, and includes the right to the lands, territories and resources which they have traditionally owned, occupied or otherwise used or acquired. Indigenous peoples' cultural values and rights associated with their ancestral lands and their relationship with nature should be regarded with respect and protected, in order to prevent the degradation of their particular way of life, including their means of subsistence, the loss of their natural resources and, ultimately, their cultural identity.[24]

The Committee on the Elimination of Racial Discrimination (CERD) has also addressed indigeneity issues in its monitoring of the *International Convention on the Elimination of All Forms of Racial Discrimination*.[25] In its *General Recommendation XXIII* on indigenous peoples, it affirmed that 'discrimination against indigenous peoples falls under the scope of the Convention' and called in particular on States parties to:

a   recognize and respect indigenous distinct culture, history, language and way of life as an enrichment of the State's cultural identity and to promote its preservation;
b   ensure that member of indigenous peoples are free and equal in dignity and rights and free from any discrimination, in particular that based on indigenous origin or identity;

---

21 Committee on Economic, Social and Cultural Rights, *General Comment No. 7: The right to adequate housing (article 11, paragraph 1, of the Covenant: forced evictions)*, 16th session (14 May 1997) [11].
22 Committee on Economic, Social and Cultural Rights, *General Comment No. 17: The right of everyone to benefit from the protection of the moral and material interests resulting from any scientific, literary or artistic production of which he or she is the author (article 15, paragraph 1 (c), of the Covenant)* 35th session, E/C.12/GC/17 (12 January 2006) [32].
23 Committee on Economic, Social and Cultural Rights, *General Comment No. 21: Right of everyone to take part in cultural life (art. 15, para. 1 (a), of the International Covenant on Economic, Social and Cultural Rights)*, 43rd session, E/C.12/GC/21 (21 December 2009).
24 Committee on Economic, Social and Cultural Rights, *General Comment No. 21: Right of everyone to take part in cultural life (art. 15, para. 1 (a), of the International Covenant on Economic, Social and Cultural Rights)*, 43rd session, E/C.12/GC/21 (21 December 2009) [36–7].
25 Opened for signature 7 March 1966, 660 UNTS 195 (entered into force 4 January 1969).

c   provide indigenous peoples with conditions allowing for a sustainable economic and social development compatible with their cultural characteristics;
d   ensure that members of indigenous peoples have equal rights in respect of effective participation in public life and that no decisions directly relating to their rights and interests are taken without informed consent;
e   ensure that indigenous communities can exercise their rights to practice and revitalize their cultural traditions and customs and to preserve and to practice their languages.[26]

The Committee against Torture has also issued a General Comment in its monitoring role of the *Convention against Torture*[27] which refers to the need for States parties to ensure that their laws are in practice applied to all persons, regardless of, *inter alia*, their 'indigenous status' or any other adverse distinction.[28]

10.2.2   Convention on the Rights of the Child

The *Convention on the Rights of the Child* is the only global United Nations human rights treaty to specifically mention indigenous children. There several provisions relating to indigenous children to consider.

10.2.2.1   Article 30

Article 30 is the principal provision in the Convention most directly relating to indigenous children: see the text of article 30 at section 3.7.9.2 in this book. There is a close linkage between article 30 of the Convention and article 27 of the ICCPR. Both articles provide for the individual's right, in community with other members of the group, to enjoy his or her own culture, to profess and practice his or her own religion or to use his or her own language. *General Comment No. 11* states that:

> The right established is conceived as being both individual and collective and is an important recognition of the collective traditions and values in indigenous cultures. The Committee notes that the right to exercise cultural rights among indigenous peoples may be closely associated with the use of traditional territory and the use of its resources.[29]

---

26   Committee on the Elimination of Racial Discrimination, *General Recommendation XXIII: The rights of indigenous peoples*, 1235th meeting, UN Doc. A/52/18 (18 August 1997) [2, 4].
27   *Convention against Torture and Other Cruel, Inhuman or Degrading Treatment or Punishment*, opened for signature 10 December 1984, 1465 UNTS 85, entered into force 26 June 1987.
28   Committee against Torture, *General Comment No. 2: Implementation of article 2 by States parties*, CAT/C/GC/2 (24 January 2008) [21].
29   Committee on the Rights of the Child, *General Comment No. 11: Indigenous children and their rights under the Convention*, 50th session, CRC/C/GC/11 (12 February 2009) [16].

Article 30 is derived from a Mexican NGO's proposal (Hodgkin and Newell 2007: 456) to dedicate an article of the Convention to the rights of indigenous children. It was subsequently agreed that the article should also encompass the rights of all minority children. The upshot was that the precedent of *minority* protection contained in the ICCPR[30] was used as the template for new provision and was extended with the addition to the stated minorities of 'persons of indigenous origin'. The Committee has read into article 30 a positive duty on States to take measures of protection.[31] It has emphasised that the cultural practices provided by article 30 must be exercised in compliance with the Convention as a whole 'and under no circumstances may be justified if deemed prejudicial to the child's dignity, health and development'; for example, if harmful practices such as early marriage or FGM are present, 'the State party should work together with indigenous communities to ensure their eradication'.[32] The Committee also recognises, in relation to the child's right to use his or her own language, that bilingual and inter-cultural curricula are important elements in the education of indigenous children.[33] This also resonates with the provision contain in the ILO Convention (see section 9.2.3) prescribing that indigenous children are taught to read and write in their own language as well as the opportunity to engage with the official language of the country.[34]

10.2.2.2 Article 17(d)

States parties are under an obligation contain in article 17(d) of the Convention to '[e]ncourage the mass media to have particular regard to the linguistic needs of the child who belongs to a minority group or who is indigenous': see text of article 17(1) at section 3.7.4.3 in this book. This provision underlines the important role that the mass media can play, for example by producing material and programmes in minority languages. Furthermore, in commenting on States' duties to disseminate material on the Convention,[35] the Committee has often emphasised the importance of ensuring translation into minority and indigenous languages, and the particular importance of the media's participation in this task (Hodgkin and Newell 2007: 224).

10.2.2.3 Article 29(1)(c) & (d)

Finally, the child's right to education provides further material protecting specifically indigenous children (in article 29(1)(c) and (d) in particular). See generally section 3.7.8.1 on rights to education.

---

30 ICCPR, art. 27.
31 *General Comment No.* 11 [17].
32 *General Comment No. 11* [22].
33 *General Comment No. 11* [62].
34 *General Comment No. 11* [62].
35 *Convention on the Rights of the Child*, art. 42.

Article 29
1   States Parties agree that the education of the child shall be directed to:
   (a) The development of the child''s personality, talents and mental and physical abilities to their fullest potential;
   (b) The development of respect for human rights and fundamental freedoms, and for the principles enshrined in the Charter of the United Nations;
   (c) The development of respect for the child's parents, his or her own cultural identity, language and values, for the national values of the country in which the child is living, the country from which he or she may originate, and for civilizations different from his or her own;
   (d) The preparation of the child for responsible life in a free society, in the spirit of understanding, peace, tolerance, equality of sexes, and friendship among all peoples, ethnic, national and religious groups and persons of indigenous origin;
   (e) The development of respect for the natural environment.

2   No part of the present article or article 28 shall be construed so as to interfere with the liberty of individuals and bodies to establish and direct educational institutions, subject always to the observance of the principle set forth in paragraph 1 of the present article and to the requirements that the education given in such institutions shall conform to such minimum standards as may be laid down by the State.

The Committee view the education of indigenous children as strengthening their ability to exercise their civil rights and contribute to the policy process for improved protection of human rights; 'the implementation of the right to education of indigenous children is an essential means of achieving individual empowerment and self-determination of indigenous peoples'.[36] It also recognises the importance of urging States parties to ensure that 'the curricula, educational materials and history textbooks provide a fair, accurate and informative portrayal of the societies and cultures of indigenous peoples'.[37]

Nevertheless, the Committee has focused specifically on questions relating to indigenous children in one of their *Days of General Discussion* in 2003.[38] It has also produced a *General Comment*[39] on this subject in 2009.

---

36 *General Comment No. 11* [57].
37 *General Comment No. 11* [58].
38 Committee on the Rights of the Child, *Day of General Discussion on 'The rights of indigenous children'*, Report on the 34th session, CRC/C/133 (3 October 2003).
39 Committee on the Rights of the Child, *General Comment No. 11: Indigenous children and their rights under the Convention*, fiftieth session, CRC/C/GC/11 (12 February 2009).

10.2.2.4 Day of General Discussion *(2003)*

In the *Day of General Discussion* the Committee on the Rights of the Child recognised that:

> indigenous children are disproportionately affected by specific challenges such as institutionalization, urbanization, drug and alcohol abuse, trafficking, armed conflict, sexual exploitation and child labour and yet are not sufficiently taken into consideration in the development and implementation of policies and programmes for children . . .[40]

It called upon States parties, UN agencies, and others to adopt a broader rights-based approach to indigenous children and encouraged the use of community-based interventions. The Committee recognised that 'the right to enjoy one's culture, may consist of a way of life which is closely associated with territory and use of its resources'.[41] It recommended that States parties strengthen mechanisms for data collection on indigenous children. Furthermore, it recommended that States parties work closely with indigenous peoples and organisations to seek consensus on development strategies, policies and projects aimed at implementing children's rights. The Committee emphasised the importance of applying the principle of non-discrimination to indigenous children in order to enjoy all of their rights equally and including equal access to culturally appropriate services including health, education, social services, housing, potable water and sanitation.[42] Importantly, it recommended that State parties, with the full participation of indigenous communities and children, 'develop public awareness campaigns, including through the mass media, to combat negative attitudes and misperceptions about indigenous peoples'.[43]

The Committee pointed out that States parties should respect the methods customarily practised by indigenous peoples for dealing with criminal offences committed by children , but only 'when it is in the best interests of the child' to do so.[44] Rights of identity by indigenous children were supported by the Committee which called upon States to, *inter alia*, ensure accessible birth registration.[45] As regards the family environment, the Committee recommended that maintaining the integrity of indigenous families and communities should be a consideration in relevant development programmes, social services, health and education programmes.[46] As

---

40 Committee on the Rights of the Child, *Day of General Discussion on 'The rights of indigenous children'*, Report on the 34th session, CRC/C/133 (3 October 2003), Preamble.
41 *Day of General Discussion on the rights of indigenous children* [4].
42 *Day of General Discussion on the rights of indigenous children* [9].
43 *Day of General Discussion on the rights of indigenous children* [11].
44 *Day of General Discussion on the rights of indigenous children* [13].
45 *Day of General Discussion on the rights of indigenous children* [15].
46 *Day of General Discussion on the rights of indigenous children* [17].

regards health, the Committee recommended that States parties take all necessary measures to implement the right to health of indigenous children, in view of 'the comparatively low indicators regarding child mortality, immunisation and nutrition that affect this group of children'.[47] Special attention should also be paid to adolescents regarding drug abuse, alcohol consumption, mental health and sex education. As regards education, States parties should 'ensure access for indigenous children to appropriate and high quality education while taking complementary measures to eradicate child labour'.[48]

10.2.2.5 General Comment No. 11 (2009)[49]

The *General Comment* consolidates, in a more forensic form, many of the recommendations developed in the *Day of General Discussion* discussed above. It also provides further analysis in particular of articles 30, 29 and 17 discussed above and announces that '[t]he specific references to indigenous children in the Convention are indicative of the recognition that they require special measures in order to fully enjoy their rights'. It emphasises that one element that prompted the need for the *General Comment* was the continued serious discrimination experienced by indigenous children.[50] Based on the recommendations provided in the *Day of General Discussion* of 2003, the objective of the *General Comment* is 'to provide States with guidance on how to implement their obligations under the Convention with respect to indigenous children.' Furthermore, it seeks to explore the challenges which impede indigenous children from fully enjoying their rights and highlights measures required by States to guarantee their effective exercise.[51] The *General Comment* then proceeds to note how the rights of indigenous children are applied within the main 'clusters' of rights used for periodic country reporting under the Convention (see section 3.5 in this book). For example, under the 'general principles' heading, the *General Comment* emphasises the importance of the non-discrimination principle (article 2) in this context, in particular the need for States parties to pursue *positive* measures of implementation, including the need for the collection and collation of data suitably disaggregated to enable discrimination to be identified.[52] As regards the 'best interest principle',[53] also perceived as requiring positive measures to implement, the Committee observes that this principle 'is conceived both as a collective and individual right, and that the application of this right to

---

47 *Day of General Discussion on the rights of indigenous children* [18].
48 *Day of General Discussion on the rights of indigenous children* [19].
49 Committee on the Rights of the Child, *General Comment No. 11: Indigenous children and their rights under the Convention*, 50th session, CRC/C/GC/11 (12 February 2009).
50 *General Comment No. 11* [5].
51 *General Comment No. 11* [12].
52 *General Comment No. 11* [23–29].
53 *General Comment No. 11* [30–3].

indigenous children as a group requires consideration of how the right relates to collective cultural rights'. However, when applied to individuals it would seem that the principle 'cannot be neglected or violated in preference for the best interests of the group'.[54] With regard to the right to life, survival and development,[55] the Committee notes with concern the disproportionate high numbers of indigenous children that live in extreme poverty and high infant and child mortality rates and recommends that States take special measures to secure an adequate standard of living for indigenous children. The Committee reiterates its understanding of the 'development' of the child as a holistic concept and in this context the use of traditional lands is seen as relevant to the indigenous child's development. It calls upon States to engage with indigenous peoples to ensure the realisation of the Sustainable Development Goals (see section 10.1.4). As regards respect for the views of the child,[56] the Committee separates out an individual child's right to express his or her views and the principle of participation, which allows children as a group to be consulted on matters involving them. It recommends that the latter collective rights are applied in particular in the school environment, alternative care settings and in the community in general. Throughout the *General Comment*, the Committee urges States parties and others to work collaboratively with indigenous groups. It concludes:

> Empowerment of indigenous children and the effective exercise of their rights to culture, religion and language provide an essential foundation of a culturally diverse State in harmony and compliance with its human rights obligations.[57]

10.2.3 ILO Indigenous and Tribal Peoples Convention

The *Indigenous and Tribal Peoples Convention*[58] ('ILO Convention of 1989') revises an earlier version ILO Convention of 1957.[59] The general frame of reference of the 1957 Convention is said to have laid in 'governments taking coordinated and systematic action to protect their indigenous peoples and progressively *integrate* them into the life of their countries' (Yupsanis 2012: 434). They point out that the 1957 Convention, which developed in tandem with the decolonisation movement,

---

54 *General Comment No. 11* [30].
55 *General Comment No. 11* [34–6].
56 *General Comment No. 11* [37–9].
57 *General Comment No. 11* [82].
58 International Labour Organization, *Convention Concerning Indigenous and Tribal People in Independent Countries 1989* (ILO Convention No. 169) (27 June 1989), entered into force 5 September 1991.
59 International Labour Organization, *International Convention Concerning the Protection and Integration of Indigenous and Other Tribal and Semi-Tribal Population in Independent Countries* (ILO Convention No. 107) (26 June 1957), entered into force 2 June 1959.

was centred on the 'ignoble primitive' image of indigenous people and 'the civilization of indigenous people, the assimilation of their retrograde cultures into modern world, is understood to be desirable and just' (Tennant 1994). It echoed an integrationist approach, commonly practised in the 1950s, and it enlisted a patrimonial and integrationist language. However, the *ILO Convention No. 107* was vital in getting recognition of indigenous people, however limited it was in recognition of indigenous customary practices and law and the right of collective land ownership (Shrinkhal 2019).

By contrast, the appearance of the *ILO Convention of 1989* marked a policy shift from assimilation to self-determination, a point supported by the text of the Convention itself.[60] *ILO Convention of 1989* is currently ratified by 23 countries, mainly in Latin America.[61] This is a disappointing number of ratifications caused perhaps by a general tendency for States to avoid subscribing to international instruments that recognise sub-groups within their territories, which may undermine national unity.

The Convention provides a description of tribal and indigenous 'peoples'. The latter are:

> (b) peoples in independent countries who are regarded as indigenous on account of their descent from the populations which inhabited the country, or a geographical region to which the country belongs, at the time of conquest or colonisation or the establishment of present state boundaries and who, irrespective of their legal status, retain some or all of their own social, economic, cultural and political institutions.[62]

Importantly, the Convention also identifies 'self-determination' as 'a fundamental criterion' for determining whether a group can rank as an indigenous people.[63] One advance achieved following the 1957 Convention was the replacement of the term 'populations' with 'peoples'. However, as the right of *peoples* to self-determination is embedded into the UN system,[64] the Convention neutralises it with the explicit recognition in the text of the Convention that the '[t]he use of the term *peoples* in this Convention shall not be construed as having any implications as regards the rights which may attach to the term under international law'.[65] Even

---

60 *Indigenous and Tribal Peoples Convention of 1989*, Preamble §4.
61 This Convention had 22 parties as at 21 November 2013. They were: Argentina, Bolivia, Brazil, Central African Republic, Chile, Colombia, Costa Rica, Denmark, Dominica, Ecuador, Fiji, Guatemala, Honduras, Luxembourg, Mexico, Nepal, Netherlands, Nicaragua, Norway, Paraguay, Peru, Spain and Venezuela.
62 *Indigenous and Tribal Peoples Convention of 1989*, art. 1(a).
63 *Indigenous and Tribal Peoples Convention of 1989*, art. 1(2).
64 See *UN Charter*, art. 1(2).
65 *Indigenous and Tribal Peoples Convention of 1989*, art. 1(3).

so, Yupsanis (2012: 438) argues that 'this restriction does not totally counteract the value of the designation of indigenous peoples as *sui generis* peoples in the context of an emerging recognition of these peoples as such'.

The Convention lays down a series of provisions establishing obligations on States parties for developing action to protect the rights of indigenous peoples and respect for their integrity.[66] Indigenous and tribal peoples also have the right to non-discrimination and governments are urged to adopt special measures for safeguarding 'the persons, institution, property, labour cultures and environment of the peoples concerned.[67] The 'cornerstone' (Yupsanis 2012: 438) of the Convention is arguably contained in articles 6 and 7 which focus on the participation of indigenous and tribal peoples at all levels of institutional and administrative decision-making. The Convention also states that 'due regard' shall be had to customs and customary laws in applying national laws to the peoples concerned.[68] The Convention contains detailed provisions protecting land and resource rights, conditions of employment, vocational training, handicrafts and rural industries, social security and health, and education and means of communication.[69] The Convention, despite the advances achieved, is not without its weaknesses. For example, the rights of consultation are arguably insufficient to prevent States from going through a procedural process of consultation without any real intent to garner participation; there was a failure to provide a right of veto by indigenous peoples over the exploration of ancestral lands and resources in article 15. Further concerns relate to the indeterminate language used in some of the provisions made perhaps more opaque by article 34, which provides that the nature and scope of the measures to be taken to give effect to the Convention shall be determined in 'a flexible manner, having regard to the conditions characteristic of each country'. Nevertheless, the abandonment of the former *individualistic* approach and the focus on recognising *collective* rights, for example to lands and resources, coupled with an emphasis on self-determination has provided, in the4 view of one commentator:

> a valuable instrument for promoting the case of indigenous peoples by establishing fundamental (and legally binding)' minimum standards' of protection, the further entrenchment of which, in scope and content, must now rely on the willingness of the countries forming the international community to recognise, respect and promote the rights of these long-suffering and most disadvantaged peoples.
>
> (Yupsanis 2012: 455–56)

---

66 *Indigenous and Tribal Peoples Convention of 1989*, art. 2.
67 *Indigenous and Tribal Peoples Convention of 1989*, arts 3 and 4 respectively.
68 *Indigenous and Tribal Peoples Convention of 1989*, art. 8(1).
69 *Indigenous and Tribal Peoples Convention of 1989*, Parts II to VI respectively.

Another commentator states that, although the Convention falls short of providing a concrete right to self-determination, it 'can be considered as a small step for indigenous persons but a giant leap for indigenous peoples' (Joonal 2010: 260).

10.2.4 United Nations Declaration on the Rights of Indigenous Peoples

The *United Nations Declaration on the Rights of Indigenous Peoples* (the *'Declaration of 2007'*)[70] was adopted by the General Assembly on 13 September 2007 with 144 votes in favour, 11 abstentions and four States against (Australia, Canada, New Zealand[71] and the United States of America), though the latter countries have subsequently endorsed it.[72] The *Declaration of 2007* is a species of 'soft law' (see section 2.2.6) but its formal, non-binding status should not be overplayed. As one commentator states, '[u]nder the complexity and dynamism of contemporary international law-making, the relevance of a soft law instrument cannot be aprioristically dismissed' (Barelli 2009: 983).

The status of the Declaration under international law

While the United Nations Declaration on the Rights of Indigenous Peoples, as a declaration, is not a formally binding treaty, it contains rights and freedoms, such as self-determination and non-discrimination, set out in binding international human rights treaty law, of which some may be considered customary international law. It reflects a global consensus on indigenous peoples' rights. Moreover, according to the Office of Legal Affairs of the United Nations Secretariat, 'a "declaration" is a solemn instrument resorted to only in very rare cases relating to matters of major and lasting importance where maximum compliance is expected'. The United Nations Declaration on the Rights of Indigenous Peoples is such a declaration deserving of the utmost respect.[73]

The question whether the *Declaration of 2007*, or at least parts of it, may be considered as (binding) customary law remains contentious. Davis asserts: '[T]he Declaration exists in an amorphous in-between state of constituting both a

---

70 General Assembly, *United Nations Declaration on the Rights of Indigenous Peoples*, resolution / adopted by the General Assembly, 61st session, UN Doc. A/RES/61/295 (2 October 2007).
71 For the impact of the *Declaration of 2007* on New Zealand, see generally, Toki (2010).
72 Office of the UN High Commissioner for Human Rights, *Fact Sheet No. 9/Rev. 2*, 'Indigenous Peoples and the United Nations Human Rights System', August 2013, New York and Geneva: OHCHR. Available at: <www.ohchr.org/Documents/Publications/fs9Rev.2.pdf> (accessed 22 November 2013).
73 Office of the UN High Commissioner for Human Rights, *Fact Sheet No. 9/Rev. 2*, 'Indigenous Peoples and the United Nations Human Rights System', August 2013, New York and Geneva: OHCHR, 8–9.

"nonbinding", influential and aspirational statement of soft law but equally an instrument that reflects already binding rules of customary international law' (Davis 2012: 19).

The *Declaration of 2007* provides a more comprehensive instrument than the ILO Convention discussed above, in particular it contains a concrete right to self-determination:

> *Article 3*
>
> Indigenous peoples have the right to self-determination. By virtue of that right they freely determine their political status and freely pursue their economic, social and cultural development.[74]

This was quite a breakthrough in international law; one commentator hails the recognition of self-determination in the *Declaration of 2007* as a 'breakthrough of great importance in the law of self-determination, probably the most important development of the right since the era of decolonization' (Barelli 2009: 2).

The right to self-determination is viewed as one which informs all the other rights in the *Declaration of 2007*. However, although self-determination by *sovereign States* is embedded in the UN system, the appearance of self-determination by an *indigenous people* within the borders of a State may pose a threat, or the perception of one, to that State. The solution to this conundrum has been the adoption of a provision in the *Declaration of 2007* that provides a right, in effect, to internal self-governance rather than outright secession.

> *Article 4*
>
> Indigenous peoples, in exercising their right to self-determination, have the right to autonomy or self-government in matters relating to their internal and local affairs, as well as ways and means for financing their autonomous functions.[75]

Autonomous self-determination if given further elaboration in a provision which provides a right of indigenous peoples to promote, develop and maintain 'institutional structures and their distinctive customs, spirituality, traditions, procedures, practices and, in the cases where they exist, juridical systems or customs'.[76] A dominant theme of the *Declaration of 2007* is the provision of equality and non-discrimination in relation to indigenous individuals and peoples.[77]

---

74 *Declaration of 2007*, art. 3.
75 *Declaration of 2007*, art. 4.
76 *Declaration of 2007*, art. 34.
77 *Declaration of 2007*, arts 1 and 2.

There are distinct political rights of participation in decision-making on matters that would affect their rights, and duties on States to consult in order to obtain their 'free, prior and informed consent' before adopting legislative or administrative measures.[78] Indigenous peoples' rights to lands, territories and resources are recognised.[79]

A further provision obliges States, subject to the participation of indigenous groups, to establish and implement a fair and independent process 'to recognize and adjudicate the rights of indigenous people's laws, traditions, customs and land tenure systems.'[80] The *Declaration of 2007*, consistently with the ICESCR, affirms indigenous peoples' economic, social and cultural rights: for example, rights to health, education, employment, housing, sanitation, social security and an adequate standard of living.[81] The *Declaration of 2007* contains several provisions to protect against discriminatory and adverse treatment on cultural grounds and positive measures to support indigenous peoples' cultures. In particular, the integrationist policy of the past is put to rest by a provision which provides indigenous peoples and individuals with 'the right not to be subjected to forced assimilation or destruction of their culture'.[82] The *Declaration of 2007* is also distinctive as an international instrument in so far as it recognises indigenous peoples' *collective* rights.[83]

Finally, there is some referencing of specifically indigenous *children* in the *Declaration of 2007*. In particular, the Preamble recognises 'the right of indigenous families and communities to retain shared responsibility for the upbringing, training, education and well-being of their children, consistent with the rights of the child'.[84] Within the framework of the 'collective right to live in freedom, peace and security as distinct peoples' there is a prohibition on 'forcibly removing children' from one group to another.[85] Further provisions spell out indigenous children's rights to education, and States' obligations to take specific measures to protect indigenous children to have access to 'an education in their own culture and provided in their own language'.[86] States are also obliges to 'take specific measures to protect indigenous children from economic exploitation and from performing any work that is likely to be hazardous or to interfere with the child's education.'[87]

Whatever the precise legal status of the *Declaration of 2007* may be, there is no doubt that it has been regarded increasingly as the 'principal benchmark' in

---

78 *Declaration of 2007*, arts 18 and 19.
79 *Declaration of 2007*, art. 26.
80 *Declaration of 2007*, art. 27.
81 *Declaration of 2007*, arts 3, 21 and 24.
82 *Declaration of 2007*, art. 8.
83 *Declaration of 2007*, Preamble §22, arts 1, 7(2) and 40.
84 *Declaration of 2007*, Preamble §13.
85 *Declaration of 2007*, art. 7(2).
86 *Declaration of 2007, art.* 14(2) and (3).
87 *Declaration of 2007*, art. 17(2).

international law for the rights of indigenous peoples. That is certainly the view[88] of the Special Rapporteur on the situation of human rights and fundamental freedoms of Indigenous people (see section 9.3.2). A comprehensive manual for national human rights institutions on the *Declaration of 2007* was produced in 2013.[89]

10.3 Indigenous peoples and United Nations mechanisms

Three principal UN mechanisms relating directly to indigenous peoples' issues are discussed in the following sections. They are:

- the United Nations Permanent Forum on Indigenous Peoples;
- the Special Rapporteur on the situation of human rights and fundamental freedoms of Indigenous people; and
- the Expert Mechanism on the Rights of Indigenous Peoples.

All three (complementary) mandates meet annually to coordinate their activities and share information. Representatives of the Permanent Forum usually attend the annual session of the Expert Mechanism and vice versa. The Special Rapporteur attends the annual sessions of both the Permanent Forum and the Expert Mechanism. In essence, the Expert Mechanism undertakes thematic studies; the Special Rapporteur undertakes country visits, addresses specific cases of alleged human rights violations through communications with Governments or others and, in addition, undertakes or contributes to thematic studies; and the Permanent Forum focuses on advice and coordination on indigenous issues within the United Nations and raises awareness about such issues. The Human Rights Council requests all three mandates to carry out their tasks in a coordinated manner. For example, all three bodies have recently participated in organising and preparing for a major World Conference on Indigenous Peoples authorised by the General Assembly,[90] to be held on 22–23 September 2014 at the UN Headquarters in New York.

---

88 See: General Assembly, *Rights of indigenous people: note / by the Secretary-General*, 67th session, UN Doc. A/67/301 (13 August 2012) [26–32].
89 Office of the High Commissioner for Human Rights, *The United Nations Declaration on the Rights of Indigenous Peoples*, August 2013, UN Doc. HR/PUB/13/2. Available at: <www.refworld.org/docid/5289e4fc4.html> (accessed 23 November 2013)
90 General Assembly, *Indigenous issues*, 65th session, UN Doc. A/RES/65/198 (21 December 2010); General Assembly, *Organization of the high-level plenary meeting of the sixty-ninth session of the General Assembly, to be known as the World Conference on Indigenous Peoples*, 66th session, UN Doc. A/RES/66/296 (17 September 2012).

10.3.1 United Nations Permanent Forum on Indigenous Peoples

The Economic and Social Council (ECOSOC), one of or the six principal bodies of the United Nations (see section 2.4.1), though losing its direct authority over the former UN Commission on Human Rights,[91] has remained the parent body of, and is advised by the United Nations Permanent Forum on Indigenous Issues (the 'Permanent Forum'). This body was established by an ECOSOC resolution in 2000[92] which noted in particular 'the striking absence of a mechanism to ensure coordination and regular exchange of information'.[93] The Permanent Forum is mandated to:

- provide expert advice on indigenous issues to ECOSOC;
- raise awareness of indigenous issues with the UN system; and
- prepare and disseminate information on indigenous issues.

The Permanent Forum has 16 members, who serve in their personal capacity for three years. Eight members are nominated by States and elected by ECOSOC, based on the five regional groupings normally used at the United Nations. A further eight are nominated directly by indigenous organisations and appointed by the President of the Economic and Social Council. They represent seven sociocultural regions to give broad representation to the world's indigenous peoples: Africa; Asia; Central and South America and the Caribbean; the Arctic; Central and Eastern Europe, the Russian Federation, Central Asia and Transcaucasia; North America; and the Pacific – with one additional rotating seat among the first three.[94]

The Permanent Forum operates annual two-week sessions. It identifies a specific theme[95] as the overall framework for its sessions, alternating with a review every other year. In recent years, the Permanent Forum has focused on

---

91 UNCHR was replaced by the UN Human Rights Council (UNHRC) in 2006, but the latter body was placed under the authority of the General Assembly.
92 Economic and Social Council, Establishment of a Permanent Forum on Indigenous Issues, Res. 2000/22 (28 July 2000).
93 Ibid.
94 Office of the UN High Commissioner for Human Rights, *Fact Sheet No. 9/Rev. 2*, 'Indigenous Peoples and the United Nations Human Rights System', August 2013, New York and Geneva: OHCHR, 12.
95 For example, the theme of the Permanent Forum's 11th session was: 'The Doctrine of Discovery: its enduring impact on indigenous peoples and the right to redress for past conquests (articles 28 and 37 of the *United Nations Declaration on the Rights of Indigenous Peoples*)'. Permanent Forum, *Report on the eleventh session: 7–18 May 2012*, UN Doc. E/2012/43 E/C.19/2012/13. The upcoming special theme for the 13th session (12–23 May 2014) was: 'Principles of good governance consistent with the United Nations Declaration on the Rights of Indigenous Peoples: articles 3 to 6 and 46'.

the implementation of the *Declaration of 2007*. The Forum also focuses attention on a specific region each year, as a means of highlighting the situation of the indigenous peoples in that region and the challenges they face. The Permanent Forum additionally undertakes studies on specific matters of concern, expert seminars and, on occasion, country visits. Its annual sessions in New York are widely attended by Member States, indigenous peoples' representatives and organisations/institutions, United Nations agencies, non-State actors and others.

10.3.2 The Special Rapporteur on the situation of human rights and fundamental freedoms of Indigenous people

While ECOSOC remains the body to which the Permanent Forum (see section 9.3.1) reports, the Special Rapporteur on the situation of human rights and fundamental freedoms of Indigenous people (the 'Special Rapporteur') and the Expert Mechanism on the Rights of Indigenous Peoples (section 9.3.3) both report back to and enter into interactive dialogue with the Human Rights Council. The Special Rapporteur[96] is a 'special procedure' of the Human Rights Council. The mandate was established in 2001 by the UNCHR and continued by the Human Rights Council. The mandate involves the Special Rapporteur in:

- examining ways to overcome existing obstacles to indigenous peoples' enjoyment of their rights;
- exchanging information about alleged violations of the rights of indigenous peoples;
- formulating proposals to prevent and remedy violations;
- liaising with other special procedures, treaty bodies and regional human rights organisations.

The Special Rapporteur assesses the situation of indigenous peoples in specific countries (see Case Study 10.1); carries out thematic studies; communicates with Governments, indigenous peoples and others concerning allegations of violations of indigenous peoples' rights; and promotes good practices for the protection of these rights. The Special Rapporteur reports annually to the Human Rights Council on particular human rights issues involving indigenous peoples and coordinates work with the Permanent Forum on Indigenous Issues and the Expert Mechanism on the Rights of Indigenous Peoples. Extracts from a recent country report on Mexico are shown in Case Study 10.1.

---

96 See, generally, the Special Rapporteur's website, available at: <www.ohchr.org/en/issues/ipeoples/srindigenouspeoples/pages/sripeoplesindex.aspx> (accessed 23 November 2013).

Case study 10.1

End of mission Statement by the Special Rapporteur on the rights of indigenous peoples on her mission to Mexico Victoria Tauli-Corpuz

17 November 2017
Available at: <www.ohchr.org/EN/NewsEvents/Pages/DisplayNews.aspx?NewsID=22411> (last accessed 11 October 2019)

Introduction

Mexico is an incredibly vast, diverse and complex country. Taking this into account and the limited time available for the official visit, I will focus in this preliminary statement on the main systemic issues and challenges I identified.

Lands, territories and natural resources

The information I received indicates that indigenous peoples who attempt to obtain land rights recognition through the agrarian systems obtain limited results that do not take into account the indigenous peoples' rights to lands, territories and natural resources. On the other hand, I have seen that the National Human Rights Commission and judicial decisions have at instances reflected international standards on lands and territories.

The official position seems to suggest, and this has been confirmed in some of my meetings with Federal and state authorities, that the agrarian reform has effectively responded to indigenous peoples' land rights demands and that no further debate on this issue is necessary. However, the information received during my visit clearly points out that this [is] a critical unresolved issue. In this sense, a more comprehensive response should be based on contemporary international standards on the rights of indigenous peoples, including the Inter-American jurisprudence which provides authoritative guidance on the legal, administrative and policy measures needed to adequately address indigenous peoples' lands, territorial and natural resource rights. These measures should be developed in full cooperation with indigenous peoples themselves.

Autonomy, self-determination and political participation

In light of article 1 of the Constitution, the concepts of self-determination and autonomy are to be interpreted and implemented according to international standards. In this sense, attention should be given to the recognition of indigenous peoples' right to self-government, the right to elect their own authorities according to their own procedures and the use of their own normative and juridical systems.

In addition to self-government, indigenous peoples have the right to participate fully if they so choose in the political life of the country. I have seen some positive advancements that could facilitate indigenous peoples' political participation in this regard, such as the possibility to register independent candidates, efforts to increase access to birth certificates and official registration to allow participation in the federal, state and municipal elections, and a call to political parties to include indigenous candidates within their lists. However, many obstacles remain to ensure full political participation of indigenous peoples. Information was received on persisting practices of undue pressures on indigenous peoples to influence their votes during electoral processes.

The right to determine development priorities

Another aspect of self-determination is the right to freely pursue economic, social and cultural development. The UN Declaration enshrines the right of indigenous peoples to 'determine and develop priorities and strategies for exercising their right to development'. Many indigenous peoples mentioned that their development priorities and strategies were not considered in the current legal and policy framework related to economic development.

During my visit, I heard consistent complaints about economic development projects that were not adequately consulted and have led to land dispossession, environmental impacts, social conflicts and criminalization of indigenous community members opposing them. These include mining, oil and gas, hydroelectric, wind, solar, infrastructure, tourism and agro-industrial projects. Repeated concerns were expressed about the 2013 energy reform and the establishment of special economic zones on indigenous lands.

In my view, there is a need for a real dialogue in equal terms between governmental authorities and indigenous peoples about the definition of the concept of development that can lead to joint decision-making about development in indigenous territories. This is the only way to ensure the achievement of the UN Sustainable Development Goals leaving no one behind and pursuing a transformative agenda.

Violence, impunity and access to justice

I would like to touch upon two vital aspects related to access to justice of indigenous peoples: the recognition of their own juridical systems and their access to the ordinary justice system.

Indigenous peoples' justice systems are recognized in the Mexican Constitution under the term 'usos y costumbres'. As discussed in my meetings with judicial and other authorities, there is still no adequate harmonization and coordination of indigenous and State ordinary jurisdictions to make that recognition effective. According to Mexican authorities, impunity in the country is as high as 98–99 per cent. Impunity adds to the suffering of the victims of human rights violations and eliminates the incentives for the perpetrators to respect the law. Effective recognition of indigenous jurisdiction could help in fighting this serious problem.

There have been advances in the recognition of different forms of indigenous justice systems, such as community police, indigenous tribunals and other conflict resolution systems . . .

However, this recognition has been made on an ad hoc basis and differs from state to state. I strongly recommend that there is an in depth discussion between the Judiciary, relevant Mexican authorities and indigenous peoples with a view to develop such harmonization. This would include mechanisms to ensure that indigenous peoples' exercise of their justice systems does not result in their criminalization.

Problems related to access to justice are also present with respect to cases of extreme violence against indigenous peoples often related to land and territorial issues. Numerous cases of serious human rights violations of indigenous peoples from different states in the country have been brought to my attention during my meetings, most of which remain unresolved. These include allegations of massacres, killings, enforced disappearances, rape, torture and forced displacement which have been attributed to actions by individuals, organized crime, paramilitary groups, law enforcement officials and the military, often in the context of development projects affecting their lands and resources.

I was informed that it is particularly difficult for indigenous peoples affected by these gross human rights violations to access the ordinary justice system for several reasons including, among others, the physical distance from justice administration institutions, language barriers, lack of adequate legal assistance, lack of economic resources to adequately pursue a case, fears of reprisals if a complaint is filed, and the lack of appropriate protection mechanisms. I was informed of a 'black number' (cifra negra) of cases which are not reported to the authorities and which have to be taken into account.

Economic, social and cultural rights

The information received during the visit indicates that indigenous peoples face huge challenges and particular obstacles for the effective enjoyment of their economic, social and cultural rights. There are many elements that contribute to this situation, but some of the key factors include the historical and structural discrimination, the conditions of multi-dimensional poverty, and the lack of sufficient and culturally adequate basic services, among others.

Official statistics from 2015 indicate that 55.5 per cent of the indigenous population resides in municipalities considered to be of 'high' or 'very high' levels of marginalization. 87.5 per cent of indigenous municipalities (where indigenous population amounts to 70 per cent or more of the population) present conditions considered to be of high or very high levels of marginalization.

With regards to education, the same statistics indicate that 16.6 per cent of the indigenous population older than 15 years had not obtained any formal school instruction, contrasting with the 6 per cent for the overall population. Similarly, only 14.6 per cent of the indigenous population had obtained advanced secondary education, and 7 per cent a higher education level, compared to a 21.9 per cent and 18.2 per cent respectively for the overall population.

In terms of health, I received various complaints with regards to the lack of adequate facilities and doctors in indigenous communities. Although it appears that efforts are made to increase the health coverage and ensure a culturally adequate perspective, challenges remain to be addressed. The recognition of and support to traditional medicinal systems, including indigenous midwives, could help in filling this implementation gap.

Various actors raised concerns about significant budget cuts that particularly affect institutions addressing indigenous peoples' issues and indigenous peoples themselves, and stressed that some of the governmental programs were not designed taking into account the worldviews and specificities of indigenous peoples and were reflecting a 'handout' (asistencialista) perspective.

Specific groups

Internally Displaced Indigenous Peoples

The situation of violence, and the general context of impunity which also affects indigenous peoples has also caused a great number of forced displacements. Information received in all States visited confirms that the presence of organized crime, 'caciques', or other armed groups has caused a climate of violence, impunity, social and cultural disintegration, ultimately leading to a large number of displacements of entire indigenous families and communities to live in urban areas or with other indigenous communities. Cases of displacement in the framework of land related conflicts, as well as direct and indirect impact of megaprojects were also brought to my attention.

Such a situation is particularly worrying and calls for an urgent action by the State, in accordance with international standards including the Guiding Principles on Internal Displacement, to ensure that all internally displaced people have the right to an adequate standard of living. This includes culturally adequate basic services. In addition, the Mexican State has the duty and responsibility to establish conditions, as well as to provide the means, to allow internally displaced persons to return voluntarily, in safety and with dignity.

Unfortunately, in many of the cases brought to my attention, displacement has been prolonged and efforts to ensure the return of displaced families and communities were insufficient. Although some Government institutions recognized this situation of displacement, there does not seem to be a comprehensive coordinated policy and response to the phenomenon. I would like, however, to stress the recent recommendation No. 39/2017 of the National Human Rights Commission regarding forced internal displacement in the State of Sinaloa that recognises this complex issue which provides an important first step in the official recognition of this problem.

Children and youth

I am also particularly worried by the situation of indigenous children and youth, in such a context of extreme poverty, violence and impunity. This raises many concerns, including malnutrition, infant mortality and human trafficking.

In different States visited, I received complaints linked to the forced enrolment of children and youth by organized crime. Given the absence of law enforcement and other state institutions in remote indigenous communities in zones affected by organized crime and drug production and trafficking, the choice left to the youth is to join these groups or to be tortured, disappeared or killed.

Migrants

I would also like to stress, although very briefly, the preoccupying situation of indigenous day labourers as well as the situation of indigenous migrants, either working in or passing through the Mexican territory. They are often confronted with multiple forms of discrimination, tend to be invizibilized [sic] in their live[s] and work, are afraid and unable to access complaint mechanisms, and are disproportionately vulnerable to discrimination, exploitation and marginalization. This requires a wholistic [sic] and adequate response.

Women

The situation of women would deserve a longer analysis, however, I like to stress in my preliminary findings that in each state visited, I had a private meeting with indigenous women, who shared their main concerns. These include feminicide, intra-communal violence against women, maternal death, obstetric violence, forced child marriage, discrimination in access to lands and the lack of inclusion in traditional and formal decision making processes.

Conclusion

I would like to conclude by saying that in view of the above, an implementation gap persists both related to the recommendations made by Special Rapporteur Stavenhagen and the UN Declaration. The Mexican Government should recognize its responsibility for the problems described above and take decisive steps to show its real commitment to fulfill the rights of indigenous peoples. This could create the necessary conditions for a sustained and inclusive dialogue with indigenous peoples addressing all these outstanding issues and provides an opportunity to establish trust and create a new relationship between indigenous peoples and the State based on equality, respect and non-discrimination.

10.3.3 Expert Mechanism on the Rights of Indigenous Peoples

The United Nations Expert Mechanism on the Rights of Indigenous Peoples (the 'Expert Mechanism') was established in 2007 by the Human Rights Council,[97] of which it is a subsidiary body. It comprises five experts on the rights of indigenous peoples, usually one from each of the world's five geopolitical regions, with indigenous origin a relevant factor in their appointment. Its mandate is to provide the Human Rights Council with thematic expertise, mainly in the form of studies and research, on the rights of indigenous peoples as directed by the Council. The Expert Mechanism may also make proposals to the Council for its consideration and approval. The Expert Mechanism has produced a number of major studies to date: one on the implementation of the right of indigenous peoples to education finalised in 2009;[98] and another appeared in 2011 which examined indigenous

---

[97] Human Rights Council, *Expert mechanism on the rights of indigenous Peoples*, Resolution 6/36 (14 December 2007).
[98] Human Rights Council, *Study on lessons learned and challenges to achieve the implementation of the right of indigenous peoples to education*, report of the Expert Mechanism on the Rights of Indigenous Peoples, UN Doc. A/HRC/12/33 (31 August 2009)

peoples and the right to participation in decision-making;[99] and further studies have been initiated on the role of languages and culture in the promotion and protection of the rights and identity of indigenous peoples in 2011–12,[100] and indigenous peoples' access to justice in 2012–13.

The rules governing participation in its annual sessions are relatively open. Hundreds of representatives of indigenous peoples' organisations, indigenous individuals and non-governmental organisations attend the annual sessions.

10.4 Concluding remarks

The *Convention on the Rights of the Child* makes a significant contribution to the corpus of international law relating to indigenous people by establishing the right of the indigenous child to enjoy his or her own culture, to profess and practise his or her own religion, or to use her own language, and by other provisions relating to cultural identity and linguistic needs. The Committee on the Rights of the Child recommendations contained the *Day of General Discussion*, taken further forward by *General Comment No. 11*, also provide a further depth to the emerging jurisprudence in this field.

The *ILO Indigenous and Tribal Peoples Convention of 1989* has been helpful in establishing rights of non-discrimination and rights of participation by indigenous people. In addition it has broadened a development of the concept and importance of *collective rights* applied to indigenous peoples. It also identified importantly *self-determination* as a fundamental criterion to assess indigeneity.

The international law relating to indigenous peoples has undoubtedly received a sharper focus with the arrival of the *Declaration of 2007*. This instrument carries forwards a human rights approach tailored to the particular needs and historical legacies of indigenous peoples. Like most international instruments, it is not perfect and will no doubt require further elaboration and development in the future. It would seem that the gathering moral authority and evidence of impact of the *Declaration of 2007* may well eclipse arcane debates about its precise international legal status. For the time being at least, it would appear that the limited notion of self-determination is sufficient to neutralise concerns about secession that might otherwise arise from further recognition of the autonomy of indigenous peoples. The tension between collective and individual rights also poses a significant challenge for the future.

---

99 Human Rights Council, *Final report of the study on indigenous peoples and the right to participate in decision-making*, report of the Expert Mechanism on the Rights of Indigenous Peoples, UN Doc. A/HRC/18/42 (17 August 2011).
100 Human Rights Council, *Role of languages and culture in the promotion and protection of the rights and identity of indigenous peoples*, study of the Expert Mechanism on the Rights of Indigenous Peoples, UN Doc. A/HRC/21/53 (16 August 2012).

The relevant UN infrastructure relating to indigenous peoples, the Permanent Forum, Special Rapporteur and Expert Mechanism, have all made significant contributions to the development of international law and policy, but there is a growing sense of the need to rationalise their respective mandates to provide a more efficient and focused institutional architecture ready to address the challenges on the horizon relating to, for example, developments in technology and climate change.

Bibliography

Abernethie, L. (1998) 'Child Labour in Contemporary Society: Why Do We Care?', 6(1) *International Journal of Children's Rights* 81–114.
ACPF (2012) *Africa: The New Frontier for Intercountry Adoption*. Addis Ababa: The African Child Policy Forum.
Agarwal, R.K. (2004) 'The Barefoot Lawyers: Prosecuting Child Labour in the Supreme Court of India', 21(2) *Arizona Journal of International and Comparative Law* 663–713.
AIVD and NCTV (2017) 'The Children of ISIS: The Indoctrination of Minors in ISIS-Held Territory'. A joint publication by the National Coordinator for Security and Counterterrorism (NCTV) and the General Intelligence and Security Service (AIVD). The Hague: Dutch Ministry of the Interior and Kingdom Relations.
Akande, D. (2003) 'The Jurisdiction of the International Criminal Court over Nationals of Non-Parties: Legal Basis and Limits', 1(3) *Journal of International Criminal Justice* 618–50.
Akdeniz, Y. (2008) *Internet Child Pornography and the Law: National and International Responses*. Aldershot: Ashgate Publishing.
Akello, G., Richters, A. and Reis, R. (2006) 'Reintegration of Former Child Soldiers in Northern Uganda: Coming to Terms with Children's Agency and Accountability', 4(3) *Intervention* 229–43.
Alexander, S., Meuwese, S. and Wolthuis, A. (2000) 'Policies and Developments Relating to the Sexual Exploitation of Children: The Legacy of the Stockholm Conference', 8(4) *European Journal on Criminal Policy and Research* 479–501.
Alexy, E.M., Burgess, A.W. and Baker, T. (2005) 'Internet Offenders: Traders, Travellers, and Combination Trader-Travellers', 20(7) *Journal of Interpersonal Violence* 804–12.
Allain, J. (2008) *The Slavery Conventions: The Travaux Préparatoires of the 1926 League of Nations Convention and the 1956 United Nations Convention*. Leiden/Boston: Martinus Nijhoff.
Allain, J. (2012) 'White Slave Traffic in International Law', 1(1) *Journal of Trafficking and Human Exploitation* 1–40.
Alston, P. (1989) 'Implementing Children's Rights: The Case of Child Labour', 58(1) *Nordic Journal of International Law* 35–53.
Alston, P. (1992) 'The Legal Framework of the Convention on the Rights of the Child', 91(2) *Bulletin of Human Rights* 1–15.
Alston, P. (2004) '"Core Labour Standards" and the Transformation of the International Labour Rights Regime', 15(3) *European Journal of International Law* 457–521.
Alston, P., Parker, S. and Seymour, J. (eds) (1992) *Children, Rights and the Law*. Oxford: Clarendon Press.

Amann, D.M. (2002) 'Group Mentality, Expressivism, and Genocide', 2(2) *International Criminal Law Review* 93–143.
American Anthropological Association (1947) 'Statement on Human Rights', 49(4) *American Anthropologist* 539–43.
Anghie, A. (2007) *Imperialism, Sovereignty, and the Making of International Law*. Cambridge: Cambridge University Press.
Anghie, A. and Chimni, B.S. (2003) 'Third World Approaches to International Law and Individual Responsibility in Internal Conflicts', 2(1) *Chinese Journal of International Law* 77–103.
Anker, R. (2000) 'The Economics of Child Labour: A Framework for Measurement', 139(3) *International Labour Review* 257–80.
Archard, D. (1993) *Children: Rights and Childhood*. London: Routledge.
Archard, D. (2010) 'Children's Rights', in Zalta, E.N. (ed.) *The Stanford Encyclopedia of Philosophy*. Available at: <http://plato.stanford.edu/archives/sum2011/entries/rights-children> (accessed 16 January 2013).
Archard, D. (2012) 'Children's Rights' in Cushman, R. (ed.) *Handbook of Human Rights*. Abingdon, Oxon: Routledge, pp. 324–32.
Ariès, P. (1962) *Centuries of Childhood*. London: Cape.
Arnstein, S.R. (1969) 'Eight Rungs on the Ladder of Citizen Participation', 35(4) *Journal of the American Institute of Planners* 216–24.
Asquith, S. and Turner. E (2008) *Recovery and Reintegration of Child from the Effects of Sexual Exploitation and Related Trafficking*. Geneva: Oak Foundation.
Aufseeser, D. (2014) 'Limiting Spaces of Informal Learning among Street Children in Peru', in Mills, S. and Kraftl, P. (eds) *Informal Education, Childhood and Youth: Geographies, Histories, Practices*. Basingstoke: Palgrave Macmillan, pp. 112–23.
Aust, A. (2010) *Handbook of International Law*, 2nd edn. Cambridge: Cambridge University Press.
Avis, W. (2017) *Data on the Prevalence of the Worst Forms of Child Labour*. K4D Helpdesk Report. Brighton, UK: Institute of Development Studies.
Badaru, O. (2008) 'Examining the Utility of Third World Approaches to International Law for International Human Rights Law', 10(4) *International Community Law Review* 379–87.
Badenhorst, C. (2011) 'Legal Responses to Cyber Bullying and Sexting in South Africa'. Occasional Paper no. 10. Cape Town: Centre for Justice and Crime Prevention.
Baker, M. (1989) *Comics: Ideology, Power and the Critics. Cultural Politics*. Manchester: Manchester University Press.
Bakirci, K. (2002) 'Child Labour and Legislation in Turkey', 10(1) *International Journal of Children's Rights* 55–72.
Ballet, J., Bhukuth, A. and Aurélie Carimentrand, A. (2011) 'Child Labor and Responsible Consumers: From Boycotts to Social Labels, Illustrated by the Indian Hand-Knotted Carpet Industry', 53(1) *Business and Society* 71–104.
Barelli, M. (2009) 'The Role of Soft Law in the International Legal System: The Case of the United Nations Declaration on the Rights of Indigenous Peoples', 58 *International and Comparative Law Quarterly* 957–83.
Bartholet, E. (2010) 'International Adoption: The Human Rights Position', 1(1) *Global Policy* 91–100.
Bartholet, E. (2011) 'Permanency is not Enough: Children Need the Nurturing Parents International Adoption', 55 *New York Law School Law Review* 781.

Bartholet, E. (2017) 'Adoption Beyond Borders: How International Adoption Benefits Children', 20(2) *Adoption Quarterly* 195–9.

Basu, K. and Zarghamee, H. (2009) 'Is Product Boycott a Good Idea for Controlling Child Labor? A Theoretical Investigation', 88 *Journal of Development Economics* 217–20.

Beah, I. (2008) *A Long Way Gone: Memoirs of a Boy Soldier*. New York: Farrar, Straus and Giroux

Bean, P. and Melville, J. (1989) *Lost Children of the Empire*. London: Unwin Hyman.

Beaulieu, C. (2008) *Extraterritorial Laws: Why They are Not Working and How They Can be Strengthened*. Bangkok: ECPAT International. Available at: <www.ecpat.net/world congressIII/PDF/Journals/EXTRATERRITORIAL_LAWS.pdf> (accessed 27 January 2010).

Beaumont, P. and McEleavy, P. (1999) *The Hague Convention on International Child Abduction*. Oxford: Oxford University Press.

Beck, U. (1992) *Risk Society: Towards a New Modernity*. London: Sage.

Beck, U. (2000) *The Brave New World of Work*. London: Polity Press.

Beck, U. and Beck-Gernsheim, E. (2002) *Individualization: Institutionalized Individualism and Its Social and Political Consequences* (published in association with Theory, Culture and Society). London/Thousand Oaks, CA: Sage.

Berelowitz, S., Firmin, C., Edwards, G. and Gulyurtlu, S. (2012) *'I thought I was the only one. The only one in the world.' The Office of the Children's Commissioner's Inquiry into Child Sexual Exploitation in Gangs and Groups: Interim Report*. London: Office of the Children's Commissioner.

Betcherman, G., Fares, J., Luinstra, A. and Prouty, R. (2004) *Child Labor, Education, and Children's Rights*. Social Protection Discussion Paper Series, No. 0412. Washington, DC: The World Bank.

Bita, B. (2012) 'Sexting Teens Risk Porn Charge'. News.com. au website (Brisbane, Australia, 1 October). Available at: <www.news.com.au/technology/sexting-teens-risk-porn-charge/news-story/4a5ffc5545de33b91d352d832cbe9a7e> (accessed 20 December 2019).

Black, M. (1986) *The Children and the Nations: The Story of Unicef*. Sydney: UNICEF.

Black, M. (1996) *Children First: The Story of Unicef, Past and Present*. Oxford: Oxford University Press.

Blagbrough, J. (1997) 'Eliminating the Worst Forms of Child Labour – A New International Standard', 5(1) *International Journal of Children's Rights* 123–7.

Blanco F., Guarcello, L. and Rosati F.C. (2017) 'Child Labour among Syrian Refugees in Jordan'. UCW Working Paper.

Boéchat, H. and Cantwell, N. (2007) *Assessment of the Adoption System in Kazakhstan*. International Social Service, December 2007.

Boezaart, T. (2013) 'Listening to the Child's Objection', 2013(3) New Zealand Law Review 357–72.

Bonnet, M. (1993) 'Child Labour in Africa', 132(3) *International Labour Review* 371–89.

Bouhdiba, A, (1982) *Exploitation of Child Labour*, E/CN.4/Sub.2/479/Rev.1, U.N., Sales No. E.82.XIV.2. New York: United Nations.

Bourdillon, M. (2017) 'Ignoring the Benefits of Children's Work: Beyond Trafficking and Slavery. Open Democracy'. Open Democracy website. Available at: <www.opendemocracy.net/beyondslavery/michael-bourdillon/ignoring-benefits-of-children-s-work> (accessed 13 December 2019).

Bourdillon, M., Levison, B., White, B. and Myers, W.E. (2006) *A Place for Work in Children's Lives?* Quebec: Canadian International Development Agency (CIDA).

Bovill, M. and Livingstone, S. (2001) 'Bedroom Culture and the Privatization of Media Use'. London LSE Research Online. Available at: <http://eprints.lse.ac.uk/archive/00000672> (accessed 13 December 2019).

boyd, d. (2008) 'Why Youth ♥ Social Network Sites: The Role of Networked Publics in Teenage Social Life', in Buckingham, D. (ed.) *Youth, Identity, and Digital Media*. Cambridge: MIT Press.

Boyden, J. (1997) 'Childhood and the Policy Makers: A Comparative Perspective on the Globalization of Childhood', in James, A. and Prout, A. (eds) *Constructing and Reconstructing Childhood: Contemporary Issues in the Sociological Study of Childhood*, 2nd edn. London: Routledge/Falmer, pp. 187–226.

Boyden, J., Prankhurst, A. and Tafere, Y. (2013) 'Harmful Traditional Practices and Child Protection: Contested Understandings and Practices of Female Child Marriage and Circumcision in Ethiopia'. Oxford: Young Lives.

Boyden, J., Porter, C., Zharkevich, I. and Heissler, K. (2016) 'Balancing School and Work with New Opportunities: Changes in Children's Gendered Time Use in Ethiopia (2006–2013)'. Working Paper 161. Oxford: Young Lives.

Breuning, M. and Ishiyama, J. (2009) 'The Politics of Intercountry Adoption: Explaining Variation in the Legal Requirements of Sub-Saharan African Countries', 7(1) *Perspective on Politics* 89–101.

Brighouse, H. (2002) 'What Rights (if Any) Do Children Have?' in Archard, D. and Macleod, C. (eds), *The Moral and Political Status of Children: New Essays*. Oxford: Oxford University Press, pp. 31–52.

Broadband Commission for Digital Development, ITU and UNESCO (2015) Geneva, Switzerland. Available at: <https://en.unesco.org/unesco-and-global-broadband-commission> (accessed 13 January 2020).

Brotherton, Vicky (2019) 'Class Acts? A Comparative Analysis of Modern Slavery Legislation across the UK', in Craig, G., Balch, A., Lewis, H. and Waite, L. (eds) *The Modern Slavery Agenda: Policy, Politics and Practice*. Bristol: Policy Press, pp. 97–120.

Brown, G. (2012) *Child Labour and Educational Disadvantage: Breaking the Link, Building Opportunity*. London: The Office of the UN Special Envoy for Global Education.

Buck, T. (2008) 'International Criminalisation and Child Welfare Protection: The Optional Protocol to the Convention on the Rights of the Child', 22(3) *Children and Society* 167–78.

Buck, T. (2012) *An Evaluation of the Long-term Effectiveness of Mediation in Cases of International Parental Child Abduction*. Leicester: Reunite. Available at: <http://hdl.handle.net/2086/6329> (accessed 13 December 2019).

Buck, T. (2014) *International Child Law*, 3rd edn. Abingdon, Oxon: Routledge.

Buck, T. and Wabwile, M. (2013) 'The Potential and Promise of Communications Procedures under the Third Protocol to the Convention on the Rights of the Child', 2 *International Human Rights Law Review* 205–39.

Buckingham, D. (2002) 'The Electronic Generation? Children and New Media', in Lievrouw, L. and Livingstone, S. (eds), *The Handbook of New Media: Social Shaping and Consequences of ICTs*. London: Sage.

Buckingham, D. (2004) 'New Media, New Childhoods? Children's Changing Cultural Environment in the Age of Digital Technology', in Kehily, M.J. (ed.) *An Introduction to Childhood Studies* Milton Keynes: Open University Press, pp. 108–22.

Bulger, M., Burton, P. and O'Neill, B.(forthcoming) *A Global Review of Evidence of What Works in Preventing ICT-related Violence, Abuse and Exploitation of Children and in Promoting Digital Citizenship, 2016–2017*. Cited in UNICEF 2017: 73.

Bunting, A. and Quirk, J. (2017) *Contemporary Slavery: Popular Rhetoric and Political Practice*. Vancouver: UBC Press.

Burke, A. and Marsh, J. (eds) (2014) *Children's Virtual Play Worlds: Culture, Learning and Participation*. New York: Peter Lang.

Burnett, J. (1983) 'The History of Childhood', 33(12) *History Today* 1–6.

Burra, N. (1995) *Born to Work: Child Labour in India*. Uttar Pradesh, India: Oxford University Press.

Burton, P. (2017) 'Risks and Harms for Children in the Digital Age'. Background paper prepared for The State of the World's Children 2017: Children in a Digital World. New York: United Nations Children's Fund.

Burton, P. and Mutongwizo, T. (2009) 'Inescapable Violence: Cyber Bullying and Electronic Violence against Young People in South Africa'. Issue Paper No. 8. Cape Town: Centre for Justice and Crime Prevention.

Bybee, C., Robinson, D. and Turow, J. (1982). 'Determinants of Parental Guidance of Children's Television Viewing for a Special Subgroup: Mass Media Scholars', 26 *Journal of Broadcasting* 697–710.

Byron, T. (2008) *Safer Children in a Digital World: The Report of the Byron Review*. London: Department for Children, Schools and Families, and the Department for Culture, Media and Sport.

Cahn, H. (2009) *Old Lessons for a New World: Applying Adoption Research and Experience to Assisted Reproductive Technology*. New York: Evan B. Donaldson Adoption Institute.

Calitz, K. (2013) 'The Failure of the Minimum Age Convention to Eradicate Child Labour in Developing Countries, with Particular Reference to the Southern African Development Community', 29(1) *International Journal of Comparative Labour Law and Industrial Relations* 83–103.

Campbell, T. (1992) 'The Rights of the Minor', in Alston, P., Parker, S. and Seymour, J. (eds) *Children, Rights and the Law*. Oxford: Clarendon Press.

Cantwell, N. (1992) 'The Origins, Development and Significance of the United Nations Convention on the Rights of the Child', in Detrick, S. (ed.) *The United Nations Convention on the Rights of the Child: A Guide to the 'Travaux préparatoires'*. Dordrecht/Boston/Norwell: Martinus Nijhoff Publishers, pp. 19–30.

Carrington, V. (2008) '"I'm Dylan and I'm not going to say my last name": Some Thoughts on Childhood, Text and New Technologies', 34(2) *British Educational Research Journal* 151–66.

Carroll, A.B. and Shabana, K.M. (2010) 'The Business Case for Corporate Social Responsibility: A Review of Concepts, Research and Practice', 12(1) *International Journal of Management Reviews* 85–105.

Catani, L. (2012) 'Victims at the International Criminal Court: Some Lessons Learned from the Lubanga Case', 10(4) *Journal of International Criminal Justice* 905–22.

Cedrangolo, U. (2009) 'The Optional Protocol to the Convention on the Rights of the Child on the Sale of Children, Child Prostitution and Child Pornography and the Jurisprudence of the Committee on the Rights of the Child'. Innocenti Working Paper No. 2009-03. Florence: UNICEF Innocenti Research Centre. Available at: <www.unicef-irc.org/publications/pdf/iwp_2009_03.pdf> (accessed 27 January 2010).

Chamberland, J. (2012) 'Whither the "Best Interests of the Child" in the 1980 Child Abduction Convention?', 2012 *International Family Law* March, 27–30.

Chase, E. and Statham, J. (2005) 'Commercial and Sexual Exploitation of Children and Young People in the UK – A Review', 14(1) *Child Abuse Review* 4–25.

Chaudhuri, S. and Dwibedi, J.K. (2016) 'Trade Sanction and Child Labour', in Chaudhuri, S. and Dwibedi, J.K. (eds) *The Economics of Child Labour in the Era of Globalization*. Abingdon, Oxon: Routledge.

Chaudron S., Di Gioia, R. and Gemo, M. (2018) *Young Children (0–8) and Digital Technology, A Qualitative Study across Europe*. Publication Office of the European Union, EUR 29070.

Chen, X. (2003) '"Parents Go Global": Report on an Intercountry Adoption Research Project', 2003(1) *Variegations: New Research Directions in Human and Social Development* 10–14.

Chiancone, J. (2001) *Parental Abduction: A Review of the Literature*. UD Department of Justice, Office of Justice Programs/Office of Juvenile Justice and Delinquency Prevention. Available at: <www.ncjrs.gov/html/ojjdp/190074/index.html> (accessed 20 January 2010).

Chiancone, J., Girdner, L. and Hoff, P. (2001) 'Issues in Resolving Cases of International Child Abduction'. Juvenile Justice Bulletin, December. Washington, DC: Office of Juvenile Justice and Delinquency Prevention. Available at: <www.ncjrs.gov/pdffiles1/ojjdp/190105.pdf> (accessed 7 January 2013).

Child Labour and Forced Labour Reports (2017) *Bangladesh: 2017 Findings on the Worst Forms of Child Labour*. Bureau of International Labour Affairs, US Department of Labour.

Child Migration Programmes Investigation Report (2018) March. A report of the Inquiry Panel. Independent Inquiry Child Sexual Abuse. Available at: <www.iicsa.org.uk/document/child-migration-programmes-investigation-report-march-2018> (accessed 20 December 2019).

Child Rights International Network (n.d.) 'Briefing: Children's Rights in the Digital Age'. Available at: <https://home.crin.org/briefing-childrens-rights-in-the-digital-age> (accessed 13 December 2019).

Child Rights International Network (2013) 'In the Matter of the Adoption of Children Act Chapter 26:01 of the Laws of Malawi and in the Matter of Chifundo James (an Infant)'. Case summary and comment. Available at: <https://archive.crin.org/en/library/legal-database/matter-adoption-children-act-chapter-2601-laws-malawi-and-matter-chifundo.html> (accessed 13 December 2019).

Chimni, B. (2006) 'Third World Approaches to International Law: A Manifesto', 8 *International Community Law Review* 3–27.

China Internet Network Information Center (2016) 'Statistical Report on Internet Development in China', CINIC, July.

Chou, S. and Browne, K. (2008a) 'Child Rights and International Adoption: A Response to Critics', 32(2) *Adoption and Fostering* 69–74.

Chou, S. and Browne, K. (2008b) 'The Relationship between Institutional Care and the International Adoption of Children in Europe', 32(1) *Adoption and Fostering* 40–8.

Choy, C.C. (2007) 'Institutionalizing International Adoption: The Historical Origins of Korean Adoption in the United States', in Bergquist, K.J.S., Vonk, M.E., Kim, D.S. and Feit, M.D. (eds) *International Korean Adoption: A Fifty-Year History of Policy and Practice*. Binghamton, NY: Haworth Press, pp. 25–42.

Chuang, J. (2014), 'Exploitation Creep and the Unmaking f Human Trafficking Law', 108(4) *American Journal of International Law* 609–49.

Chuta, N. (2014) 'Children's Agency in Responding to Shocks'. Working Paper 128. Oxford: Young Lives.

Citron, D K. and Franks, M.A. (2014) 'Criminalizing Revenge Porn', 49(2) *Wake Forest Law Review* 345–92.

Clark, L. S. (2011) 'Parental Mediation Theory for the Digital Age', 21 *Communication Theory* 323.

Cohen, S. (1972) *Folk Devils and Moral Panics: The Creation of the Mods and Rockers.* London: MacGibbon and Kee.

Coleman, J.S. (1982) *The Asymmetric Society.* Syracuse, NY: Syracuse University Press.

Coleman, J. and Hagell, A. (2007) 'The Nature of Risk and Resilience in Adolescence', in Coleman, J. and Hagell, A. (eds) *Adolescents, Risks and Resilience: Against the Odds.* Hoboken, NJ: John Wiley & Sons.

Compton, R.J. (2016) *Compton, Adoption Beyond Borders: How International Adoption Benefits Children.* New York: Oxford University Press.

Connected Nations Report (2017) *Data Analysis.* London: Ofcom.

Cooper, J. (1997) 'Child Labour: Legal Regimes, Market Pressures, and the Search for Meaningful Solutions', 52(3) *International Journal* 411–30.

Corb, A. and Grozelle, R. (2014) 'A New Kind Of Terror: Radicalizing Youth in Canada', 1 *Journal Exit-Deutschland* 32–58.

Cordova, E. (1993) 'Some Reflections on the Overproduction of International Labour Standards', 14(2) *Comparative Labor Law Journal* 138–62.

Corsaro, W.A. (2017) *The Sociology of Childhood (Sociology for a New Century Series),* 5th edn. New Delhi: Sage Publications.

Coulter, R.T. (2010) 'The Law of Self-Determination and the United Nations Declaration on the Rights of Indigenous Peoples', 15 *UCLA Journal of International Law and Foreign Affairs* 1–27.

CPS response to the Modern Slavery Act 2015 Report, December 2017.

Craft, A. (2013) 'Childhood, Possibility Thinking and Wise, Humanising Educational Futures', 61 *International Journal of Educational Research* 126–34.

Craig, G., Balch, A., Lewis, H. and Waite, L. (2019) *The Modern Slavery Agenda: Policy, Politics and Practice.* Bristol: Policy Press.

Crane, D. (2008) 'Prosecuting Children in Times of Conflict: The West African Experience', 15(3) *Human Rights Brief* 11–17.

Craven, S., Brown, S. and Gilchrist, E. (2006) 'Sexual Grooming of Children: Review of the Literature and Theoretical Considerations', 12(3) *Journal of Sexual Aggression* 287–99.

Crawford, S. (2000) *The Worst Forms of Child Labour: A Guide to Understanding and Using the New Convention.* London: Department for International Development.

Crawford, J. (2012) *Brownlie's Principles of Public International Law,* 8th edn. Oxford: Oxford University Press.

Crawford, A. (2019) 'Instagram "Helped Kill My Daughter"'. BBC News website, 22 January. Available at: <www.bbc.co.uk/news/av/uk-46966009/instagram-helped-kill-my-daughter> (accessed 13 December 2019).

Crawford, J. and Grant, T. (2007) 'International Court of Justice', in Weiss, T.G. and Daws, S. (eds) *The Oxford Handbook on the United Nations.* Oxford: Oxford University Press, pp. 193–216.

CRC General Comment No. 6 (2005) 'Treatment of unaccompanied and separated children outside their country of origin' CRC/GC/2005/6 (1 September).

Creighton, B. (1997) 'Combating Child Labour: The Role of International Labour Standards', 18(3) *Comparative Labor Law Journal* 362–96.

Crivello, G. and Van der Gaag, N. (2016) 'Between Hope and a Hard Place: Boys and Young Men Negotiating Gender, Poverty and Social Worth in Ethiopia'. Working Paper 160. Oxford: Young Lives.

Cullen, H. (1999) 'The Limits of International Trade Mechanisms in Enforcing Human Rights: The Case of Child Labour', 7(1) *International Journal of Children's Rights* 1–29.

Cumming, P.E. (2009) *Children's Rights, Children's Voices, Children's Technology, Children's Sexuality.* Congress of the Humanities and Social Sciences. Ottawa: Carleton University.

Cunningham, H. (1995) *Children and Childhood in Western Society Since 1500.* London: Longman.

Cunningham, H. (2005) *Children and Childhood in Western Society Since 1500*, 2nd edn. Harlow: Pearson Education Ltd.

Cunningham, H. (2006) *The Invention of Childhood.* London: BBC Books.

Cushman, R. (ed.) (2012) *Handbook of Human Rights.* Abingdon: Routledge.

Dachi, H. and Garrett, R. (2003) *Child Labour and Its Impact on Children's Access to and Participation in Primary Education: A Case Study from Tanzania.* No. 48, Education Papers. London: Department for International Development.

Dahlgren, P. and Olsson, T. (2008) 'Facilitating Political Participation: Young Citizens, Internet and Civic Cultures', in Drotner, K. and Livingstone, S. (eds) *International Handbook of Children, Media and Culture.* London: Sage Publications, pp. 493–507.

Daily Mail UK (2008) 'Woman Charged over MySpace Hoax "Which Drove 13-Year-Old Girl to Suicide"', 16 May. Available at: <www.dailymail.co.uk/news/article-1020171/Woman-charged-MySpace-hoax-drove-13-year-old-girl-suicide.html> (accessed 12 December 2019).

Dammert, A., de Hoop, J., Mvukiyehe, E. and Rosati, F.C. (2017) *Effects of Public Policy on Child Labour: Current Knowledge, Gaps, and Implications for Program Design.* Washington, DC: The World Bank.

Davaki, K. (2018) *The Underlying Causes of the Digital Gender Gap and Possible Solutions for Enhanced Digital Inclusion of Women and Girls.* European Parliament's Policy Department for Citizens' Rights and Constitutional Affairs. Brussels: European Parliament.

Davidson, M.G. (2001) 'The International Labour Organization's Latest Campaign to End Child Labour: Will It Succeed Where Others Have Failed?', 11(1) *Transnational Law and Contemporary Problems* 203–24.

Davies, M. (2011) 'Intercountry Adoption, Children's Rights and the Politics of Rescue', 35(4) *Adoption and Fostering* 50–62.

Davies, J. and Merchant, G. (2009) *Web 2.0 for Schools: Learning and Social Participation.* New York: Peter Lang.

Davis, M. (2012) 'To Bind or Not to Bind: The United Nations Declaration on the Rights of Indigenous Peoples Five Years On', 19 *Australian International Law Journal* 17–48.

deGuzman, M. (2012) 'Choosing to Prosecute: Expressive Selection at the International Criminal Court', 33 *Michigan Journal of International Law* 265.

De Mause, L. (ed.) (1976) *The History of Childhood.* London: Souvenir Press.

Decherney, P. and Pickard, V. (eds) (2015) *The Future of Internet Policy.* Abingdon: Routledge.

Declaration of Principles on Freedom of Expression in Africa 23 October 2002, Banjul.

Demetriou, A., Efklides, A. and Platsidou, M. (2000) *The Architecture and Dynamics of Developing Mind: Experiential Structuralism as a Frame for Unifying Cognitive Developmental Theories.* Monographs for the Society of Research in Child Development, Serial No. 234, Vol. 58, Nos 5–6, 1993. London: Wiley Blackwell.

DeNardis, L. (2014) *The Global War for Internet Governance.* New Haven, CT: Yale University Press.

Dennis, M.J. (1999) 'The ILO Convention on the Worst Forms of Child Labour', 93(4) *American Journal of International Law* 943–48.

Dennis, J. (2008) 'Women are Victims, Men Make Choices: The Invisibility of Men and Boys in the Global Sex Trade', 25 *Gender Issues* 11–25.

Department of Digital, Culture, Media and Sport (2019) *Online Harms*. White Paper Presented to Parliament by the Secretary of State for Digital, Culture, Media and Sport and the Secretary of State for the Home Department by Command of Her Majesty, April.

Detrick, S. (ed.) (1992) *The United Nations Convention on the Rights of the Child: A Guide to the 'Travaux préparatoires'*, Dordrecht/Boston, MA/Norwell: Martinus Nijhoff Publishers.

Detrick, S. (1999) *A Commentary on the United Nations Convention on the Rights of the Child*. The Hague/Boston, MA/London: Martinus Nijhoff Publishers.

Dickinson, L. (2003) 'The Promise of Hybrid Courts', 97(2) *The American Journal of International Law* 295–310.

Dijck, J., Poell, T. and de Waal, M. (2019) *The Platform Society: Public Values in a Connective World*. Oxford: Oxford University Press.

Dillon, S. (2003) 'Making Legal Regimes for Intercountry Adoption Reflect Human Rights Principles: Transforming the United Nations Convention on the Rights of the Child with the Hague Convention on Intercountry Adoption', 21 *Boston University Law Review* 179, 219.

Di Maio, M. and Fabbri, G. (2013) 'Consumer Boycott, Household Heterogeneity, and Child Labour', 26 *Journal of Population Economics* 1609.

DNA India (2015) 'Uttar Pradesh: Muslim Village Panchayat Bans Jeans, Mobile Phones for Girls', Daily News and Analysis (DNA). Available at: <www.dnaindia.com/india/report-uttar-pradesh-muslim-village-panchayat-bans-jeans-mobile-phones-for-girls-2126940> (accessed 3 January 2020).

Doek, J.E. (2003) 'The Protection of Children's Rights and the United Nations Convention on the Rights of the Child: Achievements and Challenges', 22(2) *Saint Louis University Public Law Review* 235–52.

Doezema, J. (2010), *Sex Slaves and Discourse Masters: The Construction of Trafficking*. London: Zed Books.

Doneda, D. and Rossini, C. (2015) *ICT Kids Online Brazil 2014: Survey on Internet Use by Children in Brazil*. Brazilian Internet Steering Committee, São Paulo, Brazil.

Dorr, A., Kovaric, P. and Doubleday, C. (1989) 'Parent – Child Coviewing of Television', 33(1) *Journal of Broadcasting and Electronic Media* 35–51.

Douglas, G. (1992) 'The Retreat from Gillick', 55(4) *Modern Law Review* 569.

Drislane, R. and Parkinson, G. (2016) 'Moral Panic. Online Dictionary of the Social Sciences'. Open University of Canada. Available at: <https://lawin.org/moral-panics> (accessed 4 January 2020).

Drotner, K. (2000) 'Difference and Diversity: Trends in Young Danes' Media Use', 22(2) *Media, Culture and Society* 149–66.

Drumbl, M. (2007) *Atrocity, Punishment and International Law*. New York: Cambridge University Press.

Drumbl, M. (2012) *Reimagining Child Soldiers in International Law and Policy*. Oxford/New York: Oxford University Press.

Drumbl, M. (2016) 'Shifting Narratives: Ongwen and Lubanga on the Effects of Child Soldiering'. Justice in Conflict website. Available at: <https://justiceinconflict.org/2016/04/20/shifting-narratives-ongwen-and-lubanga-on-the-effects-of-child-soldiering> (accessed 16 December 2019).

Dyer, A. (1997) 'The Internationalization of Family Law', 30 *U.C. Davis Law Review* 625–45.

Edmonds, E. (2008) 'Defining Child Labour: A Review of the Definitions of Child Labour in Policy Research'. Working paper, International Programme on the Elimination of Child Labour (IPEC). Geneva: International Labour Office.

Edwards, M. (2015) *Global Childhoods Critical Approaches to the Early Years*. St Albans: Critical Publishing.

Eekelaar, J. (1986) 'The Emergence of Children's Rights', 6(2) *Oxford Journal of Legal Studies* 161–82.

Engle, E. (2011) 'The Convention on the Rights of the Child', 29 *Quinnipiac Law Review* 793–819.

English, J. (1997) '"Imitating the Cries of Little Children": Exploitative Child Labour and the Growth of Children's Rights', 52(3) *International Journal* 431–44.

Ennew, J. (2008) 'Conference on Children's Rights', Presentation, Swansea University, 19 September.

Erikson, E.H. (1995), *Childhood and Society* [1951]. London: Vintage.

Errico, S. (2017) *The Rights of Indigenous Peoples in Asia: Human Rights Based Overview of National Legal and Policy Frameworks against the Backdrop of Country Strategies for Development and Poverty Reduction*. Geneva: International Labour Organization, Gender, Equality and Diversity Branch Regional Office for Asia and the Pacific.

European Parliament (2016) 'Adoption of Children in the European Union', Briefing, June.

European Police Office (2016) *Internet Organised Crime Threat Assessment (IOCTA) 2016*. The Hague: Europol, pp. 24–7.

Europol (2009) *Ten Years of Europol: 1999–2009*. The Hague: Europol. Available at: <www.europol.europa.eu> (accessed 14 October 2013).

Europol's European Cybercrime Centre (2015) 'Virtual Global Taskforce Child Sexual Exploitation Environmental Scan 2015'. The Hague, Netherlands: EC3-Europol, October.

Eva, B. (2006) 'Above Children's Heads: The Headscarf Controversy in European Schools from the Perspective of Children's Rights', 14(2) *International Journal of Children's Rights* 119–36.

Evans, Martin (2018) 'Twenty Men in grooming Gang are Jailed for "Inhuman" Abuse of Victims as Young as 11', *Daily Telegraph*, 19 October. Available at: <www.telegraph.co.uk/news/2018/10/19/twenty-men-grooming-gang-jailed-inhuman-abuse-victims-young> (accessed 16 December 2019).

Facer, K. (2012) 'After the Moral Panic? Reframing the Debate about Child Safety Online', 33(3) *Discourse: Studies in the Cultural Politics of Education* 397–413.

Facer, K., Furlong, J., Furlong, R. and Sutherland, R. (2003) *ScreenPlay: Children and Computing in the Home*. London: Routledge Falmer.

Farid, H. (2018) 'Reining in Online Abuse', 19(3) *Technology and Innovation* 593–99.

Faulkner, E.A. (2019a) 'The historical evolution of the international legal responses to the trafficking of children', in Jones, J. and Winterdyk, J. (eds) *Palgrave International Handbook of Human Trafficking*. Basingstoke: Palgrave Macmillan.

Faulkner, E.A. (2019b) 'The Development of Child Trafficking within International Law: A Socio-Legal and Archival Analysis', in Deplano, R. (ed.) *Pluralising International Legal Scholarship: The Promise and Perils of Non-doctrinal Research Methods*. Cheltenham, Glos: Edward Elgar.

Feinberg, J. (1980) *Rights, Justice and the Bounds of Liberty: Essays in Social Philosophy*. Princeton, NJ: Princeton University Press.

Felicini, E. (2013) 'From Domestic Labour to Commercial Sexual Exploitation: The Hidden Risk for Child Workers', *ECPAT Journal Series* No. 8. Available at: <www.ecpat.org/wp-content/uploads/2016/04/Journal_Oct2013.pdf> (accessed 4 January 2020).

First World Congress (1996) *Declaration and Agenda for Action, 1st World Congress against Commercial Sexual Exploitation of Children*. Stockholm, Sweden, 27–31 August. Available at: <www.ecpat.net/world-congress-against-commercial-sexual-exploitation-children> (accessed 24 November 2013).

Fleck, D. (2013) *The Handbook of International Humanitarian Law*, 3rd edn. Oxford: Oxford University Press.

Flichy, P. (1995) *Dynamics of Modern Communication: The Shaping and Impact of New Communication Technologies*. London: Sage.

Flichy, P. (2006) 'New Media History', in Lievrouw, L. and Livingstone, S. (eds), *Handbook of New Media: Social Shaping and Consequences of ICTs*, updated student edn. London: Sage, pp. 187–204.

Fortin, J. (2006) 'Accommodating Children's Rights in a Post Human Rights Act Era', 69(3) *Modern Law Review* 299–326.

Fortin, J. (2009) *Children's Rights and the Developing Law*, 3rd edn. Cambridge: Cambridge University Press.

Fox, M.J. (2005) 'Child Soldiers and International Law: Patchwork Gains and Conceptual Debates', 7(1) *Human Rights Review* 27–48.

Fox Harding, L. (1996) *Family, State and Social Policy*. Basingstoke: Macmillan.

Fredette, K. (2009) 'International Legislative Efforts to Combat Child Sex Tourism', 32 *Boston College International and Comparative Law Review* 1–43.

Freeman, M.D.A. (1983) *The Rights and Wrongs of Children*. London: Continuum International Publishing.

Freeman, M. (2003) *The Outcomes for Children Returned Following an Abduction*. Reunite Research Unit. Leicester: International Child Abduction Centre.

Freeman, M. (2006) *International Child Abduction: The Effects*. Reunite Research Unit. Leicester: International Child Abduction Centre.

Freeman, M.D.A. (2007) 'Why it Remains Important to Take Children's Rights Seriously', 15(1) *International Journal of Children's Rights* 5–23.

Freeman, M. (2009) 'When the 1980 Hague Child Abduction Convention Does Not Apply: The UK – Pakistan Protocol, *International Family Law* (September) 181–5. Available at: <www.reunite.org/edit/files/articles/MF_IFL%20Article.pdf> (accessed 20 December 2019).

Freeman, M.D.A. (2011) 'Children's Rights as Human Rights', in Qvortrup, J., Corsaro, W.A. and Honig, M (eds) *The Palgrave Handbook of Childhood Studies*. Basingstoke: Palgrave Macmillan.

Freud, S. (1920) *Three Contributions to the Theory of Sex* (Nervous and Mental Disease Monograph Series), 2nd edn, trans. Brill, A.A. New York/Washington, DC: Nervous and Mental Disease Publishing Company.

Fritz, M., McQuilken, J., Collins, N. and Weldegiorgis, F. (2017) 'Global Trends in Artisanal and Small-Scale Mining (ASM): A Review of Key Numbers and Issues'. Intergovernmental Forum on Mining, Minerals, Metals and Sustainable Development (IGF). Winnipeg, Canada: IISD.

Furedi, F. (2002) *Paranoid Parenting Chicago*. Chicago: Chicago Review Press.

Fyfe, A. (2007) *The Worldwide Movement against Child Labour: Progress and Future Directions*. Geneva: International Labour Office.

G8 (2003) 'Justice and Home Affairs Ministerial Meeting – Paris, 5 May: President's Summary'. Available at: <www.justice.gov/criminal/ceos/downloads/G8MinistersDeclaration20090530.pdf> (accessed 19 November 2013).

G8 (2009) 'The Risk to Children Posed by Child Pornography Offenders', Ministers' Declaration, G8 Justice and Home Affairs Ministers', Rome, 30 May. Available at:

<www.justice.gov/criminal/ceos/downloads/G8MinistersDeclaration20090530.pdf> (accessed 14 October 2013).

G8 (2013) 'Foreign Ministers' Meeting Statement, 11 April 2013'. Available at: <www.gov.uk/government/uploads/system/uploads/attachment_data/file/185944/G8_Statement_Document.pdf> (accessed 15 November 2013).

Gaer, F.D. (2007) 'A Voice Not an Echo: Universal Periodic Review and the UN Treaty Body System', 7 *Human Rights Law Review* 109–139.

Gallagher, A.T. (2010) *The International Law of Human Trafficking*. New York: Cambridge University Press.

Gallagher, A.T. (2011) 'The International Legal Definition' in *The International Law of Human Trafficking*. New York: Cambridge University Press, pp. 13–53.

Gallagher, A.T. (2017) 'The International Legal Definition of "Trafficking in Persons": Scope and Application', in Kotiswaran, P. (ed.) *Revisiting the Law and Governance of Trafficking, Forced Labor and Modern Slavery*. Cambridge: Cambridge University Press.

Gamlin, J. and Pastor, M.E. (2009) 'Child Labour in Latin America: Theory, Policy, Practice', 29(3–4) *International Journal of Sociology and Social Policy* 118–29.

Gathii, J.T. (2011) 'TWAIL: A Brief History of Origins, Its Decentralized Network, and Tentative Bibliography', 3(1) *Trade, Law and Development* 26–64.

Gathii, J.T. (2019) 'The Agenda of Third World Approaches to International Law (TWAIL)' (20 December), in Dunoff, J. and Pollack, M. (eds) *International Legal Theory: Foundations and Frontiers*. Cambridge: Cambridge University Press.

Gay y Blasco, P., Macrae, S., Selman, P. and Wardle, H. (2008) 'The Relationship between Institutional Care and the International Adoption of Children in Europe: A Rejoinder to Chou and Browne', 32(2) *Adoption and Fostering* 63–67.

Geeraerts, S.B. (2012) 'Digital Radicalization of Youth', 3(1) *Social Cosmos* 25–32.

General Comment on Children's Rights in Relation to the Digital Environment (n.d.) Committee on the Rights of the Child. Available at: <www.ohchr.org/EN/HRBodies/CRC/Pages/GCChildrensRightsRelationDigitalEnvironment.aspx> (accessed 16 December 2019).

Giddens, A. (1991) *Modernity and Self-Identity: Self and Society in the Late Modern Age*. Cambridge: Polity Press.

Gill, T. (2007) *No Fear: Growing Up in a Risk Averse Society*. London: Calouste Gulbenkian Foundation.

Gillespie, A.A. (2002) 'Child Protection on the Internet: Challenges for Criminal Law', 14(4) *Child and Family Law Quarterly* 411–26.

Gillespie, A.A. (2007) 'Diverting Children Involved in Prostitution', 2 *Web Journal of Current Legal Issues*. Available at: <http://webjcli.ncl.ac.uk/2007/issue2/gillespie2.html> (accessed 27 January 2010).

Gillespie, A.A. (2010) 'Legal Definitions of Child Pornography', 16(1) *Journal of Sexual Aggression* 19–31.

Gillespie, A.A. (2011) *Child Pornography: Law and Policy*. Abingdon, Oxon: Routledge.

Global Estimates of Modern Slavery (2017) *Forced Labour and Forced Marriage*. Geneva: International Labour Organization and Walk Free Foundation.

Global Exchange (2005) 'Human Rights Groups Say the Chocolate Industry Broke Its Promise to Eradicate Illegal Child Labor from Chocolate Production; Call for Legislation'. Press Statement, 20 June.

Goldstein, J., Freud, A. and Solnit, A. (1973) *Beyond the Best Interests of the Child*. London: Collier-Macmillan.

Goldstein, J., Freud, A. and Solnit, A. (1980) *Before the Best Interests of the Child*. London: Burnett Books Ltd.

Gonzalez Martin, N. (2015) 'International Parental Child Abduction and Mediation', 15 *Anuario mexicano de derecho internacional* 353–412.

Goode, E. and Ben-Yehuda, N. (2009) *Moral Panic: The Social Construction of Deviance*. Chichester: Wiley-Blackwell.

Graf, R. (2012) 'The International Criminal Court and Child Soldiers: An Appraisal of the Lubanga Judgment', 10(4) *Journal of International Criminal Justice* 945–69. Available at: <https://doi.org/10.1093/jicj/mqs044> (accessed 6 January 2020).

Greif, G.L. and Hegar, R.L. (1991) 'Parents Whose Children are Abducted by the Other Parent: Implications for Treatment', 19 *American Journal of Family Therapy* 215–25.

Greif, G.L. and Hegar, R.L. (1993) *When Parents Kidnap: The Families behind the Headlines*. New York: The Free Press.

GSM Association (2015) *Bridging the Gender Gap: Mobile Access and Usage in Low- and Middle-Income Countries*. London: GSMA.

GSMA and NTT (2014) 'Children's Use of Mobile Phones – An International Comparison 2013'. London and Tokyo: GSMA and NTT Docomo Inc.'s Mobile Society Research Institute.

Guarcello, L., Lyon, S. and Valdivia, C. (2015) 'Evolution of the Relationship between Child Labour and Education since 2000: Evidence from 19 Developing Countries'. Background paper prepared for the Education for All Global Monitoring Report 2015. Rome: UNESCO.

Guardian (2017) 'Screen Time Guidelines Need to be Built on Evidence not Hype', 6 January. Available at: <www.theguardian.com/science/head-quarters/2017/jan/06/screen-time-guidelines-need-to-be-built-on-evidence-not-hype> (accessed 17 December 2019).

Guymon, C.D. (ed.) (2012) *Digest of United States Practice in International Law*. Washington, DC: Office of the Legal Adviser, US State Department. Available at: <www.state.gov/s/l/2012/index.htm> (accessed 11 February 2013).

Guzman, A.T. and Meyer, T.L. (2010) 'International Soft Law', 2 *Journal of Legal Analysis* 171–225.

Haanappel, P.P.C. (2003) *The Law and Policy of Air Space and Outer Space: A Comparative Approach*. The Hague: Kluwer Law International.

Hagen, E. (2011) 'Mapping Change: Community Information Empowerment in Kibera (Innovations Case Narrative: Map Kibera)', 6(1) *Innovations: Technology, Governance, Globalization* 69–94.

Hague Conference on Private International Law '1993–2018 25th Anniversary of the 1993 Hague Convention on Protection of Children and Co-operation in Respect of Intercountry Adoption'. Brochure 'Celebrating 25 Years of Protecting Children in Intercountry Adoption'. The Hague, Netherlands: The Hague Conference on Private International Law, Permanent Bureau.

Hajdinjak, M., Kanchev, P. Georgiev, E. and Apostolov, G. (2016) *Online Experiences of Children in Bulgaria: Risks and Safety – A National Representative Survey*. Bulgaria. Available at: <www.safenet.bg/images/sampledata/files/Risks-and-Harm.pdf> (accessed 20 December 2019).

Hamilton, C. and Dutordoir, L. (2011) 'Children and Justice During and in the Aftermath of Armed Conflict'. Working Paper No. 3. New York: Office of the Special Representative of the Secretary-General for Children and Armed Conflict. Available at: <http://childrenandarmedconflict.un.org/publications/WorkingPaper3_Children-and-Justice.pdf> (accessed 10 August 2019).

Happold, M (2005) *Child Soldiers in International Law*. Manchester: Manchester University Press.

Harden, J. (2000) 'There's No Place Like Home', 7(1) *Childhood* 43–59.

Harding, L (1996) *Family, State and Social Policy*. Basingstoke: Macmillan.

Harris-Short, S. (2001) 'Listening to "The Other"? The Convention on the Rights of the Child', 2(2) *Melbourne Journal of International Law* 304–50.

Hart, H.L.A. (1984) 'Are There Any Natural Rights?', in Waldron, J. (ed.) *Theories of Rights*. Oxford: Oxford University Press.

Hart, R.A. (1992) *Children's Participation: From Tokenism to Citizenship*. Innocenti Essays No. 4. Florence: UNICEF.

Harvey, R. (2003) *Children and Armed Conflict – A Guide to International Humanitarian and Human Rights Law*. University of Essex: Children and Armed Conflict Unit/International Bureau for Children's Rights. Available at: <www.essex.ac.uk/armedcon/story_id/000044.pdf> (accessed 10 November 2019).

Harvey, A. (2015) *Gender, Age, and Digital Games in the Domestic Context*. Abingdon, Oxon: Routledge.

Hasebrink, U., Livingstone, S., Haddon, L., Kirwil, L., and Ponte, C. (2007) *Comparing Children's Online Activities and Risks across Europe*. London: EU Kids Online.

Hasebrink, U., Livingstone, S., Haddon, L. and Ólafsson, K. (2009) *Comparing Children's Online Opportunities and Risks across Europe: Cross-National Comparisons for EU Kids Online*. London School of Economics. London: EU Kids Online.

Hasebrink, U., Goerzig, A., Haddon, L. and Kalmus, V. (2011) *Patterns of Risk and Safety Online: In-depth Analysis from the EU Kids Online Survey of 9- to 16-Year-Olds and Their Parents in 25 European Countries*. London: EU Kids Online.

Haskell, John D. (2014) 'TRAIL-ing TWAIL: Arguments and Blind Spots in Third World Approaches to International Law', XXVII(2) *Canadian Journal of Law and Jurisprudence*. Mississippi College School of Law Research Paper No. 2014–07. Available at: <https://ssrn.com/abstract=2481693> or <http://dx.doi.org/10.2139/ssrn.2481693> (accessed 6 January 2020).

Hassel, A. (2008) 'The Evolution of a Global Labor Governance Regime', 21(2) *Governance: An International Journal of Policy, Administration and Institutions* 231–51.

Haufler, V.A. (2001) *Public Role for the Private Sector: Industry Self-Regulation in a Global Economy*. Washington, DC: Brookings Institution Press.

Hayes, P. (2011) 'The Legality and Ethics of Independent Intercountry Adoption under the Hague Convention', 25(3) *International Journal of Law, Policy and the Family* 288–317.

HCCH (2012) *Guide to Good Practice: Mediation*. Permanent Bureau of the Hague Conference on Private International Law, June. Available at: <www.hcch.net/upload/guide28mediation_en.pdf> (accessed 16 December 2019).

Hendrick, H. (1997) *Children, Childhood and English Society 1880–1990*. Cambridge: Cambridge University Press.

Heywood, C. (2001) *A History of Childhood: Children and Childhood in the West from Medieval to Modern Times*. Cambridge: Polity Press.

Hirst, M. (2003) *Jurisdiction and the Ambit of the Criminal Law*. Oxford: Oxford University Press.

Hjarvard, S (2013) *The Mediatization of Culture and Society*. Abingdon, Oxon: Routledge.

Ho, J. (2006) 'The International Labour Organization's Role in Nationalizing the International Movement to Abolish Child Labor', 7(1) *Chicago Journal of International Law* 337–49.

Hobbins, A.J. (2001) 'Humphrey and the High Commissioner: The Genesis of the Office of the UN High Commissioner for Human Rights', 3 *Journal of the History of International Law* 38–74.

Hodgkin, R. and Newell, P. (2007) *Implementation Handbook for the Convention on the Rights of the Child*, 3rd edn. Geneva: UNICEF. Available at: <www.unicef.org/publications/index_43110.html> (accessed 11 June 2013).

Hoffmann, S. and Hutter, K. (2012) 'Carrotmob as a New Form of Ethical Consumption. The Nature of the Concept and Avenues for Future Research', 35(2) *Journal of Consumer Policy* 215–36.

Holloway, S. and Valentine, G. (eds) (2000) *Children's Geographies: Playing, Living, Learning*. London: Routledge.

Holt, J. (1974) *Escape from Childhood: The Needs and Rights of Childhood*. New York: E.P. Dutton and Co. Inc.

Honwana, A. (2006) *Child Soldiers in Africa*. Philadelphia: University of Pennsylvania Press.

Horton, R. (2004) 'UNICEF leadership 2005–2015: A Call for Strategic Change' (editorial), 364(9451) *The Lancet* 2071–4.

Howard, N. (2017) *Child Trafficking, Youth Labour Mobility and the Politics of Protection*. London: Palgrave Macmillan.

Hubinette, T. (2006) 'From Orphan Trains to Baby Lifts: Colonial Trafficking, Empire Building, and Social Engineering', in Trenka, J.J, Oparah, J.C. and Shin, S.Y. (eds) *Outsiders Within: Writing on Transracial Adoption*. New York: Southend Press, pp. 139–50.

Hug, L., Alexander, M., You, D. and Alkema, L. (2019) 'National, Regional, and Global Levels and Trends in Neonatal Mortality between 1990 and 2017, with Scenario-Based Projections to 2030: A Systematic Analysis', 7 *Lancet Glob Health* e710–20.

Humbert, F. (2009) *The Challenge of Child Labour in International Law* (Cambridge Studies in International and Comparative Law). Cambridge: Cambridge University Press.

ILO (1996) *Child Labour: What is to be Done?* Geneva: International Labour Office.

ILO (1998) *Child Labour: Targeting the Intolerable*. International Labour Conference, 86th Session, Report VI (1). Geneva: ILO.

ILO (2002a) *Eliminating the Worst Forms of Child Labour: A Practical Guide to ILO Convention No. 182*. Geneva: ILO and Inter-Parliamentary Union.

ILO (2002b) *A Future without Child Labour, Global Report under the Follow-up to the ILO Declaration on Fundamental Principles and Rights at Work, Report of the Director-General*. International Labour Conference 90th Session. Geneva: International Labour Office.

ILO (2004) *Investing in Every Child: An Economic Study of the Costs and Benefits of Eliminating Child Labour*. International Programme on the Elimination of Child Labour. Geneva: ILO.

ILO (2006) *The End of Child Labour: Within Reach, Global Report under the Follow-up to the ILO Declaration on Fundamental Principles and Rights at Work*. Report of the Director-General, International Labour Conference 95th Session. Geneva: International Labour Office.

ILO (2010a) *Towards a World without Child Labour: Mapping the Road to 2016*. The Hague Global Child Labour Conference Report. Geneva: ILO and the Ministry of Social Affairs and Employment of the Netherlands.

ILO (2010b) *Accelerating Action against Child Labour, Global Report under the Follow-up to the ILO Declaration on Fundamental Principles and Rights at Work*. Report of the Director-General. International Labour Conference 99th Session. Geneva: International Labour Office.

ILO (2013) *Marking Progress against Child Labour: Global Estimates and Trends 2000–2012*. Geneva: International Labour Office.

ILO (2017a) *Global Estimates of Child Labour: Results and Trends, 2012–2016*. Geneva: International Labour Office.

ILO (2017b) *Global Estimates of Modern Slavery: Forced Labour and Forced Marriage*. Geneva: International Labour Organization and Walk Free Foundation.

ILO/UNICEF (2004) *Report of the MOU Project: Addressing Child Labour in the Bangladesh Garment Industry 1995–2001: A Synthesis of UNICEF and ILO Evaluation Studies of the Bangladesh Garment Sector Projects*, August. Geneva/New York: ILO/UNICEF.

International Labour Conference (2009) *General Report of the Committee of Experts on the Application of Conventions and Recommendations 2009*. 98th session. Geneva: International Labour Office.

Internet Governance Forum (2012) *Is the UNCRC Fit to Purpose in the Digital Era?* Rome: Internet European NGO Alliance for Child Safety Online.

Internet Watch Foundation (2017) *Annual Report 2016*. Cambridge: IWF, 3 April.

Invernizzi, A. and Milne, B. (2002) 'Are Children Entitled to Contribute to International Policy Making? A Critical View of Children's Participation in the International Campaign for the Elimination of Child Labour', 10(4) *International Journal of Children's Rights* 403–31.

IOM (2017) 'UN Migration Agency Warns of Trafficking, Labour Exploitation, Sexual Abuse of Rohingya Refugees'. Press Release, 14 November. Available at: <www.iom.int/news/un-migration-agency-warns-trafficking-labour-exploitation-sexual-abuse-rohingya-refugees> (accessed 16 December 2019).

IOM (2018) *Rohingya Refugee Crisis Response: Sixth Month Progress Report*. 25 February. Available at: <www.iom.int/sitreps/rohingya-refugee-crisis-response-six-month-progress-report-25-aug-2017-25-feb-2018> (accessed 20 December 2019).

IPEC (2004) *Helping Hands or Shackled Lives? Understanding Child Domestic Labour and Responses to it, International Programme on the Elimination of Child Labour*. Geneva: ILO.

IPEC (2007) 'Rooting Out Child Labour from Cocoa Farms'. Paper No. 3: Sharing Experiences. Geneva: International Labour Office.

IPEC (2013) Global Child Labour Trends: 2008 to 2012. International Labour Office, International Programme on the Elimination of Child Labour (IPEC). Geneva: ILO.

IREWOC (2010) *The Worst Forms of Child Labour in Asia: Main Findings from Bangladesh and Nepal*. Leiden: IREWOC.

Isanga, J. (2012) 'Surging Intercountry Adoptions in Africa: Paltry Domestication of International Standards', 27 *Brigham Young University Journal of Public Law* 229.

ITU (2003) *World Summit on the Information Society. Declaration of Principles, Building the Information Society: A Global Challenge in the New Millennium*. Geneva: International Telecommunication Union.

ITU (2018) 'Measuring the Information Society Report'. Available at: <www.itu.int/en/ITU-D/Statistics/Documents/publications/misr2018/MISR-2018-Vol-1-E.pdf> (accessed 21 February 2020).

Jacobsen, A.F. (2016) 'Interlinkages between the UN Convention on the Rights of the Child and the European Court of Human Rights', 24 *International Journal of Children's Rights* 548–74.

James, A. and Prout, A. (eds) (1997) *Constructing and Reconstructing Childhood: Contemporary Issues in the Sociological Study of Childhood*, 2nd edn. London: Routledge/Falmer.

James, A. and Prout, A. (eds) (2015) *Constructing and Reconstructing Childhood: Contemporary Issues in the Sociological Study of Childhood*, 3rd edn. London: Routledge.

James, A., Jenks, C. and Prout, A. (1998) *Theorizing Childhood*, Oxford: Polity Press.

Jänterä-Jareborg, M. (1994) 'Protection of Children and Co-Operation in Respect of Intercountry Adoption', 63 *Nordic Journal of International Law* 185.

Jenks, C. (1996) *Childhood*. London: Routledge.
Johnson, S.M. (1999) 'Excuse Me, but is that Football "Child-Free"? Pakistan and Child Labour', 7(1) *Tulsa Journal of Comparative and International Law* 163–76.
Johnson, C.F. (2004) 'Child Sexual Abuse', 364(9432) *The Lancet* 462–70.
Joint Committee on Human Rights (2003) *The UN Convention on the Rights of the Child*. Tenth Report of Session 2002–03 (HL Paper 117, HC 81), 24 June. London: The Stationery Office.
Jonah, J.O.C. (2007) 'Secretariat: Independence and Reform', in Weiss, T.G. and Daws, S. (eds) *The Oxford Handbook on the United Nations*. Oxford: Oxford University Press, pp. 160–74.
Joseph, S. and Kyriakakis, J. (2010) 'The United Nations and Human Rights', in Joseph, S. and McBeth, A. (eds) *Research Handbook on International Human Rights Law*. Cheltenham: Edward Elgar, pp. 1–35.
Joseph, S. and McBeth, A. (eds) (2010) *Research Handbook on International Human Rights Law*. Cheltenham: Edward Elgar.
Kaczorowska, A. (2010) *Public International Law*, 4th edn. Abingdon, Oxon: Routledge.
Kardefelt-Winther, D. (2017) *How Does the Time Children Spend Using Digital Technology Impact Their Mental Wellbeing, Social Relationships and Physical Activity? An Evidence-Focused Literature Review*. Innocenti Discussion Paper 2017-02. Florence: UNICEF Office of Research, Innocenti.
Kelly, L. (2002) *Journeys of Jeopardy: A Commentary on Current Research on Trafficking of Women and Children for Sexual Exploitation within Europe*. IOM Migration Research Series, MRS No. 11. International Organization for Migration. London: Stationery Office.
Kelly, F. (2005) 'Conceptualising the Child through an "Ethic of Care": Lessons for Family Law', 1(4) *International Journal of Law in Context* 375–96.
Kempadoo, K., Sanghera, J. and Pattanaik, B. (2005) *Trafficking and Prostitution Reconsidered: New Perspectives on Migration, Sex Work, and Human Rights*. Boulder, CO: Paradigm.
Kempadoo, K., Sanghera, J. and Pattanaik, B. (2012) *Trafficking and Prostitution Reconsidered: New Perspectives on Migration, Sex Work, and Human Rights*, 2nd edn. Boulder, CO: Paradigm.
Kempe, C.H. (1978) 'Sexual Abuse, Another Hidden Pediatric Problem: The 1977 C. Anderson Aldrich Lecture', 62(3) *Pediatrics* 382–9.
Kerry, Rittich (2017) 'Representing, Counting, Valuing: Managing Definitional Uncertainty in the Law of Trafficking', in Kotiswaran, P. (ed.) *Revisiting the Law and Governance of Trafficking,, Forced Labor and Modern Slavery*. Cambridge: Cambridge University Press.
Khair, S. (2010) 'Globalisation and Children's Rights: The Case of Child Labour', in Alam, S., Klein, N. and Overland, J. (eds) *Globalisation and the Quest for Social and Environmental Justice: The Relevance of International Law in an Evolving World Order*. Abingdon, Oxon: Routledge.
Kilbourne, S. (1998) 'The Wayward Americans – Why the USA Has Not Ratified the UN Convention on the Rights of the Child', 1998 *International Family Law* 104–12.
Kilkelly, U. (2003) 'Economic Exploitation of Children: A European Perspective', 22(2) *Saint Louis University Public Law Review* 321–58.
Kim, H. (2007) 'Mothers without Mothering: Birth Mothers from South Korea since the Korean War', in Bergquist, K.J.S., Vonk, M.E., Kim, D.S. and Feit, M.D. (eds) *International Korean Adoption: A Fifty-Year History of Policy and Practice*. Binghamton, NY: Haworth Press, pp. 131–54.
King, M. (2007) 'The Sociology of Childhood as Scientific Communication: Observations from a social systems perspective', 14(2) *Childhood* 193–213.

Kirby, M. (2010) 'Children Caught in Conflict – the Child Abduction Convention and Australia', 24(1) *International Journal of Law, Policy and the Family* 95–114.

Kolieb, J. (2009) 'The Six Grave Violations against Children During Armed Conflict: The Legal Foundation'. Working Paper No. 1. New York: Office of the Special Representative of the Secretary-General for Children and Armed Conflict. Available at: <http://childrenandarmedconflict.un.org/publications/WorkingPaper1_SixGraveViolationsLegalFoundation.pdf> (accessed 4 September 2019).

Komanovics, A. (2012) 'The Human Rights Council and the Universal Periodic Review: Is it More than a Public Relations Exercise?', 150 *Studia Iuridica Auctoritate Universitatis Pecs* 119–146.

Kotiswaran, P. (2017) *Revisiting the Law and Governance of Trafficking, Forced Labor and Modern Slavery*. Cambridge: Cambridge University Press.

Kott, E. and Droux, J. (eds) (2013) *Globalizing Social Rights: The International Labour Organization and Beyond* (ILO Century Series). Geneva: International Labour Organization.

Kramer, M.H. (1998) 'Rights Without Trimmings', in Kramer, M.H., Simmonds, N. and Steiner, H. (eds) *A Debate over Rights, Philosophical Enquiries*. Oxford: Clarendon Press, pp. 7–111.

Krauss, A. (2016) 'Understanding child labour beyond the standard economic assumption of monetary poverty', 2016 *Cambridge Journal of Economics* 1–30.

Kruger, T. (2011) *International Child Abduction: The Inadequacies of the Law*. Oxford/Portland, OR: Hart Publishing.

Kuper, J. (2012) 'The Development of International Child Law: The Definition of "the Child" and Implementation Mechanisms', in Cushman, R. (ed.) *Handbook of Human Rights*. Abingdon, Oxon: Routledge, pp. 333–48.

Lafayette, E. (2013) 'The Prosecution of Child Soldiers: Balancing Accountability with Justice', 63 *Syracuse Law Review* 297.

Lamont, R. (2008) 'The EU: Protecting Children's Rights in Child Abduction', 2008 *International Family Law* 110–12.

Lamont, R. (2011) 'Mainstreaming Gender into European Family Law? The Case of International Child Abduction and Brussels II Revised', 17(3) *European Law Journal* 366–84.

Lamont, R. (2012) 'Free Movement of persons, Child Abduction and Relocation within the European Union', 34(2) *Journal of Social Welfare and Family Law* 231–44.

Langille, B.A. (2005) 'Core Labour Rights – The True Study (Reply to Alston), 16(3) *European Journal of International Law* 409–37.

La Rue, F. (2014) 'Report of the Special Rapporteur on the Promotion and Protection of the Right to Freedom of Opinion and Expression' A/69/335. New York: United Nations General Assembly. Available at: <https://digitallibrary.un.org/record/771836> (accessed 20 December 2019).

Leathers, H., Summers, S. and Desollar, A. (2013) *Toddlers on Technology: A Parents' Guide*. Bloomington, IN: AuthorHouse.

Lee, N. (2001) *Childhood and Society: Growing Up in an Age of Uncertainty*. Milton Keynes: Open University Press.

Lee, S. (2017) 'Child's Voice vs. Parent's Control: Resolving Tension between the Convention on the Rights of the Child and U.S. Law', 117(3) *Columbia Law Review* 687–728.

Leiner, Barry M., Vinton, G., Cerf,, David D., Clark, Robert E., Kahn, Leonard, et al. (1997) *Brief History of the Internet*. Geneva: Internet Society.

Lenhart, A. (2015) *Teens, Social Media and Technology Overview 2015*. Washington, DC: Pew Research Center.

Lenhart, A., Smith, A., Anderson, M., Duggan, M. and Perrin, A. (2015) *Teens, Technology and Friendships*. Washington, DC: Pew Research Center.

Lesthaeghe, R. (2010) 'The Unfolding Story of the Second Demographic Transition', 36(2) *Population and Development Review* 211–51.

Levison, D., Hoek, J., Lam, D. and Duryea, S. (2007) 'Intermittent Child Employment and Its Implications for Estimates of Child Labour', 146(3/4) *International Labour Review* 217–51.

Liefländer, T. (2012) 'The Lubanga Judgment of the ICC: More than Just the First Step?' (1)1 *Cambridge Journal of International and Comparative Law* 191–212.

Lind, J. and Johansson, S. (2009) 'Preservation of the Child's Background in In- and Intercountry Adoption', 17 *International Journal of Children's Rights* 235–60.

Livingstone, S. (2002) *Young People and New Media*. London: Sage.

Livingstone, S. (2003) 'Mediated Childhoods: A Comparative Approach to Young People's Changing Media Environment in Europe' in Turow, J. and Kavanaugh, A.L. (eds) *The Wired Homestead*. An MIT Press Sourcebook on the Internet and the Family. Cambridge, MA: MIT Press.

Livingstone, S. (2004) Children Online – Consumers or Citizens? *ESRC/AHRB Cultures of Consumption Working Paper Series*. Available at: <www.consume.bbk.ac.uk/publications.html> (accessed 16 December 2019).

Livingstone, S. (2009) *Children and the Internet: Great Expectations, Challenging Realities*. Cambridge and Malden, MA: Polity Press.

Livingstone, S. (2010) 'From Family Television to Bedroom Culture: Young People's Media at Home'. LSE Research Online. Available at: <http://eprints.lse.ac.uk/2772> (accessed 16 December 2019).

Livingstone, S. (2011) 'Internet, Children and Youth', in Consalvo, M. and Ess, C. (eds) *The Handbook of Internet Studies*. Oxford: Wiley-Blackwell Publishing.

Livingstone, S. (2013) 'Children's Internet Culture: Power, Change and Vulnerability', in Lemish, D. (ed.) *The Routledge International Handbook of Children, Adolescents and Media*. Abingdon, Oxon: Routledge.

Livingstone, S. (2014a) 'Regulating the Internet in the Interests of Children: Emerging European and International Approaches'. LSE Research Online. Available at: <eprints.lse.ac.uk/44962/1/__lse.ac.uk_storage_LIBRARY_Secondary_libfile_shared_repository_Content_Livingstone%2C%20S_Regulating%20internet_Livingstone_Regulating%20internet_2014.pdf> (accessed 4 January 2020).

Livingstone, S. (2014b) *Report of the 2014 Day of General Discussion 'Digital Media and Children's Rights'*. Committee on the Rights of the Child. Available at: <www.ohchr.org/Documents/Issues/Women/WRGS/GenderDigital/CRC_3.pdf> (accessed 20 December 2019).

Livingstone, S. and Blum-Ross, A. (2017) 'Researching Children and Childhood in the Digital Age', in Christensen, P. and James, A. (eds) *Research with Children: Perspectives and Practices*. Abingdon, Oxon: Routledge, pp. 54–70.

Livingstone, S. and Bober, M. (2006) 'Regulating the Internet at Home: Contrasting the Perspectives of Children and Parents', in Buckingham, D. and Willett, R. (eds) *Digital Generations: Children, Young People and New Media*. Mahwah, NJ: Lawrence Erlbaum.

Livingstone, S. and Helsper, E. (2010), 'Balancing Opportunities and Risks in Teenagers' Use of the Internet: The Role of Online Skills and Internet Self Efficacy', 12(2) *New Media and Society* 309–29.

Livingstone, S. and O'Neill, B. (2014) 'Children's Rights Online: Challenges, Dilemmas and Emerging Directions'. LSE Research Online, June. Available at: <http://eprints.lse.ac.uk/62276> (accessed 16 December 2019).

Livingstone, S. and Third, A. (2017) 'Children and Young People's Rights in the Digital Age: An Emerging Agenda'. Available at: <http://eprints.lse.ac.uk/68759/7/Livingstone_Children%20and%20young%20peoples%20rights_2017_author%20LSERO.pdf> (accessed 3 January 2020).

Livingstone, S., Mascheroni, G., Ólafsson, K. and Haddon, L. (2014) *Children's Online Risks and Opportunities: Comparative Findings from EU Kids Online and Net Children Go Mobile*. London: London School of Economics and Political Science.

Livingstone, S., Lansdown, G. and Third, A. (2017) *The Case for a UNCRC General Comment on Children's Rights and Digital Media: A Report Prepared for Children's Commissioner*. London: LSE Consulting.

Livingstone, S., Tambini, D., Belakova, N. and Goodman, E. (2018) *Protection of Children Online: Does Current Regulation Deliver?* Media Policy Brief 21. London: Media Policy Project, London School of Economics and Political Science.

Loo, H. (2016) 'In the Child's Best Interests: Examining International Child Abduction, Adoption and Asylum', 17 *Chicago Journal of International Law* 609.

Lowe, N. (2007) 'The Current Experiences and Difficulties of Applying Brussels II Revised', 7(4) *International Family Law* 182–95.

Lowe, N. (2008) Statistical analysis of applications made in 2008 under the Hague Child Abduction Convention, Parts I-III (National, Regional and Global Reports). Generic reference available at: <www.hcch.net/index_en.php?act=publications.detailsandpid=5421anddtid=32> (accessed 7 January 2020).

Lowe, N. (2011a) 'A Statistical Analysis of Applications Made in 2008 under the *Hague Convention of 25 October 1980 on the Civil Aspects of International Child Abduction*. Part I – Global Report', Prel. Doc. No. 8 A of May 2011. The Hague: HCCH. Available at: <https://assets.hcch.net/upload/wop/abduct2011pd08ae.pdf> (accessed 3 January 2020).

Lowe, N. (2011b) 'A Statistical Analysis of Applications Made in 2008 under the *Hague Convention of 25 October 1980 on the Civil Aspects of International Child Abduction*. Part II – Regional Reports', Prel. Doc. No. 8 B of May 2011. The Hague: HCCH. Available at: <www.hcch.net/upload/wop/abduct2011pd08be.pdf> (accessed 7 January 2013).

Lowe, N. (2011c) 'A Statistical Analysis of Applications Made in 2008 under the *Hague Convention of 25 October 1980 on the Civil Aspects of International Child Abduction*. Part III – National Reports', Prel. Doc. No. 8 C of May 2011, The Hague: HCCH. Available at: <www.hcch.net/upload/wop/abduct2011pd08c.pdf> (accessed 1 October 2011).

Lowe, N. (2017) 'What are the Implications of the Brexit Vote for the Law on International Child Abduction?', 29(3) *Child and Family Law Quarterly* 253.

Lowe, V. and Crawford, J. (eds) (2012) *British Year Book of International Law 2011: Volume 81*. Oxford: Oxford University Press.

Lowe, N. and Stephens, V. (2017) 'Part I – A Statistical Analysis of Applications Made in 2015 under the Hague Convention of 25 October 1980 on the Civil Aspects of International Child Abduction'. Preliminary Document No. 11 A of September 2017. Globe Report of The Seventh Meeting of the Special Commission on the Practical Operation of the 1980 Hague Child Abduction Convention and the 1996 Hague Child Protection Convention – October 2017. Available at: <www.hcch.net/en/publications-and-studies/details4/?pid=6598&dtid=32> (accessed 8 January 2020).

Lowe, N., Armstrong, S. and Mathias, A. (1999) *A Statistical Analysis of Applications Made in 1999 under the Hague Convention of 25 October 1980 on the Civil Aspects of International Child Abduction*. The Hague: HCCH.

Bibliography 569

Lowe, N., Everall, M. and Nicholls, M. (2004) *International Movement of Children: Law, Practice and Procedure*. London: Family Law/Jordan Publishing Ltd.

Lowe, N., Atkinson, E. and Horosova, K. (2006) *A Statistical Analysis of Applications Made in 2003 under the 1980 Hague Convention on the Civil Aspects of International Child Abduction*, Vol. 1, *Global Report*; Vol. 2, *National Reports*; published as Preliminary Document No. 3 for the 5th Meeting of the Special Commission to Review the Operation of the Hague Convention of 25 October 1980 on the Civil Aspects of International Child Abduction. Available at: <www.hcch.net/en/publications-and-studies/details4/?pid=4867&dtid=32> (accessed 25 January 2010).

Maalla, N.M. (2008) *Report Submitted by the Special Rapporteur on the Sale of Children, Child Prostitution and Child Pornography*. UN Human Rights Council, ninth session, A/HRC/9/21, 31 July. Available at: <http://daccess-dds-ny.un.org/doc/UNDOC/ GEN/G08/148/41/PDF/G0814841.pdf?OpenElement> (accessed 27 January 2010).

Maalla, N.M. (2009) *Report Submitted by the Special Rapporteur on the Sale of Children, Child Prostitution and Child Pornography*. UN Human Rights Council, 12th session, A/HRC/12/23, 13 July. Available at: <www2.ohchr.org/english/bodies/ hrcouncil/docs/12session/A.HRC.12.23.pdf> (accessed 27 January 2010).

Maalla, N.M. (2011) *Report of the Special Rapporteur on the Sale of Children, Child Prostitution and Child Pornography*. UN Human Rights Council, 19th session, A/HRC/19/63. Available at: <http://daccess-dds-ny.un.org/doc/UNDOC/GEN/G11/175/13/PDF/G1117513.pdf> (accessed 14 October 2013).

Maalla, N.M. (2012) *Report of the Special Rapporteur on the Sale of Children, Child Prostitution and Child Pornography*. UN Human Rights Council, 22nd session, A/HRC/22/54. Available at: <http://daccess-dds-ny.un.org/doc/UNDOC/GEN/G13/102/63/PDF/G1310263.pdf> (accessed 14 October 2013).

MacCormick, N. (1982) *Legal Right and Social Democracy: Essays in Legal and Political Philosphy*. Oxford: Clarendon Press.

Maconachie, R. and Hilson, G. (2016) 'Re-thinking the Child Labor "Problem" in Rural Sub-Saharan Africa: The Case of Sierra Leone's Half Shovels', 78 *World Development* 136–47.

Mail & Guardian Online (2011) 'Mean Girls Get Meaner Online', 21 January. Available at: <https://mg.co.za/article/2011-01-21-mean-girls-get-meaner-online> (accessed 20 December 2019).

Malik, N. (2019) *Radicalising Our Children: An Analysis of Family Court Cases of British Children at Risk of Radicalisation, 2013–2018*. London: Henry Jackson Society Centre on Radicalisation and Terrorism.

Malone, D.M. (2007) 'Security Council', in Weiss, T. G. and Daws, S. (eds) *The Oxford Handbook on the United Nations*. Oxford: Oxford University Press, pp. 117–35.

Manchester Evening News (2009) 'Girl Died after Bebo Hate Campaign', 31 July. Available at: <www.manchestereveningnews.co.uk/news/greater-manchester-news/girl-died-after-bebo-hate-925836> (accessed 14 December 2019).

Marshall, D. (1999) 'The Construction of Children as an Object of International Relations: The Declaration of Children's Rights and the Child Welfare Committee of League of Nations, 1900–1924', 7(2) *International Journal of Children's Rights* 103–47.

Martin, N.G. (2015) 'International Parental Child Abduction and Mediation', 15(1) *Anuario Mexicano de Derecho Internacional* 353–412.

Marwick, A.E. (2008) 'To Catch a Predator. The Myspace Moral Panic', 13(6) *First Monday*. Available at: <https://firstmonday.org/ojs/index.php/fm/article/view/2152/1966> (accessed 16 December 2019).

Mascheroni, G. and Cuman, A. (2014) *Net Children Go Mobile: Final Report* (with country fact sheets). Milan: Educatt.

Maslow, A. (1987) *Motivation and Personality*, 3rd edn. New York: Harper & Row.

Massey, D. (1998) 'The Spatial Construction of Youth Cultures', in: Skelton, T. and Valentine, G. (eds) *Cool Places: Geographies of Youth Cultures*. London/New York: Routledge.

Masum, M. (2002) 'Eradication of Hazardous Child Labour in Bangladesh: The Need for an Integrated Strategy', 10(3) *International Journal of Children's Rights* 233–68.

Mayall, B. (2000) 'The Sociology of Childhood in Relation to Children's Rights', 8(3) *International Journal of Children's Rights* 243–59.

Mayall, B. (2003) *Childhood in Generational Perspective*. Bedford Way Papers. London: Institute of Education.

Maynard, T. and Thomas, N. (eds) (2009) *An Introduction to Early Childhood Studies*, 2nd edn. London: Sage.

McCarthy, F. (2018) 'Dynamic Self-Determinism, the Right to Belief and the Role of Collective Worship', in Cumper, P. and Mawhinney, A. (eds) *Collective Worship and Religious Observance in UK Schools: Challenges and Opportunities*. Religion, Education and Values series (13). Oxford: Peter Lang.

McCrae, D. (2012) 'The Work of the International Law Commission, 2007–2011: Progress and Prospects', 106 *American Journal of International Law* 322–40.

McEleavy, P. (2005) 'The New Child Abduction Regime in the European Community: Symbiotic Relationship or Forced Partnership?' 2005 *Journal of Private International Law* 5–34.

McEleavy, P. (2008) 'Evaluating the Views of Abducted Children: Trends in Appellate Case Law', 2008 *Child and Family Law Quarterly*, 230–54.

McEleavy, P. and Fiorini, A. (n.d.) *Case Law Analysis*. INCADAT, Hague Conference on Private International Law. Available at: <www.incadat.com/en/convention/case-law-analysis> (accessed 8 January 2020).

McRobbie, A. and Garber. (1976). 'Girls and Subcultures', in Hall, S. and Jefferson, P. (eds) *Resistance through Ritual: Youth Cultures in the Post War Britain*. Essex: Hutchinson University Library.

Melrose, M. (2010) 'What's Love Got to Do with It? Theorising Young People's Involvement in Prostitution', 104 *Youth and Policy* (June) 12–30.

Melrose, M. (2012) 'Twenty-First Century Party People: Young People and Sexual Exploitation in the New Millenium', *Child Abuse Review*, doi: 10:2002/car.2238.

Melrose, M. and Barrett, D. (2006) 'The Flesh Trade in Europe: Trafficking in Women and Children for the Purpose of Commercial Sexual Exploitation', 7(2) *Police Practice and Research* 111–23.

Melrose, M. and Pearce, J.J. (2013) *Critical Perspectives on Child Sexual Exploitation and Related Trafficking*. Gordonsville, VA: Palgrave Macmillan.

Mezmur, B.D. (2008) '"As painful as giving birth": A Reflection on the Madonna Adoption Saga', 41 *Comparative and International Law of Southern Africa* 383–402.

Mezmur, B.D. (2009) 'From Angelina (to Madonna) to Zoe's Ark: What are the "A – Z" Lessons for Intercountry Adoptions in Africa?', 23 *International Journal of Law, Policy and the Family* 145.

Mezmur, B.D. (2012) '"Acting like a rich bully"?: Madonna, Mercy, Malawi, and International Children's Rights Law in Adoption', 20(1) *International Journal of Children's Rights*, 24–56.

Mitchell, K.J., Ybarra, M.L. and Korchmaros, J.D. (2014) 'Sexual Harassment among Adolescents of Different Sexual Orientations and Gender Identities' 38(2) *Child Abuse and Neglect* 280–95.

Molfenter, C. (2011) 'Bonded Child Labour in Pakistan – The State's Responsibility to Protect from an Institutional Perspective', 5 *Vienna Journal on International Constitutional Law* 260–320.

Montgomery, H. (2008) 'Buying Innocence: Child-Sex Tourists in Thailand', 29(5) *Third World Quarterly* 903–17.

Montgomery, H (2010) 'Is Extra-Territorial Legislation the Answer?', in Botterill, D. and Jones, T. (eds) *Tourism and Crime: Key Themes*. Oxford: Goodfellow Publishing, pp. 69–85.

Montgomery, M. and Powell, A. (2018) 'International Adoptions Have Dropped 72 Percent since 2005 – Here's Why', *The Conversation*. Available at: <http://theconversation.com/international-adoptions-have-dropped-72-percent-since-2005-heres-why-91809> (accessed 20 December 2019).

Mooney, E. and Paul, D. (2010) 'The Rights and Guarantees of Internally Displaced Children in Armed Conflict'. Working Paper No. 2. New York: Office of the Special Representative of the Secretary-General for Children and Armed Conflict. Available at: <http://childrenandarmedconflict.un.org/publications/WorkingPaper-2-RightsGuarantees IDP-Children.pdf> (accessed 18 September 2019).

Moravcsik, A. (2000) 'The Origins of Human Rights Regimes: Democratic Delegation in Postwar Europe', 54(2) *International Organization* 217–52.

Morley, D. (1986) *Family Television: Cultural Power and Domestic Leisure*. London: Comedia.

Morrison, H. (2012) *The Global History of Childhood Reader*. London: Routledge.

Morrow, V. (2015) 'The Intersections of School, Work and Learning: Children in Ethiopia, Andra Pradesh, India, Peru and Vietnam', in Abebe, T. and Waters, J. (eds) *Labouring and Learning*, vol. 10 of *Geographies of Children and Young People*. Singapore: Springer.

Morrow, V. and Boyden, J. (2018) *Responding to Children's Work: Evidence from the Young Lives Study in Ethiopia, India, Peru and Vietnam. Summative Report*. Oxford: Young Lives.

Mueller, M. (2010) *Networks and States: The Global Politics of Internet Governance. Information Revolution and Global Politics*. Cambridge, MA: The MIT Press.

Mughal, S. (2016) 'Radicalisation of Young People on Social Media'. Available at: <www.internetmatters.org/hub/expert-opinion/radicalisation-of-young-people-through-social-media> (accessed 12 December 2019).

Mullerbeck, E. and Anthony, D. (2011) 'UNICEF at 65: Looking Back, Thinking Ahead'. UNICEF website. Available at: <www.unicef.org/about/who/index_60926.html> (accessed 25 February 2013).

Muntarbhorn, V. (1998) 'Child Rights and Social Clauses: Child Labour Elimination as a Social Cause?', 6(3) *International Journal of Children's Rights* 255–311.

Mutua, M. (2000) 'What is TWAIL?', 94 *American Society of International Law Proceedings* 31–8.

Myers, W.E. (2001) 'The Right Rights? Child Labour in a Globalizing World', 575(1) *Annals of the American Academy of Political and Social Science* 38–54.

Neilson, L. (2010) 'Boycott or Buycott? Understanding Political Consumerism', 9(3) *Journal of Consumer Behavior* 214–27.

Nelson, M.K. (2010) *Parenting Out of Control: Anxious Parents in Uncertain Times*. New York: NYU Press.

Newiss, G. and Fairbrother, L. (2004) 'Child Abduction: Understanding Police Recorded Crime Statistics', in *Findings 225*. London: Home Office Research, Development and Statistics Directorate.

Newman, E. (2018) 'Secretary-General', Chapter 12, in Weiss, T. G. and Daws, S. (eds) (2018) *The Oxford Handbook on the United Nations*, 2nd edn. Oxford: Oxford University Press, pp. 131–249.

NGO Group (2001) *Do You Know About the ILO Worst Forms of Child Labour Convention?* Geneva: NGO Group for the Convention on the Rights of the Child.

NGO Group (2005) *Semantics or Substance? Towards a Shared Understanding of Terminology Referring to the Sexual Abuse and Exploitation of Children*. Subgroup against the Sexual Exploitation of Children, NGO Group for the Convention on the Rights of the Child, Bangkok: ECPAT International. Available at: <www.crin.org/docs/ resources/publications/Subgroup_ Sexual_Exploitation_Semantics.pdf> (accessed 30 January 2010).

NGO Group for the Convention on the Rights of the Child (2006) *A Guide for Non-governmental Organizations Reporting to the Committee on the Rights of the Child*, 3rd edn. Geneva: NGO Group for the Convention on the Rights of the Child. Available at: <www.childrightsnet. org/docs/Reporting%20Guide%202006%20English.pdf> (accessed 6 June 2013).

Nielsen, A.E. and Thomson, C. (2009) 'Investigating CSR Communication in SMEs: A Case Study among Danish Middle Managers', 18(1) *Business Ethics: A European Review* 83–93.

Noguchi, Y. (2002) 'ILO Convention No. 182 on the Worst Forms of Child Labour and the Convention on the Rights of the Child', 10(4) *International Journal of Children's Rights* 355–69.

Noguchi, Y. (2010) '20 Years of the Convention on the Rights of the Child and International Action against Child Labour', 18(4) *International Journal of Children's Rights* 515–34.

Nyamutata, C. (2015) 'Lubanga, Child Soldiering and the Philosophy of International Law'. Unpublished thesis, De Montfort University.

Ochaíta, E., Espinosa, A. and Calvo, E. (2000) 'Child Work and Labour in Spain: A First Approach', 8(1) *International Journal of Children's Rights* 15–35.

O'Connell, R. and Bryce, J. (2006) *Young People, Well-Being and Risk On-Line*. Strasbourg: Media Division, Directorate General of Human Rights, Council of Europe.

O'Donnell, C. and White, L. (1999) *Hidden Danger: Injuries to Children at Work in Britain*. London: Low Pay Unit.

O'Connell Davidson, J. (2005) *Children in the Global Sex Trade*. Cambridge: Polity Press.

O'Connell Davidson, J. (2015) *Modern Slavery: The Margins of Freedom*. Basingstoke: Palgrave Macmillan.

O'Connell Davidson, J. (2000) 'Sex Tourism and Child Prostitution', in Clift, S. and Carter, S. (eds) *Tourism and Sex Culture, Commerce and Coercion*. London: Continuum Publishing, pp. 54–73).

O'Connell Davidson, J. (2019) 'Talking Trafficking with Jamaican Sex Workers'. Open Democracy website. Available at: <www.opendemocracy.net/en/beyond-trafficking-and-slavery/talking-trafficking-jamaican-sex-workers> (accessed 17 December 2019).

OECD (2011) 'The Protection of Children Online: Risks Faced by Children Online and Policies to Protect Them'. OECD *Digital Economy Papers*, No. 179. Paris: OECD Publishing.

OECD (2018) 'Bridging the Digital Gender Divide: Include, Upskill, Innovate'. Paris: OECD Publishing.

Oestreich, J.E. (1998) 'UNICEF and the Implementation of the Convention on the Rights of the Child', 4(2) *Global Governance* 183–98.

Office of the High Commissioner for Human Rights (2012) *The United Nations Human Rights Treaty System*, Fact Sheet No. 30/rev. 1, Office of the High Commissioner for Human Rights. New York/Geneva: OHCHR. Available at: <www.ohchr.org/Documents/Publications/FactSheet30Rev1.pdf> (accessed 1 March 2013).

OHCHR (1997) *Manual on Human Rights Reporting: Under Six Major International Human Rights Instruments*. Office of the High Commissioner for Human Rights, HR/PUB/91/1 (Rev.1). Geneva: OHCHR. Available at: <www.ohchr.org/Documents/Publications/manualhrren.pdf> (accessed 2 August 2013).

Okyere, S. (2012) 'Are Working Children's Rights and Child Labour Abolition Complementary or Opposing Realms?', 56(1) *International Social Work* 80–91.

O'Neill, B. and Dinh, T. (2018) 'The Better Internet for Kids Policy Map: Implementing the European Strategy for a Better Internet for Children in European Member States'. Available at: <www.betterinternetforkids.eu/bikmap> (accessed 17 December 2019).

Ost, S. (2009) *Child Pornography and Sexual Grooming: Legal and Societal Responses*. Cambridge: Cambridge University Press.

Oswell, D. (2002) *Television, Childhood and the Home: A History of the Making of the Child Television Audience in Britain*. Oxford: Oxford University Press.

Pakistan Bureau of Statistics (2014) *Labour Force Survey 2014–15*. Islamabad: Government of Pakistan, Statistics Division, Pakistan Bureau of Statistics. Available at: <www.pbs.gov.pk/sites/default/files//Annual%20Report%20of%20LFS%202014-15.pdf> (accessed 17 December 2019).

Palmer, T. (2005) 'Behind the Screen: Children Who are the Subjects of Abusive Images', in Quayle, E. and Taylor, M. (eds) *Viewing Child Pornography on the Internet*. Lyme Regis: Russell House Publishing, pp. 61–74.

Parkes, A. (2013) *Children and International Human Rights Law/The Right of the Child to be Heard*, Abingdon, Oxon: Taylor & Francis.

Parra-Aranguren, G. (1994) *Explanatory Report on the Convention on Protection of Children and Co-operation in Respect of Intercountry Adoption*. The Hague: HCCH Publications. Available at: <http://hcch.e-vision.nl/index_en.php?act=publications.detailsandpid=2279anddtid=3> (accessed 5 October 2019).

Parsons, T. and Bales, R. (1956) *Family: Socialisation and Interaction Processes*. London: Routledge & Kegan Paul.

Paton, J. (2012) 'The Correct Approach to the Examination of the Best Interests of the Child in Abduction Convention Proceedings Following the Decision of the Supreme Court in Re E (Children) (Abduction: Custody Appeal)', 8(3) *Journal of Private International Law*, 545–74.

Pearce, J. (2006) 'Finding the "I" in Sexual Exploitation: Hearing the Voices of Sexually Exploited Young People in Policy and Practice', in Campbell, R. and O'Neill, M. (eds) *Sex Work Now*. Cullompton, Devon: Willan Publishing, pp. 190–211.

Pearce, J.J. (2013) 'Contextualising Consent', in Melrose, M. and Pearce, J. (eds) *Critical Perspectives on Child Sexual Exploitation and Related Trafficking*. Basingstoke: Palgrave Macmillan.

Pearce, J., Williams, M. and Galvin, C. (2002) *It's Someone Taking a Part of You: A Study of Young Women and Sexual Exploitation*. London: National Children's Bureau.

Pearl, D. and Menski, W. (1998) *Muslim Family Law*, 3rd edn. London: Sweet & Maxwell.

Pereznieto, P., Jones, M. and Montes, A. (2016) 'Eliminating Child Labour, Achieving Economic Growth'. Policy paper. London: World Vision and ODI.

Pérez-Vera, E. (1980) *Explanatory Report: Hague Convention on International Child Abduction*. The Hague: HCCH Publications.

Peterson, M. J. (2007) 'General Assembly', in Weiss, T.G. and Daws, S. (eds) (2007) *The Oxford Handbook on the United Nations*. Oxford: Oxford University Press, pp. 97–116.

Phoenix, J. (2003) 'Rethinking Youth Prostitution: National Provision at the Margins of Child Protection and Youth Justice', 3(3) *Youth Justice* 152–68.

Phoenix, J. and Oerton, S. (2005) *Illicit and Illegal: Sex, Regulation, and Social Control*. Cullompton, Devon: Willan Publishing.

Piaget, J. (1952) *The Origins of Intelligence in Children*. New York: W.W. Norton and Co. Inc.

Piaget, J. (1960) *The Child's Conception of the World*. Paterson, NJ: Littlefield, Adams and Co.

Pierce, W. (1995) 'Accreditation of Those Who Arrange Adoptions under the Hague Convention on Intercountry Adoption as a Means of Protecting, through Private International Law, the Rights of Children', 12(2) *Journal of Contemporary Health Law and Policy* 535–61.

Pollock, L. (1983) *Forgotten Children: Parent – Child Relations from 1500 to 1900*. Cambridge: Cambridge University Press.

Ponte, C. and Alberto, S.J. (2009) 'Asking Parents about Children's Internet Use: Comparing Findings about Parental Mediation in Portugal and Other European Countries'. Available at: <www.fcsh.unl.pt/eukidsonline/docs/Asking%20parents-FINAL%20Paper1_27-05-09.pdf> (accessed 4 January 2020).

Postman, N. (1983) *The Disappearance of Childhood*. London: W.H. Allen.

Powell, A., Hills, M. and Nash, V. (2010) 'Child Protection and Freedom of Expression Online'. Oxford Internet Institute Forum Discussion Paper No. 17.

Prevent Duty (2015) Departmental Advice for Schools and Childcare Providers, July. Department of Education, UK.

Przybylski, A K. and Bowes, L. (2017) 'Cyberbullying and Adolescent Well-Being in England: A Population-Based Cross-Sectional Study', 1 (1) *The Lancet Child and Adolescent Health*, pp. 19–26.

Quattri, M. and Watkins, K. (2016) 'Child labour and Education: A Survey of Slum Settlements in Dhaka'. Overseas Development Institute. Available at: <www.odi.org/publications/10654-child-labour-and-education-survey-slumsettlements-dhaka> (accessed 17 December 2019).

Quigley, J.B. (2002) 'US Ratification of the Convention on the Rights of the Child', Justice for Children Project, Moritz College of Law. Cited in Peters, Jean Koh, *How Children Are Heard in Child Protective Proceedings, in the United States and Around the World in 2005: Survey Findings, Initial Observations, and Areas for Further Study*. Faculty Scholarship Series 2146, 2006. Available at: <https://digitalcommons.law.yale.edu/fss_papers/2146> (accessed 4 January 2020).

Qvortrup, J., Bardy, M., Sgritta, G. and Wintersberger, H. (1994) *Childhood Matters: Social Theory, Practice and Politics*. Aldershot: Avebury.

Qvortrup, J., Corsaro, W.A. and Honig, M. (eds) (2011) *The Palgrave Handbook of Childhood Studies*. Basingstoke: Palgrave Macmillan.

Ramcharan, B.G. (2007) 'Norms and Machinery', in Weiss, T.G. and Daws, S. (eds) *The Oxford Handbook on the United Nations*. Oxford: Oxford University Press, pp. 439–62.

Ranton, D. (2009) 'Hague and Non-Hague Convention Abductions: Notes for Reunite Website on Hague Convention Law as at 20th October 2009'. Reunite website. Available at: <www.reunite.org/edit/files/articles/Notes%20on%20Hague%20Convention%20Law.pdf> (accessed 3 January 2020)

Raz, J. (1996) 'Liberty and Trust', in George, R. (ed.) *Natural Law, Liberalism and Morality*. Oxford: Oxford University Press.

Redress Trust (2006) 'Victims, Perpetrators or Heroes? Child Soldiers before the International Criminal Court', September. Available at: <www.iccnow.org/documents/Redress_childsoldiers_report_Sep06.pdf> (accessed 20 December 2019).

Ricanek, K. and Boehnen, C. (2012) 'Facial Analytics: From Big Data to Law Enforcement', 45(9) *Computer* 95–7.

Richards, A. (2013) 'Bombs and Babies: The Intercountry Adoption of Afghanistan's and Iraq's War Orphans', 25(2) *Journal of the American Academy of Matrimonial Lawyers* 399–424.

Riiskjær, M. and Gallagher, A.M. (2008) *Review of the UNHCR's Efforts to Prevent and Respond to Human Trafficking*. United Nations High Commissioner for Refugees, Policy Development and Evaluation Service, PDES/2008/07. Geneva: UNHCR. Available at: <www.unhcr.org/48eb2ff82.html> (accessed 15 November 2013).

Rios-Kohn, R. (1998) 'UNICEF's Mission to Protect the Rights of the Child', 4 *Loyola Poverty Law Journal* 185–94.

Roberts, R.C.E. (2012) 'The Lubanga Trial Chamber's Assessment of Evidence in Light of the Accused's Right to the Presumption of Innocence', 10(4) *Journal of International Criminal Justice* 923–44.

Rosati, F., Breglia, M.G., Guarcello, L., Lyon, S. and Valdivia, C.A. (2015b) *The Twin Challenges of Child Labor and Educational Marginalization in the ECOWAS Region*. Rome: Understanding Children's Work Programme, International Labour Organization.

Rosati, F. Rosati, F.C., Guarcello, L., Lyon, S. and Valdivia, C.A. (2015a) *Understanding Child Labour and Youth Employment Outcomes in the Philippines*. Country Report. Rome: International Labour Organization and Centre for Economic and International Studies (CEIS).

Rosentahl, G. (2018) 'Economic and Social Council', in Weiss, T.G. and Daws, S. (eds) *The Oxford Handbook on the United Nations*, 2nd edn. Oxford: Oxford University Press.

Rotabi, K.S. and Bromfield, N.F. (2016) *From Intercountry Adoption to Global Surrogacy: A Human Rights History and New Fertility Frontiers*. Abingdon, Oxon: Routledge.

Roth, P. (2010) 'Child Labour in New Zealand: A Job for the Nanny State?', 12(2) *Otago Law Review* 245–63.

Rutkow, L. and Lozman, J.T. (2006) 'Suffer the Children? A Call for United States Ratification of the United Nations Convention on the Rights of the Child', 19 *Harvard Human Rights Journal* 161–90.

Sachlier, C. (1993) 'The 1993 Hague Convention on Protection of Children and Co-operation in Respect of Intercountry Adoption: A Convention in the Best Interests of the Child'. Geneva: International Social Service. Available at: <https://assets.hcch.net/docs/994654cc-a296-4299-bd3c-f70d63a5862a.pdf> (accessed 20 December 2019).

Sanghera, J. (2012) 'Unpacking the Trafficking Discourse', in Kempadoo, K., Sanghera, J. and Pattanaik, B. (eds) *Trafficking and Prostitution Reconsidered: New Perspectives on Migration, Sex Work, and Human Rights*, 2nd edn. Boulder, CO: Paradigm.

Sargent, S. (2009) 'The Best Interests of the Child in Intercountry Adoption: A Constructivist and Comparative Account'. PhD thesis, De Montfort University, Leicester, United Kingdom. Available at: <www.dora.dmu.ac.uk/handle/2086/3535> (accessed 13 November 2019).

Sarkin, J. and Pietschmann, M. (2003) 'Legitimate Humanitarian Intervention under International Law in the Context of the Current Human Rights and Humanitarian Crisis in Burma (Myanmar)', 33(2) *Hong Kong Law Journal* 371–416.

Sarri, R., Baik, Y. and Bombyk, M. (1998) 'Goal Displacement and Dependency in South Korean – United States Intercountry Adoption', 20(1) *Children and Youth Services Review* 87–114.

Savona, E.U. and Stefanizzi, S. (2007), 'Introduction', in Savona, E.U. and Stefanizzi, S. (eds) *Measuring Human Trafficking: Complexities and Pitfalls*. New York: Springer.

Sawyer, C. (2006) 'The Child is Not a Person: Family Law and Other Legal Cultures', 28(1) *Journal of Social Welfare and Family Law* 1–14.

Schabas, W. (1996) 'Reservations to the Convention on the Rights of the Child', 18(2) Human Rights Quarterly 472–91.

Schmidt, E. and Cohen, J. (2013) *The New Digital Age: Transforming Nations, Businesses, and Our Lives*. London: Knopf Publishing Group.

Schmit, A. (2008) 'The Hague Convention: The Problems with Accession and Implementation', 15 *Indiana Journal of Global Legal Studies* 375.

Schulz, A. (2008) 'Guidance from Luxembourg: First ECJ Judgment Clarifying the Relationship between the 1980 Hague Convention and Brussels II Revised', 2008 *International Family Law* 221–25.

Schuz, R. (2001a) 'Policy Considerations in Determining the Habitual Residence of a Child and the Relevance of Context', 11 *Journal of Transnational Law and Policy* 101.

Schuz, R. (2001b) 'Habitual Residence of Children under the Hague Child Abduction Convention: Theory and Practice', 13(1) *Child and Family Law Quarterly* 1.

Schuz, R. (2003) 'Returning Abducted Children to Israel and the Intifada', 2003 *Australian Journal of Family Law* 297.

Schuz, R. (2008) 'In Search of a Settled Interpretation of Article 12(2) of the Hague Child Abduction Convention', 20(1) *Child and Family Law Quarterly* 64–80.

Schwebel, S. (1984) 'Authorising the Secretary-General of the United Nations to Request Advisory Opinions', 78(4) *American Journal of International Law* 869–78.

Schwebel, S. (1988) 'Preliminary Rulings by the International Court of Justice at the Instance of National Courts', 28(2) *Virginia Journal of International Law* 495–508.

Scullion, D. (2013) 'Passive Victims or Empowered Actors: Accommodating the Needs of Child Domestic Workers', 21(1) *International Journal of Children's Rights* 97–126.

SCWG (2009) *UN Security Council's Working Group Annual Report*. Available at: <www.un.org/children/conflict/english/securitycouncilwgroupdoc.html> (accessed 14 November 2019).

Segrave, M., Milivojevic, M. and Pickering, S. (2018) *Sex Trafficking and Modern Slavery: The Absence of Evidence*, 2nd edn. Abingdon, Oxon/New York: Routledge.

Selby, J. (2008) 'Ending Abusive and Exploitative Child Labour through International Law and Practical Action', 15 *Australian International Law Journal* 165–80.

Selman, P. (2002) 'Intercountry Adoption in the New Millennium: The "Quiet Migration" Revisited', 21 *Population Research and Policy Review* 205–25.

Selman, P. (2006) 'Trends in Intercountry Adoption: Analysis of Data from 20 Receiving Countries, 1998–2004', 23(2) *Journal of Population Research* 183–204.

Selman, P. (2011) 'Intercountry Adoption after the Haiti Earthquake: Rescue or Robbery?', 25(4) *Adoption and Fostering* 41–9.

Selman, P. (2012) 'Global Trends in Intercountry Adoption: 2001–2010', 44 *Adoption Advocate* 1–17. Available at: <www.adoptioncouncil.org/images/stories/documents/NCFA_ADOPTION_ADVOCATE_NO44.pdf> (accessed 10 November 2019).

Selman, P. (2013) *Key Tables for Intercountry Adoption: Receiving States 2003–2012; States of Origin 2003–2011*. Available on request from the author at pfselman@yahoo.co.uk, or on the Hague website at: <www.hcch.net/upload/2013selmanstats33.pdf> (accessed 8 November 2019).

Selman, P. (2019) *Global Statistics for Intercountry Adoption: Receiving States and States of Origin 2004–17*. Available at: <https://assets.hcch.net/docs/a8fe9f19-23e6-40c2-855e-388e112bf1f5.pdf> (accessed 3 January 2020).

SG Report (2017) *General Assembly, Children and Armed Conflict: Report of the Secretary-General 71st session*. UN Doc. A/72/361 – S/2017/821 (24 August).

Sharma, A. and Viswanathan, H. (2011) 'Extension of the Hague Convention to Non-signatory nations: A Possible Solution to Parental Child Abduction', 4(4) International Journal of Private Law 546–59.

Shaw, M. (2008) *International Law*, 6th edn. Cambridge: Cambridge University Press.

Shaw, M. (2017) *International Law*, 8th edn. Cambridge: Cambridge University Press.

Shrinkhal, R. (2019) 'Evolution of Indigenous Rights under International Law: Analysis from TWAIL Perspective', 19(1) *The Oriental Anthropologist* 7–24.

Shuz, R. (2013) *The Hague Child Abduction Convention: A Critical Analysis*. Oxford/Portland, OR: Hart Publishing.

Siebert, J. (2007) 'Protecting Minors on the Internet: An Example from Germany', in Moller, C. and Amoroux, A. (eds) *Governing the Internet. Freedom and Regulation in the OSCE Region*. Vienna: Organization for Security and Co-operation in Europe.

Silk, J.J. and Makonnen, M. (2003) 'Ending Child Labor: A Role for International Human Rights Law?', 22(2) *Saint Louis University Public Law Review* 359–70.

Simon, L.M.J. (1997) 'Do Criminal Offenders Specialize in Crime Types?' 6 *Applied and Preventative Psychology* 35–53.

Singh, R. and Khan, S. (2016) 'Perspectives on Children's Work and Schooling: Evidence from a Longitudinal Study in Andhra Pradesh and Telangana, India'. Geneva: ILO Asia-Pacific Working Paper Series, International Labour Organization.

SIPRI (2013) *SIPRI Yearbook 2013: Armaments, Disarmament and International Security*. Solna, Sweden: Stockholm International Peace Research Institute (SIPRI). Summary available at: <www.sipri.org/yearbook/2013/files/SIPRIYB13Summary.pdf> (accessed 16 August 2019).

Sloane, R.D. (2007) 'The Expressive Capacity of International Punishment: The Limits of the National Law Analogy and the Potential of International Criminal Law', 42 *Stanford Journal of International Law* 39.

Smith, P.K. Mahdavi, J., Carvalho, M., Fisher, S., Russell, S. and Tippett, N. (2008) 'Cyberbullying: Its Nature and Impact in Secondary School Pupils', 49(4) *Journal of Child Psychology and Psychiatry* 376–85.

Smolin, D.M. (2000) 'Strategic Choices in the International Campaign against Child Labour', 22(4) *Human Rights Quarterly* 942–87.

Smolin, D.M. (2006) 'Overcoming Religious Objections to the Convention on the Rights of the Child', 20(1) *Emory International Law Review* 81–110.

Smolin, D.M. (2007) 'Child Laundering as Exploitation: Applying Anti-Trafficking Norms to Intercountry Adoption under the Coming Hague Regime', 32(1) *Vermont Law Review* 1–55.

Smolin, D.M. (2010) 'Child Laundering and The Hague Convention on Intercountry Adoption: The Future and Past of Intercountry Adoption', 48 *University of Louisville Law Review* 441–98.

Springhall, J. (1998) *Youth, Popular Culture and Moral Panics: Penny Gaffs to Gangsta-Rap, 1830–1996*. New York: St Martin's Press.

SRSG (2007) *General Assembly, Report of the Special Representative of the Secretary-General for Children and Armed Conflict, 62nd session*. UN Doc. A/62/228 (13 August).

Staksrud, E. (2013) *Children in the Online World. Risk, Regulation, Rights*. Farnham: Ashgate.

Staksrud, E. and Livingstone, S. (2009) 'Children and Online Risk: Powerless Victims or Resourceful Participants?', 12(3) *Information, Communication and Society* 364–87.

Stalford, H. (2013) 'Article 32 – Prohibition of Child Labour and Protection of Young People at Work. The EU Charter of Fundamental Rights', in Peers, S., Hervey, T., Kenner, J. and Ward, A. (eds) *The EU Charter of Fundamental Rights – A Commentary*. Oxford: Hart Publishing, pp. 869–89.

Stalford, H. and Drywood, E. (2009) 'Coming of Age?: Children's Rights in the European Union', 46(1) *Common Market Law Review* 143–72.

State of the World's Children (2017) *Children in a Digital World*, December. New York: United Nations Children's Fund.

Stearns, P.M. (2003) *Anxious Parents: A History of Modern Childrearing in America*. New York: NYU Press.

Steffen, W. (2012) 'Co-perpetration in the Lubanga Trial Judgment', 10(4) *Journal of International Criminal Justice* 971–96.

Steiner, H. (1994) *An Essay on Rights*. Oxford: Blackwell.

Steinhauer, J. (2008) 'Verdict in MySpace Suicide Case', *New York Times*, 26 November. Available at: <www.nytimes.com/2008/11/27/us/27myspace.html> (accessed 17 December 2019).

Stone, L. (1990) *The Family, Sex and Marriage in England 1500–1800*, abridged edn. London: Penguin.

Sumner, L.W. (1987) *The Moral Foundation of Rights*. Oxford: Clarendon Press.

Sunter, A. (2007) 'TWAIL as Naturalized Epistemological Inquiry', 20(2) *Canadian Journal of Law and Jurisprudence* 475–510.

Sutherland, P. (1992) *Cognitive Development Today: Piaget and His Critics*. London: Paul Chapman Publishing.

Svensson, N.L. (2006) 'Extraterritorial Accountability: An Assessment of the Effectiveness of Child Sex Tourism Laws', 28(3) *Loyola of Los Angeles International and Comparative Law Review* 641–64.

Tafere, Y. and Pankhurst, A. (2015) 'Can Children in Ethiopian Communities Combine Schooling with Work?' Working Paper 141. Oxford: Young Lives.

Taylor, M. and Quayle, F. (2003) *Child Pornography: An Internet Crime*, London: Routledge.

Telegraph (2009) 'Schoolgirl Took Overdose after Bebo Bullying, Inquest Hears', 20 July. Available at: <www.telegraph.co.uk/technology/social-media/5933925/Schoolgirl-took-overdose-after-Bebo-bullying-inquest-hears.html> (accessed 17 December 2019).

Tennant, C. (1994). 'Indigenous People, International Institutions, and the International Legal Literature from 1945 to 1993', 16(1) *Human Rights Quarterly* 1–57.

Tepelus, C.M. (2008) 'Social Responsibility and Innovation on Trafficking and Child Sex Tourism: Morphing of Practice into Sustainable Tourism Policies?', 8(2) *Tourism and Hospitality Research* 98–115.

Terre des hommes International Federation (2016) *Child Labour Report 2016, Because We Struggle to Survive: Child Labour among Refugees of the Syrian Conflict*, June. Terre des hommes. Available at: <www.terredeshommes.org/wp-content/uploads/2016/06/Child-Labour-Report-2016-ENGLISH.pdf> (accessed 20 December 2019).

Tetteh, P. (2011) 'Child Domestic Labour in (Accra) Ghana: A Child and Gender Rights Issue?', 19(2) *International Journal of Children's Rights* 217–32.

Third, A., Bellerose, D., Dawkins, U., Keltie, E. and Pihl, K. (2014) *Children's Rights in the Digital Age: A Download from Children around the World*. Melbourne/New York: Young and Well Cooperative Research Centre.

Thomas, N. (2007) 'Towards a Theory of Children's Participation', 15(2) *International Journal of Children's Rights* 199–218.

Thorp, A. (2011) *Parliament's New Statutory Role in Ratifying Treaties*. Library Standard Note SN/1A/5855, 8 February. London: House of Commons Library.

Tobin, J. (2019) (ed.) *The UN Convention on the Rights of the Child: A Commentary (Oxford Commentaries on International Law)*. Oxford: Oxford University Press.

Toki, K.R. (2010) 'What a Difference a "Drip" Makes: The Implications of Officially Endorsing the United Nations Declaration on the Rights of Indigenous Peoples', 16 *Auckland University Law Review* 243–71.

Toronto Star (2012) 'Teen's Sexting, Hacking Leads to Extortion and Porn Charges', 19 October. Cited in Sweeny, J. (2014) 'Sexting and Freedom of Expression: A Comparative Approach', 102(1) *Kentucky Law Journal* 103.

Trimmings, K. (2013) *Child Abduction within the European Union*, Oxford/Portland, OR: Hart Publishing.

Türkelli, G. and Vandenhole, W. (2012) 'The Convention on the Rights of the Child: Repetoires of NGO Participation', 12(1) *Human Rights Law Review* 33–64.

Türkelli, G., Vandenhole, W. and Vandenbogaerde, A. (2013) 'The NGO Impact on Law-Making: The Case of a Complaints Procedure under the ICESCR and the CRC', 5(1) *Journal of Human Rights Practice* 1–45.

Turow, J. and Nir, L. (2000). 'The Internet and the Family: The View of U.S. Parents', in Feilitzen, C.C (ed.) *Children in the New Media Landscape: Games, Pornography, Perceptions*. Göteborg, Sweden: Nordicom.

UK House of Commons (2016) *Radicalisation: The Counter-Narrative and Identifying the Tipping Point*. Eighth Report of Session 2016–17 House of Commons Home Affairs Committee.

UK Parliament (1942) Beveridge Report. Available at: <www.parliament.uk/about/livingheritage/transformingsociety/livinglearning/coll-9-health1/coll-9-health> (accessed 17 December 2019).

UNAIDS (2006) *International Guidelines on HIV/AIDS and Human Rights, Consolidated Version 2006*. Geneva: Office of the High Commissioner for Human Rights/Joint United Nations Programme on HIV/AIDS (UNAIDS). Available at: <http://data.unaids.org/Publications/IRC-pub07/jc1252-internguidelines_en.pdf> (accessed 1 December 2009).

UN Commission on Human Rights (1993) Programme of Action for the Elimination of the Exploitation of Child Labour, 10 March. E/CN.4/RES/1993/79.

UN Committee on the Rights of the Child (2011) *General Comment No. 13. The Right of the Child to Freedom from All Forms of Violence* (CRC/C/GC/13).

UN Committee on the Rights of the Child (2013) *General Comment No. 14. The Right of the Child to Have His or Her Best Interests Taken as a Primary Consideration* (art. 3, para. 1), 29 May (CRC/C/GC/14).

UNCRC Day of General Discussion (2014) 'Digital Media and Children's Rights'. Committee on the Rights of the Child Report. Available at: <www.ohchr.org/EN/HRBodies/CRC/Pages/Discussion2014.aspx> (accessed 17 December 2019). The resulting report is at: <www.ohchr.org/Documents/HRBodies/ CRC/Discussions/2014/DGD_report.pdf>.

UNESCO (2015) *Fixing the Broken Promise of Education for All: Findings from the Global Initiative on Out-of-School Children*. Montreal: UNESCO Institute for Statistics and UNICEF.

Unger, J. (1965) 'Hague Conference on Private International Law: Draft Convention on Adoptions', 28(4) *Modern Law Review* 463–65.

UNICEF (1997) *State of the World's Children 1997*. New York/Oxford: Oxford University Press/United Nations Children's Fund.

UNICEF (2009) *Handbook on the Optional Protocol on the Sale of Children, Child Prostitution and Child Pornography*. Innocenti Research Centre. Florence: UNICEF. Available at: <www.

unicef-irc.org/publications/pdf/optional_protocol_eng.pdf> (accessed 27 January 2010).

UNICEF (2010) *Core Commitments for Children in Humanitarian Action*. New York: United Nations Children's Fund. Available at: <www.unicef.org/publications/files/CCC_042010.pdf> (accessed 25 October 2019).

UNICEF (2012) *State of the World's Children 2012: Children in an Urban World*. New York: United Nations Children's Fund.

UNICEF (2013) *State of the World's Children 2012: Children with Disabilities*. New York: United Nations Children's Fund.

UNICEF (2017) *The State of the World's Children – Children in a Digital World*. New York: United Nations Children's Fund., December.

UNICEF (2018) *Lives in Limbo: No End in Sight to the Threats Facing Rohingya Children*. UNICEF Child Alert, February. Available at: <www.unicef.org/publications/files/UNICEF_Rohingya_Lives_in_Limbo_Feb_2018.pdf > (accessed 19 December 2019).

UNICEF (2019) *Progress for Every Child in the SDG Era: The Situation in 2019*. Available at: <https://data.unicef.org/resources/progress-for-every-child-in-the-sdg-era-2019> (accessed 20 December 2019).

UNICEF and Save the Children Foundation (2015) *Small Hands Heavy Burden: How the Syria Conflict is Driving More Children into the Workforce*, 2 July. Available at: <https://resourcecentre.savethechildren.net/node/9161/pdf/sciunicefchildlabourreport_july2015.pdf> (accessed 20 December 2019).

UNICEF India (2016) Child Online Protection in India, UNICEF India, New Delhi, 2016, p. 46.

UNICEF Sri Lanka (2015) *Keeping Children in Sri Lanka Safe and Empowered Online: A Study on Sri Lanka's Digital Landscape – Potential Risks to Children and Young People Who are Online*. Colombo, Sri Lanka: UNICEF.

United Nations (1996) *Report by Graça Machel on the Impact of Armed Conflict on Children*. A/51/306 (26 August).

United Nations (2012) 'Outcome Document of the United Nations Conference on Sustainable Development Rio de Janeiro', Brazil, 20–22 June.

United Nations Office on Drugs and Crime (2018) *Trafficking in Persons Report*. United Nations Publications, Sales No. E.19.IV.2, UNODC.

United Nations Special Rapporteur on the Sale of Children, Child Prostitution and Child Pornography (2016) *25 Years Fighting the Sale and Sexual Exploitation of Children: Addressing New Challenges*. Available at: <www.ohchr.org/Documents/Issues/Children/SR/25YearsMandate.pdf> (accessed 20 December 2019).

Unwanted in America: The Shameful Side of International Adoption (2014) Presented by Dan Rather. Available at: <https://vimeo.com/117858028> (accessed 19 December 2019).

Van Bueren, G. (1994a) 'Child Sexual Abuse and Exploitation: A Suggested Human Rights Approach', 2(1) *International Journal of Children's Rights* 45–59.

Van Bueren, G. (1994b) *The International Law on the Rights of the Child*. Dordrecht/Boston/London: Martinus Nijhoff Publishers.

Van Bueren, G. (1998) *The International Law on the Rights of the Child*. The Hague: Martinus Nijhoff/Kluwer Law International.

Van Der Bulck, J. and Van Den Bergh, B. (2000). 'Parental Guidance of Children's Media Use and Conflict in the Family', in Van Den Bergh, B. and Van Der Bulck, J. (eds) *Children and Media: Interdisciplinary Approaches*. Leuven-Apeldoorn: Garant.

Vandiver, D.M. and Walker, J.T. (2002) 'Female Sex Offenders: An Overview and Analysis of 40 Cases', 27(2) *Criminal Justice Review* 284–300.

Van Loon, H. (1995) 'Hague Convention of 29 May 1993 on Protection of Children and Co-operation in Respect of Intercountry Adoption', 3 *International Journal of Children's Rights* 463–8.

Van Loon, H. (2000) 'Globalisation and The Hague Conference on Private International Law', 2(4) *International Law FORUM Du Droit International* 230–34.

Van Loon, H (2011) 'Legal Diversity in a Flat, Crowded World: The Role of the Hague Conference', 39(2) *International Journal of Legal Information* 172–85.

Vesneski, W., Lindhorst, T. and Edleson, J. (2011) 'Judicial Implementation of the Hague Convention in Cases Alleging Domestic Violence', 62(2) *Juvenile and Family Court Journal* 1–21.

Vigers, S. (2011) *Mediating International Child Abduction Cases: The Hague Convention*. Oxford/Portland, OR: Hart Publishing.

Vivatvaraphol, T. (2009) 'Back to Basics: Determining a Child's Habitual Residence in International Child Abduction Cases under the Hague Convention', 77(6) *Fordham Law Review* 3325–69.

Vrancken, P. and Chetly, K. (2009) 'International Child Sex Tourism: A South African Perspective', 53 *Journal of African Law* 111–41.

Vygotsky, L. (1962) *Thought and Language*, ed. and trans. E. Hanfmann and G. Vakar. Cambridge, MA: MIT Press. Original Russian edn, 1934.

Vygotsky, L. (1978) *Mind in Society: The Development of Higher Psychological Processes*. Cambridge, MA: Harvard University Press.

Wakefield, J. (2019) 'Facebook Encryption Threatens Public Safety, Say Ministers'. BBC News website, 4 October. Available at: <www.bbc.co.uk/news/technology-49919464> (accessed 20 December 2019).

Walker, L. (2010) 'The Impact of the Hague Abduction Convention on the Rights of the Family in the Case-Law of the European Court of Human Rights and the UN Human Rights Committee: The Danger of Neulinger', 6(3) *Journal of Private International Law* 649–82.

Walker, L. and Beaumont, P. (2011) 'Shifting the Balance Achieved by the Abduction Convention: The Contrasting Approaches of the European Court of Human Rights and the European Court of Justice', 7(2) *Journal of Private International Law* 231–49.

Walker, K., Pillinger, C. and Brown, S. (2018) *Characteristics and Motivations of Perpetrators of Child Sexual Exploitation A Rapid Evidence Assessment of Research Centre of Expertise on Child Sexual Abuse*. Centre of Expertise on Child Sexual Abuse, Coventry University.

Ward, R. and Akhtar, A. (2011) *Walker and Walker's English Legal System*, 11th edn. Oxford: Oxford University Press.

Watkins, D. (2012) 'Intercountry Adoption and the Hague Convention: Article 22 and Limitations upon Safeguarding', 24(4) *Child and Family Law Quarterly* 389–409.

Webber, E. (2017) 'War Criminal Charles Taylor Phones Allies from Durham Prison'. BBC News website, 10 February. Available at: <www.bbc.co.uk/news/uk-38932510> (accessed 14 December 2019).

Weiner, M. (1994) 'Child Labour in Developing Countries: The Indian Case. Articles 18a, 32 and 36 of the UN Convention on the Rights of the Child', 2(2) *International Journal of Child Rights* 121–8.

Weiner, M.H. (2000) 'International Child Abduction and the Escape from Domestic Violence', 69(2) *Fordham Law Review* 593–706.

Weiss, T.G. and Daws, S. (eds) (2007) *The Oxford Handbook on the United Nations*. Oxford: Oxford University Press.

Weiss, T.G., Forsythe, D.P., Coate, R.A. and Pease, K.K. (2016) *The United Nations and Changing World Politics*. Boulder, CO: Westview Press.

Weitzer, R. (2014) 'New Directions in Research on Human Trafficking', 653(1) *The ANNALS of the American Academy of Political and Social Science* 6–24. doi: 10.1177/0002716214521562.

Wellman, C. (1999) *The Proliferation of Rights: Moral Progress or Empty Rhetoric?* Boulder, CO: Westview Press.

Westlake, B., Bouchard, M. and Frank, R. (2012) 'Comparing Methods for Detecting Child Exploitation Content Online'. European Intelligence and Security Informatics Conference, pp. 156–63.

Wilde, R. (2007) 'Trusteeship Council', in Weiss, T.G. and Daws, S. (eds) *The Oxford Handbook on the United Nations*. Oxford: Oxford University Press, pp. 149–59.

Willett, R. (2008) 'Consumer Citizens Online: Structure, Agency, and Gender in Online Participation', in Buckingham, D. (ed.) *Youth, Identity, and Digital Media*. Cambridge: MIT Press, pp. 49–69.

Wilson, J. and McAloney, K. (2010) 'Upholding the Convention on the Rights of the Child: A Quandary in Cyberspace', 16(2) *Childcare in Practice* 167–80.

Woldehanna, T. and Gebremedhin, A. (2015) 'Is Child Work Detrimental to the Educational Achievements of Children?' Oxford: Young Lives.

Wyness, M.G. (2012) *Childhood and Society*, 2nd edn. Basingstoke: Palgrave Macmillan.

Yupsanis, A. (2012) 'ILO Convention No. 169 Concerning Indigenous and Tribal Peoples in Independent Countries 1989–2009: An Overview', 79 *Nordic Journal of International Law* 433–56.

Yusuf, H. and Swann, S. (2019) 'Shamima Begum: Lawyer Says Teen was "Groomed"'. BBC News website, 31 May. Available at: <www.bbc.co.uk/news/uk-48444604> (accessed 13 December 2019).

Zhou, M. (2017) *Pakistan's Hidden Workers Wages and Conditions of Home-Based Workers and the Informal Economy*. Geneva: International Labour Organization.

Index

Note: Page numbers followed by n denote footnotes.

abduction 214, 433; by parents *see* abduction, international parental child; exploitation of children 223–4, 339–40, 451; inter-country adoption: safeguards to protect children from 407–9, 414

abduction, international parental child 335–86; best interests of child 339, 341, 369–70, 382, 386; Brexit 344; case studies 354–6, 358–61, 370–1, 378–80, 381–2; Convention on the Rights of the Child 339–40, 380, 386; European Convention 1980 340–1; habitual residence 346–7, 349, 352–61, 383, 386; Hague Convention on the Civil Aspects of International Child Abduction 1980 *see separate entry*; mediation 315, 383–5; non-convention countries 380–3, 386; Revised Brussels II Regulation 2003 341–4, 372, 374, 383, 384; statistics 337–8, 344, 368

abortion 146–7, 199

abuse 24, 215, 218, 235, 259, 266, 387, 388, 420; alternative care 174; and exploitation 429–30; homicide by 424–5; social policy 16; *see also* exploitation; torture or other punishment

activism, social 265

administrative proceedings: child's right to be heard 150, 152–4

adolescence 174, 181, 207, 264–5, 450, 460, 514; health 197–200, 201, 202

adoption 42, 89, 171–2, 177–9, 395–6; anonymity 161; best interests of child 140, 172, 177–8, 179, 387, 393, 396, 403–6, 414, 417, 420, 421–4, 427, 428; intercountry *see separate entry*; paramount consideration 172, 177–8, 396, 403, 424

Afghanistan 73, 389

Africa 273, 288, 289, 292, 293, 314, 330, 512, 539; African Charter on the Rights and Welfare of the Child 38, 267, 422, 423, 440, 472, 482–3, 506, 518; intercountry adoption 390–3, 421, 422, 423, 428; Internet 238; sub-Saharan 194, 289; *see also individual countries*

agriculture 276, 280, 283, 286, 289, 290, 308, 315, 322, 330–4

AIDS/HIV 131, 140, 148, 173, 201–2, 241, 434, 501

air pollution 196

Albania 150, 170

alcohol 222, 530, 531

Algeria 89, 242

alternative care *see* family environment and alternative care (CRC)

Andorra 393

apprenticeships 300

arbitration 51, 152, 186

Archard, D. 3–4, 6, 23, 24, 30

Argentina 89, 116, 134, 161, 264–5

Ariès, P. 2, 3, 5, 6

armed conflict and children 471–520, 530; Additional Protocols (1977) to Geneva Conventions 1949 479–81; age limits 475–6, 479, 480, 481, 482–3, 486–7, 503, 507, 508, 509, 513; child labour 292–3, 307, 308, 485; child soldiers: victims or perpetrators 512–20; CRC: art 38 89, 109, 111, 230–2, 308, 482–3, 485, 487; CRC: art 39 188, 230, 231, 232, 483–5; CRC: OPAC 93, 102–3, 104, 106–7, 109–11, 140, 188, 271, 485–93, 518; CRC: right to life 148–9; CRC: standard of living 204;

Declaration 1974 478–9; G8 436; health and access to health services 195; ILO Worst Forms of Child Labour Convention 1999 278; intercountry adoption 388–9; international criminal law *see separate entry*; international humanitarian law 473–81, 482, 483, 504, 507; internment 476–7, 485; Machel Report (1996) 471, 485, 486, 499–500, 512; non-international conflicts 477, 480; Paris Principles 498–9, 518; reasons for child soldiers 473; Security Council resolutions 493–8, 503, 504; sexual exploitation and abuse 186–7, 436; sexual violence: war crime 436; Special Representative of Secretary-General 499–502; statistics 499–500, 501, 504, 505, 509, 519; UNICEF 66
asbestos 149
Asia 303, 408, 522, 539; and the Pacific 238, 288–9; South Asian Association for Regional Co-operation (SAARC) 440; *see also individual countries*
assisted reproduction 161, 420
association, freedom of 36, 155, 162–3, 166–7, 318; digital age 267
asylum-seeking and refugee children 136, 138, 210, 211–16, 224; birth registration 159, 162; child labour 213, 214, 293; expression, freedom of 163; intercountry adoption 401–2
Australia 123, 127, 535; abduction, international parental child 375, 377; Aboriginal and Torres Strait Islander children 126, 136, 138, 218, 375; armed forces: minimum age 110, 163; birth registration 161; climate change 196; disabilities, children with 192; expression, freedom of 163; homelessness 203; information, access to 169, 170; intercountry adoption 387, 388; internet governance 259, 260; life, survival and development, right to 150; migrant children 214, 215, 387, 388; non-discrimination 136, 137, 139; sexting 252; victims, child 230
Austria 367, 395
authoritarian approach 15, 242, 243, 248, 258, 259, 263, 414
autonomy 9, 13, 14, 25–31, 34, 237, 265–6, 372

available resources 121, 124–7, 193
awareness raising 103, 128, 137, 138, 139, 153, 167, 179, 490; climate change 196; corporal punishment 183, 184, 185; disabilities 192; HIV/AIDS 202; ILO 317; indigenous peoples 530; nutrition 195; prevention of traffic accidents 149; sexual exploitation 186; substance abuse 199; vaccines 195
Azerbaijan 170

Bahrain 136, 139, 149; assembly, freedom of 167; corporal punishment 184–5; education 206, 208; mortality, child 194; nationality, right to 160; obesity 195; sexual exploitation 187; violence against children 181
Bangladesh 239, 282, 283, 290, 293, 327–8
Beck, U. 245–6, 247
bedroom culture 246–7
begging 204, 219, 291; forced child- 219, 224
behaviourist understanding of childhood 10
Beijing Rules 132, 226
Belgium 116, 122, 126–7, 128; air pollution 196; birth registration 161; disabilities, children with 192; education 207; life, survival and development, right to 150; migrant children 215; non-discrimination 136, 138, 139; sexual abuse 186; standard of living 203 4; thought, conscience and religion, freedom of 165, 166
best interests of child 28–9, 140, 180, 224, 285; abduction, international parental child 339, 341, 369–70, 382, 386; adoption 140, 172, 177–8, 179, 387, 393, 396, 403–6, 414, 417, 420, 421–4, 427, 428; CRC: art 3 20, 29, 30, 117, 140–6, 172, 393, 483; CRC: art 21 172, 177–8, 179, 396; CRC: OPAC 140; CRC: OPIC 112, 140; CRC: OPSC 108, 140; digital age 263; digital space 271, 273; family environment and alternative care (CRC) 170, 171, 172, 173, 175, 176, 177–8, 179; indigenous children 530, 531–2; inter-country adoption 140, 177, 387; migrant children 214, 215
bilateral trade agreements 328
biological parents, child's right to know 160–1

birth registration 302, 307, 492; fees 160; identity rights and 156–62, 214, 530; indigenous children 159, 530; information to include 159
blogs 264
Boko Haram 497
Bolivia 420
Bosnia and Herzegovina 129, 503, 504; adoption 179; birth registration 159; disabilities, children with 192; family environment and alternative care 176, 179; forced child-begging 219; health 195; migrant children 215; non-discrimination 137; sale and trafficking of children 224; standard of living 203
Botswana 128, 130; best interests of child 145; birth registration 159; disabilities, children with 192; expression, freedom of 163–4; health 195, 202; heard, child's right to be 154; non-discrimination 137, 139
boycotts 327–8, 329
Brazil 242, 264, 265, 280, 431
breastfeeding 197
Brexit 344
Bulgaria 242
bullying 149, 200, 207, 259; cyber- 207, 235, 248–9, 250–1, 259, 260, 261
Burma 293, 322
business sector 129; child labour 275, 290, 293, 325, 326, 327, 328–34; codes of ethics/corporate conduct 325, 326, 443, 444; corporate social responsibility 328–34; digital age 261–2, 272; sexual exploitation 442–9; UN Guiding Principles on Business and Human Rights 327

Cabo Verde 126, 128; birth registration 159; breastfeeding 197; climate change 196; corporal punishment 184; disabilities, children with 192; education 207; family environment and alternative care 176; heard, child's right to be 153; information, access to 169–70; mortality, child 194; non-discrimination 135, 137; privacy 168; street situations, children in 219–20; teenage pregnancies 199, 207
Cambodia 428, 443, 448
Canada 252, 435, 535; abduction, international parental child 345, 373; armed conflicts and children 231–2; armed forces: minimum age 110; indigenous children 218; intercountry adoption 387, 393; internet governance 260; mature minor doctrine 28; medical treatment and best interests of child 28–9; sexting 252
Central African Republic 73, 511, 515
Chad 428
child labour 275–334; agriculture 276, 280, 283, 286, 289, 290, 308, 315, 322, 330–4; apprenticeships 300; armed conflict and 292–3, 307, 308; birth registration 157, 302, 307; boycotts 327–8, 329; case study 331–3; causes of 280–1, 283–4; Convention on the Rights of the Child 220–2; covert nature of 293–4; cultural relativism, TWAIL and 284–6, 312, 324–5; definition difficulties 276–80; developed countries 275, 284, 289–90, 295, 303, 327, 328, 329, 330–4; economic benefits of elimination of 295–6; education and 275, 277, 280, 281–4, 286, 295, 298, 299, 303, 311, 312, 326; 'employment' and 'work' 298, 308; enforceability problem 324–5; extent and location of exploitative 286–91; hazardous work 130, 222, 275, 277, 278–9, 280, 281, 282, 287, 288, 292–3, 297, 302, 308–9, 310, 334, 537; ICESCR 22, 315; ILO Domestic Workers Convention 2011 313; ILO Minimum Age Convention 1973 296, 297–304, 305, 306, 308–9, 313, 315, 321, 323, 326; ILO reporting, representation and complaints procedures 319–23; ILO Worst Forms of Child Labour Convention 1999 278, 280, 296, 303–4, 305–13, 315, 323, 326, 451–2, 460, 485; ILO's wider role 316–19; indigenous children 530, 531, 537; informal economy 276, 278, 290, 293–4, 295, 309, 328; intermittent 280, 294; international legal protection of 296–323; labelling 329; light work 222, 276, 278, 279, 300–1, 321; mainstreaming child labour 306; measuring extent of 294–6; mining 280, 289, 299, 315–16; nineteenth century 18; other international instruments 22, 313–16; partnership and coordination 325–6; poverty and 281–4, 306, 311–12, 315, 317, 334; progressing

elimination of exploitative 323–34; refugees 213, 214, 293; rehabilitation and reintegration 283, 306, 311, 328; role of law 324; sale and trafficking of children 224, 278, 307, 331–3; trade–labour linkage 304–5, 326–8; 'work' and 'employment' 298, 308
child liberationists 33–4
Child Rights Connect 99–100, 112, 114–15
childhood 1, 39, 264, 275, 324–5, 512; bedroom culture 246–7; boundaries, dimensions and divisions 3–4; cocooning 244; cultural relativism 6, 36–8, 285, 286; historical perspective 2–6, 26; individualisation 245–6, 247; Internet 235, 237, 242–6, 247; psychological perspectives 4, 6–9; resilience and risk 263; risk aversion 34; risk and harm 263–4; social policy perspectives 14–17, 243, 246, 248, 258, 259, 263; sociological perspective 9–14, 16, 26, 237, 266
Children's Commissioners 127, 273
children's rights 1, 9, 14, 16, 21–3, 39, 47, 64, 92, 386; autonomy 9, 13, 14, 25–31, 34, 265–6, 372; basic interests 25–6, 265–6; cultural relativism 36–8, 285; developmental interests 25–6, 265–6; historical development of human rights 18–20; human rights and 20–1, 34, 35; international 35–6; movement 33–4, 90; participation 21, 30, 31–3; paternalism 21, 26, 30–1; theories of 23–6, 265–6
Chile 116, 420
China 57, 72, 242, 389, 393, 394, 420, 428; armed conflict and children 489–93; definition of child 130; education 284; 'one child' policy 146
chocolate 330–4
choice or will theory of rights 23–4, 26, 265–6
climate change 196, 522–3
Clinton, Bill 91
Colombia 73
Committee against Torture 527
Committee on Economic, Social and Cultural Rights 525–6
Committee on the Elimination Discrimination against Women 131, 165
Committee on the Elimination of Racial Discrimination 526–7

Committee on the Rights of the Child 20, 38, 61, 93–7, 316, 400; Concluding Observations 17, 36, 101, 105, 106, 121–3, 126, 127; delays 103–5, 470; digital environment 236–7, 272–3; exhaustion of domestic remedies 114; expeditiousness, principle of 112; General Comments 32, 94–6, 236, 272; initial reports 83, 97–8, 100, 102, 104, 120; justiciable rights 121; List of Issues Prior to Reporting (LOIPR) 105, 120–1; proposal for OPSC 109; Recommendations/Decisions 96, 103–5; reporting process: CRC *see separate entry*; reservations 46, 122, 123–4; simplified reporting procedure 104–5, 120–1; statistics 127
Committee on the Rights of Persons with Disabilities 190
companies *see* business sector
compensation 108
complaints procedures (ILO) 321–2
complaints/communications procedures (CRC) 36, 84–5, 103, 105–7, 111–20; best interests of child 112, 140; confidentiality 115; digital age 271; individual communications 112, 113–18; inquiry procedure 112, 118–19; inter-state communications 112, 119–20; time limits 115
conflict of laws *see* private international law
Congo, Democratic Republic of 73, 473, 497, 509, 511
constructivist model 9, 10–13
Convention on the Rights of the Child 5, 20–1, 22, 23, 33, 35–6, 39, 42, 49, 65–6, 86–232, 267–8, 386, 399, 422, 423, 428, 506; abduction (art 35) 223–4, 339–40, 451; abduction by parent (arts 9–11) 339–40, 380; adoption (art 21) 89, 171–2, 177–9, 395–6, 403, 421, 424; armed conflict, participation in (art 38) 89, 109, 111, 230–2, 308, 482–3; association, freedom of (art 15) 36, 155, 162–3, 166–7; background 44, 64, 88–90; best interests principle (art 3) 20, 29, 30, 117, 140–6, 172, 273, 393, 483; birth registration and identity rights (arts 7 and 8) 156–62, 214; civil rights and freedoms (art 7, 8, 13–17, 28(2) and 37(a)) 155–70; criminal responsibility, age of (art 40(3)(a)) 131–3, 226, 227,

228; cultural differences 6, 37, 38, 89, 141; death penalty 92, 150, 211; declarations 38, 46, 110, 122, 123, 133, 146–7, 165; definition of child (art 1) 1, 6, 89, 92, 129–34, 404, 451; digital era 236–7, 267–73; disability (art 23) 189–93; drafting controversies 89, 92, 129, 164, 231, 308; drugs (art 33) 189–90, 199, 222–3; economic exploitation (art 32) 220–2, 304–5; education, right to (arts 28 and 29) 204, 205–8, 282, 528–9; exploitation situations (arts 32–36) 49, 220–5; express views and participate in decisions (art 12) 30–3, 150–5, 213; expression, freedom of (art 13) 36, 151, 155, 162–4, 167; family environment and alternative care 17, 170–9, 214; general measures of implementation (arts 4, 42 and 44(6)) 121–9; general principles (articles 2, 3, 6 and 12) 134–55; Hague Conventions and 71; health and access to health services (art 24) 35, 36, 189–90, 193–202; heard, child's right to be (art 12) 30, 150, 152–5, 273; history 88–90; implementation 120–232; indigenous children (art 17(d), 29(1)(c) & (d) and 30) 216–18, 521, 527–9, 531; information, access to (art 17) 162–3, 169–70, 270; interconnected provisions 205; international customary law and 93; *jus cogens* 51; juvenile justice 92, 131–3, 143, 144, 145, 150, 154, 182, 184, 211, 225–9, 513; leisure and cultural activities (art 31) 204, 208–10; life, survival and development (art 6) 35, 38, 92, 146–50, 273; minority or indigenous group (art 30) 216–18, 527–8; non-discrimination principle (art 2) 134–40, 218, 273, 531; parental responsibilities, rights and duties (arts 5 and 14) 29, 163, 170–1; parents, contact with both (art 9) 171, 338, 339; parents and living conditions (art 27(2)) 202; participation rights (art 12) 21, 30–3, 92, 150–5, 268, 273, 342; preparatory works 44; privacy (art 16) 155, 162–3, 167–9; ratification 6, 23, 35, 43, 54, 86, 90–3; recovery and reintegration of child victims (art 39) 188, 230, 231, 232, 311, 483–5; refugee children (art 22) 210, 211–16; reporting process 83, 97–106, 120–1, 305, 469–70; reservations 38, 46, 91, 122, 123–4, 133, 146, 161, 162, 165, 218, 396, 483; sale or trafficking of children (art 35) 223–4, 339–40, 450–1; sexual exploitation and abuse (art 34) 185–7, 271, 429, 449–50, 453, 460; social exploitation (art 36) 224–5; social security (art 26) 36; special protection measures 210–32; standard of living (art 27) 35, 36, 189–90, 202–4; street children 218–20; thought, conscience and religion, freedom of (art 14) 36, 89, 162–3, 164–6; torture or other punishment (art 37(a)) 181–5, 229; understandings 46, 91; United Kingdom 54, 123, 133; United States not ratifying 43, 86, 90, 91–3; victims as criminals 460–1; violence against children (arts 19, 37(a), 34 and 39) 117, 179–88, 214, 248, 271

Convention on the Rights of the Child – Optional Protocols: armed conflict and children (OPAC) 93, 102–3, 104, 106–7, 109–11, 140, 188, 231, 271, 485–93, 518; communication procedure (OPIC) 36, 84, 103, 105–6, 111–20, 140, 188, 271; reporting regime 101–3, 104, 105–7, 108, 111, 188; sale of children, child prostitution and child pornography (OPSC) 93, 101–3, 104, 106–9, 140, 180, 188, 223, 224, 271, 336, 437, 447, 448, 449, 452–4, 456–61, 464, 465–70

corporal punishment 181, 182–5
corporate social responsibility 328–34
corporations *see* business sector
corruption 125, 265, 407, 408, 409, 428, 446
Corsaro, W.A. 9, 10, 11–13
Costa Rica 116
Côte d'Ivoire 73, 330–4, 512
Council of Europe 14, 159–60, 440–1, 453; Child Participation Assessment Tool 154
crimes against humanity 72, 149, 471, 486, 494, 502–4, 506, 511, 516–20
criminal law/justice system 211, 224, 225–9; abduction, international parental child 335–6; age of criminal responsibility 131–3, 226, 227, 228, 513; armed conflict and children 479, 513; armed groups: minimum age 111; assembly, freedom of 167; begging 291; best interests principle 143, 144,

145; birth registration 157; child labour 310–11, 452; cyber harassment 251, 260; death penalty 92, 150, 181, 211, 480, 508; disorderly conduct 251; double jeopardy 464–5; dual criminality 447, 465; encryption 261–2; extradition 42, 108, 109, 448, 465–6, 467; heard, child's right to be 154; homicide by abuse 424–5; ill treatment or torture 182, 184, 229; indigenous children 530; life imprisonment 211, 229; manslaughter 424–5; non-custodial sentences 228; pornography, child 251, 252, 431, 456, 459–60; rape 136; restorative approach 211, 226, 513; revenge porn 252; sexting 252; sexual assault 251; sexual exploitation and abuse 185–7, 251–2, 446–8, 449, 450, 453, 454, 456–64, 470; street children 218–19; tourism, sex 446–8, 449, 458; trafficking 437, 450; victims as criminals 460–1; *see also* international criminal law

cryptocurrency 431

cultural activities and leisure 204, 208–10

cultural cleansing rites 515

cultural relativism 6, 36–8, 506–7; child labour 284–6, 312, 324–5

Cunningham, H. 5, 34, 244

customary international law 42, 43, 46–9, 57, 331, 482, 535, 536; beginning of childhood 133; child soldiers 506, 507; CRC 93; Geneva Conventions 473; hierarchy of sources of international law 51; incorporation doctrine 53; *opinio juris* 46, 48; State practice 46, 47–8; UDHR 19, 74; UN Declaration on the Rights of Indigenous Peoples 2007 535–6

customary law: domestic 47, 123, 130, 150, 179; indigenous peoples 534; international *see* customary international law

cyber-bullying 207, 235, 248–9, 250–1, 259, 260, 261

databases 158, 337; adoption 179; International Child Abduction (INCADAT) 348, 353; personal data 169

De Mause, L. 3, 5

death penalty 92, 150, 181, 211, 480; ICC 508

debt bondage 278, 307, 308, 314

decentralisation 124

Declaration on the Rights of the Child 1959 22, 64, 88, 134, 140, 156, 208, 314

Declaration on the Rights of Indigenous Peoples (2007) 52, 217, 521, 535–8

definitions: child 1, 6, 89, 92, 129–34, 307, 404, 451; child labour 276–80; child pornography 459; children in street situations 219; forced labour 291; human trafficking 454–5; prostitution 450, 453, 458; worst forms of child labour 307–8, 451

democracy 267

Denmark 116, 117–18, 341, 344, 372

Dennis, M.J. 308, 311, 312

detention 180, 181, 211, 213, 214, 215, 228, 228–9, 237, 480; Guantanamo 231–2

deterministic model 9–10

Detrick, S. 37, 44, 86, 88, 121, 133, 135, 141, 155, 161, 163, 169, 209, 216, 217, 223, 304, 339–40, 395, 396, 397

devolution 124

digital age 169, 174, 198, 233–74; Convention on the Rights of the Child 236–7, 268–71; cyber-bullying 207, 235, 248–9, 250–1, 259, 260, 261; individualisation 245–6, 247; Internet *see separate entry*; natives and immigrants 245; risk society 246, 247–8, 263; typology of ICT-related harms 249, 250

disability/ies 189–93, 248; alternative care 174, 176; discrimination 138–40, 191–2; education 207; expression, freedom of 163; leisure and cultural activities 210

disappearance, enforced 161, 543, 545

discrimination *see* non-discrimination

disinformation, online (fake news) 261

domestic courts 51, 53, 54, 65; United States 92, 93

domestic and international law, relationship between 48, 49, 50, 52–5, 92, 122–3

domestic violence 368, 372

double jeopardy 464–5

drugs 189–90, 199, 220, 222–3, 261, 530, 531; trafficking 218, 222, 278, 308, 545

dual criminality 447, 465

due diligence 129

due process 213, 227, 375

eating disorders 199–200, 249; websites: pro- 235, 251

economic exploitation 22, 214, 220–2, 304–5, 537; child labour *see separate entry*; CRC: Optional Protocol 107–9; international customary law 49; *jus cogens* 51; life, survival and development, right to 147–8
Ecuador 420, 524
education 2, 6, 16; armed conflict 475, 476, 480; child labour and 275, 277, 280, 281–4, 286, 295, 298, 299, 303, 311, 312, 326; for citizenship 128; corporal punishment 182, 183; disabilities 191, 192; discrimination 139–40, 206, 207; early childhood 206, 209; indigenous children 523–4, 528–9, 531, 534, 537, 544; military training 492; peace 493; Piaget's theory and 8; privacy 167; religious signs and symbols 165–6; right to 20, 22, 143, 204, 205–8, 214, 267, 270, 282, 528, 529, 537; sex 199, 531; STEM subjects 241; Sustainable Development Goal 4 17
Eekelaar, J. 25–6, 265–6
Egypt 242, 264, 383
El Salvador 420
employment, children in 278; child labour *see separate entry*
enforced disappearance 161, 543, 545
environment: air pollution 196; climate change 196, 522–3; heard, child's right to be 154
equality 536; access to Internet and social media 209–10; before the law 218; gender 17, 240; parental responsibilities 176; of spouses during marriage 22; structural impediments to 203; *see also* inequality; non-discrimination
equity 49–50
Erikson, E. 6, 8
Ethiopia 282, 286, 387, 393, 420
ethnicity 473
ethnocentrism 37, 47, 275, 285, 286, 296, 298
European Court of Human Rights (ECtHR) 340, 350, 368–70
European Union 14–15, 70, 419–20; abduction, international parental child 341–4, 350; Better Internet for Children (BIK) 260; child labour 328; Europol 442, 467; General Data Protection Regulation (GDPR) 260–1; Revised Brussels II Regulation 2003 341–4, 372, 374, 383, 384; sexual exploitation 440, 441–2
euthanasia 150
evolving capacities of children 135, 153, 163, 170–1, 174
exploitation 210–11, 214, 220–5, 243, 276–7; and abuse 429–30; economic *see separate entry*; forced child-begging 219; intercountry adoption 388; international customary law 49; sale and trafficking of children *see separate entry*; sexual *see separate entry*; social 22, 224–5; Sustainable Development Goal 5 17
expression, freedom of 36, 151, 155, 162–4, 167; Internet 164, 234–5, 263, 266–7
extradition 42, 108, 109, 448, 465–6, 467
extraterritoriality 441, 447–8, 464–5

Facebook 249, 251, 261–2, 264
fake news (online disinformation) 261
family environment and alternative care (CRC) 17, 170–9, 203, 214, 406–7, 530; guidelines for alternative care 173, 175; individualization 172–3; judicial review 175–6; *see also* adoption
family–State relationship 15–17, 34, 35, 38, 170–6, 202–3, 246, 248
federalism 91–2, 122–3
female genital mutilation (FGM) 117, 138, 439, 528
finance industry 444–5
Finland 116
foetus 92, 133, 134
food 204, 284, 476, 479; malnutrition 90, 147, 149, 194–5, 424–5, 501, 531, 545; SDG Indicator 2.1 194
Food and Agriculture Organization (FAO) 325
forced labour 69, 224, 278–9, 291, 307, 310–11, 313, 318, 322, 331–3, 432, 433, 439; definition 291
Fortin, J. 23, 25, 26, 31, 33, 35
France 18, 57, 116, 123, 252, 393, 435; armed forces: minimum age 110; corporal punishment 183; life, survival and development, right to 147; minority and indigenous groups 218; thought, conscience and religion, freedom of 165–6
Freud, S. 6, 8
functionalist approach 10

G7/G8 435–6, 439
gender 107, 244; abduction, international parental child 336–7, 344; armed conflict and children 498–9, 501; child labour 277, 282, 290, 294, 314, 329; digital divide 240–2; discrimination 66, 136, 137–8, 139, 206; education 206, 241; equality 17, 240; forced labour 291; forced marriage 291, 292; heard, child's right to be 155; indigenous peoples 546; Islamic State (IS) 256; life, survival and development, right to 147–9; mercury and small-scale mining 316; online harms 248; rape 136; school dress 165–6; sexual exploitation 430–1, 433–4, 464; sexual slavery by non-state armed groups of Yazidi girls 148; Sustainable Development Goal 5 17, 240
generational order 13
genocide 51, 72, 494, 503–5
Georgia 73, 116
Germany 116, 208–9, 431, 435, 439; abduction, international parental child 337; armed forces: minimum age 110; definition of child 130
Ghana 282
globalisation 71, 87, 174, 275, 305, 318, 338, 397
good faith 43, 49–50, 90, 318
grooming 185, 252, 253, 442, 454, 460, 462
guardianship 50, 63–4, 214, 215, 216
Guatemala 393, 415, 420, 428
Guinea 73
Guinea-Bissau 138

Hague Conference on Private International Law 40, 64, 70–1, 346, 385, 396–7, 400; International Centre for Judicial Studies and Technical Assistance 414–19; Special Commissions 70–1, 386, 395, 396–8, 400, 401, 408–9, 416
Hague Convention on the Civil Aspects of International Child Abduction 1980 44, 335, 336, 337, 339, 340, 341, 344–80, 386, 395, 421; acquiescence 367; age limit 345; article 15 declarations 351–2; article 20 refusal 375–6, 377, 386; consent exception 367; custody, rights of 349–51; discretion, exercising 376–80; duty to make return order 361–76; exceptions from duty to make return order 363–76, 377, 386; exercising discretion 376–80; explanatory report 346; failure to exercise custody rights 365–6; grave risk of harm/intolerable situation 368–72, 380; habitual residence 346–7, 349, 352–61, 386; mediation 383, 384–5; objections of child 372–4; reservations 45–6; settlement exception 363–4, 374, 377, 386; structure of 347; time limits 345–6, 347, 361–2; wrongful removal or retention 348–61
Haiti 389, 428
Harding, F. 15
Hart, R.A. 32
hate speech 249
health and access to health services 16, 35, 36, 149, 189–90, 193–202, 544; adolescents 197–200, 201, 202; right to health 22, 35, 143, 214, 531; SDG Indicator 3.8 194
historical perspective on childhood 2–6, 26
HIV/AIDS 131, 140, 148, 173, 201–2, 241, 434, 501
Holy See 165
homelessness 203–4
Honduras 73, 242, 420
honour: -based crimes 187; killings 150
housing 203–4, 525–6
human dignity 47, 180, 317
human rights 1, 6, 47, 323, 324, 375–6; children's rights and 20–1, 34, 35; education on 207–8; evolution of enforcement 325; historical development of 18–20; mainstreaming 75; UN Guiding Principles on Business and 327; UN system for protection of 61, 74–85, 91
humidifier disinfectants 149

identity rights and birth registration 156–62, 214, 530
illegitimacy 135, 136, 157, 162
immunisation 195, 531
impact assessments, child/child-rights 124, 143, 145–6
India 72, 240, 241, 264, 380, 421, 428; armed forces: minimum age 110; child labour 283, 284, 297, 328
indigenous children 52, 126, 128, 136, 138, 211, 375, 521–48; best interests of child 530, 531–2; birth registration 159, 530; collective rights 523, 527, 531–2,

533, 534, 537, 547; CRC: art 17(d) 528; CRC: art 29(1)(c) & (d) 528–9; CRC: art 30 216–18, 527–8; discrimination 523, 526–7, 530, 531, 534, 535, 536, 537, 544; education 523–4, 528–9, 531, 534, 537, 544; expression, freedom of 163; ICCPR 524–5; ICESCR 525–6, 537; ILO Indigenous and Tribal Peoples Convention 1989 521, 528, 532–5, 547; key criteria in identifying indigenous peoples 521–2, 533; UDHR 524; UN Declaration 2007 521, 535–8, 540, 547; UN human rights treaties 524–32; UN mechanisms 538–47, 548
individualisation 245–6, 247
Indonesia 264
industry *see* business sector
inequality 10, 13, 16, 196, 281, 284; *see also* equality; non-discrimination
information, access to 162–3, 169–70, 270
inheritance rights 137
Instagram 251, 264
intercountry adoption 44, 172, 177, 179, 387–428; accreditation 409, 412, 413, 418; automatic recognition of adoption decisions 410–12; best interests of child 140, 177, 387, 393, 396, 403–6, 414, 417, 420, 421–4, 427, 428; case studies 415–19, 426–7; competent authorities, central Authorities and accredited bodies 412–14, 417, 418; conflicting perceptions on 420–7; cooperation between States and within States 410; costs and expenses 396, 408–9, 418–19; decline in 419–20; disaster situations 389, 398, 400; Hague Convention 1965 42, 394–5; Hague Convention 1993 42, 44, 45, 140, 178, 179, 389, 396–8, 399–414, 415–19, 428; safeguards to protect children from abduction, sale and trafficking 407–9, 414; sending and receiving countries 393–4, 410, 421; special needs children 402, 405, 415, 418, 419; statistics 387, 389, 390–3, 419, 427; subsidiarity principle 177, 396, 404, 406–7, 416; UNICEF's position 399–400, 420–1
interest theory of rights 24–5, 26, 265
interim measures 114, 115, 368
International Committee of the Red Cross (ICRC) 400, 475–6, 480

International Confederation of Free Trade Unions (ICFTU) 327
International Court of Justice (ICJ) 41, 48–9, 50, 56, 59, 62–5, 322; Advisory Opinions 62, 64–5; consent 62; procedure 62
International Criminal Court (ICC) 72–4, 109–10, 486, 503, 508–12; age limit 514; global norms 511; *Lubanga* case 74, 508–11, 512, 520; *Ongwen* case 509, 515–20; reparations 508; SCSL judgments and 509–10
international criminal law 502–5; expressivism 511; International Criminal Court (ICC) *see separate entry*; Special Court for Sierra Leone (SCSL) 505–8, 509–10, 513–14
International Criminal Tribunal for the former Yugoslavia (ICTY) 503–4
International Criminal Tribunal for Rwanda (ICTR) 504–5
International Labour Organization (ILO) 44, 60, 68–9, 276, 280–2, 290, 293, 295, 297, 329–30, 432; Constitution 286, 319, 321; Declaration 1998 305, 306–7, 318, 320, 326; definitions 278–80; Domestic Workers Convention 2011 313; extent and location of exploitative child labour 286–90; fundamental principles of 317; Indigenous and Tribal Peoples Convention 1989 521, 528, 532–5, 547; Minimum Age Convention 1973 296, 297–304, 305, 306, 308–9, 313, 315, 321, 323, 326; modern slavery 291, 292; reporting, representation and complaints procedures 305, 319–23; statistical data requirement 295,; trade–labour linkage 328; tripartite structure 68, 316, 320, 328; wider role of 316–19; Worst Forms of Child Labour Convention 1999 278, 280, 296, 303–4, 305–13, 315, 323, 326, 451–2, 460, 485
international law 40; customary *see separate entry*; declarations 38, 45, 46; dualism 52–3, 54; general principles of law 49–50, 51; hierarchy of sources 51; judicial decisions and publicists' writings 50–1; *jus cogens* 35, 51, 146; monism 52, 53; preparatory works (*travaux préparatoires*) 44, 133, 396; private *see separate entry*; relationship between domestic and 48,

49, 50, 52–5, 92, 122–3; reservations 38, 45–6, 67, 123–4; signature of treaty 43, 89n6, 90; soft law 52, 67, 189–90, 226, 305, 317, 318, 326, 383, 385, 498, 535; sources of 41–52, 94; Third World Approaches to (TWAIL) 284–6, 523; treaties and conventions 41–6, 48, 51, 53, 54, 67, 92, 133, 272, 346
International Law Commission (ILC) 48, 66–8; codification 67, 68; progressive development 67, 68
international parental child abduction *see* abduction, international parental child
international relations 44–5, 47
International Telecommunication Union (ITU) 238, 240, 241
Internet 168, 169, 170, 233–4, 435, 470; chat rooms 450; child pornography 107, 251, 431, 434, 436, 441, 442, 443, 444–5, 459; Convention on the Rights of the Child 236–7, 267–73; cyber-bullying 207, 235, 248–9, 250–1, 259, 260, 261; Dark Net 255, 256, 431, 433; digital divide 238–42; encryption 261–2, 431; expression, freedom of 164, 234–5, 263, 266–7; gender gap 240–2; governance 259–62; grooming 185, 252, 253, 442, 454, 460; individualisation 245–6, 247; leisure and cultural activities 209–10; moral panic 236, 243–4, 262–4; overview 234–7; personal data 249–50; radicalisation 243, 249, 252–9, 261; rights-based (participation) approach 235–6, 237, 263, 265–8, 271; risk-based (protection) approach 235–6, 237, 248–65, 271; trends in usage 237–40; Virtual Global Taskforce (VGT) 467
Interpol 448, 467
Iraq 242, 264, 389, 497
Ireland 116, 349–50, 366, 376
Islamic dress 166
Islamic law 37, 89, 116, 164, 171, 178, 380, 395
Islamic State (IS) 253–8, 473, 497
Israel 126; armed forces: minimum age 110
Italy 337, 393, 435; definition of child 130; internet governance 260

Japan 122, 123, 208, 388, 435; abduction, international parental child 373–4; adoption 178–9; best interests of child 144–5, 179; child labour 297, 315; disabilities, children with 192; education 284; heard, child's right to be 154, 155; HIV/AIDS 202; institutional care 175–6; internet governance 259, 260; juvenile justice 228, 229; life, survival and development, right to 150; non-discrimination 135–6, 138, 139; sexual abuse 186
Jebb, Eglantyne 21
Jordan 293
judicial proceedings: child's right to be heard 150, 152–4; capacity of child 152
jus cogens 35, 51, 146

kafalah 116, 171
Kazakhstan 415–19, 420
Kenya 73, 265, 512
Khadr, Omar 231–2
Korea 73, 136, 138, 139; abuse of children 184; adoption 178; best interests of child 146; birth registration 158; child labour 304–5, 329; disabilities, children with 192; education 284; intercountry adoption 388–9, 393, 394, 420; internet governance 259, 260; juvenile justice 227; life, survival and development, right to 149–50; privacy 167; sexual exploitation 431; standard of living 203; voting age 166

labelling 329
labour: child *see separate entry*; –trade linkage 304–5, 326–8
laissez-faire model 15, 242, 243, 248
Latin America 408, 533; *see also individual countries*
League of Nations 21, 60, 68, 88, 430, 481
least developed countries 238
legal aid/assistance/representation 143, 184, 228, 508, 512–13, 543
legal positivism 35
legitimate interests of child 145
leisure and cultural activities 204, 208–10
Lesotho 294
LGBT: online sexual harassment 251
liberationists, child 33–4
Liberia 150, 428
liberty right 24
liberty, right to 213
Libya 73, 512
life, right to 133, 146, 196; survival and development 35, 38, 92, 146–50, 273, 532
Locke, John 18

Lubanga Dyilo, Thomas 74, 508–11, 512, 520
Luxembourg 146–7, 161

MacCormick, N. 24
mainstreaming 75, 306, 344
maintenance, recovery of 35, 171
Malawi 162, 387, 421–4
Maldives 165
Mali 511
Malta 122, 124; birth registration 159, 160; breastfeeding 197; definition of child 130; disabilities, children with 191, 192, 193; family environment and alternative care 176; migrant children 215–16, 224; non-discrimination 137, 138; sale and trafficking of children 224
marketising of childhood 249
marriage 130–1, 138, 148, 187, 528, 546; birth registration 157; forced 148, 186, 224, 291–2, 314, 439; rape: exemption from prosecution if marries victim 187
Maslow, A. 246
media 225, 530; best interests of child 145; code of conduct 137; information, access to 169–70; minority and indigenous languages 528; parental mediation theory 244; privacy 168
mediation 152, 315, 383–5
Mexico 337, 449, 540–6
Microsoft 442
migration 116–17, 136, 138, 210, 211–16, 433; age determination 216; best interests of child 144; birth registration 157–8, 159, 162; child labour 213, 214, 290, 293; double vulnerability 213; education 207; expression, freedom of 163; heard, child's right to be 154; indigenous peoples 545; intercountry adoption *see separate entry*; leisure and cultural activities 210; life, survival and development, right to 147–8; poverty 203; sale and trafficking of children 224
Millennium Development Goals (MDGs) 56, 90, 240
minimalist State intervention 34
minority groups 216–18, 522, 528; birth registration 159; child labour 290, 293; education 207; language translations 128; non-discrimination 138; poverty 203; Roma children 204, 207

mobile phones 167, 233, 241, 242, 245, 248, 251–2, 264; sexting 252, 261
moral panic 236, 243–4, 262–4
moral rearmament groups 92
moral relativism 36
moral rights 23, 24–5
mortality rates 2, 65, 66, 90, 146, 147, 149, 194, 196, 200, 531, 532, 545
Mozambique 136, 139; association, freedom of 167; birth registration 158; disabilities, children with 192; heard, child's right to be 153; HIV/AIDS 202; information, access to 169–70; juvenile justice 228; life, survival and development, right to 149; mortality, child 194; privacy 168; street situations, children in 220
mui tsai 314
Myanmar 293, 322

name, right to a 22, 157, 159, 160, 162, 214
Namibia 130
national courts 51, 53, 54, 65; United States 92, 93
national human rights institutions (NHRIs) 75, 84, 96, 100, 127–8, 273, 490, 538
nationality 22, 157, 159, 160, 161–2, 214
natural law 18
Nepal 415, 428, 523
Netherlands 165, 252
New Zealand 535; abduction, international parental child 349, 353–7; armed forces: minimum age 110; child labour 303; intercountry adoption 387; internet governance 259–60
Nigeria 73
non-discrimination 22, 66, 74, 124, 126, 131, 134–40, 191–2, 196; active approach 134–5; digital age 273; education 139–40, 206, 207; HIV/AIDS 201–2; ILO 318; indigenous children/peoples 523, 526–7, 530, 531, 534, 535, 536, 537, 544; leisure and cultural activities 210; minority and indigenous groups 218; *see also* equality; *see also* equality; inequality
non-governmental organisations (NGOs) 17, 23, 58, 75, 108, 125, 272, 414; armed conflict and children 111, 483, 484, 495, 513; child labour 294, 295, 312, 316, 317, 325, 329; Child Rights Connect 99–100, 112,

114–15; Committee on the Rights of the Child 96, 99–100, 127, 128; CRC: OPIC 112; CRC, drafting of 86, 89, 268; intercountry adoption 400; juvenile justice 228; refugees 212; sexual exploitation 435, 437, 443, 446, 452, 467
non-refoulment 116, 216
Northern Ireland 133, 240
Norway 130
notice and take down procedures 260

Obama, Barack 93
obesity 195
older persons 21
Ombudsman/person 127, 128, 221
Ongwen, Dominic 509, 515–20

pacta sunt servanda 43, 49
Pakistan 293, 328, 329, 383, 386
Palestine 91
Panama 116
Paraguay 116, 420
parents 170, 244; abduction, international parental child *see separate entry*; contact with both parents (CRC, art 9) 171; digital age 245, 247–8; equal parental responsibilities 176; responsibilities, rights and duties (CRC, arts 5 and 14) 29; right to know 160–1
Paris Principles: armed conflict and children 232, 498–9, 518; national human rights institutions 128, 490
participation rights 21, 30–3, 92, 150–5, 273, 342; indigenous children 532; indigenous peoples 534, 537, 542, 547; Internet: rights-based (participation) approach 235–6, 237, 265–8
paternalism 21, 26, 30–1
patriarchy 137
peremptory rights/*jus cogens* 35, 51, 146
Permanent Court of International Justice (PCIJ) 50
personal data 168–9, 240–1, 249–50, 384
Peru 420
Philippines 242, 294, 523
Piaget, J. 7–9, 10, 11
Poland 88, 393
Pollock, L. 3, 5
pornography 170, 249, 263, 433; child 107–9, 251, 252, 278, 307, 431, 434, 436, 441, 442, 443, 444–5, 451, 456, 459–60; CRC: OPSC *see under* sexual exploitation; revictimisation 434
Portugal: adoption 179; breastfeeding 197; child labour 294; education 207; institutional care 176; life, survival and development, right to 149; migrant children 215; non-discrimination 136, 137, 139; sexual abuse 185–6; teenage pregnancies 199
poverty 16, 61, 65, 136, 149, 173; child labour 281–4, 306, 311–12, 315, 317, 334; child soldiers 472; education 207, 281–4; indigenous peoples 523, 532, 545; institutional care 176; inter-country adoption 387; online harms 248; sexual exploitation 434, 444, 449; single parent families 176; standard of living 203–4; Sustainable Development Goal 1 17
precedent 50, 53, 67
privacy 34, 201, 202; CRC (art 16) 155, 162–3, 167–9; detention, children in 227; online 235, 261–2, 266, 267; private and family life (ECHR, art 8) 16–17, 368–9; UDHR (art 12) 20
private international law 40; Hague Conference on *see separate entry*; ILC 67
privatisation of law enforcement 325, 326
proportionality 16, 180, 262, 274, 376, 385
prostitution 107–9, 156, 278, 307, 389, 434, 442, 445, 450, 451, 456, 458–9; CRC: OPSC *see under* sexual exploitation; definition 450, 453, 458; ECPAT (Ending Child Prostitution and Trafficking) 435
protectionism 327
psychological perspectives on childhood 4, 6–9
public budgets 124–7

racism 142, 249
radicalisation 243, 249, 252–9, 261
rape 136, 186, 187, 436, 511, 543
Raz, J. 30–1
refugee children 136, 138, 210, 211–16, 224; birth registration 159, 162; child labour 213, 214, 293; expression, freedom of 163; intercountry adoption 401–2
rehabilitation and reintegration of child victims 132, 181, 182, 188, 230; armed conflict 110, 231, 232, 483–5, 488, 494, 512, 513–14, 515, 518; child labour

283, 306, 311, 328; migrants 214; street children 219
religion, freedom of thought, conscience and 36, 89, 162–3, 164–6
reporting of child sex abuse, mandatory 187
reporting process: CRC 83, 97–106, 120–1, 305, 469–70; Optional Protocols 101–3, 104, 105–7, 108, 111, 188, 469–70
reporting process: ILO 305, 319–23
reproductive model of society 10
resilience and risk 263
revenge porn 252
rights-based (participation) approach 235–6, 237, 265–8; best interests of child 271
risk aversion 34
risk and harm 263–4
risk society 246, 247–8, 263
risk-based (protection) approach 235–6, 237, 248–65; benefits of online participation 264–5; best interests of child 271; internet governance 259–62; moral panic 236, 243–4, 262–4; typology of ICT-related harms 250, 264; virtual duty of care 261–2
ritual killings 150
Roma children 204, 207
Roman law 4
Romania 389, 394, 408, 420
Russia 47, 57, 72, 252, 393, 420, 435–6, 439, 539; *see also* Soviet Union, former
Rwanda 504–5

sale and trafficking of children 147, 157, 214, 278, 307, 331–3, 457–8; CRC: art 34 450; CRC: art 35 223–4, 450–1, 469; CRC: OPSC *see under* sexual exploitation; definition of human trafficking 454–5; ECPAT (Ending Child Prostitution and Trafficking) 435; indigenous children 530, 545; intercountry adoption 396, 407–9, 414; 'modern slavery' 431–5; sexual exploitation 430, 431–5, 437, 439–40, 450–1; street children 218; Sustainable Development Goals 17, 439–40; Trafficking Protocol 2000 437, 454–6; victims, assisting 469
Samoa 428
Saudi Arabia 242, 264, 431
Scotland 133, 240, 380
self-actualisation 246

self-determination 21, 26, 265, 268; indigenous peoples 524, 525, 529, 533, 534–5, 536, 541–2, 547
self-harm 174, 199–200, 235, 249, 261
Senegal 89
sex education 199, 531
sexting 252, 261
sexual exploitation 235, 248, 251–2, 276, 279, 290, 291, 429–70, 497; abuse and exploitation 429–30; alternative care 174; Convention on the Worst Forms of Child Labour (1999) 451–2, 460; CRC: art 34 185–7, 271, 429, 449–50, 453, 460; CRC: art 35 450–1, 469; CRC: OPSC 93, 101–3, 104, 106–9, 140, 180, 188, 223, 224, 271, 336, 437, 447, 448, 449, 452–4, 456–61, 464, 465–70; criminalisation 456–64; ECPAT (Ending Child Prostitution and Trafficking) 435, 446; emerging issue: trafficking of children and 'modern slavery' 431–5; encryption and cryptocurrency 431; extradition 108, 109, 448, 465–6, 467; gender 430–1, 433–4, 464; global bodies 435–40; grooming 185, 252, 253, 442, 454, 460, 462; indigenous children 530; industry: action against 442–9; international customary law 49; international support and cooperation 467; jurisdiction, establishing 464–6; *jus cogens* 51; life, survival and development, right to 147–8; power imbalance 430, 434–5; refugees 213; regional bodies 440–2; reporting mechanisms 469–70; social policy 16, 17; States' responsibilities 456–69; Sustainable Development Goals 17, 439–40; tourism, sex 107, 109, 276, 439, 442–4, 445–9, 458–9, 464, 465; victims, assisting 467–9; vulnerability 430
sexual harassment, online 251
sexual slavery and armed conflict 148, 436, 511
Sierra Leone 512; Special Court for (SCSL) 505–8, 509–10, 513–14
Singapore 122, 124, 129; adoption 178; best interests of child 145; breastfeeding 197; corporal punishment 184; disabilities, children with 191–2; expression, freedom of 164; migrant children 215; minority groups 218; non-discrimination 136, 137, 139, 218;

privacy 168; sex education 199; sexual exploitation and abuse 187
Slovakia 116
Slovenia 128
smartphones 167, 233, 242, 245
social activism 265
social exploitation 22, 224–5
social media 107, 210, 241, 243, 251, 252, 259, 264–5; Facebook 249, 251, 261–2, 264; Instagram 251, 264; Twitter 252–3, 256, 264
social movements 18, 33–4
social norms 285
social policy perspectives on childhood 14–17, 243, 246, 248, 258, 259, 263
social welfare 203–4, 244, 246; child benefits 203
socialisation 9, 243, 277; constructivist model 9, 10–13; deterministic model 9–10; functionalist approach 10; new sociology of childhood 13–14; reproductive model of society 10
sociological perspective on childhood 9–14, 16, 26, 237, 266
soft law 52, 67, 189–90, 226, 305, 317, 318, 326, 383, 385, 498, 535
solvents 222
Somalia 90, 497
South Africa 249, 421, 446
South Sudan 90–1, 497
sovereignty, State 91, 324
Soviet Union, former 389
Spain 116, 393
Special Court for Sierra Leone (SCSL) 505–8, 509–10, 513–14
Special Rapporteurs 57, 67, 75, 81; child labour 296; indigenous peoples 523–4, 538, 540–6, 548; sale of children, child prostitution and child pornography 223, 431, 432–3, 434n19, 435, 437–9, 443, 444, 447, 448, 450, 452, 453, 458, 460, 461, 464–5, 467, 468, 469; trafficking in persons 223
Sri Lanka 241, 445
standard of living 35, 36, 176, 189–90, 196, 202–4, 214, 532
stare decisis/precedent 50, 53, 67
statelessness 156, 157, 159–60, 162
State–family relationship 15–17, 34, 35, 38, 170–6, 202–3, 246, 248
statistics 127, 187; abduction 337–8, 344, 368; armed conflict and children 499–500, 501, 504, 505, 509, 519; child labour 281, 286–91, 292, 293, 294–5; digital age 238–42, 249, 251, 252; indigenous peoples 521, 544; intercountry adoption 387, 389, 390–3, 419, 427
stereotypes 137, 206, 276, 337, 427
street children 184, 218–20, 291
Sudan 73, 91, 497, 512
suicide 149–50, 199–200, 235, 261; cyberbullying 250–1; pro-suicide websites 235, 249, 251
surrogacy 420
Sustainable Development Goals (SDGs) 17, 56, 90, 124, 203, 439; birth registration 158; child labour 224, 275, 279, 439; child mortality, reduction of 194; education 17, 205, 208, 282; food 194; gender equality 17, 240; health 194, 201; indigenous children 532; non-discrimination 135; social protection systems 203; trafficking 17, 439–40; violence against children, ending 17, 185, 439
swimming pools 149
Switzerland 116, 395
Syria 122, 124, 136, 137, 148–9, 154, 471, 473, 497; birth registration 159; child labour 293; children in street situations 219; detention 181; health and access to health services 195; information, access to 169–70; sexual abuse 186; standard of living 204

Tahiti 524–5
Taiwan 284
television 244
terrorism 243, 252, 253, 261, 372
Thailand 445, 448
Third World Approaches to International Law (TWAIL) 284–6, 523
Thomas, N. 32–3
thought, conscience and religion, freedom of 36, 89, 162–3, 164–6
Timor-Leste 523–4
tobacco 222
tokenism 32, 152
Tonga 130, 136, 137, 139; adoption 178, 179; corporal punishment 184; education 206; family environment and alternative care 175, 178, 179; heard, child's right to be 153; life, survival

and development, right to 149, 150; mortality, child 194
torture or other punishment 181–5, 229, 331, 443, 527, 543
tourism, sex 107, 109, 276, 439, 442–4, 445–9, 458–9, 464, 465
trade–labour linkage 304–5, 326–8
traffic accidents 149
trafficking: drugs 218, 222, 278, 308, 545; sale and trafficking of children *see separate entry*; small arms and light weapons 473, 495
training 129, 138, 153, 154, 155, 207, 211, 224, 414, 418, 444, 448, 490; juvenile justice 228, 230
transparency 125, 334, 419
treaty interpretation 43–4, 272, 346
truth and reconciliation commissions 515
Tunisia 146–7
Turkey 260, 294
Twitter 252–3, 256, 264

Uganda 73, 511, 515–20
UNESCO (United Nations Educational, Scientific and Cultural Organization) 240
UNICEF (United Nations Children's Fund) 14, 23, 57, 65–6, 96–7, 106; armed conflict, children in 66, 484, 501; child labour 66, 316, 325, 327, 329; digital age 234, 237–8, 263, 272; humanitarian work 66; intercountry adoption 399–400, 420–1; juvenile justice 228; rights-based approach 65–6; sexual exploitation 66, 437, 451, 458; Sustainable Development Goals (SDGs) 17
United Arab Emirates (UAE) 162, 431
United Kingdom 18, 48, 57, 283, 508, 512; abduction, international parental child 335–6, 337, 340–1, 342, 343–4, 347, 349, 351, 357–61, 363–4, 365, 366, 367, 370–1, 372, 374, 377–80, 381–2, 383, 384, 385, 386; age of criminal responsibility 133; armed forces: minimum age 110, 483, 487; Brexit 344; bullying 249; CRC 54, 123; cyber-bullying 249; definition of child 130, 133; digital divide 240; extradition 42; *Gillick*-mature child 26–8; harassment, online 251; incorporation doctrine 48, 53; intercountry adoption 387–8, 395; internet governance 243, 261–2; nineteenth century 16, 47, 296; 'Online Harms' White Paper (2019) 243, 261; radicalisation, online 253–8; relationship between domestic and international law 48, 53, 54–5; sexting 252; sexual exploitation 431, 435, 456, 461–4; State–family relationship 15, 16; statutory interpretation 54–5; views of child 30n31, 343–4; welfare principle 30n31, 382; Welfare State 244, 246
United Nations 14, 18, 23, 47, 55–61, 323; armed conflict and children 471–2, 486, 494, 497–8, 499–502; Charter 18–19, 49, 56, 58, 59, 60, 62, 64, 66, 74; Children's Fund *see* UNICEF; Declaration on the Rights of the Child 1959 22, 64, 88, 134, 140, 156, 208, 314; Declaration on the Rights of Indigenous Peoples 2007 521, 535–8, 540, 547; Development Programme (UNDP) 69, 325; Economic and Social Council (ECOSOC) 18–19, 58–9, 60, 65, 79, 88, 105, 108, 437, 539; General Assembly 17, 48, 56–7, 58–9, 61, 62, 64, 79, 88, 105, 521; Guiding Principles on Business and Human Rights 327; High Commissioner for Refugees (UNHCR) 212, 400, 402, 484; Human Rights Committee 94, 130, 135, 147, 157, 163, 166, 167, 168–9, 217, 524–5; Human Rights Council 56–7, 59, 61, 75, 79–82, 111, 437, 438, 501, 538, 540; Millennium Development Goals (MDGs) 56, 90, 240; Office of the High Commissioner for Human Rights (OHCHR) 57, 61, 75–6, 82, 94, 228; older persons 21; Secretariat 60, 75; Secretary-General 60; Security Council 57–8, 59, 62, 64, 436, 472, 493–8, 503, 504, 505, 511, 512; sexual exploitation 435, 436–9; special procedures 75, 81; Special Rapporteurs *see separate entry*; specialised agencies 60–1, 64, 68; SRSG (children and armed conflict) 486, 494, 497–8, 499–502; SRSG (human rights and transnational corporations) 327; SRSG (violence against children) 180; Sustainable Development Goals (SDGs) *see separate entry*; treaty bodies 74–5, 82–5, 272; Universal Periodic Review (UPR) 81–2; Youth Assembly on 'Malala Day' 76–9

United States 18, 33, 47, 48, 57, 72, 535; abduction, international parental child 337, 346, 350, 368, 374; Alien Tort Claims Act 331–3; armed forces: minimum age 110, 487; child labour 275, 290, 303, 308, 311, 327–8, 328, 329, 330–4; child sexual abuse URLs 252; civil and political freedoms 155–6; Constitution 18, 33, 92; Guantanamo 231–2; ILO 316; intercountry adoption 388–9, 393, 413, 420, 424–7; Internet 242, 250–1, 252, 260; internet governance 260; not ratifying CRC 43, 86, 90, 91–3; Optional Protocols to CRC 93, 102, 107; sexual exploitation 431, 435, 449, 470

Universal Periodic Review (UPR) 81–2

Venezuela 89, 218
victims 187; assisting victims of sexual exploitation 467–9; child soldiers: perpetrators or 512–20; CRC: OPSC 108; as criminals 460–1; ICC: participation of 508; interim measures 115; rehabilitation and reintegration of child *see separate entry*; stigmatisation of 186
Vietnam 389, 393, 428, 448
views of child 30–3, 92, 150–5, 175; abduction, international parental child 342–4, 372–4; best-interests assessments 143; CRC: OPIC 112; indigenous children 532; intercountry adoption 407–8

violence 147–9, 174, 207, 209, 215, 261, 290, 545; against children (CRC, arts 19, 37(a), 34 and 39) 117, 179–88, 214, 248, 271; armed conflict and children *see separate entry*; children in street situations 220; honour killings 150; sexual exploitation *see separate entry*
vote: right to 156, 162; voting age 166
Vygotsky, L. 11, 242–3

war crimes 72, 74, 109–10, 149, 231–2, 436, 486, 494, 501, 502–4, 506, 509, 511, 513–14, 516–20; conscripting/ enlisting under 15 years 508, 514
welfare rights 24
welfarist social policy 16; digital age 242, 243, 244, 246, 248, 258, 259, 263
will or choice theory of rights 23–4, 26, 265–6
World Bank 316
World Health Organization (WHO) 64, 149, 197, 484
World Summit for Children: (1990) 61, 90; (2000) 501
World Tourism Organization (WTO) 443
World Trade Organization (WTO) 326, 327, 328

Yazidi girls 148
Yemen 471, 473, 497
Yousafzai, Malala 76–9
Yugoslavia, International Criminal Tribunal for the former (ICTY) 503–4

Zimbabwe 239, 387

Printed in Great Britain
by Amazon